THE
PRESIDENTS

250 Years of American
Political Leadership

IAIN DALE

Illustrated by
Zoom Rockman

HODDER &
STOUGHTON

First published in Great Britain in 2021 by Hodder & Stoughton
An Hachette UK company

2

Copyright © Iain Dale 2021

The right of Iain Dale to be identified as the Author of the Work has been asserted
by him in accordance with the Copyright, Designs and Patent Act 1988.

Illustrations © Zoom Rockman 2021

A CIP catalogue record for this title is available from the British Library

Hardback ISBN 9781529379525
Trade Paperback ISBN 9781529379532
eBook ISBN 9781529379549

Typeset in Bembo MT Pro by
Palimpsest Book Production Ltd, Falkirk, Stirlingshire

Printed and bound in Great Britain by Clays Ltd, Elcograf S.p.A.

Hodder & Stoughton policy is to use papers that are natural, renewable
and recyclable products and made from wood grown in sustainable forests.
The logging and manufacturing processes are expected to conform to the
environmental regulations of the country of origin.

Hodder & Stoughton Ltd
Carmelite House
50 Victoria Embankment
London EC4Y 0DZ

www.hodder.co.uk

For Daniel Forrester, Mark Milosch and Michael Fuerst

Without their friendship and introduction to life in the US, and Washington, DC in particular, my interest in American politics and the American presidency would probably never have been encouraged.

We may not see each other for years on end, but the sign of true friendship is when you pick things up again as if you'd seen each other the previous week. And that's what we do.

'The presidency has made every man who occupied it, no matter how small, bigger than he was; and no matter how big, not big enough for its demands.'

Lyndon B. Johnson

'Anybody who wants the presidency so much that he'll spend two years organising and campaigning for it is not to be trusted with the office.'

David Broder

'When you see how the president makes political or policy decisions, you see who he is. The essence of the presidency is decision-making.'

Bob Woodward

'When you get to be president, there are all those things, the honors, the twenty-one-gun salutes, all those things. You have to remember it isn't for you. It's for the presidency.'

Harry S. Truman

'I did not expect to encounter what has beset me since my elevation to the presidency. God knows, I have endeavored to fulfill what I considered to be an honest duty, but I have been mistaken; my motives have been misconstrued and my feelings grossly betrayed.'

Zachary Taylor

'Well, Warren Harding, I have got you the presidency. What are you going to do with it?'

Florence Harding

Contents

Introduction by   xi
    Iain Dale
The Office of the Presidency in History, by   xvii
    Professor Scott Lucas

1.   George Washington 1789–97, by Mitchell Reiss   1
2.   John Adams 1797–1801, by Daniel Forrester   15
3.   Thomas Jefferson 1801–09, by Alvin S. Felzenberg   28
4.   James Madison 1809–17, by Matthew Binkowski   47
5.   James Monroe 1817–25, by Brooks Newmark   59
6.   John Quincy Adams 1825–29, by Mark Fox   69
7.   Andrew Jackson 1829–37, by Simon Marks   78
8.   Martin Van Buren 1837–41, by Roifield Brown   92
9.   William Henry Harrison 1841–41, by Emma
     Burnell   104
10.   John Tyler 1841–45, by Peter Riddell   109
11.   James K. Polk 1845–49, by Brian Klaas   117
12.   Zachary Taylor 1849–50, by Michael Crick   125
13.   Millard Fillmore 1850–53, by Layla Moran   131
14.   Franklin Pierce 1853–57, by Karin J. Robinson   141
15.   James Buchanan 1857–61, by Keith Simpson   149
16.   Abraham Lincoln 1861–65, by Julia Langdon   157
17.   Andrew Johnson 1865–69, by Allie Renison   169
18.   Ulysses S. Grant 1869–77, by Bonnie Greer   178
19.   Rutherford B. Hayes 1877–81, by Robert Waller   189
20.   James A. Garfield 1881–81, by Anne Alexander   197
21.   Chester A. Arthur 1881–85, by Sue Cameron   203
22   and 24. Grover Cleveland 1885–89 and 1893–97,
     by Gerry Hassan   213

23. Benjamin Harrison 1889–93, by Rosie Ilett   226
25. William McKinley 1897–1901, by David Torrance 235
26. Theodore Roosevelt 1901–09, by Damian Collins 244
27. William Howard Taft 1909–13, by Philip Norton 259
28. Woodrow Wilson 1913–21, by Roy Hattersley   268
29. Warren G. Harding 1921–23, by Adam Boulton   283
30. Calvin Coolidge 1923–29, by Leo McKinstry   294
31. Herbert Hoover 1929–33, by Robert Buckland   304
32. Franklin D. Roosevelt 1933–45, by Neil Stockley 315
33. Harry S. Truman 1945–53, by David Blanchflower 334
34. Dwight D. Eisenhower 1953–61, by
    Peter Caddick-Adams   346
35. John F. Kennedy 1961–63, by Simon Burns   360
36. Lyndon B. Johnson 1963–69, by
    George Osborne   372
37. Richard Nixon 1969–74, by Freddy Gray   386
38. Gerald Ford 1974–77, by Andy Silvester   403
39. Jimmy Carter 1977–81, by David Owen   410
40. Ronald Reagan 1981–89, by Simon Heffer   421
41. George H.W. Bush 1989–93, by Colleen Graffy   435
42. William Jefferson Clinton 1993–2001,
    by Poppy Trowbridge   445
43. George W. Bush 2001–09, by
    Christopher Meyer   460
44. Barack Obama 2009–17, by Toby Harnden   472
45. Donald J. Trump 2017–21, by Justin Webb   486
46. Joe Biden 2021–, by Andrew Adonis   499

Ranking the Presidents, by Alvin S. Felzenberg   505
Acknowledgements   516
Index   519

Introduction

By Iain Dale

IT WAS SUMMER 1987. I was spending a month in Ann Arbor, Michigan, staying with my friend Mark Milosch, who I had met the previous year while he was interning in my office in Parliament. Mark and I connected partly through our love of books, and one of the first things he did was show me round the numerous second-hand book shops in Ann Arbor. It's the home of the University of Michigan, and I was in seventh heaven. In the first bookshop we visited I remember finding a section on presidential elections, and there on the second shelf down was a book called *Marathon: The Pursuit of the Presidency 1972–1976*, by Jules Witcover. A bargain at five dollars. It was the beginning of my love affair with the politics of the presidency and presidential elections. On that trip I bought five or six other books about previous presidential elections, and numerous biographies of presidents, some of whom from the nineteenth century I had barely heard of. I had to buy a second suitcase to carry the book loot home to the UK.

Over the following few years I became almost obsessed with reading more and more about American presidents. I became particularly interested in Richard Nixon, one of the most complex characters ever to inhabit the Oval Office. One of my first political memories came at the age of twelve when I remember seeing Richard Nixon leave the White House for the last time, climb into Marine One, and give that defiant salute.

I have read virtually every biography ever written about Nixon, as well as the books he wrote himself, all of which are brilliantly crafted and written. *Leaders*, *Six Crises* and *In the Arena* remain three of my favourite political books of all time. And so it was in early

January 1994 that I found myself at the Richard Nixon Library and Birthplace in Yorba Linda, just outside Los Angeles. Having successfully navigated the LA freeway system in the days before satnav, I intended to spend a couple of hours there, before returning to my hotel on Sunset Boulevard. It was a much more fascinating place than I ever imagined it would be. Not only were there exhibits from his time as president, but you could also listen to the Oval Office tape recordings, which contributed so much to his downfall. Not only did I spend the whole afternoon there, I returned the next morning too. The next day I drove out to Simi Valley to the recently opened Ronald Reagan Library, sat atop a mountain, with Air Force One resplendent alongside. Quite how they got it up the mountain, I still can't fathom. I have no idea how many Brits had visited before me, but I was treated like royalty, especially when I told them I had met Margaret Thatcher. A few years later I visited the JFK Library in Boston, which I'll admit was a bit of a disappointment compared to those of Nixon and Reagan. Since then, I've made plans to visit the rest of the presidential libraries. I'm even thinking of organising a group tour. I hadn't actually realised that there is a library or museum for virtually every president. And of course now, I want to visit them all . . .

There is much discussion whenever a British prime minister visits the United States about the 'Special Relationship' between our two countries. As you will read in this book, that relationship hasn't always been so special. I have built some very special friendships with Americans over the years, and none more so than with Daniel Forrester, whom I met during the British general election campaign of 1992 in Norwich. In 1995, I took him to the T.E. Utley Young Journalist of the Year awards at the Reform Club in London. Margaret Thatcher, no stranger to 'Special Relationships' of her own with American presidents, had been invited to present the awards. After she had finished her speech, Daniel whispered to me, 'I have to meet her; what should I do?' I encouraged him to go and introduce himself. In typically American style he launched into a sycophantic introduction, which immediately attracted her attention. 'Mrs Thatcher,' he began. I kicked him. 'Er, Lady Thatcher,' he hurriedly corrected himself, 'may I say how much our country misses your leadership . . .' and he continued in that vein for a few seconds. While he was speaking, the diminutive figure of the Iron Lady (for she was much smaller in height than most people imagine) stared up at him, her eyes never leaving his. When he had finally finished having his say, Lady Thatcher hardly paused for breath. 'Your president, President Clinton.' She paused, heightening the drama for our American friend. 'He is a great communicator.' Up came the forefinger, almost prodding Daniel's chest. Then, in a particularly contemptuous tone, came the *pièce de résistance*. 'The trouble is, he has absolutely nothing to communicate.' With that she was away. It was almost a flounce. Daniel eventually came down from whichever cloud he had been on – probably nine – and said, 'I'll remember that for the rest of my life.'

In 2007, I visited the White House and was shown round the West Wing. I got to stand behind the famous press room podium. I walked along the Colonnade. I got to peek inside the Oval Office, but there was a rope across the door. I gingerly put my left foot under the rope, so it was fully inside the hallowed room. I then whipped out my BlackBerry and quickly wrote a live blogpost. I claim the title of being the first person to blog from the Oval Office. Unless, of course, you know different . . .

In November 2020 my book *The Prime Ministers* was published. As soon as it came out people started suggesting I should edit a similar book on US presidents. I didn't need much persuading. The 2020 US presidential election heightened interest in presidential politics in the UK and I was delighted that my publisher, Hodder & Stoughton, felt that this book would be just as appealing as *The Prime Ministers*. In my introduction to *The Prime Ministers*, which was published to coincide with the three hundredth anniversary of the office, I confessed that there were a few of our more obscure prime ministers whom I had never heard of. I'll be honest and say that it was the same for the presidents. Even though I was familiar with most, if not all, of the twentieth-century presidents, I confess that I knew little about either William or Benjamin Harrison. Or Rutherford Hayes. I suspect I was and am not alone. And that's the joy of a book like this. You can dip into it and read about a particular president, learn the basics and then maybe undertake some further reading.

I learned so many interesting things editing this book. I learned from Damian Collins's essay on Teddy Roosevelt that the Oval Office wasn't built until 1909. Previous presidents had worked in the domestic quarters of the White House. Two of the USA's Founding Fathers, John Adams and Thomas Jefferson, died on 4 July 1826, the fiftieth anniversary of Independence Day. The fifth president, James Monroe, also died on 4 July. What are the odds of that happening? Julia Langdon writes about Abraham Lincoln's body-guard dreaming that he would die, the night before he was killed. And who knew that the S in Harry S. Truman doesn't actually stand for anything?

Editing a book with forty-six different contributors is, as readers will understand, a unique challenge. Each writer inevitably has a different style. Some, like David Owen and Sir Christopher Meyer, have had personal dealings with the presidents they have written about. David Owen was Foreign Secretary when Jimmy Carter was president and Sir Christopher Meyer was British ambassador in Washington during George W. Bush's first years in office. They bring a uniquely personal touch to their interpretations of those two pres-idencies. Colleen Graffy was Deputy Assistant Secretary of State in the George W. Bush administration, but has written a superb account of the presidency of his father. Mitchell Reiss also served in the Bush administration and went on to run Colonial Williamsburg, the uniquely atmospheric home of the Revolutionary era. His essay made me ashamed to admit how little I previously knew about America's first president. It's one of the most memorable in the book.

As with *The Prime Ministers*, I've deliberately recruited a mixture of historians, politicians, journalists and academics to write about the presidents. In some cases, I knew that the contributor had an expertise in or love of their subject. George Osborne has long been obsessed by Lyndon B. Johnson, and former MP Sir Simon Burns is known for his devotion to the Kennedys, so I was delighted when they both agreed to contribute to the book. But I made clear, this wasn't going to be a book of hagiographies, and they needed to write about their presidents warts 'n' all. And they have.

One of the most difficult presidents to allocate was Donald Trump. Everyone has a view on Trump. Like most outspoken politicians he attracts devotion and revulsion in equal amounts. I wanted someone who could be fair and nuanced, without writing a paean of praise or an outright denunciation. I think you'll agree when you read it that Justin Webb has done a brilliant job in analysing the strengths and weaknesses of American's forty-fifth president and working out where he succeeded and where he failed.

The common perception of Trump is that he was a one-off – a president without precedent. One thing this book has taught me is that perceptions like this are wrong. Go back to the presidencies of Andrew Jackson and Andrew Johnson and they were, to one degree or another, the Trump of their era. In Jackson's case, the comparisons are uncanny.

This book is intended to be a celebration of the office of the presidency and the personalities that have lived in the White House and worked in the Oval Office. But it is also a book that exposes the running sore of slavery, an issue that didn't just dominate domestic policy decisions until the presidency of Abraham Lincoln, but the long-term consequences of which still bedevil the politics of the USA today. I gained more understanding of the issue of slavery, the Confederacy and the Civil War of the 1860s than I have done reading any other single-volume book, by reading the essays here. I hope you will too.

Eleven of the forty-six contributors are American nationals, although most have a link to Britain. It may seem odd for a Brit to edit a book of essays on American presidents written by a mix of Brits and Americans, but I think it's a positive advantage and means that this is inevitably a very different read to the myriad of books published on presidents in America. A Brit writing about an American president is a positive as it brings distance and perspective, with differently informed insights given our previously hostile, but now close relationship. You, dear reader, will be the ultimate judge of whether this mix works or not. I've tried to edit with a light touch, even if it means one or two of the essays are very different in style to the rest.

It is almost a national sport in the US to rank the forty-six presidents. One of our contributors, Alvin S. Felzenberg, has also written a book on the subject called *The Leaders We Deserved (And a Few We Didn't): Rethinking the Presidential Rating Game*. His epilogue on this cottage industry is fascinating, and he gives his own rankings. Most historians rank Washington, Lincoln and FDR in the top three. Surprisingly, quite a few allow John F. Kennedy to creep into their top tens. This rather belies their liberal outlook on life, I suspect, and a tendency to buy into the Kennedy mythology. We will never know if he could have become a great president if he had lived, but to rank him so highly after only two and a half years in office, with several big failures, is preposterous. Of the dozen presidents who have held office in my adult life I think Ronald Reagan must surely count as the most transformational. As with Nixon and Watergate, Bill Clinton's presidency will always be stained by the Lewinsky scandal, but I suspect historians will rate him far more highly in terms of economic and foreign policy achievement than they do now. They will also rate him more highly than Barack Obama, whose main achievement was to be elected in the first place, as American's first president of colour. He could never have lived up to the 'hopey-changey' expectations that his campaign aroused. So with one glass ceiling shattered, there is still one that remains intact. However, I suspect it won't be long before America gets its first female president. Hillary Clinton thought it would be her but it was not to be. The current vice-president, Kamala Harris, is now in prime position to break two more glass ceilings.

Please also look out for the podcast series *Presidents and Prime Ministers* in which I will interview all the contributors about the president they have written about. The podcast series also contains interviews with the 55 contributors to my book *The Prime Ministers*.

This is not an academic book. It is aimed at the general reader, as well as those for whom politics is a part of their daily lives. The contributors were asked to tell a story, to write in an engaging way, and above all not to be afraid of giving an opinion. I am grateful to all of them in the way they have responded, and I am sure you are going to learn just as much as I have from their brilliant essays.

Iain Dale
Tunbridge Wells, September 2021

The Office of the Presidency in History

By Professor Scott Lucas

IN 1789, AS George Washington became the first US president, legislators faced the question: having waged a revolution to break from a British monarchy, what title would represent the distinction of the American experiment while proclaiming the importance of the man and the office?

Vice-president John Adams, who had spent much time in European courts as a US envoy during the Revolutionary War, maintained the royal with 'Your Highness' or 'Your Most Benign Highness'. One senator mixed monarchy with democratic republic: 'His Elective Highness'. But others raised the ante with 'His Exalted Highness' or 'His Majesty the President'. An exasperated member snapped, 'Why not call him George IV?', but Adams was not done: he suggested, 'His Highness, the President of the United States, and Protector of the Rights of the Same'.

After days of debate, one legislator reminded colleagues that the newly adopted Constitution prohibited titles. So a simple 'Mr President' was established. Washington wrote to his son-in-law, 'Happily the matter is now done with, I hope never to be revived.'

Yet for much of US history, Mr President – and perhaps in the near future Madam President – has been more important and recognised at home and abroad than any monarch. Other heads of state, with different systems of authority, may wield more power. However, the world's attention is drawn to the American presidential election and the inaugural address, rather than Xi Jinping's appearance at the Congress of the Chinese Communist Party or Vladimir Putin's State of the Nation press conference in Russia.

In 2021, both the image and the authority of the US head of state is under great scrutiny, perhaps greater than the advent of the 'imperial' presidency with Franklin D. Roosevelt, greater than the confrontation of the Civil War, greater than Washington's rejection of a royal title.

The forty-fifth president, Donald Trump, not only converted the presidency into a bully pulpit via Twitter, he used it in an attempt to dismantle the rest of the US system: Congress, the courts, government agencies, the media. The disinformation and threat would culminate in a months-long campaign to throw out the presidential election.

On 6 January 2021, several hundred of Trump's followers, spurred by his command to 'stop the steal', raided the US Capitol building. It was the first attack on the site since the British burnt the complex in 1814, and the first by US citizens on the symbol of their government.

Two weeks later, on the steps of the Capitol, the forty-sixth president put the challenge for his office, the American system and the country. Joe Biden said, 'To overcome these challenges – to restore the soul and to secure the future of America – requires more than words. It requires that most elusive of things in a democracy: Unity.'

How did the presidency get here? And where does it go?

The rise of the presidents is part of the rise of the US to global prominence, as well as its sometimes-turbulent domestic path. So the office's evolution – or devolution – can be traced in four periods: the Developing, the Recovering, the Expanding, and the Uncertain.

The Developing Presidency

From Washington's time to the Civil War, the presidency was part of a new system being established without any precedent. The president would be the representative of the people, rather than imposing authority through the claim of divine right or a personal command of the country's military. Thomas Jefferson, who would become the country's third president, wrote in 1787, 'I have no fear that the result of our experiment will be that men may be trusted to govern themselves without a master.' James Madison set out the negative side of the case for a president within a system, not at the top of it: 'The truth is that all men having power ought to be mistrusted.'

Both in myth and reality, 'checks and balances' was the distinction of the American system, with the relationship between Executive, Legislative and Judicial worked out in practice beyond the Constitution and the debates in the Federalist Papers. Even more importantly, the US was not a single entity but a federation of states, divided as much as they were united on issues such as the economy, agriculture and slavery.

The outcome in US legend was iconic Founding Fathers such as Washington, Jefferson and Madison. But development was soon marked by division. The cultural divide was embodied in Andrew Jackson, the seventh president. He was inaugurated in front of a 'vast and motley' multitude who partied at the White House late into the night. For some Americans, this was the elevation of the common man and common woman. For others, this was a drunken mob. For some, Jackson was a military hero, vanquishing the British in the War of 1812; for others, he was an 'Indian-killer'. He was to be admired or detested for his refusal to accept the Supreme Court and a US national bank.

The political divide coalesced around slavery. Some presidents, such as James Monroe and the less well-known Millard Fillmore, worked with Congress seeking compromises to navigate the issue. Others did not get the chance to pursue resolution: William Henry Harrison died in office after only thirty-one days, a victim of pneumonia. And others, like Franklin Pierce and James Buchanan, sank into ignominy beneath the approaching Civil War.

Washington was the icon of the original thirteen states, with Vermont, Kentucky and Tennessee joining during his time in office. Jefferson unlocked the potential of the continent with the Louisiana Purchase. Jackson cleared space for 'America' by removing the Native Americans. The Mexican–American War brought in Texas and the south-west US.

But taking the Inaugural Oath in March 1861, Abraham Lincoln saw a Confederacy splitting from the Union, even as he said, 'I have no purpose, directly or indirectly, to interfere with the institution of slavery in the States where it exists.'

The Recovering Presidency

Lincoln secured his legendary status by leading part of the US to victory over the other part. But he also secured his memorial and his place, from US currency to Mount Rushmore, by lifting the beacon of reunion and recovery. The wartime Gettysburg Address – 'The nation shall have a new birth of freedom' – and the Emancipation Proclamation were followed by the second inaugural address in 1865, on the brink of military triumph:

> With malice toward none; with charity for all; with firmness in the right, as God gives us to see the right, let us strive on to finish the work we are in; to bind up the nation's wounds; to care for him who shall have borne the battle, and for his widow, and his orphan to do all which may achieve and cherish a just, and a lasting peace, among ourselves, and with all nations.

But Lincoln was assassinated before the South surrendered. Amid a reconstruction that was considered an occupation by many in the South, the three presidents who followed would be impeached (Andrew Johnson), carry the mark of division (Ulysses S. Grant, the victorious Union general), and take office in a disputed election (Rutherford B. Hayes). The fourth, James Garfield, was shot three and a half months after his inauguration and died from bungled medical care two months after that.

US recovery would rest upon the denial of rights to Blacks and the final subjugation of Native Americans. This was not an American reunion for the good of all, but it was good for some as the economy grew for a rapidly expanding population moving across the continent. Between 1850 and 1930, more than 35 million immigrants entered the country.

The US presidency and America were moving beyond borders. William McKinley oversaw the annexation of Hawaii, removing the monarchy of the island. Victory in the Spanish–American War brought in territory from Puerto Rico to Guam to the Philippines, as well as a protectorate over Cuba. The 'Open Door' for China saw the possibility of breaking the spheres of influence of Russia,

France, Germany and the UK. There was even the prospect of war with Britain in 1895, over a territorial dispute between Venezuela and British Guiana.

Theodore Roosevelt, who charged up Cuba's San Juan Hill in the Spanish–American War, ascended to the presidency in 1901 after McKinley was assassinated by anarchist Leon Czolgosz. He became the face of America's global ventures with 'speak softly and carry a big stick' and the image of US power from the halls of Montezuma to the shores of Tripoli to the canal across Panama. At home, he promised the 'Square Deal' to repair the damage of an unregulated economy. The executive branch grew with agencies to monitor commerce, break monopolies and trusts, oversee railroads and public utilities, and provide for safe food and drugs.

Roosevelt heralded the new America for a twentieth-century world. He said in his second inaugural address in 1905: 'We have become a great nation, forced by the fact of its greatness into relations with the other nations of the earth, and we must behave as beseems as a people with such responsibilities.'

The Expansive Presidency

The Expansive Presidency was never one of smooth progress. Roosevelt's successor William Howard Taft may be best known for being the heaviest president, at close to 350 pounds, and getting stuck in his bathtub.

Woodrow Wilson, the university historian turned twenty-eighth president, hailed the US as a product of the reconstruction in which Black rights were sacrificed. He praised *Birth of a Nation*, the 1915 film that demonised the 'Negro' and exalted the Ku Klux Klan, as 'history writ with lightning'. His presidential reputation was built upon the invasion of Mexico and belated intervention in the First World War, with the Fourteen Points pledging open diplomacy, self-determination, freedom of trade and freedom of the seas.

The global US was checked by Congress's refusal to enter the League of Nations and the chequered presidencies of Warren Harding, felled by the Teapot Dome corruption scandal and cardiac arrest; 'Silent Cal' Coolidge; and Herbert Hoover. Thus, one of the most significant presidencies, of Franklin D. Roosevelt, rested upon seizing opportunity from the Great Depression.

Roosevelt entered office in March 1933 in a US with 25 per cent unemployment. More than 11,000 of 24,000 banks had failed. More than 60 per cent of Americans were classified as poor.

In his first inaugural address, he upheld the US system and the presidency: 'Our Constitution is so simple and practical that it is possible always to meet extraordinary needs by changes in emphasis and arrangement without loss of essential form.'

But the speech is best remembered for Roosevelt's rallying cry: 'Let me assert my firm belief that the only thing we have to fear is fear itself – nameless, unreasoning, unjustified terror which paralyses needed efforts to convert retreat into advance.' Then he promised, in the name of American ideals, a campaign to remake the US economy and society. The New Deal began with an image from the New Testament: 'The money changers have fled from their high seats in the temple of our civilisation. We may now restore that temple to the ancient truths. The measure of the restoration lies in the extent to which we apply social values more noble than mere monetary profit.'

The launch of the Expansive Presidency, with the unprecedented use of government power for a remaking of America, is commemorated with Roosevelt's Fireside Chats on radio and his 1941 'Four Freedoms': freedom of speech, freedom of worship, freedom from want and freedom from fear.

But the New Deal was nearly halted at its inception because of checks and balances. The Supreme Court ruled a series of measures unconstitutional, to the point where a frustrated Roosevelt sought the 'packing' of the bench with additional justices. If the Depression was needed to launch America's most historic initiative, the Second World War was required for the confirmation of the expanded presidential authority.

Roosevelt died from a cerebral haemorrhage on 12 April 1945, weeks before the fall of Berlin and four months before the atomic bomb ended war with Japan. Vice-president Harry Truman, a former haberdasher and undistinguished senator, told reporters, 'Boys: if you ever pray, pray for me now.'

But in their own ways, Truman and those who followed were

just as significant as Roosevelt in the expansion of the presidency. The extent of government at home would be debated, but it would never be rolled back to the 1920s. Abroad, president and nation would be joined in the image of 'superpower'.

Truman built on the New Deal with the proposals of the Fair Deal, including aid to education, universal health insurance, the Fair Employment Practices Commission, and repeal of the Taft–Hartley Act restricting labour unions. A Republican majority in Congress blocked much of the programme, but some measures were adopted. Truman also issued the first, limited edicts for civil rights, integrating the armed forces and prohibiting discrimination in federal employment.

Four days after becoming president, Truman envisaged the American mission after the war: 'The entire world is looking to America for enlightened leadership to peace and progress. Such a leadership requires vision, courage and tolerance. It can be provided only by a united nation deeply devoted to the highest ideals.'

This time, the US would not detach itself, instead joining – and leading in – the United Nations. Its military ascendancy was represented vividly, and tragically, in the image of the mushroom cloud of the atomic bomb: uranium on Hiroshima on 6 August 1945, and plutonium on Nagasaki three days later. Truman said of the presidency and the country, 'It is an awful responsibility which has come to us. We thank God it has come to us instead of our enemies, and we pray that he may guide us to use it in His ways and for His purposes.'

So the Cold War with the Soviet Union provided another opportunity. The US would finance the recovery of western Europe with the Marshall Plan, and open a military umbrella with the North Atlantic Treaty Organization. Economic and military assistance would be given to other parts of the world from the Middle East to Asia, taking over from former colonial powers in areas such as Vietnam. America would reassert authority over its Western hemisphere backyard, first claimed in the Monroe Doctrine of 1823. The CIA would fund a Cultural Cold War, supporting American art, music, journalism, labour unions, students, lawyers, and even the US Olympic Team.

Dwight Eisenhower, having led Allied forces in the Second World

War, succeeded Truman. He oversaw the hydrogen bomb, a thousand times more powerful than the atomic weapon used on Hiroshima. US conventional forces had been checked in the Korean War, but covert operations would be pursued as a cheaper alternative, with governments toppled from Iran to Guatemala and a programme to quash the incipient Cuban Revolution and Fidel Castro. US military advisers and the CIA were now entrenched in South Vietnam.

Eisenhower viewed this new world through the prism of an America with unprecedented – if unevenly distributed – economic growth. He remarked on Truman's statement about the atomic bomb: 'This great country is the greatest power on God's footstool that has been permitted to exist. A power for good, among ourselves, and in all the world . . . America's leadership in the world is necessary to the preservation of freedom and of liberty in that world.'

The presidency was handed in 1961 from one of its oldest occupants to its youngest, the forty-two-year-old John F. Kennedy. The image of American power was converted from the elderly military leader to the Camelot dynamism and celebrity of the photogenic Kennedy, his wife Jackie, and their young children. However, in his inaugural address, JFK set out the soundbites to define his mission and that of the US.

> Let the word go forth from this time and place, to friend and foe alike, that the torch has been passed to a new generation of Americans – born in this century, tempered by war, disciplined by a hard and bitter peace, proud of our ancient heritage – and unwilling to witness or permit the slow undoing of those human rights . . .
>
> Let every nation know, whether it wishes us well or ill, that we shall pay any price, bear any burden, meet any hardship, support any friend, oppose any foe, in order to assure the survival and the success of liberty.

Despite – or because of – its brevity, Kennedy's term became the repository of post-war America at home and abroad. With his assassination, the legend would be enshrined of his commitment to civil rights, his vision of the 'New Frontier' with space exploration, his support of West Germany ('*Ich bin ein Berliner*'), and his call for peace in a 1963 speech: 'In the final analysis, our most basic common link is that we all inhabit this small planet. We all breathe the same air. We all cherish our children's future. And we are all mortal.'

Yet, beyond image, Kennedy represented the post-war paradox of American presidents: they were presiding as much over insecurity as they were over security. Amid prosperity was a 'culture of fear' with an anti-communism of loyalty oaths, blacklists and McCarthyism. Its scientific and technical progress was alongside the social panic spurred by the Soviet Union's launch of Sputnik in 1957. The Statue of Liberty's assurance of an America for the tired, hungry and poor did not extend to fears of an NAACP or Martin Luther King as agents of Moscow.

So JFK's term began with the disaster of the Bay of Pigs operation trying to overthrow Cuba's Castro. It continued with a hesitancy to use the power of the presidency to intervene for civil rights. And it ended with the CIA's support of the overthrow of South Vietnam's Ngo Dinh Diem and a further descent into the quagmire that would soon suck in US troops.

The presidency could still offer not only the vision but also the economic and social programmes of Lyndon Johnson. However, they would be pulled down by the spiralling cost in resources of the Vietnam conflict, 'that bitch of a war on the other side of the world', in Johnson's words, which took away 'the woman I really loved – the Great Society'.

Richard Nixon would exploit the war to become thirty-seventh president, but his 'Vietnamisation' would not bring 'peace with honour': instead, US bombing would lead to the deaths of hundreds of thousands in Vietnam and Cambodia and the chaotic American departure in 1975. The US was still divided, and Nixon's proclaimed victory of *détente* with the Soviet Union and China – and his land-slide re-election in 1972 – was overtaken by the personal insecurity that produced Watergate and his resignation, before impeachment and conviction, in 1974.

The paradox of power could not be resolved. Gerald Ford and Jimmy Carter each presided over a Gulliver tied down abroad. The might of the US military was humbled by Kampucheans who seized a container ship and destroyed marine helicopters. The 1979 Islamic Revolution in Iran led to the seizure of the US Embassy and fifty-two Americans held captive for 444 days. Long-time US allies like Nicaragua's Anastasio Somoza fell to revolutions, and others such as Chile's Augusto Pinochet and the Philippines' Ferdinand Marcos maintained authority through martial law and mass executions and detentions. Even *détente* was fading, with the Soviet Union entering its own quagmire in Afghanistan.

At home, 'stagflation' – the unprecedented combination of soaring inflation and rising unemployment – was accompanied by oil crises that fed the 'culture of fear'. Americans worried that their post-war dream was now a perpetual nightmare. Carter's invocation, 'What is lacking is confidence and a sense of community', was converted by his opponents into a declaration of 'malaise'.

The skill of Ronald Reagan, once a famous actor, was to promise the resolution of the paradox through a 'Morning in America' after the nightmare: 'It is time for us to realize that we are too great a nation to limit ourselves to small dreams.'

But much of this was in performance, even illusion, rather than reality. 'Trickle-down economics' did not trickle down to many Americans, but fed income inequality. The wealthy became much wealthier, but the rate of poverty was the same in 1989 as it was in 1981. Civil rights were rolled back, with denunciation of affirmative action, women's right to choose, and stigmatising of the lesbian and gay community.

Far from providing security, Reagan pursued a resurgent Cold War. He emphasised a sharp escalation in military forces, including nuclear weapons. He promoted the real-life Star Wars, a fanciful notion of an anti-missile umbrella in space. He quipped on a radio soundcheck: 'My fellow Americans, I'm pleased to tell you I just signed legislation which outlaws Russia forever. The bombing begins in five minutes.' But in real life, the Soviets shot down a South Korean passenger jet, and the mistaken perception of a NATO exercise almost led to nuclear war.

Escape came from Reagan's shift in his second term, embracing the vision of the new Soviet leader Mikhail Gorbachev for a Europe free of nuclear weapons. The Soviet Union would be vanquished not by the bomb, but by its inability to sustain a viable economic system.

In an America of 'print the legend', Reagan's eventual status would be of the Man Who Won the Cold War. At the time, however, insecurity still reigned. The administration avoided some damage with the fall of Marcos in the Philippines and the beginning of Pinochet's departure in Chile. But in Lebanon, 241 US troops were killed in the deadliest suicide bombing to date. In the Caribbean island of Grenada, war was waged against Cuban contractors building an airport runway.

The complexity of America's security/insecurity from the Middle East to Central America culminated in the Iran-Contra scandal: a byzantine and illegal scheme to fund a coup in Nicaragua through arms sales to the Islamic leadership in Iran. Reagan fell from triumph to the prospect of impeachment, curbing it with the claim, 'I did not know about the diversion of funds.'

Reagan left office nine months before the fall of the Berlin Wall. The forty-first US president, George H.W. Bush, would watch as the Soviet Union finally collapsed in summer 1991. By then, however, the paradox of insecurity had spread. Pan Am 103 was blown up over Lockerbie, Scotland, killing 270 people in the air and on the ground. US troops were again at war in a small country in the Americas, this time Panama in December 1989. Just over a year later, they would lead a 'Coalition of the Willing' into Kuwait and then Iraq. By August 1991, Bush's proclamation, 'We have finally kicked the Vietnam syndrome', was replaced by criticism of supposed weakness in his 'Chicken Kiev' speech in Ukraine.

Far from celebration at home, the US was beset by a recession from 1990. The beating of Rodney King led to unrest in Los Angeles in spring 1992, with sixty-three people killed and more than $1 billion in damage. Bush fell in the 1992 election to the mantra of Bill Clinton, 'It's the economy, stupid.'

Clinton's eight years were distinguished by the resurgent American economy of the Dot-Com era. Almost 23 million new jobs were created, unemployment fell to its lowest level in thirty years, and there were 7 million fewer Americans living in poverty. Clinton worked with Russian leader Boris Yeltsin on a global economy including Moscow, and marked a high point in US–China relations – only nine years after the deadly crackdown in Tiananmen Square – with his visit to Beijing in 1998.

Still, the paradox persisted. The killing of US troops in Somalia, a US warship driven away by a group of Haitians, and American inaction when about eight hundred thousand people were killed in Rwanda: each was seen as a marker of presidential weakness. Iraq's Saddam Hussein defied sanctions and occasional air strikes, as the administration grappled with what it called 'rogue states'.

Intervention in the Balkans, from the Dayton Peace Accords to confrontation over Kosovo, recovered some of the American image. But by then, domestic tension had spiralled from the spectacle of the O.J. Simpson trial to Clinton's impeachment for sexual relations with a White House intern. The US was arguably at its most prosperous, but the rise of attack radio and TV was fuelling disinformation, conspiracy theory and constant invective against the president and First Lady.

Clinton said on 31 December 1999, 'We know the sun will always rise on America, as long as each new generation lights the fire of freedom. Our children are ready.'

The Uncertain Presidency

Less than two years later, the fire was from the blazes at the World Trade Center and the Pentagon, set by the airplanes hijacked by Al Qaeda attackers.

George W. Bush had become president eight months earlier in January 2001. He did so after the most disputed election since 1876, claiming the White House only after a 5–4 Supreme Court decision cut short a ballot recount in Florida. He walked through the Washington rain after an inaugural speech with 'a concern for civility', but partisan division had been widened.

The response of his advisers was beyond America. The project was to display the US as the world's only superpower in the 'unipolar era'. Only eleven days after the inauguration, they discussed the demonstration of that power: regime change in Saddam Hussein's Iraq.

The plan was overtaken by 9/11, but the administration quickly answered the question of National Security Adviser Condoleezza Rice, 'How do you capitalise on these opportunities?' There was an unprecedented expansion of executive power through the PATRIOT Act, including surveillance of American citizens, the suspension of the Geneva Convention and the pursuit of torture, including at the Guantanamo Bay base in Cuba.

Abroad, the 'War on Terror' quickly moved beyond Afghanistan to regime change in Iraq. By March 2002, even as US troops were killed trying to capture Osama bin Laden, vice-president Dick Cheney was proposing military operations against Saddam Hussein to UK prime minister Tony Blair. Over the next year, the Bush presidency set up the pretext for the war, manipulating intelligence and US agencies for the weapons of mass destruction that did not exist.

However, Saddam Hussein's fall was the consummate paradox: the shock and awe of US power led to the failure of the unipolar project. Bush's 'Mission Accomplished' was quickly followed by insurgency against US and UK troops and by a civil war, killing hundreds of thousands of Iraqis and almost four and a half thousand American personnel. In Afghanistan, the Taliban had been removed from Kabul, but still held sway over much of the country. Throughout the world, the image of the US suffered.

The administration tried to recover ground with a 'Freedom Agenda' promoting Iraqi elections and taking advantage of uprisings from the former Soviet republics to the Middle East. The initiative was dragged down by the ongoing killings and disorder in Iraq: the case that was meant to be the demonstration of US superpower was the marker of the weakness of the president and the country. By December 2008, the image of the American president was of George W. Bush ducking in Baghdad as an Iraqi journalist threw both of his shoes at him.

A month later, Barack Obama was inaugurated as America's first Black president. In front of 1.5 million people on the Washington Mall, he promised the Hope and Change to deal with the paradox of insecurity: 'We reject as false the choice between our safety and our ideals . . . Our security emanates from the justness of our cause, the force of our example, the tempering qualities of humility and restraint.'

Obama promoted that cause in speeches throughout 2009: in Ankara, in Cairo, and, in Copenhagen, accepting the Nobel Peace Prize. But he soon found that the world's conflicts were beyond America. An agreement to reduce US troops in Iraq did not solve the problems of violence, discrimination and poor governance. The promise of the Arab Spring was bloodied by coups and repressive leaders who killed hundreds of thousands of their people. Vladimir Putin, covering up Russia's economic problems with an aggressive foreign policy, seized part of Ukraine, propped up Syria's deadly Assad regime, and pursued cyber-warfare to disrupt elections in other countries.

Obama did join the G8 and G20 countries in the saving of the global ship amid the Great Recession of 2008. His administration pushed through the economic stimulus for a partial rebound, and brought the prospect of national healthcare to the US for the first time.

But the historic promise of a black person in the White House was not easing polarisation. To the contrary, the invective and conspiracy theory was more poisonous. Social media and broadcast outlets portrayed Obama as a communist and a dangerous Muslim. A man named Donald Trump led a movement lying that Obama was born in Kenya and thus was ineligible to be president. The polemic was feeding anger and frustration amid the uneven recovery, adding to America's entrenched damage from gun violence.

First Lady Michelle Obama maintained the resolve of 'when they go low, we go high'. But Russia was going lower with its attack on the US electoral process, and Trump was exploiting division and supposed American enemies – China, Mexicans, immigrants – to propel his capture of the Republican nomination and then the White House.

Whereas his forty-five predecessors had portrayed the beacon of the US, Trump set a different tone in his inaugural address with his reference to 'American carnage'. And he pursued a different relationship within the executive. His own agencies were foes to be vanquished: he compared the CIA to Nazis, accused the FBI of a 'witch hunt' against him, and spoke of a 'deep state' plotting his overthrow.

Pursuing a presidency by Twitter, Trump sought authority through turmoil rather than consensus. He would oversee only one major bill, the December 2017 tax cuts. But through executive orders, he banned Muslims from entering the US, threatened millions of immigrants with deportation, shredded environmental legislation, imposed punitive tariffs on both allies and rivals, and withdrew from the Paris Accords on climate change and the Iran nuclear agreement.

Trump undermined the alliances that underpinned the Expansive Presidency after the Second World War. He spoke of withdrawal from an 'obsolete' NATO, insulted leaders such as Germany's Angela Merkel and Canada's Justin Trudeau, refused to sign G7 communiqués, and sought the break-up of the European Union. Even the UK was not immune: Trump's advisers conspired for the removal of Prime Minister Theresa May and her replacement by Boris Johnson.

In contrast, there was the constant of Trump's admiration for Russia's Putin. Even as he assailed China, he fawned over 'President for Life' Xi Jinping. And he moved from the threat of 'fire and fury' against North Korea with the pursuit of photo opportunities with its leader Kim Jong-un.

Trump survived the Russia scandal through his social media tactics of shouting 'hoax' and the protection of Republicans in Congress. Attorney General William Barr misrepresented and buried the Mueller Report, despite the Special Counsel's presentation of evidence for Trump's multiple obstructions of justice.

Trump survived the Ukraine scandal. He was impeached over his blackmail of Kyiv, suspending military aid unless it proclaimed 'dirt' on Democratic nominee Joe Biden. However, Majority Leader Mitch McConnell whipped Republican senators to ensure that Trump was not convicted.

But then Trump faced his most determined and deadly foe: the Coronavirus pandemic. He initially dismissed the threat, saying there would be 'zero deaths'. He recommended unproven drugs, ingestion of bleach and ultraviolet light. He blamed China. He called his scientific advisers, such as Dr Anthony Fauci and Dr Deborah Birx, 'idiots' and a 'disaster', and sidelined them for a neuroradiologist with no experience in epidemiology or public health. He insisted on the 'reopening' of the US even as cases and deaths soared.

Even after Trump contracted the virus and fell seriously ill in October, he did not change course or rhetoric. Instead, he said his 'immunity' and 'protective glow' showed that the virus had been defeated and sneered at Joe Biden, 'So now you have a president who doesn't have to hide in a basement, like his opponent.'

When Trump left office on 20 January 2021, almost five hundred thousand Americans were dead from Covid-19. Millions had been put out of work. And Biden was not in his basement but on the Capitol steps taking the oath of presidential office.

But Trump was not accepting the defeat. Exactly two weeks earlier, he told an audience from a podium outside the White House, 'We must stop the steal.' He called on them to march to the US Capitol where legislators were gathering to confirm Biden's victory in the Electoral College. 'We fight like hell. And if you don't fight like hell, you're not going to have a country any more.'

Thousands of Trump supporters followed the lead. They made their way to the Capitol, where a mock-gallows had been erected. Several hundred swept past Capitol Police and into the building, damaging and looting it as they chanted for the hanging of Vice-president Mike Pence and members of Congress. Five people died, including a police officer who was beaten.

America was arguably in its most serious crisis since the Civil War.

Rising Anew?

In 1858, an Illinois legislator named Abraham Lincoln quoted from the Gospel of Mark: 'A house divided against itself cannot stand.'

The stories of the US presidents are the story of an America that has stood, divided, and stood again. Now it is wobbling amid division.

President Biden has not only put 'unity' at the centre of his vision for America. He has proposed the most ambitious domestic programme since Franklin Roosevelt's New Deal of the 1930s: the American Rescue Plan to deal with Coronavirus and its economic consequences; the American Jobs Plan for infrastructure and economic development linked to measures against climate change; and the American Families Plan, hoping to raise half of US children out of poverty and to provide childcare and quality education for all. Plans are being developed for immigration, the environment, voting rights, and the social issues highlighted by mass marches in 2020.

But the Republican Party, now split between 'establishment' activists and Trumpists, threatens to obstruct all of this. And Donald Trump, looking to return to the White House, continues to push misinformation that the entire US system is rigged against him.

Joe Biden told a joint session of Congress on 28 April 2021: 'In America, we never, ever, ever stay down. Americans always get up. Today, that's what we're doing. America is rising anew. Choosing hope over fear, truth over lies and light over darkness.'

The story of the US, and its presidents, is still being written.

Scott Lucas is Emeritus Professor of US Politics at the University of Birmingham and Associate of the Clinton Institute, University College Dublin.

I

George Washington

30 April 1789 to 4 March 1797
Unaffiliated
Vice-president: John Adams

By Mitchell Reiss

Full name: George Washington
Born: 22 February 1732, Popes Creek, Virginia
Died: 14 December 1799, Mount Vernon, Virginia
Resting place: Mount Vernon, Virginia
Library/Museum: Mount Vernon, Virginia
Education: College of William & Mary
Married to: Martha Dandridge Custis, m. 1759 (1731–1802)
Children: No children with Martha; they together raised her two children John Parke Custis and Martha Parke Custis
Quotation: 'Having now finished the great work assigned me, I retire from the theatre of Action.' (Address to Congress resigning his military commission, 23 December 1783)

'FIRST IN WAR, First in peace and First in the hearts of his country-men.' No American leader has ever been eulogised in such effusive terms, or received such an outpouring of widespread and heartfelt lamentation, as greeted the death of George Washington. How do we account for such esteem, bordering on reverence, with which Washington was viewed during his lifetime?

He was a former British military officer who rebelled against his sovereign; a revolutionary general who lost most of his battles; the only president elected unanimously (twice), but without any impassioned speeches, memorable writings or original political philosophy to his credit; a man with virtually no formal education whose actions and behaviour nonetheless shaped a civic culture and created precedents that have lasted centuries; a slave-holder who fanatically pursued any who escaped to freedom and yet, alone among the Founding Fathers, manumitted his slaves; and an enigmatic paternal figure who had no offspring and whose lasting memorial is a spare, pale obelisk.

Today, it seems rather old-fashioned to believe that character is destiny. Yet at the centre of Washington's personal and political life, at the core of his success, evident in his relationships with his superiors, soldiers and social contemporaries, was the irreproachable character and actions he had cultivated, shaped and refined, starting from his youth. As an adolescent, he copied by hand all 110 sayings of the *Rules of Civility and Decent Behavior in Company and Conversation*. Far more than an exercise in penmanship, this diligence and discipline suggested that young George had ambitions that extended well beyond his modest upbringing at Ferry Farms and had cultivated the self-awareness that he needed to control his emotions, as well as the maturity to understand that his reputation would rest on how well he exhibited society's notions of honour and the behaviour of a 'complete gentleman'. He would quote these maxims throughout his life.

There were few early signs that Providence had reserved a special destiny for Washington, but he started with two potential advantages that he leveraged to his benefit. First, he was born in Virginia, the most expansive territory in colonial America, the most populous, and the wealthiest; it formed an ideal political base for an ambitious young man. Second, his father died when he was eleven, denying him the benefits of the formal education in England afforded his two older half-brothers; as the third-born son, ineligible to inherit property, he had to find his own way, initially surveying the then-frontier in the Ohio Valley, which led to a military commission in the Virginia Regiment at twenty-one.

Washington's early experiences in the field yielded lessons that fundamentally shaped the course of his later military career. Inexperienced and over-eager to establish his reputation, the young Washington badly botched his first assignment, was routed by the French and returned to Williamsburg with his reputation in tatters. Over repeated engagements along the frontier, however, he learned how to command troops and lead men heroically under fire. He also witnessed first-hand the effectiveness of irregular warfare employed by the Native Americans, tactics he used to great advantage during the Revolutionary War.

This chapter in Washington's life contains one of those 'What if?' questions on which history pivots. The British refused to grant Washington a commission by the king, which meant that Washington received less pay and was effectively outranked by British officers of similar or even lower grade. Ever mindful of his honour and reputation, Washington resented the slight, which contributed to his leaving military service in December 1758. But, would Washington have led King George III's forces against the rebellious colonists for a royal commission?

In January 1759 Washington married Martha Custis, one of Virginia's wealthiest widows. He now assumed the life of a gentleman-farmer at Mount Vernon and took on his civic duties as an elected official in Virginia's House of Burgesses.

Colonial America at this time, and especially Virginia, was a source of growing political activism. In the aftermath of the French and Indian War, Britain now shouldered additional costs of defending an expanded frontier, which it viewed as directly benefiting the American colonists. This led to London enacting a series of revenue-enhancing taxes and duties over the heads of the colonial legislatures and without benefit of any American representation in Parliament. Calls for American independence started to grow.

Washington's decision to oppose the crown was years in the making. He was a *reluctant* revolutionary; a profound fear of anarchy contended with his desire for liberty. In 1767, he wrote that recourse to arms in defence of liberty should be 'the dernier resort'. Only a full seven years later, the Coercive (or 'Intolerable') Acts, followed by the unfolding crisis at Lexington and Concord, the first military engagements of the American Revolutionary War, finally forced him to choose between the terrifying disorder of revolution or the stability of despotism. Still, he wrote to a friend that spring, 'The once happy and peaceful plains of America are either to be drenched with blood or inhabited by slaves. Sad alternative!'

Washington's deep investment – politically, financially, philo-sophically – in maintaining order was exactly what made the Continental Congress feel safe in placing 'Virginia's most distin-guished soldier' at the head of an army of unruly rebels at the age of forty-three.

It is easy from today's remove to think that the victory of the American colonists over the British was inevitable, but it looked anything but a sure thing at the time. Indeed, the idea that Washington would prevail, leading a ragtag collection of citizen-militia and defeating the greatest military power in the world, commanded by some of Britain's ablest generals and most distin-guished admirals, bordered on the preposterous. In 1776, the revolutionary cause could only count on the allegiance of roughly one-third of the colonists, with one-third remaining loyal to the British and one-third not supporting either side. The British had absolute control of the seas for the first three years of the conflict, until France officially entered on the side of the colonists after the Battle of Saratoga.

The long odds against the Continental Army ensured that self-doubt, uncertainty and frustration were Washington's constant companions during the eight and a half years he served as commander in chief. Only days before his famous crossing of the Delaware River, he wrote that 'the game is pretty near up'. While encamping at Valley Forge the following winter, he confided to a friend that the army's only options were to 'starve, dissolve or disperse' unless the soldiers were resupplied immediately. That winter Washington lost almost one-quarter of his troops to typhus and dysentery, while soldiers fit for fighting fell by half.

The passionately pro-American pamphleteer, Thomas Paine, had earlier warned against the 'summer soldier and sunshine patriot' who would desert the cause when the going got tough, or worse. He anticipated critics in Congress, who now conspired to replace Washington, which plunged morale among the troops, as did the infamous treachery of Benedict Arnold. Roaring inflation undermined the rebel economy and contributed to mutinies by Pennsylvania and New Jersey Continentals over back pay in January 1781. Less than six months before the ultimate victory over General Cornwallis at Yorktown in October 1781, Washington maintained that 'we are at the end of our tether . . .'

And yet Washington persevered, holding fast to his one big idea, namely, to preserve the Continental Army by avoiding a set-piece battle with the British. Historians have referred to him as 'the American Fabius', after the Roman commander who avoided direct engagement with Hannibal's superior numbers during the Second Punic War. And when victory had been secured over the British, Washington resigned his military commission and returned to Mount Vernon to resume his life as a gentleman-farmer. When King George III was told of Washington's action, the disbelieving monarch commented: 'If he did, he would be the greatest man in the world.'

The new United States of America were initially governed by the Articles of Confederation, which established a collection of independent states loosely tethered to a weak central government. It soon proved unworkable, most notably with the inability of Congress to suppress Shays' Rebellion (ironically sparked by new taxes) in western Massachusetts. A Constitutional Convention was convened in Philadelphia in the summer of 1787, where a new constitution was drafted with much stronger central authorities, including federal courts, the power of taxation and a president as chief executive.

Washington was the consensus choice as the first president. But his understanding of honour and gentlemanly behaviour meant that he could not openly campaign for the position; besides, such ambitious public electioneering might arouse anxieties over the type of tyrannical behaviour against which the Revolutionary War had been fought. That Washington had no children of his own also reassured those who feared that the first president might launch a hereditary line of succession.

Washington assumed office in New York City at the end of April 1789, with the government renting out cramped accommodations for him, his staff and his personal retinue. (No accommodations were provided for Vice-president John Adams.) Congress had existed since 1774, but the presidency was entirely new. Washington actually had employed more people at Mount Vernon than existed in his entire executive branch. Everything was *de novo*; each action, or its absence, created a precedent. He quickly established the custom of taking the oath of office outdoors, delivering an inaugural address (deciding not to wear a military uniform), and hosting a gala party that evening. That autumn he declared the first Thanksgiving Day holiday; a few months later he delivered the first State of the Union address, which became an annual ritual.

Washington was well aware of the fragile bonds that attached the former colonies to each other. The financial interests and manufacturing strength of the north, personified by his Treasury Secretary, Alexander Hamilton, stood in tension with the more agrarian-based economy of the South, whose interests were defended by the Virginians, led by his Secretary of State, Thomas Jefferson, and James Madison. A related issue was the vexing institution of slavery, on which there were clashing opinions and irreconcilable policies. His two terms would be marked by deliberate efforts to remain above the partisan political fray, ensure cooperation and unite disparate factions at home. He was not always successful.

Washington was also aware of America's military weakness relative to the Old World empires, which still had interests in, and harboured designs on, the New World. (General fears of a standing army meant that the US had a mere 840 soldiers when Washington became president; there was no dedicated navy.) The international environment was far from serene; three months after Washington's inauguration, the Bastille was stormed, fuelling the French Revolution. (Lafayette sent Washington the key to the Bastille, which can be viewed today on a wall at Mount Vernon.) A slave rebellion erupted in Santo Domingo (Haiti) in 1781. American ships and sailors, no longer protected by the British, were seized on the high seas during all of Washington's presidency. (Congress paid $2 million in annual tribute to Barbary pirates to ensure they would not attack US vessels along the North African coast; this policy was only overturned when Jefferson became president.) America's weakness reinforced Washington's natural caution and self-restraint; as president he would exhibit a reluctance to have the United States become entangled with European rivalries that could implicate it in a conflict.

Washington also established precedents far more consequential than the ceremonial. One was to assert the president's primary authority in foreign affairs. The Founders had thought the legislative branch supreme, as a check on executive power, which was only vaguely outlined in the Constitution. A foreign policy debate soon arose over the words 'advice and consent'. In June 1789, Washington personally appeared before the Senate to present a treaty and have appointed three commissioners to negotiate with the Creek nation, a Native American tribe. The Senate insisted on understanding more about the issue before it would offer its advice, and then perhaps its consent. Washington refused to submit to this process and angrily left the chamber. It marked a turning point. According to the historian Ron Chernow, 'Washington decided that he would henceforth communicate with that body on paper rather than in person and trim "advice and consent" to the word *consent.*' From that point forward, the executive branch would maintain its lead role in determining the shape and conduct of American foreign policy, while Congress would be reduced to the subordinate, if independent, role of critic.

Much of Washington's first term was devoted to establishing the system of government finance ingeniously developed by Hamilton, trying to pacify the vehement opposition this provoked in Jefferson, and refereeing between the two.

Hamilton believed that the health of the federal government, and the ultimate prosperity and security of the country, depended on solid credit. His plan was for a central bank of the federal government to assume the debt that the states had incurred and then repay creditors over time, thus creating investment capital and a single national currency. Jefferson and Madison were staunchly opposed, fearing both for indebted Southern landowners and the creation of institutions that looked similar to Britain's (which was true). Washington directed Hamilton, Jefferson and Madison to work out

7

a compromise. The result gave Hamilton a national bank and his financial system. In return, the Virginians got the nation's capital moved to the Potomac River; it would travel from New York to Philadelphia for ten years, and then to a federal district on the Potomac, with Washington having the power to select the precise site.

This compromise was only a brief hiatus between rounds, as Jefferson continued to spar with Hamilton, secretly using proxies to undermine his fiscal policies and impugn his integrity. Washington had to devote increasing amounts of his time and declining energy to try to reconcile his two unruly Cabinet members. In the end, he sided with Hamilton. As Chernow notes, 'That Washington now identified with northern finance [and] commerce . . . would have major consequences for American history. Had he sided with Jefferson and Madison, it might have deepened irrevocably the cleavage between North and South and opened an unbridgeable chasm seventy years before the Civil War.'

Such Cabinet squabbling contributed to Washington's desire not to serve a second presidential term. By 1792, the man was physically and mentally exhausted. He admitted to Madison of 'memory lapses, poor vision and growing deafness'. Preserving his reputation was also paramount in his considerations; he was concerned that people would think him presumptuous to expect a second term, or that, for 'having tasted the sweets of office, he could not do without them'. Washington even tasked Madison with drafting a farewell address for him, despite relentless appeals from all quarters that he remain to lead the federal government. In the end, he determined that retiring from public life would cause more harm to his reputation than continuing, despite the cost to his personal health and happiness.

The first major crisis in Washington's second term involved America's posture towards Britain and France, which was now aflame with revolutionary passions. In January 1793, King Louis XVI was guillotined, and the following month France declared war against Britain. On which side should the United States stand: with its fraternal ally now championing a worldwide democratic revolution or with the new nation's largest trading partner?

Demonstrating characteristic self-restraint, Washington privileged the national interests of the young country over any sentimentality for France's aid to the colonial cause during the Revolutionary War. America would remain neutral in this conflict. His declaration warned Americans against 'committing, aiding or abetting hostilities', stating that they should 'pursue a conduct friendly and impartial towards the belligerent powers'. Significantly, Congress was not consulted, with Washington once more asserting the primacy of the executive over the legislative branch in foreign affairs.

American neutrality did not extinguish all friction between the United States and Britain, which still occupied eight forts manned by a thousand troops on territory claimed by the United States. Britain also continued to seize American ships and impress American sailors on the high seas. In May 1794, Washington sent John Jay to London to negotiate. The terms Jay won included Britain abandoning its forts and allowing a limited amount of trade with the British West Indies. In return, Britain gained very low taxes on goods exported to the US while not having to extend reciprocal privileges; Southerners did not receive any compensation for slaves who had left with the British after the Revolutionary War. The Jay Treaty was widely viewed within the government as strongly favourable to the British and greeted outside the government with violent protests after it became public. Yet Washington supported it, recognising that the unbalanced treaty, like many international agreements, reflected the genuine disparity in military and economic power between the two countries.

The Jay Treaty had both short-term and long-term significance. In the short term, Washington avoided a war with Britain that the new nation could ill afford. Longer term, Washington's refusal to honour the legislature's request for the correspondence on Jay's diplomatic negotiations created the enduring precedent of 'executive privilege'. In 1795, Washington's emissary secured from Spain a far less controversial agreement. The new western border of an expanding United States would be the Mississippi River, on which Americans would have the right to navigate and ship goods for trade in New Orleans.

Washington faced other challenges closer to home. Hamilton's plans to reduce the government's debt led to new taxes on distilled spirits. Anger erupted in western Pennsylvania in the summer of

1794, as the 'Whiskey Rebellion' turned out the largest force of armed men opposed to the government since the revolution. The president insisted on adherence to the rule of law and decided to personally command the federal troops, the only time in American history that a sitting president would lead soldiers into conflict. His public show of force, combined with deft diplomacy, defused the situation without any violence; he later exhibited leniency when the ringleaders were brought to trial.

There was little chance that the sixty-four-year-old Washington would stand for a third term. His farewell address counselled his 'Friends and Fellow Citizens' to remain united and warned them to 'steer clear of permanent alliances with any portion of the foreign world'. He then begged the country's forgiveness for any errors he had made, or 'faults of incompetent abilities', a nod to the lessons on humility and modest behaviour he had derived decades earlier from *Rules of Civility*. His departure from office cemented one last precedent: presidents would subsequently serve only two terms, until Franklin Roosevelt in 1940. And he won one last royal tribute: Washington was 'the greatest character of the age,' observed King George III.

A summary of his presidential accomplishments clearly warrants this praise. According to Chernow, Washington

> had restored American credit and assumed state debt; created a bank, a mint, a coast guard, a customs service, and a diplomatic corps . . . maintained peace at home and abroad; inaugurated a navy, bolstered the army, and shored up the coastal defenses and infrastructure; proved that the country could regulate commerce and negotiate binding treaties; protected frontier settlers, subdued Indian uprisings, and established law and order amid rebellion, scrupulously adhering to the letter of the Constitution . . . Most of all he had shown a disbelieving world that republican government could prosper without being spineless or disorderly or reverting to authoritarian rule.

Chernow rightly credits Washington not only for what he achieved, but for what he avoided.

For Washington, the personal was political. Washington's personal self-restraint was extended to the presidency. (As one perceptive friend observed in a letter to him, 'you possess an empire over yourself'.) He gave shape to a system of checks and balances to ensure that the United States would never be subject to a new dictatorship, which was a persistent fear of anti-monarchists such as Jefferson and Madison. He instilled confidence in his fellow Americans that both order and freedom could live in harmony; indeed, that they could reinforce and advance each other.

After more than twenty years of almost continuous service to his country, Washington finally was able to retire to life 'under his own vine and fig tree' as a Virginian gentleman-farmer. But his final years at Mount Vernon were far from restful, as he had to manage a collection of farms that had deteriorated in his absence, entertain a constant parade of visitors, deal with endless financial troubles, and wrestle with the original American sin of slavery as it impacted on his day-to-day operations at Mount Vernon. He was also wounded and distressed by the spiteful criticism of some of his previous friends and allies, most notably Thomas Jefferson and John Adams, who were now jockeying to establish their own claims to power and influence.

In December 1799, Washington took ill after he rode his horse for a five-hour tour of his estates during foul weather. Medical science at the time suggested that his doctors bleed him, which probably hastened his death. He died in his bed at Mount Vernon on 14 December, aged sixty-seven, and was buried in a crypt on the grounds, which visitors can see today.

From a very young age, George Washington's reputation had mattered deeply to him; sensitive to personal slights, he went to great lengths throughout his personal and professional life to ensure that he not only acted honourably and properly, but also was seen to act in this manner. (In *Hamilton, The Musical*, Washington's anxiety over how he will be remembered is perfectly captured by his character's song, 'History Has its Eyes on You'.) For example, he tried for years to track down the culprit responsible for 'spurious letters' that had first appeared in Britain in 1777 and had him 'confessing' his doubts about the merits of America's War for Independence. We also know from his own presidential correspondence how sensitive he was to criticism from the rollicking media at the time, which often reflected factional political competition and pro-France sentiments.

Every generation interprets its history anew. A year after Washington's death, the parson Mason Weems indulged in some early hagiography by publishing an account claiming that the young George Washington had chopped down his father's cherry tree, but could not tell a lie to cover up the deed. The moral lesson for the youth of America could not have been clearer. During the Civil War, the Italian artist Brumidi painted the fresco, *The Apotheosis of Washington*, in the eye of the dome in the rotunda of the United States Capitol, depicting a benevolent Washington surrounded by the goddesses Liberty and Victory and thirteen maidens, several of whom have their backs turned. When most contemporary Americans have thought about Washington, if they have thought about him at all, it was of the man with a sour expression captured in the Gilbert Stuart portrait on the $1 bill. (Washington had just had a new set of dentures implanted before the sitting; he had lost all but one tooth by that time.)

How should Washington's legacy best be viewed today?

Arguably, Washington has become *more* interesting to Americans in recent years as they witness failed revolutions overseas, and experience at home the Black Lives Matter movement, the *New York Times*'s 1619 Project, and the searing divisiveness of the Trump years.

A decade after the violence and chaos that has littered the Middle East in the wake of the Arab Spring, after the failed colour revolutions in the former Soviet space, after the crushing of dissent in Hong Kong, Myanmar and elsewhere, and given the overall decline in freedom globally during the past decade and a half, we can better appreciate in a fresh light the role that Washington played in America's initial fight for freedom and subsequent efforts to establish a representative government. For any revolution to succeed without dissolving into either anarchy or despotism, it needs leaders like Washington who can balance the inherent human desires for both liberty and stability, and harness revolutionary energies while also holding them in check. The magnitude of his achievements grows with time.

However, Washington has not escaped the harsh spotlight on

racism that has intensified recently on all the Founding Fathers who owned slaves. We know that he pursued with a vengeance any of his slaves who ran away. As president, he extended funds and arms to the French government to suppress the rebellion in Santo Domingo and even made a personal donation to help the white colonists who were fleeing from the violence there. He held on to his slaves throughout his lifetime.

Washington privately understood that slavery was immoral and sinful, and contrary to the ideals expressed in America's founding documents: the Declaration of Independence, Constitution and Bill of Rights. (He also had first-hand experience as commander in chief of the Continental Army, where Blacks comprised approximately 10 per cent of the rank-and-file soldiers.) He toyed with the then-extraordinary idea of partitioning his farms into four estates that he would rent out; the managers of these properties would then free the hundred and seventy or so slaves Washington owned and hire them as labourers; nothing ultimately came of this plan. At the end of the day, Washington could not abandon a system of free labour that he depended upon for his wealth and social standing; he may have hoped that slavery might end, but he tolerated its perpetuation.

And yet Washington never sold any of his slaves, which he knew would devastate their families. There is also no evidence that he ever slept with any of them. And alone among the Founding Fathers, Washington not only freed his slaves upon his death, but also established a fund to educate and prepare them with vocational skills so that they could sustain their freedom. Although his holding people in bondage is abhorrent by modern standards, Washington was nonetheless far more progressive on the issue of slavery than many of his contemporaries.

The past four years of the Trump administration, often distinguished by vulgar, belligerent and unprincipled presidential behaviour, and punctuated by two impeachment trials, also provide a lens through which we can better appreciate Washington's integrity. Washington's compelling sense of patriotism, his resilience and determination in the face of adversity, and his personal rectitude and self-restraint, all seem like virtues from a very different time and place. How fortuitous that he exemplified all these qualities at the birth of a new nation! Gazing back across the centuries, Washington's largest contribution to contemporary political life may be that he set the gold standard for presidential norms and public comportment. His example should always remind Americans of how essential character is to public service.

Mitchell Reiss is the former CEO of The Colonial Williamsburg Foundation and president of Washington College. He has served in the US government at the National Security Council and at the State Department, where he held the rank of ambassador.

2

John Adams

4 March 1797 to 4 March 1801
Federalist
Vice-president: Thomas Jefferson

By Daniel Forrester

Full name: John Adams
Born: 19 October 1735, Braintree (now Quincy), Massachusetts
Died: 4 July 1826, Quincy, Massachusetts
Resting place: United First Parish Church, Quincy, Massachusetts
Library/Museum: Quincy, Massachusetts
Education: Harvard College
Married to: Abigail Smith, m. 1764 (1744–1818)
Children: Six: John Quincy Adams, Abigail 'Nabby' Adams, Charles Adams, Thomas Boylston Adams, Susanna Adams (died after one year), Elizabeth Adams (stillborn)
Quotation(s): 'A government of laws, not men.'

JOHN ADAMS WAS born on 19 October 1735 in Braintree, Massachusetts, now called Quincy. The lawyer, diplomat, father, beloved husband, catalyst for American independence, two-time vice-president, and second president of the United States was raised – with his two younger brothers, Peter and Elihu – by parents of Puritan faith with no formal education. Adams's elite education would stand in stark contrast and propel his life to heights his parents could never have imagined.

Adams was a man easy to admire from afar, but difficult to like in person. He was a complicated man and fostered strife with many, including those he respected most. The spectrum of often para-doxical descriptions of him demonstrates the range of feelings he elicited. He was at once earnest, scholarly, fair, articulate, principled, inspiring, loving and tender, but he was also combative, crusty, despised, bitter, tactless, a blowhard, condescending and egotistical.

He is remembered in the birth of American history, but rarely extolled given the company of men whose personalities and accom-plishments fit more neatly into the fondness and reverence captured by the term 'Founding Fathers'. Yet when history needed a logical and persistent catalyst to galvanise scattered political will towards revolution, Adams rose as a courageous champion of freedom.

Adams's respected father, John Adams Sr., was a deacon and a farmer. Adams's mother, Susanna Boylston, was 'honored and beloved'. In his definitive biography of Adams, historian David McCullough notes John Adams Sr. was his son's idol: 'It was his father's honesty, his father's independent spirit and love of country, Adams said, that were his lifelong inspiration.' John Adams revered his father and the values that defined his life: 'He was the honestest Man I ever knew. In Wisdom, Piety, Benevolence and Charity in proportion to his Education and Sphere of Life, I have never seen his Superiour.'

The values Adams's parents instilled in him helped form his lifelong opposition to slavery. McCullough states that 'Adams was the only one of the Founding Fathers to never own a slave as a matter of principle. He saw it as an evil.'

Adams was an astute learner and showed his combativeness early while attending Braintree's Latin School, where he despised the headmaster, Joseph Cleverly. Adams thought he would follow in his father's footsteps as a farmer and leave school behind, but his father saw the value in education and forced his son to remain. The young Adams convinced his father to find an alternative headmaster, under the tutelage of whom the fifteen-year-old Adams was quickly declared ready for college within eighteen months. He was admitted to Harvard University, where he discovered his enduring love of learning. Once settled, he wrote, 'I discovered books and read forever.'

Throughout most of Adams's time at Harvard, his father hoped he would become a clergyman. However, young Adams recognised his 'faculty for public speaking', having joined a debate club that sparked an interest in his becoming a lawyer. After graduation, Adams taught for a short while and considered a medical career, but 'after attending several sessions of the local court in Worcester, Massachusetts, he felt himself "irresistibly impelled" to the law'. In 1755, he began studying as an apprentice under Worcester's leading attorney, James Putnam.

In 1758, Adams earned a master's degree in law from Harvard University, was admitted to the bar, and moved to Boston to begin his career. His work was slow at the beginning, and he lost his first case. The John Adams Historical Society captures his progress in its online chronicle of his life: 'Instead of waiting for business to come to him, he sought it. He campaigned to reduce the number of inns in Braintree, and he succeeded.' His diary shows that around this time his caseload began to increase, mostly related to inheritance issues. His first victory before a jury was in the autumn of 1760. Ensuing successes improved his confidence; as he wrote in his diary, 'I was too incautious and unartful in my proceedings, but practice makes perfect.'

Adams soon would meet the love of his life, but not before courting Hannah Quincy, the daughter of wealthy Colonel Josiah Quincy. Adams dreamt about the coquettish Hannah when not with her, and one spring night he prepared to ask her to marry him. Fate would intervene as Hannah's cousins 'suddenly burst into the room and the moment passed, never to be recovered'. Lost in love, Adams was forced to rethink the relationship and concluded they were not a good fit.

Adams first compared Abigail to Hannah and found little in

Abigail, her sisters or her parents that appealed to him, but he gradually grew quite fond of the family and realised the brashness of his initial assessment. They were a loving family known to Adams since childhood and Abigail's intelligence, wit and fondness for poetry drew him to her. Although they took their courtship slowly, Abigail quickly discovered strengths in Adams that made her fall deeply in love. From the outset, some biographers consider Adams's choice to wed Abigail as his most important life decision.

They married and had six children, one of whom died in infancy and another was stillborn.

Adams continued in his law practice, but inched towards politics. His opposition to the Stamp Act in 1765 would bring him to prominence and begin his rise as a revolutionary. After a costly seven-year war with France, the British needed revenue, so they imposed tariffs on all 'paper documents' across the colonies through the Stamp Act. The scope of the tariffs was vast and included every paper type, from deeds and contracts to playing cards. The costs attached were as high as ten pounds. Incensed, Adams penned 'The Braintree Instructions', which was read in the General Court of Massachusetts, printed, and shared throughout the colonies. Within his analysis, and for the first time in American history, Adams asserted the 'fundamental principle of the Constitution that no free man should be subjected to any tax to which he had not given his consent, in person or by proxy'. Much to the delight of Adams and other early patriots, the British reversed the Stamp Act. However, his writing and arguments summoned the ire of the British and helped galvanise New Englanders towards revolt.

Tensions continued to mount in Massachusetts as the British increased troop levels to maintain order amid growing signs of turmoil. In 1770, a Boston mob surrounded a small group of British soldiers who, while under assault, opened fire and killed five people. The soldiers were accused of murder and brought to trial. No lawyers wanted to take their case for fear it might destroy their status and livelihood. Despite his growing anger towards the British, Adams accepted the case because he believed every man was entitled to a defence. The thirty-four-year-old Adams felt a sense of duty to the law and knew he was stepping into a firestorm. Rumours swirled that he had been bribed to take the case. With Abigail pregnant at home, he knew taking the case could have grave consequences and feared for his family's safety.

Adams managed to save six of the eight soldiers from prosecution by arguing self-defence and asserting they were acting on orders from military leadership, and he secured lesser penalties for the remaining officers. He closed the case by saying, 'Facts are stubborn things; and whatever may be our wishes, our inclinations, or the dictates of our passions, they cannot alter the state of facts and evidence.' Adams remained proudest of his work in these trials throughout his life. In old age, he reflected on this event as: 'One of the most gallant, generous, manly, and disinterested actions of my whole life, and one of the best pieces of service I ever rendered my country.'

As a rising leader within the independence movement, Adams was elected to join the First Continental Congress as a representative from Massachusetts in 1774. This Congress met in response to the imposition of 'Intolerable Acts' by the British. The acts were a direct response by the British to the Boston Tea Party. The acts removed self-governing power that colonists took for granted, and many saw their imposition as a violation of the original charters and colonists' natural rights.

Over the next few years, including during the Second Continental Congress, Adams's peers dubbed him the 'Atlas of Independence' following the publication of his patriotic *Novanglus* essays. 'Novanglus', meaning 'New Englander', was the pseudonym Adams wrote under for the *Boston Gazette*. Within the essays, Adams defined the American position on the 'natural rights of individuals and the rights enjoyed by all colonial governments under British law'.

Adams's technical prowess in translating and interpreting the emerging government's work into a new government based in law, principle and structure would be overshadowed by the language, ideas and vision that Thomas Jefferson crafted into the Declaration of Independence. Biographer R.B. Bernstein captures this poignantly: 'Unlike Jefferson, Adams did not write the words or the music of the American democratic epic; he missed the chance to define his own vision of American national identity and values.'

Adams was selected as a member of the 'Committee of Five', which was tasked with drafting and presenting the Declaration of

Independence. Roger Sherman of Connecticut, Robert Livingston of New York, Benjamin Franklin of Pennsylvania, and Thomas Jefferson of Virginia joined him.

The reasons Jefferson was chosen over Adams to write the Declaration's first draft are unclear. There were no meeting minutes from the Committee of Five's proceedings. In later years, Jefferson recalled that Adams was first asked to write it. Adams recalled the assignment differently, but he would have had little time to do so because he was serving concurrently on twenty-three Second Continental Congress sub-committees. While Adams was ambitious and skilled enough to write a draft, he thought Jefferson's talents were superior. He also knew a New Englander could not carry the respect of the more powerful Virginia delegation. Adams recalled in correspondence with Jefferson, 'Reason first: You [Jefferson] are a Virginian and a Virginian ought to appear at the head of this business. Reason second: I am obnoxious, suspected, and unpopular. Reason third: You can write ten times better than I can.'

One moment in the history of the Declaration is nicely dramatised in the mini-series *John Adams*. This well-regarded interpretation of Adams's life draws heavily on the voluminous records he left and the skilful synthesis of historians. In one scene, Adams and Franklin are reading Jefferson's first draft of the Declaration in a small room in Philadelphia. This scene shows the power of political compromise and what consensus truly is. While fiction, it illustrates Adams subordinating his pride in authorship in search of something much larger than himself. For a moment Adams's and Jefferson's brewing rivalry subsides.

As Jefferson watches nervously, we hear and see,

> **John Adams:** 'This [the Declaration] is something altogether unexpected. Not just a declaration of our independence but the rights of all men. This is well said, sir. Very, very well said.'
> **Benjamin Franklin:** 'We hold these truths to be sacred and undeniable that all men are created equal . . . etc., etc. Sacred and undeniable! Smacks of the pulpit. These truths are "self-evident," are they not?'
> **Thomas Jefferson:** 'Perhaps.'
> **Franklin:** 'Self-evident, then.'

Adams: 'Self-evident.'

Franklin: 'Do not mistake me, sir. I share your sentiment.'

Jefferson: 'Every single word was preciously chosen; I assure you of that, Dr. Franklin.'

Franklin: 'Yes, but yours will not be the only hand in this document. It cannot be. They [the Congress] will try to mangle it, and they may succeed.'

Adams: 'There may be expressions which I would not have inserted had I drawn it up. But I will defend every word of it.'

Although the debate was vigorous in Congress, promoting the Declaration was left to Adams. On 1 July 1776, he took to the floor to deliver the most important speech of his life. McCullough described him as 'logical, positive, sensitive to the historic importance of the moment, and, looking into the future, saw a new nation, a new time'.

No record exists of his remarks, but Adams later described the moment as he imagined the impact on generations to come: 'Objects of the most stupendous magnitude, measures in which the lives and liberties of millions, born and unborn are most essentially interested, are now before us. We are in the very midst of revolution, the most complete, unexpected, and remarkable of any in the history of the world.'

When the Librarian of Congress asked McCullough in 2014 about Adams's legacy, he stated Adams was never afraid to be 'in the arena' (a phrase often said by Teddy Roosevelt, and later the title of a book by Richard Nixon). McCullough continues: 'Unlike Jefferson who never wanted to put his voice in public but rather through written words, it was Adams that forcefully put the Declaration of Independence over the line on the floor of the Congress. And he was damn good at it.'

While Adams was in Philadelphia, Abigail struggled to raise their children. Against the backdrop of revolution, she often made crucial decisions without any input from Adams. An outbreak of highly contagious smallpox forced her to imagine exposing her children to the disease through inoculation. She and Adams believed in the science of the day, although few understood it. The risks paid off, and she eventually wrote to her worried husband, 'This is a Beautiful

Morning. I came here with all my treasure of children, have passed through one of the most terrible Diseases to which human Nature is subject, and not one of us is wanting.'

Adams was sent to France in 1778 to seek an alliance. He was to join Benjamin Franklin, at the time the most famous American abroad. Unbeknown to Adams, Franklin had already signed a treaty before Adams arrived, which irritated Adams considerably. Their relationship would splinter further when Congress chose Franklin as the sole diplomat to France. Adams still managed to teach himself French on the long and dangerous passage and to send many letters to Abigail. Her steady affection and guidance were constant sources of balance. In a letter dated April 1778, he wrote, 'My dearest Friend I am so sensible of the Difficulty of conveying Letters safe, to you, that I am afraid to write, any Thing more than to tell you that after the Fatigues and Dangers of my Voyage, and Journey, I am here in Health.'

In 1779, Congress nominated Adams as minister plenipotentiary to begin negotiations with the British in France to end the war. Adams took his sons Charles and John Quincy with him on the trip. The war would not formally end until the Treaty of Paris in 1783. Within the treaty, shrewdly negotiated in part by Adams, Britain recognised American independence and even fishing rights along the New England coast – a priority for Adams because of its impact on the local economy.

In 1785, Adams was chosen as the first American Minister to Great Britain, where he was granted an audience with King George III. Towards the end of their brief meeting, King George said to the nervous Adams that he had been told Adams was not 'the most attached of all [his] countrymen to the manners of France'. Adams replied, 'That opinion, sir, is not mistaken. I must avow to your Majesty, I have no attachment but to my own country.' The king replied, 'An honest man will never have any other.'

In the 1789 presidential race, Adams came in second to the unanimously selected Washington – a testament to Adams's relative popularity. Consequently, Adams served as America's first vice-president from 1789 to 1797. As vice-president, Adams's main role was to serve as leader of the Senate, only using his vote to break legislative ties. He despised the job. In a letter to Abigail, he complained: 'But my Country has in its Wisdom contrived for me, the most insignificant Office that ever the Invention of Man contrived, or his Imagination conceived: and as I can do neither good nor Evil, I must be born away by Others and meet the common Fate.'

Adams narrowly won the 1796 election against Jefferson, the Democratic-Republican candidate, by an Electoral College vote of 71–68. He served as second president of the United States with Jefferson as his vice-president. Adams ran as a member of the Federalist Party, one of the two prominent political parties at the time, the other being the Democratic-Republicans. The Federalists believed in stronger centralised government over states' rights, higher tariffs, a national bank, and a US dollar; they also emphasised commercial and diplomatic harmony with Britain. The Democratic-Republicans, led by Jefferson and James Madison and composed of mostly New York and Southern farmers, supported states' rights, a weaker central government, and a stricter interpretation of the Constitution.

It was the dawn of political parties, and their stark personality differences struck a schism between Adams and Jefferson. That tension would cast a shadow on their relationship until the ends of their political careers. Merely a few months into Adams's presidency, Jefferson noted to a French diplomat that President Adams was 'distrustful, obstinate, excessively vain, and takes no counsel from anyone'. Weeks later, Adams shared his personal contempt for Jefferson, writing privately that Jefferson had 'a mind soured, yet seeking for popularity, and eaten to a honeycomb with ambition, yet weak, confused, uninformed, and ignorant'.

Adams was tested early in his presidency. He led the nation through the XYZ Affair, which highlighted the young nation's struggles with the traditional powers of Old Europe. As a remnant of unresolved diplomatic tensions during the Washington administration, French forces began attacking American ships and seizing cargo. To set things right with France and make the seas safe again for American ships, Adams sent three commissioners to France: Charles Pinckney, the US senator and Minister to France; John Marshall, a lawyer from Virginia and future Supreme Court Justice; and Elbridge Gerry, future vice-president under Madison.

When the three commissioners arrived, three agents of Foreign Minister Charles Maurice de Talleyrand met them. Instead of giving their names in their official report, the commissioners labelled these men X, Y and Z, hence the scandal's name. The French agents demanded a $250,000 bribe to meet with Talleyrand and a $12,000,000 loan. Political bribes were normal at the time, but this type of bribe was considered insulting and preposterous. Pinckney's response to the men was, 'No, no, not a sixpence!'

When the commissioner's report to Congress was made public, Americans were outraged. Even the Democratic-Republicans, who had staunchly supported the French, joined in the rallying cry: 'Millions for defense, but not one cent for tribute.' Many people wanted war, especially Adams's fellow Federalists, but Adams deftly avoided open conflict with the far more powerful France. Some described his leadership during this time as his finest moment – doing the right thing despite overwhelming public scrutiny.

If the XYZ Affair showed his diplomatic skills and temperament, Adams's signing into law the Alien and Sedition Acts deeply harmed his presidency. The Alien Enemies Act allowed the government to arrest and deport citizens of an enemy nation during war, and the Alien Friends Act allowed the government to deport any non-citizen who plotted against the government during peacetime. The Sedition Act, the more controversial of the two acts, criminalised people who spoke out against the Federalist government or the president. These acts targeted immigrants and political opponents of the Adams administration, triggering public indignation. As historian R.B. Bernstein describes it: 'The controversial acts of the Adams presidency – signing the Alien and Sedition Acts into law and enforcing the Sedition Act – made him look like an enemy of the freedom of speech and press.'

Adams faced a tough re-election campaign in 1800. The Federalists were severely split over his foreign policy. Adams fired two members of his Cabinet, the Secretary of State and the Secretary of War, because they failed to support his foreign policies. The Democratic-Republicans nominated Jefferson and Aaron Burr as their candidates. During the divisive campaign, the Federalists depicted Jefferson as a godless nonbeliever, whereas the Democratic-Republicans cast Adams as a monarchist.

On 1 November 1800, the day of the election, Adams arrived in the new capital city of Washington, DC, to take up a short, inaugural residency in the White House. The unfinished building was cold, damp, dirty, and far from the beacon of democracy the building now represents. Adams wrote home, 'Before I end my letter, I pray Heaven to bestow the best of Blessings on this House and all that shall hereafter inhabit it. May none but honest and wise Men ever rule under this roof.'

As American trade and influence grew, so did tensions with the British and French. Adams signed into law the creation of the US Navy and authorised the strengthening of the US Army. Adams managed to convince Washington to come out of retirement to oversee this military expansion. Adams avoided war with France by securing the Treaty of Mortefontaine in 1800, but this high-profile diplomatic win that finally secured much-needed peace with France came too late to engender goodwill during the election. Jefferson would defeat him.

Adams was the first outgoing president to skip an incoming president's inauguration. Adams quietly left the White House at 4:00 a.m. on 4 March 1801, the morning of President-Elect Jefferson's inauguration. The pain of the loss and the recent death of his son Charles surely weighed on his decision.

Historian C. James Taylor captures the contradictions and conflicts that consistently followed Adams: 'On the one hand, his aloofness and refusal to enter directly into political conflict probably undermined his effectiveness and cost him his reelection in 1800. His stubborn independence left him politically isolated and alone. Even his own Cabinet opposed his policies much of the time. He valued no one's opinion half as much as his own, except for that of his wife, Abigail.'

After his tumultuous presidency, Adams retired to Quincy, Massachusetts, to focus on securing his legacy. There, he spent time with his beloved Abigail; mostly managed to avoid politics; and relished watching his son, John Quincy Adams, grow in prominence and eventually become president in 1824. Two of the Adams's three sons were alcoholics – something he never wrote about nor confronted in the thousands of documents and records that survive him.

Abigail, John's wife, best friend and source of strength, died of typhoid fever on 28 October 1818. They were married for fifty-four years. Upon her death, Adams wrote, 'I wish I could lay down beside her and die too.'

In retirement and no longer in the rough-and-tumble of politics, Adams sought to repair his relationship with Jefferson. He and Jefferson exchanged 158 letters throughout their retirement. 'You [Jefferson] and I ought not to die before we have explained ourselves to each other,' Adams wrote.

Friction between the two eased over time, and Jefferson wrote, 'Crippled wrists and fingers make writing slow and laborious. But while writing to you, I lose the sense of these things, in the recollection of ancient times, when youth and health made happiness out of everything.'

The two remained in contact until their deaths on 4 July 1826. The date marked the fiftieth anniversary of the Declaration of Independence, and many Americans saw their simultaneous passing as a divine symbol. Adam's son, John Quincy, captured his last spoken words in a diary entry: 'Thomas Jefferson survives.' But Jefferson had died earlier that afternoon in Virginia.

Adams was ninety years old.

Founding Fathers are often memorialised in Washington, DC, with grand statues and historic sites, but Adams is not. The Library of Congress was authorised by law under Adams and was given a $5,000 appropriation to purchase 'such books as may be necessary for the use of Congress'. Adams never could have imagined that it would one day be the largest library in the world.

Although there is no Adams memorial, there is a sprawling, nondescript government building on Capitol Hill named after him that now forms part of the Library of Congress. Appropriately and symbolically, it is filled with 180 miles of books (something Adams would have relished) and mostly scholars toil there. In one last symbol of the tension that characterised their relationship, the Adams Building stands deeply in the shadow of the lavish and majestic Jefferson Building—one of the most beautiful, celebrated and visited federal buildings ever imagined.

Daniel Forrester is an author, strategist and entrepreneur. He has advised the Library of Congress, Washington National Cathedral, the United States Marine Corps, the Architect of the US Capitol and the Colonial Williamsburg Foundation.

3

Thomas Jefferson

4 March 1801 to 4 March 1809
Democratic-Republican
Vice-presidents: Aaron Burr 1801–05,
George Clinton 1805–09

By Alvin S. Felzenberg

Full name: Thomas Jefferson
Born: 13 April 1743, Shadwell, Virginia
Died: 4 July 1826, Monticello, Virginia
Resting place: Family graveyard, Monticello, Charlottesville, Virginia
Library/Museum: Charlottesville, Virginia
Education: College of William & Mary; private tutelage under George Wythe, Esquire
Married to: Martha Wayles Skelton, m. 1772 (1748–82)
Children: Six; two daughters, Martha and Maria, survived to adulthood

Quotation: 'Sometimes it is said that man cannot be trusted with the government of himself. Can he, then, be trusted with the government of others?'

THOMAS JEFFERSON REMAINS one of the most significant Americans, not only because of what he achieved as president, but also because of arguments he advanced in the Declaration of Independence to justify America's separation from the United Kingdom in 1776:

> We hold these truths to be self-evident that all men are created equal, that they are endowed by their Creator with certain unalienable rights, that among these are life, liberty, and the pursuit of happiness – That to secure these rights, governments are instituted among men, deriving their just powers from the consent of the governed.

When the Second Continental Congress named a committee to draft the Declaration, John Adams argued that Jefferson, who had already shown an 'elegance with a pen', should be its principal drafter. The choice was fortuitous. As Margaret Thatcher would observe, 'Europe was created by history. America was created by philosophy.' Jefferson was the most articulate proponent of the philosophy that all persons were equal in the eyes of the law and before each other and that they came into the world with rights governments must respect.

Benefiting from one of the finest educations in the American colonies, Jefferson had studied the classics, history and law. He thought about how governments should be organised to allow freedom to flourish. The historical record of the few democracies and republics that had been established prior to 1776 was discouraging. Free societies eventually succumbed to tyranny. The arc of Jefferson's life was a mission to prevent the young United States from suffering a similar fate.

The roots of the man Jefferson became can be traced back to the Piedmont region in Virginia, the largest of the thirteen American colonies. Thomas Jefferson was born on 13 April 1743 at Shadwell plantation in Albemarle County to Peter Jefferson and Jane Randolph Jefferson. Peter named Shadwell after the parish in London, England, where Jane was christened. Thomas's parents influenced their first-born son in profound, but different ways.

Born in Virginia, Peter, the son of a Welsh sea captain, was a self-educated surveyor, cartographer, sheriff and justice of the peace. Late in his life, he was elected to the Virginia House of Burgesses. Peter charted the first map of Virginia and surveyed its border with North Carolina. In 1739, he married Jane Randolph, a member of one of Virginia's most prominent families. Jane was the daughter of Isham Randolph, who had emigrated from England, where he had been a prominent merchant, shipper and colonial agent. In Virginia, he became a successful planter.

Thomas inherited Peter's athleticism, drive and intellect. Although Peter had become a successful planter and entered Virginia's gentry through his marriage to Jane, Thomas romanticised his father as an ideal yeoman farmer in whose care the future United States could be safely entrusted. Peter's library contained Rapin-Thoyras's multi-volume history of England, which celebrated the Glorious Revolution of 1688 as the triumph of parliamentary democracy over royal absolutism. Both sides of Jefferson's family looked upon the Glorious Revolution as a 'golden age.'

Thomas came to exhibit his Randolph grandfather's intellectual curiosity, especially about politics and science, and an appreciation for the gracious hospitality his parents showed their guests. Although Jefferson downplayed in his autobiography the influence the Randolphs had on his career, he made ample use of family connections as he made his way to the top of Virginia's hierarchical society.

When Thomas was nine, Peter entrusted his education to a local rector, who taught him French and Latin. After Peter died during Thomas's fourteenth year, the Reverend James Maury tutored Thomas in the classics, which young men, presumed destined to rule, were expected to master. At seventeen, Thomas enrolled in the College of William & Mary in Williamsburg, Virginia's colonial capital. While he was away, Jane administered Peter's estate of sixty-six slaves and 2,750 acres. On this land, Jefferson would later build his home, Monticello.

In Williamsburg, Jefferson acquired three powerful mentors: William Small, George Wythe and Francis Fauquier. Small, a Scotsman and the sole non-cleric on the William & Mary faculty, taught mathematics and moral philosophy and exposed Jefferson to the Scottish and French enlightenments. Wythe, perhaps the most prominent and respected lawyer in the colony, prepared Jefferson for the bar. (Jefferson spent five years under Wythe's tutelage after having completed two years at William & Mary.) British-appointed Lieutenant Governor Francis Fauquier, whose principal avocations were science and hosting grand receptions, made Jefferson a regular at his table, where the younger man conversed freely with luminaries of Williamsburg society. Another pillar of the political establishment who looked out for Jefferson was his mother's cousin, Peyton Randolph, Speaker of the House of Burgesses and President of the First Continental Congress. As Jefferson came of age, he demonstrated extraordinary self-confidence, determination and an expectation to have his way.

While in Williamsburg, Jefferson spent time observing the proceedings of the House of Burgesses. He recalled standing in the doorway listening to Patrick Henry denounce King George III during the Stamp Act crisis. Lacking a flair for the dramatic and disdaining personal confrontation, Jefferson decided that he would rely upon writing, rather than oratory, as his principal means of political persuasion. His capacity to compress complex materials into simple language and write speedily served him well.

Jefferson learned a valuable lesson when Henry almost succeeded in getting vacillating Burgesses to approve a radical anti-British resolution he had introduced, only to see it fail the next day, when a determined group of moderates employed several parliamentary manoeuvres to defeat it. Subsequently, Jefferson paid close attention to legislative precedent, history and procedure. Other than *Notes on Virginia*, the only book Jefferson wrote was *Jefferson's Manual*, detailing US Senate procedure.

In 1767, Jefferson began practising law. Two years later, he won election to the House of Burgesses. On 1 January 1772, Jefferson married Martha Wayles Skelton. She shared his love of literature and music and had Jane's knack for managing a large plantation. After Martha received a substantial inheritance following her father's death on 28 May 1773, Jefferson, already a man of wealth, could afford to concentrate on politics. During their ten-year marriage, Martha bore Jefferson six children, two of whom, Martha and Maria, lived into adulthood.

In 1774, Jefferson drafted instructions for the Virginia delegates to the First Continental Congress. In this document, he advanced the premise that, as the American colonies had been settled solely under the authority of the crown, their locally elected legislatures, rather than the British Parliament, had exclusive authority over their governance. The document was published in pamphlet form in England under the title, *A Summary View on the Rights of British America*. Members of Parliament sympathetic to the colonists' cause cited it and Jefferson became regarded as a figure of note in Britain and throughout the colonies.

On 27 March 1775, Virginia's Second Revolutionary Convention elected Jefferson as a delegate to the Second Continental Congress. His fame for his *Summary View*, and his participation in drafting the Declaration of the Causes and Necessity for Taking Up Arms in June 1776, may have made Congress predisposed to act favourably on Adams's suggestion that Jefferson draft the Declaration of Independence.

On 9 September 1776, Jefferson returned to Monticello and was soon elected to the Virginia House of Delegates. The General Assembly passed Jefferson's bill to abolish primogeniture, through which the eldest son inherited all of his father's estate, and its twin bill, 'entail', which discouraged the breaking up of large estates by restricting the inheritance of property to direct descendants of the initial owner. Jefferson also authored bills to establish public schools and ensure religious freedom. His measure to assure religious freedom passed the General Assembly on 16 January 1786 well after he departed the House. The Virginia Statute for Establishing Religious Freedom disestablished the Anglican Church as Virginia's official church, banned public support for any religion, and allowed people of all faiths to practise or not practise their religion as they wished. Jefferson considered this act, which became the model for the First Amendment to the US Constitution, among his three greatest achievements, along with his authorship of the Declaration of Independence and his founding of the University of Virginia, after he had retired as president.

Jefferson's work on this bill drew him into close contact with fellow delegate, James Madison, twelve years his junior and much his equal in intellect. Their collaboration, which endured for the remainder of Jefferson's life, proved one of the most productive in US history.

The General Assembly elected Jefferson for a one-year term as governor on 1 June 1779 and re-elected him for a second one-year term on 2 June 1780. When British forces under turncoat general Benedict Arnold arrived in Virginia in January 1781, Jefferson was slow to call the militia. Jefferson fled Richmond, Virginia's new capital, and retreated to Monticello. Facing little resistance, Arnold captured and torched Richmond. When British forces under Lieutenant Colonel Banastre Tarleton approached Charlottesville in June 1781, the General Assembly, which was meeting there, moved to Staunton. Narrowly escaping capture at Monticello, Jefferson abandoned the General Assembly after his term expired and fled to his second home, Poplar Forest, in Bedford County, leaving Virginia without a governor for eight days. Many Virginians condemned Jefferson's conduct as cowardly. The General Assembly investigated, but exonerated him on 12 December 1781, after Generals George Washington and Nathaniel Greene, who commanded US forces in the Southern states, had vouched for him.

Tragedy struck on 6 September 1782 when Martha died in childbirth. On her deathbed, she extracted a promise from her husband that he would not remarry. After Martha's mother, who she never knew, had died, her father had remarried twice, and Martha's relationship with her two stepmothers had been unpleasant. For weeks, Jefferson suffered interminable grief and showed signs of depression.

On 4 May 1784, the Continental Congress designated Jefferson as a minister along with John Adams and Benjamin Franklin to negotiate treaties of amity and commerce with European powers. Jefferson arrived in Paris on 6 August 1784. When Franklin returned to America, the Continental Congress elevated Jefferson to minister plenipotentiary to France on 10 March 1785. During his five years in France, Jefferson excelled at diplomacy. A young American who visited him in Paris recalled that, 'although Mr. Jefferson was the plainest man in the room, and the most destitute of ribbons, crosses, and other insignia of rank . . . he was the most courted and most attended to'. During 1787, Jefferson exceeded his diplomatic role and advised the Marquis de Lafayette on drafting the Declaration of the Rights of Man and the Citizen.

Because Jefferson regarded the French Revolution as the product of the Enlightenment and witnessed only its more moderate phase, he held a romanticised view of what was actually unfolding during and after his stay in Paris. His comment in a letter to Adams's son-in-law that 'the tree of liberty must from time to time be refreshed with the blood of patriots and tyrants' caused Jefferson considerable embarrassment in his presidential campaigns.

When he returned to Monticello on 22 December 1789, Jefferson found President George Washington's letter inviting him to serve as the first Secretary of State waiting for him. Jefferson accepted on 14 February 1790. As Secretary of State, Jefferson came into conflict with Alexander Hamilton, the first Secretary of the Treasury, over the direction the fledgling nation was to take. Their conflict was inevitable given their differences in background, beliefs and vision and the overlapping jurisdictions of their respective departments.

Jefferson viewed economics through the prism of Henry St John, the First Viscount Bolingbroke, who led the Tory opposition among the English gentry to the reforms of Whig prime minister Robert Walpole – monetisation, a funded debt, and a government respon-sible to the House of Commons instead of the king – in the early eighteenth century. Bolingbroke lauded seventeenth-century Britain where the king ruled, agriculture dominated the economy, wealth arose from land ownership, guilds regulated craftsmen, and the peasants knew their place. By replacing gold and silver with paper currency, Walpole, Bolingbroke charged, had 'corrupted' Britain by creating wealth through 'dishonest' banking, manufacturing and trade rather than 'honest' agriculture. Bolingbroke lamented that peasants were leaving the estates of the English gentry to work for wages in growing cities. Indeed, Walpole's reforms had ignited the Industrial Revolution. Rapid economic growth resulted, and English bankers, industrialists and merchants gained economic and political influence at the expense of the gentry.

Identifying with the English gentry, Jefferson shared Bolingbroke's critique of Walpole's England, except for his nostalgia for an unconstrained king. Jefferson wanted to prevent Bolingbroke's twin serpents of money and ministers from spoiling America as an agricultural paradise.

Born out of wedlock in Nevis, in what was then the British West Indies, and orphaned at a young age, Hamilton rose from poverty through his drive, intellect and good fortune. Beginning as a clerk in an international trading firm in St Croix, Hamilton earned a scholarship to King's College (now Columbia University). He left early to became an aide-de-camp to General Washington during the Revolutionary War. After the war, Hamilton became one of New York City's most successful lawyers and politicians. Hamilton proved Jefferson's match in intellect and writing skills and his superior in debate and finance.

Hamilton admired the very economic policies of Walpole that Bolingbroke so disdained and set out to transform the US in a similar manner. Hamilton sought to (1) fund the existing debt from the Revolutionary War with tariffs and excise taxes, (2) establish a hybrid central-commercial bank issuing a national currency along the lines of the Bank of England, (3) foster manufacturing, and (4) build canals and roads. As a youth in the Caribbean, Hamilton observed agricultural economies evolve into societies of a wealthy land-owning few and an impoverished many. Hamilton supported manufacturing and urbanisation because they created a path through which intelligent young men, born to poor families, would be able to rise. Hamilton's vision ran smack up against Jefferson's idealised agrarianism.

The new nation's first economic challenge was the Revolutionary War debt – $11 million incurred by the Continental Congress to foreign lenders, $40 million incurred by the Continental Congress to domestic lenders, and $25 million incurred by states to domestic lenders. Hamilton proposed 'funding and assumption' through which Congress would authorise the assumption of the Revolutionary War debts incurred by the states at face value, the refinancing of both continental and state debt at lower interest rates, and tariffs and excise taxes to pay interest costs.

There were two politically sensitive issues. First, some soldiers received promissory notes in lieu of pay. While about 40 per cent of promissory notes were held by their original owners, some veterans sold their notes to speculators at substantial discounts. Veterans were enraged that speculators would profit when the Treasury redeemed these notes at face value. Second, some states were unable to service their debts; others had used more or less fraudulent means to retire most of their debts (e.g., selling public land in exchange for promissory notes at their face value); others had serviced their debts honourably. The states that serviced their debt resented bailing out those that had not.

Jefferson and Madison, now a rising leader in Congress, arranged a compromise through which Hamilton received the necessary votes for funding and assumption in exchange for locating the nation's capital in what would become Washington, DC. The conflict between the two Cabinet officers erupted again when Hamilton proposed chartering the Bank of the United States. When Congress passed legislation enabling this, Jefferson raised concerns with Washington about the bank's constitutionality. Washington asked both men to submit legal briefs.

Jefferson argued that the Constitution's 'necessary and proper' clause limited the government's implied powers to only what was essential to carrying out enumerated functions set forth in Article I, and not what might be merely useful. Since Congress could collect taxes, borrow money, pay debt, and coin currency without a bank, he insisted that Hamilton's bank was not absolutely essential and was therefore outside the scope of implied powers. In this brief, Jefferson produced the first legal argument for a 'strict constructionist' interpretation of the Constitution.

Hamilton countered that since (1) the bank would help Congress perform its enumerated powers, (2) its establishment was not expressly prohibited by the Constitution. By this reasoning, chartering a bank was an implied power and therefore constitutional. This became known as the 'expansive interpretation' doctrine. Washington agreed with Hamilton and signed the enabling legislation into law on 25 February 1791. At this juncture, Jefferson decided to thwart his rival through other means. While in Washington's Cabinet, he began building an opposition from within the administration.

Jefferson and Madison established what became known as the Democratic-Republican Party (the antecedent of today's Democratic Party). At Jefferson's initiative and manned by a full-time employee Jefferson retained at the State Department (a friend of Madison's from his student days at Princeton), a newspaper came into being that promulgated Jefferson's grievances. Hamilton responded by establishing a pro-administration newspaper and founding the Federalist Party. (Hamilton funded his newspaper by directing government advertising its way.) When Hamilton complained that Jefferson had misused government funds to set up an opposition newspaper, Jefferson swore to Washington 'in the presence of heaven' that his Secretary of State did not establish the paper and had not tried to influence its contents. Meanwhile, he was instructing Madison to 'take up' his pen and 'tear' Hamilton to 'pieces', presumably through this newspaper.

During Washington's second term, with the French Revolution entering its most radical and violent phases, France sent Edmond-Charles Genêt to press for American assistance under the Treaty of Alliance of 1778. Determined to keep the United States neutral, Washington held that this treaty was no longer in force since it had been signed with France's pre-Revolutionary government. After Genêt began to organise US privateers to attack ships of other nations and foment revolution within remaining European colonies in North America, Jefferson denounced Genêt and embraced Washington's neutrality policy. He resigned as Secretary of State on 31 December 1793.

When Washington announced his retirement in 1796, with the first contested presidential election approaching, Jefferson prepared to oppose vice-president John Adams for the nation's highest office. The Federalists selected Charles Pinckney of South Carolina as Adams's running mate, while the Democratic-Republicans selected Aaron Burr of New York, Hamilton's in-state rival, as Jefferson's. During the campaign, the Federalists castigated Jefferson as an atheist and a Jacobin, while the Democratic-Republicans mocked Adams as a monarchist.

Prior to the passage of the Twelfth Amendment years later, the Constitution provided that when the Electoral College convened, each elector would cast two undifferentiated votes. The candidate that received the highest number of votes would be elected president and the candidate receiving the second highest number of votes would be elected vice-president, with the House of Representatives deciding ties, each state's delegation casting one vote. Adams received seventy-one votes to Jefferson's sixty-eight. On 4 March 1797, Adams became president; Jefferson, vice-president. The results put Jefferson in the awkward position of simultaneously being in the Adams administration, while leading the opposition to it.

Adams sought to avoid war with France. In response to pro-French agitation among some Democratic-Republicans, Congress passed the Alien and Sedition Acts. The Alien Act allowed the imprisonment and deportation of any alien deemed a security threat in time of war. The Sedition Act permitted the arrest and imprisonment of anyone who published or said anything that held the US or its president up to disrepute. (Many who were prosecuted under these laws were French émigrés and Irish immigrants.) In response, Jefferson and Madison drafted the Virginia and Kentucky Resolves through which these states declared that they would not comply with these laws in their jurisdiction.

Adams and Jefferson faced each other again in the presidential election of 1800. The Democratic-Republicans defeated the Federalists, but Jefferson and his running mate Aaron Burr tied at seventy-three votes each in the Electoral College. (Only five states selected their electors through some form of popular vote.) Because no candidate emerged with a majority, it fell to the outgoing Federalist House of Representatives to determine the winner. In the House, each of the sixteen state delegations would cast a single vote, with nine needed to win. Although the Democratic-Republicans intended that Jefferson should become president and Burr vice-president, Burr, seeing a chance to become president, hoped to attract votes from Federalists, who considered Jefferson their implacable enemy. Federalist James Bayard, Delaware's single member of the House of Representatives, was among those who considered Burr the lesser of two evils. To Bayard, Jefferson was both a hypocrite (claiming to be the 'high priest of liberty' while profiting from slave labour) and an impractical dreamer.

After thirty-five ballots, the tally remained Jefferson with eight votes, and Burr with six, with several abstentions. At this juncture,

Jefferson received unexpected help from Alexander Hamilton, who beseeched Federalist Representatives to acquiesce to having Jefferson as president. 'He is by far not so dangerous a man; and he has pretentions to character,' Hamilton wrote. Jefferson 'was as likely as any man to temporize – to calculate what will be likely to promote his own reputation and advantage; and the probable result of such a temper is the preservation of systems though originally opposed, which being once established could not be overturned without danger to the person who did it.'

Behind the scenes, Jefferson surrogates bargained with Bayard and others. The Federalists demanded that Jefferson keep Hamilton's financial legacy, maintain neutrality in any war between France and the United Kingdom, preserve the US Navy, and retain Federalist officials (beneath Cabinet rank) in their positions. Although Jefferson insisted that he would not go in with his 'hands tied' and would long maintain that no deals had been made, his subsequent actions argue to the contrary. Assured that the agreement would stick, Bayard and several of his colleagues cast blank ballots, allowing for Jefferson to win.

In his inaugural address, Jefferson made unity and compromise his major themes: 'We are called by different names brethren of the same principle. We are all Republicans, we are all Federalists.'

As would Lincoln more than a half-century hence, Jefferson proclaimed the American republic 'the world's best hope', and predicted that it would not, on his watch, die for want of energy.

With Democratic-Republican control of both Houses of the Seventh Congress that was elected in 1800 and convened on 1 December 1801, Jefferson pressed for the enactment of his agenda. By the end of his first year in office, he had eliminated all internal taxes, cut spending, and made headway on reducing the national debt. Over eight years, he lowered it from $83 million to $57 million. He pardoned persons who had been convicted of violating the Alien and Sedition Acts. Jefferson increased sales of public lands, but in smaller lots than had his predecessors, to promote settlement along the frontier. He signed legislation to create the United States Military Academy at West Point.

Jefferson asked Secretary of the Treasury Albert Gallatin to investigate whether the Bank of the United States was corrupt and should be dismantled. Finding nothing, Gallatin persuaded a reluctant Jefferson that the bank was necessary for Jefferson's goal of reducing the federal debt. 'It mortifies me to be strengthening principles which I deem radically vicious,' Jefferson wrote. But the bank stayed in place.

On the international stage, the war Jefferson waged against the Barbary pirates, however popular at home, proved a short-term victory in what would be a protracted struggle. His acquisition of the Louisiana territory proved an unqualified success, while the embargo he placed on trade with warring belligerents was an unmitigated disaster.

For centuries, Morocco and the quasi-independent Ottoman provinces of Algiers, Tunis and Tripoli had practised piracy in the Mediterranean. In order for their ships and passengers to sail through unmolested, European kingdoms routinely paid considerable tribute. From 1784 to 1800, the United States had paid more than $1 million to free captured American sailors and protect American merchant ships. Jefferson had long opposed the practice of paying tribute to those who threatened, detained or harmed US citizens.

On 4 March 1801, the day Jefferson took office, Tripoli was demanding tribute of $250,000 and an annuity of $25,000. Jefferson refused and sent three frigates and a schooner to the Mediterranean with instructions to sink pirate ships. Tripoli declared war on the United States on 10 May 1801. With help from the Kingdoms of Sicily and Sweden, the US Navy, led by Commodore Edward Preble, imposed a blockade on Tripoli. On 31 October 1803, Tripoli captured the USS *Philadelphia*, which had run aground, and took its crew hostage. US marines led by Captain Stephen Decatur overwhelmed Tripolitan sailors on the captured vessel and sank it on 16 February 1804. British admiral Horatio Nelson described this as the 'most bold and daring act of the age'. An American force led by US Army captain William Eaton and US marine Lieutenant Presley O'Bannon captured the Tripolitan city of Derna on 13 May 1805.

Negotiations ensued to end the war. Jefferson agreed to pay $60,000 in ransom, Tripoli released the American captives, and hostilities ended. Jefferson tried to put as best a face as he could on this costly 'victory'. It would not be long before threats against American merchant ships and sailors in the Mediterranean resumed.

Jefferson argued that nations, like individuals, should be held to a common moral standard and eschewed the realpolitik approach of paying tribute as too cynical for a nation committed to protect the natural rights of its citizens. 'Under a government bottomed on the will of all, the life and liberty of every citizen become interesting to all,' he wrote.

From his days as Secretary of State, Jefferson sensed that whatever country governed New Orleans would control the Mississippi River and a large part of North America. The Treaty of Paris of 1783, which ended the Revolutionary War, established the Mississippi River as the western boundary of the United States and allowed Americans to navigate it and use New Orleans, which Spain governed, as a port of deposit. Over the next two decades, Spain did not consistently honour these commitments.

Hoping to re-establish a French empire in the Americas, Napoleon sent troops to suppress a slave uprising in the sugar-producing colony of Saint-Domingue (now Haiti) and sought to reacquire the former French colony of Louisiana, then under Spanish rule, as a source of food, lumber and other supplies for Saint-Domingue. Under French pressure, Spain ceded New Orleans and the rest of Louisiana to France in 1802.

In early 1803, Napoleon, preparing for war against the United Kingdom, was in need of funds. Napoleon realised that, once hostilities commenced, the British Navy would prevent France from supporting troops in Saint-Domingue or from occupying New Orleans. Jefferson had already realised that a French-controlled New Orleans could threaten US security. Delaying French occupation of New Orleans was much on Jefferson's mind when he resisted demands from Southern planters, fearful that a successful slave revolution then underway in Saint-Domingue would inspire similar uprisings in the United States, that he help France put it down.

Early in 1803, Jefferson instructed US ambassador Robert R. Livingston and James Monroe, his personal emissary, to offer up to $10 million to purchase New Orleans and surrounding coastal area (totalling 45,000 square miles). On 11 April 1803, Napoleon offered to sell all of Louisiana (a total of 827,937 square miles) to the United States for $15 million. Livingston and Monroe accepted his counter-offer. The purchase treaty was signed on 30 April 1803, and the Senate ratified it by a 24–7 vote on 20 October 1803. The House of Representatives and the Senate quickly appropriated the necessary funds.

Jefferson achieved his great accomplishment because the demands of the moment necessitated his bypassing his own principle of strict constructionism. The Constitution does not authorise Congress power to purchase new territories. Ironically, Jefferson paid Hamilton a much-delayed tip of the hat when he accepted arguments his erstwhile rival had made about implied powers. (The Constitution had allowed for the governance of territories, but had not specifically authorised purchase of them.) Jefferson considered pressing for a constitutional amendment to allow for the purchase, but bowed to the need for speed. He would not, he said, let this opportunity pass in observance of 'metaphysical subtleties'.

Jefferson's philosophical and religious opinions differed substantially from those of other founders. John Locke, Francis Bacon and Isaac Newton were his intellectual heroes. Jefferson rejected traditional Christianity. Reason was his god. Human nature, in his eyes, was not forever fixed. It could be improved by the accumulation and dissemination of knowledge over time. Jefferson looked to history not as evidence of mankind's propensity to fail, but as a guide to what could be avoided. 'I like the dreams of the future better than the history of the past,' Jefferson wrote to Adams.

Most founders believed that humans, if left to their own devices, would prove aggressive, avaricious and selfish. The US Constitution delineates federalism, separation of powers, and checks and balances as the means to prevent one person or faction from gaining total control of the government. As James Madison wrote in defence of the Constitution drafted in 1787: 'what is government itself, but the greatest reflection on human nature? If men were angels, no government would be necessary. If angels were to govern men, neither external, nor internal controls on government would be necessary.'

While he shared Madison's pessimism about the then current state of human nature, Jefferson believed that it could change. In 1816, Jefferson wrote to a friend: 'I know also that laws and institutions must go hand in hand with the progress of the human mind. As that becomes more developed, more enlightened, as new discoveries are made, new truths disclosed and manners and opinions change with the change of circumstances, institutions must advance also, and keep pace with the times.'

Jefferson was a 'physiocrat' who held that agriculture was the source of all wealth and governments should not interfere with an agrarian economy. His wealth arose from a large slave-operated plantation, selling tobacco and wheat on world markets. Yet he held a romanticised view of an agrarian future with self-governing communities of self-sufficient yeomen farmers operating free of government regulation. In reality, colonial Virginia bore little relationship to Jefferson's vision, though he tried to make it so. Land ownership was highly concentrated in a few gentry families; slaves provided agricultural labour; banks and paper currency did not exist; gold and silver coins were rare; transactions often involved barter; and taxes were paid in tobacco. Over his life, Jefferson tried to make land ownership more diverse, but he never reconciled himself with the emergence of a diversified, market-oriented economy.

Jefferson regarded himself primarily as a philosopher. Biographers, poring over his voluminous correspondence, in which he voiced countless opinions on every subject imaginable, made the mistake of believing that he actually was. Unlike most philosophers, Jefferson enunciated few principles, other than the universality of natural rights and the power of reason to change human nature, to which he adhered for the better part of his life. Jefferson would articulate positions and disregard them, depending on circumstances and what seemed to him most pressing at any particular time. Jefferson's inconsistencies continue to stymie more than a few who study him.

No consideration of Jefferson's significance to his country and the world can be complete without mention of two paradoxes in his legacy. Jefferson had so eloquently proclaimed the universality of natural rights and equality of all persons before the law. Yet, in the course of his life, he kept 609 human beings in bondage. Moreover, none of the advances in human knowledge he so anticipated and praised proved sufficient to persuade him either to stop living a contradiction, or to use the power at his command to destroy the institution of slavery, which he found abhorrent.

As a young legislator, Jefferson tried and failed to convince his fellow Burgesses to put slavery on a path to extinction. He tried and failed to persuade the Continental Congress to include in the Declaration of Independence Britain's participation in the slave trade among the colonies' grievances against the crown. Before he departed for France, Jefferson proposed in the Confederation Congress what became the Northwest Ordinance of 1787, which barred slavery in US territory north of the Ohio River and west of Pennsylvania. This marked the only time he helped ban slavery anywhere. Jefferson did not try to prohibit slavery in any of the territory acquired by the Louisiana Purchase. Instead, he hoped to reduce racial tensions in existing slave states by encouraging planters to move there with their slaves and manumitted slaves to relocate to the new territory.

Jefferson doubted that Blacks and Whites could live together peacefully, enjoying equal status, because of 'deep rooted prejudices entertained by the whites' and 'ten thousand recollections, by the blacks of the injuries they have sustained'. He described the entire relationship between masters and slaves as 'a perpetual exercise of boisterous passions, the most unremitting despotism on one part and degrading submissions on the other'. In *Notes on Virginia*, Jefferson 'trembled' for his country when he reflected that 'God is just' and that 'his justice cannot sleep forever'.

During his life and upon his death, Jefferson freed no more than ten of his slaves. All were of the same family, which had close personal, if not familial, associations with Jefferson and his deceased wife, Martha. Martha Jefferson and the slave Sally Hemings shared the same father. Sally Hemings and several of her relatives joined Jefferson's household either when he and Martha wed or as part of Martha's father's estate. Sally and many in her family played an important role in the Jefferson household, whether as artisans, cooks, carpenters or domestic servants.

In 1998, DNA studies of Sally's descendants and collateral male descendants of Jefferson suggested that Jefferson had fathered at least one of Sally's children. Based on this study and evidence that Jefferson had included in or omitted from his 'Farm Book', most contemporary Jefferson scholars and the Thomas Jefferson Memorial Association (which operates his home, Monticello) accept that Jefferson fathered the six children that Sally Hemings bore.

After the Missouri Compromise of 1820, which admitted Missouri

as a slave state and Maine as a free state and established the 36°30'
parallel as the dividing line for slavery in the remainder of the
Louisiana Territory, Jefferson likened the slavery issue to a person's
holding a wolf by the ears: 'We can neither hold him, nor let him
go.' He left it to future generations to eradicate what he and several
of his successors considered the 'original sin' in the settling and
founding of his country.

To decode the riddle of Thomas Jefferson, who one biographer
referred to as 'The American Sphinx', one must understand that
Jefferson was in actuality a pragmatic politician, albeit with a philosophical bent. While Jefferson professed that he was happiest when
he was at Monticello surrounded by his books, he devoted much
of his time during his few retreats back to his mountaintop home
to politics.

The legacy Jefferson left behind was primarily political and
substantial. He headed the first 'loyal opposition' in US history. He
founded America's first political party. The Democratic Party, as it
is now known, remains the oldest continuous political party in the
world. He founded it while leader of his country's first loyal
opposition. As its leader, Jefferson exhibited extraordinary organisational and communication skills. He founded partisan newspapers
to spread his message to supporters and controlled their contents.
He established political clubhouses to mobilise the faithful and get
supporters to the polls. And, in what historians refer to as the
'Revolution of 1800', his ascension then to the presidency signified
the first transition of presidential power to an opposition party by
means of an election.

As president, Jefferson exercised power adroitly and strategically
and proved an excellent administrator. On occasions when he
circumvented the separation of powers to advance his agenda,
Jefferson maintained the fiction that he was following the will of
Congress or the public. (Often he handed legislators drafts of bills,
which they sponsored.) In orchestrating what history knows as 'the
Louisiana Purchase' (which included the city and port of New
Orleans and the western half of the Mississippi River basin),
Jefferson, through a series of moves worthy of a master chess player,
doubled the size of the United States without waging a war of
conquest. Without question, Jefferson was the second most conse-

quential president during the nineteenth century behind Abraham Lincoln.

Leaders in multiple fields would benefit from studying Jefferson's management style. He deftly used symbolism to promote 'republican values' in a world dominated by kings and potentates. The British ambassador referred to Jefferson's manner as 'negligence actually studied', after the president received the king's representative in slippers. Jefferson greeted visitors with handshakes. His concept of protocol was to encourage dinner guests to take the nearest or most available chair. People competed for White House invitations so they could hear Jefferson regale them with stories about deceased Revolutionary War figures, palaeontology, French cuisine, archaeology, art, architecture and science.

The only topic he avoided at these gatherings was politics. To minimise conflict, he hosted people of different political persuasions on alternate evenings. He had discerned early in life that what people most liked to discuss was themselves. A perceptive Williamsburg hostess recalled Jefferson as a young man questioning her about how her best meals were prepared. 'I know this was half to please me,' she said, 'but he won't throw away anything he learns worth knowing.'

In what was probably the greatest tribute any American president paid a predecessor, John F. Kennedy described an assembly of Nobel Laureates as 'the most extraordinary collection of talent, of human knowledge that had ever gathered at the White House, with the possible exception of when Thomas Jefferson dined alone'. As president, though, Jefferson did some of his best work while charming others.

Alvin S. Felzenberg served in two presidential administrations and as spokesman for the 9/11 Commission. He is author of The Leaders We Deserved . . . Rethinking the Presidential Rating Game; *and* A Man and His Presidents: The Political Odyssey of William F. Buckley, Jr., *among other works.*

4

James Madison

4 March 1809 to 4 March 1817
Democratic-Republican
Vice-presidents: George Clinton 1809–12,
Elbridge Gerry 1813–14. Otherwise post was unfilled.

By Matthew Binkowski

Full name: James Madison Jr
Born: 16 March 1751, Belle Grove Plantation, Port Conway, VA
Died: 28 June 1836, Montpelier, Virginia
Library/Museum: Orange, Virginia
Resting place: Montpelier, Virginia
Education: Princeton University
Married to: Dolley Todd, m. 1794 (1768–1849)
Children: Adopted son, John Payne Todd
Quotation: 'The advancement and diffusion of knowledge is the only guardian of true liberty.'

JAMES MADISON WAS a porcupine. He was socially prickly, sharply grounded in principle, and exceptionally good with a quill. Nicknamed the Father of the Constitution, Madison is one of the few American presidents whose influence, and therefore future prestige, preceded his tenure as commander in chief. His brilliance in shaping the core of the republic should be heralded, as its influence has endured to this day. Yet Madison's early principles were not without fault. As with all young-minded thinkers, he suffered from a lack of experience. His beliefs about the power of the federal government, the role of political parties, states' rights and foreign affairs would see radical shifts as he matured from a young American statesman to president of the United States. As president, Madison's idealism nearly cost him his country. Miraculously, by the end of his tenure he would emerge from the fire of war as America's most popular president.

Madison grew up in the Piedmont region of western Virginia on his parents' tobacco plantation overlooking the Blue Ridge Mountains. John Madison, James's great-great-grandfather, procured the family plot of over 600 acres in 1653, as part of the Headright System – an immigration incentive programme that originated in Jamestown in 1618. Four generations and 4,675 acres later, James Madison was born into the elite planter class of colonial society, as the eldest of twelve children. He received about as good an education as one could expect in the rural back-country of a royal colony in the 1760s. Madison's early schooling by clergymen schoolmaster Donald Robertson was quite traditional. James was educated in the basics of Greek philosophy and literature, geometry, geography, Greek, Latin and French. Yet it wasn't until 1767, when his father, James Madison Sr, hired the Reverend Thomas Martin to continue James's education, that a new transformational shift in ideology took seed in James's mind.

The Madisons were deeply rooted members of the Church of England. James Madison Sr was a member of the vestry and a church warden for St Thomas' Parish in Orange County, VA. Attending church, which included a three-hour ride by horseback, occupied most of the family's time on Sunday and was an integral part of the family's portrayal of prestige and standing in the community. It was a surprise then that James Madison was never a pious individual. As an adult, he never attended church and did not value the role of institutionalised religion in society. Thomas Martin could be partially to blame. He was a Presbyterian educated at Princeton University, and although a religious man, he taught James the value of religious toleration and influenced his decision to attend Princeton University, instead of the prescribed path for a wealthy Virginia Anglican: the College of William & Mary.

When Madison decided to attend Princeton University in 1769, he could not have known how formative his experiences would be for the development of the future United States of America. Attending Princeton meant following in the footsteps of those such as Jonathan Edwards and Aaron Burr, but it also meant placing Madison in a position that he had never been in his entire life: a minority. Princeton University was a less expensive school than William & Mary, and therefore attracted the merchant class of white colonial men. They went to school to become 'gentlemen', whereas one could argue that, because of Madison's family wealth, he was already one. Princeton was also primarily Presbyterian, placing James in the religious minority.

Madison was in a strange and undesirable position; one in which he would be seeking tolerance from others rather than granting it. Ultimately, he found himself welcomed with open arms. John Witherspoon, the president of Princeton, said of Madison that he 'never knew him to do, or say an improper thing'. Madison would go on to graduate from Princeton in two years, rather than the usual four, and spend a third year under the private tutelage of Witherspoon. Madison's graduate year with Witherspoon would see an education emphasising European Enlightenment thinkers. The works of Montesquieu, Locke, Rousseau, Hume and Hobbes were required readings that carried with them a new philosophical approach to religion, rule and human purpose. Madison was indoctrinated in radical new reasonings that would eventually serve as the basis for the American Constitution. Montesquieu's *The Spirit of Law* would conceive the idea of the three branches of government; Rousseau's *Social Contract* would help establish democratic principles through majority consent; and Locke's ideas on Liberal Theory (life, liberty and property) can be directly seen in the Declaration of Independence. These lessons would prove to be substantive in the future development of the nation, but also in James's mind be linked to his biggest takeaway from Princeton University: the importance of religious liberty.

By the time James graduated from Princeton University in 1773, the colonies were displaying acts of open defiance against British rule. In December of the same year, events such as the Boston Tea Party, and the lesser-known Philadelphia Tea Party, validated in Madison's mind the connection between institutionalised religion and blind obedience to the state. Pennsylvania, since the days of William Penn, had been a beacon of religious freedom. And although Massachusetts hadn't always been as religiously tolerant, the diffusion of Enlightenment ideals coupled with religious revivals of the early eighteenth century pushed Massachusetts' parishes to elect their own ministers, instead of state-appointed leaders. Madison couldn't help but compare these states, where the people were capable of questioning the absolute rule of the monarchy, to his home state of Virginia, where obedience to England's absolute rule still went widely unchallenged. Virginia's established religion of the Church of England was so ingrained in society that the taxes Virginians were paying were not only going to support the royal colony but were also paying for the church. To Madison, the fusing of church and state had positioned England next to God and made the government unchallengeable.

Although Madison never saw combat in the Revolutionary War, he was commissioned in 1775 as a colonel in the Orange County Militia and served as second in command to his father before being elected as a committee member to the Fifth Virginia Convention. Madison helped Virginia declare its independence and establish a working Virginia state constitution. He was most adamant about adding provisions within the state constitution that pushed for 'equal entitlement' of religious rights, rather than mere toleration. As its youngest member, Madison served in the Second Continental Congress until the war's end and then was elected to the Virginia House of Delegates in 1787. Madison's diminutive stature (5 foot 4 inches), frail appearance and shy personality made it difficult for him to push his political agenda, but it was here that Madison would establish his famous nationalist opinions that defined his legacy as the Father of the Constitution.

When the First Constitutional Convention was called in 1787, the realisation that the United States government was in serious need of radical revision was evident to many of the Founding Fathers, but the solution to fixing it was not transparent. For fear of past tyrannical rule, some wished to keep power in the hands of the individual state legislatures. Others, like Madison and Alexander Hamilton, came to understand that the nation's survival depended deeply on the ability of state governments to cooperate with one another, and not drift to follow their own sectional differences. Other nations, creditor nations, would never take the United States seriously if the country functioned as thirteen separate pieces, rather than as a cohesive entity, and no one would fear a nation that could not raise its own army or levy its own taxes. In order to achieve these goals, a stronger federal government was necessary. To this end, Madison would spend his time arguing for a strong federal government; one that could help gravitate the states towards a central authority.

Within the first week of the Constitutional Convention, Madison introduced 'The Virginia Plan' to the delegates. Madison's Virginia Plan would call for a federal legislative branch composed of representatives from each of the thirteen colonies. The number of representatives would be proportional to the population of each state. Large states, such as Pennsylvania and Virginia, were accepting of the plan, but smaller states such as New Jersey, who were advocating equal representation, threatened to leave the convention if a compromise could not be found. Madison didn't like it, but was forced to accept a bicameral legislature with both forms of representation. He distrusted state legislatures and believed there needed to be a way to check the selfish abuses of individual states in order to do what was in the national best interest. Madison proposed the concept of a federal veto power that could overrule the actions of state governments if they did not align with national policy. Although this idea was voted against by the convention's delegates, its concept would be later adapted in the form of the Supreme Court's power of judicial review.

At the start of the convention, Madison had been against adding a Bill of Rights, but nearing ratification, he changed his mind. Madison would go on to pen the Bill of Rights, ensuring they would agree with his political sentiments. The Bill of Rights was necessary to get the votes for ratification, but he also looked at it as an opportunity to add what he learned to believe was the most important right of citizens. In the very first line of the First Amendment to the Constitution, Madison wrote: 'Congress shall make no law respecting the establishment of religion, or prohibiting the free exercise thereof . . .'

Initially, Madison and Hamilton were in agreement on the size and scope of the federal government. They co-wrote the *Federalist Papers*, which were a series of eighty-five essays and articles that provided a persuasive argument for the ratification of the Constitution with a strong federal government. Yet while Hamilton's motivations for federal power were to control the flow of money and credit, Madison believed that a large federal government might help prevent the rise of political parties. He believed that political factions would be detrimental to the United States. Whichever political party took office would oppress the constituents of the other. Madison believed that by expanding the size and reach of a central government, political parties would not be necessary because the diverse multitudes of regional interests would prevent two major parties from forming.

Madison would hold on to his strong federalist philosophies throughout the beginning of Washington's presidency, but began to take a more centrist point of view after witnessing what he perceived as a series of federal abuses. Perhaps most egregious was Alexander Hamilton's creation of a national bank. A national bank was not explicitly granted in the Constitution and, like Jefferson, Madison would come to see it as an elitist organisation that could suppress the rights of rural farmers. He would realise that federal leaders (who were eastern elites) would act in their own self-interest, completely alienating a vast portion of the population.

This realisation was a pivot point in Madison's political ideology. He would be forced to help create the very thing he had been hoping to avoid for his new country – a new political party to challenge the over-reach of the Federalists. Madison would join Thomas Jefferson in creating the Democratic-Republican Party in 1792.

On 15 September 1794, Madison married Dolley Payne Todd.

To many this came as a complete surprise. Dolley was introduced to James at a party in Philadelphia by Aaron Burr and she was said to have fallen for his respectful treatment of women. Dolley was only twenty-six to Madison's forty-three and they couldn't have been more different from one another. Dolley was a charismatic but bossy extrovert, while Madison was hardly noticed in a room. It may have been exactly what Madison needed as his political career blossomed into the presidency. It was said that Dolley was the voice of the president in the White House.

Throughout John Adams's presidency, Madison remained an activist for Democratic-Republican ideals. When the Adams administration passed the Alien and Sedition Acts, a series of laws limiting free speech, Madison penned the Virginia Resolutions. These were a collection of formal political statements that set a precedent for states to consider federal laws nullified if they found them to be unjust. By writing the Virginia Resolutions, Madison shifted his beliefs even further away from his original federalist point of view and showcased his commitment to the Constitution and now the rights of states.

When Thomas Jefferson was elected as the third president of the United States in 1801, James Madison became his Secretary of State. Madison would prove to be one of Jefferson's closest advisers in foreign affairs. He supported Jefferson's decision to fight against the Barbary pirates of Tripoli, and advised Jefferson to proceed with the Louisiana Purchase. But Madison also helped Jefferson commit one of the biggest political blunders the young country had ever seen.

Madison soundly believed in a government that was centred around democracy. Upholding these republican values meant conducting the affairs of the country differently than the authoritarian models of the world. Imperialist countries had strong militaries, therefore he wished to limit the size of the American Army and Navy. Just two years into Jefferson's presidency, the Napoleonic Wars would pit France and Britain against each other in a twelve-year conflict. As a neutral country, America wished to profit from both countries by trading with whomever they could. Neither Britain nor France was willing to see American merchant goods flow to their enemy and would seize American ships bound for opposing ports. The need for sailors would force both countries to take American merchantmen off their vessels and press them into service in their respective navies. The practice of impressment would be challenged by the United States several times; but how can one convince a foreign power to bend without the perceived threat of force? Madison believed the answer to be in economic sanctions. He advised Jefferson to pass the Embargo Act of 1807, which restricted American trade by prohibiting American merchants from travelling to any foreign port. The hope was that at least one of the countries would stop interfering with American merchants. The effect of the Embargo Act proved to be nothing more than self-imposed sanctions. It crippled New England merchants and did little to stop Britain or France, because they greatly underestimated the economic reach of both nations.

With Jefferson following Washington's custom of two terms in office, Madison would run as the Democratic-Republican candidate in the presidential election of 1808. His opponent would be Federalist candidate Charles C. Pinckney of South Carolina. Pinckney was a Revolutionary War hero and successful Minister to France. Federalists hoped they could take advantage of the economic blunders of the Jefferson administration to win the election. While many voters in New England who were affected by the embargo voted for Pinckney, most of the country had not forgotten the First Amendment abuses of the Adams administration and voted for Madison. He won 122 Electoral College votes to Pinckney's 47.

Madison became the fourth president of the United States on 4 March 1809 in the midst of an economic and foreign crisis. He would feel pressure from New England merchants to lift the economic embargo that was crippling their livelihood. Warhawks in the Democratic-Republican Party who hoped to expand the American frontier into Canada were calling for war with Britain. The national bank, which Madison initially despised, was due for rechartering in 1811. France and Britain were still impressing sailors and, without a strong military, America's appearance on the world stage was utterly laughable.

Madison's inaugural speech emphasised American neutrality in the Napoleonic conflict, and called those countries involved to respect America's rights on the high seas. In an attempt to appease

New England merchants after the disaster of the Embargo Act, Madison quickly pushed through Congress a milder Non-Intercourse Act, which allowed American merchants to trade with all countries except Great Britain and France.

It is important to note that although Madison had no love for Great Britain or France, he had no great desire to go to war with either country. Great Britain had the largest navy in the world, and Napoleon's ruthless tenacity and sizeable armies were a threatening prospect. Pressure from Madison's own party, however, would eventually force his hand. Organised Indian attacks on north-western settlers would be blamed on the British, as they had provided them weapons in trade. Warhawks like Henry Clay of Virginia would see this as nothing more than a secret attempt by the British to regain parts of what they lost during the American Revolution. This exacerbated the call to invade Canada and establish an American-dominated North America. So when Napoleon promised to stop impressing American sailors and respect its neutral shipping (a promise he did not keep), Madison lifted the embargo on France while keeping it on Britain.

Warhawks pushed Madison to see that the only way to defend American integrity would be to fight a 'Second American Revolution'. Harry Lee, an old friend and colleague who served with Madison in the Fifth Virginia Convention, said to him, 'Take us out of the odious condition of half war by drawing the sword.' By May of 1811, the Republican Congressional Caucus met to decide who would be the Democratic-Republican candidate in the 1812 election. Led by Henry Clay, the members bluntly informed Madison that his candidacy depended 'upon him screwing his courage to a declaration of war'. On the first of June, Madison asked Congress for a declaration of war. The war bill passed the Senate by nineteen votes to thirteen on 17 June 1812. Madison handily won a second term in office over Federalist candidate De Witt Clinton and became America's first wartime president.

Ironically, the British had sent a message to the United States on 2 June in which they agreed to yield to American neutrality and stop harassing shipping. If this had been the internet age, or even the era of the transatlantic telegraph cable, war probably would have been avoided. But in 1812, it took a month to cross the Atlantic Ocean.

Because of Madison's democratic idealism, the United States was no better suited for war with England than they had been against the Barbary pirates of Tripoli. America was armed with local and state militia and five frigates. The plan for war would be a three-part invasion of Canada with forces under the command of either retired Revolutionary War veterans or greenhorn cadets fresh out of military academies. America had to wonder why a war, whose pretext was in defence of free trade and maritime rights, was being fought by invading Canada. Madison soon realised that although militias were great for defending a nation against localised attacks (such as Indian attacks on the frontier), they were not suitable for offensive invasions. An entire militia of 3,000 men refused to cross the border of New York and Canada because they were not contracted to do so. An invading force was able to capture the Canadian capital of York (present-day Toronto), but undisciplined militia burnt many government buildings to the ground. This action would serve as just cause for the British invasion of Washington, DC and the subsequent burning of the White House in August of 1814.

The invasion of Canada ultimately failed and Madison knew that America's chances of respectably ending this war would depend on its ability to stop British naval advances on the Great Lakes and the eastern seaboard. With the British Navy having 219 ships-of-the-line and 296 frigates at her disposal, Madison would have to find an alternative tactic to fighting ship to ship.

In 1813, Congress passed the Torpedo Act, which gave any American citizen who was able to sink a British ship by use of 'torpedoes, submarine instruments, or any other destructive machine whatever', one-half of the value of the ship. This blurred the lines between who were enemy combatants and who were innocent civilians. Traditional military warfare was between professional armies and navies. With the passage of the Torpedo Act and the offensive use of militia, the consequences of Madison's refusal to build a substantial military were made apparent. Madison wanted a country ruled for the people, and by the people, but now the people were being used as national defence. British attacks on civilians in coastal towns such as Stonington, Connecticut, or Baltimore, Maryland, were a direct result of British retaliation on an ambiguous enemy.

The war became so unpopular in New England that the New England states threatened to secede from the Union. New Englanders were bitter over years of economically crippling, self-imposed sanctions, and a war they never supported. A convention was held in Hartford, Connecticut, in December 1814 to discuss the matter. Madison could have easily found just cause to crush this convention as a treasonous act, but instead he let it happen. Madison saw similarity in the Hartford Convention to his own penned Virginia Resolutions back in 1798 and believed states' rights were supported by a powerful Constitution that would see an eventual solution to this crisis. One might also argue that Madison somewhat agreed with New Englanders. Although he would never admit it, he was depressed by this war and eager to see its conclusion.

After having fought either the French or the Americans since nearly the beginning of the century, the British were also war weary. Neither side was able to make substantial gains in Canada and the Great Lakes region, so peace talks came in mid-February of 1815. Although there were no concessions made by either side at the Treaty of Ghent (including sailors' rights), the people of the United States were ecstatic with their moral victory. They had stood toe-to-toe with the might of Great Britain and felt they had earned America's place among the powerful nations of Europe.

As for James Madison, the outcome of the war had propelled him into the embrace of a grateful nation. Madison stood at the peak of his popularity. The Hartford Convention, having convened just a few months before the official end of the war, looked treasonous in the eyes of the American people and doomed the Federalist Party. By the time Madison stepped down from public office in March of 1817, he had unwittingly created a United States with no competing political parties and ushered her into 'The Era of Good Feelings'.

So what is James Madison's legacy? James Madison was not a very good president. Domestically, he didn't do much. He let the charter for the national bank expire in 1811, but begrudgingly supported its recharter in 1816. His inability to prevent a war the country was not ready to fight almost doomed the Union. His shy and introverted personality left many of his decisions to be made without proper consultation from those around him. He even had a portion of the nation ready to secede if their economic grievances were not heard. By modern standards, his treatment of Native Americans was barbaric and inherently racist. We cannot forget that, throughout Madison's entire life, he owned well over a hundred slaves and they were never freed. Even though Madison emerged a national hero, his positive legacy will never be in how he handled the war of 1812, but in the development of a balanced Constitution. His legacy is a Madisonian democracy with emphasis on checks and balances, states' rights and religious liberty.

Matthew Binkowski is a historian and American history teacher at Stonington High School in Connecticut, USA.

5

James Monroe

4 March 1817 to 4 March 1825
Democratic-Republican
Vice-president: Daniel D. Tompkins

By Brooks Newmark

Full name: James Monroe
Born: 28 April 1758, Westmoreland County, Virginia
Died: 4 July 1831, New York City
Resting place: Hollywood Cemetery, Richmond, Virginia
Library/Museum: Fredericksburg, Virginia
Education: College of William & Mary (1774–76), Virginia Bar (1782)
Married to: Elizabeth Kortright, m. 1786 (1768–1830)
Children: Three: Eliza, James (died in infancy) and Maria
Quotation: 'It is the knowledge that all men have weaknesses and that many have vices that makes Government necessary.'

JAMES MONROE WAS the last Founding Father and the last of the Virginia Dynasty (four of the first five presidents came from Virginia) to serve as president of the United States. Monroe had a long distinguished career as a soldier, diplomat, governor, senator and Cabinet minister, and as Francis Walker Gilmer – a contemporary of Monroe's – noted in 1816, Monroe had 'successfully occupied almost every station of public confidence which his native state or the national government could confer', making him one of the most qualified candidates to run for president in the young republic's history. Monroe, the fifth president, served from 1817 to 1825, and oversaw a period in early US history that is referred to as the 'Era of Good Feelings'. One of his lasting achievements was the Monroe Doctrine, still a major plank of US foreign policy.

James Monroe was born in 1758 into a family of wealthy Virginia landowners. His parents died when he was in his teens, leaving the young James and his siblings (two brothers and a sister) the family estate, which was run by his uncle. Monroe was educated at a local school in Virginia run by the Reverend Archibald Campbell and was a contemporary of John Marshall, who later became Chief Justice of the United States. After graduating from school in 1774 he enrolled at the prestigious William & Mary College in Williamsburg and soon found himself caught up in the independence movement. An enthusiastic revolutionary, he raided the British governor's mansion with a group of his classmates, took 200 muskets and 300 swords and presented them to the Virginia militia. He then joined the Continental Army as an officer in 1776 and served in Washington's army in New York. He served with distinction in several key battles in the War for Independence, including Monmouth, Brandywine and Germantown, and was severely wounded at the Battle of Trenton. Promoted to captain, then major, he served on General William Alexander's staff, before resigning from the Continental Army in 1779 and joining the Virginia Army as a colonel. General Charles Lee was one of the first people to recognise the potential of the young James Monroe, writing in a letter to him in 1780: 'you wou'd appear one of the first characters of this country, if your shyness did not prevent the display of the knowledge and talents you possess.'

Following the war and his return to Virginia, Monroe became close to and studied law under Governor Thomas Jefferson, passed the bar in 1782 and was elected to the Continental Congress in 1783. While at the Congress, convened in New York at that time, he met Elizabeth Kortright, the daughter of a local merchant. A year later they were married; he was twenty-seven, she was seventeen. They moved to Fredericksburg, Virginia, to bring up a family. They had three children, Eliza, James (who died in infancy) and Maria. By all accounts James Monroe was a devoted father, who strongly believed in the importance of education for girls as well as boys. The education of a new generation of Americans was a critical platform of future president Monroe: 'In a representative republic, the education of our children must be of the utmost importance.'

Monroe's political journey continued when he began serving in the Virginia Assembly in 1787. He started to make a name for himself when he was selected as a delegate to the Virginia state convention to consider the ratification of the new US Constitution. He voted against the ratification and argued for direct elections of future presidents and senators and, perhaps more importantly, the inclusion of a Bill of Rights in the Constitution. Eventually, Monroe and his supporters won the day, with the Bill of Rights becoming the first ten amendments when the new republic's Constitution was ratified in 1791.

Although Monroe narrowly lost his first congressional election to James Madison (who was later to become his predecessor as the fourth president of the United States), the Virginia legislature appointed him to the US Senate. As a new senator he allied himself with his fellow Virginians James Madison and his mentor Thomas Jefferson (who was soon to become the third president). Madison, Jefferson and Monroe put themselves up against the Federalist faction led by vice-president John Adams and Treasury Secretary Alexander Hamilton.

President Washington made Monroe Minister to France in 1794. During his time in Paris, Monroe won the release of Thomas Paine – the British pamphleteer and supporter of the American Revolution, who had been imprisoned for speaking up against the execution of Louis XVI – and sheltered him in the ministerial residence. While

Monroe sought to maintain Washington's position of neutrality between Britain and France, his task was not helped when the French government heard that the US had signed a new accord with Britain – the Jay Treaty. The Federalists blamed Monroe for the deterioration in relations with France and persuaded Washington to recall him to the US in 1797.

Monroe returned to his estate in Virginia and in 1799 was elected governor, where he pushed hard to improve public education and campaigned for his mentor and fellow Virginian Thomas Jefferson in the presidential election of 1800. In 1803, President Jefferson sent him back to France to negotiate the Louisiana Purchase. Monroe then stayed on in Europe as Minister to Britain from 1803 to 1807. During his time in that role Monroe sought to end the British policy of impressments – the practice of capturing US sailors and forcing them to serve in the British Navy. Monroe signed a treaty with Britain in 1806 to end this policy, but Jefferson refused to take it to the Senate for ratification on the grounds that it did not call for an outright ban on impressments. Monroe had a temporary falling-out with both Jefferson and Madison over the issue as he felt that his treaty was a step in the right direction towards improving relations with Britain, which remained tense. Dissident Republicans persuaded Monroe to oppose his friend Madison for the Democratic-Republican nomination in 1808, which he reluctantly accepted, but his heart wasn't in the campaign as, other than foreign affairs, there was little he differed on with his friend, and Madison won the election easily. Monroe was re-elected governor of Virginia in January 1811, but found himself back in the capital by April as President Madison's new Secretary of State, a post he held until 1817, when he ran for president.

Madison sought to keep some semblance of neutrality with France and Britain, who were at war with one another, but Britain in particular continued to target American commercial ships and to seize and impress American sailors into service with the Royal Navy. In 1812, the US declared war on Britain. From the US's standpoint, the war was a disaster from the start. The US Army was equally ill-equipped and ill-prepared to fight an increasingly professional British military. The Minister for War resigned and Monroe took on this role in addition to that of Secretary of State in December

1812. This new role suited Monroe's military and organisational skills. He reorganised the US military and gave it a new energy. Notwithstanding this, the British troops continued their advance on the US capital, and when they reached the mouth of the Potomac in August 1814, Monroe stayed in Washington, DC to organise the city's evacuation. The British attacked the capital and burnt all the government buildings, including the presidential mansion and Capitol, to the ground.

When Madison stood down after two terms, Monroe was seen as his natural successor as the candidate for the Democratic-Republicans (and was in fact the last presidential candidate of the Democratic-Republican alliance). Monroe was popular, seen as an energetic member of Madison's government, and was hugely respected among war veterans. The Federalists, on the other hand, were so out of favour with the public – viewed as unpatriotic for opposing the war – that Monroe won a resounding victory in 1816 over his Federalist opponent Rufus King and the Federalist Party thereafter all but disappeared.

Monroe began his presidency in 1817 with a national tour of the northern states over a period of fifteen weeks. This was followed by a tour of the Chesapeake Bay area in 1818 and the south and west in 1819. By the end of his tour most Americans had seen more of the new president than any of his predecessors. According to Richard Beale Davis's 'Sketches of American Statesmen', Monroe was praised for his 'captivating frankness . . . [and] disqualifying humility . . . which went straight to the heart'. Monroe was even praised and applauded in Massachusetts, where the *Columbian Centinel* described his reception in the state as the beginning of the 'Era of Good Feelings', a phrase still used to define the Monroe presidency.

Monroe's first task was to form a Cabinet. He was the first president to really think through how he could pull together a broad church from across the nation: John Quincy Adams, from Massachusetts, was made Secretary of State; William Crawford, from Georgia, Secretary to the Treasury; John Calhoun, from South Carolina, Secretary of War; and William Wirt, from Maryland, Attorney General. Monroe's Cabinet was seen as a strong and talented team. The president had a reputation as a good listener, sought out everyone's opinion, but always made the final call and expected his Cabinet to support and implement his decisions.

Monroe's first term as president was dominated by three major issues. First, the panic of 1819 and the subsequent depression. This was caused by falling trade and a collapse in agriculture prices, and was the first depression since the 1780s. The country was faced with high unemployment and an increase in foreclosures and bankruptcies. Monroe was perceived as not responding quickly and effectively to the economic crisis, but he believed that it would be short-lived (which indeed it was, ending in 1823) and was a function of the growing pains of a new country. The president, with the support of Treasury Secretary Crawford, sought to soften the economic impact by relaxing repayment terms on mortgages on property bought from the government, while at the same time instituting stricter and more conservative financial regulations through the Bank of the United States.

The second crisis was the entrance of Missouri into the Union. As a slave-owning state (16 per cent of the population were slaves), the inclusion of Missouri in the Union was seen as potentially disruptive to the legislative balance between the North (which controlled the House of Representatives) and the South (which controlled the Senate). Matters were not made easier when Congressman James Tallmadge from New York attached two amendments to the bill to admit Missouri into the Union: the first barred new slaves from entering into the new state; and the second emancipated all Missouri-born slaves after admission upon their twenty-fifth birthday. In other words, Tallmadge and his supporters would only admit Missouri into the Union as a free state. The Senate insisted on the opposite. Monroe feared the dispute would divide the nation. However, he also respected the Constitution and the right not to set conditions on the admission of any potential state. He navigated this potential crisis by negotiating a compromise through a new Congress convened in the winter of 1819 in which Massachusetts allowed its northernmost counties to, in essence, secede from the state and apply for admission to the Union as the new free (non-slave) state of Maine. After further debate there was an additional compromise in which the Southern-dominated Senate agreed to outlaw slavery in the western territories of the Louisiana Purchase above the 36°30' northern latitude. On today's map of the United States that line would allow slavery in Arkansas and Oklahoma but forbid it in nine other states. What became known as the Missouri Compromise was signed into law by Monroe on 6 March 1820. In *The Missouri Compromise and Its Aftermath: Slavery and the Meaning of America*, Robert Forbes – a leading authority on the Missouri crisis – praises Monroe's role in shaping the outcome and depicts him as an 'anti-slavery pragmatist' who saw how slavery had the potential to tear the Union asunder. While Monroe sought to lead the new nation down an anti-slavery path, Martin Van Buren (the eighth president of the United States) and the pro-slavery Democrats who took over the new party once the Republic-Democratic Party split at the end of Monroe's term as president in the mid-1820s, up-ended Monroe's ambitions and relaid the foundations for the Civil War forty years later.

The third crisis the new president had to deal with in his first term was raiding by Seminole Indians on American settlements on the border with Florida (then controlled by Spain). Monroe sent General Andrew Jackson (later to become seventh president), the hero of the Battle of New Orleans (the only battle the US won against the British in the War of 1812), deep into Spanish-controlled territory in Florida to deal with the Seminole Indians, but taking advantage of weak Spanish defences General Jackson took it upon himself to capture a strategic Spanish fort. Secretary of War John Calhoun felt that Jackson had gone well beyond his remit in not only capturing the Spanish fort, but also deposing the Spanish governor and executing two British spies who he accused of inciting the Seminoles to raid American settlements. Calhoun and a number of Congressmen and diplomats wanted Jackson to be punished. However, Secretary of State John Quincy Adams came to Jackson's support and declared he had acted well within his remit to end the Indian raids. Monroe agreed with Adams, and like his Secretary of State recognised that Spain had little real control over the territory.

Monroe sent Adams (later to become sixth president) to negotiate and pressure Spain into selling Florida to the new republic, and to drop its claims to the Louisiana Territory and Oregon. In return the United States would relinquish its claims on Texas and write off claims of $5 million against Spain. The Adams–Onis Treaty (named after the two negotiators, John Quincy Adams and the Spanish minister Luis de Onís) was signed in 1819 and was publicly well received.

As Spain's dominion in the Americas began to disintegrate, this third crisis spilled over into Monroe's second term (he was re-elected in 1820 unopposed by either his own party or the opposition, the first time this had happened since the election of President Washington forty years earlier) when other European countries threatened to form an alliance with Spain to protect its lands. The Spanish colonies in Central and South America sought to break away from Spain, their spirit of revolution and independence engendering considerable support in the United States. Monroe didn't wish to antagonise Spain and trod a fairly neutral line until 1822, when he finally recognised Argentina, Chile, Colombia and Mexico as independent countries. Rumours circulated that Spain (or even Britain) might want to reassert themselves in their old colonies. Monroe, with the support of Adams, decided to formally address this threat in a message to Congress on 2 December 1823, in which, first, he reasserted the United States' neutrality in European conflicts. Second, he said he would not accept the recolonisation of any colony in the Americas, though he would not interfere in the affairs of existing colonies. Finally, he declared that the Western hemisphere was not open to further colonisation (a message aimed at Russia, which had ambitions on the Pacific North West, as well as Britain and Spain). Although Britain at the time recognised the importance of keeping the young nation out of European affairs, they supported Monroe's policy and gave the country certain protections through the Royal Navy. Furthermore, Britain secured assurances from France not to support Spain's ambitions to recover their colonies. Monroe's declared aim to resist European intervention in the Western hemisphere and to offer protection to the new Latin American republics became the foundation of US foreign policy that has lasted until this day, becoming known as the Monroe Doctrine, and it remains one of the president's most lasting achievements.

On the domestic front Monroe's legacy is wide and varied. During his tenure as president, five states joined the Union (Mississippi, Illinois, Alabama, Maine and Missouri) and by 1820 25 per cent of the population lived west of the Appalachian Mountains. America's increasingly mobile population identified less with their countries or states of origin and saw themselves as American first. Transportation links improved, with over sixty steamboats on the Mississippi alone. In fact Monroe was the first president to travel by steamboat. Further, he authorised the building of a canal between the Hudson River and Lake Erie, thereby opening a continuous water link between New York City and the north-west, and subsequently sanctioned the construction of the Erie Canal, which stretched for 364 miles. The introduction of steam looms in factories led to the employment of thousands of young women from the countryside in the production of cloth, with New York increasingly becoming the national commercial centre for ready-made clothes. Protecting US manufacturing interests, especially in textiles, led to the controversial tariff of 1824, which once again caused a rift between North and South, with New England manufacturers supporting the act and Southern cotton growers opposing it, fearing British retaliation. Finally, domestically there was a diminution of states' rights following the US Supreme Court's ruling against the state of Maryland in *McCulloch vs Maryland*, in which the court found that states could not tax federal agencies.

Monroe wished during his presidential tenure to oversee the end of political parties, which he believed to be divisive and old world, but the election of 1824 that followed his presidency demonstrated that partisan politics was alive and kicking. In the end, he became the last of the Democratic-Republican presidents; the Federalists disappeared and the Democratic-Republican Party split between the Democrats and the Whigs. This eventually formed the basis of the two-party system that still exists today.

Monroe, following the precedent set by Washington, Jefferson and Madison, served only two terms and retired from politics in 1824 following the election of John Quincy Adams as the sixth president of the United States. Monroe returned to his estate in Virginia; however, he faced significant financial problems, having received only a small salary as president while taking personal responsibility for many presidential expenses. He petitioned the government to repay him for his services, which the government did in part. Monroe served on the Board of the University of Virginia, which was founded by his fellow Virginian and friend

Thomas Jefferson. He started to write, first a book comparing the US government to the governments of ancient and modern nations, then his autobiography. Neither book was completed, as he became increasingly concerned by his wife Elizabeth's poor health – she died in 1830. Monroe's health also quickly declined. He moved to New York to live with his daughter and died there on 4 July 1831, the third of the first five presidents to die on Independence Day.

Monroe was the most qualified person to become president to date. He had been a soldier, a governor, a senator, a Cabinet minister and a diplomat before being elected to the highest office. A personable and engagingly straightforward character, as president he sought to reach out to all regions of the new republic. His first Cabinet reflected this broad coalition while maintaining a strong team around him. He was a strong nationalist and sought to prevent division in the new nation. The Missouri Compromise was very much emblematic of his skills in keeping the Union together and avoiding a sectional crisis. His foreign policy was on the whole a success and culminated in the acquisition of Florida from Spain and the neutralisation of Britain and the European powers in their activities in the Western hemisphere. The historian John Garraty called the Monroe Doctrine 'the final stage in the evolution of American independence'.

Brooks Newmark was Minister for Civil Society and MP for Braintree (2005–15). He is currently a Visiting Academic in the Department of Politics & International Relations at Oxford University.

6

John Quincy Adams

4 March 1825 to 4 March 1829
Democratic-Republican/National Republican
Vice-president: John C. Calhoun

By Mark Fox

Full name: John Quincy Adams
Born: 11 July 1767, Braintree (now Quincy), Massachusetts
Died: 23 February 1848, Washington, DC
Resting place: United First Parish Church, Quincy, Massachusetts
Library/Museum: Quincy, Massachusetts
Education: Harvard
Married to: Louisa Johnson, m. 1797 (1775–1852)
Children: Four: George, John, Charles, Louisa
Quotation: 'Always vote for principle, though you may vote alone, and you may cherish the sweetest reflection that your vote is never lost.'

JOHN QUINCY ADAMS was one of the most extraordinary and gifted people ever to be the president of the United States. He possessed a natural intellect and intelligence, which he cultivated throughout his long life. His public career as a politician and as a diplomat is unmatched by any other person to have occupied the presidency. His record of service is unsurpassable. In addition to serving as president for four years, he also served terms in both the Senate and the House of Representatives; was his country's representative to no fewer than four other nations; and, prior to being elected president, was Secretary of State for seven and a half years. He brought to public affairs a huge experience of national and international affairs.

At times a reluctant participant in politics, Adams was prone to bouts of depression and introspection, a person who found companionship and comfort in books. Nevertheless, his upbringing and interests demanded and required that he play his full part in the public and political life of his emerging country. In a sense, Adams was born to this. His father, John Adams, was one of the United States' Founding Fathers, serving as first vice-president and second president. Adams junior grew up as a child of and witness to America's struggle to be free from Great Britain. As a youngster he travelled with his father on diplomatic missions overseas, and in doing so he broadened his understanding of the world and learned the art of international diplomacy.

Adams's life spanned the establishment of America as an independent country from Britain through to the beginning of its expansion from the original colonies across the continent to ultimately include all the land in the north between the Atlantic and the Pacific. He would enter politics before the party system evolved fully, but would be defeated in his bid for a second presidential term by emerging party factions, some of which he himself would belong to during his long career. Initially he would oppose the US Constitution, but he came to be a staunch defender of it. A man ahead of his time, he understood well the corrosive effect of slave owning – despite its general popularity – on the spirit and life of the new country, and proceeded to devote his considerable authority to ridding the new country of the scourge of slavery. His would not be the final word on the subject in American life, but without him the task would have been much harder and taken much longer.

As with many who reach the highest political office, Adams's time as president was not the most successful or satisfying part of his political career. He would not be the last to perhaps find his post-presidency more productive than the actual thing itself.

Adams came from a large and well-established family long involved in politics and he was in part named after his great-grandfather John Quincy, who had been a long-serving member of the Massachusetts Legislature. His parents, to whom he was close, ensured he had an excellent education, and it was both education and travel that marked his early years.

In 1778 and 1780, he travelled with his father to Europe, spending the time in between at school in Paris and university in the Netherlands. As well as travelling with his father, he also travelled as private secretary with Francis Dana, who was charged with establishing diplomatic relations with Russia in 1781. Adams was fourteen years old. Dana was ultimately unsuccessful in his mission, but Adams was able to spend an extended period in the country. The following year he travelled to Paris to join his father by way of Hanover and Scandinavia. He could then have remained, as his father had been appointed America's representative to Great Britain. Young Adams chose to return home instead. By the time he enrolled at Harvard he had seen more of the world than most Americans at that time, watched diplomacy at the highest international level, and lived closely with several other peoples and cultures. He had, in other words, seen the world. In the years that lay ahead, this early experience would prove to be invaluable. In the meantime, he needed to earn a living.

Graduating second in his class in 1787, he then spent the next two years training as a lawyer. It was while trying to establish his legal practice that he turned his hand to writing a series of newspaper articles commenting on current events. At first, he wrote in support of a British style of government as opposed to the French system. He was unsure initially about the new US Constitution, but eventually came round to supporting it. However, it was his support for President George Washington's policy of US neutrality when war broke out between England and France in 1793 that earned him the notice of the president and resulted in his first public appointment. As with so many before and since, the law and journalism had brought him both a living and public notice. This relatively conventional start to a political career provided the launch pad for what would be anything but a conventional path thereafter.

Adams's public life can easily be split into three parts: the first period when he undertook several diplomatic appointments and became a senior and respected figure in American public life; the second period when he served for four years as president; then the third and perhaps most glorious period when he served as a member of the House of Representatives until his death.

Between 1794 and 1801 he served in the Netherlands, Portugal and Prussia. In each posting he diligently promoted his country's interests and immersed himself in the local culture and language. The Prussian appointment opened him to charges of nepotism, but both he and his father, the newly elected president, who appointed him, brushed these off and no lasting reputational damage was done. With his father's defeat in the presidential election of 1801, however, his appointment came to an end and he returned home.

Elective politics beckoned, and, swiftly after he returned home, he successfully ran for the Massachusetts Senate. Local politics was never going to be enough to retain his sole interest, and within two years, in 1803, he won election to the United States Senate, following an unsuccessful campaign for the House of Representatives.

In the Senate he allied himself with the Federalists, but found them uncomfortable bedfellows and over the following five years voted against them as often as he voted with them. During this time, he found time to be a professor at both Brown and Harvard Universities, lecturing on logic, rhetoric and oratory. His period in the Senate had failed to impress his electors and as soon as they elected his successor, he resigned the office. He was not unemployed for long and accepted President Madison's invitation to become the US representative to Russia. Indeed, Madison thought so highly of Adams that he nominated him to a position on the Supreme Court, a proposition that was unanimously endorsed by the US Senate, but he declined the offer.

During his time in Russia, Adams worked hard to avoid conflict between Britain and the US, and in 1815 Madison appointed him to be America's representative to Britain. Already Adams had enjoyed a remarkably varied and influential career. He had earned the trust of successive presidents and politicians at local and national level, escaped from the shadow of his distinguished father, and established himself as an independent force. His time in London would last for barely two years. James Monroe, the newly elected president, was looking for a Secretary of State and it was Adams to whom he turned.

Adams would serve nearly eight years as Secretary of State and be closely involved at the highest level with some of the most significant issues of the time, at least one of which would settle American policy for decades to come. This period would also set him firmly on course for the presidency itself. His general policy was to seek to reduce tensions and avoid wars. Adept at responding to circumstances as they arose, he was able as a result to agree treaties and accords that helped ease relations with Latin America, settle border disagreements with Canada and Alaska, and do much to expand the borders and territories of the United States itself.

Perhaps the most significant development during these years was the publication of the Monroe Doctrine. Based very largely on Adams's thinking, the doctrine was the most vigorous statement of US foreign policy laid out to that date. It set out the country's views on the kind of influence it felt it should have in its own region and was the clearest signal to that point of the country's views being more than just European in focus. It was a significant shift in national focus and a strong statement of the growing strength and confidence of the new country.

The four years of Adams's presidency were perhaps the least productive of his long time in American public life. A popular and respected choice for president, Adams, with his three opponents, saw the election decided by the House of Representatives. Upon his election, he set out to build a Cabinet of appointees from across factional and geographical lines. In this he was largely successful. He sought to establish the federal government in a more activist role in helping to bind the emerging country together. His broad interpretation of the Constitution in supporting him in this endeavour caused a degree of controversy. As his term progressed it became clear that he would be the last of the non-party candidates to hold the presidency, as the emergence of fixed party allegiances gained pace during his time in office and would eventually help to deny him a second term.

Domestically he focused on infrastructure investment and the establishment of several new national institutions, including the national observatory, the naval academy and a university. His infrastructure investments were aimed at improving links between major national cities and territories. In his domestic plans it is possible to discern a strong sense of nation building and strengthening. Adams was personally and politically committed to the expansion of the nation's borders westwards. He strongly championed a policy of assimilation rather than annihilation of the indigenous Native American population, which, at the time, was very much a minority view. It was, however, true to his personal belief and foreshadowed his personal commitment to other oppressed peoples that would be a major part of his post-presidential career.

If peace, tolerance and investment at home were his key themes, so was expanding trade and commercial opportunity abroad. In this he was partially successful, and by the end of his tenure US trade and exports had increased. Apart from an unsuccessful attempt to buy Texas from Mexico, Adams generally pursued a policy of peaceful neighbourliness to the South.

His four years as president saw the United States generally at peace and increasing in prosperity. He faced some political opposition to some of his policies, but nothing more than any person in such a job might expect to face. Nevertheless, the nature of domestic US politics was rapidly changing. This was foreshadowed in the congressional elections of 1826. Adams's opponents were organised and formed a recognisable political grouping. They easily defeated allies of the president and formed a formidable and co-ordinated opposition once elected. Adams resisted using the powers of his office to strengthen his own political position. He clung wilfully and obstinately to the notion of non-party politics and the ideal of good people coming together in good faith to serve the nation. His was the older and the founding ideal, but his successors would increasingly cling to party support and identity, which would in time come to be more important to those seeking the presidency than arguably the interests of the nation itself. The divisive and polarising party politics of today's presidential politics in the United States would surely have appalled those who were there at the birth of the nation.

Adams had met his wife, Louisa, during an early visit to London, and they were married on 26 July 1797, at All Hallows-by-the-Tower, in the City of London. Their marriage was opposed by both families, but turned into a long and successful union that lasted until his death in 1848. They had four children – George, John, Charles and Louisa – of whom the first three survived into adulthood. The middle two followed their father into politics and the eldest child followed him into a legal career. Throughout their long marriage, the couple were devoted and affectionate. There is plenty of evidence that Louisa found her husband's public life and the entanglements that inevitably arose a strain, and she suffered physically as a result. Nevertheless, when he was called to serve abroad, she nearly always made the effort to join him, most notably in 1814 when she travelled for forty days across Europe to Ghent to join him for the peace negotiations following the Napoleonic war that had left the continent desolated. Having been born and brought up in London, she is said to have found America somewhat provincial and unsophisticated, and perhaps the happiest time they had together was when Adams was appointed to be the US ambassador to the Court of St James. She died in 1852 aged seventy-seven, four years after her husband, in Washington, DC. A loyal and loving companion, as well as successful First Lady, she served her adoptive country with considerable distinction.

Having resisted partisanship throughout his presidency, in 1828 Adams duly went down to defeat by a well-coordinated opposition, led by Andrew Jackson. Adams did not attend his successor's inauguration – one of only four presidents who failed to do so.

Following his defeat, President Adams had planned to retire from public life, but he was prevailed upon to run for the House of Representatives in 1830, where he would serve nine successive terms up to his death. During this period, he sought election as governor of Massachusetts and a return to the Senate, losing on both occasions, and after 1835 he concentrated his formidable focus on the House of Representatives.

Adams was fully involved in the issues of the day and opposed the Mexican–American War of 1844–48. During this period, however, it is perhaps his staunch opposition to slavery that was the most notable of all his political activities. Time and again he attacked slave owning and sought to undermine its hold on the politics of the time, but it was not until 1841 that he was to have the chance to land a decisive blow on the practice that would have profound consequences for the United States in the years that would follow.

On 24 February 1841, he argued for four hours in the case of *United States v The Amistad* in front of the Supreme Court, of which he had refused membership, in favour of a group of African slaves who had revolted against their captors. He won; the slaves were freed and returned home. It was a decisive moment in American history and a shining victory for the, by this time, veteran and ailing statesman.

Ever mindful of cultural improvement and the importance of learning, Adams had long dreamt of establishing a national centre and museum. In 1846 – after a protracted process of safeguarding the funds, dealing with constitutional questions about federal authority, and securing the legacy of British scientist James Smithson – Congress voted to establish the Smithsonian Institution. This was a huge and personal victory for Adams, who had taken on the leadership of the cause and done so much to see his vision realised. His career in public life always involved much more than mere party politicking or international intrigue. Here was an example of the establishment of a national institution that has outlasted much of the policy that absorbed Adams and his contemporaries in his lifetime.

Adams had not expected his career in the House of Representatives, but he took it on with gusto. Despite attempts to sideline and marginalise him, he became an authoritative and effective member of the House, and it was there, while making a vigorous intervention, that he collapsed on 21 February 1848. He was taken to the Speaker's Room where two days later, in the company of Louisa, he died. It was perhaps fitting that he should die in the building that housed the young republic's political heart.

Adams had served his country with immense distinction and wisdom, not always being right or on the winning side, but always with integrity and insight. Few of those who have come after him as president have matched the depth and breadth of his learning, and fewer still can match the number of positions in which he served. He remains the only former president to hold elected national office following the presidency.

John Quincy Adams is rightly considered one of America's greatest public servants and statesmen, but more probably for what he did either side of the presidency than while occupying the presidency itself.

Mark Fox has had a varied career in business, journalism and politics. He is currently the Chief Executive of the Business Services Association and Deputy Chairman of Reaction Digital Media.

7

Andrew Jackson

4 March 1829 to 4 March 1837
Democrat
Vice-presidents: John C. Calhoun 1829–32,
Martin Van Buren 1833–37

By Simon Marks

Full name: Andrew Jackson
Born: 15 March 1767, Waxhaw Settlement, border region of
North and South Carolina
Died: 8 June 1845, Nashville, Tennessee
Resting place: The Hermitage, Nashville, Tennessee
Library/Museum: The Hermitage, Nashville, Tennessee
Education: Sporadic, informal
Married to: Rachel Donelson Robards, m. 1791 (1767–1828)
Children: Three: Andrew Jr, Lyncoya, Hutchings (all adopted)
Quotation: 'I have only two regrets: that I did not shoot Henry
Clay and did not hang John C. Calhoun.'

IN THE RACE for the coveted title of 'America's Most Controversial President', Andrew Jackson is assuredly a front-runner. Revered and reviled even during his two terms in the White House, America's seventh president left a legacy that remains controversial to this day.

When President Donald Trump moved into the White House almost two centuries after Andrew Jackson's first inauguration in 1829, one of his first acts was to hang the seventh president's official portrait in the Oval Office. But in an indication of the arguments raging over Jackson's legacy, the US Treasury was simultaneously preparing to remove Jackson's image from the face of the $20 bill.

That one man can be considered worthy by some of occupying wall-space in the most powerful office in the world but unworthy by others of featuring in Americans' wallets is a consequence of Jackson's storied life and his controversial record.

The first self-made man to reach the top of America's greasy political pole, he shocked society with populism, championing the rights of working-class Americans, provided they were both white and male. He was America's beloved war hero, whose military triumphs were secured thanks to the efforts of Native Americans fighting alongside him, but whose lands he later brutally expropriated. His personal fortune was built off the backs of slaves long after he knew slavery's immorality was America's central, gnawing issue. Quick to fury, he challenged scores of opponents to duels, killing at least one of them, and bearing the bullets from two encounters for the rest of his life: one lodged in his chest, the second embedded in his left shoulder.

Jackson knew little of forgiveness. Family losses during the War of Independence left him bearing a deep-seated animus towards Britain. Later in his career, when military tribunals spared the lives of mutineers, Jackson had them shot anyway. He believed rules were made to be broken and legal judgments could be ignored whenever he disagreed with them. The creator of the Democratic Party, he became the first American politician to use the media tools of his age in relentless self-promotion. He was also the only president ever formally censured by the Senate, the first president to face an assassination attempt and the first to survive one. An early biographer called him 'An urbane savage. An atrocious saint.'

A later chronicler concluded: 'If you were his friend, you were his friend forever. If you were his enemy, God help you.'

Andrew Jackson was born into the same poverty his parents hoped to escape when they departed Ireland for a new life in the Carolinas. In 1767, his twenty-nine-year-old father died in a logging accident just three weeks before his third son's birth on the Ides of March.

Andrew was eight when the War of Independence began, turning the Carolina frontier into a deadly battleground. Like other young boys in the region, Jackson put his knowledge of the Carolina backwoods to good use, conveying handwritten orders to the patriots' front lines.

In 1781, advancing British troops captured him and his older brother Robert. The British had no idea that they were about to write the first chapter in a future president's personal legend.

As Jackson's first biographer John Eaton writes: 'Andrew was ordered in a very imperious tone, by a British officer, to clean his boots which had become muddied in crossing a creek.' Jackson refused. The officer struck him with a sword, leaving him with scars on his hand and his head that would never heal. Robert suffered a head wound that would eventually prove fatal. Elizabeth Jackson secured her sons' freedom in a prisoner exchange. But the war would leave Andrew orphaned, his mother and brothers succumbing to heatstroke and disease.

For several years Jackson was adrift, drinking and gambling away the few funds available to him. A small inheritance from his grandfather was squandered the very weekend it was received. But by the age of twenty, maturity – and the need to earn an income – led Jackson to become a lawyer's apprentice and then advance a legal career of his own.

In 1788, Jackson moved to a new outpost on the edge of America's frontier, becoming a prosecutor in the new settlement of Nashville. There he met the woman who would forever change his life and that of the nation.

Historians invariably describe Rachel Donelson Robards as 'vivacious', but unfortunately for Jackson she was also already married. A loveless relationship with her absent husband and an unfulfilled promise of divorce contributed to the wagging of tongues in

Tennessee. But Andrew and Rachel's next step raised eyebrows even further as they flouted eighteenth-century convention.

They eloped, marrying in the Spanish-governed territory of Natchez. When they returned to Nashville six months later, their union was deemed adulterous and bigamous. They would never overcome the scent of scandal, and decades later the nation would revel in it.

In 1796, Tennessee became the sixteenth state to join the Union, and Jackson – who had served on the committee drafting its constitution – accepted an offer to become the state's first representative in Congress.

He loathed Washington's clubby atmosphere of backroom deals brokered by members of the wealthy, aloof and learned elites. Within twelve months he quit. 'I was born for the storm,' the rugged frontiersman raged, adding 'the calm does not suit me.'

Returning home, he immersed himself in horses, gambling, whiskey and Rachel. But 'the storm' he craved was on the horizon and heralded events that would eventually return Jackson to Washington in triumph.

In 1812, the US declared war on Great Britain. This 'Second War of Independence' would turn Jackson into the single most famous American of his generation.

As commander of the Tennessee militia, Jackson established a reputation for ruthlessness, a willingness to disobey orders he found objectionable, and voiced a clarion call on his fellow volunteers to back the war effort. 'We are the free-born sons of America,' he proclaimed as he rallied them to confront the British: 'the citizens of the only Republic now existing in the world and the only people on earth who possess rights, liberty and property that they dare call their own.'

In the cold swamps of the south-east, Jackson's militia was tasked with defeating Creek Indian tribes allied with the British. The climax of the crisis came at the Battle of Horseshoe Bend in the Mississippi Territory. By sunset, 27 March 1814 had become the bloodiest single day in Native American history, with more than a thousand Creek Indians slaughtered by Jackson and his men. The skin was peeled from their bodies and used to fashion celebratory bridle reins for the families of Jackson's troops.

Elsewhere, the British were making headway. Having laid waste to the White House and the Capitol in Washington, they planned to cause further humiliation by conquering America's celebrated port of New Orleans. Then, they would march up the Mississippi Valley and meet conquering colleagues heading south from Canada.

As a British flotilla of sixty warships gathered in the Gulf of Mexico, American forces suddenly needed a commander buccaneering enough to stave off the British advance.

Secretary of War James Monroe turned to the man whose 'punishing hand' had devastated the Creek Indians at Horseshoe Bend. Jackson was tasked with securing victory in a battle the US government feared was unwinnable.

Jackson assembled a motley crew of militiamen and irregulars, supplementing them with the forces of French pirate Jean Lafitte and the Cherokee Indians. He rounded out this 'army' by pledging to free any black slaves who signed up for the battle and survived it.

On 8 January 1815, Jackson ordered his vastly outnumbered men to stand their ground and shoot directly at the oncoming British troops. It was a bloodbath, the British sustaining more than two thousand casualties to just sixty on the American side. Without a single day of military training, Jackson had brought unprecedented humiliation upon the world's greatest naval power. A popular engraving captured the moment of victory and spread across the United States propelling Jackson to national prominence.

Not everyone was impressed. In a portent of fiery conflicts ahead, the Speaker of the House of Representatives, Henry Clay, declared: 'I fail to see how the killing of 2,000 English persons in New Orleans qualifies a person for the difficult and complicated duties of the Presidency.'

By the time Jackson swore the presidential oath on 4 March 1829, he had been battle-tested in both the military and political spheres. His first bid for the presidency in 1824 was a searing experience. No less a figure than Thomas Jefferson called Jackson 'the most unfit man imaginable for the office', a conclusion influenced by Jackson's determination to end the elite's traditions of crony corruption.

'It is not necessary that we look exclusively to the mental qualifications of a candidate,' wrote Jackson's friend John Eaton in an open letter to voters. 'It is strength of character, a perseverance of purpose, that makes a distinguished man.'

The voters responded, delivering their hero a big victory in the popular vote and shocking the learned patricians in Washington. But in a four-horse race, Jackson failed to secure a majority of delegates in the Electoral College. The election was thus resolved in the House of Representatives, where Washington's insiders denied the outsider the keys to the Oval Office, handing them instead to John Quincy Adams.

Jackson spent the next four years furiously choreographing his comeback. He accused Adams of becoming president thanks to a 'corrupt bargain' struck among lawmakers. He also correctly surmised that – for two reasons – the 1828 campaign would be a historic turning point and also a unique opportunity.

The year 1828 saw the first election in which the majority of white males had been granted the franchise: their earliest opportunity to participate in a process that – until then – had been the preserve of the educated and the gentry.

Second, Jackson understood that the media tools of the age could deliver his message straight into the homes of first-time voters. He flooded the country with lithographs depicting his heroism in battle. The first political rallies held in America were those promoting Jackson's populist candidacy. Newspaper owners saw him as their golden ticket, telling readers that for the first time they could elect a legendary man of the people.

It was, however, a newspaper loyal to President John Quincy Adams that almost derailed Jackson's campaign. The *Cincinnati Gazette* printed the court record of Rachel Jackson's divorce, alongside an editorial that thundered: 'Ought a convicted adulteress and her paramour husband be placed in the highest offices of this free and Christian land?' The newspaper also falsely alleged that Jackson's mother was a whore.

Furious, Jackson accused Henry Clay – the president's Secretary of State and a friend of the *Gazette*'s editor – of orchestrating the attack. He inveighed the publisher of the *New Hampshire Patriot* to attack Clay's management of the president's re-election, calling him a 'shyster, pettifogging in a bastard suit before a country squire'. Jackson also falsely asserted that the president had procured prostitutes for the Tsar when serving as US Envoy to Russia.

After engaging in the first utterly ruthless election campaign, dominated by libel, slander and bile, Jackson won in a landslide. But for his wife Rachel, the campaign had devastating consequences. 'Who has been so cruelly tried as I have?' she asked a friend in December 1824. 'Our enemies have dipped their arrows in wormwood . . . and sped them at me. Almighty God, was there ever anything equal to it?'

Within days, she was dead – the victim of a heart attack that Jackson blamed squarely on his political rivals. 'May God Almighty forgive her murderers,' he thundered at her funeral, vowing: 'I never can.'

So the Jackson presidency began in grief and rage. But it also started with a near-riot at the White House. Jackson's supporters poured into Washington in their thousands to celebrate his inauguration. 'What a scene we did witness,' wrote socialite Margaret Bayard Smith. 'Cut glass and china to the amount of several thousand dollars was broken in the struggle to get the punch. Ladies fainted, men were seen with bloody noses and such a scene of confusion took place as is impossible to describe.' Jackson escaped by a rear exit, retiring to a nearby tavern.

The mob's presence reignited fears among Jackson's opponents that the new president was determined to up-end Washington. In one of his first acts, he fired dozens of long-term federal officials he regarded as corrupt, replacing them in a blatant act of patronage with his own supporters and friends.

The elite struck back in what was to become Washington's first full-blown sex scandal. Jackson appointed John Eaton, his friend and biographer, to serve as Secretary of War. But Eaton's dalliance with Peggy O'Neill, the unhappily married wife of a US Navy officer, soon became the talk of the town. When her husband died at sea, rumours falsely claimed he had committed suicide over Peggy's affair.

When Eaton married Peggy nine months after her husband's death (by contemporary standards, another scandal), the couple was ostracised, with the wife of vice-president John C. Calhoun leading demands for their removal from Jackson's inner circle.

In 1830s Washington, power gravitated to social events in the mansions of Georgetown, which served as vital settings for political conversations, bargaining and dialogue. When those doors closed to the Eatons, Jackson refused to betray his long-time friend. The scandal of the so-called Petticoat Affair brought political activity in the city to a standstill, dividing Jackson and Eaton from the rest of the Cabinet and thus torpedoing the president's ability to advance his first-term agenda. For Jackson, the affair reeked of the attacks that had killed his wife, and while the newspapers called Mrs Eaton 'The Doom of the Republic', Jackson was determined not to allow gossip to determine the composition of his Cabinet.

It took mass resignations to break the deadlock. Only the Postmaster General survived and Jackson seized the chance to imbue his Cabinet with personalities uninvolved in the scandal. But half of his first term in office had been frittered away.

What Jackson had lost in the opening two years of his presidency, he made up for during the second half of his first term. A stand-off over slavery suddenly presented Jackson with a stark choice and decisive test: would he protect the interests of slave-owners like himself, or save America's nascent federal system from collapse as it came under unprecedented threat?

Congress had banned the import of new slaves in 1808, and – with slave-owners rapidly becoming a minority – the country's slave-owning vice-president John C. Calhoun sought to shore up the economic viability of Southern plantations. When Congress voted to protect factories in the slave-free north by imposing heavy tariffs on the cheap, imported materials that plantation owners in the South used to clothe their slaves, Calhoun – a native of South Carolina – sought to ensure the taxes did not kill the plantations.

His extraordinary proposal was called 'nullification', he claimed any state could ignore ('nullify') within its own borders any federal law that it deemed locally unconstitutional. It was an astounding gambit that – if enacted – would tear the US from its federal moorings.

Calhoun urged Jackson to back him. After all, the president owned more than a hundred slaves, used their labours to create his personal wealth and had even brought some of them to Washington to toil at the White House. Surely he agreed the South required protection?

The president's decision came during a dramatic congressional dinner in April 1830. After Calhoun offered several toasts in support of nullification, Jackson raised his presidential glass and uttered seven pre-planned words severing himself from his fellow Southerners and propelling the country to the brink of civil war: 'Our federal union. It must be preserved.'

The pronouncement caused uproar. Calhoun accused the president of treachery and stopped speaking to him. In South Carolina, lawmakers voted to ignore what they called the 'Tariff of Abominations', and warned that the state would leave the Union if Jackson attempted to collect the tax. Jackson, contemplating the possibility of military action, warned South Carolinians they had been 'seduced . . . by ambitious, deluded and designing men'. But he also warned darkly: 'Disunion by armed force is treason. Are you ready to incur its guilt?'

Henry Clay – now a senator from Kentucky – forged the compromise that postponed America's date with civil war. He won legislative support for a dramatic reduction of the tariffs, in turn allowing Jackson and the lawmakers of South Carolina to stand down.

The crisis revealed the extent of Jackson's commitment to America's federal experiment, but many of his other decisions would be decidedly less idealistic.

With slavery now the country's central political issue, Jackson viewed the work of abolitionists with alarm. He urged northerners to abandon their efforts to raise Southern consciousness about slavery, and quietly and illegally ordered postmasters across the South to destroy abolitionist campaign leaflets mailed from the north.

Among those anxiously observing Jackson's treatment of the abolitionists was another group of people in the president's sights: thousands of Native Americans who comprised the Cherokee Nation. In 1830, Jackson signed the Indian Removal Act into law, a move that in later times would be widely regarded as an act of genocide. The law terminated the government's earlier commitments to respect the rights of the indigenous population. George Washington himself had asserted that the settlers' approach to Native Americans would be guided 'entirely by the great principles of justice and humanity'. The new law was guided by neither.

Jackson viewed the presence of the Cherokee on lands east of the Mississippi as irreconcilable with the expansion of the American frontier, and the growth of slave plantations in the South. Although the Cherokee had emulated America's new European immigrants – creating their own alphabet, town councils, even a newspaper – the president had no interest in compromise. His calculation was callously simple: for America to thrive, it needed westward expansion and white, slave-owning Southerners needed more land. The Cherokee sat on valuable prairies that Jackson now moved to expropriate. 'What good man,' he asked, 'would prefer a country covered with forests and ranged by a few thousand savages to our extensive republic, studded with cities, towns and prosperous farms?'

Two missionaries brought the Native Americans' case to the US Supreme Court. On 3 March 1832, in a stunning rejection of the president's position, the justices ruled 5–1 that the displacement of the Cherokee was unconstitutional and must stop. In events that today would be inconceivable, Jackson called the court ruling 'still-born' and ignored it. Over the next twenty years, up to a hundred thousand Native Americans were evicted by soldiers at gunpoint and forced along the so-called 'Trail of Tears' to present-day Oklahoma.

Jackson faced no sanction for his illegal, unconstitutional and deadly actions. Plantation-owners in the South grabbed the expropriated land in Georgia, Mississippi and Alabama. Evan Jones, a missionary who travelled with the Cherokee on their journey, wrote: 'Multitudes were not allowed to take anything with them other than the clothes they had on. Well-furnished houses were left prey to plunderers who – like hungry wolves – follow the progress of the captors and rifle the houses and strip the helpless. For what crime, then, was this whole nation doomed to almost unheard-of suffering?' Among the Cherokee, Jackson became known as 'the Devil'.

As industrialisation began in an expanding America, Jackson feared his supporters were at risk of economic exploitation. Factories were destroying the activities of small-scale artisans and then offering them the only low-paid employment many could find. Jackson focused his trademark rage on the financial institution that was facilitating industry: The Second Bank of the United States, or as his supporters called it, 'The Monster Bank'. Created by Congress in 1816, the bank handled all fiscal transactions for the US government, its largest single shareholder. The remaining 80 per cent was owned by 4,000 private investors, and – controversially – 3,000 of them were Europeans.

Jackson viewed the bank as an all-powerful monolith overseen by unelected managers who controlled the nation's credit and put America's stability at risk. He also despised their enthusiasm for new-style businesses known as 'corporations', which he considered to be money-grabbing behemoths lacking any semblance of soul. Cartoons depicted him intent on slaying multi-headed corporate monsters that delivered profits for shareholders while caring little about their employees. In this, Jackson was a visionary antecedent of left-wingers to come. He viewed the corporate profit motive with suspicion and believed big business threatened 'to influence [the] judgements and control [the] decisions' of working Americans.

The more the bank's president, Nicholas Biddle, used his clout to dig in, the more Jackson became determined to up-end the institution. In 1832, Biddle tried to force the president's hand by seeking the bank's premature congressional reauthorisation. But Jackson vowed: 'The Bank is trying to kill me. But I will kill it.'

On 10 July 1832, Jackson vetoed a congressional decision to renew the bank's charter. Henry Clay – running against the president as the candidate of the newly formed National Republicans – believed the move risked economic meltdown and would cost Jackson that year's election. Again, he underestimated his foe.

Jackson used the campaign to demand a thumping mandate to destroy the bank. 'We can . . . take a stand,' he urged, 'against the prostitution of our government to the advance of the few at the expense of so many.'

If those words sound like they could fall from the lips of modern-day Democrats, it's not coincidental. Within weeks, Jackson formed the Democratic Party as a vehicle to bash the bank and win re-election.

Even the party's symbol – the donkey – has roots in Jacksonian populism: for years, the president's opponents lampooned him as a jackass. But in rural areas the donkey was a symbol of hard work and reliability. The image started proudly appearing on Jackson's re-election campaign posters.

The result: a landslide. Jackson secured 219 delegates in the Electoral College to Clay's 49. The frontiersman's instincts had paid off again.

Jackson's second term was dominated by the final act in the 'Bank War', and by his determination that US expansionism should not create a national debt to weigh on future generations.

Winning a mandate to destroy the Bank of the United States proved easier than shuttering the institution. Jackson hunkered down, ordering the US government's money to be removed from the bank. But that only created a fresh stand-off. His Treasury Secretary refused to implement the order, insisting it was illegal, and when Jackson fired him all hell broke loose on the floor of the US Senate. Jackson was accused of usurping the Constitution and creating an all-powerful presidency verging on a dictatorship. Henry Clay told his fellow senators: 'We are in the midst of a revolution, hitherto bloodless, but rapidly tending . . . to the concentration of all power in the hands of one man.'

'Jackson took joy in the fight,' writes biographer Jon Meacham, citing a letter written by the president's cousin Andrew Donelson: 'This Bank excitement has restored his former energy,' observed Donelson, 'and gives him the appearance that he had ten years ago.'

The fight made history: on 28 March 1834, Jackson became the only president ever censured by the Senate in a motion that accused him of assuming 'authority and power not conferred by the Constitution'. Characteristically, Jackson shrugged it off. He refused to renew the bank's charter, and in 1836 it closed forever.

By then, Jackson had achieved something else no other president ever managed. On 8 January 1835 he paid off the national debt entirely by selling land that he'd stolen from the Cherokee and reducing government expenditure. For the next twelve months – and for the only year in its history – the nation would be entirely debt-free. The celebrations, though, proved premature. Two years later, Jackson's actions sparked the longest depression in American history. But by then, he was gone from Washington.

Jackson's presidency almost ended early. On 30 January 1835, as he departed a congressional funeral, Richard Lawrence – an unemployed painter with a long history of mental illness – accosted him. Brandishing two pistols, Lawrence falsely claimed Jackson had killed his father, and launched America's first attempted presidential assassination. Astoundingly, both guns misfired, the gunpowder inside them being too damp to ignite. In a fury, Jackson pummelled his would-be assassin into submission with the hickory cane that was not only his trademark but had also given rise to his nickname: 'Old Hickory'.

Jackson retired to Tennessee on 4 March 1837, leaving the White House in the hands of Martin Van Buren, his handpicked successor. In a vivid symbol of the pace of American change, eight years after Jackson arrived in Washington aboard a horse-drawn carriage, he departed on a train pulled by a locomotive.

He spent his remaining eight years at The Hermitage, where – until his death – he continued owning dozens of slaves. His papers leave no indication that he ever regretted owning other human beings, nor that he believed any of them should enjoy their own political or economic rights.

The same applied to women: Jackson is buried alongside his beloved Rachel, whose reputation he defended throughout his life. But he never believed that any woman should enjoy the right to vote, and he dismissed early demands for gender equality in America.

Today, debate rages over Jackson's legacy and he defies categorisation. To many, he's the architect of the ethnic cleansing and genocide of the Cherokee, a lawless tyrant who destroyed the lives of anyone and anything that got in the way of his determination to further the interests of white supremacy and extend the life expectancy of institutions that relied entirely on the labours of slaves.

To others, he's a man of his time who – judged by the standards of that time – challenged unaccountable elites who despised the working classes, saved America from an early date with civil war, prevented its federal system from collapsing entirely, and advanced the universal rights of only white males in ways that would then inspire women and minorities to demand equal treatment.

Jackson's admirers include later presidents of dramatically distinct viewpoints: little unites the outlook of Abraham Lincoln, Franklin Delano Roosevelt and Donald Trump other than the admiration they expressed for elements of Jackson's record.

Today, towns like Jacksonville, Florida, and Jackson, Mississippi remain named after America's seventh president, yet his image will soon disappear from the face of the country's $20 bill.

At the instigation of President Barack Obama, he's to be replaced by Harriet Tubman, heroine of the 'Underground Railroad' that freed a hundred thousand slaves whom Jackson raised not a finger to liberate.

Simon Marks is a veteran Washington correspondent whose reports are broadcast by TV and radio networks worldwide. He's the founder and Chief Correspondent of broadcast agency Feature Story News and hosts the podcast 'Simon Marks Reporting'.

8

Martin Van Buren

4 March 1837 to 4 March 1841
Democrat
Vice-president: Richard Mentor Johnson

By Roifield Brown

Full name: Martin Van Buren, born Maarten Van Buren
Born: 5 December 1782, Kinderhook, New York
Died: 24 July 1862, Kinderhook, New York
Resting place: Kinderhook Reformed Church Cemetery, New York
Library/Museum: Kinderhook, New York
Education: Kinderhook Academy, Washington Seminary
Married to: Hannah Hoes, m. 1807 (1783–1819)
Children: Five: Abraham, John, Martin Jr, Smith, Winfield
Quotation: 'There is a power in public opinion in this country – and I thank God for it: for it is the most honest and best of all

powers – which will not tolerate an incompetent or unworthy man to hold in his weak or wicked hands the lives and fortunes of his fellow-citizens.'

M ARTIN VAN BUREN sits at a unique inflection point of American history. Shaping the modern American political system like no other historical figure, he pointed to an alternative future and authored a narrative for an America that could have been but never was.

Born in Kinderhook, New York, to a Dutch American family, the young Martin grew up speaking his mother tongue, as was customary among town inhabitants. Though the history of the first white people to successfully colonise New York made an indelible mark on the American landscape, it was in Van Buren's ascendance to the office of presidency that we were given glimpses of an altogether different America – one where English was not the official language of the new nation, and where the United States was anything but united.

Van Buren was the first president to have been born after the American Revolution. Being one of America's many nineteenth-century mutton-chopped forgotten presidents, his lasting legacy of the creation of modern American political duopoly and the notion of national politics has remained largely unremembered. His legacy doesn't stop there, however. He also helped usher in the post-Founder phase of the American presidency, and was a key architect of the modern Democratic Party. It certainly is peculiar that a president whose contributions are so deeply woven into the fabric of American society should be so buried and forgotten.

Kinderhook was a small town south of Albany, New York, where Dutch was exclusively spoken during the eighteenth century despite the residents' status as fifth-generation Americans of Dutch ancestry. Van Buren's father, Abraham, had fought in the Revolutionary War and served as a captain in the Albany County Militia's 7th Regiment. He was a man steeped in the politics and mission of the new republic. Abraham, a Jeffersonian Republican, served as the town clerk and was the proprietor of a local tavern. At the time, taverns were very much at the centre of local politicking, with men entering the establishments to discuss the news of the day as much as they came to imbibe. It was in this environment that the young Martin was first educated in politics and began to understand what was required to acquire political power and wield influence.

It was not until he was seven years old that Van Buren began speaking English. He attended a one-room schoolhouse in Kinderhook until the age of fourteen, marking the end of his formal education, as he did not go on to attend college. As the town clerk, Martin's father had extensive local contacts and was able to find his son a clerk position at a lawyer's office, where he would remain for seven years, running errands by day and studying the law by night. The hard work paid off – in 1803, at the age of twenty-one, Martin gained admission to the New York state bar.

After a year in New York, Van Buren returned to Kinderhook to open up a law practice. It was during this time that flickers of his future politics could begin to be seen. The law practice was successful in boosting his reputation locally, where he championed the common people rather than the landed elite in property cases. His future populist politics of the late 1820s were clearly visible, alongside a desire for limited federal government and defence of individual liberties.

In the early years of the nineteenth century, America's two political parties were the Democratic-Republicans and the Federalists, each doggedly fighting to navigate the direction of the republic's future. New York state was very much at the centre of the competing political factions. Van Buren, believing in small national government, aligned himself with the Democratic-Republicans and was rewarded with a county official's post in 1808. At the time, his political allegiance was at best fluid, leaving his detractors to call him unprincipled as he shifted alliances while accruing local political power.

With a reputation bolstered by a slew of courtroom victories, Van Buren ran for New York's State Senate in 1812, beating the Federalist opponent. He ran a campaign opposing the Bank of the United States while supporting the impending war with Great Britain. This was his first electoral success and the beginning of an earnest paving of the road towards the White House.

The war of 1812 against the British started badly for the Americans, resulting in vicious infighting among Democratic-Republicans and the pushing of personal rivalries to the fore. Wanting party discipline, Van Buren formed his own faction within the party known as the 'Bucktails' and committed himself to the defeat of the local Federalists. The Bucktails also railed against New York's most powerful politician and fellow Democrat-Republican, DeWitt Clinton, whom they believed was not strident enough in his defence of limited federal government. Such was the enmity between Van Buren and Clinton that their rivalry became the centrepiece of New York state politics during the 1810s. By the end of the decade, Van Buren, now thirty-two, was appointed the state of New York's Attorney General. With the role as New York's leading Democratic-Republican now fully formed, his total control of the party during this time came to be known by his detractors as the 'Albany Regency'.

Politically powerful in New York state, Van Buren won election to the United States Senate in 1821. Upon arrival in Washington, DC, he cultivated an air of sophistication and adopted the dress of a dandy to accompany his ready wit and unfailing tact. His warnings in the corridors of power about the lack of party discipline marked him out as an up-and-coming political force.

With the end of the James Monroe administration in 1825 and the Federalists vanquished around the nation, politically the Democratic-Republicans stood supreme across America, but the price they were to pay for this victory was the erosion of political party unity. This period saw key Federalist economic programmes and institutions adopted by the Democratic-Republicans. National tariffs came in 1816 and a Second Bank of the United States was incorporated. These policies were anathema to many Democratic-Republicans. Elements of the party, including Van Buren, found the developments worrisome. Van Buren also warned that such policies weakened the primacy of Southern slaveholding interests, enfeebling the national party's political foundation.

The creation of cabals was the unintended consequence of wide-single party identification rather than a fostering of political harmony among Democratic-Republicans. On the eve of the 1824 election, there were at least three distinct factions in the party – the Adams–

Clay Republicans, the Jacksonians and the Old Republicans – with each promoting their own candidate. In addition to factional candidates, the party was increasingly riven by regional concerns, with separate parts of the country backing different candidates for commander in chief. This made a true national consensus around a candidate almost impossible.

In the election, Van Buren threw his support behind Secretary of the Treasury William Crawford of Georgia, a man of impeccable Jeffersonian credentials. Secretary of State John Quincy Adams dominated the vote in New England and won some support elsewhere. Clay dominated in his home state of Kentucky and won majorities in two neighbouring states. Crawford won the Virginia vote and did well in neighbouring North Carolina. General Andrew Jackson won in Tennessee, his home state, and in Pennsylvania. Of all the candidates, Jackson had the broadest geographical support.

The two candidates with the most votes in the election, Jackson and Adams, both fell short of the Electoral College votes needed to claim the presidency. The rules of the Constitution mandated that the presidency be decided in the House of Representatives where the fourth-place finisher, Senator Henry Clay, threw his votes to Adams, who was then crowned victor. The supporters of Jackson were outraged, believing a 'corrupt bargain' had been hatched between Adams and Clay, which had cost their man the White House. They, along with Van Buren, vowed to win back the White House in 1828.

Van Buren believed that Adams was a secret Federalist, pointing to the new president's intention to strengthen the federal government's role in economic development as a prime example. He brought together the factions of the Democratic-Republicans hostile to Adams under Jackson's standard. The Jackson–Van Buren coalition was formed, with the populist Jackson promising a return to smaller federal government and a protection of state rights.

In 1827, in the run-up to the 1828 election, Van Buren wrote to Virginia newspaper editor Thomas Ritchie, a Jeffersonian political leader in the state. Van Buren argued that the time had come for South Carolinian John C. Calhoun's idea of a national nominating convention to choose a presidential candidate before the 1828 elections.

The idea of a convention would be a key milestone towards the formation of a new political party and would put an end to the political regionalism that had marked the 1824 election. Van Buren thought a party convention would help focus the opposition to the incumbent president and solidify politics around principles rather than personal coteries and local interests. Lastly, he opined that the divide between the Northern and Southern states could be healed by creating a national political coalition, something that a convention would aim to create.

Though a supporter of Jackson, Van Buren thought that a congressional caucus or general convention would help rein him in were he to become president. Van Buren worried that Jackson's personal popularity meant that he might govern with little thought of the Democratic-Republican Party or party policy in general, so a convention would be a prudent way to keep him on message.

In the letter to Thomas Richie, Buren stated:

I have long been satisfied that we can only get rid of the present, and restore a better state of things, by combining General Jackson's personal popularity with the portion of old party feeling yet remaining. The sentiment is spreading, and would of itself be sufficient to nominate him at the Convention.

The call of such a convention, its exclusive Republican character, & the refusal of Mr. Adams and his friends to become parties to it, would draw new the old Party lines and the subsequent contest would re-establish them; state nomination alone would fall far short of that object.

Van Buren's letter to Richie was one of the most farsighted documents in American political history. It set in place an American political system that still stands today. Forming a national party system was needed to stop the factionalisation of American politics. Van Buren united the planters of the south and the Republicans of the north around a united political identity.

Van Buren saw the 1828 election as an opportunity to restore the party to its 'first principles' of limited federal government. 'If General Jackson will put his election on old party grounds, preserve the old systems, avoid if not condemn the practices of the last campaign,' he said, 'we can by adding his personal popularity to the yet remaining force of old party feeling, not only succeed in electing him but our success when achieved will be worth something.'

By the start of 1828, Van Buren had created his campaign to put Jackson in the White House. It was customary at the time for actual candidates not to go on the stump, leaving Van Buren in the position of chief fundraiser, strategist and political mouthpiece for Jackson. With some states expanding their franchise, there were new voters to win. With his large parades, rallies and fiery speeches, Van Buren targeted first-time voters, who he saw as vital to obtain the presidency.

Van Buren's most difficult challenge during the campaign was persuading the candidate to suffer in dignified silence as the Adams' camp levelled virulent attacks on Jackson's wife's character. His wife was called an adulteress and a bigamist, much to Jackson's distress and anger. While keeping Jackson's temper in check was one problem, another was the protectionism growing strong in the west and north-east. Van Buren had to be mindful of the Southern planters' more free-trade leanings if his candidate was to triumph in the election. Courting both camps, he kept his coalition together through the 1828 tariff, known in the South as the 'Tariff of Abominations'. This kept westerners on his side where they might have voted for the sitting president, while kicking the issue down the road for Southerners.

During the campaign, Van Buren was elected governor of his home state of New York, a position he had sought in order to improve Jackson's chances of winning that state in the election and securing its Electoral College votes.

The 1828 United States presidential election was held from 31 October to 2 December. Jackson's victory over Adams is widely heralded as a triumph of the 'common man'. Significantly, it also started a newly reformed Democratic-Republican Party that gave birth to the modern Democratic Party. With nearly all white men eligible to vote, 9.5 per cent of the nation cast a vote, compared with only 3.4 per cent in 1824. Jackson won the Electoral College vote 178 to 83.

With twenty Electoral votes for Jackson secured in New York

state, Van Buren resigned from the governorship and joined the Jackson administration as Secretary of State. In Jackson's Cabinet, Van Buren shone as the most capable member among a sea of men who were personal friends of Jackson. During his tenure as Secretary of State, he became one of the president's most trusted confidants and an adviser who Jackson knew he could trust, in contrast to hangers-on who were dubbed the 'Kitchen Cabinet'.

Jackson came to office to entrench white interests, and key to this goal was the Indian Removal Act of 1830. This act gave the president power to negotiate removal treaties with Indian tribes living east of the Mississippi. The Indians were to give up their ancient land, leaving their schools and community for the promise of land to the west. The prize of citizenship was offered to those who wanted to stay. The act was to lead to the 'Trail of Tears', an act of calculated genocide and a grave stain on the young republic. However, it was President Van Buren who most brutally enforced Jackson's Indian Removal Act, not the populist president.

In his new role as Ambassador to the United Kingdom, Van Buren sailed for England in 1832. Always well mannered, he was popular in London's diplomatic circles – the ending of the border dispute in Maine with Britain being one of his accomplishments while abroad.

In late February 1832, the Senate rejected Van Buren's nomination to continue as UK Ambassador, with vice-president John C. Calhoun casting the deciding vote. This angered Jackson, but after reflection, Calhoun's act gave him ample reason to remove him from the ticket in the coming presidential election. Jackson decided that his adviser Van Buren was to be his next vice-president, saying that 'the people in mass would take you up and elect you vice-president!'

After returning to the US political fray in July 1832, Jackson needed Van Buren's help in drafting the president's message to Congress explaining his proposed veto to the recharter of the Second Bank of the United States. Getting rid of the bank was an article of faith to both Jackson and Van Buren. The lack of a national bank was to have grave consequences for the country later in the decade and Van Buren's impotence during the forthcoming Depression was to be one of the many blemishes on his presidency. He helped pen a ringing denunciation of the bank, calling it an 'instrument of privilege'. The future of the bank was to be a key election issue, and the Jackson–Van Buren ticket easily won re-election on an anti-bank platform, sealing the bank's fate.

The re-elected Jackson had now rid himself of Calhoun, eliminated the national bank, and brought Van Buren just one step away from the presidency. During Jackson's second term, Van Buren was as 'close to the president as a blistering plaster', as one critic put it.

The transfer of government deposits from the doomed bank to state depositories and private institutions dominated the administration. Jackson rejected a more cautious course than Van Buren proposed, which would have been sensitive to political sensibilities and would have minimised financial repercussions of a hasty withdrawal of government funds. Wall Street, however, added pressure on the administration, as it wanted the bank closed so that private banks and institutions would receive government deposits. Against this backdrop, Van Buren withdrew his opposition to a more orderly transition of government assets and the gradual closing of the bank.

The confrontation between the state of South Carolina and the federal government was the other pressing issue at the end of Jackson's first term and into the start of his second. The Nullification Crisis nearly brought the secession of South Carolina from the Union. Southern states were uncomfortable with the 1828 and 1832 national tariffs, but South Carolina went the furthest, declaring the federal tariffs to be unconstitutional, null and void within the state. The crisis put the state courts and the US Supreme Court in opposition with the state government. Such were the inflamed passions around the issue that Governor Hayne of South Carolina assembled two thousand mounted minutemen and an infantry of twenty-five thousand who were ready to assert the state's policy in the face of federal forces in Charleston.

During the crisis, Van Buren always counselled a policy of conciliation to South Carolina, not wanting to inflame an already volatile situation. Though nullification and the limits of states' rights were the overt reason for the crisis, after its de-escalation Jackson declared: 'the tariff was only a pretext and disunion and Southern Confederacy the real object. The next pretext will be the negro, or slavery question.'

In Jackson's second term, the real clear demarcation of party-political lines came into view. Van Buren's idea of a creation of parties around policy, conventions and clear alliances saw the Democratic-Republicans start to refer to themselves as simply 'The Democrats'. In opposition were the followers of the former vice-president Calhoun, who went on to form the Whig Party.

The 1835 Democratic National Convention chose Van Buren and Richard Mentor Johnson of Kentucky. Van Buren was Jackson's candidate. The Whig Party's *raison d'être* was to oppose Jackson, but the party was too new to have the same organisational rigour as the Democrats. Riven by regionalism, the Whigs ran multiple candidates. Former Senator Harrison of Ohio represented the north, Senator Lawson White of Tennessee carried the hopes of the South along with Daniel Webster of Massachusetts and Willie P. Mangum of South Carolina. The strategy was to try to deny Van Buren an Electoral College victory and to turn the election to the House.

Despite facing multiple candidates, Van Buren became the third incumbent vice-president to secure an election win, earning a majority of the electoral vote and taking most of the popular vote in both the South and the North. Van Buren's idea of a national party and a coalition of interests was vindicated; he had won election on policy grounds, as everyone agreed he did not have the popular appeal of his predecessor. It was through endorsement and the strength of the party that victory had been delivered.

Van Buren's inaugural address was a discourse about the American experiment being an example to the people of the world. America was a land of unlimited freedom and prosperity. Less than three months later, the economy had spectacularly crashed in the panic of 1837, dispossessing tens of thousands of their land and homes. For the next five years the United States was wracked by the worst depression in its short history. Van Buren's reputation as a political wizard was to end in ruins before the end of his term in office. He was labelled 'Van Ruin', and whatever could go wrong in the next four years did.

On the day that Van Buren formally became the eighth president, one of the nation's most prominent trading houses suspended payments, prompting a wave of brokerage failures to sweep the nation. The fiscal policies of the Jackson administration and a national trade imbalance contributed to the country's depression. Van Buren declared that the panic was due to the easy availability of credit, his main concern during the crisis being the maintenance of the national government's solvency to avoid elevating the actual crisis. Deflationary policies extended and prolonged the depression. Van Buren had inherited a situation that he could not understand or fix.

'No man ever entered upon the execution of an official duty with purer motives, firmer purpose or better qualifications for its performance,' Van Buren wrote in his memoirs of President Jackson. 'We were perhaps in the beginning unjustifiable aggressors' towards the Indians, but 'we have become the guardians and, as we hope, the benefactors'.

Shortly after Congress approved the Indian Removal Act of 1830, the government started enforcing it in earnest. Tribes in the south-east were the first to be removed. After 1832 it was the turn of the Chickasaw, Choctaw and Creek to be forced to move east of the Mississippi. In office Van Buren continued to brutally enforce the act. The costly Second Seminole War in Florida that was to last until 1842 was a direct outcome of this policy. The 'Trail of Tears' is another of Van Buren's enduring stains on American history, with a quarter of those forced to leave their homes and march thousands of miles perishing on the journey.

The problems continued to mount. The white settler situation in Texas meant that relations with Mexico became increasingly strained, leading to a war between Mexico and Texas in 1835–36. Many Americans were disappointed that the Jackson and the Van Buren administrations did not act forcefully on behalf of the new Texan government or admit Texas to the Union. His refusal to do the latter represented an attempt to avoid upsetting the balance of slave and free states across America, part of Van Buren's opposition to the expansion of slavery.

With the nation beset by myriad problems, Van Buren lost his 1840 re-election bid. The Whig William Henry Harrison triumphed. The Democratic Party asked Van Buren to be its candidate again in 1844, but his opposition to the incorporation of Texas in the Union halted these plans. Van Buren's anti-slavery leanings led him to head the Free Soil Party ticket in 1848, but this too was to be another lost election.

Martin Van Buren died in Kinderhook in July 1862, aged seventy-nine. He passed during the Civil War, which was fought over the issue of slavery, an institution that he had gently pushed against during his political career. He left America with a political system that in large part is still in place today. A two-party system with national conventions, clear policy platforms and in which political campaigns can be fought around policy and not just personality.

Roifield Brown is a podcaster on politics, history and culture. The host of six podcasts, he teaches podcasting at UC Berkeley.

9

William Henry Harrison

4 March 1841 to 4 April 1841
Whig
Vice-president: John Tyler

By Emma Burnell

Full name: William Henry Harrison
Born: 9 February 1773, Charles City County, Virginia
Died: 4 April 1841, Washington, DC
Resting place: North Bend, Ohio
Library/Museum: Berkeley Plantation, Charles City, Virginia
Education: Hampden-Sydney College
Married to: Anna Symmes, m. 1795 (1775–1864)
Children: Ten: Elizabeth, John Cleves, Lucy, William Henry Jr, John Scott, Benjamin, Mary, Carter, Anna and James
Quotation: 'Times change and we change with them.'

WILLIAM HENRY HARRISON is probably most famous as the president who died of machismo. Having been taunted about his age throughout the campaign, he was determined to prove his mettle at his inauguration, so he spoke for nearly two hours in the rain without an overcoat. The next month he died of pneumonia. He was the first president to die in office.

Harrison was born in Virginia to what counts as American aristocracy. His father Benjamin had been a highly influential politician and a signatory of the Declaration of Independence. In fact he was reverently known to the family as 'The Signer'. The family lived comfortably on a Virginia plantation.

However, as the youngest of seven, William Henry was neither entitled to much nor expected to go far. In those days first sons were advantaged by inheritance. The second son – Carter – had a career mapped out for him in law. By the time they got to William Henry, there was little interest left. He made a brief attempt to join the medical profession (you didn't need formal qualifications so he simply studied under a family friend) but showed little interest. He finally found his way when he joined the army in 1791.

Harrison was involved in a number of battles, including Fallen Timbers – where he first fought the Shawnee warrior Tecumseh, who would figure prominently in the legend of Harrison's time in the military.

When Harrison was governor of the Indiana Territory, Tecumseh (Shooting Star) and he went toe-to-toe at a three-day council discussing the disputes between the Native Americans and the white settlers over land. As Tecumseh and his prophet brother built a settlement at the mouth of the Tippecanoe River, the white settlers were getting increasingly nervous and angry.

The Battle of Tippecanoe was against the Shawnee, but they were led during it by Tecumseh's brother, who had set himself up as a spiritual leader. Tecumseh was actually away travelling when the decision was made to gather a thousand men and march on the native settlement in autumn 1811. Harrison was not necessarily expecting conflict – anticipating, perhaps, that the natives would surrender. A delegation of chiefs was sent to suggest a council between the two sides the following day. Harrison then disastrously took his troops off to camp on a nearby hill. It was a trap and the natives attacked the unfortified camp. The white soldiers were easy to pick off against their campfires. It was only as dawn broke that the dynamics of the fight changed and the much greater numbers of the white army turned the fight to their advantage.

While the details of the initial stages of the battle are unfavourable to Harrison (who had failed to fortify his troops' position, leaving them vulnerable to the attack), his victory became famous and it was this battle that earned him the nickname Tippecanoe when he ran for president.

While his political opponents tried to paint Harrison as a coward during the election (he left the army for politics before the official end of the war), this was not a version that anyone who served with or under him recognised. Harrison was renowned for being at the front of the fight, riding up and down the line issuing commands and holding the troops together. His mistake on the night in question was softened by a resounding victory during the day. Tecumseh himself was finally killed at the Battle of the Thames, where the forces were led by Harrison – further enhancing his reputation as a great military leader.

Harrison had a number of business ventures that failed, so he was always poor and, as a result, always seeking promotion. John Quincy Adams once wrote of him: 'This person's thirst for lucrative office is absolutely rabid.' As such, he went in and out of political office.

He was first elected a delegate to the House of Representatives in 1799, was appointed governor of the Indiana Territory in 1800, went to the House again from 1816 to 1819, and was elected to the Senate in 1825 but immediately traded up to become the US envoy to Columbia.

His political instinct was usually to split the difference. For example, he was against the slave trade, and would emphasise this when speaking with abolitionist northerners, but would always make clear to southerners that he did not believe the trade could be ended until it was decided by the slaveholding states.

Andrew Jackson had become such an unassailable president that his style led to the creation of two separate parties: his own Democrats and the newly formed Whigs. The Whigs weren't agreed much on what they were for, but were united in their opposition to Jackson.

They were generally in accord not on political principles, but on formats. They rallied around Henry Clay's call for a strong federal government where power was centred on the Congress and not the president. But they had strong factions for and against the key issues of the day: slavery and banking.

William Henry ran unsuccessfully (after Clay declined) to be president in 1836 against Jackson's deputy Martin Van Buren, but was one of many on a split Whig ticket and lost resoundingly.

However, 1840 was a much more opportune moment as, just weeks after Van Buren's swearing in, the country had been plunged into panic due to the financial catastrophe of 1837, which saw banks close their doors and workers failing to get paid. Clay was determined to secure the nomination, but Harrison's supporters got out of the traps early, passing resolutions as early as 1837 in favour of him running again. This sort of early internal jostling was new to politics and a sign of further innovation to come on the campaign trail. Clay was also a Kentuckian and a slave-owner. Given the Whigs' strength in abolitionist New York, this made his path all the harder, and New York editor and Whig organiser Thurlow Weed was clear he wouldn't win the all-important state and so worked against him.

Nevertheless, there were still a number of candidates in the race when it came to the USA's first nominating convention. In both a first and a sign of things to come, the press were given prime seats on the floor. The race was largely between Clay and Harrison. Clay had been a towering figure in the Senate, which was an impressive but double-edged achievement. Where William Henry could split the difference, or simply tell different factions slightly different stories (so little known were his real views), Clay was on the record on the most contentious issues of the day. So while Clay led on day one, his support faded as the balloting continued. On the third ballot, Harrison was elected with 148 votes.

Harrison set himself up as the 'ordinary' guy against the 'elitist' Martin Van Buren. That William Henry had grown up in a Virginia mansion the son of a 'signer' and Van Buren was the self-taught son of a tavern-owner didn't seem to have much effect on this narrative. Harrison was painted as the 'log cabin' candidate. (While it was true that the house his family lived in had once been a log cabin, it had since been vastly improved on.)

In this they had been helped by a tin-eared attack from the Democrats, which said that Harrison would rather be in his log cabin sipping hard cider than running the country. Many hard-working – and hard-drinking – voters saw this as an elitist attack, and the Whigs adopted the imagery wholesale. There was hard cider at many campaign events and practically anything that could be renamed log cabin was.

There was a carnival-like atmosphere throughout the campaign with vast rallies and parades – something unheard of before. There were speeches by the candidate – another first. Average Americans had difficult lives. The primary employment was farming and any excuse to get out and do something different was welcomed with open arms. The Harrison campaign released songs such as 'Tippecanoe and Tyler too' (Tyler was his running mate) and – somewhat inexplicably – rolled giant balls across the country as entertainment.

It may be that this 'man of the people' stance contributed to Harrison's death. As he made his journey from North Bend to Washington after his victory, crowds would camp outside every place he stayed, carousing well into the night and ensuring the travelling party had no sleep. Consequently, by the time he made that long, exhausting speech in the rain, he was severely run down.

Having died just a month into office, Harrison did not leave much of a legacy in terms of legislation. However, much of his run for office could be considered the birth of modern political campaigning. Though predecessor Andrew Jackson had worked to appeal to an extended franchise, it was nothing compared to the tactics and techniques that would be used in the Harrison campaign, many of which have echoes in today's politics.

Emma Burnell is a journalist and communications and political consultant. She is also a playwright and director.

IO

John Tyler

4 April 1841 to 4 March 1845
Whig
Vice-president: None

By Peter Riddell

Full name: John Tyler
Born: 29 March 1790, Charles City, Virginia
Died: 18 January 1862, Richmond, Virginia
Resting place: Hollywood Cemetery, Richmond, Virginia
Library/Museum: Sherwood Forest Plantation, Charles City, Virginia
Education: College of William & Mary, Williamsburg
Married to: (1) 1813, Letitia Christian (1790–1842), they had eight children; (2) 1844, Julia Gardiner (1820–89), they had seven children
Quotation: '[The annexation of Texas] shall crown my public life . . . I shall neither retire ignominiously nor be soon forgotten.'

JOHN TYLER WAS a more consequential president than his usual historical image as a slave-owning champion of states' rights and national expansion who looked back to the era of Thomas Jefferson.

He was caught in the turbulent cross-currents of American politics in the middle decades of the nineteenth century leading up to the Civil War, and was widely reviled during much of his time in office. At his death, he was the only former president to be treated as a traitor since he was a citizen of the Confederacy and buried in its flag. But Tyler made a significant mark both on the office of the presidency and on the size and future of the United States. He was the first vice-president to become a president between elections, and he immediately asserted his right to take over in the face of initial opposition and doubts.

Tyler defended the powers of the presidency against the claims of Congress, not always successfully. His term also featured important treaties with the UK over the boundaries with British North America, now Canada, and with China in opening up access to the treaty ports for American business. His most memorable, and final, achievement was to push for, and to secure, the annexation of Texas.

His presidency was full of incident, not least his second marriage to a New York beauty thirty years his junior, who was a forerunner of Jacqueline Kennedy in redecorating a dowdy and run-down White House. She produced seven of his fifteen children, a record for any president. Pearl, the last, was born in 1860 when he was seventy, and only died in 1947. And at the time of writing his last surviving grandchild was still alive, 231 years after Tyler was born, a year after George Washington was inaugurated.

Tyler never escaped his origins as part of the plantation, and slave-owning, aristocracy of English ancestry of Virginia and he looked the part with his striking Roman nose. He revered the generation of the Founding Fathers that produced four great presidents from Virginia: Washington, Jefferson, Madison and Monroe. He was the fifth president from Virginia. His father had been a classmate and friend of Jefferson at the College of William & Mary in Williamsburg and became a Virginia legislator and governor with spells in between as a state and then federal judge.

Tyler followed closely in his father's footsteps, growing up on a

1,200-acre slave plantation. Like many prominent politicians, he lost a parent, his mother Mary Armistead, when he was young, only seven. He was educated by tutors at home and then, between the ages of twelve and seventeen, at the College of William & Mary, reading Adam Smith's *Wealth of Nations* and developing a lifelong love of Shakespeare. He then studied law and was admitted to the Virginia bar at the precocious age of nineteen.

For the following three decades he alternated between the law and politics – the former to finance his rapidly growing family after he married in 1813, the same year as his father died. That year also marked his brief involvement in military matters, after the British invasion of Hampton on the coast during the war of 1812 led to him becoming captain of a militia company to help defend Richmond – though he never saw action.

From 1811, Tyler served five single-year terms in the Virginia House of Delegates before being elected to the US House of Representatives in December 1816 and serving four years. After two bored years at home, he successfully sought re-election in 1823 to the Virginia House, then two years later was elevated to the largely ceremonial position of governor.

Tyler followed a consistent approach during this period – a strong defence of the rights of individual states and hostility to Washington initiatives, whether during the recurrent debates over a national bank or about centrally financed infrastructure projects (which he believed should be initiated by states). He presented this as a strict defence of the US Constitution. His attitude to the 'peculiar institution', as slavery was known, was less explicit, perhaps more hypocritical, than the full-blooded defence offered by politicians from the cotton-producing Deep South. He never sought to justify slavery but also never spoke against it and rejected claims that Congress could regulate or end slavery. He bought slaves himself, and never freed any.

The ambiguities in his position emerged in the late 1820s when he was narrowly elected by the Virginia legislature in early 1827 as a US senator. (Senators were indirectly elected by state legislatures until 1913.) This was the time when the party system was splintering between the National Republicans of incumbent president John Quincy Adams and the Democrats of Andrew Jackson, who defeated him in 1828. Despite frustrations over some of Jackson's actions, and his style, Tyler backed him up to, and after, his re-election in 1832. But he then moved into opposition over proposals to force states to comply with the federal lead and voted for motions of censure on the president, in the process aligning himself with the newly formed Whig Party under Henry Clay, which made him president pro tempore of the Senate.

The Whigs were a broad coalition including both abolitionists and supporters of slavery. But with the Democrats in control in Virginia, Tyler's position was becoming increasingly untenable and he resigned as a senator in February 1836. He became a candidate for the vice-presidency in the very confusing politics of 1836, but came third in a vice-presidential election decided by the Senate.

Despite returning to private law practice for the third time, he could not resist the lure of politics, being re-elected in 1838 to the Virginia House of Delegates. He had become a national political figure, being put forward to return to the Senate, and then emerging as the vice-presidential candidate again in 1840. This was because of a lack of alternative candidates to attract Southerners to the Whig ticket headed by William Henry Harrison, a former general and hero of the Indian wars in 1811, hence the campaign slogan of 'Tippecanoe and Tyler too'. The campaign was rumbustious as Democrat jibes that the elderly Harrison could retire to his log cabin and drink hard cider were turned to his advantage. Tyler made some non-committal campaign speeches, and following the landslide victory of the Whigs he returned to his home in Williamsburg, making only a brief visit to Washington to be sworn in as vice-president on 4 March 1841.

With Congress not in session, Tyler was at home when woken on 5 April to be told that the sixty-eight-year-old Harrison had died the previous morning from pneumonia and pleurisy, not helped by the medical treatment of the time. This was the first time a sitting president had died in office and there was uncertainty about whether the Constitution meant that the office of the presidency now transferred to Tyler, or just its powers and duties. The immediate response of many in the Harrison Cabinet and in Congress was that Tyler was 'vice-president acting president'. Tyler, who travelled to Washington in the very rapid time of twenty-four hours, was decisive in claiming that the Constitution gave him the full powers of the president and got himself immediately sworn in in his hotel room, becoming the youngest president until then at fifty-one. His critics, including former president John Quincy Adams and Henry Clay, initially described him as a regent or caretaker, and some of his critics continued to describe him as 'His Accidency'. Adams said that Harrison's death had brought to the presidency 'a man never thought for it by anybody'. But Congress quickly accepted his succession and an important precedent was set for the orderly transfer of power on the death of a president, as has occurred several times since then. The legal position was formally clarified in the Twenty-fifth Amendment, adopted in 1967.

The views Tyler held on states' right and limits to federal power were not accepted by many Whigs, but he started by retaining Harrison's outgoing Cabinet, though quickly asserted that he was in charge and would not be bound by their opinions. He repeatedly clashed with Clay, who himself wanted to be the effective national leader as the dominant figure in the Whig Party. A confrontation on legislation about national banking, the symbol of federal versus state power, led first to the resignation from the Cabinet in September 1841 of all but Secretary of State Daniel Webster, and then, the same month, to Tyler's expulsion from the Whig Party.

Tyler had continuing battles with the Whig-dominated Congress over tariffs, an important source of revenue in view of the continued weakness of the economy following the collapse of 1837. Tyler vetoed a number of bills, challenging Congress's claims to have the initiative over policy. This led in turn to discussion of possible impeachment. Moreover, a record four of his Cabinet nominations were rejected by the Senate, as were a similar number of his nominations to the Supreme Court. His early years in office were also overshadowed by the death of Letitia, his first wife, in September 1842. She had been an invalid for much of her time in the White House and Tyler was helped by some of his adult children in looking after her.

The Tyler administration did, however, achieve some significant successes internationally. In particular, the Anglophile Secretary of State Daniel Webster negotiated a treaty with Lord Ashburton (of the Baring family and with an American wife), which addressed several of the disputes with the UK over the USA's northern border, especially between Maine and New Brunswick and in the Great Lakes. The north-western boundary in what was then Oregon was dealt with later. It tends to be forgotten now how fraught relations were between Washington and London over border disputes. Naval clashes occurred for much of the first seventy or eighty years after the USA became independent and anti-British feeling ran high. The 1842 treaty, with careful compromises that turned out to favour the US side in Maine because of mineral deposits, lowered the temperature. The administration also negotiated an important trade agreement with the Qing dynasty in China: the Treaty of Wangxia, which remained in effect for a century and challenged the dominance of Britain by clarifying issues of extra-territoriality and gave American businesses access to the treaty ports. Tyler also asserted American interests across the Pacific.

His other main achievement dominating the end of his presidency was relations with Texas, which had become independent from Mexico in 1836 thanks to the leadership of Sam Houston after the debacle of the Alamo. Tyler was a strong believer in the expansion of the United States, taking his cue again from Jefferson, and from the doctrine of Manifest Destiny: the belief that the economic and political power of the country would be strengthened by extending its borders. As with so much else in that era, the question was bound up with slavery, which existed in Texas. Tyler was suspicious of British intentions to develop links with Texas to free slaves, and saw annexation as a route to re-election as an independent in 1844. In making Texas a priority, Tyler dispensed with Daniel Webster. Texas was promised military protection against an invasion from Mexico, though this was kept secret to avoid stoking congressional opposition.

A day after the completion of the treaty, on 28 February 1844, came the disaster of the USS *Princeton*. She was on a cruise down the Potomac to show off the 'Peacemaker', the world's largest gun, in front of four hundred guests, including the whole Cabinet. After several successful firings, the captain decided on one more shot. But the gun exploded, killing several people including the Secretaries of State and the navy, as well as Armistead, Tyler's personal black slave. Among the other casualties was David Gardiner, one of whose daughters, Julia, was already being courted by Tyler, who was unharmed after remaining below decks. He carried Julia, who had fainted, to safety. They married four months later and she became a glamorous hostess in the final months of the Tyler presidency as well as the mother of his seven further children.

The Princeton catastrophe and the death of Secretary of State Abel Upshur ended both the hopes of ratifying the treaty by the November election date and Tyler's own chances. He did not help himself by appointing as Upshur's successor John C. Calhoun of South Carolina, an outspoken defender of slavery. This angered abolitionists, and both the Whigs and the Democrats opposed annexation. After being expelled by the Whigs, and being rejected by his old party the Democrats, Tyler then set up a new party, the Democrat-Republicans, which duly nominated him. But when after lengthy wrangling the Democrats nominated James K. Polk, a supporter of annexation, Tyler recognised that he had no chance of re-election and that the best hope of achieving his goal of including Texas was by backing Polk. The Senate rejected the annexation treaty by a two-to-one majority. But after Polk was narrowly elected as president in November 1844, Tyler pressed ahead during the then four-month transition with legislation requiring a simple majority, rather than the two-thirds margin needed for a treaty. This passed both Houses and was signed into law by him three days before he left office in March 1845.

Annexation meant that Tyler's final weeks in office were marked by celebrations, with a final official ball attended by three thousand people. The politically partyless Tyler said: 'They cannot say now that I am a president without a party.'

Tyler then returned to a plantation on the James River, which he renamed Sherwood Forest since he had been outlawed by his old party, the Whigs. He farmed, raised another large family and socialised. As the threat of secession by a majority of slave-owning states approached, he played a leading role in an unsuccessful peace conference in Washington, but he ended up voting against compromise and becoming a prominent backer of the secession of Virginia and a member of the Confederate Congress.

Never in good health throughout his life – suffering from persistent stomach complaints – he died of a stroke in Richmond.

He was given a full ceremonial funeral there, but his death was ignored in Washington.

Tyler has generally been rated in the bottom quarter of American presidents, with the positive achievements of his four years – the decisive way he took over the office, the treaties with Britain and China, and the annexation of Texas – being overshadowed by the bitter political divisions of the time that limited his effectiveness and, above all, by his defence of slavery and his final support for the Confederacy. As recent biographer Gary May concluded: 'Tyler found himself on the wrong side of history, left the Union and died a traitor, his good deeds forever tainted by his final years.'

Regarded in his time as the accidental president, he has become the forgotten one – remembered, if at all, for the number of his offspring and their longevity – and by the city of Tyler in Texas.

Peter Riddell was US Editor and Washington Bureau Chief of the Financial Times *during the presidency of George H.W. Bush before joining* The Times. *He was Commissioner for Public Appointments for five years between 2016 and 2021.*

II

James K. Polk

4 March 1845 to 4 March 1849
Democrat
Vice-president: George M. Dallas

By Brian Klaas

Full name: James Knox Polk
Born: 2 November 1795, Pineville, North Carolina
Died: 15 June 1849, Nashville, Tennessee
Resting place: Tennessee State Capitol, Nashville
Library/Museum: Columbia, Tennessee
Education: University of North Carolina
Married to: Sarah Childress, m. 1824 (1803–91)
Children: None
Quotation: 'No president who performs his duties faithfully and conscientiously can have any leisure.'

JAMES K. POLK is the most consequential American president that you've never heard of. When he first emerged as a 'dark horse' candidate to lead the Democratic Party in the 1844 presidential election, his main opponent in the Whig Party dismissed him. He was so unknown to most voters that the Whigs adopted a jeering campaign slogan: 'Who is James K. Polk?' Today, most people could ask the same question. He is largely unknown outside the pages of history books, an invisible president whose name has faded over time.

Yet, if you've been to California, Texas, Arizona, New Mexico, Nevada, Utah, Idaho, Oregon, Washington state, or certain parts of Wyoming, Montana, Oklahoma and Kansas, you've stood in territory that wasn't part of the United States before Polk acquired it through conquest and diplomacy. American folklore often speaks of the United States stretching 'from sea to shining sea', a reference to an uninterrupted expanse of land from the Atlantic to the Pacific oceans. That line was made possible by James K. Polk. In the comparative blink of his four years in power, the United States added one million square miles of territory – an area that is equivalent to *eleven* times the land area of the entire United Kingdom. Polk quite literally reshaped America, and in the process, he reshaped American history.

Polk also did something that many politicians say they'll do but few actually accomplish: he fulfilled every major domestic and foreign policy promise that he made during his presidential campaign. That, many historians argue, surely qualifies him for exceptional recognition in the pantheon of American presidents. Sure enough, when historians are occasionally asked to rank presidents, Polk routinely ends up near the top tier.

But fulfilling short-term goals can sow the seeds for long-term problems. And that's precisely what Polk's presidency did. America got bigger under his leadership. But adding territory without addressing key social questions – most notably whether to allow people to be legally enslaved – just meant that there was a larger land area that was even more divided than before. Polk's presidency foreshadowed a national calamity that would see the newly enlarged territory break in half: the American Civil War.

But before there was power, there was piety. Polk was born into a religious Presbyterian family in North Carolina in 1795, shortly after America had gained its independence. They taught Polk that the 'gospel of duty' demanded hard work. Polk mostly grew up in Tennessee, where his father had taken the family. There, they became prosperous. His family owned fifty enslaved people. But Polk later returned to North Carolina to study mathematics and classics at the University of North Carolina at Chapel Hill. By 1820, he had gained additional qualifications in law, but he decided to launch a political career instead. Polk picked a pivotal moment to do so.

He was first elected to the Tennessee House of Representatives in 1823 as a Democrat. Two years later, he made it to Congress. As a result, Polk's political rise would coincide with Andrew Jackson's ascent to the presidency. Jackson was one of America's first populists, positioning himself as a champion of the common man against a corrupt elite. At the same time, though, Jackson began enthusiastically and brutally removing Native Americans from their lands, expanding settlement of territory through any means necessary. Polk was mesmerised. He had found his political inspiration.

Polk relentlessly promoted Jackson. While Jackson was known as 'Old Hickory', some of Polk's associates dubbed him 'Young Hickory'. Jackson, in turn, made Polk a political protégé. In 1835, in the final years of Andrew Jackson's second term, Jackson had the chance to show that the loyalty went both ways. Jackson supported Polk's bid to become the Speaker of the US House of Representatives. With a powerful friend in the White House, Polk got the post.

But by 1839, Polk had set his sights on a new prize: the governorship of Tennessee. In a close race, he narrowly defeated the Whig candidate, Newton Cannon. The euphoria from victory was short-lived. Polk's tenure as governor was largely a failure. He achieved none of his signature priorities. Nonetheless, Polk hoped that his gubernatorial experience would make him the logical choice as vice-president to join the ticket of Democratic president Martin Van Buren in his bid for re-election in 1840. The Tennessee governorship could, Polk hoped, act as a springboard to high national office. Instead, Polk was snubbed, left to continue his lacklustre tenure as governor of Tennessee. With little to show from his two-year term, Polk was defeated in his bid for re-election in 1841. Undeterred, he prepared to rise phoenix-like from the ashes of defeat in the 1843 election. Again, he was defeated. From Speaker of the US House of Representatives, Polk's star had fallen. He was now the failed, twice-defeated former governor of Tennessee – a candidate who hoped to be a Jacksonian man of the people, only to find that his people wanted someone else.

There are few ironclad rules in American politics, but it is close to an ironclad rule that successful candidates for the presidency are people who are climbing the political ladder rather than tumbling down it with a crash. Polk was at a low point in 1843. He had fallen, in just a few years, to being an obscure political figure who couldn't even win over his home state. Polk seemed destined to be a minor footnote in American history.

It was profoundly surprising, then, when Polk was selected to represent the Democratic Party in the 1844 presidential election. The presumptive favourite had been Martin Van Buren, a man who had already served as president from 1837 to 1841. But when Van Buren openly opposed annexation of Texas, it opened up a split in the party. Southern Democrats and expansionists who wanted to enlarge the Union abandoned Van Buren. Suddenly, the nomination was wide open. There were plenty of obvious alternatives. None of them were James K. Polk.

But after seven ballots at the party convention, Democrats had not been able to agree on who should represent them. On the eighth ballot, one delegate proposed Polk as a consensus candidate, a little-known, long-forgotten figure who didn't inflame passions as much as the more prominent names. Polk was known for being an expansionist, someone who favoured pushing America's borders further south and west. He won the nomination. It stunned everyone, including Polk himself.

When the Whig candidate, Henry Clay, heard the news of who his opponent would be, he lamented that the Democrats had not picked someone who was 'more worthy of a contest'. It was widely believed that Polk would lose in a landslide. Instead, Polk won.

Upon entering the White House, Polk tried to replicate the ethos of Jacksonian democracy. On Mondays, Wednesdays, Thursdays and Fridays, he received visitors (without an appointment) until noon. They would simply turn up and ask him for a favour, complain about some grievance, or demand a job. Polk's diaries are filled with complaints about these insufferable meetings that guaranteed the 'useless consumption of time'. Occasionally, even on days or times in which Polk had given explicit instructions to allow no visitors, he would enter his office to find someone waiting for him. In one instance, Polk was startled to find a trespasser, who had convinced a White House porter to let him inside. The intruder demanded that Polk make him a brigadier general in the army. (The Secret Service, which is charged with protecting the president, wasn't formed until 1865.)

His mornings taken up with frivolous demands and grifting political climbers, Polk often worked late into the night. 'No president who performs his duties faithfully and conscientiously can have any leisure,' he wrote. But Polk took being a stern workaholic to its limits. When jugglers came to the White House, he wrote that it distracted him and lamented that others were amused by it when they should have been thinking about more important matters. He was equally adventurous and fun-loving when it came to food. When attending a breakfast in his honour in Louisiana, where Southern cuisine was at its most exotic, Polk wrote: 'I could see nothing before me that I had been accustomed [to] . . . I took a cup of coffee and something on my plate to save appearances, but was careful to eat none of it. As soon as an opportunity offered, I asked a servant in a low tone if he could give me a piece of corn-bread and broiled ham.' Summing up his notoriously charmless personality, one of Polk's contemporaries said of him that he was a 'victim of the use of water as a beverage'.

It turns out, however, that having a charismatic, fun-loving personality is not a prerequisite for presidential achievement. Polk set out to fulfil four main goals, which he called the 'four great measures'. First, end the ongoing dispute with Great Britain over the Oregon territory on the Pacific coast. Second, reduce tariffs – something the Democratic Party had long favoured. Third, establish an independent treasury. And finally, acquire California from Mexico. Despite being waylaid by the incessant flow of opportunists visiting the White House, Polk successfully achieved all four – and also acquired Texas.

Polk had been swept up in the newest craze in Democratic circles: the mantra of Manifest Destiny. The notion, a precursor to American exceptionalism with religious overtones, suggested that America was destined to spread across the North American continent. This belief provided a convenient justification for both territorial expansion and the removal of Native Americans from their lands. Polk pursued both.

In 1846, Polk signed a treaty with the British government that granted the United States control over the Oregon territory (which includes not just Oregon but parts of modern-day Washington, Idaho, Wyoming and Montana) so long as it was south of the 49th parallel. There was, however, one exception: Vancouver Island dipped below that line, but remained under British control.

With the northern dispute settled peacefully, Polk still had a far thornier territorial question to resolve. Immediately before Polk was inaugurated, President Tyler had put the wheels in motion to annex Texas, which had been effectively operating as an independent republic. Mexico, however, claimed Texas as its own territory. So, when Polk recognised the annexation of Texas and formally admitted Texas as America's twenty-eighth state in December 1845, Mexico objected. Polk offered $30 million (a little under $1 billion in today's value) to buy huge swathes of land claimed by Mexico, including Texas. The Mexican government refused. Polk sent a garrison to enforce the annexation, setting out the Rio Grande River as America's new southern border with Mexico (as it largely is today). War soon broke out. Polk suspected it would be a quick campaign, as America's weak enemy to the south would swiftly capitulate. History would prove him wrong.

Whigs, many northerners, and abolitionists opposed the war, fearing that it would create more power for the bloc of Southern slaveholding states. Abraham Lincoln, then a young anti-war statesman in the House of Representatives, accused Polk of abusing his power, circumventing Congress, ignoring the Constitution, even acting like a dictator. But perhaps most prescient was Henry David Thoreau, the transcendentalist writer who wrote the now-famous essay *Civil Disobedience* about refusing to pay taxes that funded Polk's war with Mexico. 'The United States will conquer Mexico,' he predicted, 'but it will be as a man who swallowed the arsenic which brings him down in turn. Mexico will poison us.' History would prove him right.

The war lasted for nearly two years. The United States won, but more slowly than Polk had anticipated. All told, roughly thirteen thousand Americans and twenty-five thousand Mexicans died as a result of the conflict. On 2 February 1848, Mexico and the United States signed the Treaty of Guadalupe Hidalgo, which gave the United States control of territories that make up the modern-day states of Arizona, California, Colorado, Nevada, New Mexico, Utah and Wyoming. In exchange, Polk agreed to pay the Mexican government $15 million, substantially less than the pre-war offer that Mexico had refused. The California Gold Rush followed soon afterwards, quickly attracting greater numbers of settlers out to America's new western territories.

Whether in the south-west or north-west, these borders were moved and territory was acquired without consulting the Native Americans who lived on the land. Polk had backed Andrew Jackson's vicious Indian Removal policy decades earlier – and continued America's long history of seizing indigenous land.

Polk's legacy, however, isn't just one of territorial expansion. It's also of leaving the great question of the nineteenth century – slavery – totally unresolved. Instead, Polk, who himself was a plantation-owner who owned slaves, let the dispute fester. During his time in the White House, he bought an additional nineteen enslaved people from the profits of his plantation – a plantation he had relocated to the state of Mississippi to make it harder for anyone to escape to free states in the north. But Polk, who was aware of the risks of a public outcry in the north against his slaveholding, mostly kept that plantation business secret. In a letter to his cousin – a man who purchased enslaved people – Polk wrote: 'There is nothing wrong [in] it, but still the public have no interest in knowing it, and in my situation it is better they should not.'

Nonetheless, Polk did publicly defend slave-owners with the twisted logic of nineteenth-century Democrats, framing the issue as one related to *the plantation owners'* individual freedom. In speaking out against the Wilmot Proviso (a measure that would have ensured that slavery was banned in territories acquired from Mexico), Polk said the ban would mean 'the blessings of liberty may be put in jeopardy or lost forever'. Meanwhile, thirteen of the nineteen enslaved people Polk bought during his presidency were children.

Polk did nothing to defuse tensions around slavery in America. Instead, his territorial expansions only further inflamed them. And in the process, he laid the groundwork for America's bloodiest conflict: the Civil War. He unwittingly provided tactical training for it too. Most of the generals in both the Confederate and Union armies had previously fought side by side in Polk's Mexican–American War. A little over a decade later, slavery would divide them on opposite sides of the battlefield.

Polk, who had pledged to serve only one term, made good on that promise and left the White House on 4 March 1849. He, along with his wife Sarah, made a sort of meandering post-presidency departure tour through several Southern states, travelling on riverboats and being toasted at lavish banquets. On one of those boats, or in one of those banquets, Polk contracted an illness – believed by historians to have been cholera. He died on 15 June, just over three months after the end of his presidency, aged fifty-three. His wife Sarah lived for another forty-two years.

Of all the presidents who have largely been forgotten by history, James K. Polk was certainly not the most virtuous, but he was the most consequential.

Dr Brian Klaas is an Associate Professor in Global Politics at University College London, a columnist for the Washington Post, *an author, and the host/creator of the 'Power Corrupts' podcast. His latest book is* Corruptible: Who Gets Power and How It Changes Us. *He is originally from Minnesota.*

Zachary Taylor

4 March 1849 to 9 July 1850
Whig
Vice-president: Millard Fillmore

By Michael Crick

Full name: Zachary Taylor
Born: 24 November 1784, Barboursville, Orange County, Virginia
Died: 9 July 1850, Washington, DC
Resting place: Zachary Taylor National Cemetery, Louisville, Kentucky
Library/Museum: Louisville, Kentucky
Education: By his mother, and at schools in Kentucky
Married to: Margaret 'Peggy' Mackall Smith, m. 1810
Children: Six: Ann Mackall Wood; Sarah Knox Davis (briefly married to future Confederate president Jefferson Davis); Octavia Taylor; Margaret Taylor; Mary Elizabeth Dandridge; Richard Scott Taylor

Quotation: 'The idea that I should become President seems to me too visionary to require a serious answer. Such an idea never entered my head, nor is it likely to enter the head of any sane person.' (Letter to brother, 1846)

ZACHARY TAYLOR WAS not a political creature. He is one of five presidents who had never held public office before. He was reluctant to be president and knew little of how politics worked. He was no great speaker and did not campaign for votes. And he lasted just sixteen months in office – the third shortest spell of all.

Taylor was born in 1784 on a plantation in Orange County, Virginia, not far from the birthplace of the fourth president James Madison, his second cousin. The Taylors were a prominent Virginia family, but when Zachary was only eight months old, they moved five hundred miles west, to a spot near a tiny new settlement in Kentucky called Louisville. His father had obtained 400 acres on Beargrass Creek on the Ohio River, part of a generous bonus he'd received for his service as an officer during the War of Independence, and Louisville's rapid expansion helped them prosper.

Despite this well-to-do background, Zachary had only a rudimentary education, and his early writing is full of spelling mistakes. At twenty-three, he joined the army and spent the next forty years as a soldier, but with regular visits back home to oversee the family plantations, which eventually extended to 10,000 acres, worked by hundreds of slaves. The rugged, weather-beaten face in Taylor's portraits came from a life spent mostly outdoors, whether as a soldier or a planter.

Like Washington and Andrew Jackson before him – and Grant and Eisenhower subsequently – Taylor reached the presidency through military exploits that brought fame and popularity. He fought briefly in the war of 1812 against Britain, and for many years defended the western frontier against Native Americans. Taylor achieved distinction as a colonel in the 1832 Black Hawk War against American tribes, and then, from 1835 to 1842, during the Second Seminole War in Florida, when he earned the nickname 'Old Rough and Ready', for his willingness to share the poor conditions of his men.

Taylor's military reputation rests, however, on his leadership during the Mexican–American War of 1846–48, which followed the annexation of the republic of Texas in 1845. His victories at the Battles of Palo Alto and Resaca de la Palma drove the Mexicans out of Texas. Taylor pressed on south into Mexico, and had further success at the Battle of Monterrey in 1846, which prompted the first talk of him as a presidential candidate. But it was the Battle of Buena Vista that made Taylor – by now a general – a serious prospect for the White House. Disobeying orders from above, he ventured further into enemy territory and, despite being outnumbered, achieved a famous victory that caught the public imagination, partly because his forces were mostly volunteers. He was now a national hero, celebrated in art, poetry and music.

Yet few would claim that Taylor was an outstanding commander. 'I thought well of him as a general but never for a moment regarded him as a great one,' said William Marcy, the War Secretary throughout the conflict. 'His bravery and steadfastness of purpose are the summary of his high qualities as a commanding officer.' It helped that the Mexicans were often disorganised and lacked resources.

'Old Zack' was an unpretentious officer, with typical Southern courtesy, though he could flare into a rage over something trivial. He hated wearing uniform, so people sometimes mistook him for a farm labourer. One officer wrote in his diary: 'Taylor is short and very heavy, with pronounced face lines and grey hair, wears an old oil cloth cap, a dusty green coat, a frightful pair of trousers, and on horseback looks like a toad.'

The war resulted in the conquest of a third of Mexico – and the US gained a great swathe of territory from the Atlantic to the Pacific – about a fifth of the contiguous area of the modern USA – including all of California, Nevada and Utah; most of New Mexico, Arizona and Colorado; and segments of several other states.

Towards the end of the Mexican War, however, Taylor fell out with President James Polk, who began starving him of supplies and men, and transferred his soldiers to Major-General Winfield Scott. Polk seemed wary of Taylor's military prominence, and fearful of a potential rival. Taylor had never, in fact, voted in his life or even expressed any political views, but groups lobbied the reluctant general to run for the White House. When a visitor to his tent hailed him as 'the next US president', Taylor is said to have responded: 'Stop your nonsense, and drink your whiskey.'

Zachary Taylor eventually agreed to try for nomination by the Whigs, even though they had opposed the war. His main rival was the legendary statesman Henry Clay (also from Kentucky), who was against the extension of slavery, and derided Taylor as a 'mere military man'. Taylor was backed, however, by most southern Whigs, who wanted to preserve and extend slavery (and also by a new congressman, Abraham Lincoln, who admired his military achievements). At the convention in Philadelphia, Taylor was preferred over both Clay and his army rival Winfield Scott. Taylor hadn't attended the convention, and didn't hear of his success for six weeks. When party officials wrote to tell him, Taylor had been tardy to respond to the letter notifying him of his nomination.

In the election, Taylor won 47.3 per cent of the vote and beat the Democrat contender, Lewis Cass of Michigan, 163–127 in the Electoral College. The outgoing Democrat president James Polk dismissed his successor as 'wholly unqualified for the station' and warned he would be manipulated by his devious Whig colleagues.

Taylor had made clear he would 'feel bound to administer the government untrammelled by party schemes'. Once in the White House, he abandoned much of the Whig programme, and declared that his party's cherished policy of re-establishing a national bank was 'dead', and 'will not be revived in my lifetime'.

The biggest issue, however, was slavery, and Southern fears that the new territories would upset the delicate political balance between their slavery interests and the abolitionist north. Taylor owned slaves himself – the last president to do so in office – but the driving principle of his administration was a middle course: slavery should be protected, but not extended to the new territories. Amid growing talk of secession, Taylor urged settlers in New Mexico and California to push quickly for statehood so that they could decide the issue for themselves. Naïvely, Taylor hoped Congress would simply not discuss the issue; instead, they did so in fierce debates involving Daniel Webster, John Calhoun and Henry Clay – the 'Great Triumvirate' of historic statesmen who had dominated US politics for thirty years. Each represented different interests: northern business (Webster), Southern slave-owners (Calhoun) and western settlers (Clay).

Taylor opposed the package of slavery measures, known as the Compromise of 1850.

Then, in July 1850, just sixteen months into his presidency, Zachary Taylor was suddenly taken ill after attending Independence Day festivities, and a ceremony for the new Washington Monument. It was a hot, sweltering day and Taylor is said to have eaten cherries and drunk iced milk, then cold water back at the White House. He soon suffered severe stomach cramps, diarrhoea and dehydration, which were probably caused by the milk or water, at a time when sanitary standards were poor and Washington still had open sewers. He died five days later, of a bacterial infection of the small intestine, his doctors said. He was sixty-five, and left 131 slaves in his estate. The Compromise of 1850 was passed soon afterwards.

For almost a hundred and fifty years subsequently there were suspicions that Taylor was poisoned, perhaps by pro-slavery Southerners. In 1991, his body was exhumed from the mausoleum at Zachary Taylor National Cemetery in Kentucky, but analysis found no evidence of poisoning. It was probably a gastric ailment, the study concluded, though his corpse was too decomposed to be certain. The experts reckoned, however, that the president 'would probably have recovered if left alone', but instead his doctors had overloaded him with medication.

What if he'd lived? Some argue that as a Southern slave-owner who opposed the expansion of slavery Taylor might have acted as a compromise figure and helped avoid the Civil War that broke out eleven years later. He was a friend of the Confederate president Jefferson Davis, who was very briefly married to his daughter Sarah, and also a distant cousin of the Confederate general, Robert E. Lee.

But Zachary Taylor was probably too ignorant and innocent of the ways of politics ever to have changed history or been a distinguished president. He was a true outsider to Washington, and the first president whose party didn't have a majority in either the Senate or the House throughout his time in office. He and his Cabinet refused to negotiate with the legislature. Taylor didn't seek out the counsel of Clay or Webster, and failed to recruit other shrewd advisers who might have compensated for his shortcomings.

Taylor's one significant accomplishment was the 1850 Clayton–Bulwer Treaty with Britain, which was meant to enable both countries jointly to build a canal across the Panama isthmus. Symbolically, it was a part-renunciation of the Monroe Doctrine to limit European involvement in the Americas, and of Manifest Destiny, the idea that the US was bound by God to expand throughout the continent. It took a second treaty and sixty-four years, however, before the Panama Canal was actually built, but the treaty paved the way for a relationship between the two English-speaking countries that *did* change history.

Zachary Taylor was a poor president, unread, untutored in political ideas, lacking the art of persuasion or the judgement of character to succeed in high office. His determination to stick to a battle-plan may have brought success in war, but inflexibility is a handicap in politics. He was out of his depth, one of a string of mediocrities to occupy the White House in the twenty-four years leading up to the American Civil War.

Michael Crick is a broadcaster with Mail Plus and former ITN Washington Correspondent. He has written biographies of Arthur Scargill, Jeffrey Archer, Michael Heseltine, Michael Howard and Sir David Butler, and his biography of Nigel Farage will be published shortly.

13

Millard Fillmore

9 July 1850 to 4 March 1853
Whig
Vice-president: None

By Layla Moran

Full name: Millard Fillmore
Born: 7 January 1800, Moravia, Cayuga County, New York
Died: 8 March 1874, Buffalo, New York
Resting place: Forest Lawn Cemetery, Buffalo, New York
Library/Museum: East Aurora, New York
Education: No formal education
Married to: Abigail Powers, m. 1826 (1798–1853), Caroline McIntosh, m. 1858 (1813–1881)
Children: Two: Millard and Mary
Quotation: 'God knows I detest slavery but it is an existing evil, and we must endure it and give it such protection as is guaranteed by the Constitution.'

THIRTY-FIVE PER CENT of American college students can't pick him out as a former president even when shown his name in a list. This rises to 92 per cent when no list is shown. So known is Millard Fillmore for being forgettable that the Millard Fillmore Society was founded in 1963 with the sole purpose of commemorating his anonymity. On 7 January, his birthday, the society handed out awards such as the 'Medal of Mediocrity' to honour 'mediocrity to combat the rising tide of over-achievers'.

While we may jest about his forgettability, there is much about Fillmore that is truly remarkable, as well as so odious that there is no joke in it. But without doubt his story has resonance today.

Millard Fillmore was purportedly declared by Queen Victoria to be 'the handsomest man she had ever met', though his beginnings were so humble that one would struggle to believe he could rise to such heights as to find himself in the admiring gaze of a queen. This is a true rags-to-riches story, emblematic of the cherished 'American dream'.

Millard was born on 7 January 1800 in the Finger Lakes area of upstate New York. In his early childhood his father, Nathaniel Fillmore, a farmer, and his mother, Phoebe Millard (his first name was derived from her surname, a tradition at the time), struggled to put food on the table. His childhood was spent working the land and he received no formal schooling, though he was taught to read the Bible.

When Millard was thirteen, his father, convinced that his eldest son (of eight children) should learn a trade to improve the outlook of the family, apprenticed him to a clothmaker one hundred miles away. Pauper apprenticeships at that time were commonplace, and essentially child labour.

As an indentured servant Millard was, by law, tied to the mill in which he worked unless he could buy himself free. He hated it. He longed to learn and would take pleasure in occasionally being allowed to help with the books, as he had basic reading and writing skills. He dreamt of how he could leave this life of menial work and make more of himself.

How, and exactly when, he came to be free of the mill changes depending on the source you consult. Almost all the stories say he walked the one hundred miles home on foot following the mill's temporary closure. Whether he saved the money or took out a loan, he did pay off the mill-owner (around $30) and never went back. At seventeen, he bought himself a dictionary and spent his spare time studying it, then enrolled in a local academy. There he met a remarkable red-headed teacher two years his senior called Abigail Powers, and fell deeply in love with her.

Abigail was well spoken, smart and educated. She herself is note-worthy as she was the first ever First Lady of the United States who worked before and after her marriage. It would not be until the latter half of the twentieth century that this became normalised, and as such Abigail herself should be considered a trailblazer. She would also go on to create the White House Library and took great joy in selecting the books in it. This was a surprisingly modern woman for the age.

Millard, however, decided he needed to prove himself to Abigail before asking for her hand. He studied hard, and his parents decided they wanted to help him get on. His father contacted a friend and got Millard a job as a clerk. The family then moved to Aurora, a town near Buffalo, where his talent and studiousness were recognised by other lawyers. In fact, they petitioned the court for him to be fast-tracked to the bar. Millard had made it!

By 1823 he was six foot tall, handsome, and he dressed the part of a middle-class man of means and education. Not a hair was out of place, nor would an un-ironed shirt ever betray his roots. He was desperate to be accepted and seen as worthy. Scholars suggest that this deep personal insecurity haunted him for the whole of his life and is one of the defining characteristics of his presidency. In 1826, he finally married Abigail, and they went on to have two children, Millard and Mary.

By the time Millard was almost thirty, he was well respected and getting noticed. At the time, the Freemasons were powerful in US politics, with most ruling politicians having some kind of connec-tion with them. A man called William Morgan had broken ranks and was ready to expose the inner working of the secretive organ-isation, but was kidnapped before he could do so and never seen again. There were suspicions that the Masons were behind the disappearance, and so a fledgling new party arose called the Anti-Masonic Party.

Fillmore joined, and he was elected to New York's state legislature for the first of three terms in 1828. While there, he fought to pass legislation that forbade debtor imprisonment, no doubt an issue close to his heart given his childhood experiences. He was popular with the electorate and was elected to the US House of Representatives in 1833. His party then joined the Whigs in 1834, a new party that stood opposed to President Andrew Jackson and his Jackson Democrats. They borrowed their name from the British Whigs, who were broadly anti-monarchy, portraying Jackson as a 'king' and themselves as closer to the common man. Millard served as the Whig congressman for Buffalo from 1837 to 1843.

Another feature of Millard's career was his great rivalry with former New York governor William Seward, against whom he 'harbored a jealousy that had in it something of the petulance of a child'. Seward was a close ally of the then party leader, Thurlow Weed, and his upbringing and outlook was very different to Fillmore's. Seward's father owned land and also slaves, and gave Seward a childhood of plenty. Yet his son took a strident anti-slavery stance and, when governor, enacted laws that helped African Americans. Millard, who, let's remember, had an altogether more difficult background, had a less dogmatic view of slavery. You get the sense that he viewed Seward's easy charm and care for minorities as a luxury that only someone who had never known poverty or had to graft could afford. While Millard claimed to be personally against slavery, he felt it was a pragmatic part of life and that compromise was the right approach.

So, in 1844, he decided (partly to stop Seward getting the position) that he wanted to be vice-president of the United States. He sought the nomination and failed.

As it happens, Seward did not even go for it. Millard then ran for governor of New York, and failed at that too. Naturally, he blamed the anti-slavery voters, who had previously supported Seward when he was governor from 1839 to 1842, and the newly immigrated Catholics for his lack of success.

Finally, he was successfully elected in 1847 as Comptroller of New York by a sizeable margin.

Being a man of great practical skill, he excelled at the job and was popular with the electorate. He was also sufficiently redeemed from his past failures for him to be taken seriously again as a contender for a leadership position in his party. So, in 1848, when the Whigs needed to decide their presidential ticket, Fillmore was in the running.

Zachary Taylor, a celebrated general who had made his name in the Mexican–American War, won the presidential nomination despite having never been elected to any position before in his life. He was a slave-owning Virginian, and the Whig Party sought to balance the ticket by putting a northerner as his running mate. Millard seized his chance. He and his campaign manager went around the convention that year promising anything to anyone.

It was this propensity to put pleasing people before holding to any principle that, many argue, is a significant factor in explaining why he is not well remembered. As we shall see, his fluidity of position was the only permanence of his approach.

Millard won the nomination. Not only did he tick the northerner box, but his moderate stance on slavery was electorally attractive as it wouldn't scare off the Southern states.

The Taylor–Fillmore ticket, never even meeting one another until three days before their inauguration, went on to win by a narrow margin. And so Fillmore, from his dirt-poor roots, achieved his life's dream. He was headed to the White House. But not all was to turn out as he had hoped.

Vice-presidents at that time were not as powerful or influential as they can be nowadays, so the fact that nothing of note happened for Fillmore in the first years of his tenure comes as little surprise. However, another factor was the relationship between Taylor and Millard's nemesis Seward. Taylor held Seward in very high regard, far higher than any he felt for Millard. Seward became Taylor's effective right-hand man and sat in his Cabinet.

Millard became increasingly irritated with his lack of influence and instead concentrated on being a fair and diligent president of the Senate, but the animosity grew and festered. He even aligned with Senator Clay – a long-time opponent of Taylor who remained aggrieved for having not won the Whig presidential nomination – to pass an Omnibus Bill that Taylor was opposed to.

Lady Luck was to intervene, for Fillmore anyway. Less so for Taylor, who had served only sixteen months as president when, in

July 1850, he fell ill. He went to a 4 July parade and died. Whether it was the heat, the fact he weighed 300 pounds, or likely gastro-enteritis caused by the unsanitary conditions in Washington, is unclear. But, as a result, Millard Fillmore, now fifty years old, became president of the United States. And as he said himself, to say he was surprised would be an understatement.

The man from humble beginnings had risen to the top through quiet determination and, most of all, a willingness to say and do whatever it took.

His first act as president was motivated by pure spite. It had been customary for the Cabinet of a former president to write letters of resignation to the incoming president, who would then politely decline and allow a level of continuity before replacing them. Against all advice, Fillmore accepted them all, and spent his first twenty-one days putting a Cabinet together rather than getting on with the job.

What Millard would go on to do as president was not driven by his own beliefs as much as by a desire to continue and complete the work started under Taylor. Without doubt, his greatest political feat was to pass the Compromise of 1850, which included the controversial Fugitive Slave Act. The fact that the act contained the word 'compromise' was fitting some might say, given Fillmore's inability to take a position and stick to it. However, this rather oversimplifies a complex issue that obsessed the political class at the time: the country's relationship to slavery and the strain this was putting on the Union, with some Southern states actively making overtures towards seceding.

At this point, we should bear in mind that the American Civil War would start just eleven years later, and the Emancipation Proclamation would be signed by Lincoln just two years after that. Perhaps only a man of fluid principle could stand by an act that was so obviously going to be both a sticking plaster and an aggra-vating thorn in that great existential battle that led to bloodshed, and that still reverberates in America and its politics today. If pol-itics is the art of the possible, then Fillmore was a master practitioner.

The Compromise itself was designed to dampen disquiet in four areas: the recent acquisition of vast areas of land following the Mexican War of 1848 and whether or not these new states should allow slavery; the petition by California to join the Union as a state that would be free to determine its own position on slavery; a land dispute pushed by Texas that claimed land all the way to Santa Fe; and, finally, Washington, DC's status as the nation's capital, it being also the largest slave market on the continent.

Five new laws were proposed. The newly acquired territories of New Mexico, Nevada, Arizona and Utah would be able to take their own decisions regarding slavery when they eventually applied for statehood. Texas would relinquish its claim to disputed land at her northern and western boundaries following the Mexican–American War, and, in return, would receive ten million dollars and use this to pay off its debts to Mexico. Washington, DC would outlaw the slave trade, though slavery was still permitted, and California would join the Union as a free state (as opposed to a slave state). That last part was particularly problematic as Congress had taken great pains to keep a balance between free and slave states until this point, and California tipped the country into imbalance.

A fifth bill was introduced to placate the slave-owning lobby, which was called the Fugitive Slave Act. It is this act that stained Fillmore's life and legacy even in his own times, let alone from the enlightened perspective of today. In fact, so obviously problematic was it at the time that his wife Abigail told him not to sign it as it would split the Whig Party. And she was right.

The new Fugitive Slave Act 'improved' on the former Fugitive Slave Act of 1793. It was already the case in the US that, should a slave escape, the local authorities had a duty to find and return them, but this was weakly enforced, not least because many Americans did not agree with slavery, especially if they lived in a free state. So, if an enslaved African American did cross the state line, they could live in relative freedom knowing they were unlikely to be hunted down. However, the new act meant that it was now a responsibility of the federal rather than state government to enforce the return of the slave, and there were fines for officials who did not comply. Emerging from this were the 'slave catchers', who would hunt down escaped slaves across the country for money.

Not only did Fillmore sign this act, but he also went on to enforce it with extraordinary vigour. He did this even though he had said that, on a personal level, he detested slavery. The presidential nomination for 1852 was uppermost in his mind and he knew that if he wanted to win it, he needed the support of the Southern states. So, yet again, his personal ambition superseded any sense of principle that he might have possessed. He would widely claim that he himself wasn't pro-slavery or anti-immigration, but it suited him to ally politically with those we now consider racists and bigots, who would eventually find themselves on the wrong side of history.

The consequences of the Fugitive Slave Act reverberated through the African American community. Stories of defiance were rife across the country, especially in areas that rejected slavery. Fillmore even threatened to send troops to dampen down protests in regions that refused to comply. The revolt spread to Buffalo, his hometown, which was at the end of a railroad and a gateway to Ontario, Canada, where a community of former slaves had sprung up.

Locals in Buffalo would frequently seek to help slaves escape, and it was a town well known for harbouring fugitives. This included a judge who, in 1851, issued a writ of habeas corpus in favour of a slave from Kentucky to give to him to escape a bounty hunter. The slave succeeded. But many did not. An estimated one hundred people were condemned because of the Fugitive Slave Act, but many more spent their lives looking over their shoulder living in fear of the blossoming industry of the professional slave catcher.

The next few years were characterised by loss and tragedy.

In 1852, despite his best efforts, Fillmore lost the Whig presidential nomination. A year later, his beloved wife Abigail died, having caught a cold at the inauguration of Democrat Franklin Pierce. This developed into pneumonia and, just twenty-six days after leaving the White House, she died. Fillmore was devastated. His daughter Mary took over his household, but she too passed in 1854 from cholera. Millard decided to go on a tour of Europe, a long-standing wish of Abigail's while she was alive.

In 1855, during a visit to the UK, he was offered an honorary degree by Oxford University. He declined it with the words: 'No man should, in my judgement, accept a degree that he cannot read' (the wording of the certificate would have been in Latin). And it is stories like these that make me wonder what I would have made of the man at the time, for it seems he was capable of deep principle, just perhaps not when it really mattered. While away, his ego buoyed perhaps by Queen Victoria's flattery, he decided to throw his hat into the ring for president once more.

Fillmore joined the Know-Nothing Party. Its name derived from the fact that when it was set up it was secret, so its members, if asked about it, would say they 'knew nothing'. It was also known as the 'Native American Party'. But this was not a pro-indigenous people's party; rather, a nativist, anti-Catholic, anti-immigration, populist movement that held some surprisingly progressive views on labour and women's rights, and was 'neutral' on slavery. Its platform, politically muddled then and certainly from our perspective, must have chimed with Fillmore's propensity for contradiction.

He won the 1856 presidential nomination for the now-named 'American Party', but failed to be elected. It was curtains for his time on the national stage.

The rest of Fillmore's life was spent in Buffalo. In 1846, he founded Buffalo University (UB), becoming chancellor, a position he held until his death in 1874; arguably his greatest achievement outside of his presidency. The university started as a medical school, and in 1862 it merged with the State University of New York. Today, it is the largest public college in New York state, educating more than thirty thousand people each year. One must only reflect on Fillmore's humble childhood, and how education provided the foundations of his success, to understand his motivation here.

In 1858, Fillmore married a wealthy widow called Catherine Carmichael McIntosh. From 1862 to 1867, he served as president of the Buffalo Historical Society, and in 1870 he became president of Buffalo General Hospital. He died of a stroke on 8 March 1874, and was buried at Forest Lawn Cemetery in Buffalo, NY. His last words, presumably referring to something he was eating, were 'the nourishment is palatable'.

For fifty-four years, the city of Buffalo, in partnership with the University of Buffalo, commemorated Millard Fillmore in a ceremony at his graveside. However, in January 2020, the University of Buffalo said that they would no longer co-sponsor the commemoration ceremony, even though they did recognise he 'played a complex role in the history of slavery in the US'. On 3 August 2020, they decided to remove his name from an academic centre, 'a decision that aligns with the university's commitment to fight systemic racism and create a welcoming environment for all'.

There is something poignant in this. The president, famous for being forgotten, fades further into the shadows due to decisions he made over a hundred and fifty years ago. The founding of Buffalo University is an extraordinary legacy that should not be forgotten, but neither should his acts as president. All of them, the good and the bad, deserve to be remembered and reflected on.

In his life, Fillmore rose from the bottom of the heap to the very top of the pile, but along the way he fractured his party and enacted one of the most oppressive laws in the United States' history. It was only very recently that his full part in that history was acknowledged.

Millard Fillmore was many things. He embodied the classic rags-to-riches success story, and he was tinged with good luck, contradictions, some great decisions, some terrible ones and some that were simply deadly. This very forgettable president has so much we can all learn from. The American dream is real, but the cost of compromise for political gain can lead to both infamy and anonymity.

Layla Moran is Liberal Democrat MP for Oxford West and Abingdon and speaks on foreign affairs for the party.

14

Franklin Pierce

4 March 1853 to 4 March 1857
Democrat
Vice-president: William R. King 1853. None thereafter.

By Karin J. Robinson

Full name: Franklin Pierce
Born: 23 November 1804, Hillsborough, New Hampshire
Died: 8 October 1869, Concord, New Hampshire
Resting place: Concord, New Hampshire
Library/Museum: Hillsborough, New Hampshire
Education: Philips Exeter Academy, followed by Bowdoin College
Married to: Jane Appleton, m. 1834 (1806–63)
Children: Three: Franklin Junior (died in infancy), Frank Robert (died of typhus at the age of four), Benjamin (Benny, died in a train crash at the age of eleven)
Quotation: 'There is nothing left to do but get drunk.'

FRANKLIN PIERCE'S TWO-FOLD political passion was to prevent division among both the Union and the Democratic Party – he failed at both. During his time in office, America's movement towards the looming Civil War accelerated rapidly. He is widely regarded as a failed president.

But Pierce did possess many of the personal qualities that could have made him successful in the White House. Those who knew him described him as charming and personable. He was bright but not scholarly, personally loyal and capable of inspiring loyalty in others, and free from the types of corruption and graft that dogged other presidents during this period in history. If only he had not also been cursed with extraordinary bad luck. If only he had not come to power at a time of intractable national crisis. And if only he had not so consistently erred in deferring to the interests of the slave-owning South.

Franklin's father Benjamin was a war hero of the American revolution, and a successful local politician, who would eventually serve two terms as Governor of New Hampshire.

Young Franklin was a popular boy, fond of fishing and skating – and less fond of books. But his stern father made sure that he received a top-notch education, sending him to Bowdoin College, Maine, where he continued to be more interested in play than work. It was here that Franklin met novelist Nathaniel Hawthorne, who would become an important and lifelong friend.

After graduation, the young man threw himself into politics and, at just twenty-four years old, he became the Democratic Party's nominee for his New Hampshire House district. Pierce won an overwhelming victory and went to Washington, DC to begin his career in national politics.

During this period he became engaged to Jane Appleton, daughter of a wealthy and powerful family. Jane was painfully shy, physical frail, deeply devout, and strongly opposed to the consumption of alcohol and tobacco. In many ways she was a surprising choice for Franklin – a heavy-drinking, gregarious politician fond of vigorous outdoor exercise. Nevertheless, in 1834, the couple married, and within thirty minutes of the cere-mony, they departed for Washington, DC, a city that Jane quickly came to detest.

By the time her husband began his second term in the House, pregnant Jane chose to stay in her hometown of Amherst, leaving Franklin to a bachelor-like existence of hard work and heavy drinking in the Capitol. Jane's pregnancy resulted in a boy, who only lived three days. Franklin never met his first-born son.

It was at this time that Pierce first faced head-on the conflict between the interests of slave-owning Southern states and the growing abolitionist movement in the North. Although Pierce was never officially pro-slavery, from the start of his political career he maintained a dislike of abolitionism, finding the fervour and religiosity of the movement off-putting, and believing it to be a threat to the Union. He also cultivated many close and deep friendships with Southern lawmakers, including Jefferson Davis – a frequent drinking buddy who would later serve in Pierce's Cabinet as Secretary of War. Over his time in Washington, his desire to prevent discord between North and South evolved into something that looked more like a decided preference for Southern interests.

An abolitionist newspaper in his home state published an attack on Pierce calling him a 'doughface' (slang for a Northerner with Southern sympathies). This charge would follow him for the rest of his career, but it didn't prevent northern New Hampshire from electing him to the Senate in 1837. At thirty-two years of age, this made Pierce the youngest senator yet elected.

In both the House and Senate, Pierce was more concerned with committee work than legislation, and was seen as a competent but not exemplary legislator. When he found himself in the minority after the Democratic Party was ousted by Whigs in the 1840 election, it made sense to listen to Jane's pleas that he should leave political life and return to live with her and their second-born son, Frank Robert. Possibly another factor in this decision may have been the temperance pledge that Franklin had recently been persuaded to take, delighting Jane, but making it impossible to continue the kind of carousing Washington life that Franklin had been leading. He declined to run for re-election.

He did, though, enjoy the good graces of the Democratic President James Polk, who offered him a role as US Attorney General, which Pierce was forced to decline out of concern for

Jane, who was in a deep depression at the time. Four-year-old Frank had recently died of typhus.

But against the pull of his family obligations and his grief, Pierce also felt called to military service. Since boyhood, he had longed to match his father's military prowess – so in 1847, enthusiastic to make his mark on the war, Pierce persuaded Polk to send him into action and departed for Vera Cruz, Mexico.

What followed was an unlucky and unimpressive term of military service. In his first battle, Pierce's horse bolted at the sound of gunfire, leading the fresh-faced brigadier general to injure his groin on the pommel and pass out. To his men, it looked like their leader had fainted in the face of enemy fire. In his second battle, he twisted his knee and his men marched past their fallen leader – by the time he limped to the front, the fighting was over.

Back home, there was a political fight brewing that would define Pierce's future and bedevil his presidency. The subject was the question of whether slavery would be allowed to expand to the new territories as the country grew.

The US had acquired a large amount of territory through the Mexican–American War, and the Southern states wanted those territories admitted as slave states, while the anti-slavery forces in the North wanted the institution banned everywhere, and certainly not expanded.

The Southern states considered it essential not only to their political but also to their economic interests to expand the institution of slavery. Whereas in the industrial North, accrued wealth tended to be in the form of cash or goods, in the agrarian South, wealth was mostly in the form of non-fungible land. So 'human livestock' offered a source not just of free labour but also of ready cash. More slave states meant a bigger market for selling these 'goods', increasing their value.

Eventually, Congress would settle on the 'Compromise of 1850', which, among other things, decreed that the new states should determine themselves whether they would be slave or free. This violated the terms of the earlier Missouri Compromise. The Compromise of 1850 also included the Fugitive Slave Act, which mandated that escaped slaves be returned to their owners even if they had arrived on free soil.

Pierce's Democratic Party were strong supporters of the compromise, believing that it was essential to preserve the Union, and Pierce himself, though out of office, had campaigned hard for it in state and local elections, making barnstorming speeches and vigorously backing pro-compromise candidates in New Hampshire.

With the Whigs divided along North/South lines, the 1852 presidential election looked like it was the Democrats' to lose, which raised the stakes for the party's nomination. Among the prime candidates were Stephen Douglas, who had been instrumental in drafting and passing the Compromise of 1850, and former Secretary of State James Buchanan, who was popular with Southern Democrats. But not Franklin Pierce, who proclaimed his total lack of interest in running, writing in a public letter that: 'The use of my name in any event before the Democratic National Convention at Baltimore . . . would be utterly repugnant to my tastes and wishes.'

This did not prevent a cabal of Pierce's influential friends from circulating his name as a possible compromise candidate. But for this campaign to succeed, Southern Democrats wanted reassurance that Pierce would strongly support the Fugitive Slave Act. Having been persuaded to go along with his friends' plan, Pierce duly wrote a private letter, which he allowed to be circulated among delegates, expressing his support for the constitutionality and desirability of the controversial Act.

When the convention convened, on 1 June, it was quickly clear that no candidate could win outright. Support switched back and forth between three front-runners, until the thirty-fifth ballot, when Pierce received his first set of votes. By the forty-ninth and final ballot, Pierce had emerged as the surprise compromise choice, helped along by strong support from the Southern delegations, and he won overwhelmingly.

Pierce himself was not at the Convention. He and Jane had spent the week in Boston, and they were returning from a horseback ride through Cambridge when a rider met them with the shock news of his nomination. Jane fainted.

At the general election, Pierce's Whig opponents were so divided between their pro- and anti-slavery wings that they instead leaned on personal attacks – falsely accusing Pierce of anti-Catholic bias and intimating (more accurately) that he was a drunk.

Pierce himself, following the traditions of that time, did no personal campaigning. The turnout at the election was low, and many southern Whigs abstained from the election altogether. In the end, Pierce won all but four states. The new president, elected almost by accident, would enter office with a nation deeply divided, but with his own party convincingly dominant, having won both Houses of Congress.

However, tragedy struck the Pierces once again. On 6 January 1853 the couple had been travelling to attend the funeral of one of Jane's uncles, accompanied by eleven-year-old Benny Franklin, their sole surviving child. The family were making a short train journey from Andover back to their home in Concord when, just a mile outside the station, the train derailed and the carriage broke apart. The portion of the carriage that contained the Pierce family plummeted twenty feet down a culvert, landing on its roof. Both Jane and Franklin were bruised but not seriously injured. Benny, who was sitting opposite his parents, was killed instantly – decapitated.

The effect of this trauma on his grieving parents was profound. Jane, who had always been a shy, quiet, religiously devoted woman who loathed both Washington, DC and her husband's political calling, chose to remain in Andover and withdrew from public sight. She did not attend her husband's inauguration.

Unlike his wife, Franklin could neither avoid the public nor find comfort in religion. Indeed, he came to believe that his misfortunes represented a direct punishment by God, who he must have angered in some way. For this reason, he refused to use a Bible for his swearing-in. He opened his inaugural remarks by telling the assembled nation, 'I ought to be, and am, truly grateful for the rare manifestation of the nation's confidence; but this, so far from lightening my obligations, only adds to their weight. You have summoned me in my weakness; you must sustain me by your strength.'

Apart from this mark of personal trauma, the inaugural speech was noteworthy for the new president's hope that the Compromise of 1850 would end the conflict between the states. He declared that the institution of slavery itself was 'constitutional' and that he would rigorously enforce the Fugitive Slave Act.

He did. Two years into his administration, Pierce sent in federal troops to assist in the return of an escaped slave from Massachusetts to Virginia. This inflamed abolitionists across the country. But it was the Kansas–Nebraska Act that ultimately did the most damage to Pierce's presidency. One key purpose of the act was to organise territories the US had acquired in the war with Mexico. The perennial difficulty was the question of whether these new territories would be admitted as slave states or free.

Since 1820 there had been a fixed rule that slavery would not be permitted in any new Northern states. However, offering the opportunity to Kansas and Nebraska to potentially become slave states would overturn this rule. It would be a big step backwards for slavery's opponents, and a big victory for slavers. Pierce believed that by allowing the voting residents of new states to directly decide the slavery question through 'popular sovereignty' by those 'immediately interested' in the issue, Congress could sidestep the need to resolve its divide.

Of course, enslaved people themselves were not included in this formulation of those 'immediately interested' in their own freedom. Nor were women in the territories, who were more likely than men to support the abolitionist cause.

But the slave-owning faction in Congress were not content merely to allow the Missouri Compromise to be disregarded – a group of Southern Democrats convinced Douglas to add an amendment that would formally repeal it. After some reluctance, Pierce agreed, making support for the amended act a matter of party loyalty for Democrats. After a rancorous debate in Congress the bill narrowly passed, thanks to Pierce's support.

Franklin Pierce signed the Kansas–Nebraska Act into law on 30 May 1854. The effect was to transform congressional debates into a series of violent confrontations in the new Kansas territory. Slave-owning 'border ruffians', mostly from neighbouring Missouri, poured into the state, as did 'Free Staters' from the east. Clashes between the two become so commonplace and deadly that the events became known as 'Bleeding Kansas'.

The political impact of this and the now very unpopular Kansas–Nebraska Act led directly to the creation of the anti-slavery Republican Party, which quickly overtook the still-divided Whigs as the main opposition to Pierce's Democrats.

In this tense environment, President Pierce began to prepare his plan for re-election, with former Secretary of State James Buchanan as his most serious rival for the nomination. Buchanan, in his role as ambassador to the UK, had been able to escape the political firestorm of the Kansas–Nebraska Act.

Pierce entered the Democratic National Convention confident of his re-nomination, but it was not to be. Although the convention was divided, Buchanan was ahead of the incumbent president from the first ballot and Pierce's numbers fell with each round. Buchanan won the nomination.

Pierce left office on 4 March 1857. To this day, he is the only serving US president to seek and lose his party's nomination.

When the Civil War began, Pierce did not support secession, but bitterly opposed it, writing in a letter to Jane: 'I will never justify, sustain or in any way or to any extent uphold this cruel, heartless, aimless, unnecessary war.' Nor was he shy about criticising President Lincoln's actions during the war, making a number of speeches in opposition to Lincoln's wartime suspension of habeas corpus and other measures.

In December 1863, Jane Pierce died of tuberculosis. Following her death, Franklin bought land and dedicated himself to becoming an 'old farmer'. But without the constraints of office, his life having already been well lubricated, the liquor now flowed liberally, and by 1869 he had returned to Concord, suffering from cirrhosis of the liver. He died on 8 October at the age of sixty-four with no family present – a disappointing end to a disappointing life.

Historians have come to rank Pierce as one of America's worst presidents. His support for the Kansas–Nebraska Act, and the perception that he prioritised Southern interests more generally at a time when abolitionism was on the rise, did a great deal to unravel the uneasy peace of the pre-Civil War era.

Teddy Roosevelt, born four years after the end of the Pierce presidency, summed up the harsh judgement of the next generation when he described him as 'a small politician, of low capacity and mean surroundings, proud to act as the servile tool of men worse than himself but also stronger and abler. He was ever ready to do any work the slavery leaders set him.'

Karin Robinson is Strategy Director at Edelman UK and she is a former Vice Chair of Democrats Abroad in the UK. She hosts the 'Democratically: 2020' podcast.

15

James Buchanan

4 March 1857 to 4 March 1861
Democrat
Vice-president: John C. Breckinridge

By Keith Simpson

Full name: James Buchanan Jr
Born: 23 April 1791, Cove Gap, Pennsylvania
Died: 1 June 1868, Lancaster, Pennsylvania
Resting place: Woodward Hill Cemetery, Lancaster, Pennsylvania
Library/Museum: Lancaster, Pennsylvania
Education: Dickinson College, Carlisle, Pennsylvania
Unmarried, no children
Quotation: 'I am the last President of the United States! Whatever the result may be, I shall carry to my grave the consciousness that I at least meant well for my country.'

JAMES BUCHANAN WAS the fifteenth president of the United States and when he was elected in 1857 he was the oldest holder of the office. He has regularly been counted by American politicians, journalists and academics as the worst holder of that office and responsible for failing to prevent the outbreak of the Civil War. Some have portrayed him as an elderly, weak and prevaricating president buffeted by the crisis over slavery and states' rights. But that interpretation ignores the fact that Buchanan was one of the most politically experienced candidates who appeared to have all the virtues required and a commanding personality. So the question to be asked is: why does Buchanan come bottom of every poll that rates presidents?

James Buchanan Jr was born in a log cabin, something that was fairly common in the early years of the United States. His family were Ulster Scots and worked hard to establish a comfortable lifestyle. Despite some early bad behaviour at school Buchanan qualified as a lawyer and slowly earned a substantial income. During the war of 1812 he served in the local militia. He remains the only president with military service who did not serve as an officer.

Buchanan was a tall man, but a squint in one eye meant that his head tended to rest at an angle, which was disconcerting to those engaging in conversation with him. From an early age he had political ambitions and he used his contacts through his legal profession to further them. In 1820, he was elected to the House of Representatives, where he was a staunch supporter of President Andrew Jackson and helped to organise the New Democratic Party. From the beginning of his political career, Buchanan was a staunch defender of the Constitution and states' rights.

In 1832, Jackson appointed Buchanan as the US Minister to Russia, where he served for eighteen months and helped to negotiate maritime and trade treaties. On his return to the United States, Buchanan was elected to the Senate. Here his political views were developed, and he became an advocate of what was known as the Manifest Destiny of the United States, which meant territorial expansion. He believed that the issue of slavery, that 'peculiar institution', was a matter for individual states. He detested the abolitionists and what he saw as their attempts to limit states' rights.

Before the 1844 presidential election Buchanan tried to become the Democratic candidate, but it went to James K. Polk, who, on his election as president, offered him the position of Secretary of State. Buchanan helped to almost double the territory of the republic and his reputation was enhanced. In 1848, he had once again hoped to be the Democratic candidate, but it was not to be and the Whig, Zachary Taylor, was elected as president.

Buchanan returned to private practice, and though he worked hard to become the 1852 presidential candidate, he again failed. But he was offered and eventually accepted the office of Minister to Great Britain. He was out of the country for three years and thus avoided the increasingly violent debate over the Kansas–Nebraska Act. Finally, his perseverance and networking, particularly in the South, succeeded, and after seventeen ballots he was nominated as the Democratic presidential candidate and elected in 1857.

Buchanan was no seeker of compromise and from the start of his presidency he denounced the new Republican Party as one comprised of dangerous abolitionist radicals, making it clear that he was a firm supporter of Southern states' rights.

As a young man, Buchanan had shown an interest in a young woman, but nothing came of it and she died. After her death Buchanan never courted another woman. There had been rumours of his emotional attachment to an Alabama politician, William Rufus King, but nothing was proven and King died in the 1840s.

Although without a wife, Buchanan – a comparatively wealthy man – supported twenty-two nephews and nieces, providing financial support and lobbying his political friends for patronage appointments. His favourite niece was Harriet Lane, and when he moved into the White House in 1857 she officially became his First Lady, designated as such because she was not his wife but rather his official lady and provided him with social support at dinners and receptions.

On becoming president, Buchanan was determined to exercise real authority over his Cabinet, as he remembered with horror the squabbling and lack of cohesion in the Cabinet of Andrew Jackson. He appointed four Southerners and three Northerners to his Cabinet, with the Northerners regarded as Southern sympathisers. Like his predecessors, Buchanan used his patronage to appoint friends and supporters to offices that required presidential nomination.

Buchanan used his Cabinet as a sounding board, more for them to listen to him than to initiate discussion, and for the first two years the Cabinet met every afternoon, apart from Sundays, for several hours. Frequently, Buchanan asked the Cabinet to dinner, as he regarded them as part of his wider political family. He was quite capable of both criticising and bullying Cabinet members, particularly those who were lazy or corrupt. But as the crisis over slavery and states' rights intensified, it became more difficult to hold the Cabinet together. His relations with Congress became more difficult, especially after Republican electoral successes, with tensions on both sides.

Whoever became president in 1857 would have faced serious crises with no easy solutions. But Buchanan's personality and political views meant that it was difficult for him to either act decisively or work for a compromise. Unfortunately for Buchanan, he faced several concurrent crises in his first three years that overlapped in timing and intensity.

The first crisis was one that would have been beyond the capabilities of any president, given Buchanan's limited powers and the economic thinking of the time. The panic of 1857 saw the collapse of nearly fifteen hundred state banks and some five thousand businesses. This had a major impact in Northern states but less in the South, where people were critical of over-speculation. Buchanan was prepared to carry out reform but not give relief, and it took several years for the economy to recover, accompanied by a rise in the federal deficit.

The immediate crisis facing the Buchanan administration was the decision of the Supreme Court over the Dred Scott case. The aged Chief Justice, Roger Taney, delivered the judgment over an enslaved petitioner's request for freedom. The ruling broadly stated that Congress had no constitutional power to exclude slavery in the territories, a ruling that Buchanan supported. This ruling enraged the Republicans and gave succour to the South. Buchanan's position on the Dred Scott case and his public statements revealed a president determined to uphold states' rights and to appear to be sympathetic to the South while rejecting the opinions of many Northerners.

The second crisis centred on the Utah territory, where Brigham Young and his followers rejected the federal government, harassed officials and deterred outside settlers. Buchanan was offended by the behaviour and religious views of Young and in 1857 was able, through the good offices of others, to appoint a new governor and establish peace.

The third and most inflammatory crisis that Buchanan faced was over what became known as 'Bleeding Kansas'. The Kansas–Nebraska Act of 1854 created the Kansas territory and allowed the settlers there to decide whether to allow slavery. Two factions were violently opposed to each other: the Free Soilers, who were anti-slavery, and the pro-slavery settlers. Both factions received political and material support from neighbouring states. Kansas ended up with two governments, the pro-slavery one at Lecompton and the anti-slavery counterpart at Topeka. Under Buchanan's predecessor there had been widespread violence over securing a majority of residents in support of a constitution relating to the admission of Kansas as a state that could be formally presented to Congress.

In the unfolding events, as the rival factions attempted to secure votes for their constitution and to influence Congress and the president, Buchanan's partiality was obvious to all. From the beginning, he supported the pro-slavery faction and tried to get their constitution accepted by Congress.

The Lecompton government sent a pro-slavery constitution to Buchanan, but without having it certified through a referendum. Eventually Buchanan accepted this constitution despite many vocal local protests, and sent it to Congress for approval. He did everything he could to have Congress validate the pro-slavery constitution, including using patronage and offering bribes. The Lecompton constitution won the approval of the Senate in March, but was defeated in the House. Buchanan refused to accept the vote and offered Kansas immediate statehood if it accepted the Lecompton constitution, but this was rejected.

The arguments over Kansas showed where Buchanan's sympathies lay, but despite wielding what presidential powers he had, he was unable to get his way. Many in the South drew the conclusion that despite Buchanan's sympathies the president would not be able to uphold what they believed were their rights. The issue also split the Democratic Party, with most Southern Democrats and some Northern sympathisers, known as 'Doughfaces', on one side, and on the other the mainly Northern Democrats with their formidable presidential candidate Stephen Douglas and his support of popular sovereignty.

By 1858, with the mid-term elections, Buchanan found his presidential powers and his ability to get his legislation through Congress constrained. It was Douglas Democrats (adherents of Stephen Douglas), who won seats in the North but few in the South, which enabled the Republicans to win a plurality of the House in 1858. A frustrated Buchanan used his veto on six pieces of Republican legislation on the grounds that they were unconstitutional.

In early 1860, Buchanan's administration found itself being investigated for corruption and malpractice by a congressional committee, which ultimately failed to find grounds to impeach Buchanan. The divisions within the Democratic Party became very obvious in 1860 when Stephen Douglas won the presidential nomination but with virtually no support in the South. With the Democrats fatally divided and Buchanan unable or unwilling to work for conciliation, the Republicans selected Abraham Lincoln as their candidate. The Commanding General of the US Army, Winfield Scott, warned Buchanan that the election of Lincoln would cause at least seven states to secede from the Union. He recommended strengthening the Union's military forces, but was ignored by the president.

With tensions rising and threats of secession, Buchanan attempted to straddle the divisions with his final speech to Congress in which he denied the rights of states to secede but admitted that the federal government had no powers to prevent them. He really didn't have any proposals that would satisfy a deeply divided Union. As Southern states slowly began to secede and members of his Cabinet resigned, Buchanan continued to consult Southern politicians. He was even prepared to appease secessionists in the South by surrendering the federal Fort Sumter, but reconsidered when faced by opposition from within his Cabinet. By this time, he had run out of authority with President-Elect Lincoln in place.

Two months after Buchanan's departure from the White House, the Civil War had begun in earnest. Despite his sympathies and actions as president, Buchanan supported Lincoln and the Union in the ensuing conflict. He became very upset by the attacks made upon him in retirement, writing letters to the press defending his presidency and drafting a memoir entitled 'Mr Buchanan's Administration on the Eve of the Rebellion', which was published in 1866. In 1868, he caught a cold and died at the age of seventy-seven, having outlived the assassinated Lincoln.

As he left the White House, Buchanan believed that calm reflections concerning his presidency would show it had its merits. Subsequently, assessments of his presidency have had their ups and downs in critical opinion. Even during the Civil War many people referred to it as Buchanan's War. Although he had shown his Southern sympathies, Buchanan had few supporters from that region prepared to speak up in his defence. Of course, the Buchanan presidency is completely overshadowed by the Lincoln presidency, and despite Lincoln's failures and miscalculations the latter is still seen as one of the great presidents, able to surmount the immense difficulties he faced.

Buchanan entered the White House as president with considerable political and administrative experience. He knew how the somewhat limited American government worked and was familiar with those men who could help or hinder him. His personality was rather restrained and he lacked the aggressive attributes of Andrew Jackson or the natural empathy of Lincoln. He never married and, while capable of being avuncular, never really relaxed in female company. During a relatively calm period of American history, even one with a foreign war, Buchanan could have probably exercised presidential authority reasonably effectively. But in 1858 he was faced by a multiplicity of crises and on the central question of slavery and states' rights he appeared to sympathise with the South.

In the crucial months of November and December 1858 and January to March 1860 he seemed unable or unwilling to try to bring the Union together. He made no attempt to use the abilities of Stephen Douglas, and he viewed the Republican Party with complete distaste. In the choice of his Cabinet, he looked for men who would support him and not offer alternative advice, and the balance within his Cabinet favoured the Southern states. He used patronage and financial inducements to try to influence Congress, but without much success.

Even President Kennedy had some sympathy for Buchanan, as

he revealed when talking with a group of political scientists, observing that it wasn't until you sat in the Oval Office and experienced the challenges facing the president that you could understand the pressures – even for Buchanan. By the time of Lincoln's inauguration, Buchanan was exhausted and depressed, and as he accompanied Lincoln to that ceremony he said to him: 'If you are as happy in entering the White House as I shall feel on returning to Wheatland, you are a happy man indeed.'

Keith Simpson is a military historian and served as Conservative MP, first for Mid Norfolk, then Broadland from 1997 to 2019. He served on the Intelligence & Security Committee and the Commonwealth War Graves Commission.

16

Abraham Lincoln

4 March 1861 to 15 April 1865
Republican/National Union
Vice-president: Hannibal Hamlin 1861–65,
Andrew Johnson 1865

By Julia Langdon

Full name: Abraham Lincoln
Born: 12 February 1809, Sinking Spring Farm, Hodgeville,
Kentucky
Died: 15 April 1865, Washington, DC
Resting place: Oak Ridge Cemetery, Springfield, Illinois
Library/Museum: Springfield, Illinois
Education: Attended school intermittently on three occasions
amounting to less than twelve months
Married to: Mary Todd, m. 1842 (1818–82)
Children: Four: Robert Todd, Edward Baker (Eddie), William
Wallace (Willie), Thomas (Tad)

Quotation: 'Four score and seven years ago our fathers brought forth upon this continent, a new nation, conceived in liberty, and dedicated to the proposition that all men are created equal . . . that this nation, under God, shall have a new birth of freedom and that government of the people, by the people, for the people, shall not perish from the earth.'

W HAT MADE ABRAHAM Lincoln remarkable when he took office as the sixteenth president, one month and ten days before the shots that heralded the start of the American Civil War rang out at Fort Sumter in South Carolina, was that he became the first in his country's eighty-five-year history to have taken the iconic words of the Declaration of Independence as the foundation of his own political philosophy. His legacy was thus not only to win the four-year bloody war against the Confederate states, to save the Union and bring an end to slavery, but also, in doing so, to have successfully defended the precept that all men are created equal and to have defeated those who had sought instead to build a nation in which some people would have been considered better than others.

The circumstances of his own life, as a child of the frontier whose formal schooling could be counted in months, precisely exemplified the equality of opportunity envisaged by the Founding Fathers. His election as president was itself an illustration of the potential of the American dream. And his assassination just five days after the surrender of the Confederate Army at Appomattox Court House would guarantee his immediate status as a martyr whose extraordinary achievements were destined to resound forever through the pages of history.

Yet it is important to distinguish between the legend of Lincoln, the mythologised martyr, revered as he is today as one of the greatest of all presidents, and the profoundly difficult circumstances of his presidency. He was a brilliant man, a superb political strategist and a politician of rare principle. He was not, however, a popular man when in office, and although he had just secured a hard-won second term, the tragedy of his murder was enhanced by the fact that he would not live to carry out his vision of reconstruction 'with malice toward none, with charity for all . . .' as he had himself set it out days earlier in his second inaugural address. The words of that imposing speech, together with his unforgettable oration at the dedication of a new national cemetery at the scene of the Battle of Gettysburg, can be found now carved in the marbled memorial of the neo-classical temple erected in his honour at the western end of the Washington Mall, but it would be many years after Lincoln's death before the value of his new vision of American politics would secure the reverence his name has come to command.

Now, however, all this time later, a new currency can be attached to that name. For the fears of Abraham Lincoln, the president who realised democracy itself was at stake when the Confederate states attempted to pervert the principle of equality, are the same fears that were recently recognised in Minneapolis, Minnesota, about the principle of equality before the law. In 2021, a white police officer stood trial and was convicted of the murder of an African American man on whose neck he had kneeled for nine minutes and twenty-nine seconds. In 1858, in Chicago, Illinois, as the prospect of war rolled closer, and Lincoln sought to return to national politics, he rejected the arguments of those who had defended enslavement, in any form, in all the ages of the world. Among the words he used? 'They always bestrode the necks of the people,' he declared.

But it wasn't actually his hatred of slavery, which he had always abhorred, that got this oddball into politics in the first place and then, quite unexpectedly, elected as the first Republican Party president. It was, rather, his belief that an efficiently functioning economy did not have to depend upon an underclass with strong backs and weak minds: what is known as the mudsill theory. Instead, it should be based on the idea that anyone could go 'onwards and upwards', that it should be possible for a hard-working man to rise, to achieve what he termed 'individual, social and political prosperity and happiness'. It was that which brought the Republicans into existence and Lincoln into the White House. More than sixteen thousand books have been written about this man – reportedly a larger number of books written about any single person in history except Jesus Christ – and that is because he was someone in a position to know exactly what he was talking about. He knew what it was like to have been in the mudsill.

Everyone always thought he was odd. It started with his own father, the itinerant Thomas Lincoln, a shiftless drifter who left Kentucky for Indiana and then Illinois, who scoffed at book-learning, as many did on America's nineteenth-century frontier. Young Abraham was unusual because he stood out against that prejudice and because he learned very quickly not to care what other people thought of him. He looked odd, too, as he grew into a strong young man who was exceptionally tall for those times. His height of 6 foot 4 inches is considered tall today; it was extraordinary then. The word 'gangly' was what the contemporary accounts of him repeatedly record, and, of course, he could never find clothes to fit him. His trousers were always too short and his sleeves never reached his wrists. If he lost a button he might substitute a peg. His braces were often found wanting. By the time he was distinguished enough to have important papers, he would keep them in his battered top hat. Later, he would make a joke of pulling a speech out of his hat to get a laugh from the crowd. He was uncouth and awkward and he had a small head and a scraggy neck. It was only shortly before his election as president that he grew the beard of the mind's memory, of the famous Memorial statue, of the authenticated images captured in his lifetime by the coming new wonder of photography.

He was indifferent to his appearance although, oddly enough, the presidential beard arrived a month after a letter from an eleven-year-old girl suggested that if he 'wore whiskers' it might be to his benefit. He charmingly responded, writing back: 'Would it not be a silly affectation?' But he took the advice. His young correspondent had remarked also, if not in her letter, on his 'sadly pathetic eyes', and she was clearly a perceptive child. Throughout his life Lincoln carried with him an all-pervasive air of melancholy that was probably his most characteristic feature, apart, that is, from standing a head above the crowd.

Among many other things, he suffered from depression, a condition that would have been continually exacerbated by the personal tragedies of his life. For a start, pioneer life was hard. He had malaria twice: in 1830, when the family first arrived in Illinois, 'the Prairie state', and then again, in 1835, during his first experience of politics as a member of the Illinois state legislature. He got frostbite in the winter of 1830 when the temperature famously didn't rise above freezing for three months and all the wild animals, except the wolves, died of cold. He was kicked in the head by a horse as a child, whipped and beaten by his father, and hit by his wife.

If the president of the United States looked particularly miserable when he delivered the 272 words of the most famous speech of his life – what was billed as 'a few appropriate remarks' and became the Gettysburg Oration – it was because he had incipient smallpox. It was noted that he looked sad, mournful and haggard. The crowd, having just stood through a two-hour address before hearing Lincoln's two minutes, didn't know what they had heard. A nineteen-year-old girl who stood a few yards away thought 'it seemed short'; there was no applause, but an impressive silence was reported. His words were whisked off to the press and got a mixed reception: *The Times* of London noted them as 'the luckless satires of that poor President Lincoln'. The ailing president travelled by train back to Washington and took to his bed shortly afterwards. His valet contracted smallpox at the same time and died.

Tragedy stalked him from the first. He was born the middle of three children of Thomas and his wife, Nancy Hanks, about whose antecedents little is known but from whom he is assumed to have inherited ability. Abraham, named after his paternal grandfather who had been killed by an Indian in Kentucky, had a younger brother who died days after birth in 1812. His mother died when he was nine and his elder sister, Sarah, died with her baby in childbirth ten years later. His first love, Ann Rutledge, to whom he was about to become engaged, died aged nineteen in 1835, as Lincoln set out in politics. Abraham's depression was understandably bad at this time and his misery such that his friends were anxious for his own life.

Things scarcely improved when he met Mary Todd, the accomplished, sharp-tongued, educated woman who would become his wife. She was pretty as a young woman. 'Molly', as she was known, was said then to have the looks to make a bishop forget his prayers. She was also pretty ambitious. And she spotted brilliant potential in Abraham Lincoln, despite his gloomy air and a 'poor white' social status so far below her own. In the face of her family's objections, she accepted his proposal of marriage, refused to allow him to rescind it when he tried to break it off, and even though he failed to show up on their wedding day, still married him anyway, albeit nearly two years later. The putative bridegroom, who had professed himself 'the most miserable man living' in this interim as a result of his own behaviour, did not cheer up. Asked where he was headed on the day they did marry, a question prompted by his uncharacteristically smart attire, he retorted: 'To hell, I reckon.'

But the man who Mary married, who became the politician to fulfil her ambition, had already shown himself as someone who was on his way. The hunger and hardship of his childhood was not a matter of myth. The log cabin in Kentucky had not been much improved on by the family's migration westward to Indiana in 1816. There they lived in what was called a half-faced camp, a hut with three sides, the fourth providing window, door and hearth, a mile from the nearest well. But what did improve for Abraham was the arrival, in 1819, of a stepmother, Sarah Johnston, who came bearing books. She brought *Aesop's Fables*, *The Pilgrim's Progress*, *Robinson Crusoe* and *Sinbad the Sailor*. Another passing relative brought an etymological dictionary. There was a Bible.

The child embarked on what would be a lifetime of learning. He learned to read and write and spell. He read everything. His father thought him lazy because he would rather read, recite or talk. He learned the power of language. He started to write poems. In the arithmetic book from one of his short spells in a schoolroom he wrote: 'Abraham Lincoln – his hand and pen – he will be good – but God knows when.' And he started to tell stories. He mastered language as a tool and he practised telling jokes and anecdotes. He noticed when people laughed and he began to use humour, not least to cheer himself. 'If I didn't laugh, I would die,' he once said. He discovered Burns and Shakespeare – *Macbeth* was his favourite play – and he imbibed the rhythm of language from the King James Bible. It was said of him, years later in Washington, that his mastery of language was such that he could have made the proposition that Texas and New Hampshire should forever be bound by a single post office sound like something out of Genesis.

He left home, of course. After the move to Illinois, he escaped the father he despised. In due course he would pay off Thomas Lincoln's debts, but afterwards he declined an invitation from a stepbrother to visit Thomas before he died. There was nothing that could be said that wouldn't be painful, he observed. In 1831, he had been offered a job as a store clerk in a little place called New Salem, a pioneer village of fifteen houses, on a bluff above the Sangamon River, the kind of settlement that started up in those days and sometimes made it. He was by now a personable young man, and recognised as popular and honest, for all his oddities. He told a lot of stories and was known to be kind and courageous, if not the saint as subsequently depicted. When he enlisted in the militia to fight in the brief Black Hawk War against Native Americans in the spring and summer of 1832, he was elected captain by his company, something of which he was always profoundly proud, more so, he would say, than of other later distinctions. He was acquiring ambitions, but he said, at this time, that he had 'no other so great as that of being truly esteemed of my fellow men'. Lincoln was gratified by this military service. What he could never have imagined, however, was that one Robert Anderson, a colonel of the Illinois Volunteers who mustered Lincoln into service, would come into his life again. He was the man in charge of the Union troops at Fort Sumter, Charlottesville, nearly thirty years later, as the Civil War broke out.

Back in New Salem meanwhile, Lincoln took his first steps into politics and ran unsuccessfully for the state legislature. His vote was remarkably high for a newcomer and he was encouraged to try again. For a couple of years he pursued all sorts of jobs: he opened his own store, engendering debts that took twenty years to clear; worked as the postmaster, which was neither demanding nor financially rewarding; learned the rudiments of surveying; studied the law. In 1834, he was elected on an all-party ticket with the second highest poll in Sangamon County. He was off to the capital, Vandalia, a town with a hundred houses, and now his education made real progress. He had access to men of ability and to the ways of the world in what became known as the Old West. A Whig in the lower house of the legislature, he swiftly showed himself to be politically adroit and campaigned for lavish public works and for the capital of Illinois to be transferred to the bigger and more important town of Springfield. On the day after that vote was triumphantly achieved in 1837, Abraham Lincoln was admitted to the Illinois Bar, and a month later he settled in Springfield himself. For the next four years he was happier than at any other time in his life and this was the man that Mary Todd wouldn't allow to escape.

Marriage with Mary was difficult. She was ambitious for her husband and was politically astute herself, but she was not a home-maker and she was bad-tempered. By the time of their wedding in late 1842, Lincoln's political popularity had waned. He had not been re-nominated for the legislature and although he was now aiming for Congress, he was passed over twice. Practising as a circuit lawyer and spending much time away from home, he felt himself to have been politically eclipsed and 'dripped melancholy'. When he did secure election to the House of Representatives for one two-year term in 1846, he was unpopular in Illinois for his oppos-ition to the Mexican–American War and was regarded as obstreperous in Washington. He undertook not to seek a second term and returned to Springfield.

It was the issue of slavery that changed everything. The passage of the Kansas–Nebraska Act in 1854, which allowed settlers to vote for slavery if they wanted it, was an abomination to Lincoln. The Southern slave-owners controlled the Democratic Party and were seeking to control the national government. The Whig Party, which had promoted the interests of urban professionals, was wrecked. The newly formed Republicans came into existence to oppose slavery as an economic system that meant that ordinary free labourers could not compete and thus prosper. It was Lincoln who linked this proposed extension of slavery to a violation of the principle of equality in the Declaration of Independence and who argued, what's more, for equality to include access to education. He ran for the Senate in 1855 and again the following year, and, while he lost, he had made a national name for himself by then. In 1858, he took part in seven historic debates, standing for the Senate against the incumbent Democrat Stephen Douglas, the five-foot-tall 'Wee Giant', who had pushed through the Kansas–Nebraska Act.

The power of the language of those debates is truly remarkable. Lincoln was witty and wise, and the cadences of his beautiful biblical rhetoric drew massive crowds throughout the state. The speeches were widely reported in newspapers and published in pamphlets. Douglas was, however, also a terrific orator and, portraying his opponent as a dangerous radical, he won that Senate election. Yet the debates had established Lincoln's reputation. He was chosen as the presidential candidate for the upstart Republicans in 1860 and gangly 'Honest Abe' beat the 'Wee Giant' standing for the Democrats in the North. In the South, the vote was split between two candidates and thus, although winning less than 40 per cent of the popular vote, Lincoln won the White House by carrying the Electoral College.

'Mary! Mary! We are elected!' he cried, but he knew there was little joy in this victory. Today it takes twelve hours to drive from Springfield to the nation's capital. The newly elected President Lincoln spent two weeks, in anguish, travelling by train for his inauguration the following year, 1,800 miles of a whistle-stop tour around the North, stopping to meet the people and seeking to promote national unity, appealing as he put it in his first inaugural address to 'the better angels of our nature'. And still the war came. By the time of his inauguration seven Southern slave states had seceded from the Union and the inevitable war was weeks away. By the time of his second inauguration, exactly four years later, six hundred thousand men had lost their lives in battle and $5 billion had been spent.

Lincoln is the only president of the United States who was not a member of any church. It was, as he said, a tax on his personality, but he never directly identified himself as a Christian. His brutish father became a Baptist, but Abraham Lincoln was never baptised. He was sceptical as a youth, outraging opinion in the Bible-fearing frontier on one occasion by saying that the Bible was 'just a book'. He never denied the Scriptures and he cited God and the Bible often. He was, however, much more comfortable with Euclid, whose work he studied to improve his logic: 'It's true because it works!' But in the course of his presidency he came to use God in his arguments.

After his death, an unpublished meditation was found, a fragment in his papers, written in 1862. He rehearsed here the arguments with God that he would later reflect in his second inaugural address: if both sides claimed to act in accordance with the will of God, then one of them must be wrong. Then, as the weary years of the war progressed, he began also to assert a belief that it was God's will to end slavery, although previously he had insisted that the paramount object of the war was to save the Union – not either to save or to destroy slavery. It was this apparent change of view that led him to issue the Emancipation Proclamation, freeing all the enslaved people in the rebel states, which took effect in 1863, and then to push through Congress the Thirteenth Amendment to the Constitution, which abolished slavery and servitude within the jurisdiction of the United States.

Lincoln believed that this was the best thing he achieved in office. It passed in January 1865, after he had won – to his own surprise – the second term he would never complete. He pushed it through Congress before the end of the war and the return of the Southern states to the federal government. In his first term, as well as running the war, he had built on the Democrats' readiness to pursue a bipartisan approach and embarked upon policies intended to extend economic opportunity as envisaged by the new Republican Party. These policies included new national taxes; a Homestead Act to help farmers buy land, hire workers and put an end to the mudsill theory; the Pacific Railway and National Bank Acts; and a Land Grant College Act to establish funding for state universities. It was an ambitious programme.

Lincoln didn't keep a diary, but he wrote a great deal. He wrote to the newspapers to try out his ideas in public. He wrote letters, replying to those who wrote to him, and penned others that he didn't send but that got feelings off his chest. After the Battle of Gettysburg, which looked like it might begin to turn the war in favour of the Union and stop the dreadful rollcall of death, he wrote to his general commanding the Army of the Potomac upbraiding him for failing to pursue the defeated Confederate Army. 'Your golden opportunity has gone and I am distressed immeasurably because of it,' he wrote. On the envelope he wrote: 'Never sent or signed.' Lincoln was still reading and learning, of course, ever the auto-didact, and now he was studying military strategy. In 1862, he borrowed from the Library of Congress a sort of do-it-yourself manual on the principles of war theory. He kept it for two years, then returned it two weeks after General Ulysses Grant took command of the Union Army, when he could see that, perhaps at last, he had found a military leader who could bring an end to all this misery.

Lincoln still had tragedy at his heels. There were four sons born of his marriage to Mary, only one of whom, their eldest, Robert, was to reach adulthood. Their second son, Eddie, died of tuberculosis in Springfield before he reached his fourth birthday and their favourite, Willie, died of typhoid aged eleven, in his bed at the White House. Tad, the baby of the family, survived typhoid and outlived his father, but died aged eighteen of a heart condition. Mary had become increasingly mentally fragile in the course of their marriage and suffered appalling migraine attacks after a carriage accident in 1863. Robert would consign her to an institution for her troubled last years. Robert himself would live until 1926 and the age of eighty-two, but the Lincoln line ended in 1985 with the death of his grandson, Abraham and Mary's great-grandson, Robert Todd Lincoln Beckwith, who married three times but had no children.

And now the tragic fate that befell the great man himself. He had survived five failed assassination attempts before John Wilkes Booth shot him in the back of the head as he laughed at one of the sallies in the comedy *Our American Cousin* at Ford's Theatre that night. Abraham Lincoln had always loved the theatre, of course, and he had his own silk-lined rocking chair in the state box, but he hadn't wanted to go that night. He had told the Cabinet earlier in the day about the dream he had the night before, the same dream that had recurred in advance of some of the big battles of the war, and it had discomfited him. 'I seemed to be in a singular and indescribable vessel,' he said of it, 'but always the same, and to be moving with great rapidity towards a dark and indefinite shore.' As it happened, he had also that day signed a bill that would create what came to be known as the Secret Service, but this would be of no use to him. A solitary policeman had escorted him and Mary to the theatre, but the policeman wasn't there as a guard, which wasn't his job anyway. Wilkes Booth, the actor who Lincoln admired and whom he had previously (unsuccessfully) invited to visit him at the White House, met no resistance in his murderous pursuit of salvaging the Confederate cause.

Lincoln was carried across the street, where he was laid on a bed in the Petersen Boarding House and where he died the following morning, the great length of him still lying awkwardly at a diagonal across the small divan. He lay in state on a black-draped catafalque in the East Room at the White House and then it was back on the train on a solemn and heart-breaking reprise return journey, 1,800 miles, the long way round to Springfield, Illinois, and his place in history.

The world that Abraham Lincoln left behind would be a very different one from that into which he had been born. Emancipation would change it for those many millions previously enslaved and for all those born after his death. Through an odd quirk of historical coincidence, two men born on the very same day, albeit on opposite sides of the Atlantic Ocean, Abraham Lincoln and Charles Darwin, would between them rewrite the agenda for the future of human history. The passage of time would win them both credit for the understanding they brought to the truth they both held to be self-evident. The immediate tragedy for the evolution of the New World that would be ushered into being by the legacy of Lincoln was that his early and untimely death robbed America of his inclusive style of government, his political flexibility and his personal magnanimity, which might otherwise have speeded the process of reconstruction. It would take many years to redress the manifest inequalities that had caused the Civil War and the economic devastation that ensued. It would be even longer still before Abraham Lincoln would achieve his sole ambition of 'being truly esteemed' – not only by his fellow men and women but by all the generations to come.

Julia Langdon is a political journalist, author and broadcaster.

17

Andrew Johnson

15 April 1865 to 4 March 1869
Democrat
Vice-president: None

By Allie Renison

Full name: Andrew Johnson
Born: 29 December 1808, Raleigh, North Carolina
Died: 31 July 1875, Elizabethton, Tennessee
Resting place: Andrew Johnson National Cemetery, Greeneville, Tennessee
Library/Museum: Tusculum, Tennessee
Education: No formal education
Married to: Eliza McCardle, m. 1827 (1810–76)
Children: Five: Martha (1828), Charles (1830), Mary (1832), Robert (1834) and Andrew Jr (1852)
Quotation: 'Outside of the Constitution we have no legal authority more than private citizens, and within it we have only

so much as that instrument gives us. This broad principle limits all our functions and applies to all subjects.'

THE STORY OF Andrew Johnson – a man routinely topping the list of worst presidents – is one of tragic circumstance made worse by personal conviction and contradiction. It serves to enhance his predecessor's ideals by comparison, and further mourn what could have been following the Civil War. Yet it is also a cautionary tale about the tension between political failure – wrongdoing even – and constitutional redress. As such, the implications and lessons drawn from a presidency gladly forgotten by many have subsequently made him a talking point once more.

The stubborn and selective approach of Johnson – the unexpected successor to Lincoln – to safeguarding the Union, as a Southern Democrat of the era, yielded disastrous results, cementing the very divide that had torn it apart. The reconstruction period that followed the war went from missed opportunity to firmly embedding Confederate ideals on race and discrimination under his tenure, going far beyond the states' rights agenda it was wrapped in.

This also underpinned the clash between the executive and legislature that marked Johnson's presidency. A stance that had previously combined fierce opposition to secession with robust defence of slavery led to his subsequent refusal to compromise with the predominantly Northern Unionists in Congress after the war. They wanted to go further and faster to right the wrongs of the Confederacy and extend the Lincoln ideals of freedom to civil liberties for the formerly enslaved.

Johnson, who grew up poor and illiterate but developed a flair for political rhetoric, identified with fellow Tennessean Andrew Jackson's limited government agenda and felt the impoverished Southern states needed to be treated leniently with self-determination to help restore the Union. The divide accelerated as public opinion in the North grew stronger concerning the need to ensure the South fully acknowledged the errors of its ways. Progressives saw the president's light-touch approach as emboldening state governments in the South to act as if the war had been fought over nothing.

Compromise attempts failed and gave way to open conflict,

presidential vetoes and congressional overrides, including contentious legislation to limit Johnson's ability to dismiss those in his own Cabinet – many of whom were Lincoln holdovers. His move to fire one such member eventually resulted in the first impeachment in US history, and while rancour over his relationship with Congress was widespread, questions about whether his actions amounted to high crimes and misdemeanours persisted. The Senate's subsequent narrow vote to acquit him clearly reflected a divide over whether the pursuit of the president rested on overly partisan and spurious grounds.

Ultimately, the contradictions of Andrew's Johnson's position as a Southern Unionist – the same contradictions that saw Abraham Lincoln appoint him as his running mate in an attempt to restore national unity – proved to be his undoing. His failure to acknowledge that slavery and not just secession had been justly defeated laid the foundations for segregation and racial divides that continue to this day. But his legacy remains varied due to an age-old debate about constitutional over-reach and whether political ends are justified by questionable means. Accordingly, even if the man himself may often be forgotten, the issues and debates underpinning his legacy will certainly endure.

The poverty in which Andrew Johnson was raised could have made his working-class, rags-to-riches path to political fortune the hallmark of his legacy. He was in fact one of the few US presidents never to have received any formal education. His humble origins did serve to inform his policy platform across his political life, including as he saw it the reasoning among others for defending slavery.

Advocating for poor Whites of the South became a focal point, with the planter class often as much in his sights as the abolitionist movement. His campaign for the 'common man' took as a prerequisite that Blacks were destined to come below the lowest White man in society, in order to allow the latter to retain some advantage and preference in the social hierarchy.

Johnson long maintained his justification of bondage and supported contentious federal administrative legislation such as the Fugitive Slave Act. This came despite his professed aversion to such trampling of states' rights elsewhere, and despite having fled far across state lines as a bound apprentice to escape capture and fulfilling indentured service himself.

With a bounty on his head, the young Johnson left North Carolina and settled in Tennessee, where his future young wife – herself educated – taught him to spell and write as he honed his tailor's craft. She also helped him with financial literacy as his business acumen grew, and he invested in surrounding farmlands, which fortified his connection to settlers and the South's agrarian economy.

Despite his initial illiteracy, Johnson became a voracious reader and particularly enamoured with famous orators, arousing his interest in political dialogue just as he began rising through local political ranks. As his populist tell-it-like-it-is tack further cemented his appeal to the labouring classes, he moved from town alderman and mayor to the state legislature, and entered Congress as a thirty-five-year-old in 1843.

Having initially had no real allegiance to anything other than Andrew Jackson, who he revered, Johnson found his stump speeches fitted well with the burgeoning Southern Democrats. As the issue of slavery became a more prominent demarcating line, they began to split across multiple fronts. Not only did they sharply splinter with Republicans – old Jeffersonian Republicans – who they had once joined against the more centralising Federalists; they also drifted from more moderate Democrats who feared the geographic and constitutional schism the issue was accelerating.

Ensuing stints as Tennessee governor further helped Johnson to project his combination of common-man appeal with high political office, and he moved into the US Senate off the back of support from small farmers and tradesmen in particular. While they comprised much of the Tennessee electorate, he was less connected with the planter class who ran much of the Southern Democrat establishment. Unsurprisingly, much of his time in the Senate focused on procuring land for small-farmer expansion in order to compete with large plantation landowners.

When the planter class – and by extension the leadership of the Democrats – moved towards secession following Lincoln's election, Andrew Johnson saw it as a conspiracy of Southern elites. This viewpoint enabled him to focus less on the substantive issue of slavery, which he saw as a natural dividing line to keep poor Whites in the South on a level playing field with their richer counterparts. Slavery was not a moral question to him, but one of inevitability, a natural prerequisite for uniting citizens by excluding others from that citizenship. And in a further contradictory view, it was one of the policy differences that held the political party sectionalism (disliked by the Federalist Founding Fathers) of the Union together – even though this nearly destroyed it in the end.

While his fiercely pro-Union sentiments led to Lincoln appointing him Governor of the Union during the Civil War, it has been argued that this position was easier to adopt in light of Johnson's long-standing disconnect with the Southern leadership. Lincoln further rewarded him by putting him on his re-election ticket in 1864, in an attempt both to stave off radical Republicans impatient with progress on ending the war and slavery and to appeal to Democrats.

Even as the new national unity ticket secured the election and moved the country towards the conclusion of the war, no resolution to any differences between Lincoln and Johnson on how to address reconstructing the South was to be forthcoming. Following the former's assassination in April 1865, Johnson was sworn in as president.

Lincoln's rapid elevation to martyr status hid the reality of a likely more flexible approach to the Confederate states compared to the true victor's approach that Republican radicals wanted him to take. Johnson's lack of political nous and stubborn attachment to the baseline fundamentals that he saw as separating poor Whites and Blacks, however, inflamed these tensions.

His ultimate aversion to support for congressional legislation to enforce emancipation in the South, and extend enfranchisement and other basic civil rights to Blacks, angered both moderate and radical Unionists. This was further compounded by his desire to rapidly welcome back Confederates into the Union fold.

Contending that they had never been constitutionally entitled to secede anyway, Johnson shrugged off the need for any process of retribution or reconciliation. He swiftly moved to pardon the Confederate leadership as well as rewarding its soldiers with redistributed land. It stood in stark contrast to the vigour with which he had taken against secessionists before and during the war.

When he further turned a blind eye to state governments in the South enacting 'Black Codes' that severely restricted the activities of freed slaves while vetoing federal bills that sought to assist them, many in Congress and public opinion in the North had had enough. Instead of embracing the savvy compromise of Lincoln, Johnson doubled down to capitalise on his newfound collective popularity among Southern White elites and 'plebians' alike.

His intemperate remarks further drew a wedge between the executive and legislature, all the while fanning the flames of a North–South divide over race that only intensified following the war aimed at ending its worst injustices. The 'Reconstruction' era consequently did little to reconstruct true freedom for Blacks in the South, cementing instead the division of the Union across a plethora of new fronts.

Thrust into the national spotlight at a moment of immeasurable consequence, Johnson was hopelessly unprepared and politically incapable of the savvy needed to navigate the concurrent end of the Civil War with the momentous needs of its after-effects. The circumstances in which he found himself called for healing and compromise. Instead, his naïve attempt to pursue swift and unilaterally enforced forgiveness rendered it ever more difficult to ensure reconciliation.

Johnson consolidated this by picking fights with an angry Congress over the basic constitutional ideal the country had waged war over, namely that *all* men are truly created equal. In seeking to forcibly restore the Union, he glossed over and indeed expanded the basis over which it had nearly torn itself apart

This emboldened the legislature to reach for any means at their disposal to try to remove him. In this, Andrew Johnson became the architect of his own downfall as well as setting a precedent for future battles between the branches of government.

In relatively short order, Congress moved from an initial reluctance to confront the president to an all-out battle with Johnson. Buoyed by the unprecedented demands of reconstruction and a man at the helm of the executive who came to see the open conflict as purely a battle with the legislature's more radical elements, big-picture thinking soon gave way to procedural skirmish.

Johnson conceptualised and even internalised the struggle as one of allowing the Southern states their sovereignty back, believing it would somehow advance both reconstruction and the balance of the

Union. He almost seemed to relish trading presidential vetoes with congressional overrides on legislation to federally enshrine basic civil rights for freedmen, and the back and forth carried on apace.

But the weariness and consequent support from moderates that he anticipated would come did not materialise as expected. When his absolutist veto stance extended against compromise in the perpetual name of states' rights, without much regard for the substance of extending any freedoms, wider rancour across Congress developed beyond Thaddeus Stevens's radical Republicans.

Johnson separately calculated this would help unite the various White class factions of the South behind him, and provide a boost to his [re-]election fortunes. Not only did it further alienate moderates in Congress, it also was seen as costing his party votes in the 1866 mid-term elections from those who had joined forces across the divide to elect him and Lincoln on a joint ticket. His working-man stump speeches became more emphatically focused on his own persona.

One impromptu oratory to supporters marching on the White House referred to himself hundreds of times and even decried his political opponents as akin to traitors. It was seen as virtually a declaration of war, and moderates on both sides and among the public rapidly fell away from seeing Johnson as a unifier. Republicans subsequently swelled their numbers in Congress to levels that would easily provide for continued, consistent overrides of presidential vetoes on their preferred reconstruction policies and conditions.

In upping the ante, Stevens and other radicals went further to propose replacing Southern governments in the South with military districts managed under martial law. To maximise the defenestration of Johnson's veto, the bill was passed on a congressional override in tandem with a Tenure of Office Act that drew added controversy. Created in response to reports that the president was considering dismissing Cabinet members who disagreed with him, the legislation drew consternation from senators that its constitutional basis in requiring Senate approval for such an executive function was questionable at best.

Things came to a head when Johnson and his Secretary of War Edwin Stanton soon disputed the question of whether those placed in command of military districts could in fact override civil authorities in the South. With Congress out of session, Johnson moved to fire Stanton, over the objections of his subsequent replacement, one Ulysses S. Grant, who would eventually replace him in the next presidential election as well.

Following a back and forth with Congress, including the Senate, over this apparent violation of the Office of Tenure Act, the House of Representatives – having been mulling over the idea for some time – moved to adopt eleven articles of impeachment against Johnson.

It is important to stress that not all eleven dealt with the contentious Office of Tenure legislation, which became a significant point of contention – both during the Senate trial on the scope of its application and after as to its questionable legal basis. John F. Kennedy even commended the vote of Republican senator Edmund Ross, which narrowly prevented the required two-thirds majority to convict the president, as a heroic independent rebuke to the partisan politics apparently at play.

Recent historians have contended that while this ultimately became a central factor in the Senate's vote to acquit the president, it does not render the entire process of impeachment as simply partisanly dubious, given the range of charges levied. And yet the broad interpretive thrust of some of the other articles – particularly the Omnibus Article – still raises the question of whether and to what extent being unfit for office can or should be a check on the executive's continued function.

Despite the numbers to convict falling just short of the requisite majority, and the bitter disappointment of Stevens and the radical Republicans, the outcome was not entirely unexpected. Johnson was reported to have promised that he would do less to interfere with reconstruction policies in Congress, and there were concerns that his removal could impinge on the likely victory of his eventual successor Grant.

The remaining months of the presidency saw his influence almost non-existent, although some superficial conflict with Congress continued. Despite generating support among all classes of Whites across the South, where, before, his Union support had divided them, he failed in his bid to obtain the Democratic nomination for the looming presidential election. In addition to becoming the first sitting president to be impeached – but not convicted – Johnson, like John and John Quincy Adams before him, and Donald Trump much later, refused to attend his successor's inauguration.

Bidding to preserve some vestige of personal triumph as well as exact political revenge, he subsequently made several attempts at returning to Congress, successfully doing so in 1875 as a senator for Tennessee. He served in just one short-lived special session, speaking only once to criticise Grant for using the military to support Louisiana state's pro-reconstruction government. Upon his subsequent return home, a series of strokes and resistance to medical intervention led to his death at the age of sixty-six – stubborn to the last.

The tension between narrow and broad readings of the US Constitution encapsulated in the Johnson precedent continues to this day, well beyond the strictures of impeachment proceedings too. It is naturally most acute when it involves the interplay between the various branches of government, but all go to the heart of constitutional proceduralism clashing with politics and elected governing.

Neither one nor the other is more reflective or representative – for better or worse – of American democracy. The Constitution continues to evolve, as much a function of the law-making it affords as the interpretations US judges pass it through. Checks and balances swing in roundabouts, and if there is one beneficial thing that the tale of Andrew Johnson gives us it is a reminder that they reinforce the peaceful transitions of power that have largely guided America since the Civil War that once tore it apart.

But that tale also reminds us of the other legacy that was left behind. A divide steeped in war and discrimination that still reverberates across American society. While not being utterly consumed by the past, we must remember it to understand how the need to move forward for progress began – and still continues today.

Allie Renison was born and raised in Washington, DC by British-American parents. She is one of the UK's leading experts and commentators on the trade aspects of Brexit.

18

Ulysses S. Grant

4 March 1869 to 4 March 1877
Republican
Vice-presidents: Schuyler Colfax 1869–73,
Henry Wilson 1873–75, vacant 1875–77

By Bonnie Greer

Full name: Hiram Ulysses Grant
Born: 27 April 1822, Point Pleasant, Ohio
Died: 23 July 1885, Wilton, New York
Resting place: Grant's Tomb, Morningside Heights, New York City
Library/Museum: Starkville, Mississippi
Education: John Rankin's Academy, United States Military Academy
Married to: Julia Dent, m. 1848 (1826–1902)
Children: Four: Frederick, Ulysses Jr, Nellie, Jessie
Quotation: 'The art of war is simple enough. Find out where

your enemy is. Get at him as soon as you can. Strike him as hard as you can, and keep moving on.'

IT IS QUITE possible that the presidency of Ulysses S. Grant was what we would now call 'cancelled'. By that I mean that his two terms, in a time of great turbulence, were written off, debased, ridiculed by powers that saw him as a threat to their way of life. Because he was.

The way of life that he threatened was quite simply the racial segregation and second-class citizenship that was the reality of my ancestors, for all African Americans – a reality that lasted close to a hundred years and, to some extent, is trying to return.

In the late 1950s to mid-1960s when I was growing up in America, Westerns were the very staple of television. In them, and in the movies, too, Ulysses S. Grant was depicted as a hard-drinking no-nonsense general – a one-dimensional human being. Above all, he was an utterly corrupt president, perhaps the most corrupt of them all.

He was often depicted as stubby and blunt, a kind of rude mechanical compared to his more elegant and refined opponent in the US Civil War, Robert E. Lee. But the reality was very different, in that it was he, not Lee, who prevailed.

Those who promoted this view of the eighteenth president of the United States were largely proponents of what is known as 'The Lost Cause': that complex set of beliefs that held that the American Civil War was primarily what my African American nuns from Baltimore called at school 'The War of Northern Aggression'. Some of them even saw the Civil War as federal over-reach at its most extreme level, and Grant, a Unionist, as a kind of devil.

Gone with the Wind is peak 'Lost Cause', the novel even more than the masterpiece of a film. Grant and his soldiers intruded on that world where enslaved women were casually given the names of heroines from Shakespeare and rape was not that, but a gift.

When Reconstruction, the set of laws and constitutional amend-ments designed to give my ancestors their rights as human beings and American citizens, began to be chipped away in the administrations that followed Grant's, his own reputation began to be chipped away too.

The corruption that engulfed both his terms in office, while inexcusable, had at its root his own political naïveté, as well as a desire to help family and friends.

Hiram Ulysses S. Grant was born in Point Pleasant, Ohio, on 27 April 1822. His father was a tanner and the smell of the tannery would disturb Grant all of his life. This battlefield soldier preferred his food well-cooked because he could not stand the smell of blood.

His paternal ancestors had landed at Massachusetts Bay Colony in 1620, making him what passes for a kind of aristocrat in the United States, just without money and status. His mother was descended from Protestant immigrants from County Tyrone. Grant was born less than a year after his parents married. They drew his name 'Ulysses' out of a hat and named him Hiram after his grand-father. Five more children followed and by then the Grant family was living in Ohio.

Grant's uncanny ability with horses was evident from an early age, an affinity that saved him from life in the family tannery. He drove his father's wagons and learned to ride well. Horses loved him. Quiet and reserved, he expressed no desire to make his religion a public matter, an unusual thing for an American at that time. No one bothered him about church-going and it was assumed that he was agnostic. He liked to keep them assuming.

After his father wrote to a congressman asking that he be appointed to the prestigious United States Military Academy at West Point, Grant was recommended and was admitted in 1839. He was enlisted as 'Cadet U.S. Grant' by an indifferent clerk. So as not to make a fuss, Grant allowed it to stand. He became known as 'Sam' to his friends, after 'Uncle Sam', one of the popular names for the US.

Indifferent to military life except for the horses and the high jumps, it was at West Point that Grant discovered an even greater love for them. To escape the rigid military routine, he studied the art of the Romantic Age, and read James Fenimore Cooper. Sundays were devoted to drills and going to church. Grant was indifferent to both.

He graduated in the middle of his class in 1843, not a great showing, and had grown five inches from his original five foot two. His plan was to stay in the military for four years and then to get out.

Long afterwards, he once wrote to a friend that the two happiest days of his life were when he left West Point and when he left the presidency. His intention after the Academy was to teach.

It was at this point that Julia Dent, the daughter of a slave-owner, came into his life, much to the disapproval of Grant's abolitionist parents. But he was in love. His parents refused to attend the wedding due to the slavery-supporting activities of Julia's parents, but later came round. Ulysses and Julia went on to have four children. His family was everything to him, so he decided that, all things considered, a career in the military might be a safer bet than working on the farm as his father had done. To Grant, the United States was his family too, as were the enslaved people of the South, even if their humanity had been stripped away from them in 'the land of the free and the home of the brave'.

Ulysses Grant distinguished himself in the Mexican–American War of 1846–48, although he despised it. He wrote later that it was clear to him that the American intent was the annexation of Mexican land. This included the state of California, and the whole thing was about extending slavery.

As assistant quartermaster, he learned about battle, how to wage it, the importance of logistics and supply lines, and how to win. He became quite good at war.

After the Mexican War, Grant returned to civilian life, but he struggled to support his family and he was a wretched businessman. The whole world of commerce bored him. At one time he even turned to farming, owning a farm called 'Hardscrabble'. It was at this time that he also developed a drink problem.

Before that, Grant had acquired an enslaved man called William. He bought a manumission deed and set him free, an act that would have cost Grant plenty.

He subsequently moved his family to Galena, Illinois, and worked in his father's leather goods business, but the question of slavery still plagued him.

Abraham Lincoln, the wily country lawyer from Illinois, was elected in 1860. There he was, the living signal to the South that the question of slavery, which they couched in states' rights, would not be settled in their favour.

Fort Sumter in Charleston Harbour, South Carolina, was fired upon by a Confederate battery on 12 April 1861. In the dark. The Stars and Stripes were lowered, and the Confederate flag raised. It was war.

Grant set about helping to raise militias, but he knew that he had to do more. He was appointed a brigadier general of volunteers and ended up delivering the Union its first victory at Fort Donelson in 1862. His drinking was becoming an issue and complaints were made, but Lincoln promoted him because he was not afraid to fight.

On 2 March 1864, President Lincoln promoted Grant to lieutenant general. The last man to hold that rank had been George Washington. Grant was also given command of the Union Army, the largest military on the face of the earth.

It was in May and June 1864 that Grant really made his name. He oversaw the terrible battles waged over seven weeks in Virginia against the Confederate forces of Robert E. Lee. At the beginning, the Union forces suffered huge losses. But it was here that Grant's tactical genius – and experience of supply-line management – came to the fore. He was renowned for his ability to focus and also to understand battle at a deep level. Grant knew where Lee's weakest point was: at Cold Harbor, near Richmond. But he delayed attack, allowing Lee's reinforcements to arrive and to build new fortifications. On the morning of 3 June, two days after he had initially planned, Grant's forces of more than a hundred thousand men launched their attack. Lee's fifty-nine thousand men were outnumbered.

Lee then moved his army south towards Petersburg, which doubled as Virginia's most important railroad hub. Grant laid siege to the town for nine months. In July, he endured a setback, suffering three and a half thousand casualties compared to Lee's one thousand. But in spite of victories in Savannah and Nashville, Lee's ability to hold out at Petersburg was ebbing away. He had extended his lines to thirty-five miles, but his troops were starting to desert their posts due to hunger and illness. At the end of March 1865, President Lincoln met with Grant and Generals Sherman and Porter to discuss how to take the surrender of the Confederate armies. On 2 April, Grant's forces finally took

Petersburg, with Richmond falling the following day. Lee sent a letter of surrender. The formal surrender document was signed at Appomattox Court House on 9 April. Grant said: 'The war is over; the rebels are our countrymen again.'

Five days later, President Lincoln invited Grant and his wife to attend the theatre, with him and Mary Lincoln, on that fatal evening in April 1865. But Grant declined. He had other plans.

After Lincoln's assassination, Andrew Johnson, Lincoln's vice-president, and now president, urged a speedy return to normal life for the South, but Grant did not believe that the former Confederacy was anywhere near ready.

Grant's opposition to Johnson's pro-South views, and the latter's support for the continued suppression of African Americans, became more and more vociferous. Within a year their relationship had ruptured. Grant had spent an unhappy few months as Secretary for War, a position he had only accepted in order to prevent a more conservative lieutenant of Johnson's getting the job and reversing Reconstruction. However, Congress then voted to reinstate his predecessor Edwin Stanton. Johnson was furious and accused Grant of lying and duplicity. The whole episode led to Johnson being impeached and put on trial in the Senate. He survived by one vote.

In 1868, the Republican Party, the party of civil rights for African Americans, selected Grant as their nominee for president. The impeached Andrew Johnson was not nominated by his party, the Democrats, who instead chose Horatio Seymour. Johnson only received four votes, all from Tennessee.

The anti-Semitic General Order No. 11 became a factor in Grant's campaign when the public learned that Grant had accused the Jewish community, during the war in parts of the South, of profiteering. The Order commanded the expulsion of all Jews from the areas under his command. Pogroms resulted. Later, by way of a kind of apology and admission of guilt, Grant appointed more than fifty Jews to federal office: deputy postmasters, district attorneys, consuls. He also made Edward S. Salomon territorial governor of Washington. No Jew had ever held this position. All of this was his apology, in a sense, for an unspeakable act. But the damage was done. General Order No. 11 is an indelible stain on Grant's legacy.

But it is what Grant did for African American civil rights that caused Southern revisionists to cancel his military achievements post-Reconstruction and highlight his presidential failures.

The 1868 election campaign was the first election after the ratification of the Fifteenth Amendment, which protected the voting rights of all male citizens. In addition, Texas, Mississippi and Georgia were readmitted to the Union.

Grant kept his head down and did not campaign, but the Republican Party were able to win on his name alone and the fact that he supported the Fifteenth Amendment. The Democrats gained seats in Congress, but the Republicans continued to hold the majority. Grant won the popular vote by more than three hundred thousand out of 5.7 million votes cast. In the Electoral College he won by 214 votes to Horatio Seymour's (the Democratic candidate) 80. Grant had received the votes of more than five hundred thousand African American men. He was forty-six years old, and the youngest man to ever hold the office.

Grant was sworn in as the eighteenth president of the United States on 4 March 1869. He urged all Americans to support the voting rights of all citizens. This meant men, because women had not yet won the right to vote. He also backed the drive that supported bonds issued during the war being paid in gold, and that indigenous Americans, some day, might have citizenship. What lay before Grant was the overwhelming reality of Reconstruction.

Reconstruction was a series of laws and executive actions whose intention was two-fold: to end any vestiges of the Confederacy and to eradicate it completely as a warning to both the present and the future. The old Southern landed gentry, some of whom believed that their allegiance was to the state that they were born in, rather than to the Union formed out of *all* of the states, had to be made to understand that their way of life was over. Grant had defeated them not only on the battlefield, but also at the ballot box.

The Confederacy, rooted in a kind of romanticism, in which a *faux*-Walter Scott world mixed in with distortions of Anglo-Saxon history, helped to fuel a credo that white people were a superior race.

Those who came from the North to live in the region, some to help enforce federal law, were considered mortal enemies. The genre of the Western emerged from all of this – sagas of deep longing to leave a defeated land and search for freedom away from the central-isation of Washington.

The Thirteenth, Fourteenth and Fifteenth Amendments centre on the citizenship and enfranchisement of African Americans. The old South felt threatened, and it led to a variety of state interpret-ations. The priority of many was to roll back change in order to defeat federal power. And to keep African Americans second-class citizens. This battle continues today.

The North saw the South as needing to be continually supervised and watched. The Ku Klux Klan began a reign of terror, the first homegrown terrorist organisation in the US. Their allies, whether knowingly or not, began to perpetrate the myth that the South would rise again.

Grant had forced the majority of Republicans to understand that protecting the voting rights of African Americans was also in their interest. He believed this not only because of his abolitionist back-ground but because he had seen the African American man in battle. Ulysses Grant was also a Unionist. The war had been fought to hold on to the union of states and the sovereign right of these states as an indivisible nation called the United States, assembled in Washington, to make law and to govern as one.

Grant had seen first-hand what the South could do and what it would do if it had been allowed to perpetuate the kind of country it had so desired.

So the Enforcement Acts protected freedmen, the collective name of the formerly enslaved, and enabled them to have their rights guaranteed them by the new amendments. The federal government could intervene when rights were breached. Grant knew that he was at war with white supremacy, which had never been defeated. And it now had an enforcement wing: the Ku Klux Klan.

Grant implanted the federal government, for a time, as the occu-pying power. This was never forgotten in the South.

When Reconstruction started being rolled back under his successor, Grant was remade as a monster, a cesspool of corruption, a man who had reversed his legendary military status and been disgraced. Yet it can be said that his rather narrow military mind, his absolute trust in friends and family, his fear of leaving his family in poverty, also played a role in what happened to him.

Some of the scandals associated with Grant have an air of Victorian farce. All of them were damaging. For example, there have been many Black Fridays in history, but the gold scam of 24 September 1869 lives on in infamy as an example of the corruption of what became known as 'The Gilded Age'.

Grant was releasing gold slowly to pay for the nation's debts in order to bring some stability to the economy. His brother-in-law persuaded him not to do this, through the urging of two financiers, one of them railroad mogul Jay Gould. This would increase the sales of agriculture products overseas, thereby aiding Gould's shipping business. Grant was assured that a high price for gold helped farmers.

At the same time, a friend of Grant's, who had been his nominee for Secretary of the Treasury, gave him the same advice. Grant's wife, Julia, got involved too, as did his sister. But it was Jay Gould who reaped the benefits as his business got richer and richer.

The Secretary of the Treasury suspected that the market was being manipulated. The market crashed when the manipulation was exposed and the price of wheat and corn dropped, devasting the agricultural sector for years to come. The men who started the whole thing for their own benefit hired the best lawyers and were never prosecuted.

The Gold Exchange was obligated to take in all debts. There was an investigation, but it was never quite accepted that Grant himself did not profit from this, even though he died broke.

In 1872, Grant ran against the great newspaperman Horace Greeley. Greeley owned the *New York Tribune*, which supported 'the Liberal Republicans' who broke away from the Republicans and fought Grant over his prosecution of the Klan. The Democrats threw their lot in with the Liberal Republicans, as they saw them as the best hope of defeating Grant. They called what Grant did, and what he was, 'Grantism' – his nod to women's suffrage; full voting rights for African American men; the continued occupation, in some parts, of the renegade South.

Grant won the Electoral College in a landslide – 286 votes to Greeley's 66. Greeley was to die twenty-four days after the election. Taxes were low; the economy was coming back; and African Americans voted for Grant in the South. It would be more than a century before they could vote with that measure of freedom again.

Grant continued to work for a strong dollar, but the economy needed fixing and the changes in economies around the industrialised world caught the United States too; so there he was: the man who had saved the Union and was saving it again, trying to hold it together.

The Democrats gained a majority in the House after the 1874 elections and began to search for what they were sure was hidden corruption. Grant tried to reform the Justice Department and formed a Civil Service Commission. He believed in big government as the ultimate protector of ordinary people.

And then there were the wars with Native American communities in the West. The Sioux were prepared for a battle to the death after the constant infringement of their sacred Black Hills by gold hunters. The Sioux leader, the mystic warrior Sitting Bull, refused to relocate his people. On 4 July 1876 it was announced that General Custer and his entire 7th Cavalry had been wiped out at the Battle of the Little Big Horn. Many demanded retribution, but President Grant felt that Custer had brought the massacre on himself. In October 1876, Grant managed to convince the Sioux to relinquish their lands and Congress ratified the agreement a few days before he left office.

In his lifetime Grant's reputation remained intact. He once said: 'Failures have been errors of judgement. Not intent.' He had spent eight years in the office of president and was done. He took two years away, embarking on a world tour to Europe, Africa, the Middle East and India, encountering along the way Queen Victoria, Otto von Bismarck and the Pope.

When Grant realised he was broke, he wrote a bestselling memoir, which remains in print to this day. He lived until 1885 and is buried in the eponymous tomb in upper Manhattan along with his wife, Julia.

When Lincoln was told by some of his more obsequious generals that Grant had a drink problem, Lincoln is reported to have said that he wished he knew the booze that Grant drank so that he could give it to the rest of his generals, the ones reluctant to fight.

Ulysses S. Grant died of throat cancer, maybe as a result of his constant cigar smoking. His last word was said to have been 'water'.

Grant took the job of president because the job had to be done, not because he wanted it. He saw life as a pageant, as Lincoln did.

It is easy to dismiss Grant as a man surrounded by people smarter, slicker than he was. He was an ordinary man who managed an extraordinary time. In his way, he understood what America is meant to be.

Not a great president, he was what Lincoln understood about him: the man who would fight.

In many ways, Ulysses S. Grant was ahead of his time.

Bonnie Greer is an American-British playwright, novelist, broadcaster and former Deputy Chair of the British Museum

19

Rutherford B. Hayes

4 March 1877 to 4 March 1881
Republican
Vice-president: William A. Wheeler

By Robert Waller

Full name: Rutherford Birchard Hayes
Born: 4 October 1822, Delaware County, Ohio
Died: 17 January 1893, Fremont, Ohio
Resting place: Oakwood Cemetery, Fremont, Ohio
Library/Museum: Fremont, Ohio
Education: Methodist Norwalk Seminary (Ohio), Webb
Preparatory School (Connecticut), Kenyon College (Gambier,
Ohio), Harvard Law School
Married to: Lucy Ware Webb, m. 1852 (1831–89)
Children: Eight: Birchard, Webb, Rutherford, Joseph, George,
Fanny, Scott, Manning

Quotation: 'Nothing brings out the lower traits of human nature like office-seeking.'

RUTHERFORD HAYES, THE single-term Republican Party president from 1877 to 1881, began his period in office clouded by the most controversial and disputed election in United States history, bar none, not even 2000 or the stormy events of 2020–21. Not only did Hayes lose the popular vote to his Democratic opponent, but he only managed to triumph in the Electoral College by a highly dubious and seedy compromise manoeuvre.

His stewardship is noted most of all for the decisive end to the reconstruction period after the Civil War, and the restoration of power to Southern white supremacists and thus the inauguration of the many decades of 'Jim Crow' segregation and oppression of the African American population. One of the very few ways his period in government is in any way widely remembered is that his wife would not serve alcohol in the White House, and thus became known as 'Lemonade Lucy'. It is hard to find evidence of any major positive achievements.

One aspect of Rutherford Hayes's life that was unusual is that he was born after his father died – actually one of three presidents for whom this was the case, the others being Andrew Jackson and Bill Clinton. His father, a successful merchant and landowner, had moved the family west to Ohio from Vermont, but had been struck down by a fever two and a half months before Rutherford's birth in October 1822; the last-born child became even more the apple of his mother's eye when his only brother Lorenzo died at the age of nine when he fell through thin ice while skating.

Rutherford was well provided for by his mother and his wealthy lifelong bachelor uncle Sardis Birchard, attending private schools and college in Ohio. However, Rutherford's route through employment was far from unusual. He was one of no fewer than twenty-six of the forty-six presidents to date to have been lawyers, at least in some part of their careers. Uncle Birchard paid for Rutherford to attend Harvard Law School, after which he returned to Ohio to practise law and then serve as city solicitor for Cincinnati from 1858. He may have remained in such a comfortable if unspectacular position had his life not been turned upside down, as for so many Americans, by the Civil War.

Hayes is one of seven presidents who saw active service in the US Civil War, all on the Union (northern) side, and, as with some of the others (notably Ulysses S. Grant), his eventual advance to the highest office was clearly assisted by conspicuous bravery and good fortune. Hayes served in, and from 1862 led, the 23rd Ohio Volunteer Infantry Regiment, participating in battles such as Fox's Gap and Cedar Creek. He took five bullets in all and had four horses shot from under him. Although he was never responsible for significant strategic or tactical decisions, by the end of the war he had reached the rank of brevet (acting) major general and had already been elected in absentia in November 1864 to the US House of Representatives for the second district of Ohio.

Hayes's record in the lower house of Congress was undistinguished. He did not even attend before December 1865, a year after he was elected, as he argued his military service was more important, and after two terms he exchanged the House for his first executive experience. Largely on his solid war record, he was chosen by the Republican Party as their candidate for governor of Ohio. In all, sixteen presidents have previously been state governors. Hayes served in this capacity from 1868 to 1872, when he was term limited, and again from 1876. He had little impact in this role, partly because for the vast bulk of the time the Democrats controlled the state legislature. He wrote during his time in the governor's mansion in Columbus that there was 'not too much hard work, plenty of time to read, good society etc.'.

The year 1876 saw the centenary election after the US Declaration of Independence, and it did not provide a healthy or positive impression of the development of American democracy. In June, at the Republican Convention to pick their candidate, there was a bitter split between factions: the front-runner, Senator James Blaine of Maine, was one of the moderates known as 'Half-Breeds'. The leader of the other faction, the 'Stalwarts', was Roscoe Conkling of New York. As neither faction was willing to let the other prevail, the selection eventually resolved on a compromise candidate – Rutherford Hayes, who was the governor of the state in which the convention was held, but who hadn't even figured in the top four candidates in the early ballots. The Democrats, keen to regain the presidency, nominated Governor Samuel Tilden of New York.

In the popular vote Tilden seemed the clear winner. The final tally gave him 4,284,757 votes to Hayes's 4,044,950 – one of the five occasions when the loser of a presidential election received more than the eventual winner. The other presidents who failed to gain even a plurality, never mind a majority, were John Quincy Adams, Benjamin Harrison, George W. Bush and Donald Trump. What is more, in 1876, whether Hayes had a majority of the Electoral College was also contested. Tilden had clearly won 184 of the EC votes, but 185 were needed for victory. The most disputed states were all in the South, and both the Republicans and Democrats in South Carolina, Louisiana and Florida claimed victory there and submitted separate sets of voting results. Tilden seemed to have taken more votes in these states, but the Republicans alleged voter fraud and intimidation of their voters, including African Americans.

Furious Democrats around the nation claimed the election was being stolen from them (another echo of 2000 and 2020–21). In Columbus, a bullet was fired through Governor Hayes's parlour window, passing through two rooms and burying itself in the library wall.

Meanwhile, some Republican and Democrat politicians searched for a deal or a compromise solution. In January 1877 Congress appointed a fifteen-man Electoral Commission to settle the result. What happened therein was secretive and arcane and the final decision was delayed until early March, just before the inauguration. After a series of 8–7 votes by the Commission in Hayes's favour, the Democrats eventually accepted a compromise solution – recognising Hayes as president in return for the withdrawal of federal (that is, Northern) troops from the remaining Southern states still occupied to maintain the reconstruction system. This was the notorious Hayes Compromise. In the end, the Electoral College ratified Hayes as victor by 185 votes to 184.

Many Democrats still fumed as the decision turned against them, insisting that Hayes had stolen the election and had no right to be president. He was widely called 'His Fraudulency' and Ruther*fraud* B. Hayes. However, the fury of the Democrats was somewhat mollified as, now he was in office, Hayes kept the terms of the

Compromise. On 3 April 1877, Hayes instructed the Secretary of War to remove the troops from the State House of South Carolina. When he ordered the same in Louisiana, it can be said that reconstruction came to an end. Republicans packed their carpetbags and returned to the North, and the party was to be reduced to scarcely any presence in the Deep South for the best part of a century. Black Americans were now to be stripped of the rights and gains they had made in the reconstruction period, as 'Jim Crow' measures of discrimination and oppression were imposed in the South – overwhelmingly prevalent segregation, vote suppression through poll taxes, literacy tests and blatant intimidation. Such was the meaning of the Hayes Compromise for African Americans. It was to be a shameful legacy of Hayes's presidency.

One of the reasons why Rutherford Hayes achieved so little in the way of positive legislative achievement is a perennial problem affecting the American presidency: he did not have a sympathetic majority in Congress. Unlike the British system of parliamentary government, in which the executive government and the prime minister at its head are not separately elected, but in fact derive their power from their control of the House of Commons, there is no guarantee that the president has a majority in the legislature. Hayes found that the opposition Democrats held a majority in the lower House in the forty-fifth Congress (1877–79) and in both Houses in the forty-sixth (1879–81). It is true that at this time voting on party lines was far from universal, but Hayes also did not manage to gain reliable support from either of the two powerful Republican Party factions, the Half-Breeds and the Stalwarts, as he was in essence alienated from the leaders of his own party as well. As a result, his legislative influence was reduced to the negative – twelve successful vetoes in all, such as that on 1 March 1879 of a bill to restrict Chinese immigration to the United States. However, his veto of the Bland–Allison Silver Act (which required the government to buy silver and use it in the currency) on 28 February 1878 was overridden by a two-thirds majority in both Houses on the very same day. This is an indicator that Hayes as president had one of the weaker positions in relation to Congress. His influence was perforce largely restricted to 'executive action'.

The main attempted executive measure associated with the

presidency of Rutherford Hayes concerns reform of the civil service, as he was determined to weaken the 'spoils' system ('to the victor the spoils') whereby a victorious president rewarded supporters by allocating jobs in the executive branch. Instead, Hayes favoured appointment on merit by open examination. However, this conflicted with the expectations of the 'Stalwart' branch of his Republican Party and Congress in general, who were accustomed to wielding patronage over political appointments. Therefore, Hayes could not persuade Congress to outlaw the spoils system, though he did issue an executive order forbidding federal officeholders from making campaign contributions. His initiative also paved the way for the Pendleton Act of 1883, during Chester Arthur's term, which went some way towards creating a career civil service based on merit, and stood unchallenged until October 2020, when Donald Trump issued an executive order that meant that a large number of the federal workforce could be fired for political reasons, including lack of loyalty to the president.

At the time of Hayes's period of office, the late 1870s, many regarded the dominant aspect of United States history to be the rise in power of the great industrialists, in iron and steel, mineral extraction, and railway construction. The period is often described as the 'Gilded Age', characterised by rapid growth and the creation of huge fortunes for 'millionaires', but also of massive inequality and widespread poverty. In some cases, new trade ('labor') unions resisted the industrial 'barons', resulting in bitter and frequently bloody strikes. One such year of disruption was 1877, Hayes's first as president. With workers driven to desperation by a concerted campaign by railway companies to cut wages, strikes paralysed six to seven thousand miles of track by July. Despite personally expressing some sympathy for the strikers, and despite the tradition of non-intervention by presidents in labour disputes, Hayes also proclaimed that workers had no right to interfere with business. He sent federal troops into West Virginia on 18 July, Pennsylvania on the 21st of the same month, and Maryland on the 23rd, and crushed the strikes. Therefore it is clear that Hayes sided more with the naked capitalism of the Gilded Age than with trade union rights.

Was the presidency of Rutherford Hayes marked by any 'notable firsts'? It is hard to find major innovation in policy or procedure. Although prohibition of alcohol is usually associated with the 1920s, the evils of strong drink had been challenged for much of American history, and from 1877 Rutherford's wife broke new ground by refusing to serve alcohol in the White House. As the Secretary of State remarked ironically after one dinner: 'it was a brilliant event; the water flowed like champagne.' After Thomas Edison's demonstrations of the phonograph in 1878 and his electric lightbulb in 1879, Hayes was quick to use them in the White House for the first time, and the same applied in the case of Alexander Graham Bell's telephone, and, indeed, running water in the plumbing. To credit these as presidential domestic achievements is perhaps to take a very literal view of that phrase.

Although, in general, presidents have had more freedom in foreign than domestic policy, Hayes made very little impact on world affairs. Perhaps his only lasting legacy is that after Hayes arbitrated in their favour in a border dispute with Argentina in 1878, Paraguay named the province they had gained after him: Presidente Hayes Department is still on the map, and its capital is Villa Hayes. This constitutes a rather thin international legacy.

What can we say in a positive sense about Rutherford Hayes? First, he did not take an active part in his highly controversial election process, and most historians have concluded that he probably would have won clearly in 1876 under a free and fair electoral system in which African Americans in the South were not already disbarred or intimidated. Second, what came to be called the Hayes Compromise that ended reconstruction and initiated the slide into the Jim Crow period in the South was probably inevitable, as neither the will nor the practical circumstances existed for a permanent Northern occupation. Hayes himself clearly hoped that black citizens in the South would not suffer reverses denying their rights and was sorry when this process started even in his own presidency. After he left office he expended effort supporting African American education. Finally, although Hayes could claim very few clear achievements in the four years of his office, the verdict of the voters does not appear to have been overly damning.

We cannot judge if he would have been re-elected if he had not kept to his pledge to serve a single term, but he did hand over the office to a favoured successor. James Garfield was a fellow Republican and a fellow Ohioan.

In retirement, Hayes suffered an almost immediate blow when his friend Garfield was shot on 2 July 1881, and died from the resulting infection on 19 September. Hayes himself never played an active role in politics again, acting as a director of a bank and trustee of Ohio State University. He was much saddened when his fifty-seven-year-old wife Lucy suffered a fatal stroke in 1889. Rutherford Hayes himself died at his home, Spiegel Grove, in Fremont, Ohio, on 17 January 1893. He was seventy years old.

Rutherford Hayes was by most accounts a pleasant, thoughtful and well-meaning man. Unfortunately, his presidency generated no positive legacy to counter the grim turning point of the 'Hayes Compromise' with its reversal of the advances and denial of the hopes of African Americans. Hayes must therefore be placed in the bottom half of any ranking of presidents. It is quite possible that he should never have been awarded the office in the first place; he did little of positive note in his single term, and if he is remembered for only one thing, it was his election in 1876 with its parallels to 2000 and 2020. As in 2000, the candidate with the popular majority of votes lost. In both cases the problem of racial discrimination at the polls influenced the controversial result, and in each, also, the state of Florida played a crucial role. In both 1876 and 2020 there was a widespread lack of acceptance of the legitimacy of the man who was to move into the White House, however unjustified in the latter case. This sullied the whole of the Hayes presidency.

Dr Robert Waller is a former tutor and lecturer at Oxford University. He is the author of eight editions of The Almanac of British Politics *and of the 'Ramsay MacDonald' chapter in Iain Dale (ed.)* The Prime Ministers *(2020).*

20

James A. Garfield

Republican
4 March 1881 to 19 September 1881
Vice-president: Chester A. Arthur

By Anne Alexander

Full name: James Abram Garfield
Born: 19 November 1831, Orange Township, Ohio
Died: 19 September 1881, Elberon, New Jersey
Resting place: Lake View Cemetery, Cleveland, Ohio
Library/Museum: Mentor, Ohio
Education: Williams College, Massachusetts
Married to: Lucretia Rudolph, m. 1858 (1832–1918)
Children: Seven (two died in infancy): Harry Augustus 'Hal',
James Rudolph, Abram, Mary 'Mollie', Irwin McDowell, Eliza
Arbella, Edward 'Neddie'
Quotation: 'I never meet a ragged boy in the street without

feeling that I may owe him a salute, for I know not what possibilities may be buttoned up under his coat.'

T HE TWENTIETH PRESIDENT of the United States can be summed up in one word: potential. James Abram Garfield – orator, lawyer, preacher, linguist, general, congressman, senator-elect, president – only served six months in office.

Garfield was shot by Charles J. Guiteau at the Baltimore and Potomac Railroad Station in Washington, DC in July 1881, conferring on him the dubious distinction of being the second commander in chief to suffer an untimely death at the hands of an assassin. Abraham Lincoln had been the first, having been assassinated sixteen years earlier.

When the delusional Guiteau opened fire with his Webley & Son British Bull Dog revolver, he did so believing he was owed a government job in return for what he considered to be crucial support he had given Garfield during his presidential election campaign, under the 'spoils' system, where political allies were rewarded with plum civil service posts.

It was an increasingly discredited system, which Garfield had set his sights on reforming. As it happens, his premature death – he died from an infection two months after the shooting – though tragic in cutting short the promise of his presidency, almost certainly hastened the reform he had campaigned for, with the posthumous setting up of the foundations of the modern US civil service.

A little under fifty years before the fateful encounter with Guiteau, Garfield had been born into poverty in Ohio, and might have been expected to live a modest and unremarkable life. But this boy – the last president to be born in a log cabin – would defy his humble beginnings, rising to the highest position in the land, in many ways epitomising the American dream.

Garfield's father – one of five children – died when he was a toddler, and his mother remarried, then divorced (a scandal at the time) and raised him and his siblings mostly alone. He was a teenager when he was baptised into the Disciples of Christ Church, which influenced his personal and political life.

Encouraged by his strong-willed, doting mother, and with a fierce intellect and work ethic, he got an education against the financial odds. He worked to support himself, including taking jobs as a tutor and a janitor.

Garfield studied at local institutions before gaining a place at the prestigious Williams College in Williamstown, Massachusetts, before returning to his home state of Ohio where he became president of Hiram College as a scholar of Greek and Latin. He later trained as a lawyer.

It was his experience in Massachusetts in the mid-1850s that likely broadened the young Garfield's mind and this was probably where he began to consider politics as a career, becoming more politically aware in the school's anti-slavery atmosphere.

When, years later in 1861, Garfield joined the Union Army in the Civil War, he saw it partly as a Christian and moral crusade against the evil of slavery, in contrast to some of his contemporaries who saw abolition more as a means to a political end.

Though Garfield was doubtless a supporter of abolition, and later during reconstruction, of black suffrage, he still had, at best, a patronising attitude towards black people, and at worst, white supremacist views, typical of the time. He said in 1865 in a private letter that he had a 'strong feeling of repugnance when I think of the Negro being made our political equal'. However, publicly, he continued to support the vote for African Americans: 'Let us not commit ourselves to the senseless and absurd dogma that the colour of the skin shall be the basis of suffrage . . .' he said in a speech the same year.

By the time he was excelling as a military leader in the Civil War, he was already an Ohio State senator, having been elected in 1859.

Garfield had played a major role in recruiting Ohio's volunteer regiments, using his speaking skills and evangelistic fervour he had honed as a preacher with the Disciples. He later saw battle action, and rose to the rank of major general. His post-Civil War and reconstruction years as a member of the House of Representatives, to which he was elected in 1863, were marked by a journey from the radical wing of the Republican Party to a more moderate stance.

He had, in the immediate post-Civil War years, advocated a hard line against the South, including confiscation of Southern plantations and even exile or execution of rebellion leaders, but his position later softened.

He served nine terms as a congressman, becoming an expert on fiscal matters as chairman of the House Committee on Appropriations.

Garfield marked himself out as a unifying figure in Congress, bringing together opposing factions within his own party.

His experiences growing up, moving from a small town in the mid-West to mixing with an eastern elite in Massachusetts as a student, appear to have instilled a certain confidence in him and developed his ability to relate and engage with people from a range of backgrounds and views. These social and diplomatic skills were major drivers in him winning the Republican nomination for president in June 1880.

But his rise from the House of Representatives to the White House was accidental, if you fully believe Garfield's protestations that he had not sought the presidential nomination at the fractious Republican Convention. Nor did he deliberately betray his political ally John Sherman, whom he had originally backed for president.

Even before the 1880 convention began, Garfield had been whispered about as a potential nomination pick. He had been elected to the Senate in January 1880, though his term was not scheduled to commence until 1881. Garfield never took up his seat.

With the convention split over who to back, Garfield's stirring speeches in support of his man Sherman actually ended up convincing his colleagues to name him as their nominee instead of the lacklustre subject of his speeches.

Garfield accepted the nomination, and conducted, as was tradition, a so-called 'front porch' campaign, focusing on his rags-to-riches life. He narrowly beat his Democrat rival, Winfield Scott Hancock, in the popular vote, though comfortably under the Electoral College system.

He remains the only sitting member of the House of Representatives to have been elected president and also the only person to be a representative, senator-elect and president-elect at the same time, if only briefly.

On his election as president, Garfield, who had worked to hold together the warring Republican factions of the so-called stalwarts and moderates, almost immediately faced a confrontation with one of the leading backers of the patronage system.

Senator Roscoe Conkling of New York felt the burn of the new president when Garfield refused to install Conkling's choice for the powerful Collector of the Port of New York. Garfield said, as he fought Conkling over the nomination: 'This . . . will settle the question whether the President is registering clerk of the Senate or the Executive of the United States . . . shall the principal port of entry . . . be under the control of the administration or under the local control of a factional senator?'

Garfield refused to back down and he prevailed.

In taking on and defeating the influential Conkling, Garfield enhanced the power of the office of the presidency and marked the beginning of an era of the return of presidential authority. One of his first moves was to launch an investigation into corruption in the Post Office. The Star Routes scandal exposed large contractors, an ex-US representative and senior post office employees who were involved in a bribery ring involving the awarding of lucrative postal delivery contracts. It was shut down, though not resolved until after Garfield's death. There were few convictions, but the affair caused enough of a public outcry to have a significant impact on the campaign to clean up the government.

That scandal, plus Garfield's assassination, would be used to help push through reform. The campaign for civil service reform had been gathering pace for some years. The National Civil Service Reform League argued that the spoils system had played a major role in the assassination of Garfield, and this gained traction.

In 1883, Congress passed the Pendleton Civil Service Reform Act, which ended the spoils system and established the basis of a federal employment system based on merit rather than on political party affiliation. It provided for the selection of some government employees by competitive exams, and made it illegal to sack or demote government officials for political reasons.

The act initially only applied to a relatively small proportion of federal employees, but it now covers most employees. It was instrumental in the creation of a professional civil service. It also had an impact on campaign finance, as the parties were forced to look for new sources of campaign funds.

Ask most laypeople who James Abram Garfield was, and they would probably struggle for a coherent answer. He has been consigned to the 'also ran' category of the history of the occupants of the White House. This may be understandable because of his very short tenure. However, when examining his service in the war, in politics, and his role in helping to unify the Republican Party, he helped bring some stability at a time when the future of the Union was by no means guaranteed.

Had Garfield lived beyond the age of forty-nine, it's entirely possible he could have ranked as one of the great transitional leaders of the nineteenth century.

Anne Alexander is the senior political producer for ITV's Good Morning Britain. *She's been a journalist for twenty-five years, and has specialised in politics for the past nineteen. She's contributed to two books, and is a patron of Women in Westminster: The 100.*

21

Chester A. Arthur

19 September 1881 to 4 March 1885
Republican
Vice-president: None

By Sue Cameron

Full name: Chester Alan Arthur
Born: 5 October 1829, Fairfield, Vermont
Died: 18 November 1886, New York City
Resting place: Albany Rural Cemetery, Menands, New York
Library/Museum: Fairfield, Vermont
Education: Union College, Schenectady, New York
Married to: Ellen Herndon, m. 1859 (1837–80)
Children: Three: William, Chester and Ellen
Quotation: 'Men may die but the fabrics of free institutions remain unshaken.'

CHESTER ARTHUR SPENT much of his career cheerfully embroiled in all kinds of political corruption, from jobs-for-the-boys to cash-for-favours. Dubbed the unexpected president, he had neither sought nor wanted the highest office in the land. Yet once in the White House he underwent a Damascene conversion that saw him cracking down on graft, reforming the civil service, modernising the country's dilapidated navy and championing the rights of minorities. Congress often blocked him and much of what he started remained unfinished or was only brought to fruition by others. Some historians say that he achieved little and note that he has been largely forgotten. Yet that was not the verdict of his contemporaries. As Alexander K. McClure of the *Philadelphia Times* said: 'No man ever entered the Presidency so profoundly and widely distrusted as Chester Alan Arthur and no one ever retired . . . more generally respected by political friend and foe.'

What is remarkable is that until he became vice-president, Arthur had never stood in any election. He rose to power through his mastery of the 'spoils system' – a form of political patronage based on the maxim 'to the victor the spoils'. Electoral victory allowed party bosses to hand out thousands of government jobs in return for votes plus contributions to party funds. As Thomas Reeves explains in his biography of Arthur: 'Virtually every office had a price tag and all public officials who owed their jobs to the bosses were expected to spend time and money on behalf of party candidates, under threat of dismissal.' The jobs the bosses controlled included street sweepers, post office workers and top judicial appointments – with endless opportunities for graft along the way. Many public officials were able to keep a portion of the fines and taxes they collected on behalf of the government. For example, the legendary lawman Wyatt Earp wanted to be County Sheriff not so much in the interests of justice but because it was a plum post in the spoils system. The sheriff's share of the takings would have brought in thousands of dollars annually – hundreds of thousands today – at a time when most cattlemen were on one dollar a day.

The spoils system was not new but in Chester Arthur's day it thrived as never before. He became president at an extraordinary time in his country's history. This was Mark Twain's 'Gilded Age' when a thin layer of fabulous wealth as personified by the Vanderbilts,

the Rockefellers and Carnegies – the billionaires of their day –
overlaid the grinding poverty of millions. The US population had
surged from around 35 million after the Civil War to 50 million in
the decade up to 1880. Immigrants flooded into the big cities –
400,000 in New York alone – only to be hit by economic collapse.
The country was ravaged by the 'Long Depression' that ran from
1873 to 1879, with unemployment ranging between 24 and 40 per
cent. Party bosses and their political machines could help loyal
families with jobs or small payments for food and fuel – always in
return for votes. The rich were tapped for large contributions to
party funds in return for fat contracts and business-friendly legislation. At election times the spoilsmen were ruthless. As Arthur, a
Republican, later recalled: 'Political leaders had organised gangs of
ruffians at their command and could impose obedience at caucuses
. . . ballot boxes were stuffed almost openly.' Arthur's job was to
deliver votes for the Republican Party in the key city of New York
and he was impressively good at it.

Chester Alan Arthur – Chet to his friends – was born in 1829.
His mother, Malvina Stone, was from Vermont. His father, William,
an Irish immigrant, was a Baptist minister and a passionate opponent
of slavery, as his son would be. Young Arthur went to Union College
and became a lawyer in New York. Slavery there had been abolished
in 1827, but racism was rife. In 1854, Lizzie Jennings, a young, black
schoolteacher, was ordered off a 'white' streetcar. She sued and
Arthur represented her – one of several anti-discrimination cases
he fought. They won and the case helped end segregation on New
York public transport.

Now in his twenties, Arthur was tall, personable and with an
impressive set of mutton-chop whiskers. He met Ellen Herndon,
known as Nell, the daughter of a well-connected Virginian family.
Her uncle noted: 'He's a fine-looking man and we all like him very
much.' The two married in 1859. Meanwhile Arthur had become
active in Republican politics and through party contacts he was put
on the staff of the New York governor. Already a member of the
state militia, during the Civil War he proved a talented administrator,
fitting out over two hundred thousand men for the Union Army
and ending with the rank of brigadier general. By then New York's
Republican Party was dominated by Senator Roscoe Conkling – a

brilliant orator but pompous, humourless and a shameless believer in political patronage. He was a spoilsman to his fingertips – and proud of it. 'We are told the Republican Party is a machine,' he said. 'Yes. A government is a machine, a church is a machine . . . every organisation which binds men together for a common purpose is a machine.'

Arthur became his lieutenant and in 1871 he was made Collector of the New York Custom House – the most important and lucrative post the Republican machine could offer. The Collector controlled hundreds of jobs that could be given to party supporters. He was also entitled to a cut of all Custom House fines and forfeitures, which took his pay from a basic $12,000 to some $50,000 – over $1m today. Arthur was now earning as much as the president and his newfound wealth was reflected in his lifestyle. He bought an elegant brownstone house on Lexington Avenue, he loved good food, fine wines and the best cigars – and staying up late into the night talking politics. Yet calls for the reform of the spoils system were steadily mounting. Supporters of civil service reform wanted public appointments to be based on merit rather than patronage. The Republican Party split. Those against reform, including Arthur and Conkling, were known as Stalwarts. President Rutherford Hayes, loathed Conkling, who always referred to him as 'Rutherfraud' and spoke of the 'snivel service'.

Hayes launched an investigation into the New York Custom House. It found 'inefficiency and corruption' that was 'perverting the powers of government to personal and party ends'. Hayes seized the opportunity to remove Arthur as Collector. At the 1880 Republican Convention, there was a stand-off between Stalwarts and reformers over who to nominate as presidential candidate. After a record thirty-six ballots, they compromised on James Garfield, a reformer. To bring the factions together and hold the New York vote, Arthur was nominated as vice-president. The Garfield/Arthur ticket won – but only just. Then, on 2 July 1881, an office seeker who had been denied the job he wanted shot President Garfield at a Washington railway station, shouting: 'I am a Stalwart and Arthur will be President.' The assassin, Charles Guiteau, was hanged.

The prospect of Chester Arthur in the White House caused widespread dismay. Many expected him to be Conkling's puppet and the cry went up: 'Chet Arthur president of the US! Good God!' Whatever the doubts, Arthur won respect for his dignified demeanour. When sworn in, he paid tribute to his predecessor's 'noble aspirations', including measures to 'correct abuses'. Weeks later, he broke with Conkling. 'For the vice presidency I was indebted to Mr Conkling,' he said. 'For the Presidency of the United States, my debt is to the Almighty.'

In his first address to Congress, Arthur pledged support for civil service reform. The Stalwarts were dismayed, the reformers delighted and just about everyone was surprised. So why the radical change of mind? As an astute politician, Arthur recognised that public outrage over Garfield's murder by an avowed Stalwart meant reform had become imperative. As president he was at last his own man – he didn't have to please Conkling or anyone else. It was as if he had gained a new sense of freedom. A civil service reform bill had already been introduced by Democrat senator George Pendleton. It required civil servants to be appointed on merit as decided through competitive exams – similar to the system in Britain.

In 1883, Arthur signed the Pendleton Act into law and followed it up by appointing an effective Civil Service Commission to oversee the new rules. Initially the Act applied to only some 10 per cent of federal posts, but it changed attitudes. Over time a more professional civil service developed. Political patronage did not disappear. It still exists today; the US ambassador to the United Kingdom is usually a political appointment. Yet the US public service did start to become more identified with the public interest and not just the interests of machine politicians. Arthur himself said his reforms had been successful in 'securing competent and faithful public servants'.

He cracked down on other forms of government graft. In 1882, he vetoed the Rivers and Harbours Bill. Designed to fund $19m worth of construction projects, the bill was denounced – rightly – as a piece of 'legislative pork', aimed at 'the advancement of local jobbery'. Congress overturned his veto, but his principled stand won plaudits. He also insisted that racketeers in the post office be prosecuted 'with the utmost vigour'. There was public anger when none of them was sent to prison, but the trials and the outcry brought the frauds to an end.

With his knowledge of shipping and trade, Arthur was horrified at how obsolete and totally neglected the US fleet had become since its success in the Civil War. 'Never,' said one observer, 'was there such a hopeless, broken-down, tattered, forlorn apology for a navy.' There were far too many officers, some of them drunks. In his first address to Congress, Arthur insisted that 'national safety, economy and honour' necessitated total modernisation of the navy. Old wooden sailing ships were duly retired and four new, steel-hulled vessels were built. The change of approach was far more significant than these numbers suggest. What mattered was the president's commitment and in 1884 he ordered the creation of a national Naval War College, at Newport, to develop the strategic training of officers. America's 'new navy' was born. In the next four years, money was found for another thirty new vessels. America was poised to become a naval superpower.

From the outset, Arthur was very conscious of the need to raise the standing and prestige of the presidency, which had been badly tarnished by the corruption of the Grant administration and the inadequacy of President Hayes. The White House itself was shockingly run-down. To set a new tone, Arthur ordered it to be completely refurbished before he moved in. Twenty-four wagonloads of furniture, carpets and curtains, some dating back eighty years, were removed before a revamp overseen by Louis C. Tiffany, one of the top designers of the day. The new look included jewelled glass screens and gold wallpaper. Once installed, Arthur entertained lavishly. Dinner guests would enjoy fourteen courses at a cost of $10 a plate. One spoke of 'the flowers, the damask, the silver, the attendants all showing the latest style'. Thousands attended receptions, waiting for their chance to shake the president's hand. As historian Zachary Karabell put it: 'Chester Arthur was the closest thing to Jacqueline Kennedy that Washington would see until Jacqueline Kennedy.'

As president, Arthur invariably looked the part. Tall and impressive, he was always beautifully dressed. His coats were ordered from London and he once tried on twenty pairs of trousers, all made to his measurements, before choosing. His manners were impeccable. Out walking in Washington or riding in his elegant dark green carriage, he would raise his hat and bow to those he met, however humble. Then, as now, appearances matter and Arthur knew it.

The new-look White House and the glamour that went with it enhanced the image of the presidency and raised it in public esteem. The only sadness for Arthur was that his wife, Nell, had died of pneumonia, aged only forty-two, the year before he became president. One of his sisters, Mary Arthur McElroy, acted as his hostess.

Since President Lincoln's administration, the balance of power between Congress and president had tilted significantly in favour of the former and would remain so for the rest of the century. This constrained Arthur's freedom of manoeuvre, but having spent most of his life as a fixer, he was always ready to compromise. Nor was he afraid to challenge Congress or his own party. While most Republicans favoured the very high tariffs that had protected the industrialised North since the Civil War, Arthur's political antennae told him tariff cuts would increase competition, lower the cost of living and be a vote winner. He set up an independent commission that called for tariff cuts of 20 to 25 per cent. Congress brought the final tariff reductions right down to 1.5 per cent. Nobody blamed Arthur and many congratulated him. He had taken an independent line and appointed a conscientious commission not in thrall to vested interests. The 1.5 per cent cut he secured was the only one for more than a decade.

Any understanding of Arthur has to reflect not just his pragmatism and capacity for compromise but the values instilled in him during his youth. These are most evident in the way he consistently championed the rights of ethnic minorities. In 1883, he was horrified when the Supreme Court effectively nullified the Civil Rights Act of 1875, pivotal legislation designed to ensure equal rights for African Americans. Arthur made a passionate plea to Congress for new laws guaranteeing equal civil and political rights for *all* citizens, saying that such legislation would 'receive my unhesitating approval'. He was furious when they rejected his plea. He was ahead of his time. Only in 1964 would there be the kind of new Civil Rights Act he had envisaged.

In Arthur's day, the American West was still, well, wild. In his first address to Congress, delivered only weeks after that gunfight at OK Corral, Arthur spoke of 'armed desperadoes, known as "cowboys" . . . committing acts of lawlessness and brutality' in Arizona. He also spoke of the need to protect white settlers from attack by Indians (as Native Americans were then known), but made a passionate plea for tough new laws to stop the settlers encroaching on Indian lands. Those who did should face prison, not just fines. He called for Indians to be given the same protection of the law as other citizens and said 'frontier collisions . . . had led to frequent and disastrous conflicts between the races' costing thousands of lives. He managed to secure money from Congress for Indian education though not as much as he had hoped for.

Inevitably, Arthur also clashed with Congress over Chinese immigration. Apart from the race issue, the Chinese provided cheap labour, undercutting other workers on the railroads. Feelings were very strong. So Congress passed an Exclusion Bill banning Chinese immigration for twenty years, despite a treaty guaranteeing free movement between China and the US. Arthur vetoed the bill saying it would be 'a breach of our national faith'. Ever the pragmatist, he said he would accept a ten-year ban and signed the amended bill into law in 1882. It marked the end of America's once-proud policy of offering a haven to all peoples, but Arthur had at least managed to halve the exclusion period and limit the diplomatic fallout.

Arthur also did his bit to improve the status of women by toughening laws against what he called 'the odious crime' of polygamy. This had been introduced into Utah by the Mormons, whose leader, Brigham Young, had fifty-five wives. Arthur's 1882 Anti-Polygamy Act banned those who practised this 'barbarous system' from voting or holding public office.

On the political front, the similarities between Arthur's time and now are almost eerie. Even at the beginning, his opponents falsely claimed that he was ineligible to be vice-president because he had been born in Canada, not the US as the Constitution requires. Similar false accusations were made about Barack Obama. Arthur's story resonates with the politics of today in other ways. He was an early campaigner on climate change, telling Congress: 'The condition of the forests of the country and the wasteful manner in which their destruction is taking place give cause for serious apprehension. Their action in . . . modifying the extremes of climate . . . is now well understood.'

Yellowstone National Park – the first of its kind – had been established in 1872, but Arthur was the first president to go there. His party, which included 175 pack animals, was greeted by huge crowds. At Lafayette, black American citizens gave him a plaque thanking him for supporting 'justice to an oppressed people': Indian chiefs and 500 of their warriors staged a sham battle for him; and he was able to indulge in his favourite sport, fishing. In one day he and a companion caught 105 lbs of fish.

The trip, which he described as 'better than anything I ever tried before', was aimed at boosting interest in Yellowstone itself and spreading awareness of the concept of national parks. It received huge publicity, which helped save Yellowstone from plans for damaging commercial development.

Arthur's health had deteriorated rapidly during his presidency. He knew from his second year in office that he had a fatal kidney disease. He was determined to conceal it, fearing that he would become a lame-duck president if word got out or if he failed to stand for a second term. He made only a token effort to secure nomination and failed to do so. He took no part in the 1884 election.

In March 1885, Chester Arthur left the White House for the last time, dying in November 1886. Two days before his death he ordered all his private papers to be burnt. At his death there was widespread praise for his presidency. One newspaper said he had risen 'steadily in the esteem and respect of the nation'. Another called him 'one of the most successful and meritorious in our whole list of presidents'. Mark Twain said, 'it would be hard indeed to better President Arthur's administration'. Yet today, few have even heard of him.

It is not so much that history has been damning of his record – it has just forgotten him. Why? Admittedly history has not had much to go on. By destroying his papers, he left us with little insight into his thinking and motivation. He didn't serve even one full term as president. He was notoriously suspicious of journalists, telling one reporter: 'I hope you are not interviewing me – I believe that is the word – or intending to quote what I have been saying.' They did, of course, under the headline 'A Chat with Chet', but true to form he hadn't given anything away.

Scott S. Greenberger, in his 2017 biography of Arthur, says: 'The social, political and economic changes that shook America in the 1870s and 1880s were the birth pangs of the society we have today.'

Chester Arthur presided over a period of huge technological change and innovation: his era saw the arrival of the electric light-bulb, the telephone, the skyscraper, refrigeration – and Coca-Cola. In his three and a half years as president, Arthur brought stability to the nation. He exuded reliability and decency, giving people a new sense of security. He strengthened civil society, laid the foundations for the country to become a global superpower, and started to restore the status and prestige of the presidency itself. Others would take up where he left off and win greater renown, perhaps deservedly so, yet it was Arthur's work that they built on. Nobody would claim that he should be in the top rank of US presidents, but he deserves more study and much more recognition. In many ways he was the right man for the time.

Sue Cameron is a writer and broadcaster. She is a former presenter of BBC Newsnight *and has been a columnist on the* Financial Times *and the* Telegraph.

22 and 24

Grover Cleveland

4 March 1885 to 4 March 1889 and
4 March 1893 to 4 March 1897
Democrat
Vice-presidents: Thomas A. Hendricks 1885,
vacant 1885–89, Adlai Stevenson 1893–97

By Gerry Hassan

Full name: Stephen Grover Cleveland
Born: 18 March 1837, Caldwell, New Jersey
Died: 24 June 1908, Princeton, New Jersey
Resting place: Princeton Cemetery, New Jersey
Library/Museum: Caldwell, New Jersey
Education: Fayetteville Academy; Clinton Liberal Academy
Married to: Frances Folsom, m. 1886 (1864–1947)
Children: Five: Ruth, Esther, Marion, Richard, Francis
Quotation: 'A government for the people must depend for its

success on the intelligence, the morality, the justice, and the interest of the people themselves.'

G ROVER CLEVELAND IS unique among US presidents – being the twenty-second and twenty-fourth president – and to this day the only person elected twice in non-consecutive elections. Not only that but in all three elections as the Democratic Party nominee he won the popular vote – in 1884 when he became president, 1888 when he lost to Benjamin Harrison due to the Electoral College, and in 1892 when he returned to office, beating Harrison. Cleveland's winning margins, especially in the southern states, coincided with and were rendered possible by the complete disenfranchisement of African Americans in the South, a process begun with the final dismantling and end of Reconstruction in 1877.

Cleveland is also the sole Democrat elected in a sea of Republican dominance – stretching from the middle of the nineteenth century to the early twentieth century. Between the election of James Buchanan in 1856 before the onset of the American Civil War and Woodrow Wilson in 1912 prior to the First World War, Cleveland was the only successful Democratic candidate who managed to win the White House.

Stephen Grover Cleveland – the fifth of nine children – was born in Caldwell, New Jersey, on 18 March 1837; his father was Richard Falley Cleveland, Congressional and Presbyterian minister, and his mother was Ann Neal. His family on his father's side was of English descent, having emigrated from Cleveland to Massachusetts in 1635. His father's maternal grandfather fought at the Battle of Bunker Hill in 1775 in the American War of Independence.

In 1853, Cleveland's father died and, aged sixteen, he left school to find employment. Shortening his name to Grover Cleveland, he worked in a shop while he trained and then qualified to be a lawyer in Buffalo. In 1863 he first stood for public office, running for assistant District Attorney of Erie County for the Democrats, losing to the Republicans. Eight years later, in 1871, he became the Sheriff of Erie County, where he came to public attention by carrying out two public executions – earning him the moniker 'the Hangman of Buffalo' and another first as the only US president to serve as a public executioner.

In 1881, he was elected Mayor of Buffalo on an anti-corruption platform. This he was true to, vetoing various appropriations from the city council, popular and unpopular, bringing him to the notice of Democrats looking for a candidate with a clean reputation. Thus in 1882 he became Democrat candidate for the Governorship of New York, was successfully elected, and governed on the ticket he was elected on, earning the opprobrium of many Democrats associated with the Tammany Hall machine of the party.

Cleveland continued with his stance of standing against corruption, but also against measures that extended government powers or responsibilities even when popular. Thus, he vetoed a bill that would have reduced fares on New York's elevated trains. At the same time Cleveland consistently opposed appointments of Tammany Hall Democrats, the rationale of which was focused on party favouritism, with Cleveland's stance earning their opposition. This was offset by the support of reform-minded Republicans, including Theodore Roosevelt – an alliance that stood Cleveland in good stead in his first presidential election and subsequent term.

Cleveland may have stood apart from Tammany Hall, but that did not mean he failed to recognise the importance of allies within the Democrats and beyond. The first group contained well-respected New York Democrat leaders such as Daniel Manning, who was close to Samuel J. Tilden, the party's defeated presidential candidate in 1876, and William C. Whitney, who had stood up to the Tammany Hall faction. In the second group were a section of reform Republicans who became known as 'the Mugwumps', who believed that corruption and cleaning up politics was important and were prepared to support Cleveland.

Yet winning the Democratic Party nomination at the 1884 National Convention in Chicago was not automatic. On the first ballot Cleveland was ahead with 390 votes to Thomas Bayard's 170, which in the final tally saw Cleveland win the nomination with 683 votes to 81.5 for Bayard and 45.5 for Thomas A. Hendricks; Hendricks from Indiana had been the Democrat vice-presidential candidate in 1876 and accepted this position again.

The 1884 contest was one of contrasting styles and personalities.

Republican candidate, James G. Blaine of Maine, was the opposite of Cleveland in many ways. Cleveland had at this point no experience of national office whereas Blaine was steeped in Washington, having been Speaker of the House of Representatives, US Senator, and Secretary of State. Cleveland was also not a natural campaigner or public speaker, seen as stiff and sometimes blunt, but fastidiously honest and straight dealing. Blaine, on the other hand, was an experienced insider politician, larger than life, full of energy and ideas, and adept at deals. This contrast contributed to a significant group of prominent Republicans supporting Cleveland.

In contrast to the above, Blaine had significant appeal to Irish-Americans, traditionally Democrat supporters, because he was perceived to be anti-British – Republicans calling Cleveland 'the British candidate'. With the Irish-American constituency more in play alongside the wary support of the Tammany Hall machine for Cleveland, both camps judged, correctly, that New York would be a close contest.

The Democrat campaign emphasised Cleveland's honesty and stand against corruption, calling Blaine 'the continental liar from the state of Maine'. Republicans countered by raising Cleveland's fathering of an illegitimate child with the phrase: 'Ma! ma! Where's my pa? Gone to the White House, Ha! Ha! Ha!' Adding to this he was also vulnerable to attack for avoiding service in the Civil War by nominating a substitute – a perfectly legal, if morally questionable action.

The result was close in the popular vote, Cleveland winning 48.9 per cent to Blaine's 48.3 per cent: a lead of 23,005 – one of the narrowest victories in a US presidential election to this day. This translated into an Electoral College margin of 219 to 182. While Cleveland and the Democrats swept the South, Connecticut, New Jersey and Indiana, the Republicans held the rest outside New York (183 for Cleveland; 182 for Blaine), leaving this state as the critical one that would put either side over the top.

New York, then the biggest state in the US with thirty-six votes, split narrowly for Cleveland by 1,149 votes, giving him victory. Critical had been remarks made by Samuel G. Burchard, a Presbyterian clergyman at a New York meeting with Blaine near to polling day, when he said, in an act of political folly: 'We are Republicans and don't propose to leave our party and identify with the party whose antecedents have been rum, Romanism and rebellion.'

Blaine did not fully grasp what Burchard had said, but a reporter recorded the remarks and gave them to the Democrats. Eventually Blaine disowned the comments, calling them 'an unfortunate and ill-considered expression', but by then Democrats had printed and distributed posters with the remarks, and wooing by Republicans of the Irish-American vote in New York was thrown into chaos. On such matters tight elections can turn, and Blaine after the result blamed his defeat on 'rum, Romanism and rebellion', along with the weather.

Cleveland's first administration began on 4 March 1885 and reflected his personality: honest, informed by the importance of public service, deeply conservative and often unimaginative. His first Cabinet contained men, informed by a sense of public duty, who aimed to do their jobs in a business-like way. These included Thomas F. Bayard, who became Secretary of State; David Manning, Secretary of the Treasury; Augustus H. Garland, Attorney General; and L.C.Q. Lamar, Secretary of the Interior – the latter two of whom made history post-Civil War. Garland was from Arkansas and Lamar from Mississippi, and they represented the first Southerners to fill Cabinet posts since the Civil War, and with Cleveland being the first Democrat to occupy the White House since the Civil War, many other Southerners filled up junior posts.

The Democratic administration had many expectations to meet, one of which was the pressure from prominent supporters for government jobs. However, Cleveland's campaign and demeanour led reform-minded Republicans to think he might be different and instead expand the scope of the Pendleton Civil Service Act of 1883 and refrain from sacking Republicans in government posts to make room for his own people.

Cleveland had little idea how to square this circle, or a constructive view of how national government should work and be staffed. He attempted to find a middle position, declaring that no one would be fired without due cause and only properly qualified people would replace those leaving government. This meant that his administration took up immense time and political capital in micro-management, with Cleveland complaining of 'the damned, everlasting clatter of office'.

Cleveland had a restricted idea of what the president should do and presidential authority. He stated: 'The office of the President is essentially executive in its nature.' From this he went even further in embracing constraints, declaring that he did not think it proper 'to meddle' with legislation, writing in December 1885: 'It don't [sic] look as though Congress was very well prepared to do anything. If a botch is made at the other end of the Avenue, I don't mean to be a party to it.' This outlook was not going to prove adequate when later economic storm clouds gathered and resulted in depression.

Cleveland had a passion for keeping government out of things and vetoing bills, even popular ones. One of the most controversial vetoes he undertook was that of the Dependent Pension Bill of 1887. This measure would have granted pensions to the parents of men who had died while in service, who were in need of support.

Several important pieces of legislation were passed in his first term. Nearly all of them had nothing to do with Cleveland. These included the Interstate Commerce Act of 1887, the Dawes General Allotment Act of 1887 (an act that invested Indians with American citizenship and gave them land on an individual not tribal basis), and legislation giving the Department of Agriculture Cabinet status. Cleveland opposed none of these, giving them his presidential signature, but had no real involvement.

Cleveland's qualities did not help him be a successful president. He was not a good public speaker or orator, had a dislike of crowds and public gatherings, and to add to all that had a deep disdain for campaigning and building relationships with the media. None of these were aided by the death of the vice-president, Thomas A. Hendricks, in November 1885, a mere eight months into the post, which remained vacant for the rest of his term. Some of Cleveland's characteristics were softened by his marriage at the age of forty-nine to Frances Folsom, aged twenty-one, the daughter of his former law partner; they were married in the White House – the only president to this day to have been so.

By far the most challenging issue facing Cleveland in his first term was the economy and the government's finances driven by the expansion of wealth, industry and commerce along with population. Yet the supply of money in circulation did not keep pace with this growth, resulting in long-term deflation that adversely affected those in debt, including farmers and those in rural communities. In response, Congress passed the Bland–Allison Act of 1878, which increased the amount of money in circulation by purchasing and coining significant amounts of silver. Such a measure was opposed by conservatives, including Cleveland, who believed that 'inflating' the currency would harm investors and business.

Instead, Cleveland proposed to end government purchases of silver and reduce tariffs on imports with the aim of reducing prices for consumers. Congress opposed tariff reduction, and Cleveland decided to take a stand, summoning the Democratic leadership of Congress to a series of meetings known as the Oak View Conference, held at Oak View, Cleveland's summer residence outside Washington. He persuaded fellow Democrats to come up with a tariff reduction and in his annual address to Congress on 6 December 1887 devoted most of his speech to the subject. He said that the current rate of tariffs was a 'vicious, inequitable, and illogical source of unnecessary taxation'. Not only that, but manufacturers protected by these high duties were making 'immense' profits, and if duties were lowered, 'the necessaries of life used and consumed by all the people . . . should be greatly cheapened'.

This was a defining point in his presidency – one where he brought an issue to national attention and associated himself with it. Unfortunately, as an ill-at-ease campaigner he failed to build on his own actions. In July 1888, Roger Q. Mills of Texas, Democratic Chairman of the House Ways and Means Committee, introduced a bill removing duties on raw wool, lumber, copper, ore, tinplate and many other materials, and reducing them on iron and steel, sugar and woollen cloth. This was the agenda Cleveland had set forth in his speech, but he did nothing to advance the bill and its cause, even refusing to make speeches or public statements in support of the bill. The Mills bill was passed by the House but defeated in the Senate, setting up tariff reform as one of the defining issues of the 1888 presidential election and Cleveland's re-election campaign.

As a sitting president, Cleveland was unanimously endorsed by the Democratic National Convention in June in St Louis, Missouri, while the vice-presidential slot, having been vacant for three years, was won by Allen G. Thurman from Ohio. His Republican opponent was

Benjamin Harrison, a senator from Indiana, with Levi P. Morton from New York as his vice-presidential candidate. They fought an animated campaign and defended the principle of protective tariffs.

Again, Cleveland showed his aversion to campaigning – a disadvantage for any presidential candidate. Harrison was energetic, speaking at more than one hundred events on a vast array of subjects, from tariffs and veterans' pensions to the example of Abraham Lincoln. There was scandal and controversy, with the Republicans portraying Cleveland as pursuing a pro-British policy if re-elected – aided by the British minister in Washington, Lionel Sackville-West, who was tricked into writing a private letter indicating his preference for Cleveland, which many assessed cost the Democrats support among Irish-American voters.

The election was another close contest, with Cleveland winning 48.6 per cent and Harrison 47.8 per cent – a lead for Cleveland of 100,456 votes. Yet in the Electoral College Harrison won 233 votes to 168 for Cleveland – a lead of 65 votes. Cleveland won all the Southern states with large majorities, but Harrison took New York's 36 Electoral College votes with a lead of 14,373 votes and Indiana's 15 votes by a 2,348 margin.*

In the aftermath of Cleveland's defeat, many senior Democrats thought Cleveland would have won if he had waited until after the election to bring up tariffs; others if he had followed through on the issue; while some thought if he had campaigned more thoroughly the result could have been different. Cleveland saw it differently, stating: 'I did not wish to be re-elected without having the people understand just where I stood. Perhaps I made a mistake from the party standpoint; but damn it, it was right.'

Post-office, he set up a family home in New York City and joined the Wall Street law firm of Bangs, Stetson, Tracy, and MacVeigh, who handled some of the interests of the J.P. Morgan empire, which resulted in him becoming relatively wealthy aided by stock speculation. This influenced Cleveland's view of the world, and as he began to develop a more pro-corporate business outlook than usual

---

*There is some discrepancy about final vote totals in nineteenth-century US presidential elections, and all electoral and popular vote totals are based on data from the United States Office of the Federal Register and *Congressional Quarterly's Guide to US Elections*, 4th edn (2001).

for Democrats, he attracted the interest of leading financiers in thinking that he might be worth supporting in 1892.

The Republican administration proceeded to raise tariffs while engaging in sizeable public works and expanding pensions. In the 1890 congressional elections, the Democrats swept back to control the House while making gains in the Senate, putting the party in an optimistic mood for the future presidential election.

Cleveland saw himself as a man of principle, and when many Democrats voted for a bill providing for the unlimited coinage of silver in 1891, he spoke out unambiguously against the measure, despite pressure from many in the party for him not to do so. This typically frank approach could have worked against Cleveland in the party, but instead many noted his undoubted personal qualities and straight talking.

The June 1892 Democratic Convention held in Chicago, Illinois saw Cleveland win the necessary two-thirds majority on the first ballot: 617 votes, with David B. Hill from New York on 114 and Horace Boies from Iowa on 103; subsequently, Cleveland was then selected unopposed and unanimously with 910 delegate votes; Adlai E. Stevenson of Illinois emerged as the vice-presidential candidate.

The campaign of 1892 turned into a three-way contest with the arrival of the Populist Party, which nominated James B. Weaver of Iowa as its presidential candidate and supported a range of reforms including direct election of US senators, a federal income tax and state ownership of railways as well as unlimited silver coinage.

This was Cleveland's third campaign, and he kept true to his character of engaging in the minimum campaigning while mending fences with senior Democrats, including the Tammany Hall faction. In the South, the Democrats played the race card with Southern white voters, playing on fears that Republicans would protect voting rights of Blacks and aid racial mixing in schools and society. They also rewarded their southern supporters handsomely on patronage and in policy. All four of Cleveland's Supreme Court appointments, two of whom had fought for the Confederacy, voted in favour of the 'separate but equal' Supreme Court Plessy v. Ferguson decision, which sanctioned legal segregation. With Cleveland happy to preside over a coalition wide enough to include Tammany Hall supporters and white voters in the South with racial fears, the party was in a good position to win.

Cleveland won 46.0 per cent of the vote to Harrison's 43.0 per cent, with Weaver on 8.5 per cent – a comfortable lead of 380,810 compared to the previous two contests; the Electoral College was even more emphatic, with Cleveland on 277 to 145 for Harrison and 22 for Weaver. New York returned to Cleveland with a 45,518 lead and the Democrats won control of both Houses of Congress.

On 4 March 1893 the second Cleveland administration began, with Walter Q. Gresham of Indiana as Secretary of State, John G. Carlisle as Secretary of the Treasury, Daniel S. Lamont as Secretary of War, Hoke Smith as Secretary of the Interior, and J. Sterling Morton as Secretary of the relatively new Department of Agriculture.

The Democrat victory was aided by the economic troubles afflicting the country and by the Depression, but they were as ill-equipped to deal with them as the Republicans. The first weeks of Cleveland's presidency saw bank closures, collapse of corporations, and a decline in the supply of gold in the US Treasury as citizens exchanged paper currency for gold.

Cleveland's minimalist government and legislative outlook was ill-suited to this climate and he believed the economy would improve if confidence could be restored, aided by repealing the Silver Purchase Act of 1890. He believed the advance of silver-based money was undermining the economy's prospects via inflation and curbing investment. Congressional opposition to repeal was strong, with the Democrats split on the issue – many Southern and Western Democrats were squeezed by price deflation and viewed silver as the only hope of improving this situation – and the party hoped Cleveland would compromise.

Instead, repeal for the president became a matter of principle and opposition was considered 'shameful'. Cleveland, the arch anti-corruption crusader, turned to methods he had long condemned. He used patronage and the threat of its withdrawal to win allies and support. When Democrat congressman William Jennings Bryan of Nebraska warned that repeal of the act would 'injure the party' in his state, Cleveland refused to appoint Bryan allies to state offices.

The repeal of the Silver Purchase Act on 30 October 1893 marked a turning point in Cleveland's career. What he portrayed as a stand for principle and sound economy policy, others, including in his own party, saw as arrogance and economic conservatism. Some Democrats were furious: Bill Tillman, a senator from South Carolina, compared his 'betrayal' of the party to that of Judas and his betrayal of Jesus. Cleveland was also having health problems, having to undergo an operation for mouth cancer that saw him lose considerable weight during his convalescence.

The act's repeal did not change the economy for the better, and things continued to get worse. Cleveland could have made the case that the Depression began under Harrison. Instead, he insisted that government could do little in the context of depression, beyond making sure that a nation's currency was 'sound'. Such orthodox thinking about government and the economy was not unusual at this time, but Cleveland clung to non-intervention like a worn-out dogma, declaring: 'While the people should patriotically support their government its functions do not include the support of the people.' This was terrible economics and worse politics.

After repeal, Cleveland had little influence left with members of Congress who opposed his policies. He was still passionate about lower tariffs, and the unpopularity of the McKinley Tariff of 1890 gave him a target. A new bill outlining this was passed by the House in 1894, but in the Senate it ran into opposition from protectionists, Cleveland losing the support of many Democratic senators. Cleveland raged against those in the party opposing him, and the new Wilson–Gorman Tariff became law without his support.

Cleveland's lack of a political touch was shown in his disastrous handling of the Pullman strike in 1894. Pullman manufactured and operated sleeping and dining cars on US railways, and its workers went on strike in May in protest at wage cuts. The American Railway Union, acting in solidarity, refused to move trains carrying Pullman cars. Cleveland delegated dealing with the strike to Attorney General Richard Olney, who had been a railway lawyer, was stridently anti-trade union and wanted to break the strike.

After consulting with railway owners, he sought and got an injunction forbidding the strikers from interfering with the movement of mail. The strikers ignored this, with the situation in Chicago becoming more tense. Olney ordered federal troops to be sent to Chicago and on 3 July, the day after the injunction was issued,

Cleveland ordered troops into the city to preserve order: he remains the only US president to this day to send in troops without the invitation of the governor. This was a major misjudgement: it did not preserve order and for two days there were disturbances in Chicago, it bitterly divided Democrats, and once the strike was broken it did not facilitate good relations between workers and employers. Cleveland throughout had shown his inflexibility, declaring: 'If it takes the entire army and navy of the United States to deliver a postcard in Chicago, that card will be delivered.'

On foreign policy, Cleveland had a tense stand-off with the UK over defining the proper boundary between Venezuela and the colony of British Guiana. This was really about the Monroe Doctrine, the American sphere of influence over Latin America and how the British Empire understood it. The end result was an arbitration that favoured the British, but on the larger canvas, the British had to take the US seriously as a global power while American politicians noted the limits of playing up the anti-British card.

Cleveland's second term was anything but a success. Whether it was the economy, the role of the government, or management of the Democratic Party, it was widely seen as a failure, and it was little surprise that Cleveland did not run in 1896. He did see the election of Republican William McKinley as a not unwelcome development, commenting that it gave adherents of 'the cause of sound money . . . abundant reason for rejoicing'.

In post-presidential life, Cleveland settled in Princeton, New Jersey, and wrote a book on the issues he had encountered in the White House, *Presidential Problems* (1904), which was not noted for great insights. Contemporary commentators observed that, post-White House, his writings on two of his favourite activities – hunting and fishing – displayed more passion; he produced a volume on the subject, *Fishing and Shooting Sketches*, in 1907. Cleveland lived to the age of seventy-one and died in Princeton on 24 June 1908.

Cleveland's reputation has gone up and down depending on the political weather. In the 1920s and pre-New Deal, he was seen as one of the presidents who stood for limited government, anti-corruption and championed economic orthodoxy and conservatism. After the Great Depression, the onset of the New Deal and the Second World War, his reputation crashed and he was seen as having inadequate insights, skills and politics for his age. He was viewed by scholars as having held back the march of wealth and innovation, spending time and political capital trying to maintain the gold standard.

In the Reaganite era, his place in the presidential pantheon altered again, as Republicans talked about limited government and balanced budgets, while not practising them when in the White House. Now, in the era of post-Trump and a world ravaged by Covid, where the role of state, government and regulation are pivotal, Cleveland seems from another age, trying to hold back the dam of progress.

Cleveland claimed many firsts while US president and displayed admirable qualities – honesty, standing up to corruption including in his own party, and a belief in public duty. But he was a politician who struggled to understand the America emerging in the late nineteenth century, filled with industry and commerce and go-getting, alongside immense concentrations of corporate wealth and 'robber baron capitalism' that demanded that the state and lawmakers have a more interventionist role. Cleveland showed that personal qualities are necessary to be president but are not enough on their own.

Professor Gerry Hassan is a writer, commentator and academic at Glasgow Caledonian University. He is author and editor of more than two dozen books on Scottish and UK politics, including The Strange Death of Labour Scotland *and the recently published* Scotland after the Virus

23

Benjamin Harrison

4 March 1889 to 4 March 1893
Republican
Vice-president: Levi P. Morton

By Rosie Ilett

Full name: Benjamin Harrison
Born: 20 August 1833, North Bend, Ohio
Died: 13 March 1901, Indianapolis, Indiana
Resting place: Crown Hill Cemetery, Indianapolis, Indiana
Library/Museum: Indianapolis, Indiana
Education: Miami University, Ohio
Married to: Caroline Lavinia Scott, m. 1853 (1832–92); Mary Lord Dimmick, m. 1896 (1858–1948)
Children: Three: Russell, Mary (with Caroline); Elizabeth (with Mary)
Quotation: 'No other people have a government more worthy of their respect and love or a land so magnificent in extent, so

pleasant to look upon, and so full of generous suggestion to enterprise and labor.'

FIFTY-FIVE-YEAR-OLD BENJAMIN HARRISON became the twenty-third president – the sixth Republican to hold the office – on 4 March 1889. Sandwiched between Democrat Grover Cleveland's two terms, Harrison is often called 'the most forgotten president'.

Born on 20 August 1833 near the Ohio River, Harrison was the second of Elizabeth and John Harrison's six surviving children. His parents were farmers of English Presbyterian stock; his father a president's son and sometime Republican congressman. Three other American families contained two presidents, but Harrison remains unique as the grandchild of another. His grandfather (William Henry Harrison) died soon after becoming the ninth president – the first to do so in office and the shortest-serving. Grandfather Harrison was great-grandson of Benjamin Harrison V, Founding Father and signatory to the 1776 Declaration of Independence, after whom this Benjamin was named. One of his many nicknames – 'Grandfather's Hat' – reflects this dynasty.

Benjamin was educated locally, attending college near Cincinnati aged fourteen until sixteen where he met future wife Caroline Scott. From 1850 to 1852 Harrison studied law at Miami University, Ohio, and completed legal training in Cincinnati, and in 1853, aged twenty, he married Caroline. The newlyweds moved to Indianapolis the next year, where Harrison joined a law firm, and took up paid and pro bono roles in the Federal Court, US Court of Claims, and Presbyterian Church. In 1856, when the Republican Party arose from the Whig Party, Harrison joined.

In 1862, Harrison answered President Lincoln's call for more Union troops to fight in the Civil War. Although recently appointed Reporter to Indiana's Supreme Court and with Caroline pregnant, he offered to raise a regiment. Lieutenant 'Little Ben' Harrison fought in over thirty battles (the nickname referred to his small stature); for bravery at Resaca and Peach Tree Creek he became a brevet brigadier general – the rank he held when the war ended.

Post-war, Harrison returned to Indiana as Supreme Court

Reporter. Failing in 1872 to become Republican nominee for Indiana governor, he secured it four years later, narrowly losing to his Democratic rival. In 1877, as nationwide rail strikes escalated, Harrison attempted to reconcile workers and management to prevent further disruption; in 1879 he was appointed to the Mississippi River Commission, and in 1881 the Indiana General Assembly elected him senator. He chaired committees on transport and territories; promoted war pension reform; advocated for better education for black Southerners; highlighted often-competing rights of indigenous Americans and incomers; and opposed the 1882 Chinese Exclusion Act.

Harrison was a one-term senator, failing to get re-elected in 1887. The next year he won the Republican presidential nomination with Levi P. Morton as his running mate. Harrison took on incumbent Democrat president Grover Cleveland in the campaign. Ignoring traditional methods, Harrison only spoke to delegations at his Indianapolis home – the 'Front Porch Campaigner' becoming another nickname. The campaign's main focus was the tariff – with Harrison presenting Republican views on government intervention to promote economic growth. The final vote was controversial – Cleveland won the popular vote by approximately ninety thousand while Harrison took the Electoral College by 233 to 168. Allegations of voter suppression and fraud beset Harrison, who was accused of buying votes.

Ambiguity aside, Harrison became the twenty-third president on 4 March 1889 and John Philip Sousa's Marine Band entertained the large crowd at his inauguration. Harrison praised the contribution of education and religion to industrial and economic power, exalted states to industrialise, and promised to restrict foreign imports. He highlighted war pensions, expanding the Union and the US Navy, continuing the Monroe Doctrine, and maintaining non-interference in foreign governments.

A large Harrison entourage entered the White House – his wife Caroline; his father-in-law; his adult children, Russell and Mary; and Mary's family. A menagerie of animals including a goat, two opossums and various dogs also moved in. This was a family home as well as the site of presidential power, as Harrison highlighted at the inauguration:

There is only a door – one that is never locked – between the president's office and what are not very accurately called his private apartments. There should be an executive office building, not too far away, but wholly distinct from the dwelling house. For everyone else in the public service, there is an unroofed space between the bedroom and the desk.

Many noted the warmth and informality of Harrison's White House. In 1891, the *New York Times* reported on the 'Indianapolis simplicity' of the president's table, noting that codfish balls, fried steak and flapjacks were hardly 'effete New York epicure'. Harrison worked on presidential business until noon to then spend time with his family, and, as a Presbyterian, did not work on Sundays.

With his thirty years' experience as a Republican, Harrison's Cabinet choices disappointed the party hierarchy. Expectations that James G. Blaine – long-standing senator, ex-Secretary of State and Speaker of the House, who had unsuccessfully run against Cleveland in 1884 – would immediately become Secretary of State were quashed. Harrison eventually offered him the role, but the delay caused consternation, as did the fact that only one Republican boss – Redfield Proctor as Secretary of War – was initially appointed. Harrison's Cabinet comprised those who reflected his interests, background and allegiances – war veterans, those from Indiana, lawyers or Presbyterians – with government or political experience not always necessary.

Harrison's campaign promoted tariffs to prevent cheap, foreign goods undermining American farmers and manufacturing, and in 1890 he introduced the McKinley Tariff Act that placed protective rates on agricultural products and compensated farmers. Harrison oversaw some aspects, including powers to impose duties on imported sugar, molasses, tea, coffee and hides if their exporting nations imposed unreasonable duties on American goods. Harrison's diligence failed, as inevitable prices rises were not predicted. However, Harrison and Blaine negotiated reciprocal deals that modified tariffs with key global trading partners. Encouraging competition to ensure high wages and profits was another campaign pledge, again involving farmers' interests. The Sherman Antitrust Act 1890 responded by restricting monopolies, trade restraints and trusts to mitigate the impact of the Tariff Act. However, the presi-. dent failed to rigorously enforce the legislation, Congress failed to make funds available to investigate trusts and only seven cases occurred during Harrison's presidency.

As industrialisation continued, debt increased, including among farmers. The Populist Party and others began to champion free coinage for silver as a way forward. Harrison was supportive, but as a 'bimetallist' who supported expanded paper currency backed by silver, rather than backing the gold standard, maintaining rela-tions with 'Silver Republicans' critical of him was equally important. Treasury Secretary William Windom and Harrison developed the Sherman Silver Purchase Act 1890 authorising the issue of treasury notes linked to silver bullion – to facilitate not free coinage but increased silver coin production. Despite attempts at a compromise, opposing free coinage lost Harrison the support of many free-silver Republicans.

Harrison's campaign promoted civil rights for the black popula-tion and as president he needed to also improve Republican support in the South. The 1890 Lodge Bill aimed to protect black voters' rights in Southern elections but divided Republican legislators, while black leaders demanded that Harrison championed 'free speech, a free ballot and a fair return of votes at the South'. The bill passed the House, but fell victim to a filibuster in the Senate. This led Harrison to continue the Republican tradition of honouring individual black leaders, giving, for example, N. Wright Cuney the post of Collector of the Port of Galveston, while former slave Frederick Douglass became US Minister Resident and consul general in Haiti – the first African American to hold government office. Harrison also wanted black postmasters appointed to Southern cities, but was stopped by the Senate, although his efforts received approval from the black press and black leaders. Harrison called for federal legislation to outlaw lynching.

As a Union soldier Harrison supported veteran welfare, declaring that the USA should not use 'an apothecary's scale to weigh the rewards of the men who saved the country'. To deliver this, he appointed Corporal James R. Tanner as Commissioner of Pensions. Tanner's proposal to support soldiers without proof of need was felt too generous – and possibly illegal. Harrison encouraged Tanner's resignation but in 1890 oversaw an even more liberal pension law. The Dependent and Disability Pension Act ensured financial support for soldiers who had served for at least three months and could not now undertake manual labour whether linked to war service or not, and expanded entitlement for their widows, children and parents.

Unsurprisingly, claims massively increased, as did the funding needed. Between 1891 and 1895 (after Harrison was president) pensioner numbers increased from 676,000 to 970,000 and the cost from $81 million to $135 million, costing the government over $1 billion. Responding to the critical term the 'Billion-Dollar Congress', Speaker Thomas B. Reed replied, 'Yes, but this is a billion-dollar country.' The impact was serious; before the end of Harrison's administration the treasury surplus had evaporated, and American government was much less financially secure.

The domestic agenda challenged President Harrison, while foreign affairs offered opportunities. In 1889, Harrison and Blaine expanded an idea from the Cleveland era – for a meeting of Latin American countries to discuss trade – and shaped the first Pan-American Congress. This successful event in Washington attracted delegates from seventeen countries, and led to the Pan-American Union being established. A recording by Harrison describing the Congress is the earliest existing voice record of any president: 'As president of the United States, I was present at the first Pan-American Congress in Washington, DC. I fully believe that with God's help, our two countries shall continue to live side by side in peace and prosperity.'

Harrison's other pan-American ventures included advocating for a Central American canal and increased US presence in Latin America. Other policies inherited from the previous Democrat administration included the Bering Sea controversy – a long-standing dispute between the US, Canada and Britain over Alaskan fishing rights, specifically the killing of seals for fur. America claimed the sea in 1881, and Congress authorised Harrison on election to seize encroaching vessels (mainly Canadian hunters), following this with complex diplomacy that outlived his administration.

Harrison also dealt with Pacific Ocean issues, including the Samoa Islands where Britain, Germany and the US contested ownership.

Blaine's negotiating skills at the Berlin Conference in April 1889 helped Harrison take credit for preserving the Samoan ruling dynasty and avoid further conflict by establishing a three-way arrangement, although without Britain and Germany's full approval.

In 1891, the Chilean government was overthrown. Harrison disapproved of the victorious rebels who 'do not know how to use victory and moderation', and initially refused to recognise their authority. Simultaneously, two USS *Baltimore* sailors on shore leave were killed by a local mob. Chilean leaders failed to punish the assailants quickly enough and Harrison told Congress in December 1891 that unless he was satisfied with Chilean investigations, further action was possible. The Chilean foreign minister then insulted Harrison, who instructed the US Navy to standby, whereas Blaine advocated caution. As American public opinion increasingly turned against Chile, a new more conciliatory Chilean foreign minister apologised. Harrison remained resolute and in January 1892 effectively sought congressional approval for action. The liberal press accused Harrison of warmongering; and Blaine's intervention, the spirit of the Pan-American Congress, and further Chilean expressions of regret clipped his ambitions.

Harrison also became involved in the Hawaiian Islands, which he wished to annex to the US. After an American-supported revolution overthrew Queen Lili'uokalani in 1893, the US sent troops to protect American lives and interests, and Harrison sought Senate support for annexation near the end of his presidency, arguing that if another country took over, 'such a possession would not consist with our safety and with the peace of the world'. The Senate's Democratic majority disagreed, although most House Republicans supported Harrison, as did those who wanted an expanded navy – and America. President Cleveland later withdrew the treaty.

Despite evidence that Harrison did not enjoy being president, with the political tide turning and little support from Republican hierarchy, he stood for re-election at the 1892 Republican National Congress (the first that women attended) after surviving an attempt from Blaine to become the candidate. Many opposed Harrison's re-nomination, with senator W.D. Washburn from Minnesota exemplifying that view: 'There are two serious objections to Harrison's re-nomination; first, no one cares anything for him personally, second, no one, as far as I know, thinks he could be elected if nominated.'

Harrison secured party backing and became presidential candidate, with the Democrats having recently regained the House of Representatives. In a repeat of 1888, he faced Grover Cleveland, this time supported by Adlai Stevenson. Harrison chose college friend Whitelaw Reid as running mate instead of sitting vice-president Morton. Also from Ohio farming stock, Reid was a Republican grandee, having held various posts including ambassador to France. First Lady Caroline was gravely ill with tuberculosis throughout the campaign, and having Reid on the ticket reflected Harrison's need for someone to do the heavy lifting and provide personal support. Sadly, Caroline died on 26 October 1892 – less than a fortnight before the vote.

On Election Day on 8 November, President Harrison was resoundingly defeated. Cleveland gained nearly four hundred thousand more in the popular vote, and nearly two-thirds of the Electoral College (277 to 145). Leaving office, Harrison returned to his previous employment as a lawyer in Indianapolis and took up speaking engagements, with a selection of his lectures published in 1901. Newly widowed, he began a relationship with his late wife's niece, Mary Lord Dimmick, who had attended her aunt during her final illness, and was nearly twenty-five years younger. The two married in 1896 when he was sixty-two, with a child Elizabeth born the following year. In 1901, Benjamin Harrison died from pneumonia at his home in Indianapolis. His body laid in state in the state capital, escorted to its destination by the 70th Indiana, his former Civil War regiment. Then President William McKinley accompanied his funeral procession.

Benjamin Harrison was not a popular president – the narrowness of his presidential win, the McKinley Tariff Act that made imports more expensive, the perhaps over-generous pension reforms, his allegiances to the elite and not the whole country were much criticised. However, he supported various liberal policy and legislative areas, and argued for equality for black voters. His attitudes to foreign affairs reflected changing American society, industrialisation and the recent reconstruction. Harrison wanted a global United States, but always sought support from Congress and others before acting – and was well aware of public opinion. However, his foreign interventions were rated mostly as ineffective.

Benjamin Harrison was a unique president in many ways. He remains the one most connected to the office through family history, was the last Civil War general to serve, was the smallest in height, the last to have a full beard and the first whose voice can still be heard. Being president does not seem to have satisfied Harrison, and he told his family that the White House felt like prison. He saw himself as destined for greatness, but lacked charisma and people skills, and failed to build alliances. Yet another nickname – 'the Human Iceberg' – suggests how he seemed to others.

Dr Rosie Ilett is a retired NHS manager and librarian with research experience in nineteenth-century America. After having lived in Glasgow for thirty years, she now lives in Kirkcudbright in south-west Scotland.

25

William McKinley

4 March 1897 to 6 September 1901
Republican
Vice-presidents: Garret Hobart 1897–99, vacant 1899–1901,
Theodore Roosevelt 1901

By David Torrance

Full name: William McKinley Jr
Born: 29 January 1843, Niles, Ohio
Died: 14 September 1901, Buffalo, New York
Resting place: Canton, Ohio
Library/Museum: Canton, Ohio
Education: Poland Seminary, Allegheny College and Albany
Law School
Married to: Ida Saxton, m. 1871 (1847–1907)
Children: Two: Katherine and Ida
Quotation: 'We need Hawaii just as much, and a good deal

more, than we did California. It is manifest destiny.' (To his personal secretary George B. Cortelyou in March 1898)

A FEW YEARS AGO, I boarded a flight from John F. Kennedy Airport for Buffalo, an unfashionable city in upstate New York. If tourists go there at all it is as a stopping off point en route to Niagara Falls. Few linger, for Buffalo is not the wealthy metropolis it once was. Not only am I drawn to faded urban glory, but I was also keen to track down a couple of notable but usually overlooked presidential sites.

After checking out some architecture (Art Deco) and a handful of excellent museums, I headed to Fordham Drive between Elmwood Avenue and Lincoln Parkway in the northern suburbs of the city. Without much difficulty I located a small boulder in the middle of the road, to which was attached a bronze plaque. This reads: 'In the Pan-American Temple of Music which covered this spot, President McKinley was fatally shot Sept. 6, 1901.'

It is a modest memorial for a generally forgotten US president. Unveiled by the Buffalo Historical Society nearly two decades after the assassination, that it took so long speaks to how quickly William McKinley faded from the public memory. The theatre where Abraham Lincoln was assassinated is a much-visited site, largely on account of being located in Washington, DC, but even the road in Dallas, Texas, where JFK met his fate is a well-known presidential site. While McKinley was neither as significant as Lincoln nor as charismatic as Kennedy, he was nevertheless a significant occupant of the White House. So, what happened?

McKinley, like several other US presidents, was of Ulster-Scots descent. Centuries earlier, the family name 'Finlay' had become MacFinlay ('son of'), McKinlay and, finally, McKinley. The McKinleys moved from Scotland to Ulster – present-day Northern Ireland – during the Plantation and became tenant farmers. From there they emigrated, like many before and since, to the United States.

William McKinley Jr was born on 29 January 1843 in Niles, Ohio, the seventh of nine children. His education was patchy and unremarkable. Later, McKinley found work as a postal clerk and as a teacher near Poland, Ohio. The American Civil War (1861–65), however, set him on a different path. McKinley was lucky in that Rutherford B. Hayes, a future president, became his mentor both during and after the conflict. Hayes wrote in his diary that his new second lieutenant was 'an exceedingly bright, intelligent, and gentlemanly young officer'.

McKinley rose through the ranks, ending up as major. Along with two others, he later published a twelve-volume work on Ohio's role in what they called the 'War of the Rebellion'. Having survived the defining event of America's first century, Major McKinley settled upon a legal career. At first, he found work with a local firm before enrolling at Albany Law School. On returning home, McKinley was admitted to the bar in Warren, Ohio. In 1869, he was a surprise victor in the race to become prosecuting attorney of Stark County, losing to a Democrat two years later.

In early 1871, McKinley married Ida Saxton. Their family life began serenely. On Christmas Day that year, Ida gave birth to Katie, and was pregnant again by the end of the following year. But when Ida's mother passed away, the McKinleys' fortunes began to change. Their second daughter, also Ida, died from cholera at five months old; her mother then suffered an accident that affected her ability to walk; then, in June 1875, Katie developed scarlet fever and died. Ida suffered a nervous breakdown. For the next quarter-century, a not inconsiderable part of William McKinley's energies were devoted to caring for his wife's fragile health.

Ida McKinley therefore played little part in her husband's first congressional campaign. He won, as did his mentor Rutherford B. Hayes in his race for the White House. McKinley first took his seat in October 1877, but his early career was unsettled on account of repeated attempts by Democrats to redistrict (or gerrymander) him out of Congress. He was unseated in 1882, re-elected in 1884 and lost again in 1890. When not fighting for political survival, McKinley made his mark as a member of the influential House Ways and Means Committee (of which he became chairman) and as a specialist on protective tariffs, which he viewed as central to the United States' economic fortunes. Though not an original thinker, he proved adept at absorbing masses of intricate detail.

A dramatic intervention during the 1888 Republican National

Convention had also put McKinley in good stead for his post-congressional career. Responding to an attempt to place his name on the ballot as nominee, McKinley gracefully declined. 'You gained gloriously,' judged Hayes. 'A better crown than to have been nominated.' His reward a few years later was a lesser crown, the governorship of Ohio. The McKinleys moved to Columbus where, twice each day, William would pause on the steps of the Capitol and doff his hat in the direction of Ida's hotel window. A financial scandal in 1893 threatened his otherwise unblemished reputation (he was guilty of carelessness rather than corruption), but friends rallied round and got his affairs in order. After completing a second term, William and Ida returned to Canton in January 1896.

McKinley was short, with broad shoulders and a large, expressive face. A kindly man, he was not an obvious contender for high office, but quietly, and in concert with his associate Mark Hanna, he planned his bid during 1895 and early 1896. During a key meeting at Hanna's home, McKinley suggested the slogan 'The Bosses Against the People' (later modified to 'The People Against the Bosses'). Aptly, he began his nomination fight by rejecting the demands of eastern Republican political 'bosses' lest he be hamstrung once in office. By the time of the convention in St Louis, there was no contest.

Remarkably, the man who wanted to be president did not leave Ohio during the campaign that followed. While the Democratic candidate William Jennings Bryan traversed the nation, McKinley pursued what became known as the 'Front Porch strategy'. Over several weeks he welcomed hundreds of delegations from thirty states, to whom was imparted carefully crafted campaign rhetoric. On election day McKinley won 271 Electoral College votes to Bryan's 176, sweeping the battleground states of the upper Mid-West. His has some claim to being the first modern campaign in that the literature distributed across the country was tailored to targeted demographic groups.

Office appeared to transform McKinley, as had the Civil War thirty-five years earlier. Those encountering the new president found him sharper and more decisive than they expected. As his first Secretary of State, McKinley named long-serving Ohio senator John Sherman, author of anti-trust legislation that bears his name. This conveniently opened up a Senate seat for his loyal associate Mark Hanna. The new president, the nation's twenty-fifth, hoped to focus on domestic politics, as he had in Congress. In his inaugural address on 4 March 1897, McKinley stated his belief that 'peace is preferable to war in almost every contingency'. This was doubtless sincere, but proved a poor guide to what followed.

The 1896 election came to be seen as a realigning contest, in which a stronger central government sought to bolster American industry via protective tariffs and a stable currency. Usefully, rapid economic growth marked McKinley's first term following a deep depression. He promoted the 1897 Dingley Tariff to protect manufacturers and factory workers from foreign competition and, in 1900, secured the passage of the Gold Standard Act, which stripped away decades of ambiguity and defined the dollar in relation to gold.

McKinley's first term also continued the innovative techniques of the campaign that preceded it. Part of the White House was set aside for journalists, who reported on the president's extensive travels and speeches, a departure from the more modest activity of his predecessors. In those days, the president's official residence was considered a public building in which sightseers could roam freely until 2 p.m. each day. Public receptions were packed and rowdy affairs. Rather as a British monarch perceives their position, McKinley was of the view that America's commander in chief had to be seen to be believed.

McKinley had no intention of being drawn into territorial conflicts, but the ongoing Cuban rebellion left him with little choice. By 1895, a sporadic campaign for independence from Spanish colonial rule had grown into a war. As Spanish reprisals grew, US public opinion sided with the Cuban underdogs. Although McKinley – consistent with his inaugural rhetoric – favoured a peaceful solution, when it became clear that Spain had no intention of granting Cuba any degree of autonomy, he agreed to send the battleship USS *Maine* to Havana following reports of riots.

On 15 February 1898 the *Maine* exploded and sank with the loss of 266 American lives. McKinley resisted the jingoistic fervour whipped up by newspapers owned by William Randolph Hearst, but when a naval inquiry concluded that an underwater mine was responsible, Congress declared war rather than follow McKinley's call for 'neutral intervention' to safeguard US interests in Cuba. He wasted little time, however, in embracing his unexpected role as a wartime president. 'While we are conducting war and until its conclusion, we must keep all we get,' McKinley scribbled on a scrap of paper; 'when the war is over we must keep what we want.'

An overwhelming US military victory in Manila expanded the scope of the conflict into a full-blown Spanish–American War that determined the fate of all Madrid's Pacific and Caribbean colonies. When the Treaty of Paris was signed in December 1898, the US was left with the Philippines, Guam and Puerto Rico, for which it compensated Spain to the tune of $20 million. US sovereignty over Cuba was brief – its flag was raised on 1 January 1899 and lowered in May 1902 – but the Philippines became the more enduring focus of American imperialism.

There were rather tortuous efforts to differentiate this colonialism from the British variety. McKinley told a group of Methodists that he wanted to 'uplift and civilise' the Filipinos, and later talked of 'benevolent assimilation', promising that the US would 'come, not as invaders or conquerors, but as friends'. A military governor-general, future president William Howard Taft, was installed in Manila, while a commission later pledged 'the largest measure of home rule and amplest liberty' consonant with US aims. Unconvinced, the Democrat-dominated American Anti-Imperialist League accused McKinley of hypocrisy.

Even before the US went to war with Spain, McKinley had sought to complete the US's westward expansion by annexing Hawaii. US business interests had behaved badly – arguably illegally – by deposing Queen Lili'uokalani in 1893, but McKinley quickly became convinced of the islands' strategic value. 'We need Hawaii just as much and a good deal more than we did California,' his secretary George Cortelyou recalled the president declaring in March 1898. 'It is manifest destiny.' The Republic of Hawaii became a US territory on 8 July that year.

The new American Empire was not all plain sailing. When Puerto Rico lost its long-standing markets in Spain and Cuba on coming under US sovereignty, it raised ambiguities as to its constitutional status; in short, did the Constitution follow the flag? McKinley was of the view that it could be governed as a domestic territory, others disagreed. The US Supreme Court later vindicated the president. There was also trouble over an 1850 treaty with the UK that prevented either country establishing exclusive control over a proposed Central American canal. While McKinley was satisfied with new terms that allowed US control provided it was open to all, the Senate disagreed, and it was not until after McKinley's administration that what became the Panama Canal would be agreed to American satisfaction.

Events in China, however, confirmed American supremacy. In the past, US interests and citizens in the Middle Kingdom had relied on the casual protection of other global powers, but the Philippines meant it now sent ships and troops in defence of its ministers, missionaries and merchants when the Boxer Rebellion threatened foreigners in China. The US was a major player in the international China Relief Expedition of June 1900, which later produced an 'Open Door Policy' in which all nations could trade freely with China in return for a pledge not to violate its territorial integrity.

Another foreign policy success of McKinley's presidency was improved relations with the UK, leading to the much mythologised 'Special Relationship' of the twentieth century. Lord Salisbury, British prime minister between 1895 and 1902, seemed relaxed about the US's new role. And when Queen Victoria died in early 1901, McKinley dispatched a splendid wreath that reflected this new accord between the US and its former colonial master.

Despite having made private noises about not standing for a second term, in late 1900 McKinley's re-election campaign centred on imperialism and protectionism. Voters liked what they heard (although the president only made one public speech during the campaign) and McKinley won 292 Electoral College votes to William Jennings Bryan's 155. The Republicans also made gains in both the House and Senate. 'I can no longer be called the president of a party,' the second-termer told his secretary. 'I am now the president of the whole people.'

Though not for much longer. In 1898, McKinley's cousin had articulated fears that the president might fall victim to an anarchist's bullets, and indeed when William planned an extensive post-election tour culminating at the Pan-American Exposition in upstate New York, a second-generation Polish-American anarchist by the name of Leon Czolgosz sensed an opportunity to leave his destructive mark. McKinley was impatient with such concerns. He loved shaking hands and found it hard to believe that anyone would wish to harm him. On 6 September 1901, the day after a typical second-term speech focused on fair trade and the Central American canal, Czolgosz simply lined up to shake hands with his president at the Temple of Music.

When McKinley reached out to shake Leon's left hand (his right had been injured), his assassin pressed a .32 calibre pistol against the president's chest and fired twice. 'Am I shot?' McKinley asked a detective into whose arms he fell. 'I fear you are, Mr President.' Even in his distress, McKinley made a point of instructing those who had apprehended Czolgosz not to hurt him. Initially, the president seemed likely to recover, but unknown to his doctors the second bullet had caused gangrene to grow on the walls of his stomach, which slowly poisoned his blood. 'It is God's way,' McKinley whispered to his wife as he slipped away. 'His will, not ours, is done.'

William McKinley died at 2:15 a.m. on 14 September 1901. His assassin – who had been motivated by disgust at economic inequality – was executed in the electric chair six weeks later. According to one of his biographers, Lewis L. Gould, the US experienced 'a wave of genuine grief' at the news. Theodore Roosevelt, McKinley's vice-president, had hurried to Buffalo but did not arrive until after his chief's death. He took the oath of allegiance at his friend Ansley Wilcox's home, one of only four instances outside of Washington, DC. The house still stands today, preserved as one of Buffalo's two presidential sites. I visited it shortly after tracking down the McKinley assassination memorial on the other side of the city.

Unlike John F. Kennedy, however, the manner of McKinley's death did not enhance his reputation, and Czolgosz failed to acquire the macabre notoriety of John Wilkes Booth before him or Lee Harvey Oswald after. On the contrary, a popular and substantial US president quickly faded from the public consciousness, while Roosevelt's colourful legacy and more dominant personality came to absorb that of his predecessor. The achievements of 1896–1901, whether domestic or foreign, came to be viewed as inevitable. Although it was true that McKinley had often responded to events rather than proactively shaped them, that hardly devalued the skilful way in which he had commanded them, for that is the essence of political leadership.

Only after the 1950s did biographers and historians come to upgrade McKinley's undeservedly middling reputation. Gould called him the 'first modern president', while H. Wayne Morgan concluded that 'he could not advertise his methods without destroying them'. Robert W. Merry, McKinley's most recent biographer (2017), has convincingly argued that his subject paved the way for the American Century. The largely uncontested territories of Guam and Puerto Rico are testament to that, as is the United States' enduring role as an economic and military superpower.

David Torrance is a political biographer, historian and clerk at the House of Commons Library. He has visited all but one of the official US presidential libraries.

26

Theodore Roosevelt

14 September 1901 to 4 March 1909
Republican
Vice-president: Vacant 1901–05, Charles W. Fairbanks
1905–09

By Damian Collins

Full name: Theodore Roosevelt Jr
Born: 27 October 1858, 28, East 20th Street, Manhattan, New York City
Died: 6 January 1919, Sagamore Hill, Oyster Bay, New York
Resting place: Youngs Memorial Cemetery, Oyster Bay, Long Island, New York
Library/Museum: Dickinson, North Dakota (under construction)
Education: Harvard University
Married to: Alice Lee, m. 1880 (1861–84); Edith Carrow, m. 1886 (1861–1948)

Children: Six: Alice, Theodore Roosevelt III, Kermit, Ethel, Archibald, Quentin

Quotation: 'It is not the critic who counts; not the man who points out how the strong man stumbles, or where the doer of deeds could have done them better. The credit belongs to the man who is actually in the arena, whose face is marred by dust and sweat and blood; who strives valiantly; who errs, who comes short again and again, because there is no effort without error and shortcoming; but who does actually strive to do the deeds.' (From his speech, *Citizenship in a Republic*, delivered at the Sorbonne in Paris on 23 April 1910)

T HOUSANDS GATHERED AT Montauk Point on Long Island, New York, to greet the troopship *Miami* and celebrate the return of the Rough Riders; the 1st United States Volunteer Cavalry regiment. The *New York Times* reporter observed: 'Colonel Theodore Roosevelt . . . standing on the bridge . . . was at once recognised by his many friends who were waiting near the dock, and the cheering at once began.' At around noon, when he walked down the gangplank, 'the last ultimate climax of the possibility of cheering was reached.' He was, in the opinion of one of the troop captains, Schuyler McGinnis from Kansas, 'the biggest man that it is my pleasure to know personally. He is a good fighting American.'

It was 15 August 1898, and their heroics in Cuba during the short but victorious Spanish–American War had made the Rough Riders known to the world. This thousand-strong regiment of prairie cowboys, Rocky Mountains miners, professional hunters and a few university men who enjoyed 'rough outdoor sports' had been created by Theodore Roosevelt. He'd resigned as Assistant Secretary of the navy in President McKinley's government in order to oversee their training and mobilisation, and would later command them in battle. On 1 July 1898, only fifty days after Roosevelt had left his desk in Washington, DC, he personally led them in an uphill charge under heavy fire, to capture the Spanish redoubts on top of the San Juan heights, and with them, the imagination of the American people. In what he called his 'crowded hour', Roosevelt's courage, coolness and leadership would see him nominated for the

Congressional Medal of Honour. From the top of San Juan Hill, the American forces had clear sight of the route to the port city of Santiago, and for Theodore Roosevelt there opened another path, one that would take him to the presidency of the United States in a little over eleven hundred days.

The 'Bull Moose', 'Teddy Bear', 'T.R'., 'damned cowboy' or New York City 'dude', whatever label was chosen for Theodore Roosevelt he was a completely different personality from the typical politicians of his time. He was a massive ball of energy, constantly expressing that he was 'dee-lighted' when a situation looked promising, and reflecting how 'bully' (as in good fun) was some great activity in which he'd participated. The war in Cuba had been a 'bully fight', and the presidency would be a 'bully pulpit'.

At 5 foot 10 inches tall, with his sturdy walk and bull-like frame, along with a great moustache, 'double row' of white teeth, and gold pince-nez glasses, he was instantly recognisable. In an era when political leaders didn't talk to the press, he'd give morning briefings to journalists while being shaved at home by his barber. His friend, the newspaper editor William Allen White, observed of Roosevelt that, 'every inch of him was over-engined'. Horse riding, wild water swimming, tennis, boxing and jiu-jitsu were all part of his vigorous regime. He had a photographic memory, and was a speed reader who could get through up to three books a day, as well as great volumes of government papers. He wrote thirty-eight books and over a hundred and fifty thousand letters. While presidents like Garfield, Harrison and McKinley had been elected by a 'front porch' campaign where people came to visit them at home, Roosevelt as a candidate travelled more miles, visited more states and gave more speeches than anyone had ever done before. His style didn't please everyone and the writer Mark Twain thought he was 'the Tom Sawyer of the political world of the twentieth century; always showing off; always hunting for a chance to show off; in his frenzied imagination the Great Republic is a vast Barnum circus with him for a clown and the whole world for audience'.

Theodore Roosevelt's upbringing made him an unlikely shaker-up of the established order. His father Theodore Senior, whom he thought 'the best man I ever knew', was a wealthy philanthropist who had founded New York Orthopaedic Hospital and was a

Director of the Metropolitan Museum of Art and the American Museum of Natural History. His mother Martha Bulloch Roosevelt was a Southern belle, the daughter of a wealthy planter family from Georgia, who is believed to have been one of the influences for the character of Scarlett O'Hara in Margaret Mitchell's novel, *Gone with the Wind*. As a boy Theodore had been physically weak and suffered greatly with asthma, so to compensate he focused on building up his body with physical exertion. He enrolled at Harvard University in October 1876, where he was a member of the elite Porcellian Club, and one contemporary remembered that 'when it was not considered good form to move at more than a walk, Roosevelt was always running'. It was also while at Harvard that he met his first wife, Alice Hathaway Lee. Upon his graduation in 1880, he and Alice married, and Theodore purchased 155 acres of land at Oyster Bay, Long Island, which overlooked the bay and the Long Island Sound. Here he would commission the building of Sagamore Hill, named after the Algonquin tribe's word for chief, which after its completion in 1885 would be his family home for the rest of his life. In 1880, he also decided, much to the dismay of his family, to start attending political meetings at Morton Hall, 'a large barn-like room over a saloon' that served as headquarters for the New York Twenty-first District Republican Association.

Roosevelt took an interest in the debates at Harvard, but his first real insight into politics came through his father. Politics then was an unseemly trade for a gentleman, but when President Rutherford B. Hayes asked him to clean up corruption at the port of New York, he accepted. However, the local Republican bosses, fearing the change, blocked the appointment. Theodore Senior wrote to his son warning, 'The "machine politicians" have shown their colors . . . I feel sorry for the country however as it shows the power of partisan politicians who think of nothing higher than their own interests, and I feel for your future. We cannot stand so corrupt a government for any great length of time.' Two months later, on 9 February 1878, Theodore Senior died, aged just forty-six years, and that letter was one that his son would often keep on his person as a 'talisman against evil'.

The debates at Morton Hall soon brought Roosevelt to the attention of Joe Murray, an Irish-American political street fighter, who organised for Roosevelt to be elected to the New York state assembly in 1881, aged just twenty-three. There he made an instant mark, speaking out about allegations of fraud and corruption against the railway magnate Jay Gould, whom Roosevelt accused of being part of the 'wealthy criminal classes'. Personal tragedy struck, though, on 14 February 1884, when two days after the birth of their first child, Alice was taken gravely ill as the result of an undiagnosed kidney failure. As she fought for her life, Theodore's mother lay dying in the same house from typhoid fever. He would lose them both within a few hours and wrote in his diary that 'the light has gone out of my life'. Theodore named the baby Alice Lee Roosevelt and placed her in the care of his elder sister Bamie. He called the child Baby Lee, and never mentioned her mother's name again. In the autumn of that year, he stood down from the New York assembly and, with his grief still raw, left for the Badlands of North Dakota, where he purchased a cattle ranch at Medora. On leaving he told a friend, 'Black care never sits behind a rider whose pace is fast enough.'

At Medora, Roosevelt worked alongside the cowboys on his ranch, sharing with them the arduous work on the round-up. In that harsh environment a man was valued most for his honest character and physical bravery, and he earned their respect. Roosevelt made prolonged visits home in 1885 after the completion of Sagamore Hill, and during that period began a relationship with a former childhood sweetheart, Edith Carrow. The following year they were married and set up home in Oyster Bay. Edith would adopt young Alice as her daughter, and together with Theodore they would have a further five children.

Roosevelt was part of the first generation of Republican Party politicians to have been too young to serve in the Civil War. They had reached adulthood during the 'gilded age' when patronage and the financial power of big business had corrupted politics. Theodore Roosevelt wanted to break the system. As he rose through the ranks as a reforming member of the Civil Service Commission in Washington, DC, and as president of the New York City Police Commission, he was frequently in conflict with the party bosses.

In 1896, following the surprise nomination of the populist William Jennings Bryan as the Democratic Party presidential candidate,

Senator Mark Hanna, William McKinley's friend and the boss of his campaign, wanted powerful speakers who could travel across America to challenge Bryan. Roosevelt was happy to oblige and, after McKinley's victory, was appointed Assistant Secretary to the navy. He championed building up the armed forces and in 1897, during a speech to the Naval War College in Rhode Island, stated that 'no nation can hold its place in the world . . . unless it stands ready to guard its rights with an armed hand . . . Diplomacy is utterly useless when there is no force behind it.' In response, the *Washington Post* exclaimed, 'Well done, nobly spoken . . . Theodore Roosevelt, you have found your place at last.'

It was the mysterious explosion in February 1898, sinking the USS *Maine* while docked in the harbour at Havana, that provoked war with Spain. After the declaration, McKinley called for 125,000 volunteers to swell the ranks of the American Army, which was only 28,000 soldiers strong. Roosevelt responded by recommending the formation of the Rough Riders volunteer cavalry regiment. Those who saw him up close in Cuba in the days before his heroic charge up San Juan Hill believed the war had changed him. The reporter Edward Marshall observed him in combat at Las Guasimas on 24 June and noted as he entered that battle, 'he left behind . . . all those unadmirable and conspicuous traits which have so often caused him to be justly criticised in civic life, and found on the other side of it, in that Cuban thicket, the coolness, the calm judgement, the towering heroism, which made him, perhaps, the most admired and best loved of all Americans in Cuba'.

In August, when Roosevelt returned, there was open speculation that he would stand to be the next Republican governor of the state. The *New York Times* published an editorial stating:

> the machine will not name Colonel Roosevelt if it can be helped. It might possibly name him as the only alternative to defeat . . . It is because of his fidelity to principle . . . that they are afraid of him . . . he would let no man steal or waste the people's money for the pretend benefit of the party, that he would enforce the civil service law with the sole purpose of getting the best service for the State and not to get patronage for the machine, and that

his appointees, while they would be Republicans, would be men of the highest character and efficiency . . . he would be far and away the best candidate the party has put up for Governor since the close of the Civil War.

Senator Thomas Platt, the boss and self-proclaimed 'political godfather' of the New York Republicans, agreed, due to his popularity, to secure Roosevelt the nomination, but was uneasy about it, confiding in an aide, 'If he becomes Governor of New York, sooner or later, with his personality, he will have to be President of the United States . . . I am afraid to start that thing going.' Theodore Roosevelt won, something no other Republican could have achieved in New York that year, but Platt was soon complaining about his new governor: 'I can't do what I want with him, he is wilful as Hell.' In 1900, he saw an opportunity to rid himself of Roosevelt, by getting him nominated for the vice-presidency on William McKinley's re-election ticket. Mark Hanna was against the appointment and Roosevelt told friends that he didn't want the job, believing the vice-presidency would be an 'irksome, wearisome place where I could do nothing', and instead had wanted to carry on as governor of New York. Platt threatened to block his re-nomination and, with reluctance, Roosevelt agreed he would not turn down the vice-presidency. Hanna though was fearful of the consequences of that 'damned cowboy' being a heartbeat away from the White House, and told McKinley, 'your duty to the country is to live for four more years'.

On Friday 6 September 1901, McKinley was shot while visiting the Pan-American exhibition at Buffalo. Initially, his condition wasn't considered dangerous and, after visiting the president, Roosevelt joined his family on holiday in the Adirondacks. However, infection got into the president's wounds and his condition quickly deteriorated. On 13 September, while on an expedition on Mount Marcy, Roosevelt received a message that he should urgently return to Buffalo. That night he completed a seven-hour journey on a buckboard wagon to the railway station at North Creek, where a train was waiting at full steam. There he was presented with a telegram from John Hay, the Secretary of State, which read, 'The President died at two-fifteen this morning.' Theodore Roosevelt, aged forty-two, was now the youngest ever holder of the office of president of the United States.

On arrival at Buffalo, Roosevelt was met by his old friend, the lawyer Ansley Wilcox, and it would be in his home at 641 Delaware Avenue, in a borrowed frock coat and silk top hat, that he would take the oath of office that day, witnessed by members of the Cabinet. One notable absentee was Mark Hanna, who had been at the dying president's bedside the night before. Roosevelt may now have been the leader of the nation, but as far as Hanna was concerned, he still controlled the Republican Party, and at a meeting with the new president later that afternoon he pointedly told him, 'Do not think anything about a second term.' Yet, as president, Roosevelt would become the master of his own fate and at the 1904 election secured a unanimous nomination from the Republican National Convention on the first ballot, before defeating the Democrat Alton B. Parker by a landslide, winning every state outside of the old South.

Roosevelt initially promised to carry on the policies of McKinley, and made no alterations to the Cabinet. From the start though, he began the process of reshaping the presidency. He made 'The White House' the official title of the president's home, and commissioned the design and construction of the West Wing, so that office staff could be moved out of the main residence, creating more space for his large family. The Oval Office was not added until 1909 and Theodore worked in the current-day Roosevelt Room in the West Wing.

Roosevelt believed 'the Constitution was made for the people, and not the people for the Constitution', and it was his role as president to act in their interests. During his two terms he would sign 1,081 executive orders, just over two hundred short of the total of those presented by all of his twenty-five predecessors combined. The novelist Henry James commented that his initials TR really stood for 'Theodore Rex', but the president would later be indignant that, 'While President . . . I have not cared a rap for the criticisms of those who spoke of my "usurpation of power" . . . I have felt not merely that my action was right in itself, but that in showing the strength of, or in giving strength to, the executive, I was establishing a precedent of value.'

On 3 December 1901, Theodore Roosevelt's first 'State of the Union' address was delivered to Congress. At the start of the twentieth century, industrial production in America had never been higher or the profits greater. However, the power of America's major industries had become increasingly concentrated into the hands of a few 'captains of industry', like the oil magnate John D. Rockefeller and the financier J. Pierpont Morgan, and it was these men who the president had in his sights. The combinations of companies they controlled could be used to suppress business competition, and fix prices and wages in ways that could be detrimental to the public interest. Roosevelt did not object to big businesses in principle, but believed that 'combination and concentration should be, not prohibited, but supervised and within reasonable limits controlled'. He told the Congress,

> Great corporations exist only because they are created and safeguarded by our institutions; and it is therefore our right and our duty to see that they work in harmony with these institutions . . . the Government should have the right to inspect and examine the workings of the great corporations engaged in interstate business . . . There would be no hardship in such supervision; banks are subject to it.

On 13 November 1901, J.P. Morgan had incorporated Northern Securities, a trust company that held an effective monopoly on the railroad routes from Chicago and the Great Lakes, through to the Pacific Ocean. Roosevelt asked the Attorney General Philander Knox to investigate whether action could be taken against the company for violating the 1890 Sherman Antitrust Act. He believed that it could and, on 18 February 1902, without any warning, the Department for Justice filed its case. Four days later, Morgan came to the White House to meet with the president and Knox, the banker complaining that he'd had no warning of this action, and adding: 'If we have done anything wrong send your man to my man and they can fix it up.' However, the Attorney General replied, 'We don't want to fix it up. We want to stop it,' with Roosevelt reportedly adding, 'I am neither a bull nor a bear in Morgan stock. I am president of the United States, and am sworn to execute the law.'

The case was finally settled in Roosevelt's favour by the Supreme Court in 1904, and led to the dissolving of the trust. He'd shown other businesses that if he could take on and win against J.P. Morgan, then no trust was safe. Over the following seven years, forty-four other federal antitrust cases would be brought, leading to the break-up of other companies, including Rockefeller's Standard Oil.

Roosevelt's progressive domestic policy during his presidency was based on his 'square deal'. This he would later explain meant 'not merely that I stand for fair play under the present rules of the game, but that I stand for having those rules changed so as to work for a more substantial equality of opportunity'. His 'trust-busting' programme showed his determination to intervene to prevent the abuse of market power by big businesses. In the summer of 1902, he also made an unprecedented intervention to help settle the anthracite coal strike in eastern Pennsylvania, fearing the conse-quences for the country if the strike ran into the winter. Further legislation was passed, including the 1903 Elkins Act and the 1906 Hepburn Act, which introduced fair and transparent pricing on the railways. The 1906 Pure Food and Drug Act protected consumers by requiring manufacturers to accurately label the goods they sold. Roosevelt also protected the nation's natural resources, establishing one hundred and fifty national forests, fifty-one federal bird reserves, four national game preserves, five national parks and eighteen national monuments on over two hundred and thirty million acres of public land.

If Theodore Roosevelt's policies at home were based on the 'square deal', in foreign affairs he led with a 'big stick'. He would often quote the West African proverb, 'Speak softly and carry a big stick; you will go far.' This was evidenced by his expansion of the navy from sixth place in the world, to second only behind Great Britain. In 1907, Roosevelt demonstrated the strength of the United States Navy by sending sixteen modern battleships along with support vessels on a fourteen-month tour of the globe. The peaceful mission of what became known as 'The Great White Fleet' sent a powerful message to other nations.

However, American security also required the building of the Panama Canal, so that the fleet, and other shipping, could move easily between the Atlantic and Pacific oceans. For this an agreement was required with the Colombian government, which controlled the canal zone at that time, so that the Americans could construct and operate the canal. When the deal was blocked by the Colombians, Roosevelt took advice that an 1846 treaty between the United States and Colombia had guaranteed them free transit across the Panama isthmus 'upon any modes of communication that now exist, or that may hereafter be constructed'. This suggested that the United States could take control and build the canal anyway. However, there were also reports of revolutionary tensions in Panama that could lead to an uprising against Colombia. On 10 October, Roosevelt met Philippe Bunau-Varilla, a French solider and engineer who was also in contact with the Panamanian rebels, and intimated that he could support an independent Panama. Five days later, Secretary John Hay told Bunau-Varilla that a squadron of navy vessels from San Francisco would soon be off the Pacific coast of Panama, and the press was reporting American naval movements in the Caribbean. It was enough to persuade the revolutionaries to rise up, which they did on 3 November 1903. Roosevelt ordered the navy to 'prevent [the] landing of any [Colombian] armed force with hostile intent'. This they did and on 6 November the United States recognised the new Republic of Panama. Bunau-Varilla, now the official representative of the new state, commenced negotiations with Secretary Hay on the Canal Treaty and the agreement was signed on 18 November. This was American imperialism, but Roosevelt justified his actions believing the securing of the Panama Canal would benefit the whole world. In December 1904, he included in his annual address to Congress what became known as the Roosevelt Corollary to the Monroe Doctrine, which not only prevented European powers from interfering in the Western hemisphere, but gave the United States the responsibility to intervene in other nations in the Americas to preserve order and protect life and property. He also asserted American interests in the Pacific, by successfully mediating to end the 1904–05 Russo-Japanese war, for which he was awarded the Nobel Peace Prize.

In November 1898, just after his election as governor of New York, Roosevelt's friend Rudyard Kipling presented him with his then-unpublished poem, 'The White Man's Burden', as a call for the United States to accept the responsibilities of empire after its occupation of the Philippines. The poem urged America to 'send forth the best ye breed – / Go bind your sons to exile / To serve your captives' need'. Roosevelt thought Kipling's work made 'good sense from the expansion standpoint'. However, if America was now asserting the right to intervene in the affairs of other nations on the grounds of security or human rights, people would question their own policies on civil rights.

Roosevelt believed in individual merit regardless of race or religion, and in the first weeks of his presidency asked Booker T. Washington, an influential African American leader, to dine with him at the White House. This was the first time such an invitation had ever been extended to a black man, and caused an outrage in the Southern states. Roosevelt appointed black men to federal office, and was the first president to publicly condemn the 'inhuman cruelty and barbarity' of lynchings. However, he also believed that black people were 'altogether inferior to the whites', but unlike many of his contemporaries thought in time it would be possible for African Americans to achieve equality. His prejudice was exposed in his handling of the 1906 case in Brownsville, Texas, where a white barman and police officer were wounded by gunshots after a late-night incident. White residents of the town blamed a black regiment of 'Buffalo Soldiers' stationed nearby. An army investigation found no hard evidence against them, but as none of the soldiers had confessed to taking part in such an action, the army's inspector general claimed there was a 'conspiracy of silence' about the affair and recommended to the president that he dismiss all 167 men. Roosevelt approved this action on 5 November 1906, but the announcement was held back for four days so that the decision wouldn't be public until after voting in that year's congressional elections. In time, thirteen of the soldiers would be reinstated, but the rest lost their pensions and were denied any opportunity to work again in the military or civil service. One of them had served with Roosevelt in the Rough Riders at the Battle of San Juan Hill. Booker T. Washington thought the president had 'blundered', but told friends he was prepared to forgive him for 'one mistake'.

After his re-election as president in 1904, Roosevelt stated that he wouldn't seek his party's nomination for a third consecutive term, honouring the precedent first established by George

Washington. As his first term was not the full four years, he could have made an exception and there was certainly nothing in the Constitution that could have prevented him. He was hugely popular and his re-election in 1908 would have been assured. However, he believed it would damage the presidency for the power and patronage of that office to be extended to one man across three consecutive terms. That did not mean though, in his mind, that having been out of office for at least four years, a former president could not stand for election again.

He was just fifty years old when he left the White House, and having seen the safe election of his chosen successor, his great friend and War Secretary, William Howard Taft, Roosevelt left the country to embark on a year-long African safari and tour of capitals of Europe. He was treated as an honoured guest wherever he went, and great crowds greeted him. When he returned to the United States on 18 June 1910, over one million people turned out for his official reception and parade through the streets of New York City. He'd chosen to spend his first year abroad after leaving the White House to avoid being drawn into politics, but he simply found it impossible to leave the arena and retire to Oyster Bay.

In August, Roosevelt delivered a major speech in Kansas, on the 'New Nationalism', in which he championed 'practical equality of opportunity for all citizens'. To achieve this he regarded the federal government and 'executive power as the steward of the public welfare'. Roosevelt challenged Taft for the Republican nomination in 1912, and in the first ever primary elections won nine of the thirteen contested states. However, at the convention itself where the majority of the delegates had been selected by party bosses, Taft won. Roosevelt walked out, followed by his supporters, and accepted instead the nomination of the Progressive Party to run for president, which then became known as the 'Bull Moose Party'.

The Bull Moose manifesto proposed electoral reforms, including votes for women, limiting campaign contributions and creating a register of lobbyists. There were also policies for old-age pensions and social insurance for workers, very much in line with the reforms the leading Liberal and future prime minister David Lloyd George had introduced in Britain. The two men had met in London in 1910 and Roosevelt 'took a real fancy to' Lloyd George, who also thought the former president's political convictions were based on a 'stern and dauntless Radicalism [that] always appealed to me'.

The most dramatic moment of the presidential campaign came in Milwaukee, when, while leaving the Gilpatrick Hotel to board a motor car waiting to take him to a speaking engagement, Roosevelt was shot at close range by John Schrank. The bullet penetrated TR's thick overcoat, steel glasses case, and the manuscript of a fifty-page speech folded over twice, before lodging in his chest, a quarter of an inch from his heart. Roosevelt, seeing that he was not coughing any blood, decided that the bullet had not penetrated his lungs and so decided to continue and give his speech before going to hospital. He spoke for eighty-four minutes, revealing his bloodstained shirt to the audience and telling them, 'It takes more than that to kill a bull moose.' At the election on 5 November, Roosevelt secured the strongest ever showing for a third-party candidate, and won more states and votes than Taft. However, his candidacy split the Republican vote and allowed the Democrat, Woodrow Wilson, to win with just 41 per cent of the popular vote.

In the summer of 1914, the First World War arrived out of a clear blue sky. Roosevelt was resolute in his support for Britain and France against Germany, and was critical of Wilson's failure to bring America in sooner on their side, particularly after German U-boats sank the transatlantic Cunard ocean liner, the RMS *Lusitania*, in 1915. However, anti-war sentiment in America would also rule out his seeking the nomination from the Republican Party to stand against Wilson at the 1916 election. He wrote to his English friend, Arthur Lee, a letter that he asked to be shared with Lloyd George, explaining, 'I don't believe there is any chance of my being nominated . . . unless the country was in heroic mood. If they put "Safety First" ahead of honour and duty, then they don't want me.'

It was the commencement of unrestricted submarine warfare by the Germans on Atlantic shipping in 1917 that would eventually bring America into the war. Roosevelt urged his four sons to get into the action, which they all did, but his youngest Quentin, a pursuit pilot in the Army Air Service, was killed in action on 14 July 1918, aged twenty. On hearing the news, Theodore wrote to his son Archie: 'He died as the heroes of old died: as brave and fearless men must die when a great cause calls. If our country did not contain such men it would not be our country.'

By the end of the war in November 1918, Roosevelt was reconciled once again with his old party, and was seen as a certainty for the nomination to run for the presidency in 1920, an election he would have been expected to easily win. He was still only sixty, but was in increasingly poor health, worn down by his vigorous life. In the early hours of 6 January 1919, at home at Sagamore Hill, he died suddenly in his sleep. The vice-president, Thomas Marshall, remarked that, 'Death had to take Roosevelt sleeping, for if he had been awake, there would have been a fight.'

Carved from the rock on Mount Rushmore in South Dakota, the image of Theodore Roosevelt stares out alongside fellow presidents Washington, Lincoln and Jefferson. Yet our view of him in history has been somewhat obscured by the crises that came after his time, particularly the Great Depression and the Second World War, which were addressed by his fifth cousin President Franklin Delano Roosevelt, who thought TR was 'the greatest man I ever knew'. Theodore Roosevelt's example, however, still remains a benchmark for the presidency, as one of the great holders of that office in the twentieth century.

Damian Collins has been the Member of Parliament for Folkestone and Hythe since 2010. He is the former Chair of the Digital, Culture, Media and Sport Select Committee, and the current Chair of the Joint Select Committee on the Online Safety Bill. He is also the author of Charmed Life: The Phenomenal World of Philip Sassoon.

27

William Howard Taft

4 March 1909 to 4 March 1913
Republican
Vice-president: James S. Sherman 1909–12, vacant 1912–13

By Philip Norton

Full name: William Howard Taft
Born: Cincinnati, Ohio, 15 September 1857
Died: 8 March 1930, Washington, DC
Resting place: Arlington National Cemetery, Washington, DC
Library/Museum: Cincinnati, Ohio
Education: Woodward High School, Cincinnati; Yale College;
Cincinnati Law School
Married to: Helen ('Nellie') Herron, m. 1886
Children: Three: Robert, Helen, Charles
Quotation: 'Politics make me sick.'

WILLIAM HOWARD TAFT had three careers during more than fifty years of public service. He held high office in all three: as a lawyer, concluding his career as Chief Justice of the United States; as an administrator, serving as Governor-General of the Philippines; and as a politician, being elected president of the United States in 1908. However, he felt fulfilled in only two. He spent three productive years establishing civil government in the Philippines, four uncongenial years in the White House, and nine contented years at the top of the judicial tree. He was dedicated to the law and, left to his own devices, would likely have never moved outside a career in the legal profession. That he did so was through the prompting of three people: President William McKinley, who appointed him to his post in the Philippines, President Teddy Roosevelt, who selected him as his successor in the White House, and his wife, who was ambitious for him to achieve public prominence.

Taft was born into a prominent Ohio family that was steeped in the law, the work ethic and public service. His grandfather and father were judges. He married the daughter of a judge. His father, Alphonso, also served in public office as War Secretary and Attorney General, as well as ambassador to Austria-Hungary and Russia. His parents pushed him to work hard and succeed.

After attending Woodward High School, Taft gained admission to Yale. Though not regarded as an intellectual, he proved a diligent student. He then returned to Ohio to study law at Cincinnati law school, complementing his studies by working for a local newspaper, *The Cincinnati Commercial*, covering court cases. He graduated in 1880 – second in his class out of 121 – and the same year took and passed the state bar exam.

He had a successful career as a lawyer. His success appears to have been helped by the fact that he was popular – he mixed easily with others – and by his engagement in Republican politics. He appears to have soon come to the attention of leading Republican politicians, including President Chester A. Arthur and the State Governor, Joseph B. Foraker. After a year spent as assistant prosecutor of Hamilton County (covering Cincinnati), he was appointed by Arthur as Collector of Internal Revenue for Ohio's First District. He bolstered a reputation for integrity by refusing to dismiss employees who were doing their jobs effectively but were out of favour politically. After a year, he resigned in order to begin private practice.

While in practice, he met Helen (Nellie) Herron and in 1884 they married. They were a devoted couple, Nellie proving a loving, but ambitious, wife. She was keen for her husband to succeed in public life. Whereas he was happy mixing with fellow lawyers, she was more interested in ensuring he mixed with those who could advance his political career. The couple were to have two sons and a daughter.

Taft's ultimate ambition was to serve on the US Supreme Court. The first step to achieving that goal was achieved in 1887, when – aged twenty-nine – he was appointed by Governor Foraker to fill a vacancy on the Superior Court of Cincinnati. The vacancy was for just over a year. On completion of the term, Taft sought election for a full five-year term, Ohio being one of the states where state judges are elected. He was successful and got his first substantial experience on the bench.

Although he was young and still relatively inexperienced as a judge, this did not stop him lobbying for nomination to the US Supreme Court. When a vacancy on the court occurred in 1889, Taft urged Foraker to put his name forward to the president. Although Foraker did promote his case, President Harrison decided instead to appoint Taft to the vacant post of Solicitor General. At the age of thirty-two, Taft arrived in Washington, DC. He appears to have seen it as a way of advancing his judicial career; Nellie still seemed more intent on pushing him to mix with Washington's political elite.

In 1892, he was appointed as a judge of the US Sixth Circuit Court. On the bench, he was generally seen as pro-business, holding secondary strikes to be illegal, but he was not uniformly anti-labour: he upheld the right of workers to join a union and to strike. Significantly, in terms of the stance he was later to take in the White House, he handed down judgments to enforce antitrust legislation. He also took up a post as professor of law at his old law school, a position that required him to give two one-hour lectures a week. By all accounts, it was a particularly happy time for Taft, enabling him to devote his energies to what he enjoyed.

In 1900, he was summoned by President McKinley, but not for

the purpose, as Taft hoped, of offering him a place on the Supreme Court; rather, to ask him to serve on a commission to set up a civilian government in the Philippines. Although the offer may have been as compensation for the fact that McKinley had not appointed Taft to the Supreme Court two years earlier, when a vacancy had arisen, it proved an inspired choice. Taft accepted on condition he headed the commission. He proved an effective and empathetic governor. He treated Filipinos as social equals and prepared the ground for eventual self-government. He oversaw reforms in public works, education, law, health and banking. His dedication to completing his work led to him turning down the offer of a place on the Supreme Court, made by McKinley's successor, Theodore Roosevelt.

Taft had got to know Roosevelt when both were working in Washington, DC. Each appeared to hold the other in high regard and, once he had completed his work in the Philippines, Taft accepted Roosevelt's invitation in 1904 to become his Secretary of War. In office, he travelled to Panama to initiate work on constructing the Panama Canal, to Cuba where he served briefly as provisional governor, and Japan where he achieved various commitments, including to reduce the number of passports to work in the USA. (This 'gentlemen's agreement' had the effect of holding down Japanese immigration to the west coast of the US) However, his principal role was to act as a confidant and legal adviser to Roosevelt. The relationship between the two appeared to be close.

Taft twice turned down offers to join the Supreme Court when vacancies occurred, apparently having his eye on the position of Chief Justice. Roosevelt, however, moved from seeing Taft as a potential member of the court to designating him as his successor in the White House, believing he would continue his policies. He used his political leverage to ensure that Taft received the party's nomination, which he did on the first ballot at the Republican Convention in Chicago in June 1908.

Taft was not a particularly enthusiastic, or effective, campaigner – he described the campaign as 'one of the most uncomfortable four months' of his life – but benefited from Roosevelt's support. He faced Democrat William Jennings Bryan, making his third attempt to enter the White House. Taft achieved a majority of the popular vote, 7.6 million votes to 6.4 million for Bryan, and a substantial victory in the Electoral College, by 321 votes to 162. The divide was essentially between the North and South, Bryan's strength coming from Southern states. Taft was inaugurated as the twenty-seventh president on 4 March 1909. The event was distinctive for two reasons. A snowstorm forced the ceremony to be held indoors and Nellie became the first First Lady to travel with her husband from the inauguration to the White House.

In office, Taft was by no means a poor president – historians tend to rate him as a middle-ranking holder of the office – but he suffered by virtue of being Roosevelt's successor and differing from him in three basic respects. First, he lacked Roosevelt's flair and oratorical skills. Second, he had a very different view of the office of president. Third, he pursued policies that were not those embraced by Roosevelt. Taft was far more conservative than Roosevelt in his interpretation of the powers of the president and in his approach to public policy.

Taft's skills were essentially legal and administrative. He was not a natural politician, and disliked conflict. Roosevelt had adopted a rhetorical style and believed that a president was free to make of the office what he wanted, limited only by any explicit prohibitions specified in the Constitution. Taft was not a platform orator and took a narrow view of his constitutional powers, believing that the president could only do that which he was empowered to do by the constitution.

His presidency was not without some successes. As Harold Laski noted, when it came to 'trust busting', Taft's record was actually better than his predecessor's, with ninety-nine cases brought in his four years in office (more than double the number during Roosevelt's tenure). He oversaw the introduction of the US Postal Savings System. The Mann–Elkins Act of 1910 expanded the power of the Interstate Commerce Commission. Taft was also kept busy in foreign affairs, not least by unrest in Latin America and East Asia. He extended US influence through 'dollar diplomacy'. His approach to conflict reflected his legal approach, favouring arbitration over armed conflict. It was an approach not favoured by Roosevelt.

However, his biggest problems were in domestic politics. He failed to live up to Roosevelt's expectations, proving more conservative than expected. He clashed with progressives in the party over his stance on tariffs, signing the Payne–Aldrich Act of 1909 that, instead of lowering tariffs, was seen as a protectionist measure. He sided with his Interior Secretary, Richard Ballinger, in a clash with the Roosevelt-appointed Chief Forester Gifford Pinchot, his dismissal of the latter dismaying Roosevelt. He also failed to follow Roosevelt in his policy on civil rights. Roosevelt resisted pressure from local white citizens to dismiss African Americans from public office. Although supporting the right of African Americans to vote (and vetoing a bill imposing a literacy test for unskilled labourers), Taft succumbed to such pressure. Further trouble came in the 1910 mid-term elections with the Democrats gaining control of the House of Representatives. Thereafter, as Denis Brogan recorded, the president was 'bombarded with bills that expressed less the considered legislative views of Congress than the tactical views of Democratic politicians'.

Teddy Roosevelt's criticisms wounded Taft deeply. The estrangement was so severe that Roosevelt decided to stand in the 1912 presidential election. Taft was able to use his powers to secure the Republican nomination, seeing off a challenge by his rival. Roosevelt had grassroots support, but Taft controlled the party machinery, so Roosevelt decided to form and stand under the label of the Progressive Party. Taft knew he was likely to lose, and did not help his chances by maintaining the tradition that presidents seeking re-election do not campaign. He was beset by problems, not least in mobilising money and in crafting an effective campaign organisation. The contest was dominated by the battle between Roosevelt and the Democratic candidate, Woodrow Wilson. Roosevelt's intervention served to split the Republican vote and deliver the presidency to Wilson. Taft came a poor third in the contest, carrying only two states (Utah and Vermont), which between them delivered eight Electoral College votes.

Although the loss of office was a disappointment, it was also a relief. As he told Wilson, 'I'm glad to be going. This is the lonesomest place in the world.' After leaving the White House, he returned to academic life, as a law professor at Yale. While there, he wrote *Our Chief Magistrate and His Powers*, which developed his views of the presidential office. He served briefly as joint chairman of the National War Labor Board.

After the 1920 presidential election, the Republican president-elect, Warren Harding – like Taft, from Ohio – invited Taft to meet him and asked whether he would accept appointment to the Supreme Court. Taft said he would accept, but only if he were Chief Justice. Harding made no commitment. The Chief Justice, Edward White, died in office on 19 May 1921. Taft's nomination was not a foregone conclusion; Harding apparently considered a proposal to appoint Justice William Day for a short period before he retired from the bench, but in June he announced Taft's nomination. It easily gained Senate approval (by sixty-one votes to four) the same day.

Taft entered the most satisfying period of his public life. He had achieved his life's goal. He had served at one end of Pennsylvania Avenue, but had always wanted to serve at the other end. (At the time, the Supreme Court still met in the Capitol building.) He was sworn in as Chief Justice of the United States on 11 July 1921.

Taft was not an outstanding Chief Justice in terms of developing the jurisprudence of the court, but he was a reforming one. As well as pressing for greater efficiency in dealing with cases, he was instrumental in achieving passage of the Judges' Act 1922, giving the power to create new judgeships and to enable him as Chief Justice to move judges temporarily to help reduce the substantial backlog of cases. He also pressed successfully for legislation, the Judiciary Act (1925), giving the Supreme Court greater discretion in deciding its cases, enabling it to focus on those of national importance.

More than two hundred and fifty cases were heard during his tenure. The court in its judgments tended to limit government, especially federal government, but also upheld the authority of both president and Congress in exercising certain powers. In 1922, in *Bailey v. Drexel Furniture Co.*, Taft authored the court's opinion striking down a law that taxed certain corporations making use of child labour, contending that it was designed not to raise money, but to regulate matters reserved to the states. However, in *Myers v. United States* (1926), Taft led in holding that Congress could not require the president to gain Senate approval before removing an appointee, as no such restriction existed under the Constitution. In *McGrain v. Docherty* (1927), a unanimous court held that Congress had the power to conduct investigations – enabling it to subpoena documents – as auxiliary to its legislative function. The picture was mixed in dealing with the rights of citizens. In *Olmstead v US* (1928) the court allowed warrantless wiretaps of phone conversations to be used against defendants. Against this apparently illiberal judgment, it had three years earlier delivered a landmark opinion in *Gitlow v New York* (1925), holding that the Fourteenth Amendment 'due process' clause extended the First Amendment provisions protecting freedom of speech and freedom of the press to the governments of the US states.

Taft clearly felt fulfilled on the bench in a way that he had never been in politics. In 1925, he wrote: 'The truth is that in my present life I don't remember that I was ever President.'

By the end of the 1920s, his health was declining, and at the beginning of 1930 he became seriously ill. Before resigning, he obtained from Hoover an assurance that his successor would be Charles Evans Hughes, a former Republican candidate for the presidency, and not the more liberal Justice Harlan F. Stone. He resigned on 3 February, at the age of seventy-two, and died just over a month later, on 8 March. He became the first president and first member of the Supreme Court to be buried at Arlington National Cemetery.

Taft became president having not sought the office. His son, Robert, was elected senator for Ohio and did have designs on the presidency, on no fewer than three occasions seeking the Republican nomination, but never achieved his ambition.

As president, Taft has two historical distinctions to his name. One is that he is the largest man ever to have held the office. He weighed over twenty stone and was the subject of a story, apparently apocryphal, that he once got stuck in a bathtub. The second is that he is the only president to have served as Chief Justice of the United States. He was relaxed about jokes made about his girth. The best known at his expense was when he was serving in the Philippines and cabled the Secretary of War to say he had ridden twenty-five miles on horseback, receiving the reply: 'How is the horse?' The fact that he was the only man to have served in two of the highest offices in the United States is something that, as a man dedicated to public service, he would have been enormously proud, even if he would have preferred to have served in only one of them.

His biggest misfortune was being stuck not, as alleged, in a bathtub, but between two presidents noted for radical policies and rhetoric. He was overshadowed by both his predecessor and his successor, who was to be a dominant figure in US politics. Unlike them, Taft was not one to carry a 'big stick', his conservative and low-key approach achieving some benefits but not raising him to the ranks of the great presidents. His rating as a Chief Justice of the United States was much higher and that would have given him the greatest satisfaction.

Philip Norton is Professor of Government at the University of Hull and sits in the House of Lords as Lord Norton of Louth.

28

Woodrow Wilson

4 March 1913 to 4 March 1921
Democrat
Vice-president: Thomas R. Marshall

By Roy Hattersley

Full name: Thomas Woodrow Wilson
Born: 28 December 1856, Staunton, Virginia
Died: 3 February 1924, Washington, DC
Resting place: Washington National Cathedral, Washington, DC
Library/Museum: Staunton, Virginia
Education: College of New Jersey (which became Princeton), University of Virginia Law School, Johns Hopkins University
Married to: Ellen Louise Axson, m. 1885 (1860–1914); Edith Bolling Galt, m. 1915 (1872–1961)
Children: Three: Margaret, Jessie, Eleanor
Quotation: 'If you want to make enemies, try to change something.'

PRESIDENT WOODROW WILSON secured his place in history with an idea that he hoped would change the world. The change was not as great as Wilson wished. But, thanks to him, some international disputes – which once would have ended in war – are now solved by negotiation. The United Nations organisation and the League of Nations, by which it was preceded, are memorials to an achievement of such importance that credit for their creation overshadows everything else that Wilson said or did. Yet Woodrow Wilson's presidency was the great bridging passage in the history of the United States. During his eight years in the White House, America awoke from economic and diplomatic hibernation and began to act like a great world power.

Thomas Woodrow Wilson was born in Staunton, West Virginia, on 28 December 1856. His father – a third-generation American – and his mother – Jesse Woodrow, who had emigrated from England with her family when she was a child – were pillars of the Presbyterian Church. In 1858, his father, who had begun his working life as a printer, was appointed pastor of the First Presbyterian Church of Atlanta, Georgia. Although a Northerner by upbringing, Joseph Ruggles Wilson felt at home in the Deep South. When Georgia seceded from the Union, he supported the Confederacy with as much evangelical fervour as he displayed at Sunday services and enrolled as chaplain to the state's volunteers.

Until he reached his early teens, Tommy, as his family called him, was a slow learner. In consequence, when Joseph Wilson was appointed a professor in the Columbia Theological Seminary and the whole family moved to South Carolina, Tommy was registered in Davidson College in the northern sister state, a small and academically undistinguished institution that provided cut-price education for young men of limited ability.

Life at Davidson College was hard. Students washed their own clothes and drew their drinking water from an ancient well. Within weeks of enrolment, Wilson determined to leave Davidson College and worked at his studies with such fierce determination that, before the end of his freshman year, he was able to transfer to New Jersey College in Princeton. He chose to study history and political philosophy. It was the beginning of his preoccupation with the business of government – a subject that absorbed him, in theory and practice – for the rest of his life.

Tommy became Tom as soon as he arrived in New Jersey. His contemporaries disagree about whether the college can take credit for his metropolitan demeanour or if he arrived in Princeton already a homogenised American. However the transformation came about, when he left New Jersey College he no longer bore the marks of his Southern upbringing – except in one particular. Throughout his life Wilson believed that the White race was superior to the Black. He was not a man to hesitate in acting on his beliefs. So, he diverted black students from the universities in which he taught to what he regarded as 'more suitable' institutions. Then, first as governor of New Jersey and subsequently as president of the United States, he methodically replaced black public servants with white.

Immediately he graduated from New Jersey College, Tom Wilson enrolled in the Virginia University Law School. Despite the first attack of the mysterious sickness from which he suffered all his life, he completed the course, was admitted to the Georgia Bar and opened a law office in Atlanta. After ten unhappy months, he decided that he was a scholar, not a lawyer, and that a doctorate would secure him a place in a senior common room. And so it proved. Six months after he was awarded a PhD by Johns Hopkins University, he joined the history faculty at Bryn Mawr, a women's college in Pennsylvania.

The security that comes with tenure enabled him to marry Ellen Louise Axson, the daughter of a Presbyterian preacher. It was the beginning of a thirty-year partnership that survived her husband's brief infatuation with a Massachusetts socialite, which began when he was taking a recuperative holiday alone in Bermuda. Ellen Wilson became, as did the couple's three daughters, an essential part of the Wilson political entourage. It was his dependence on her to which Wilson's friends attributed his second marriage barely a year after her death.

Wilson was on his way. His first published work, *Congressional Politics*, confirmed him as an expert on the American Constitution and guaranteed his ascent up the academic ladder. He had taught for two years in the Wesleyan University in Middletown, Connecticut, when the New Jersey College, about to be reborn as Princeton University, offered him the chair of Jurisprudence and Political Economy. He remained at Princeton for twenty-two years. For ten he was president of the university. During that decade Princeton increased in stature to the point at which it rivalled Harvard and Yale, and Tom became Woodrow, taking on his mother's maiden name.

The new president of Princeton had no doubt that his primary duty was to secure improvement in the university's academic standards – if necessary at the expense of its social standing. Usually, Wilson listened politely to criticisms of his plans for change and then went ahead as if he had secured a mandate for reform. But two of his proposals – first the siting of the new Graduate School within the main campus and then a reorganisation of student accommodation to make it less confined to the sons of the rich – met with implacable opposition from the university's trustees and the Princeton alumni – both sources of indispensable revenue. Wilson's plans were rejected. Even before that humiliation, the Princeton presidency – indeed the whole business of college management – had lost its charm. At an academic dinner, held three years before the Graduate School siting snub, he had told the assembled college presidents that they were, in effect, managers of country clubs. The double defeat brought the simmering dissatisfaction to the boil. There was no thought of dramatic resignation. That was not Wilson's way. Instead, he calmly and privately decided to seek a different occupation. The escape route that he found most attractive was some sort of elected office. Woodrow Wilson became a politician not because of sudden ideological passion or long-held conviction but because politics offered alternative and more congenial employment opportunities.

By happy coincidence, at the time when Woodrow Wilson was looking for a new career, the New Jersey Democrats were looking for a new candidate to nominate as governor of the state. The Republican Party had won the last five gubernatorial elections and in the early months of 1910 there seemed every likelihood of their winning a sixth. The Democrats were hopelessly divided between self-styled 'conservatives' and 'progressives', and while they wrangled about the direction of state policy, New Jersey became notorious for allowing price fixing by companies that moved into the state expressly to avoid the trust-busting provisions of the Sherman Act. Petty corruption infested both parties. But it was the New Jersey Democrats – guilty by association with the Tammany Hall-dominated party across the Hudson River in New York – whose reputation suffered the most. To New Jersey Democrats, desperate for reform, the discovery that Woodrow Wilson might become their candidate for governor seemed like the chance to make a fresh start.

The notion that Woodrow Wilson was not a typical politician – an electoral asset throughout his political career – owed much to his austere appearance and his penchant for the formality of top hat and frock coat whenever it was appropriate – and sometimes when it was not. The myth that he was different from the usual grubby seeker after office was encouraged by his Princeton years. At the end of his second term in the White House, cartoonists still depicted him wearing a mortar board and academic gown.

Woodrow Wilson had supported the Democrats since, as a Princeton undergraduate, he had campaigned in the presidential election of 1876. Twenty years later he had broken ranks and endorsed a no-hope deserter rather than William Jennings Bryan, who had barnstormed his way to the Democrat nomination with the accusation that America was being 'crucified on a cross of gold' – his description of orthodox monetary policy. Wilson's supporters argued that his apostasy in 1896 proved that he was the man of independent conviction that the party needed in 1910. His accept-ance speech at the state convention confirmed their claim. 'I did not seek this nomination . . . I made absolutely no pledge of any kind to prevent me from serving the people of this state with singleness of purpose.' The assumption that he would favour the 'conservative' faction within the party was banished with the promise to promote a revision of tax rates and the 'control of corporations'.

Woodrow Wilson was elected governor of New Jersey with a 10 per cent majority of the votes cast. In office he moved even closer to the 'progressive' wing of the Democratic Party. State bills promoted compensation for injuries at work, regulated the employ-ment of women and children, and created a State Board of Education that set minimum standards for teaching in public schools and possessed the power to inspect and demand improvements.

On the day that he was elected governor of New Jersey, Woodrow Wilson became the favourite to win the Democrat nomination for president of the United States. But the Democratic Party's convention, which met in Baltimore on 25 June 1912, was presented with a list of eight prospective candidates from which to make its choice. Wilson only just survived the first round of voting. On 5 July, he won the nomination on the forty-sixth ballot.

The 1912 presidential election was a three-horse race. Theodore Roosevelt – who had declined to run for re-election to another consecutive term in 1908 – stood as an independent with the determined intention of preventing the party's official candidate, William Howard Taft, from winning a second term. Roosevelt made most of the running until he was wounded by an assassination attempt that would have killed him had the bullet not lodged in the thick wodge of speaking notes in his coat pocket. He described himself as the prophet of 'New Nationalism', a claim that Wilson countered with the announcement that he offered America a 'New Freedom' – the protection of the ordinary citizen from the tyranny of big business, the banks and trusts. The proclamation of citizens' rights was turned into practical policies. But Woodrow Wilson, the student of politics, remembered that most American voters believed that 'the government is best which governs least'. A week before polling day he told a rally in Madison Square Garden, 'I do not want a government that takes care of me. I want a government that makes others take their hands off me so that I can take care of myself.' Seven days later he won 435 votes in the Electoral College but only 42 per cent of the popular vote – 100,000 fewer votes than Bryan won in 1908.

Surprisingly, President Woodrow Wilson found the appointment of Cabinet members an unrewarding occupation and, in consequence, performed the uncongenial task with an uncharacteristic casual incompetence. William Jennings Bryan agreed to become Secretary of State on the understanding that his duties would not require him to drink alcohol. William Gibbs McAdoo – a New York railway magnate who was notorious for his dislike of bankers – became Treasury Secretary and later the president's son-in-law. The other members were chosen with the assistance of Colonel Edward M. House – a Texan who held an honorary commission in a phantom regiment and became Wilson's closest adviser throughout his White House years. The unintended result was a Cabinet that was dominated by the old South. So was the Senate and the House of Representatives.

Wilson's apologists have always claimed that the overt and continual racial discrimination that was a feature of his first four years in office was the unavoidable consequence of pressure from the Deep South. Within weeks of taking office, Postmaster General Albert S. Burleston ordered the segregation of post office employees and prohibited Black Americans from holding positions of authority over white junior officials. But Wilson let it happen. Active racial discrimination was wholly consistent with his long-held and openly expressed view on white superiority. The record speaks for itself. The 'reconstruction' that followed the end of the Civil War had included the promise to promote the emergence of a black middle class by the recruitment of black executives to work in the federal bureaucracy. By the end of his first term Wilson had made nine 'special appointments'. President Taft, his Republican predecessor, had been heavily criticised for appointing 'only' thirty-one. One of the paradoxes of Woodrow Wilson's presidency was the philosophical conflict between his racial prejudice and his domestic agenda, which confirmed, beyond doubt, his status as a 'progressive' Democrat.

The new president set out his plans for four years of reform in a speech to a joint session of Congress. It was, at the time, the most comprehensive legislative programme in American history and, since then, it has only been exceeded in size and originality by Franklin D. Roosevelt's 'New Deal'. Wilson described his proposals in the language of his election campaign. The 'New Freedom' would protect the citizen from the tyranny of 'great bodies of astute men [who] seek to overcome the interests of the public for their private profit'. The first candidates for emancipation would be consumers who paid prices that were kept artificially high by the imposition of indefensible import duties. For a time, it seemed that a rebellion by Democratic senators, closely associated with the protected industries, would prevent the passage of the tariff reduction bill. But Wilson endorsed the proposal that the Senate investigate the relationship between its members and vested interests within their states. When it was revealed that, in the recent general election, sugar producers had contributed $5 million to the election expenses of selected candidates, the urge to demonstrate integrity swept through the Senate, and the 1913 Revenue Act, which reduced the average import tariff from 40 per cent to 26 per cent, was passed into law.

The next item on the progressive agenda was banking reform. Again, vested interests in the Senate seemed likely to derail the creation of a Federal Reserve. Mid-Western farmers were particularly exercised by the prospect of their credit status, and therefore the cost as well as the extent of their borrowing, being determined in the big cities on the east coast. Wilson shared their view and allayed their fears. The banking system he proposed would be 'public not private and [its authority] would be vested in the government itself so that the banks would be the instruments, not the masters, of business'. The Senate voted in favour of the Federal Reserve Bill by fifty-four votes to thirty-four − a virtual landslide.

Initially, President Wilson thought that his ambition to reinforce the largely ineffective Sherman Act of 1890 could be achieved by legislation that prohibited a list of specified anti-competitive practices. The list − which included discriminatory pricing, overlapping directorships and exclusive dealing − was by no means comprehensive, and experience suggested that the giant railroad and bank monopolies would find ways of circumventing even the explicit prohibitions. Wilson concluded that enforcement of the law required a constitutional innovation − the creation of a government agency with powers to investigate and identify anti-competitive practices and ensure that those who practised them were prosecuted. The Federal Trade Commission Act was passed by Congress in the spring of 1914 − the third of the major reforms that reflected America's gradual emergence as the world's most powerful industrial economy.

An attempt to describe the Woodrow Wilson philosophy of government would probably conclude that 'interventionist' − although an imperfect definition − is as near as a single word could get. He certainly chose to involve himself in the progress of the American economy in a way that no president who preceded him − and few who were to follow − would have even contemplated. But his economic policy was driven more by instinct than by ideology. However, his foreign policy owed more to principle than personality. He was profoundly antagonistic to the idea of empire. So, in the early days of his presidency he joyfully assisted towards full independence the numerous island states that America had semi-colonised. But his excursions into foreign policy were less sure-footed than his advances into new areas of economic management. That was because diplomacy takes time and, by nature, Wilson was always in a hurry. Mexico taxed his patience to near breaking point.

In a permanent state of economic chaos and political turbulence, Mexico descended into quasi-anarchy during the autumn of 1913. An army coup had deposed the democratically elected president Venustiano Carranza and installed, in his place, General Victoriano Huerta. The riots that followed were said to endanger the lives of the many thousand Americans who lived south of the Rio Grande. When the expatriates' demands were reinforced by United States oil companies, with multi-million-pound investments in Mexico, prevarication was no longer possible. The State Department judged that formal recognition of the Huerta regime would restore stability. But Wilson insisted that the Monroe Doctrine – which committed the United States to promoting democracy in the American hemisphere – justified, indeed demanded, action to depose the dictator. Invasion, economic sanctions, supplying arms to the 'constitutionalist' opposition and imposing punitive tariffs on Mexican ships that plied their trade in the recently opened Panama Canal were all considered. None of them was judged to be feasible.

Then, three American sailors – taking part in a naval exercise in Tampico Bay – were arrested by the Mexican police and imprisoned. They were quickly released. But what began as a minor incident escalated into a major crisis that Wilson initially believed would justify American military intervention. Rumours of Mexican troop movements were used to justify three thousand American soldiers and marines being sent to occupy Veracruz with the announcement that the United States' complaint was against General Huerta, not the Mexican people. Unfortunately, Carranza did not agree. He denounced the American action as imperialist aggression. Disappointing though that was, it caused Wilson nothing like the visible distress that followed his discovery that 1,700 Mexicans and

5 United States soldiers had died in the sporadic fighting. For almost four years, Mexico – although not forgotten – was officially ignored.

Even during the years of diplomatic silence, Wilson could not forbear from expressing the occasional opinion about the ebb and flow of Mexican democracy. One of his more unwise comments included a favourable reference to Francisco 'Pancho' Villa, the revolutionary bandit whose activities Wilson chose to describe as reminiscent of Robin Hood. If Villa knew of the flattering comparison, he showed no sign of gratitude. In March 1916, a contingent of his followers crossed the frontier into America and raided Columbus, a near-deserted relic of the frontier wars in New Mexico. It was the first invasion of the United States since the war of 1812. The president had no option other than to sanction what became known – in the language of nineteenth-century colonialism – as a punitive expedition, which, Wilson again insisted, was directed against undesirable elements in Mexico, not the whole nation. A force of four thousand officers and men, under the command of General John J. Pershing, made virtually unimpeded progress deep into the country. In Washington, there was some agitation for all-out war, which Wilson rejected out of hand. His alternative solution was 'conciliation' – a process that he agreed with Carranza, who had become Mexico's democratic, though essentially temporary, president. Negotiations were still going on when Pershing began a gradual withdrawal. Wilson and his administration had become preoccupied with a bigger conflict. The war in Europe had raged on for nearly two years and there was no sign of it coming to an end.

In the words of one delegate, the Democratic Party's national convention of 1916 'went crazy for peace'. Woodrow Wilson – whose second-term nomination was agreed by acclamation – shared the party's passion. At the beginning of the year, he had been categoric, at least in private: 'If being re-elected as president depends upon me getting into the war, I don't want to be President.' It was a principle to which he remained stubbornly faithful even as the course of the war changed and with it the mood of the American people.

Until the end of 1916, both the Allies and the Central Powers chose – or were forced – to fight a static war. Germany, no less than Great Britain and France, hoped for a great breakthrough. Both sides suffered great losses, but neither gained or lost much ground. Determined to end the stalemate, Great Britain decided to blockade German ports and starve the Central Powers into surrender. President Wilson made a formal protest but – largely because America did so little trade with Germany – took no action to prevent or deter the Royal Navy from intercepting American cargo ships. Then Germany – rightly concluding that Britain would be particularly vulnerable to enforced isolation – announced that its submarine fleet would seek out and sink any ship from any nation that was carrying cargo bound for Britain. Three American ships were sunk in 1915 and in May of that year, the British liner *Lusitania* was torpedoed in mid-Atlantic. The casualty list included the names of 1,198 American citizens. Inevitably there were strident and persistent calls for retaliation – all of which Wilson resisted. There was, he said, in a moment of uncharacteristic whimsy, 'such a thing as being too proud to fight'.

Then, in a moment of madness, the German High Command committed an act of folly that made America's continued neutrality impossible. Arthur Zimmerman, the German Foreign Minister, cabled his ambassador in Mexico City with instructions to make an offer to Wilson's old adversary, Venustiano Carranza. If Mexico joined Germany in the war against America, the certain victory of the new alliance would be followed by the gift to Mexico of Texas, New Mexico and Arizona.

American troops arrived in Europe during the early winter of 1918 – in time to help in the rebuttal of Germany's last 'big push and to take part in the allies advance on Berlin'. Germany capitulated. An Armistice was signed on 11 November. Two months later, the leaders of the victorious allies met in Versailles to agree the terms of the peace treaty that was to be imposed on Germany. Georges Clemenceau of France and Lloyd George had a virtually identical view of the task that lay before them. The distribution of the spoils of war – German colonies in Africa and the Ottoman caliphate in the Middle East – had already been agreed, but needed the bogus respectability that would follow by their incorporation in a treaty. Germany's punishment must ensure that it was rendered incapable of ever again making war and must pay 'reparations' – a word that the allies invented to include the cost of going to war and the value of the damage that war had done to the nations that resisted its aggression. Woodrow Wilson arrived in France with a ready-made plan to secure and maintain world peace.

The dream, as it turned out to be, of an international alliance of countries that promised to preserve the peace, had excited Wilson long before the war broke out. Colonel House had attempted, in a tour of Europe during 1913, to test the plausibility of what the president called 'the great idea' and had been encouraged by sympathetic conversations with the Kaiser and Edward Grey, the British Foreign Secretary. The assassination of Archduke Franz Ferdinand at Sarajevo and its consequences did nothing to dampen Wilson's ardour for an international peace pact. As the war raged on, he spoke of his need to end it 'in peace without victory' and on 8 January 1918 he set out his plan for a new world order. The specific proposals included the re-creation of an independent Poland and self-determination for the subject peoples of the Ottoman and Austro-Hungarian empires. But it was the creation of an alliance for peace – to be known as the League of Nations – that caught the public imagination. The League was to encourage or enforce fourteen points that embodied and ensured the rule of international law. The Fourteen Points – as the plan was known – were submitted by Wilson to the Peace Conference as the blueprint for the guarantee of lasting peace.

Woodrow Wilson must have known that the Fourteen Points would not be acceptable to his allies. For over a hundred years, Britain had asserted the Royal Navy's right to stop and search any vessel anywhere in the world. His Britannic Majesty was not going to forgo that right because point two of an American plan for world peace guaranteed 'the freedom of the seas'. Point three – the removal of trade barriers – was equally unacceptable to a nation that maintained 'imperial preference' – tariffs imposed on imports from outside its empire. Seven of the Fourteen Points asserted the sanctity of 'self-determination' and 'autonomous development' – two imperatives that, had they been respected, would have denied France and Great Britain the spoils of victory.

Lloyd George and Clemenceau, despite their mutual dislike, were united in their opposition to the Fourteen Points, which the president of France chose to ridicule with the question, 'Why fourteen? The Good Lord required only ten.' But America had to be paid due respect and the price of that essential commodity was Woodrow Wilson's appointment as chairman of a sub-committee that examined the future relationship of the world's major nations. The committee drafted what it called the Covenant of the League of Nations. Nations that endorsed the covenant would be obliged to settle international disputes through the machinery of the International Court of Justice. Wilson presented the sub-committee's report to the sceptical French and British delegations with all the moral certainty that had characterised his determination to improve Princeton's academic record and to break up the trusts that forced up domestic prices in New Jersey. Unless there was agreement to create the League of Nations, he would not sign – and in consequence there could not be – a treaty.

Wilson had come to Versailles determined to resist the imposition of a punitive settlement on the defeated enemy. No doubt distracted by his preoccupation with the League, he had allowed Lloyd George to persuade him to support impositions that were consistent with the promise, made during the British general election, to 'squeeze Germany till the pips squeak'. When Lloyd George lost his nerve, Wilson argued for consistency – even though the penalties imposed on the defeated enemy violated the principles laid down by the Fourteen Points. However, Wilson was in a mood to celebrate success rather than to regret failure. He left France reassured by the belief that he had 'been present at one of the most vital things that has happened in the history of nations'.

His enthusiasm was not a reflection of American public opinion. The war being won and the cost counted, the attractions of isolation were reinforced by a reluctance ever again to become involved in distant wars. Yet by signing the League of Nations Treaty, America would make a solemn promise to come to the aid – if necessary, by force of arms – of countries that faced even the threat of aggression. Only a handful of senators favoured outright rejection, but forty or so asserted that commitment to the principles of the Charter amounted to the sacrifice of America's national sovereignty. Their support depended on the treaty being amended to ensure that

America could decide for itself whether or not it went to war.

So the hope of America signing the treaty rested on Wilson's ability to persuade and his willingness to compromise – two expedients that Wilson, even at his best, did not employ with great enthusiasm. But the president was not at his best. He had been ill in France with what was later thought to be Spanish flu and had suffered what, again weeks after it occurred, was diagnosed as a small stroke. On his return to America in the late summer of 1919, he pronounced himself fully fit and began what he intended to be a barnstorming tour of the West Coast. Most of his speeches were judged by both his staff and the attendant journalists to be failures. In late September, his health had so far deteriorated that the tour was cut short and Wilson returned to the White House. On 2 October he suffered a second stroke and his nationwide campaign in support of the treaty was over.

Some of Woodrow Wilson's closest friends insist that the second stroke – as well leaving him partially paralysed – did irrevocable damage to his political judgement. The alternative explanation of his conduct is that with age, what had once been a reluctance to temporise or dissimulate had become a pathological inflexibility. Whatever the cause, he began to argue that an amended treaty would certainly be no better than no treaty at all and might be worse. On 17 November 1919, he drafted a letter for circulation among his supporters in the Senate. It claimed that the amendment, which was tabled by Henry Cabot Lodge, the Leader of the Republican Senators, 'provides for nullification not ratification' and concluded with 'the sincere hope that the friends and supporters of the treaty will vote against the Lodge resolution of ratification'. By design, mistake or malevolence, the letter reached the press before it was received by most Democratic senators. Hopes of ratifying the treaty were dead.

It would have been reasonable to expect that a man of Wilson's age and health – with eight years in the White House, the consolation of a Nobel Peace Prize and a bitter humiliation behind him – would think that the time had come for dignified retirement. Not Woodrow Wilson. He announced his intention to seek a third term. For a time, it seemed that the Democrat National Convention would not even consider his nomination. He was eliminated on the first ballot. Bitter at rejection, he thought his destiny was unfulfilled. But, thanks to him, 'the great idea' of an alliance for peace made its first faltering steps from hope towards achievement.

Wilson's last year in the White House amounted to little more than marking time until his presidency was done. But, freed from the burdens of office, he made a recovery of sorts, bought a house in Washington and opened a law firm. The venture was always destined to fail. Wilson retreated into the dignified obscurity that is the usual refuge of retired presidents. Lloyd George paid him a visit. So did Georges Clemenceau. Respect was not an adequate substitute for the responsibility of office. So the bitterness at rejection remained. President Warren Harding's invitation to take the place of honour at the burial of the Unknown Soldier in Arlington Cemetery was declined.

To his wife and coterie of closest friends he talked about his work being the beginning of a century of progress rather than a transient success that briefly caught the headlines and public imagination and was then abandoned and forgotten. And that was surely true. Thanks to him, 'the great idea' of an alliance for peace made its first faltering steps from hope towards achievement and America began to develop the institutions and, more important, the psychology of a superpower. Woodrow Wilson was not a Washington, a Roosevelt or a Johnson. But he was one of the architects of modern America.

There is a sad postscript to the Woodrow Wilson story. In the years that followed his death, Princeton – conscious that he had made it one of the Ivy League's most respected universities – named new faculties in his honour. Most famous among them was the Woodrow Wilson School of Government. Because of his aberrant belief in racial segregation, the now–multi-racial institutions no longer bear his name.

Lord Hattersley is a historian, biographer and former Deputy Leader of the Labour Party. He served as a Member of Parliament from 1964 to 1997.

29

Warren G. Harding

4 March 1921 to 2 August 1923
Republican
Vice-president: Calvin Coolidge

By Adam Boulton

Full name: Warren Gamaliel Harding
Born: 2 November 1865, Blooming Grove, Ohio
Died: 2 August 1923, San Francisco, California
Resting place: Harding Tomb, Marion, Ohio
Library/Museum: Marion, Ohio
Education: Ohio Central College, Iberia, Ohio
Married to: Florence Mabel Kling, m. 1891 (1860–1924)
Children: One: Elizabeth Ann Christian (with Nan Britton)
Quotation: 'America's present need is not heroics, but healing; not nostrums but normalcy.'

'I KNOW ABOUT THAT woman on K Street!' America's long-disregarded twenty-ninth president first came to my notice thanks to the dramatised fury of his betrayed First Lady in a tawdry 1980s TV mini-series. I was living nearby on Q St Northwest, Washington, DC at the time. A century after his inauguration, when he is remembered, Warren Gamaliel Harding is mocked as 'the worst president' and, even more frequently, 'America's Horniest President'. He is discounted for fathering at least one child with mistresses, while his explicit love letters laced with cringeworthy poetry are more likely to be quoted than his political speeches:

> I love your poise of perfect thighs
> When they hold me in Paradise . . .
> I love the rose your garden grows
> Love seashell pink that over it glows.

Yet in 1920, when he was elected to the White House, Harding received the largest personal plurality for a century, winning 60.3 per cent of the popular vote and 404 seats in the Electoral College compared to his Democratic opponent's 127. His beloved Republican Party made big gains in both Houses of Congress, regaining firm control of the Senate after a decade of bitter splits. 'It wasn't a landslide, it was an earthquake,' moaned Joseph Tumulty, private secretary to the outgoing Democratic president Woodrow Wilson.

Less than three years later, when Harding died in office aged fifty-seven while on a trans-continental speaking tour, he was still one of the most popular presidents ever. There was a national outpouring of grief. More than three million people turned out to watch his funeral train make its way from California via the District of Columbia back to his home state of Ohio. Three of the industrialists who made modern America – Thomas Edison, Henry Ford and Harvey Firestone – joined the mourners at Marion Cemetery in August 1923.

By 1931, however, the two Republican presidents who followed Harding – his vice-president Calvin Coolidge and Herbert Hoover, his Commerce Secretary – were reluctant to take part in the dedication of the completed Harding Tomb because of the scandals that had come to light following Harding's death. In the end Coolidge stayed away but Hoover attended and participated.

In 1929, his Secretary of the Interior, Albert Bacon Fall, became the first US Cabinet minister to be sent to prison, for accepting bribes over the privatisation of three federally owned oil wells, including the Teapot Dome concession in Wyoming, which gave the scandal its name. Two years before that, Nan Britton published the first presidential kiss-and-tell memoir, *The President's Daughter*. Britton alleged that Harding had fathered her daughter Elizabeth while a US senator and continued to enjoy trysts with her in a closet off the Oval Office, while a functionary stood guard against the appearance of the First Lady. DNA tests in 2015 confirmed Harding's paternity.

The paradox of Harding's popularity and his subsequent fall from grace says more about the vantage points in time from which he is looked at than about the man himself. Harding was neither the lazy, priapic buffoon dismissed today, nor the ingenuous accidental president he pretended to be. He was an ambitious and hard-working career politician from the so-called 'Presidential State' of Ohio.

Harding was a leader at a hinge moment in American history, when the US emerged from the Great War as the reluctant world superpower and struggled at home with rapid social change, from race relations to industrialisation to alcohol to women's rights. Harding recognised, experienced and addressed the epochal challenges confronting his country, domestically and abroad.

He was a president who faced in two directions, attempting to accommodate traditional Republican prejudices to the rapidly evolving future of the US in the twentieth century – albeit habitually seeking compromise, with a small 'c', at a time of intense constitutional activism. As he wrote to Harry Daugherty: 'I think you know me well enough to know that I incline to a middle of the road course.' (One of his critics on Capitol Hill was less flattering, diagnosing 'that vertebral weakness which is the one material infirmity in his character.')

Harding benefited from luck and the misfortunes of others, but not without hard work. His standpat Republican conservatism was complemented by his openness to changing times. He was one of the first in his town to own an automobile. He was in the first batch of US senators elected by the popular vote rather than through party patronage, going on to secure the presidency in the first federal election in which women had equal suffrage. He was the first serving president to visit Alaska.

He was also the first, and so far only, newspaper editor to win the White House. His campaign was the first to comprehensively exploit modern media techniques. Thanks to the PR guru Albert Lasker and heavy spending by RNC chairman, Will Hays, newsreels, telemarketing, and 'grip and grin' handshake photo opportunities with out-of-state supporters were unleashed on the electorate. Once in the White House, he was the first president to install a radio there and the first to use the new medium to broadcast to the nation. He and his Commerce Secretary Herbert Hoover were the first to attempt to encourage and regulate broadcasting and aviation.

The US Census in the year Harding became president pinpointed change. For the first time 'the average American' lived in an urban setting, not a rural one. Harding followed this trajectory himself, but as the British polymath Andrew Sinclair wrote in his biography *The Available Man*, published after Harding's papers became newly available in the early 1960s, Warren Harding rose to power riding on the nostalgic 'myths' Americans treasured about their post-Civil War democracy: 'of the Country Boy, the Self-Made Man, of the Presidential State, of the Political Innocent, of the Guardian Senate, of America First, of the Dark Horse, of the Smoke-filled Room, of the Solemn Referendum and of The Best Minds'.

Warren Harding's roots conformed to the type of many presidents who had preceded him since the reconstruction. He was the eldest of eight children in a staunchly abolitionist WASP (White Anglo-Saxon Protestant) family with antecedents in Great Britain and Holland. The future president's father Tryon, a sometime farmer and schoolteacher who eventually became a medical practitioner, would outlive him. His mother Phoebe was a state-licensed midwife.

The family moved a short distance from the country into the small town of Marion in Warren's late teens. On graduating from two years of college where his only distinction was being good at spelling long words, eighteen-year-old Warren raised $300 to buy the least successful of Marion's three newspapers, the *Marion Daily Star*. A free pass on the railroad was the top perk for the budding editor and publisher's political ambitions. He used it to attend the 1884 Republican National Convention.

Marion was a Democratic town surrounded by Republican counties. Harding, a lifelong believer that thriving businesses were the key to his country's future, was a natural Republican, and he inclined his newspaper – which had previously been sympathetic to the Democrats – towards the party, expanding it with a new, overtly partisan, weekly edition. His newspaper business only really prospered after his wife Florence, a divorcee five years older than Warren, took over its financial management. Providentially, the population of Marion grew from three thousand to thirty thousand during Harding's proprietorship.

Warren Harding was considered emollient, charming and strikingly good looking. 'He was a handsome dog, a little above medium height, with a swarthy skin, a scathing eye and was meticulously clad in mourning clothes with a red geranium in his boutonniere, and he had the harlot's voice of the old-time political orator,' William Allen White, an ally of Theodore Roosevelt, conceded through gritted teeth when Harding arrived in the US Senate. 'I distrusted him . . . He represented the tip of the salient on the right.'

It was Harding's good fortune to hail from Ohio, the Buckeye (Horse Chestnut) State. Many currents in America blended there from east, west, north and south. What had been a predominantly agrarian state was rapidly industrialising along with the east coast. Ohio was also a melting pot, attracting German, Irish and Italian immigrants, with an established African American community.

The state's favourite sons had accounted for seven of the twelve presidents since 1869. Harding would be the eighth and, so far, last Ohio president. He climbed the state's promising greasy poll diligently, friendly to all Republicans, and trying to stay clear of bosses and factions. Two terms as state senator were followed by election as lieutenant governor. His emerging national profile led William Howard Taft to ask him to deliver his nomination speech at the 1912 Republican Convention. Harding's silver-tongued oratory was in demand, though he never seemed to say much, relying on repetition and alliteration. Thanks to Harding, the useful word 'Bloviate' entered the American lexicon – 'an army of pompous phrases moving across the landscape in search of an idea' as defined by Woodrow Wilson's son-in-law and Treasury Secretary William McAdoo.

'I found him like a turtle sunning himself on a log, and I pushed him into the water,' was Harry Daugherty's account of Harding's decision to run for national office in the US Senate. Harding's charm and luck were crucial as, for the first time, both state Republicans and then Ohio, statewide, were holding votes to choose their next senator. Harding's 'sweetness and light' style won him the primary against an Old Guard candidate. His next stroke of luck was to have a Roman Catholic as his Democratic opponent at a time of growing nativist anxiety.

'No one could be as much a senator as Harding looked' was soon a *bon mot* on Capitol Hill. Here again, Harding avoided controversy by giving all sides the impression that he agreed with them. Pledging to follow the wishes of his state, he supported the Nineteenth Amendment for women's suffrage and the Eighteenth Amendment to prohibit the liquor trade. Harding was a drinker, but the Anti-Saloon League was powerful in Ohio. His uncharacteristic stab at partisanship misfired badly when he attempted a smear suggesting falsely that he had evidence that President Wilson had mishandled the war effort.

In the presidential election cycle of 1920, six sometime presidents jockeyed for office. Events and timing favoured Harding again. President Woodrow Wilson's hopes of re-election for a third term were effectively ended by a severe stroke in October 1919. Former president Theodore Roosevelt was favourite for the Republican nomination, having quit his breakaway Progressive Party, but died unexpectedly in January 1919. This contest proved too soon for three other future presidents. Teddy's cousin Franklin Delano ran as the vice-presidential nominee on the unsuccessful Democratic ticket. Massachusetts governor Calvin Coolidge would become Harding's running mate and successor, with Herbert Hoover joining Harding's Cabinet.

First, Harding had to secure the nomination at the Republican Convention. He arrived in Chicago as an outsider dark horse candidate. He came sixth in the initial ballot of delegates. Days and nights of hard bargaining followed in 'smoke-filled rooms' – the first time that cliché of machine politics entered common parlance. Harding was despondent, 'dishevelled, with a two-day beard, a little drunk, his eyes bloodshot', but his wife Florence rallied him: 'Give up? Not until the convention is over. Think of your friends in Ohio.'

Senators, bosses and other grandees thought they were in control, but most delegates were unbound. Popular suffrage rescued Harding again, along with the fallback tradition of the Republican candidate coming from Ohio: ten of the last thirteen presidential nominees had done so. Fortuitously, Senator Harding was also the only Republican from Ohio in high office that summer. Many harkened to the appeal of the state's delegation leader: 'Say, boys and girls too – why not name as the candidate the man whose record is the platform of the party.'

Harding pulled ahead only on the ninth deadlocked ballot, but won overwhelmingly on the tenth. Anxious to head home on a Saturday afternoon, the delegates quickly elected Calvin Coolidge as their vice-presidential nominee.

The Democrats also struggled to find a strong candidate, eventually alighting on Governor James M. Cox. Almost incredibly, American voters faced a choice for president between two newspaper proprietors from Ohio; the differences being that Cox was colourless, physically unappealing and much richer than Harding. Excessive wealth was considered an electoral disadvantage back then.

The Republican nominee stayed mainly at home in Marion for the campaign, using many aspects of the mass media to get out his message. He built a bungalow for journalists opposite his McKinley-esque front porch, and would frequently go over to shoot the breeze, ever mindful, as a newspaperman himself, of deadlines and the hunger for a story. Once, while he was talking to his long-time mistress Carrie Phillips on the porch, household items, starting with a feather duster and ending with a piano stool, were hurled out of a window in her direction, presumably by Mrs Harding. It was also noted that Phillips's husband's store downtown was one of the few not decorated with bunting in support of the local boy.

During the campaign there were racist smears against Harding, alleging that he had black ancestry. Leaflets depicting the White House with the caption 'Uncle Tom's Cabin?' were distributed and a respected Ohio college professor published what he claimed was evidence, laced with racist epithets, that Harding had a black great-grandmother. The smear was widely believed, with Harding's own father-in-law, the German-speaking Amos Kling, remarking, 'My daughter has married a n_ _ _ _ _ but he's a smart n_ _ _ _ _.'

Harding said nothing. The Democrats were the party of segregation in the South. The black vote went Harding's way, as did those of the immigrant communities offended by Wilson's internationalist foreign policy. Germans and Italians thought Wilson too harsh on the old country, Russians not hard enough on the Reds, and the Irish resented his wartime alliance with the British. After Wilson's long absence in Europe at the Versailles peace negotiations, Harding promised that 'the next American president will stay in America'.

Republican Party Chairman Will Hays outspent the Democrats four-fold on the national campaign, a record total of over eight million dollars. Nan Britton received more than $20,000 hush money from the Republicans.

Harding won handsomely with the homely slogans 'Return to Normalcy' and 'Let's be done with wiggle and wobble'. Turnout was below 50 per cent for the first time in a century, but this was most likely due to Harding being the runaway favourite by the time voting started and because women proved hesitant in using their newly granted right to vote.

The twenty-ninth president was the first sitting senator to be elected to the White House. He was inaugurated in a modest ceremony the following March. He quickly snubbed his would-be patrons in the Senate with his Cabinet appointments. The top jobs went to 'Great Minds' rather than party hacks. They were expected to think and act independently. Charles Evans Hughes, who resigned temporarily from the US Supreme Court, became Secretary of State; the billionaire banker Andrew Mellon went to the Treasury; and Herbert Hoover, who had served in the Wilson administration, to Commerce.

However, Harding gave way to his desire to please with other appointments. He imported 'the Ohio Gang' to Washington, DC. Their corrupt actions would be partly responsible for his posthumous disgrace. Harry M. Daugherty, who would be implicated but not convicted in the Teapot Dome scandal, was made US Attorney General. His first action was to ask for control of redistributing property confiscated during the war. Another crony would later tarnish the establishment of veterans services begun by Harding, who insisted that black professionals should be employed in veterans hospitals and in the Federal Service.

Harding decided to address the race question in a notable speech delivered before a segregated audience in Birmingham, Alabama. The Blacks cheered and the Whites stayed silent as he argued that 'politically and economically there need be no occasion for great and permanent differentiation, for limitations of the individual's opportunity, provided that on both sides there shall be recognition of the absolute divergence in things social and racial'. Harding proposed legislation to make lynching a federal crime and managed to steer it through the House of Representatives, although it fell in the Senate.

Harding was elected on a platform opposing American participation in Wilson's League of Nations, although he had cautiously supported the idea earlier. He objected to Article X, which, like Article 5 of the NATO treaty, could potentially force America into another war automatically. In spite of their 'America First' mantra, Hughes and he engaged in international diplomacy, proposing to join in the World Court on a voluntary basis and hosting a successful Washington Disarmament Conference where the US, Britain and Japan were among countries who agreed to cut their battleship fleets. Unlike Wilson, Harding deliberately included senior senators from both sides of the aisle in the US negotiating team, thus ensuring speedy ratification of the treaty.

In the 1920 election, the Socialist candidate Eugene V. Debs had managed to garner 3.4 per cent of the vote while imprisoned for opposing the war effort. President Harding had this founder of the 'Wobblies' (the Industrial Workers of the World) released and invited him for what turned out to be a cordial visit to the White House.

As an editor, Harding was said to leave his office at Christmas time with pockets stuffed full of gold coins to give to the less fortunate. He believed in personal charity, but he and Treasury Secretary Mellon opposed handouts, notably to veterans and farmers. They cut taxes and raised tariffs instead. By the time Harding died, the American economy was booming, although it is argued that the measures taken helped precipitate the Great Depression.

The president's pleasures included golf, yachting, drinking, poker and, of course, women – those last three often at the House in

K Street, laid on for the Ohio Gang by a lobbyist. Yet, long-serving White House aides reported that Harding worked harder than any other president they had observed.

Unwittingly contributing to his poor posthumous reputation, he was also prone to self-doubt and depression, the first to agree with grandees who looked down on his lack of education, and, in their view, intellect. In his memoirs, the president of Columbia University and Nobel Peace Prize-winner Nicholas Murray Butler recalls being invited to the White House at short notice in the early summer of 1923. He never found out the particular thing Harding said he wanted to discuss, but records the president damning himself with the words: 'I am not fit for this office and never should have been here.'

Like others, Butler noted that Harding seemed to have some sort of premonition of approaching death around this time. The president wrote a will and sold the *Marion Star* paper for a generous price of more than half a million dollars. He and his wife had previously nursed each other through serious illnesses, in his case due to a weak heart. At the Chicago Convention, Florence had already warned melodramatically: 'I can see but one word written over the head of my husband if he is elected and that word is "tragedy".'

Harding's final 'Voyage of Understanding', as those planning his re-election bid billed it – a 15,000-mile speaking tour of America including the trailblazing visit to Alaska – ground to a halt in California when his health gave way. He died in his hotel bed while Florence was reading a favourable newspaper article headlined 'A Calm Review of a Calm Man'. His last words were, 'That's good! Go on, read some more.' The enduring strength of the marriage between Warren and Florence, who herself died little more than a year later, is another aspect of his life that is often misunderstood. There were even unfounded suggestions that she and his personal doctor, from Ohio naturally, had poisoned the president.

President Harding was a colourful Jazz Age figure, who partici-pated fully in the hypocritical self-indulgence of the Prohibition era. His term coincided with the publication of major American works of fiction. Many saw parallels between him and the small-town boosters in Sinclair Lewis's novels *Main Street* and, above all, *Babbitt*. F Scott Fitzgerald lampooned him openly as the supremely average president Jerry Frost in the play *The Vegetable*, which flopped on Broadway. Fitzgerald can hardly have known that 'Jerry' was Harding's pet name for his penis in his love letters, but the lines 'I don't want to be President. I never asked to be President' echo Harding's complaint: 'I haven't had a happy moment in this job.'

Harding was better than that. There were significant achievements during his brief thirty-month presidency that helped to stabilise his country. Fitzgerald's masterpiece, *The Great Gatsby*, published in 1925, is set in the summer of 1922. There is something of Warren Harding in its Great American Anti-Hero – the elegant, snobbishly despised, self-made Joe Average from Nowheresville, mid-West, complete with a murky past and misguided love life.

During the 1920s, America built monuments as if to consolidate its burgeoning imperial status. President Harding presided over the dedication of the iconic statue of the greatest Republican president at the Lincoln Memorial. He wept in Arlington Cemetery at the burial of America's first Unknown Soldier. The Greek-style Harding Tomb would be the last of its kind. Presidential libraries were instigated instead. It is a mark of America's ambivalence about its first president in modern times that the Harding Presidential Library was still not opened officially a century after he took office.

Adam Boulton is a British broadcaster and journalist specialising in UK and US politics, mainly for Sky News, TV-am and The Sunday Times. *His books are* Tony's Ten Years *and* Hung Together. *He wrote on David Cameron for* The Prime Ministers.

30
Calvin Coolidge

2 August 1923 to 4 March 1929
Republican
Vice-president: Vacant 1923–25, Charles G. Dawes 1925–29

By Leo McKinstry

Full name: John Calvin Coolidge Jr
Born: 4 July 1872, Plymouth Notch, Vermont
Died: 5 January 1933, Northampton, Massachusetts
Resting place: Plymouth Notch Cemetery, Vermont
Library/Museum: Northampton, Massachusetts
Education: Amherst College
Married to: Grace Anna Goodhue, m. 1905 (1879–1957)
Children: Two: John and Calvin
Quotation: 'No man ever listened himself out of a job.'

TACITURNITY IS NOT a quality usually associated with politicians. Verbal fluency and an enthusiasm for discourse are meant to be central ingredients of their craft. But Calvin Coolidge was a remarkable exception to this pattern. Throughout his career in public office, which culminated in his presidency during the 1920s, he was renowned for his terseness. This brevity with words brought him the nickname of 'Silent Cal' and remained a source of astonishment to the political observers. The journalist Edward Lowry wrote that Coolidge 'is the oddest and most singular apparition that Washington has ever known: a politician who does not, will not and seemingly cannot talk. A well of silence, a centre of stillness.'

His reticence extended from the political realm into his social life. Perhaps the most famous story about Coolidge refers to the occasion at a White House dinner, when a gushing female guest, sitting beside him and aware of his reputation, said, 'You must talk to me, Mr President. I have made a bet today that I can get more than two words out of you.' Coolidge looked at her for a moment, then replied laconically, 'You lose.' When the writer and wit Dorothy Parker was told of his death, she asked, 'How could they tell?'

Yet there was a fundamental paradox about Coolidge's restraint. Although a shy man, he was not an inarticulate one. When he chose to, he could be a fine, lucid speaker, who was all the more powerful because of his succinct prose. In her superb biography of Coolidge, the historian Amity Shlaes described how in 1923 he delivered his first presidential speech to Congress 'in artillery style' with a 'clear voice', impressing not just his audience in Washington, but millions of listeners in their homes on the new medium of radio. Indeed, it was partly his gift for spartan, punchy rhetoric that had propelled him so far in politics as he moved up the Republican hierarchy.

Nor was he a reclusive president, despite his habitual reserve. In fact, he was a highly visible figure who successfully cultivated the media and was happy to exploit the new arts of public relations. During his 67 months in office, he held no fewer than 520 press conferences, gave a radio broadcast to the public at least once a month and enjoyed being photographed by the press, sometimes even dressing up for the camera, as when he wore a cowboy hat and leg protectors on a visit to Dakota in 1927, prompting one critic to wail, 'The President of the United States has become a pitiful puppet of publicity.'

The contradictions in Coolidge did not end there. His verbal frugality matched his financial outlook. 'I am for economy and after that I am for more economy,' he once said, words that encapsulated his insistence on prudence in both his government and his own domestic life. Yet he presided over an era of prosperous excess, as the 'Roaring Twenties' heralded unprecedented consumption and stock market rises. Similarly, Coolidge harked back to the austere, old-fashioned values of his rural Vermont upbringing, yet during his presidency America saw an astonishing embrace of modernity, reflected in aviation, architecture, energy, the motor car, the cinema, engineering and the radio. With a wide-eyed boyish streak, Coolidge was fascinated by technological advances. Incongruously, Silent Cal was the first president to appear in a talking film – a recording of one of his own speeches – while perhaps the highlight of his time in the White House was the homecoming welcome he gave to the brave aviator Charles Lindbergh after he made his solo flight across the Atlantic in 1927.

Paradoxes can be found everywhere. Once, when asked if he had any interests, he replied, 'holding office', and, over the years, Coolidge ran for elected positions seventeen times, probably a higher total than any other president. Yet he dramatically quit the presidency before seeking a second full term, an election he would have won easily. He deeply believed in the conservative traditions of liberty and small government, yet he accepted Prohibition, one of the greatest intrusions on freedom in American history. He was praised for his racial tolerance, particularly over the rights of Native Americans, and was even compared to Abraham Lincoln after a speech that praised the black contribution to the USA, but he did little to counter the revival of the Ku Klux Klan in the 1920s. Nor, despite his severe objections, did he veto legislation that specifically excluded Japanese immigrants from America. Even his marriage had dichotomy at its heart, for in contrast to his dour, clipped manner, his attractive wife Grace was warm and vivacious. 'I don't see how that sulky, red-haired little man ever won that charming, pretty woman,' said one Washington hostess.

In all its complexities, Coolidge's character was forged in the tough environment of Plymouth Notch, a remote hamlet in Vermont, where he was born on 4 July, Independence Day, in 1872. He inherited many of his traits, especially duty, perseverance, respectability and abstemiousness, from his father John, a storekeeper, farmer and public servant. His mother Victoria was more poetic and romantic, but she died when Calvin was just twelve. 'The greatest grief that can come to a boy came to me,' he wrote later. For the rest of his life, he carried with him a locket of her hair, and his first action on entering the White House was to place her photograph on his desk in the Oval Office. This tragedy was compounded five years later when his beloved sister Abigail also died, probably from appendicitis.

During his youth, Coolidge gave little indication that he was destined for the political summit. At high school he was a diligent but not outstanding student. Then, at Amherst College, he was initially classed as an '*ouden*' – from the Greek word meaning 'nothing' – because of his academic, sporting and social limitations. In his final year, however, he impressed not only with his oratorical skill but also with his historical writing, winning a national prize for an essay on the US Constitution. After graduation, having served his apprenticeship in a law firm, he set up his own successful legal practice in Northampton, Massachusetts. The city was also the base for the start of his political career. Following his father's example of long public service, he won his first election as a Northampton councilman in 1899, rising inexorably over the next sixteen years to the local General Court, the Mayoralty, the Massachusetts State Senate, and then, in 1915, the presidency of the Senate. His short inaugural address in this post was typical of his style. In just forty-four words, he exhorted his colleagues to 'be brief, above all things be brief', words that he elevated into a political principle. By then he was widely recognised as the best vote winner in the state. His growing stature enabled him to win two terms as the lieutenant governor from 1916, and, from 1919, to serve as the Governor of Massachusetts. Although a committed Republican, reflecting the Plymouth Notch conservative ethos of self-reliance, he was neither a partisan nor a reactionary but backed several progressive causes, such as women's suffrage, the expansion of education and improved conditions for labour.

Coolidge also found domestic contentment, when in 1905 he married Grace Goodhue, a teacher for the deaf in Northampton. 'Other men found her stunning and were stunned to find she favoured the quiet lawyer,' wrote Shlaes in her biography of Coolidge. Helped by Grace's generous personality, and her ability, through her profession, to cope with silences, theirs was mostly a happy marriage that produced two sons, John and Calvin. With his brusqueness and quick temper, however, Coolidge could be a difficult husband, sometimes treating Grace with coldness or indifference. He himself admitted that he could be 'hard to get along with'.

He might have remained in state politics had it not been for an event that gave him a national profile and transformed his political fortunes. In 1919, the police in Boston went on strike, fuelling serious public disorder and crime in the city. As Massachusetts governor, Coolidge took a tough line, which saw the state guard mobilised and the strikers dismissed from their jobs. In one of his most famous utterances, he declared that 'there is no right to strike against public safety by anybody, anywhere, at any time'. In the febrile mood of the country, where there was genuine concern about revolution, he became a hero. The *Boston Herald* described him as 'the pilot who weathered the storm'. Even the Democrat president Woodrow Wilson sent him his congratulations. The widespread admiration for his robust stance encouraged him to seek the Republican nomination for the presidency in 1920. At the party's convention in Ohio, he failed in that bid, as the gregarious, loquacious Ohio senator Warren Harding emerged triumphant. But when it came to the vote on Harding's running mate, the name of Coolidge was yelled by one state delegation before it spread like wildfire through the convention centre. By popular acclaim, Coolidge had forced himself onto the Republican ticket.

The pair had a landslide victory with over 60 per cent of the vote in November 1920, one of the most lopsided contests in history. Yet the vice-presidency turned out to be a frustrating time for Coolidge. Confined to ceremonial duties in the Senate, he had little influence on policy nor much support from colleagues. In particular, Henry Cabot Lodge, the grand senator from Massachusetts, held him in open contempt. Some lunchtimes, the lonely figure of Coolidge could be seen eating his home-made sandwiches in a corner of Congress on his own.

The victims of snobbery and slights, he and Grace did not even have their own official accommodation but had to live in Washington's

Willard Hotel, whose bills Coolidge found exorbitant on his $12,000 annual salary. Both animal lovers, they were banned from keeping pets in their quarters, with the result that Grace, in her distressed isolation, even resorted to feeding the mice for some company. Nor did her husband enjoy any fame, despite his position. One magazine said that he 'presided like a sphinx' over the Senate. His anonymity was graphically illustrated by an incident in the spring of 1922, when there was a fire at the Willard Hotel and all the guests were evacuated. Once the emergency was over, Coolidge tried to re-enter the building, only to be stopped by a security guard. 'I am the vice-president,' he protested. 'Vice-president of what?' asked the guard.

But Coolidge soon had his unexpected revenge. On the night of 2 August 1923, while staying in his old family home at Plymouth, he learned that President Harding had died suddenly from a heart attack during a tour of the west. The news was brought to Coolidge by telegram, since there was no phone in the house. Nor was there any electricity, so his father, a local notary, swore his son into the office at 2:47 a.m. by the light of a kerosene lamp. The homely, modest scene became an enduring symbol of his unpretentious presidency. With astonishing coolness, after the ceremony had been completed, Coolidge then went back to bed and back to sleep.

Once he was ensconced in Washington, his initial aim was to maintain 'meticulous continuity' with Harding's policies and personnel, including most of his Cabinet. Differences did assert themselves, however, as Coolidge focused relentlessly on tax cuts as a means of enhancing prosperity. Although he was unable to secure the agreement of Congress to his entire fiscal package in December 1923, he was able to signal clearly his intentions, with his Revenue Act reducing the top rate of tax from 58 to 46 per cent. He also supported two other welcome measures: the Washington Naval Treaty, which attempted to halt a maritime arms race; and the award of US citizenship to all Native Americans. In addition, his natural integrity, helped by his membership of the Congregational Church, brought a higher moral tone to the White House after the Harding years, which, as a series of scandals was revealing, had been tainted by cronyism and corruption. Coolidge proceeded slowly with his investigations into the squalid, hard-drinking culture of his predecessor's rule, but the sheer force of his unblemished personality restored public trust in the White House. The writer Alice Longworth, daughter of Theodore Roosevelt, memorably wrote that the atmosphere under the new occupants was 'as different as a New England front parlour is from a backroom in a speakeasy'.

At first Coolidge was regarded as nothing more than a stop-gap. 'If the country has reached the state where Coolidge is the right sort of person for president, then any office boy is qualified to be chief executive,' sneered the progressive Harold Ickes. Such critics badly underestimated Coolidge, whose pithy broadcasts, detached style, pro-business beliefs and air of personal rectitude suited the mood of the moment. Moreover, he was a canny operator, with sufficient self-confidence and subtlety to thwart all his potential challengers, whose number included the car-maker Henry Ford. As the historian David Greenberg has written: 'Coolidge's team carefully stage-managed' the Republican Convention in Cleveland, Ohio, in June 1924, turning the event 'into a veritable coronation'. Coolidge easily saw off the last of his opponents, Hiram Johnson and the progressive Robert La Follette, to win the nomination on the first ballot. Soon afterwards, a far more intense contest for the vice-presidential nomination saw Charles Dawes, the distinguished banker, diplomat and financial administrator, elected as his running mate after three ballots. The smoothness of the Republican process was in stark contrast to the chaos of the Democrats' convention in New York, which was still in stalemate after no fewer than 103 ballots before a compromise candidate, John W. Davis, was accepted.

But after this promising start, Coolidge's campaign for re-election was suddenly overshadowed by personal tragedy, when a month afterwards his second son, Calvin Junior, aged just sixteen, died after contracting a lethal infection in his foot while playing tennis on the White House lawn. In the age before antibiotics, there was no treatment for such a problem, and his parents had to watch in agony as their child slid away. Coolidge was shattered by the loss, which accentuated his introspection and lessened his affection for office. 'When he went, the power and the glory of the Presidency went with him,' he wrote later.

Nevertheless, he proceeded to win an overwhelming victory in November, gaining 54 per cent of the popular vote against an opposition that was badly split between Davis and La Follette, who decided to run on a radical progressive ticket. There had been some concerns among Republicans that Coolidge might be rhetorically outgunned on the campaign trail; during one radio test, his voice was so quiet that the equipment had to be adjusted to pick it up. But Coolidge's message of prosperity, combined with thrifty management, resonated across America. The slogan 'Keep Cool with Coolidge' proved a winner. His 15.7 million votes compared to 8.39 million for Davis and only 4.8 million for La Follette. He was now back in the White House on his own terms.

Over the next four years, the dominant theme of his presidency was the pursuit of cuts in both taxation and expenditure. He triumphantly succeeded in that goal in partnership with his Treasury Secretary Andrew Mellon, the rich Pittsburgh industrialist who was another taciturn individual; it was joked that the two men communicated largely by pauses. They were certainly effective. By the end of his presidency the top rate had been reduced to 25 per cent and only the highest 2 per cent of earners paid any federal income tax at all. At the same time, with the economy booming and revenues buoyant, the budget surplus grew from $100 million in 1925 to $599 million in 1927. The intensity of Coolidge's focus on this issue was revealed when, in recognition of his devotion to animals, he was given two lion cubs by Johannesburg Zoo. He called the pair 'Budget Bureau' and 'Tax Reduction', and insisted to their White House keepers that they be kept exactly the same weight.

His fiscal success reinforced his conviction that small government was best. Hostile to large-scale federal intervention, he believed that his duty was to create the right environment for enterprise to flourish. 'The chief business of the American people is business,' he told a group of editors in 1925. He had little faith in regulation or legislative activism. 'It is much more important to kill bad bills than pass good ones,' he argued. In his mind, subsidies were as harmful as federal bureaucracy. Even though he hailed from a farming background, he vetoed the bill put forward by Republican Congressmen Gilbert Haugen and Charles McNary to provide more government support to agriculture, claiming that modernisation would be more beneficial. In the same vein, when there were severe floods in Mississippi and Vermont, he refused to become involved in the rescue efforts because he believed this was mainly a state, not a federal responsibility, though he did send his energetic Commerce Secretary Herbert Hoover, the supposed 'Wonder Boy' of the Cabinet, to both disaster areas.

Coolidge's passive approach was mirrored in his personal style at the White House. There was nothing frenetic about him as president. He took long naps in the afternoon and went to bed early in the evening. A good delegator, he trusted his Cabinet members to get on with their jobs. When the Secretary of Labor James J. Davis once submitted some papers to him, seeking presidential advice, Coolidge said to an assistant, 'You tell ol' man Davis that if he can't do his job, I'll get a new Secretary of Labor.' The journalist H.L. Mencken wrote that 'his ideal day is one in which nothing whatever happens'.

Contradicting his stern, icy image, Coolidge loved to play practical jokes in the White House, like pressing his bell to summon a staff member, then hiding under his desk or behind the curtains so that, amid mounting alarm, he could not be found. For all his shyness, he relished meeting the ordinary public, including visitors to the White House. He often shook thousands of hands a day, and remained hugely popular across much of America. When he and Grace visited the town of Hammond in Indiana in 1927, fifty thousand people gathered to hear him give a lecture about conservative values and religious faith. Part of his secret was the sense of calm security that his government exuded. In 1926, the journalist Walter Lipmann wrote shrewdly that 'this active inactivity meets the mood and certain of the needs of the country admirably. It suits all the business interests to be left alone. And it suits all those who have become convinced that government in this country has become dangerously complicated and top heavy.'

But by mid-1927, even his minimalist routine was becoming a burden. Concerned about his health, still grieving his lost son, devoid of any lust for power, he announced, without consulting Grace, that he would not run again for the presidency in 1928. Given both his connection to the public and the prosperity of the economy, his move caused a severe national shock, but he refused to reverse his decision, anxious to be 'relieved of the pretensions and delusions of public life'.

His final period in office was not entirely fruitless, especially in foreign affairs, in which he had previously taken little interest.

Neither an isolationist nor interventionist, his attitude was essentially pragmatic. Before 1928, the main foreign achievement of his administration had been a deal negotiated by Charles Dawes to give Germany partial relief from post-war reparations. The last year of his presidency witnessed a number of developments, including: an agreement with France, concluded by his Secretary of State Frank Kellogg, to outlaw war as an instrument of diplomacy; the normalisation of ties with post-revolution Mexico; and an improvement of relations with Latin America, helped by Coolidge's trip to Cuba, his only visit overseas. But what had always mattered much more to him was the economy. Here he had an enriching story to tell. From 1921 to 1928, unemployment had been cut from 5.7 million to 1.8 million. Manufacturing was up by a third over this period, while iron and steel production had doubled. At the same time, the national debt had fallen from $28 billion to $17.65 billion.

On his departure, he was succeeded by Herbert Hoover, someone he had never liked. 'For six years he has given me unsolicited advice – all of it bad,' complained Coolidge. Hoover was soon engulfed by the stock market crash, followed by the Great Depression, events that cast a long shadow over Coolidge's economic legacy and his reputation for building prosperity. In fact, Coolidge himself had worried about the economy overheating during his final spell as president. 'Disaster' could be looming, he privately warned. Amid economic meltdown in the early 1930s, his retirement did not last long. Having written a dry autobiography as well as a syndicated newspaper column, he began to experience worsening health and fatigue. 'I no longer fit in with these times,' he told a friend. On 5 January 1933, just before Franklin Roosevelt's inauguration, he died from heart failure, aged just sixty. He never had the chance to express any view about the New Deal, which was the antithesis of his *laissez-faire* approach. In keeping with his character, his funeral was a simple one, with just two hymns and no eulogy. He left his entire estate to his beloved Grace.

Leo McKinstry is an author, historian and journalist. He appears regularly in the Spectator, New Statesman, Daily Express *and* Daily Mail. *He has also written twelve non-fiction books, including an award-winning biography of the UK Liberal prime minister Lord Rosebery.*

31

Herbert Hoover

4 March 1929 to 4 March 1933
Republican
Vice-president: Charles Curtis

By Robert Buckland

Full name: Herbert Clark Hoover
Born: 10 August 1874, West Branch, Iowa
Died: 20 October 1964, New York City
Resting place: Hoover Presidential Library, West Branch, Iowa
Library/Museum: West Branch, Iowa
Education: Friends Pacific Academy, Oregon; Stanford University
Married to: Lou Henry, m. 1899 (1874–1944)
Children: Two: Herbert Hoover Jr and Allan Henry Hoover
Quotation: 'This is not a showman's job. I will not step out of character.'

Mister Herbert Hoover
Says that now's the time to buy
So let's have another cup o' coffee
And let's have another piece o' pie!
(From 'Let's Have Another Cup of Coffee' by
Irving Berlin 1932)

WHEN PRESIDENT FRANKLIN Delano Roosevelt officially dedicated the vast concrete dam that sits on the Colorado River
on the Arizona–Nevada border in 1935, both he and Interior Secretary
Harold Ickes had a political objective in mind. They wanted the
Boulder Dam, as they called it, to be a reflection of the course of
US economic policy since the new administration took office in
1933. This was a shining example of what the federal government
could achieve with investment and energy; it was all part of the
New Deal that marked a decisive break with the *laissez-faire* policies
of the previous president. Yet the man who had actually brought
about this enormous project in the late 1920s, and during whose
presidency the work began, wasn't even invited to the ceremony. It
took a Joint Congressional Resolution in 1947 to give the massive
edifice its proper name: The Hoover Dam. In sharp contrast to such
reticence, Roosevelt and the Democrats were all too happy to see
the shanty towns of the Depression labelled 'Hoovervilles' in mock
tribute to their Republican opponent, and to continue to campaign
against the thirty-first president, long after he had left office, with
resultant damage to Herbert Hoover's reputation.

What a reputation it could have been. Elected by a landslide,
one of the greatest humanitarians of the age and a politician with
a successful Cabinet career under presidents of both parties, Herbert
Hoover made a fortune in mining in his twenties, living outside
the USA for lengthy periods as his family grew. Born to a Quaker
family in West Branch, Iowa, this man rose from the most humble
of backgrounds to preside over the greatest expansion in federal
government programmes in the history of the US up to that time,
in response to the onset of what became a horrendous economic
depression. He was the first president to have been born west of
the Mississippi and the first surveyor or engineer to enter the White
House since George Washington.

Born in a tiny cottage to Jesse and Huldah Hoover, the young Bertie Hoover did not have an easy childhood. Orphaned at ten, he was split from his siblings and adopted by his maternal uncle, who was superintendent of the Friends Pacific Academy in Newberg, Oregon. It was out in the far West that Hoover's essential character began to emerge. Industrious, self-disciplined, serious and with a Quaker reserve that had been exacerbated by the loss of his parents, this was a man who found expressions of emotion and affection very difficult. In small groups, however, he was a good communicator, with clear principles, yet also with the ability to compromise. Having already proved himself invaluable to his uncle in helping to manage the family land company in the state capital, Salem, Bert Hoover decided on two things in the late 1880s: first, that he would pursue a career in engineering that would require a degree; and second, that he was a progressive Republican. He had also acquired a love of fishing, which he never lost.

In the early 1890s, US senator Leland Stanford was using some of his railroad fortune to set up a new university near to Palo Alto, California. It caught Bert's imagination and he became a Geology and Mining student in Stanford's inaugural year of 1891. The entrance-exam process was not straightforward; he struggled with English composition and spelling. This persisted throughout his life, right through to his unfortunate misspelling of FDR's surname in a message to the president-elect during the 1932–33 transition period. This, however, was Stanford's very beginning and students were needed. They made the right decision, as Bert flourished. He excelled at his course, at student politics and even managed the university football team, before falling in love in his final year with the erudite and attractive Lou Henry, a fellow Iowan who was Stanford's first female Geology major and, in her turn, one of the most accomplished women ever to enter the White House as First Lady. It was in his summers, though, that Bert gained invaluable knowledge about surveying, when he worked for the US Geological Survey in the California Sierras for the well-known geologist, Ralph Lindgren, who said: 'Never have I had a more satisfactory assistant.'

Bert's graduation coincided with the economic 'panic' of the mid-1890s, which meant that he literally had to start at the bottom, taking a job as a 'mucker' working underground in the northern goldfields of California. It was then that he had his first break, with the French mining consultant Louis Janin. Working as his clerical assistant, Hoover made himself more than useful and was soon being remunerated handsomely.

It was on Janin's recommendation that Hoover went in 1897 to the goldfields of western Australia to work for Berwick Moreing, a British mining company with major global interests. The job specification had stated they were looking for someone of at least thirty-five. Quickly, however, the twenty-three-year-old Hoover was being called 'Chief' by his men, and his successful identification of the Sons of Gwalia mine as a profitable future source of gold meant that, by 1898, he was earning $15,000 a year, making him one of the world's leading mining engineers.

The next move was to China and, after he had married Lou in California on the way, the Hoovers arrived in Tianjin in spring 1899 just in time for the Boxer Rebellion. They both emerged unscathed with a few adventures along the way, and, after a not uncontroversial transfer from Chinese ownership of coal-mining operations in Kaiping, the Hoovers left China for London at the end of 1901, where his two sons were born and spent their early years. From then until the Great War, Hoover travelled the world as a roving partner and then consultant, building up a considerable fortune and the sort of foreign experience that no previous US president had ever acquired, but keeping in touch with his American base. The Hoovers were a serious couple. Their idea of relaxation was to entirely translate Georgius Agricola's sixteenth-century treatise on mining from a version of Latin into English, which took them five years. Even Hoover's beloved fishing took a back seat to this labour of love.

The outbreak of the First World War and the humanitarian crisis in Belgium proved to be his finest hour. After Hoover had success-fully organised the repatriation of thousands of Americans home from Britain and Europe in the early days of the war, the US ambassador in London suggested that he take on another, bigger project: the relief of hunger in Belgium. Hoover, spurred on by his deep Quaker sense of obligation to the next generation, set up and chaired the Commission for the Relief of Belgium, which fed and supported hundreds of thousands of children and families in Belgium and occupied northern France who were facing destitution. The fact that he did this unpaid, while securing millions of dollars in support from, among others, the British and French governments, speaks volumes for the man. He burnished his diplomatic credentials on both sides too, capped by Lord Kitchener's (politely declined) offer of a peerage and a Cabinet post as Minister for Munitions, if Hoover agreed to become a British citizen.

After successfully setting up and running the Food Administration on President Wilson's invitation to join the Cabinet after the US entered the war, and then as head of the international American Recovery Agency (ARA), providing food relief to Eastern Europe and vigorous political support for America's membership of the League of Nations, Hoover was establishing himself as a national figure in domestic affairs. When the ARA's federal mandate expired in mid-1919, Hoover carried it on as a private charity, and it brought aid to Germany, Austria and even the starving, fledgling Soviet Russia in the early 1920s. Millions of lives were saved by the intervention of the man who became known as 'The Great Humanitarian'.

By now, Hoover had become a contender for the presidency, and due to his service to Wilson, both parties thought they had a claim to him. Franklin Roosevelt, himself to be vice-presidential candidate for the Democrats in 1920, had sought to recruit Hoover to be at the top of the ticket, describing him as 'a wonder, and I wish we could make him president . . . there could not be a better one'. Hoover then made it clear to the world that he was, in fact, a Republican.

When President Harding offered Hoover a place in his Cabinet in 1921, he chose Commerce, a relatively new department but one that he led with vigour and expansiveness. It led to him be described as 'Secretary of Commerce and the undersecretary of Everything Else'. The department's reach soon extended into technology, safety standards and housing, to name but a few areas. Hoover once again showed his humanitarian credentials with his strong leadership on federal relief during the 1927 Mississippi floods, and ensured that the legislation to allow construction of the Hoover Dam could be passed.

After Coolidge's typically laconic decision not to run in 1928, Hoover's ascent to the Republican nomination was effortless. He stood in stark contrast to his Democrat opponent, New York governor and product of the Tammany Hall system, Al Smith. Smith, a robust 'wet' when it came to Prohibition and the first Roman Catholic candidate for president, was the original 'Happy Warrior', a nickname coined by FDR in his memorable 1924 convention nomination speech, but Smith's cheerful brand of urban politics, with one foot on the rail of the saloon bar and his campaign theme 'The Sidewalks of New York' was not what America, and particularly rural America, was looking for in that year of continued prosperity. In the 1928 presidential election, the very first elected office that Hoover had ever stood for, he won by 444 Electoral College votes to Smith's 87 and by 17 percentage points, carrying forty of the forty-eight states. In doing so, however, he had to allay suspicion of his political views by assuring the likes of Senator William Borah of Idaho that he would not buckle on Prohibition.

Hoover's Cabinet was very much in his mould, with only one member having held elected office. In a sign to business that there would be continuity at the top, Andrew Mellon continued as Treasury Secretary. The trouble was that in his mistrust of the political animal, engendered no doubt by his direct experience of the corrupt Harding administration, he managed to select a group of people singularly out of touch with ordinary Americans. This was to cost him dear in the years ahead.

Once installed in the White House, an energetic and driven Hoover adopted a demanding work schedule and made changes. He closed the White House stables, had a phone installed in the Oval Office, and let go of the presidential yacht. This was an industrious president; after rising at 6 a.m., a typical day involved a morning game of 'Hooverball' on the south lawn, and then desk-work from 8:30 a.m. through to past 6 p.m. The evenings were busy, as Lou Hoover always ensured that many guests were enter-tained at the White House.

Hoover lost no time in warning Wall Street about the danger of excessive speculation and in discouraging excessive tax avoidance too, marking a clear departure from his predecessor. The Federal Reserve increased interest rates in order to take the heat out of the spiral of speculation. This was a president who wanted to follow in the footsteps of Teddy Roosevelt's progressivism. Hoover expanded the civil service and made decisive moves on increased conservation, with greater federal parks and forests. He also took a close look at criminal justice, and started important prison reforms. Hoover launched a series of antitrust suits, more than under any prior president. His work to advance the rights of black people in education was significant, and he did more than anyone before to protect the interests of Native Americans, whose children he had played with as a boy in Iowa. As a final line drawn under the Teapot Dome scandal, he cancelled oil leases on federal land.

The Republicans enjoyed initial majorities in both Houses of Congress, but by the early 1930s, the Republican majority in the House had evaporated. It soon became clear that the Western Progressive caucus would increasingly call the shots in the Senate, too. Perhaps Hoover's greatest political mistake was to have encouraged moves to tariff reform and then to have called a special session of Congress in the first few months of 1929, but without the essential clarity or leadership. Politics abhors a vacuum, and it was promptly filled by Congressman Hawley, Senator Smoot, their protectionist tariff legislation, and the very noisy Senator Borah. By the time the president made a public statement on his wish for an element of flexibility in the proposed tariff regime, Senator Borah led the charge in attacking Hoover for presuming to interfere in congressional matters. Hoover declined to take up the debate and so the die was cast. In the words of one Republican congressman, 'He didn't know where the votes came from.' This was a president with neither a network on, nor experience of, Capitol Hill, and it showed, resulting in tariff reforms that sent the wrong signal at the wrong time to the world, heralding a wider move to protectionism at a time of economic recession.

The dramatic events in Wall Street during October 1929 are viewed as the moment when Hoover and the Republicans lost the 1932 election. Defeat, however, was not inevitable. More accurately, the Great Crash proved to be the political hinge of his presidency, after which things were never 'glad confident morning' again for him. Hoover, already keen to draw a line under Coolidge economics, worked immediately to contain the stock market crash and to protect the rest of the economy, by announcing new federal investment programmes and tax reductions. By the end of the year, he was being hailed as the man who had prevented contagion spreading to jobs and wages. The underlying facts, however, pointed to a decline in industrial activity and consumer spending in late 1929 with an upturn in 1930. This was still looking to be a bump in the road, rather than a calamitous downturn.

But 1930 brought only a hint of early promise and then, growing economic misery. A broiling summer in the South meant disaster for many farmers, and this time the continued decline in stocks was met by an inexorable rise in unemployment. By the beginning of 1931, five million Americans were out of work. Hunger was becoming a reality for many families. By the end of his second year in office, unemployment had risen further and there was more than a hint that the underlying instability of too many of America's tens of thousands of small banks was beginning to show.

It was at that point that Hoover made the political decision to use federal power as an adjunct to, not as a replacement for, state or private initiative. While his approach was a world away from Coolidge, his decision to veto bills to create more federal unemployment relief agencies and an infrastructure project at Muscle Shoals on the Tennessee River, and another to allow war veterans to borrow against compensation due, were examples of the political course that he had set. The veterans' bonus issue was to culminate in protests and unrest in Washington, DC in 1932, although the effect of this on Hoover's re-election prospects has been exaggerated.

There was another false economic dawn in early 1931, but the increasing woes being experienced by the major European economies, from Germany to Britain, brought home the reality that the US economy was not an impregnable island. Hoover's correct analysis was a moratorium on war debt, but thanks to French intransigence, this was watered down and proved insufficient to stem a financial collapse in Germany. To add to Hoover's misfortune, the drought of 1930 was repeated in 1931, piling more misery onto rural communities. The decision by Britain in September 1931 for sterling, still the world's leading reserve currency, to come off the gold standard meant that the flow of gold into the US soon became a flood the other way as international investors pulled out, and the value of British and German assets held by US banks collapsed.

This was the moment when recession became Depression, with unemployment soaring to over 23 per cent in 1932.

Hoover's banking plan in response to this calamity was hailed as the end of non-interventionism, and his decision to cut public spending and raise taxes marked a decisive break with the Coolidge–Mellon economics of the mid-1920s. His response in late 1931 culminated in what was the most successful and enduring of his initiatives, the Reconstruction Finance Corporation, providing financial loans to businesses, mortgage lenders, banks and railroads to get the system moving. The RFC is remembered as a key part of the New Deal, but it was all started by Hoover.

By the end of 1932, what had been a stock market crash had turned into a full-scale banking crisis. The near collapse of the banking system across the US was what brought the Great Depression to the doorstep. It wasn't just someone you knew who had lost their job, it was you and your family who had lost their income and savings. The widespread sense that, by then, Hoover was completely out of touch was reflected in Irving Berlin's lyrics for the opening number of his 1932 musical *Face The Music* that are quoted at the beginning of this chapter. What really nailed the Hoover presidency, however, wasn't Roosevelt or the Depression, but Prohibition. As the country increasingly saw the ill-effects of the Eighteenth Amendment, and the rise of organised crime, not even the conviction and imprisonment for tax evasion of Al Capone, the notorious Chicago gangster, was enough to turn the tide of public opinion against the ban on booze. Hoover's failure to grasp this was a major error.

It is perhaps typical of a fine engineer but lousy campaigner that after, rather than before, his defeat, Hoover commissioned the first ever US national election opinion poll. The Democrats had held a sizeable lead among decided voters, with Prohibition repeal being the key driving force from Republican to Democrat. Republican voters were deeply divided on the issue, but a clear link between repeal of the Eighteenth Amendment and economic recovery was being made. The Depression itself was decisive to a much lesser extent. Sixty-eight per cent of respondents believed that Hoover had done something to make the Depression less severe, and the Reconstruction Finance Corporation was strongly supported. The vast majority of those polled believed that the Depression was over. Hoover's opposition to the federal dole was a very marginal issue among respondents. His stance on tariffs, however, was not popular, with 70 per cent of Republican deserters objecting to existing rates.

Most fundamentally, however, the election was a question of leadership. The contrast between Hoover, who projected an increasingly gloomy persona, with an inability to empathise or communicate effectively, and Roosevelt, the greatest campaigner of them all, who exuded confidence and who wore a smile that matched his 'Happy Days Are Here Again' campaign theme, made it a wholly unequal contest by the autumn of 1932. Hoover's Olympian detachment and his refusal to even enter the fray until after Labor Day contrasted with Roosevelt's punchy and aggressive campaign, tempered with a message of optimism, however vague the details might have been in reality. The result was a hammering: 472 Electoral College votes for Roosevelt to Hoover's 59. In terms of the popular vote, it was an almost complete reversal of 1928, with Roosevelt winning by 18 percentage points.

In the Transition Period, FDR refused all of Hoover's requests for co-operation to meet the extreme economic conditions, and after Inauguration Day in March 1933, the two never met again. Hoover enjoyed a much better relationship with Truman, Eisenhower and Kennedy. Never an orator, Hoover became a more powerful and accomplished public speaker after his term of office, and found a greater coherence to his ideas and thinking that had been somewhat lacking during his presidency. Truman invited Hoover to set up a commission in the late 1940s to help drive greater federal government efficiency. A similar effort under Eisenhower yielded fewer positive results, but right up until his death at the age of ninety, Hoover continued to write and speak about conservative politics and gained a reputation for opposing excessive federal bureaucracy and the dangers of selfish big business. As the country moved towards bigger government as a result of depression and world war, Hoover remained a remarkably constant voice.

Was Herbert Hoover a desperately unlucky president, or just not up to the level of the events that faced him? Probably both. It is beyond any reasonable doubt that his character and temperament were ill-suited to the emergency that faced the United States in the early 1930s. His responses to the downturn were bold by the standards of his immediate predecessor, but in both style and substance he did not prove to be capable of dealing with the greatest crisis to afflict the Republic since the Civil War. What would have been a satisfactory response in normal times was insufficient for a challenge that required inspiration and guile. Yet the old adage that history is written by the victors does apply here. His life up to the presidency was one of huge achievement. This was a man of real substance and quality, whose successes at disaster relief should have prepared him for the emergency that he faced. He never fully understood, however, that a truly effective chief executive needs a cooperative legislature to get things done. His failure at politics meant a failure of policy. It is with a heavy heart that I place Hoover below the halfway mark when it comes to his presidency.

Rt Hon. Robert Buckland QC MP was Lord Chancellor and Secretary of State for Justice from 2019 until September 2021. Prior to entering the Cabinet, he served as Minister of State for Justice and Solicitor General and has been Conservative MP for South Swindon since 2010. A criminal barrister, Robert also served as a Recorder of the Crown Court. He wrote the chapter on Lord Melbourne for The Prime Ministers.

32

Franklin D. Roosevelt

4 March 1933 to 12 April 1945
Democrat
Vice-presidents: John Nance Garner 1933–41,
Henry A. Wallace 1941–45, Harry S. Truman 1945

By Neil Stockley

Full name: Franklin Delano Roosevelt
Born: 30 January 1882, Hyde Park, New York
Died: 12 April 1945, Warm Springs, Georgia
Resting place: Springwood, Hyde Park, New York
Library/Museum: Hyde Park, New York
Education: Harvard University (AB); Columbia Law School
(attended)
Married to: Anna Eleanor Roosevelt m. 1905 (1884–1962)
Children: Six: Anna, James, Franklin, Elliott, Franklin, John

Quotation: 'The only thing we have to fear is fear itself – nameless, unreasoning, unjustified terror which paralyses needed efforts to convert retreat into advance.'

FRANKLIN D. ROOSEVELT – FDR – was the most significant president of the twentieth century. He took office as the United States was in the depths of the Great Depression, the country's biggest crisis since the Civil War. The innovative programmes of his 'New Deal', combined with Roosevelt's optimistic and confident leadership, saved the country from economic and social disaster and paved the way for its eventual recovery. During the Second World War, the greatest conflict in human history, he led the United States and its Allies to victory over Nazi Germany and imperialist Japan. Over a record twelve years in office, he transformed the federal government by building a welfare state and turning the United States into the world's pre-eminent power.

Franklin Delano Roosevelt's confidence and optimism can be easily traced back to his patrician background and comfortable upbringing. He was born on 30 January 1882, in Hyde Park, New York, to James Roosevelt, a wealthy landowner and businessman, and his second wife, Sara. Their forebears were early immigrants who prospered in New England and joined its wealthy elite; Theodore Roosevelt was a distant cousin of James.

By all accounts, young Franklin was a happy, pleasant child, who was at the centre of the family's life. His mother closely supervised his interests and hobbies. With no siblings, he did not have to compete with anyone for his parents' attention – or learn how to deal with conflict.

Franklin was tutored at home until at the age of fourteen, when he went to Groton, an Episcopal boarding school in Massachusetts. He then attended Harvard University. During his first semester, Franklin's father suffered a fatal heart attack. Roosevelt was an average student, more interested in extracurricular activities, most notably writing for the *Harvard Crimson*, of which he eventually became managing editor. After Harvard, Roosevelt began studying at Columbia Law School but dropped out in 1907 after passing the New York Bar Examination. He then joined a New York City law firm.

In March 1905, Franklin married Eleanor Roosevelt, the daughter of Theodore's younger brother Elliott. To many people it seemed an unusual match. Whereas Franklin was handsome, ebullient and frivolous, Eleanor was plain, shy and serious. She was also intelligent, educated, and involved in social causes. The marriage soon came under pressure. By 1916, Franklin and Eleanor had six children, of whom five, one girl and four boys, survived. Nearly all the burdens of child-rearing fell on Eleanor. She also had to contend with the matriarchal Sara, who controlled the trust funds that the couple relied upon to finance their lifestyle.

In his mid-twenties, Roosevelt concluded that he had no interest in practising law. Having developed a deep admiration for cousin Theodore and his accomplishments, FDR decided to go into politics. He chose his father's Democratic Party as his political vehicle, but otherwise Roosevelt followed almost the same path to the White House as the twenty-sixth president. In 1910, he ran for the New York state Senate seat representing his native Dutchess County. It was Republican territory, but after running an effective local campaign, Roosevelt won handsomely.

As a state senator, FDR made his name by vigorously opposing the Tammany machine over the nomination of William F. 'Blue-eyed Billy' Sheehan for the United States Senate. The long, bitter row ended in the selection of another Tammany man, but Roosevelt claimed it as a victory. During his successful re-election campaign in 1912, Roosevelt was supported by Louis Howe, an unusual-looking journalist with a flair for political strategy and campaigning. For the rest of his life, Howe placed his considerable talents at Roosevelt's disposal.

In 1913, Roosevelt joined the Wilson administration as assistant secretary of the navy. When war broke out in Europe the following year, he argued that the United States should join the conflict on the side of Britain and France, which put him at odds with the administration's pacifist stance. After the United States entered the war, in 1917, Roosevelt worked energetically to supply and organise American naval forces. The assistant secretary was an innovative and imaginative problem solver – 'a great trial and error guy', as one admiral observed.

In autumn 1918, Roosevelt faced a personal crisis, when Eleanor discovered that he had been having an affair with Lucy Mercer, her part-time social secretary. He refused Eleanor's offer of a divorce after Sara threatened to withdraw his financial support and Howe warned that it would jeopardise his political prospects, but Roosevelt agreed to cut all ties with Mercer, a promise he eventually broke. His physical relationship with Eleanor ended, however, and their somewhat joyless marriage became more a political partnership, albeit one that was overlain with a deep friendship. Eleanor then began to develop her own public profile as an advocate for feminist and labour causes.

Roosevelt experienced two electoral defeats during his time at the Navy Department. In the summer of 1914, he contested the New York Democratic nomination for the United States Senate, but Wilson did not support him against the Tammany-backed candidate, James W. Gerard, the United States ambassador to Berlin. Gerard trounced Roosevelt in the primary but went on to lose the general election.

In 1920, the Democrats chose FDR as their vice-presidential running mate to Ohio governor James Cox. The ticket campaigned enthusiastically for progressive policies, including the League of Nations, but war-weary voters wanted neither and gave the Republican nominee, Warren G. Harding, a landslide victory. Still, Roosevelt gained valuable political experience and a national profile in the Democratic Party.

After leaving Washington, FDR found employment with a surety bonding firm in New York City and started to plan the next stage of his political career. Disaster struck in August 1921 when, during a family holiday at his holiday home in Campobello, off the coast of Maine, Roosevelt suddenly found himself paralysed from the waist down and suffering from acute pain. He had poliomyelitis and would never walk again.

Roosevelt began years of rigorous physical therapy to regain the strength in his arms and upper body, and slowly mastered his braces, crutches and wheelchair. He was amply supported by Eleanor and Howe, but it was Roosevelt's remarkable courage, determination and positivity that ultimately sustained him throughout this ordeal. An upbeat sense of geniality and cheerfulness became a key part of FDR's persona.

FDR made an audacious return to public life at the 1924 Democratic National Convention, when he nominated his sometime New York ally, Governor Alfred E. Smith, for president. Roosevelt made his way to the platform on his son James's arm and gave an electrifying address, describing Smith as 'the Happy Warrior of the political battlefield'.

FDR's political comeback was confirmed four years later. Even though Republican Herbert Hoover won the presidency by a wide margin, Roosevelt was narrowly elected as governor of New York after waging a spirited campaign across the state. By 1930, the sharp economic downturn and rising unemployment presented Governor Roosevelt with huge challenges. Moved by first-hand stories of people's suffering, he pushed for the construction of hydroelectric power plants and supported lower taxes for farmers. He became the first governor to champion old-age pensions funded by contributions from government, employers and workers.

The following year, as the economic crisis worsened, FDR persuaded the Republican legislature to introduce a state programme of unemployment insurance and a public work scheme for jobless citizens. Roosevelt's comprehensive relief programme became a model for other states and established him as the type of compassionate leader people wanted in a depression. With around 15 per cent of the labour force out of work and the country mired in despair, Hoover became deeply unpopular. Roosevelt's contention that the state should do its share to help jobless citizens 'as a matter of social duty' contrasted with Hoover's insistence that private enterprise, local government and charities should be relied upon to ease economic distress.

FDR became the front-runner for the Democratic Party's presidential nomination in 1932, but it was by no means a foregone conclusion. When the Democratic National Convention gathered in Chicago to select its presidential nominee, he topped the first ballot, but fell 104 votes short of the two-thirds majority needed. Smith, still resentful at the way Roosevelt had sidelined his key aides in Albany, rallied his successor's more conservative opponents, including John Nance Garner of Texas, the Speaker of the House. A deal was done: Roosevelt became the party's presidential nominee, with Garner his vice-presidential running mate.

To project himself as a man of action, Roosevelt broke with convention and travelled to Chicago. In a confident address, he promised 'a new deal for the American people'. He then campaigned across forty-one states in the general election campaign, speaking in bland generalities that promised happier days ahead. His specific solutions were hard to pin down, however. In one speech, he promised to balance the budget through a 25 per cent cut in government spending. In another, Roosevelt argued that Americans should work together to overcome the economic crisis and hinted at a bigger role for government in reviving the economy. He also suggested that he might run deficits to provide relief to the jobless and the needy. An increasingly desperate Hoover called Roosevelt 'a chameleon on plaid'.

One explanation for this ambiguity was the diversity of views among the 'brains trust' that the candidate assembled to advise him. Roosevelt himself had not worked out exactly how he would end the Depression. Another was FDR's strategy, which was to frame the election as a referendum on Hoover's dismal record. By the end of 1932, around a quarter of the workforce was unemployed; Hoover's *laissez-faire* approach to economic management offered no hope. With such a weak opponent, Roosevelt wanted to avoid having to defend a raft of detailed policies. Voters still had a choice, however. 'If Roosevelt's program lacked substance,' says William Leuchtenberg, 'his blithe spirit – his infectious smile, his warm voice – his obvious ease with crowds – contrasted sharply with Hoover's glumness.'

On election day, Roosevelt won 22.8 million votes (57.4 per cent) and 472 Electoral College votes to 15.7 million (39.7 per cent) and 59 Electoral votes for Hoover, with the Democrats gaining huge majorities in both Houses of Congress.

FDR could not become president for another four months. Shortly after the election, Hoover tried to persuade him to endorse an international debt settlement, but Roosevelt declined. FDR assembled a Cabinet made up of Democratic Party regulars and some progressive Republicans, including Harold Ickes, who became Secretary for the Interior and went on to be a major figure throughout his presidency. Another notable appointment was Frances Perkins, the new Secretary of Labor and the first woman Cabinet member in United States history. Roosevelt's incoming White House team had a more obviously liberal tinge: Harry Hopkins, for instance, had run New York's programme for the unemployed. The president-elect still gave little away about his plans, even after a new round of bank failures in the days before his inauguration.

On 4 March 1933, Roosevelt took the oath of office and in a masterful inaugural address reassured the American people in their time of peril that 'The only thing we have to fear is fear itself – nameless, unreasoning, unjustified terror which paralyses needed efforts to convert retreat into advance.' He rejected both fear and paralysis. 'This nation asks for action, and action now,' he declared.

Within three days of taking office, Roosevelt issued a proclamation declaring a four-day national bank holiday, closing every bank in the country and embargoing all shipments of gold and silver. He then summoned Congress into a special session to pass legislation providing the liquidity that would enable most banks to reopen.

On Sunday 12 March, Roosevelt used his first radio 'fireside chat' as president to explain, in simple language, how the banks would be strengthened and deposits guaranteed. He then called on citizens to return their savings when the banks reopened the next day. Over the following weeks, Americans returned nearly $1 billion to the banks. The combination of the national bank holiday, the emergency legislation and Roosevelt's projection of optimism and confidence had worked.

Then, in a whirlwind hundred days, Roosevelt sent to Congress fifteen major pieces of legislation, all of which were passed: permitting the sale of beer and light wines; dispensing farm relief and credit; providing job relief to the states; establishing federal oversight of securities sales; bringing in protections against small-home mortgage foreclosures; ending the gold standard; and reforming the railways.

The legislation created an 'alphabet soup' of new federal agencies: The Federal Deposit Insurance Corporation (FDIC); the Civilian Conservation Corps (CCC), providing 250,000 young men with work planting trees and tidying up forests; the Agricultural Adjustment Administration (AAA), paying subsidies to reduce farm surpluses; and the Civil Works Administration (CWA) and Public Works Administration (PWA), providing jobs for the unemployed; and many others. Thus, the New Deal was born.

The programme was a triumph of ambition, experimentation

and improvisation, best exemplified by the Tennessee Valley Authority (TVA), which harnessed the natural resources of seven Southern states to provide cheap hydroelectricity and new job opportunities to millions of people, many of whom had lived in poverty. Roosevelt was prepared to change course and adapt his policies, as when he reversed the initial securities legislation, a move that led eventually to the creation of the Securities and Exchange Commission (SEC), one of the enduring and most admired legacies of the New Deal.

There was, however, no grand strategy or governing philosophy. Roosevelt claimed, for example, that his priority was to provide relief for the unemployed. The CWA spent almost $1 billion on public works projects but was closed after only four months because of its cost, for Roosevelt was determined to keep his campaign promise to balance the budget. The CCC, TVA and AAA were partly financed by cuts in veterans' invalid pensions and benefits (which were soon reversed), and reductions in federal salaries of up to 15 per cent. Prohibition was abolished, partly to provide new revenues from beer and wine duties. The New Deal did not end the Depression, though there were signs of modest recovery by 1934.

More importantly, Roosevelt provided the American people with the kind of leadership they wanted. The former Supreme Court Justice, Oliver Wendell Holmes, is said to have described him as 'a second-class intellect; a first-class temperament'. The second quality manifested itself in the optimism and sense of vitality that Roosevelt conveyed; in his tremendous political instincts; and in his uncanny ability to connect with the public. FDR was a talented political teacher, who used his regular Sunday night 'fireside chats' on radio to explain his policies and keep up the spirits of an anxious American public. Roosevelt cast himself as a benevolent leader of a newly active government, working to solve the nation's problems. His charm and personality dazzled nearly everyone with whom he came into contact; Winston Churchill later said that meeting President Roosevelt was like uncorking your first bottle of champagne.

In rolling out the New Deal, FDR projected himself as a non-partisan leader, putting forward policies that would benefit all sections of society, regardless of class or political affiliation. He took care to embrace business. The National Industrial Recovery Act (NIRA) sought to encourage government, business and workers to work together and revive the economy. It created the National Recovery Administration (NRA), which called on businesses to draft fair codes of competition setting prices and wages. Section 7(a) of the act guaranteed unions the right to organise and bargain collectively. In return, the NIRA suspended antitrust laws that business leaders had opposed since the beginning of the twentieth century.

Roosevelt's big tent soon showed signs of wear and tear. With the banking crisis resolved, business leaders and conservatives in both parties began to bristle at the prospect of more deficit spending and resented the influence of liberal thinkers within the administration. In the summer of 1934, a group of wealthy Republicans joined with conservative Democrats and formed the American Liberty League to protect private property and the Constitution from what they saw as FDR's rampant liberal agenda. People from Roosevelt's own social background now bitterly denounced him as a class traitor and reviled him as they had few previous presidents.

There was also discontent from the populist left. Senator Huey Long, a Louisiana Democrat and an early supporter of the New Deal, soon accused FDR of being captured by business interests. Long promised a 'share our wealth' scheme to heavily tax the rich and 'make every man a king'. Another early supporter of the New Deal, Father Charles Coughlin, commanded huge radio audiences and demanded the use of 'free silver' to end the Depression. Dr Francis Townsend, a California general practitioner, advocated generous pensions for everyone over the age of sixty.

The NRA came under fire from all sides. The price codes were often favourable to big business and frequently resulted in price fixing. Labour unions complained that businesses ignored provisions that guaranteed workers' wages and hours. The enactment of section 7(a) was followed by a wave of union militancy. By 1935, as the economy remained flat, the New Deal lost momentum and Roosevelt's popularity suffered.

In May 1935, the Supreme Court delivered a body blow to the New Deal. In *Schechter Poultry Corp. v. United States*, the court struck down the NIRA on the grounds that Congress had improperly delegated its powers to the Executive and that the act unconstitutionally interfered with intra-state commerce. Roosevelt angrily rejected the court's decision, which, he said, took the Constitution back to the 'horse and buggy' era.

FDR was determined to preserve and advance the New Deal, and with a presidential election looming, he felt the need to show strong leadership. In the spring and summer of 1935, he engineered the passage of a fresh round of progressive legislation.

In the wake of *Schechter*, FDR threw his weight behind the Wagner National Labor Relations Act, which he had previously opposed. By guaranteeing employees the right to organise and bargain collectively, and establishing the National Labor Relations Board to enforce these rights, the Wagner Act provided the foundation for a unionised American workforce.

Picking up a concern from his Albany days, and to neutralise the left-wing populists, Roosevelt secured the passage of the Social Security Act, which brought in old-age pensions for people over the age of sixty-five, unemployment insurance and benefits for children. The legislation as finally agreed had its flaws. The schemes were funded through deductions from workers' pay packets and some workers were excluded, at least initially. Unemployment insurance was administered by state governments, leaving variations in provision. Nevertheless, for the first time, the federal government took responsibility for the economic security of some of the most vulnerable Americans.

Roosevelt also set aside his pledge to balance the budget, as he tried to stimulate the economy. In April 1937, Congress approved the Emergency Relief Appropriation Act, providing $5 billion to create the Works Progress Administration (WPA), which, under the active leadership of Harry Hopkins, paid three million people to build schools, hospitals and airports and financed theatre productions and public art works. The WPA did not bring about economic recovery, but its legacy included La Guardia Airport and Triborough Bridge in New York and Chicago's Lake Shore Bridge.

FDR did not achieve all his aims. He had to compromise with Congress on his plan to eliminate the holding companies that dominated electric utilities. And when he proposed a Revenue Bill that raised taxes for wealthy Americans and large corporations, conservatives in Congress removed the inheritance tax and left only a mild graduated corporate income tax.

This so-called 'Second New Deal' alienated the business community, with some seeing the new bills as an attack on individual liberty and private enterprise. Once again, Roosevelt seized the political opportunity. Running for re-election in 1936, he cast himself as being on the side of the 'little people' against 'big business'. The inclusive narrative of his first two years in office was forgotten as Roosevelt railed against the 'powerful forces' and vowed 'they are unanimous in their hatred of me, and I welcome their hatred'.

FDR buried his colourless Republican opponent, Alf Landon, the governor of Kansas, by nearly 11 million votes and carried every state except for Maine and Vermont, with the Democrats increasing their majorities in both Houses of Congress. The electoral coalition that Roosevelt had created, of newly unionised blue-collar workers, urban immigrants in the big cities, senior citizens, the poor, middle-class progressives, farmers and African Americans, many of whom saw their lives transformed by his social programmes, sustained the Democratic Party for some forty years.

Roosevelt's second term was much less productive than his first. His second inaugural speech, on 20 January 1937, proclaimed, 'I see one-third of a nation ill-housed, ill-clad, ill-nourished.' The president was all too aware, however, that during the Supreme Court's 1936 term it found all seven cases dealing with the New Deal unconstitutional. Fearing that the Social Security Act might be next in the firing line, Roosevelt decided that drastic action was required.

The result was the biggest defeat of his presidency. In February 1937, FDR suddenly sent to Congress a proposal to reorganise the Supreme Court. He claimed that the court's workload had become too great for nine justices to handle and proposed the appointment of an additional justice for each one aged seventy years or over. This transparent plan would have installed six new Roosevelt-appointed justices, providing a comfortable majority that could be expected to uphold the New Deal.

Much of the press, and conservatives in both parties, immediately came out against the proposal, as did some New Deal Democrats and progressive Republicans in Congress, who saw it as a crude attempt to 'pack the court'. Chief Justice Hughes demolished Roosevelt's case by releasing figures showing the court 'fully abreast of its work' with 'no congestion of cases'. The justices spiked

Roosevelt's guns by validating key pieces of New Deal legislation, including the Wagner Act and the Social Security Act. By the summer, it was clear that Roosevelt lacked the votes in the Senate to pass the bill.

Even though he was able to fill seven court vacancies over the next few years, guaranteeing pro-New Deal rulings, the 'court packing' fiasco was a major humiliation for Roosevelt and damaged his credibility. Republicans and conservative Democrats in Congress became more prepared to block or amend his legislation. In spring 1938, FDR secured the passage of the Fair Labor Standards Bill, but had to accept regional variations in minimum wages. He was also defeated on an executive branch reorganisation bill as conservatives claimed that he was seeking dictatorial powers.

Roosevelt then tried to remove conservative Democrats from Congress by supporting more liberal candidates in the party's primaries. The 'purge' failed; of the ten Democrats he targeted for defeat, only one lost. The Democrats maintained their congressional majorities in the 1938 mid-term elections, but the Republicans made impressive gains.

To add to the president's burdens, a sharp economic downturn began in 1937, and unemployment climbed to more than 11 million. The 'Roosevelt recession' largely resulted from new cutbacks in federal spending, after Secretary of the Treasury Henry Morgenthau convinced the president that he should make a new drive for a balanced budget. After some hesitation, Roosevelt sided with Hopkins and other advisers who called for higher spending to 'prime the pump' and create jobs. He asked Congress for a $5 billion relief programme, which passed in the summer of 1938.

The nation remained stuck in a depression, however, with nearly a fifth of the workforce still unemployed by 1939. The continuing slump and his weakened political authority led Roosevelt to acknowledge in January of that year that the New Deal was now on hold; economic recovery was now the administration's priority.

By this time, FDR and the nation were increasingly concerned by ominous developments abroad. The Spanish Civil War broke out in 1936 and, the following year, Japan attacked China and occupied Shanghai. Having taken power in Germany in 1933, Adolf Hitler moved his troops into the Rhineland in 1936, then into

Czechoslovakia and Austria, and in September 1939, into Poland, precipitating the Second World War. In the spring of 1940, Hitler's armies conquered western Europe and began to prepare for an invasion of Britain.

Roosevelt had been an internationalist and an interventionist for almost his whole political life. He was also an anti-fascist who understood the dangers to the Americas posed by a Nazi defeat of the Allies. But Roosevelt, the consummate politician, was convinced that public opinion remained isolationist. He was also hamstrung by the anti-interventionist Congress, which passed a series of Neutrality Acts that forbade American involvement in foreign conflicts. He took therefore a cautious approach to international affairs. When Britain declared war on Germany in September 1939, FDR promised to uphold United States neutrality but added that he could not 'ask that every American remain neutral in thought as well'.

FDR began providing Britain with all support 'short of war'. In autumn 1939, he secured a repeal of the arms embargo, on the condition that belligerents could buy arms in the United States under 'cash and carry'. In September 1940, the United States agreed to loan Britain fifty mothballed destroyers in return for the use of eight British defensive military bases, but this followed some foot-dragging.

As ever, political considerations were at the front of Roosevelt's mind. For most of his second term, he had been undecided whether to seek an unprecedented third mandate in 1940. In the spring, he told confidants that he would run only if the situation in Europe deteriorated further and his fellow Democrats drafted him as their candidate. The first box was ticked with Nazi Germany's successful invasion of western Europe in the spring of 1940. The second was ticked in July, when the Democratic National Convention nominated him once again, after Chicago mayor Ed Kelly had organised a none-too-subtle draft. Roosevelt had already drawn out potential rivals. In place of Vice-President Garner, who strongly opposed his decision to seek re-election, FDR had a new running mate, Secretary of Agriculture Henry Wallace, once a progressive Republican, but now a New Dealer.

The general election campaign became a contest over which candidate would keep the United States out of foreign conflicts.

The Republican nominee, Wendell Willkie, rounded off a solid campaign by calling Roosevelt a 'warmonger'. After campaign strategists warned that he might lose, FDR promised: 'We will not participate in foreign wars and we will not participate in foreign wars outside of the Americas except in case of attack.' Then he pledged simply: 'Your boys are not going to be sent into any foreign wars.' American voters decided that they trusted FDR to deal with the growing international crisis. He defeated Willkie by 27 million popular votes (54.8 per cent) to 22 million (44.8 per cent) and 449 Electoral College votes to 82.

Roosevelt continued to play both sides of the war issue, while waiting on 'events' to let him justify a more interventionist stance. In a 'fireside chat' in December 1940, he denounced appeasement of Hitler but promised 'to keep war away from this country and its people'. He also declared, 'we must be the great arsenal of democracy.' In his State of the Union speech of January 1941, Roosevelt affirmed his Four Freedoms: freedom of speech, freedom of religion, freedom from want and freedom from fear, with the elimination of national acts of aggression against peace-loving countries everywhere in the world. The following March, FDR finally won enactment of a $7 billion Lend-Lease programme that loaned the British and other Allies American arms and supplies that they could repay at the end of the war.

Hitler suddenly became very useful. Having failed to invade Britain from the air, the German leader instructed Nazi submarines to attack British shipping in the North Atlantic, thereby stopping American supplies of military equipment. FDR ordered the American Navy to 'patrol' the North Atlantic and later to 'escort' British ships. When Hitler launched a massive invasion of the Soviet Union, FDR extended Lend-Lease aid to that country.

Roosevelt built an effective working relationship with the British prime minister, Winston Churchill. In August 1941, on a battleship off Newfoundland, the two leaders crafted a joint statement, the Atlantic Charter, in which they committed their countries to the goal of achieving 'the final destruction of the Nazi tyranny' and set out their nations' post-war aims, which included the formation of an international peacekeeping organisation, the United Nations. Just as importantly, the two nations' service chiefs met and began planning in earnest for the coming war. Back home, however, Roosevelt denied that the United States was any closer to entering the conflict and was evasive about the difference between the nation being 'short of war' and 'at war'. The following month, after a German submarine fired on an American destroyer, Roosevelt ordered the navy to shoot on sight any German ships in the North Atlantic.

The decisive shock came from Asia. FDR's strategy, agreed with other Western leaders, was to contain an increasingly aggressive Japan using limited economic sanctions. He did not want to provoke Japan into war and encouraged the State Department to keep up a dialogue with Tokyo. In July 1941, Japan invaded Southern Indochina to secure industrial supplies. The Roosevelt administration responded by freezing Japanese assets and imposing an embargo on aviation fuel against Japan. Relations between the two countries rapidly deteriorated.

Roosevelt's ambiguities over the war ended on 7 December 1941, when Japan launched a surprise attack against the United States at Pearl Harbor naval base in Hawaii. Congress declared war on Japan on 8 December; three days later, Germany and Italy declared war on the United States, which the US Congress acknowledged in a resolution accepting the state of war. The American public's opposition fell away quickly. Roosevelt was determined to lead the nation to victory.

FDR was clear and consistent on his strategy: to defeat Germany as the priority and then to conquer Japan, while supporting the Soviet Union. He soon dominated the Allied leadership. At the Casablanca conference with the British in January 1943, Roosevelt made a tactical concession to Churchill over launching an assault on Sicily and Italy. They also agreed on preparations for invading France in 1944 and assisting Russia to the fullest. But Roosevelt bounced Churchill when he suddenly announced at a press conference that the Allies would seek the unconditional surrender of Germany, Italy and Japan, one of FDR's key aims.

The Tehran Conference at the end of 1943 saw FDR's first meeting with Joseph Stalin, the Soviet leader. With his country suffering terrible losses in the East, Stalin wanted a second front to be opened in western Europe. Roosevelt charmed the Soviet leader and supported him in persuading Churchill to commit to an invasion of France by the middle of 1944. Roosevelt also convinced Stalin that a post-war peacekeeping organisation should be a world-wide body, effectively overruling Churchill, who favoured a set of regional organisations.

FDR was prepared to deal with Stalin and the Chinese leader, Chiang Kai-shek, despite their ruthless treatment of domestic opponents and general indifference towards democratic values. Roosevelt described himself as a foreign policy 'realist' who recognised that both countries were essential to winning the war with minimal loss of life. He also needed Stalin and Chiang to help deliver his vision of a permanent United Nations organisation that would assure peace, fulfil Woodrow Wilson's dream of collective security and foster international cooperation after the war. Learning from Wilson's experience with the League of Nations, he wanted to see the new institutions in place before the conflict ended. Roosevelt may have been a realist in foreign policy, but he was also an idealist.

On military strategy, FDR was steady and disciplined. He stayed focused on his central objective, the launch of an Allied attack on Nazi Germany from the west. Unlike Churchill, he did not interfere with their operational decisions of his military commanders. His self-confidence and level-headedness were vindicated with the success of Operation Overlord – the invasion of France – in June 1944.

Roosevelt's diplomatic dominance was fortified by his successes in scaling up a huge fighting force and building a massive industrial war machine that Germany and Japan could not beat. In 1942, the United States armed forces grew nearly four-fold, from 1.6 million to 5.4 million. Four weeks after Pearl Harbor, FDR set challenging targets for building thousands and thousands of aircraft, tanks, anti-aircraft guns and merchant ships within two years.

As FDR himself said, 'Dr New Deal' became 'Dr Win the War'. New agencies were set up to oversee war production. Business leaders became 'czars' of mobilisation and government and industry became entwined as never before. The president and his advisers took charge of the distribution of tens of billions of dollars as federal spending reached record levels. To keep inflation down, FDR introduced war bonds, price and wage controls and stabilised farm prices. Nearly all consumer goods were rationed. He settled industrial disputes and batted away isolationist criticisms. Staying above the political fray, FDR visited tank assembly plants, aircraft assembly lines, naval training stations and shipyards all over the nation. In the end, all his production targets were met.

The industrial mobilisation for war achieved what the New Deal had not: economic recovery and an end to national unemployment alongside rising living standards. But some Americans were left behind. Millions of women entered the workforce but were still paid less than men. African Americans also moved into new jobs, which often paid poorly. Roosevelt's attempts to prohibit discrimination in government agencies had little impact and the armed forces remained largely segregated.

A larger stain on Roosevelt's domestic record was his decision to have 120,000 Japanese Americans herded into prison camps in the California deserts and Utah flatlands, where they lived in basic conditions. In taking this unconscionable step, he was influenced by the military's dubious warnings of possible sabotage and espionage, and the outburst of racist emotions that followed Pearl Harbor.

Throughout Roosevelt's presidency, this sensitivity to public and congressional opinion on racial matters had unfortunate outcomes. In his first term, FDR chose not to progress anti-lynching legislation, calculating that it would cost him the support of Southerners in Congress that he needed to pass New Deal bills. Fear of anti-immigration sentiment, and of the anti-Semitism that was prevalent in the late 1930s and 1940s, led the administration to limit the entry of Jewish refugees from Nazi Germany. It was not until 1944, when he was faced with the potential loss of Jewish votes in New York, a key state, that Roosevelt allowed more European Jews to be rescued.

After some indecision, FDR sought a fourth term. He wanted to achieve final victory, establish the United Nations and launch new reforms at home. Having concluded that the left-leaning Wallace was an electoral liability, Roosevelt chose Senator Harry S. Truman of Missouri as his running mate. He campaigned as an experienced war leader and on the promise of an 'Economic Bill of Rights', including full employment underpinned by government spending, public healthcare for all, generous pensions, better education, more electrification in rural areas, and fair employment rights for minorities.

The 1944 election campaign began shortly after the liberation of Paris and a string of American victories in the Pacific, but Roosevelt faced a burst of red baiting from his opponent, Thomas Dewey, and Republican-inspired rumours about his health. (The latter were well-founded. During the previous spring, an independent, secret health assessment found that Roosevelt was suffering from hypertension, an enlarged heart, congestive heart failure, pulmonary disease and acute bronchitis.) Roosevelt took to the campaign trail with gusto, culminating in his famous four-hour ride in an open car, braving cold and rain, across New York City's five boroughs.

Roosevelt was re-elected with 53.5 per cent of the vote to 46 per cent for Dewey, which delivered a 432–99 victory in the Electoral College. It was the tightest of his presidential election victories, but voters were prepared to keep him in the White House so long as there was a war to be won.

FDR was visibly tired and frail when the Big Three met again at Yalta in January 1945, with victory in Europe all but assured. For decades, Republicans criticised his conduct at Yalta as the product of naïveté about Stalin and communism. He and Churchill accepted Stalin's agreement to allow representatives from other political parties into the communist-dominated provisional government in Poland. Stalin also promised to sanction free elections there and to permit free elections in all territories in Eastern Europe liberated from Nazi occupation. But Stalin quickly broke his promises and interpreted the Yalta arrangements as granting him a free hand to set up puppet governments throughout the region. For more than forty years, millions lived under the Soviet yoke.

The criticism ignored the realities that Roosevelt and Churchill faced: their need to keep together the fragile Allied coalition as the fighting raged on and the brutal truth that the Red Army dominated in Eastern Europe by early 1945. Stalin also agreed at Yalta that Soviet forces would join the Allies' final push to defeat Japan, which was expected to cost thousands of lives. Roosevelt secured Stalin's commitment to Soviet participation in the United Nations, on the basis that permanent Security Council members would have a veto. These were both significant achievements, central to FDR's objectives for winning the war and shaping the post-war world.

Roosevelt did not live to see the Allies' final victories in Europe and Japan or the foundation of the United Nations. On 12 April 1945, just weeks before the German surrender, the president collapsed and died at his 'little White House' in Warm Springs, Georgia. The cause of death was a massive cerebral haemorrhage.

Nearly eight decades on, FDR's legacy endures. For all the ambiguities of the New Deal, he created a welfare state, guaranteed a minimal standard of living for all Americans and ensured that the benefits of prosperity were shared more fairly. With the election of Ronald Reagan in 1980, a powerful surge from the right dominated American politics for nearly thirty years. Yet none of FDR's successors has rolled back social security or any of his other landmark achievements. His central notion, that the federal government should play a major role in ensuring the economic security of the American people, remains a core value of American politics.

During the Second World War, Roosevelt's leadership of the Allies played a vital part in the victory of freedom and democracy. By the time he died, the United States was a global leader that was taking on global responsibilities. His successors had many triumphs and made many mistakes, but the United States eventually prevailed in the Cold War and became the world's only superpower. Roosevelt ensured that the wartime allies cooperated in creating the United Nations, the central pillar of the post-war order, which, for all its faults, has made a massive contribution to maintaining peace and security and improved the lives of millions. Despite all the momentous changes of the last eighty years, we still live in the world that Franklin D. Roosevelt built.

Neil Stockley is a communications consultant and a regular contributor to the Journal of Liberal History.

33

Harry S. Truman

12 April 1945 to 20 January 1953
Democrat
Vice-president: Vacant 1945–49, Alben W. Barkley 1949–53

By David Blanchflower

Full name: Harry S. Truman
Born: 8 May 1884, Lamar, Missouri
Died: 26 December 1972, Kansas City, Missouri
Resting place: Harry S. Truman Presidential Library and Museum, Independence, Missouri
Library/Museum: Independence, Missouri
Education: Spalding's Commercial College, Kansas City
Married to: Bess Wallace, m. 1919 (1885–1982)
Children: One: Margaret
Quotation: 'You know, it's easy for the Monday morning quarterback to say what the coach should have done, after the

game is over. But when the decision is up before you – and on my desk I have a motto which says The Buck Stops Here – the decision has to be made.' (from his speech at the National War College, 19 December 1952)

'GIVE 'EM HELL' Harry S. Truman was the thirty-third president of the United States. He was born on 8 May 1884 and died at age eighty-eight on 22 December 1972. Of note also is that VE Day occurred on Truman's birthday on 8 May 1945. He had no middle name. His parents gave him the middle initial, 'S', to honour his grandfathers, Anderson Shipp Truman and Solomon Young. He married his wife Elizabeth 'Bess' Wallace on 28 June 1919; he had previously proposed in 1911 and she turned him down, but they finally got engaged in 1913. She had been in his class at school when he was six and she was five, and she sat at the desk immediately behind him. The couple had one child, Mary Margaret Truman.

Harry was a little man who did a lot, standing just 5 foot 9 inches tall, which is short for a president. In height terms he was joint thirty-third, with Millard Fillmore, out of forty-five. In modern times only Jimmy Carter comes close at 5 foot 9½ inches. James Madison was the shortest at 5 foot 4 and Abraham Lincoln was tallest at 6 foot 4. FDR was 6 foot 2, Joe Biden is 5 foot 11½ and Trump was 6 foot 3. The tallest candidates in presidential elections tend to get more votes. Thomas Dewey, who Truman defeated in 1948, was 5 foot 8 inches tall, so Truman fits the taller takes-all rule. FDR was taller than all four of the contenders he beat. Obama was taller than McCain; Reagan was taller than Mondale; Kennedy was taller than Nixon; Clinton was taller than Dole; Trump was taller than Hillary; but Kerry was taller than G.W. Bush; and Gore was taller than Clinton and George H.W. Bush, who tie for fifth place at around 6 foot 1½ inches tall.

Neither George Washington nor Harry Truman went to college. Every other president since the twenty-fifth POTUS, William McKinley (1897–1901), has graduated from university. Truman's formal education ended after a year at Spalding's Commercial College in Kansas City. He served in the National Guard from 1905 to 1919. In the First World War, as a captain in the army, he served in France, and in subsequent years he was in the Army

Reserve. He had a number of business ventures, including opening a haberdashery.

Truman was a Democrat. With the help of the Kansas City Democratic machine led by Tom Pendergast, he was elected in 1922 as County Court judge of Jackson County's eastern district. He had no legal training although he did start courses towards a law degree and in business college at several different points in his life, but he never formally graduated or completed a degree. Truman lost his 1924 re-election campaign in a Republican landslide. He spent two years selling automobile club memberships, which he didn't like much, so he ran for presiding judge in 1926 and won with the support of the Pendergast machine; he was re-elected in 1930. Then he was elected senator for Missouri in 1934. He won re-election narrowly in 1940 without FDR's support. Truman was sometimes called 'The Senator from Pendergast'. In 1939, Pendergast was convicted of income tax evasion and served fifteen months in a federal prison. During his decade as a senator, Truman was the chairman of the Committee on Military Affairs Subcommittee on War Mobilisation, which gained him a good deal of publicity saving large amounts of money and even getting him on the cover of *Time* magazine on 8 March 1943 under the headline 'Investigator Truman: A Democracy Has to Keep Its Eye on the Ball'.

Harry Truman became vice-president of the United States on 20 January 1945, although he did not campaign for the job. Henry Wallace was the sitting vice-president, but he was regarded as too liberal by many of Roosevelt's advisers. Truman was the compromise candidate and in the short time he was vice-president Roosevelt rarely contacted him and they met alone only twice. As vice-president he did attend Pendergast's funeral.

Unexpectedly, Truman became the thirty-third president eighty-two days later on the death of Franklin D. Roosevelt at age sixty-three during his fourth term as president. Roosevelt was at his Warm Springs, Georgia, retreat where he had gone on doctor's advice, to recover from what was believed to be exhaustion, along with his mistress Lucy Mercer. At about 1 p.m. the president suddenly complained of a terrific pain in the back of his head and collapsed unconscious. He was pronounced dead at 3:30 p.m., apparently having suffered a massive cerebral haemorrhage.

Truman had spent his time as vice-president presiding over the Senate, and he was meeting with his friend, Texas congressman Sam Rayburn, the forty-third Speaker of the US House of Representatives, after the Senate had finished its business. A call came from the White House to go immediately to its Pennsylvania Avenue entrance. Truman was met by Eleanor Roosevelt and told the president had died. Offering his condolences, Harry Truman asked, 'Is there anything I can do for you?' Mrs Roosevelt responded, 'Is there anything we can do for you? For you are the one in trouble now.' Ultimately, Truman designated Eleanor Roosevelt as his representative to the United Nations and 'First Lady of the World'.

The White House press agency sent out an official bulletin at 5:47 p.m., that President Roosevelt had died two hours earlier from a cerebral stroke. Supreme Court Chief Justice Harlan Stone was then called to the White House to issue Truman's presidential oath of office in the Cabinet Room at 7 p.m. in front of Bess Truman, Rayburn, and several Cabinet members.

Truman served two terms. Roosevelt was the first and only president to serve more than two terms. The Twenty-second Amendment was passed by Congress in 1947 and was ratified by the states on 27 February 1951; it says that a person can only be elected to be president two times for a total of eight years.

Under the language of the amendment, the president at the time of its ratification was exempt from the two-term limitation, so Truman could have served a third term. He seriously considered a run but decided not to do so after a big loss in New Hampshire and poor polling. Prior to the ratification of the Twenty-fifth Amendment in 1967, no constitutional provision existed for filling an intra-term vacancy in the vice-presidency. So Truman had no vice-president until he appointed Alben W. Barkley in his second term after his victory in 1948.

Famously, Truman was behind in the polls in November 1948, when he took on Republican governor of New York, Thomas Dewey, with Strom Thurmond as a third candidate on the Dixiecrat ticket. In addition, Truman's predecessor as vice-president, Henry A. Wallace, ran under the Progressive party label. Truman was widely considered to be the underdog in the race, and virtually every prediction indicated that he would be defeated by Dewey.

The polls predicted a Dewey victory of between 5 and 15 percentage points. In the end, Truman won the election with 303 Electoral College votes to Dewey's 189. He also won 49.6 per cent of the popular vote compared to Dewey's 45.1 per cent. The headline from the Republican-supporting *Chicago Daily Tribune* newspaper on the night of the election, 'Dewey Defeats Truman', was not a high point in journalism or of pollsters.

Just before the pandemic I visited the Little White House in Key West, the southernmost point of the United States and a hundred miles as the crow flies to Cuba, which is now a museum and is where Truman stayed for 175 nights while he was president. It was originally part of a US Navy submarine base and was nicely secure and warm all year round, but in the summer too much so. After nineteen months in office, Truman was exhausted and went there for some rest and recuperation. It is reported that Truman liked to start his days with a nice, brisk walk and a shot of Old Grand-Dad bourbon followed by a glass of orange juice. Cabinet members and foreign officials were regular visitors for fishing trips and poker games, especially in the winter months. It is alleged Truman loved to tell and hear dirty jokes. In subsequent years while in office, Truman went there every November to December and February to March. Truman also loved to swim and was a frequent user of the pool that FDR had installed in the White House in 1933 as therapy for his polio.

There were two assassination attempts on Truman's life while he was in office. Zionist terrorists tried to assassinate him by letter-bomb in 1947. According to his daughter Margaret: 'A number of cream-colored envelopes, about eight by six inches, arrived in the White House, addressed to the president and various members of the staff.' They were found to contain 'powdered gelignite, a pencil battery and a detonator rigged to explode the gelignite when the envelope was opened'. The White House mail room discovered the letters and had them defused by Secret Service bomb experts. The second attempt, by militant Puerto Rican pro-independence activists Oscar Collazo and Griselio Torresola, occurred on 1 November 1950 while President Truman resided at Blair House during the renovation of the White House. Torresola mortally wounded White House police officer Leslie Coffelt, who killed him in return fire. Secret Service agents wounded Collazo. Truman escaped unscathed, but after that the Secret Service took the president to various undisclosed locations for his daily walk. Several assassination attempts were made after Truman left office.

Under Truman, the Marshall Plan and the North Atlantic Treaty Organization (NATO) committed the United States to a role of world leadership and brought it out of its years of isolation, the country having entered both world wars late, the latter only in 1941 when it was attacked at Pearl Harbor. That night, Churchill said he had never slept so well. 'Being saturated and satiated with emotion and sensation, I went to bed and slept the sleep of the saved and thankful,' he wrote.

At the time, NATO was a military alliance established in 1949 to provide a common defence against potential Soviet and later Communist Chinese military aggression, and it was the first peacetime military alliance the US had ever joined. In 1947, Truman also established the Central Intelligence Agency (CIA).

Implemented in 1947 and 1948, the Marshall Plan provided more than $15 billion to help finance rebuilding efforts in Europe. Named after its designer, US Secretary of State George C. Marshall, it was a four-year plan to reconstruct cities, industries and infrastructure heavily damaged during the war and to remove trade barriers between European neighbours – as well as foster commerce between those countries.

Others have written on the importance of the Truman Doctrine and his foreign policy initiatives. On 11 May 1945 Truman ended Lend-Lease to Russia. George Herring argues that Stalin saw this as an attempt to extort political concessions by economic pressure. This looks like an early start to the Cold War. Truman oversaw a major confrontation with the Soviets, the Berlin airlift in 1948 that carried food, fuel and other supplies into West Berlin by plane. In March 1948, Britain, France and the United States decided to combine their sections of Berlin into one unified West Berlin. In June 1948 the Soviet Union, whose territory fully surrounded the capital, cut off all ground traffic into and out of West Berlin in an attempt to force the Allies to abandon the city. The blockade of Berlin had begun. The lift went on through April 1949.

The Truman Doctrine in 1947 established that the United States would provide assistance to all democratic nations under threat from external or internal authoritarian forces. It effectively reoriented US foreign policy, away from its prior isolationist stance to one of possible intervention in overseas disputes.

A low point was Truman's announcement on 27 June 1950 ordering US troops to South Korea, under General Douglas MacArthur, to help them defend against an invasion from the north of the peninsula. He did not consult Congress for a declaration of war. Almost forty thousand Americans died in that war, with around a hundred thousand casualties, and the North Korea problem has still not been resolved. The fighting ended on 27 July 1953 when the Korean Armistice Agreement was signed. The agreement created the Korean Demilitarised Zone (DMZ), a 155-mile-long, 2.5-mile-wide zone to separate North and South Korea and allowed the return of prisoners. A notable side effect is that the DMZ has become an unintentional major wildlife preserve and bird sanctuary.

We of course must deal with the dropping of the two atomic bombs ordered by Harry Truman, which are certainly among the most monumental decisions made by any president ever. In retrospect the decision seems even more consequential for humanity than the declaration of war by FDR on 8 December 1941, after the attack on Pearl Harbor – the day, he famously said, 'that will live in infamy'.

Apparently, Truman didn't know fully about the existence of the Manhattan Project or the bombs until he was briefed on 24 April 1945. The project was so secret that FDR had not informed his fourth-term vice-president that it existed. But Truman did have some suspicions that something highly secretive was going on. As part of his 1943 senatorial investigations into war-production expenditures, he asked questions about a suspicious plant in Minneapolis, which was secretly connected with the Manhattan Project. Truman received a call from FDR's secretary of war, Harry Stimson, warning him to back off. When President Roosevelt died on 12 April 1945, Truman was informed by Stimson of a new and terrible weapon being developed by physicists in New Mexico. In his diary that night, Truman noted that he had been informed that the US was perfecting an explosive great enough to destroy the whole world.

Truman went to Potsdam, Germany, to meet with Stalin and

Churchill from 17 July to 2 August 1945 to discuss how Germany, which had surrendered nine weeks earlier, was to be administered. Notably, France was excluded from the discussions. Lessons had clearly been learned from the First World War that showed what not to do at a peace conference. Keynes had been part of the UK delegation to the Versailles Conference but resigned and wrote about the inevitable consequences of the overly harsh reparations imposed on Germany set in the Treaty of Versailles that they would never be able to pay if the terms were too severe. By the end of the Potsdam Conference, Churchill had been voted out of office.

The successful Trinity test of the hydrogen bomb was conveyed to Stimson at Potsdam. As Diana Preston notes, the next day Stimson sent a note to Churchill saying: 'babies are satisfactorily born', which Churchill failed to understand and had to have it explained explicitly. With Churchill's agreement they told Stalin, who, it turned out, already knew, as Soviet intelligence had been receiving information about the project since 1941. The Potsdam Declaration for Japan outlined terms of unconditional surrender and threatened if they did not accede that they would meet 'prompt and utter destruction'. Japan rejected the terms but ultimately accepted them after the dropping of the two nuclear bombs and the intervention of the Russians in the Pacific theatre.

The enriched uranium bomb Little Boy was dropped by the *Enola Gay*, a Boeing Superfortress B29 bomber, on Hiroshima, Japan, on 6 August 1945. The UK gave permission for the attack, as was required by the 1943 Quebec Agreement. Truman was informed of the project's success in the Atlantic on his way home from Potsdam. The Fat Man plutonium bomb was dropped from a B-29 named *Bockscar* on Nagasaki on 9 August 1945, causing less damage than the first bomb. On the same day, as agreed with the Allies at the Tehran Conference in November 1943 and the Yalta Conference in February 1945, the Soviet Union entered the war in the Far East within three months of the end of the war in Europe. The invasion of Manchuria began on 9 August 1945. The Soviet entry into the war and the defeat of Japan's Kwantung Army was a significant factor in the Japanese government's decision to surrender.

The second bomb was dropped not least to prove that the US had more than one bomb and to save the many allied lives that would have been lost in any invasion of mainland Japan. When asked about the decision to drop the bomb and how hard it was, in an interview Truman said, 'I went to bed and got a good eight-hour sleep.'

Diana Preston further reported that Truman addressed the American people on 10 August 1945 in a nationwide radio broadcast:

> Having found the bomb, we have used it. We have used it against those who attacked us without warning at Pearl Harbor, against those who have starved and beaten and executed American prisoners of war, against those who have abandoned all pretence of obeying international laws of warfare. We have used it in order to shorten the agony of war, in order to save the lives of thousands and thousands of young American lives.

Compelling stuff.

Apparently, the US had a couple more bombs available in August, with more being prepared. The surrender of Imperial Japan was announced by Japanese Emperor Hirohito on VJ Day, 15 August. The surrender documents were formally signed by the Japanese and General MacArthur at a twenty-three-minute ceremony on 2 September, on the deck of the 45,000-ton battleship USS *Missouri*, named after Truman's home state. The ceremony took place in Tokyo Bay before representatives of nine allied countries, including Admiral Sir Bruce Fraser for the UK. The bombs worked, along with the Soviet intervention, which in the end some academics have argued was even more important than the bombs. The Second World War was over. The *Missouri* sits today as a permanent museum in Pearl Harbor, Hawaii.

McCarthyism raged during the final two years of Truman's second term. Wisconsin senator Joe McCarthy of 'Have you no decency, sir?' fame, in a speech in February 1950, had claimed he had a list of 'members of the Communist Party and members of a spy ring' who were employed in the State Department. In succeeding years after his 1950 speech, McCarthy made additional accusations of communist infiltration into the State Department, the administration of President Harry S. Truman, the Voice of America, and the US Army. Inevitably, McCarthy and Truman clashed frequently. At a news conference in Key West, Truman was asked about McCarthy.

Q: 'Do you think that Senator McCarthy can show any disloyalty exists in the State Department?'

The President: 'I think the greatest asset that the Kremlin has is Senator McCarthy.'

Truman was known for having a sharp tongue.

In August 1946 HST created the Council of Economic Advisers (CEA) to the president, which has an audience of one. It provides POTUS with his own economic advice and analysis. Many great economists have been appointed to its chair, including Nobel laureate Joseph Stiglitz; Martin Feldstein, creator of the National Bureau of Economic Research – where I have been a research associate for thirty years – and ex-Fed chairs Alan Greenspan and Ben Bernanke, along with four distinguished labour economists: current US Treasury Secretary and another ex-chair of the Federal Reserve and President of the San Francisco Fed, Janet Yellen, and the current incumbent Ceci Rouse, along with two dear labour economist friends who recently passed away: Eddie Lazear and Alan Krueger.

The CEA has been remarkably successful, and being a member and especially its chair has been a launching pad for the careers of many economists.

Wartime recoveries are always rapid and tumultuous. America had the benefit that little of its territory had been devastated, but much of the rest of the world had been and there was much rebuilding to do as the troops came home. Memories of the Great Depression were still in people's minds, as the war and pre-war spending had brought full employment. The female participation rate had risen during the war and expectations were that this would continue an upward trajectory, which it has done in subsequent years.

A labour economist has to talk about labour markets. The war brought full employment; in 1935 US unemployment rates were 20 per cent; by 1945 they had fallen to 1.9 per cent. The month that Truman won re-election, November 1948, the unemployment rate was 3.8 per cent, having been 4 per cent or lower every month that year. In November 1952 it was 2.7 per cent: between March 1952 and September 1953 it was below 3 per cent in thirteen months, reaching 2.5 per cent in May and June 1953.

But in the immediate post-war years, Truman struggled to deal with a wave of strikes. In 1946, this included one by the United Auto Workers as well as among railroad workers, coal miners and steel workers. In 1947, Congress responded to the strike wave by passing, over President Truman's veto, the Taft–Hartley Act, restricting the powers and activities of labour unions. The act is still in force as of 2021. In the 1940s, around a third of private sector workers were members of unions compared with 5.3 per cent in 2020.

In 1944, the world came to talk to J.M. Keynes in Bretton Woods, at the Mount Washington Hotel up the road from my Dartmouth office in New Hampshire. Keynes wasn't well and wanted to get out of the bad air of New York City, so he came to the Great North Woods. The meeting resulted in the establishment of both the World Bank and the IMF. In his great book on the summit, Ed Conway tells the tale of why the US appoints the head of the World Bank and Europe gets to appoint the head of the IMF.

It turns out it is a spy-story, and it goes like this. On Keynes's recommendation, Truman nominated Harry Dexter White, who was a senior US Treasury official and senior representative of the US at the summit, as executive director of the IMF. But White had been under surveillance by the FBI since November 1945 due to his connections with Russian intelligence. Conway notes that shortly afterwards, Truman was notified that White was involved with Soviet espionage.

J. Edgar Hoover, Director of the FBI, was concerned that even though White was unfit, removing his nomination, which had already been approved by the Senate, would cause an unholy mess. In the end, the top job at the IMF at its establishment in 1948 went to a Belgian, Camille Gutt.

When Truman retired, he moved back to his hometown of Independence, Missouri, where he lived for the remainder of his life and established his presidential library, in which he spent a lot of time through the mid-1960s until his health deteriorated. Truman famously had financial difficulties and did not make money from his presidency. He taught occasional classes at universities including Yale and survived from selling an inheritance he had received from his mother. He also published a two-volume set of his memoirs, which sold well.

Nuclear bombs, the CEA, the CIA, NATO, the Marshall Plan, the Berlin airlift; war and peace. Plus, he recognised the state of Israel. Truman made a lasting impact on the world, and the institutions he created have stood the test of time. As time has gone by, Truman's reputation has risen. When he left the presidency, Harry was one of the most unpopular presidents ever. 'His conduct of foreign policy, tackling the Soviets, has endured well.' He converted the US economy from a war footing to a peacetime economy and advanced civil rights by desegregating the military and banning discrimination in the civil service. Truman even called for a national health service and a minimum wage. A number of polls have been taken in recent years among voters and scholars on which presidents Americans believe were the best, and Truman generally ranks in the top ten. He even has a nuclear-powered Nimitz-class aircraft carrier named after him, which was commissioned in 1998. Its battle flag has the phrase 'Give 'em hell' on it. It didn't hurt that Harry S. Truman had the greatest labour market ever. Not bad for a college dropout.

David Blanchflower is the Bruce V. Rauner 78 Professor of Economics at Dartmouth and the University of Glasgow, a Bloomberg TV Contributing Editor, a Research Associate at the NBER and an ex-member of the Bank of England's Monetary Policy Committee.

34

Dwight D. Eisenhower

20 January 1953 to 20 January 1961
Republican
Vice-president: Richard M. Nixon

By Peter Caddick-Adams

Full name: Dwight David Eisenhower
Born: 14 October 1890, Denison, Texas
Died: 28 March 1969, Washington, DC
Resting place: Dwight D. Eisenhower Presidential Library
Museum and Boyhood Home, Abilene, Kansas
Library/Museum: Abilene, Kansas
Education: West Point
Married to: Mary 'Mamie' Doud, m. 1916 (1896–1979)
Children: Two: Doud and John
Quotation: 'We are going to have peace, even if we have to
fight for it.'

DWIGHT DAVID EISENHOWER was the Supreme Commander of the Allied Expeditionary Force that invaded Normandy and defeated Germany, later becoming thirty-fourth president. In the Anglo-Saxon world Ike – as he was universally known – remains at least as celebrated for his achievement of pioneering victory in Europe in 1944–45 as for his two-term presidency of 1953–61. For many Americans, these were happy, confident years when America settled down to enjoy the growth and prosperity that the hard years of the 1940s had brought.

Yet Ike remains an enigma. He reached the very pinnacle of military command in the Second World War, despite possessing no combat experience of his own. Almost without exception, his military and political contemporaries from all nations had seen action in earlier wars, many being wounded. Even his predecessor, Harry S. Truman, an unlikely military figure, had served under fire in France with the Missouri National Guard. Likewise, Ike came to the presidency with no previous experience of public office or politics. Until 1948, Eisenhower had never even voted. Nothing in his earlier life remotely shouted future Supreme Military Commander, or president. So, what were the special qualities that enabled him to step into the shoes of the great, twice over?

Ike arrived on 14 October 1890 as the third of seven sons born to David Jacob Eisenhower and Ida Elizabeth, née Stover. One of his younger siblings, Paul, died aged ten months, but Ike remained closest to the youngest surviving son, Milton (1899–1985), whose advice he sought and respected. After a period of government service, the latter also became a president – of three universities in succession, Kansas State; Pennsylvania State; and Johns Hopkins. The boys grew up in Abilene, Kansas, a town of under three thousand citizens. His parents had suffered financial embarrassment and his early years were spent in straitened circumstances, under the influence of his excessively devout mother.

Through the intercession of his local senator, and to his mother's disappointment, Dwight was accepted for West Point in 1911 and commissioned into the infantry, class of 1915, famous for producing fifty-nine generals out of one hundred and sixty-four graduates. However, as an instructor preparing young Tank Corps officers (including the future novelist F. Scott Fitzgerald) for the European war, he missed being posted overseas himself.

The young Ike met 'Mamie', Mary Geneva Doud, at a military function in 1915 and they married the following year when he was nineteen. She understood the necessity of supporting her husband as he rose through the ranks, with the result that she fitted naturally into the role of First Lady and is generally regarded as being one of the most successful, if overshadowed by her successor, Jacqueline Kennedy. By the end of Ike's presidential career, the couple had moved twenty-eight times. One of their two sons, Doud, died young of scarlet fever, but John was commissioned from West Point on 6 June 1944 (D-Day prevented his father from attending his graduation), and rose to become a soldier, ambassador and respected author.

As always with high achievers, it is instructive to peer behind the mask to discover their mentors. In 1922, Captain Eisenhower reported to Panama on the staff of Major General Fox Conner, who instilled in him a love of military history. Often credited as 'the man who made Eisenhower', Conner gave his protégé directed reading, would test him on his observations, and together they would critique the great battle captains of the past. Ike's efficiency also caught the eye of US Army Chief of Staff, General Douglas MacArthur, when serving as an aide on his staff, and attracted the patronage of the future US Army Chief of Staff during the war, George C. Marshall, who similarly mentored the rising star.

His aptitude for staff work was demonstrated in 1926, when he graduated first out of 275 at the US Army's Command and General Staff School, Fort Leavenworth, Kansas, and again in 1928, when he attended the Army War College, at Carlisle, Pennsylvania. Major Eisenhower drew his own conclusions about what was then termed the Great War in 1929, when attached to the American Battle Monuments Commission in France, to write *A Guide to the American Battle Fields in Europe*, a work still in print. In this role he was directed by General 'Black Jack' Pershing, commander of the AEF during the war and another influential patron. Ike's passion for history, shared by his later subordinate (though five years older), George S. Patton, was such that he and Mamie would retire not to his native Kansas, but adjacent to the Gettysburg battlefield in Pennsylvania.

His analysis of the American experience in France of 1917–18 taught him the necessities of a resolute political coalition, overwhelming superiority in men and materiel, and thorough training. His inter-war military education involved much study of military history, which brought Ike deep insights into human nature. He and his contemporaries were urged to realise they were not delving into the past for its own sake, but to understand that while weapons and technology change, soldiers and commanders do not. Through the generations, they are the same individuals, motivated by similar hopes and fears. Ike found this good ammunition for judging people, both as a general and as a president.

Having gained a private pilot's licence in his spare time, by 1940 Lieutenant Colonel Eisenhower had demonstrated all the qualities needed in a hard-working staff officer, but not necessarily a great general. At this stage, America's 180,000-man army ranked nineteenth in the world, slightly smaller than Portugal's. France was considered the world's military superpower, and it was the humbling of that country in May 1940 that initiated the US Army's massive growth. Partly overseen by Eisenhower, five years later the army would contain nearly 8.3 million in uniform.

The rapid expansion brought incredible opportunities and promotion. After staff posts in Washington, DC in June 1942, Marshall promoted Ike over 366 senior officers to be a lieutenant general, Commander of US troops in Europe, based in London. He had risen from lieutenant colonel to lieutenant general in sixteen months. This rapid elevation worked due to Eisenhower's personal charm and tact, where a lesser man would have excited envy or bitterness. His ambitious deputy, who was prone to stir emotions, was the future commander in Italy, Mark Clark.

Ike's personal qualities, as well as Marshall's patronage, were surely the key to his success. He was the ultimate 'team player', able to reconcile different national interests, as well as being an outstanding staff officer, while radiating calm and inner confidence. In command of the Anglo-American landings in French North Africa, he oversaw US forces in combat for the first time. It was here, during Operation Torch, that Eisenhower very nearly came unstuck.

To neutralise enemy opposition, he negotiated a pact with the local Vichy French commander, Admiral Darlan, which caused uproar among the Free French led by de Gaulle. Roosevelt and senior allied commanders backed him, appreciating the strategic benefits this created, if temporarily complicating geopolitics, but it brought Ike his first insights into the politics of building coalitions. Tunisia, his first combat command, was marked in February 1943 by the US setback at the Kasserine Pass, where a subordinate was defeated by Erwin Rommel. With necessary ruthlessness, Ike replaced him with the thrusting George Patton. Thereafter, Patton discreetly referred to Eisenhower in his diaries as 'Divine Destiny', after the initials of his forenames.

As Supreme Allied Commander Mediterranean, Ike went on to oversee the July 1943 landings on Sicily (Operation Husky), and that September at Salerno (Operation Avalanche). With his hands-on experience of leading an Anglo-American-Canadian coalition against formidable German forces, assisted by numerous other allies, involving air, land and maritime forces, encompassing extensive amphibious operations, it is not difficult to see why Eisenhower was appointed as head of SHAEF (the Supreme Headquarters Allied Expeditionary Force) in December 1943. His task was to lead the Normandy invasion the following summer.

Many of the winning Mediterranean team accompanied him to London, including Bernard Montgomery ('Monty'), who would initially command all land forces. The latter may have thought he was in the running for Eisenhower's job, but he little understood the military-political level of war. Their first meeting in March 1943 was difficult, with Monty noting afterwards:

> Eisenhower came and stayed a night with me. He is a very nice chap. I should say he is probably quite good on the political side. But I can also say, quite definitely, that he knows nothing whatever about how to make war or to fight battles; he should be kept away from all that business if we want to win this war. The American Army will never be any good until we can teach the generals their stuff.

It was a private opinion, never really revised, and would shape their relationship – and that of their respective armies – for the rest of the war. Montgomery was the subject of an Eisenhower oil painting. Like

Churchill, Ike used painting as a stressbuster, along with playing bridge, and was widely known as an accomplished player throughout the US Army, especially during the run-up to D-Day and during his presidency.

Although Field Marshal Alan Brooke, British Chief of the Imperial General Staff, had been promised the Allied Commander's post by Churchill, and General George C. Marshall, his opposite number in Washington, DC, had a similar understanding with Roosevelt, the two premiers came to an accord. Eisenhower's successors in the Mediterranean became British appointees, leaving that theatre dominated by London. In exchange, the invasion of north-west Europe would be American led. As Roosevelt preferred to keep Marshall, his trusted confidant, in Washington, the job went to his protégé, Eisenhower. Brooke, bitter at losing out, was of the Montgomery school of thought: 'The main impression I gathered was that Eisenhower was no real director of thought, plans, energy or direction. Just a coordinator, a good mixer, a champion of inter-Allied cooperation, and in these respects, few can hold a candle to him. But is that enough?'

Even King George VI was won over by the Kansan's charm. On their first meeting the monarch perceptively asked how he got along with Montgomery. 'Fine, your Majesty, except I always think Monty is after my job.' Quick as a flash came the regal retort: 'You relieve me greatly, General Eisenhower. I always thought he was after mine.' Despite Ike having the credit for choosing the time and place of the successful D-Day invasion under his belt, the north-western European campaign nevertheless twice strayed seriously off course.

First was the defeat of Operation Market Garden, the partially successful airborne operation that ended in failure at Arnhem. Although the initiative came from Montgomery, it was Ike who allowed it to proceed. Second was the December 1944 German offensive in the Ardennes (the Battle of the Bulge), which caught him and his intelligence team completely by surprise. However, he reacted quickly, controversially gave Montgomery temporary command of US units, and within the month had stabilised the front. After that, the course of the European war was predictable.

From VE Day for the rest of 1945, Ike was Military Governor of the American Occupation Zone in Germany, which included Karlsbrunn in the Saar, from where his ancestor, Nikolaus Eisenhauer, had migrated to Pennsylvania in 1741. Meanwhile, Eisenhower had gained his fifth star as General of the Army, and succeeded his last mentor, Marshall, as Chief of Staff in late 1945. He had risen to the very top as a professional staff officer; the concept is anathema to the British, who interspersed staff work with regimental duty and combat command.

Ike continued until 1948, when he was succeeded by his wartime contemporary and confidant, Omar Bradley. He was then elected president of Columbia University, establishing its Institute for War and Peace Studies, and it is here that his wider education began. He was given leave to continue working at NATO, established in April 1949, but from Columbia he learned how to debate rather than order, and of the world outside the military, that included international relations, economics and politics. Fund-raising for Columbia also brought him into contact with big business and the backers of his future presidential campaigns.

At this stage Eisenhower had no thoughts of political life, explicitly stating his hostility to any thought of seeking public office. Yet, as the election year of 1948 neared, Truman, who had still to win a term as president in his own right, privately approached Ike with an astonishing offer: that they campaign together on the Democratic ticket, with Eisenhower as the presidential candidate and Truman as his running mate. Ike's rejection of this unique opportunity underlined how little he regarded a life in politics, and how dedicated he was to containing the Russians, for in June 1948 Stalin had sealed off East Germany from the West, necessitating the Berlin airlift, lasting the next eleven months. On leave from Columbia, Ike gave priority to limiting the Soviet menace in Europe and overseeing the creation of NATO in 1949. Subsequently recalled to active duty, Eisenhower served as its first military head, SACEUR (Supreme Allied Commander Europe), in 1951–52, succeeded by Matthew Ridgway, one of his wartime subordinates.

Truman went on to win re-election in 1948, but during the Korean War grew increasingly unpopular due to its military stalemate, and for firing Douglas MacArthur as commander of UN forces. As the 1952 election approached, Eisenhower was busy with his NATO duties, but the Republicans were in disarray. Senator Taft of Ohio had become the leading candidate for the GOP nomination, but represented a revival of inter-war, isolationist thinking towards inter-national affairs, opposing American involvement in both NATO and the UN. Realising that much of the new world order now looked to America to continue the Truman doctrine of insulating commun-ism, other Republicans believed that leading the international community was the only viable approach to winning the Cold War.

Enter Senator Henry Cabot Lodge Jr of Massachusetts, who had fought with great distinction in the Second World War, being the first senator to resign his seat to serve since the Civil War. In 1944, he was appointed to the US Sixth Army Group as chief liaison officer to the French. As a respected soldier and a Republican with an internationalist outlook, Lodge led a behind-the-scenes lobby to spark Eisenhower's interest in politics. Publicly, Ike remained aloof from America's domestic wrangles, but privately he began to listen to Lodge's arguments during the latter's visits to NATO's Fontainebleau headquarters that a Taft presidency would essentially undo all Eisenhower had achieved in the European war and at NATO. The result was Eisenhower's acceptance that he would run against Taft, though he began his campaign only on leaving NATO in June 1952.

With Lodge as his campaign manager, Ike beat Taft for the Republican nomination in the first ballot. Some thought he would choose Lodge for his running mate, but Eisenhower's gaze fell on thirty-nine-year-old Senator Richard Nixon of California, an able 'fixer', with a presence in states and communities beyond Ike's reach. Nixon had recently won national attention for his role in a congres-sional investigation of Alger Hiss, a former State Department official accused of spying for the Soviets. Though in many ways the two men were chalk and cheese, their joint ticket widened the appeal of each of them, with Ike's grandson, Dwight David II, eventually marrying Nixon's daughter Julie.

Ike's popularity was such that when New Hampshire's governor sent a telegram stating he was ready to start to fire up his state, he had but one question: 'to which political party does General Eisenhower belong?' The said general proved an excellent campaigner, blessed with his naturally sunny countenance − the legendary grin − and his ability to deliver off-the-cuff speeches full of plain talk, as he had done to millions of troops during the Second World War. He managed a forty-five-state tour by train, speaking to large crowds, who were as entranced by his war record as they were by his 'I like Ike' slogan. Equally adept on television (1952 was the first time TV commercials played a role in a presidential election), he never mentioned his opponent, Adlai Stevenson, by name, and pushed home his simple recipe for victory, K1C2 (Korea, Communism and Corruption).

On 4 November 1952, Eisenhower won 55 per cent of the popular vote and a landslide in the Electoral College, with 442 votes to Stevenson's 89. However, the vote was for the man, not his adopted party, and Republicans won the House of Representatives by three seats, and the Senate by just one. One of the unfortunates, who had neglected his Senate seat to run Ike's campaign, was Henry Cabot Lodge, who lost Massachusetts to John F. Kennedy, and deserves more credit as 'the man who made President Ike' than he has received.

Eisenhower spent the first two years of his tenure dealing with the charges levelled by Senator Joe McCarthy of communist infiltration into government agencies. Republicans had benefited from his allegations that Truman was 'soft on the Reds', but his attacks continued into Eisenhower's Republican administration. Public interest was significant, fuelled by the media, though the claims never led to indictments or convictions. The president stayed his hand for several reasons. He felt that public criticism would demean his office, or might work to McCarthy's advantage, and was reluctant to alienate influential Republicans, who viewed the claims as true, even if they disliked the senator's methods.

During the election, some felt that Ike had not spoken out to protect his own mentor, Marshall, whose State Department had initially excited McCarthy's attention. However, in 1954 the senator turned his attention to alleged communist influence within the US Army, an institution Ike had served all his adult life. Colleagues meanwhile began to conclude that the senator was a troubled, vindictive soul, with an exaggerated war record, consumed by a drink and morphine addiction, chasing bogeymen who did not exist. Eisenhower was behind the move to let television cameras follow the senator at work, bullying and ranting. Immediately, McCarthy lost public support, and at the end of 1954 the Senate censured him, but in avoiding a confrontation and being slow to react, Ike was perceived as weak by some observers.

Four years later, as the end of his first term drew near, Ike having originally stated he was a 'one-term-man', it was uncertain whether he would run again, and in September 1955 he suffered a major heart attack. After a lengthy convalescence, he was pronounced fit by his cardiologist and his election campaign swung into full gear, with the Eisenhower–Nixon team easily winning the GOP nomination. Yet behind Ike's robust bonhomie there lurked his frail health. He was a heavy smoker (a sixty-a-day man), and his heart attack in the first term was followed by a stroke in the second, with gastrointestinal surgery in between. The demands on a president's health in this era were excessive by today's standards; for example, it took twenty-two hours to fly from Washington to Paris. Part of the dynamic tension of the eight-year Eisenhower–Nixon partnership was triggered by the possibility that at any stage Nixon might become president. Ironically, of the two, the vice-president was probably the more militarily hawkish, in favour of involvement in Vietnam as early as 1954.

Ike's gravitas as a cautious statesman played out to his advantage in the 1956 campaign. While the result was probably never in doubt, Ike's lead widened when he dealt with not one but two foreign crises. At the end of October, Israel, Britain and France attacked Egypt to win back the Suez Canal from President Nasser, who had nationalised it in July. Eisenhower was personally stung that two of his staunchest NATO allies had planned the move in secret without consulting him. He immediately condemned the action and imposed sanctions that forced the invaders to withdraw.

At the same moment, Soviet troops invaded Hungary. Earlier in the year, Nikita Khrushchev had exposed Stalin's crimes and appeared to be liberalising Russia's approach to its Warsaw Pact neighbours. This encouraged the self-determination of the Eastern bloc, particularly in Hungary. Rather than see the disintegration of communism, Khruschev's uncompromising response was to crush the uprising with military force, killing hundreds, while two hundred thousand fled abroad. Faced with the reality of a nuclear-armed Soviet Union and a distracted Britain and France, Eisenhower limited his response to condemning the invasion and assisting Hungarian refugees.

With their president having proved himself able to rebuff international friends and enemies alike, Americans rallied behind him, and on Tuesday 6 November 1956, even more turned out for Eisenhower than four years earlier. He won forty-one states and received nearly 58 per cent of the popular vote, slicing deep into even African American support for Adlai Stevenson, the former Illinois governor, whom he defeated for the second time. This time, however, the Democrats retained control of Congress, which they had secured in the mid-term elections of 1954. Again, 1956 proved a personal triumph for Eisenhower, if not for his party.

It is easy to forget that Ike himself had risen to great heights from a poor background and had encountered many soldiers from worse circumstances. He thus pioneered what he called Modern Republicanism, which promoted individual freedom and the positive aspects of a market-driven economy, and appealed to moderate Republicans. However, he defied the conservative old guard in refusing to roll back Roosevelt's New Deal programmes or diminish government regulation of the economy. Less inclined to slash taxes as loud voices in the GOP demanded, Eisenhower also understood the wisdom of balancing government spending. Treading a middle path between 'the unfettered power of concentrated wealth and the unbridled power of statism or partisan interests', he signed legislation that expanded Social Security, increased the minimum wage, and created the Department of Health, Education and Welfare.

Against some Republican instincts, he saw the advantage of directing state spending into infrastructure. Remembering his 1945 advances through Germany along the Third Reich's autobahn networks, Eisenhower initiated the Interstate Highway programme, creating a 41,000-mile road system. This also stimulated the economy and made driving long distances faster and safer. In partnership with Canada, he invested in a system of canals, locks and channels that linked the Great Lakes to the Atlantic – the St Lawrence Seaway. These were very public achievements, initiated and completed during his presidency, which directly affected the lives of millions, and won him great support. For those who had suffered in the Great Depression of the 1930s, these policies were seen to bring economic security and stability throughout the decade.

Under Eisenhower, personal income soared by around 45 per cent, which brought many the power to eat out, buy an automobile, own their own home, invest in kitchen appliances, and above all, acquire a television. This was the era when TV really expanded in America, at least a decade before the rest of the world.

Seen as the author of all this largesse, which none of his Republican or Democrat rivals would have delivered in the same fashion, or as fast, Ike earned approval ratings throughout his two terms that consistently hovered in the seventies.

Taking off the rose-tinted spectacles, the revisionist view of the Eisenhower years is that although America's poverty rate declined during his two terms, maybe one in five – chiefly within the African American communities – were not admitted to the prosperity of the era. Many had left the South for the urban sprawls of Detroit, Chicago and Cleveland where unskilled, low-paid jobs replaced their previous agricultural work. However, these people had no voice – they would find it in the 1960s – and their financial and racial inequality rarely made the news, leaving the American dream confined to a larger demographic, but a white, middle-class one. Although the same accusation can be levelled at his Democratic rivals, Eisenhower was only a limited supporter of black civil rights. While not necessarily against, he urged caution and osmosis rather than swift change, arguing – probably correctly – that successful integration required a change of hearts and minds. Thus, he had argued against desegregation within the US military during the 1948 debate before Truman's Executive Order No. 9981.

Ike's attitude reflected less outright hostility, but more the limited horizons of his upbringing in a small Kansas town, and the lack of black representation in the US officer corps he knew so well. His reluctance to advance radical social change was of its time: few among his contemporaries thought it important enough to champion. However, it is significant that on only a single occasion did he meet African American leaders, and he failed utterly to use his tenure to build popular support for racial integration, which would have given his 'hearts and minds' argument more credence. Although this was the era of Brown versus the Topeka Board of Education, in which the Supreme Court in 1954 ruled that racial segregation of children in public schools was unconstitutional, when Eisenhower left the White House, only 6 per cent of African American pupils were attending integrated schools.

Yet at the time, many judged Eisenhower's presidency by the integrity of his earlier wartime record, when seemingly he rarely put a foot wrong. It was outlined in his bestselling 1948 narrative of those days, *Crusade in Europe*, largely ghost-written by his naval aide, Commander Harry C. Butcher. Most were drawn to the story, later related by Butcher, of Ike having taken the difficult decision to proceed with D-Day. About to return to his headquarters, Eisenhower had paused, drawn out a pen and scrawled a quick note. It was a press release, a memo to himself, the tension still evident in his handwriting. 'Our landings in the Cherbourg-Havre area have failed to gain a satisfactory foothold and I have withdrawn the troops,' it began. 'My decision to attack at this time and place was based upon the best information available. The troops, the air and the navy did all that bravery and devotion to duty could do. If any blame or fault attaches to the attempt it is mine alone.' Sixty-six words; it contained several insertions and crossings out; distractedly, he dated it 5 July, rather than June, and folded it untidily into his wallet. Butcher found it months later and was allowed to keep it.

Those sixty-six words explain why the modest Kansan became Supreme Commander and, later, a two-term president. He had no pretensions; was prepared to take the blame if things went wrong. Eisenhower had no use for distinguishing badges, other than the stars of his rank, a single line of medal ribbons above his left breast pocket, and his SHAEF shoulder patch. In the eyes of a majority of his troops, and later his citizens, there was no swagger or bluster about him. It was his self-effacing humility of character that those around him recalled, rather than his bearing or the trappings of his office. A born listener equally to generals and corporals, he had no need for flags, framed certificates or signed photographs of the great to remind him of his job. Throughout his life, Eisenhower acted as the conductor of an orchestra. He resolved discord and produced winning harmony, to the intense satisfaction of his many audiences.

Ike's tenure was immediately eclipsed by the youthful energy of John F. Kennedy, and historians rushed to condemn his presidency as dull, quiet and old-fashioned. In the twenty-first century this analysis has been reversed to conclude he was rather successful. Eisenhower was one of the few who achieved what he set out to do, remained his own man, and resisted powerful lobbies. Well-organised, analytical, steady, Ike was the polar opposite of presidents seen as reactive, bouncing between crises and controversies.

In his farewell address of 17 January 1961, Eisenhower famously warned that America had created an unhealthy 'military–industrial complex', akin to a permanent war economy, arising via the Second World War and Korean conflict, which he had failed to limit. We have lingered over his army record because that is how and why he became president, courted by both political parties. The army defined him, and on his stepping down from office, it was military business and his wartime and NATO roles that claimed his attention. On 6 June 1964, he and Walter Cronkite, both giants in their respective fields of expertise, released a still fondly remembered ninety-minute documentary, *D-Day Plus Twenty Years*. As a sage, his foreign affairs advice was sought by his successors: Kennedy over Cuba and Lyndon B. Johnson over Vietnam. In truth, though, he rapidly slowed, devoting most of his time to his family, writing memoirs and painting.

It is intriguing to consider Eisenhower's career had he accepted Truman's offer in 1948. Doubtless he would have won, and been re-elected in 1952, but the Twenty-second Constitutional Amendment had meanwhile been ratified in February 1951, still limiting him to two terms in office. His reputation would have been marred, as was his predecessor's, by the stalemate of Korea, bringing him into confrontation with his old boss, MacArthur, who he had never liked. As usual in his illustrious career, Dwight David Eisenhower made the correct decision, declining an offer very few would have been capable of resisting. Consequently, with no ambitions for public office, he shines through still today as that rare, honourable individual who put duty to one's country before self.

Ike's health declined rapidly when he stepped down from office, aged seventy, and by the time of his passing, he had suffered a total of seven heart attacks. Extremely popular until the end, few were surprised at his death from heart failure on 28 March 1969. He was interred in the chapel of the Eisenhower Presidential Center in Abilene, Kansas.

Peter Caddick-Adams is a professor of military history at Cranfield University.

35

John F. Kennedy

20 January 1961 to 22 November 1963
Democrat
Vice-president: Lyndon B. Johnson

By Simon Burns

Full Name: John Fitzgerald Kennedy
Born: 29 May 1917, 83 Beals Street, Brookline, Massachusetts
Died: 22 November 1963, Dallas, Texas
Resting place: Arlington National Cemetery, Washington, DC
Library/Museum: Boston, Massachusetts
Education: Edward Devotion School, Noble and Greenough Lower School, Dexter School, Riverdale Country School, Canterbury School, Choate; Princeton and Harvard Universities
Married to: Jacqueline Lee Bouvier, m. 1953 (1929–94)
Children: Four: Caroline, John Jr, Arabella (stillborn), Patrick
Quotation: 'Ask not what your country can do for you – ask

what you can do for your country.' (Inaugural Address,
20 January 1961)

IT IS REMARKABLE that, though his presidency lasted a mere
thousand days, with relatively few domestic achievements to its
credit, John F. Kennedy still inspires many in America, who hark
back to a time before the Vietnam War, Watergate and the Iraq
War, when government was trusted and cynicism had not corrupted
the body politic.

At forty-three years old, Kennedy was the first president born
in the twentieth century and is the youngest person to have been
elected president (Theodore Roosevelt was forty-two when he
took office, but that was due to the assassination of William
McKinley and not by election) and he was succeeding the oldest
man up until then to have been so, Dwight D. Eisenhower. With
a young and beautiful wife and two young children, his family
captured the imagination of the nation and came to epitomise the
hopes for the 1960s, in contrast to what was considered the dour
and stagnant 1950s, by projecting an image of vigour and excitement not usually associated with politicians, and an optimism,
which Ronald Reagan embraced so effectively two decades later,
that America's best years were ahead of it.

Behind the immense charm and projected image, Kennedy was
a paradox. He was a gifted politician often reacting to events he
did not anticipate or understand, dealing with some well and others
badly. He was intelligent, often detached, inquisitive and candid,
even if he could be careless and disorganised. By nature, he was
very impatient, addicted to excitement and with a self-belief that
his charm would always win over others in any one-on-one
encounter − a notion that proved disastrous when he first met the
Russian premier Khrushchev in Vienna in June 1961.

Kennedy was decisive, but with a reluctance to take a decision
until the last minute and, even then, mostly opting for the most
moderate option. He was unencumbered by ideology beyond anti-
communism, conservative economic policies and a strong belief in
proactive government. Unlike his brothers Robert and Edward, he

was fairly unemotional and instinctively compartmentalised his life. As his friend Charlie Bartlett said: 'No one ever knew John Kennedy, not all of him.'

Richard Reeve, in his biography of President Kennedy, wrote:

All his relationships were bilateral. He was a compartmentalised man with much to hide, comfortable with secrets and lies. He needed them because that was part of the stimulation: things were rarely what they seemed . . . his White House organisation would look like a wheel with many spokes and himself at what he called "the vital centre." It was instinctive at first. Kennedy said: "I had different identities, and that was a useful way of expressing each without compromising the others."

But it was the influence of his father, Joseph Kennedy Sr, and his tight-knit family that shaped the man he was to become. Joseph Kennedy was both a Catholic and of Irish descent in a Boston controlled by Brahmin Protestants, and the prejudice he encountered haunted his outlook throughout his life. Although he was a very successful businessman who amassed a considerable fortune from an early age, the motivation for his success was always for family – the wealth and the power that that brought him were the means to fulfil a desperate need to elevate his and his family's status.

No one believed more fervently in family than Joseph Kennedy. Of all the lessons he taught his children, there was none more important – family took precedence over everything else. In his memoirs, Edward Kennedy wrote: 'From our earliest days I think all the Kennedy children were made to feel that our father's principal interest in life was his family.'

As the second of nine children, John Kennedy was inculcated with this philosophy from a young age, as were his siblings. But it was a two-edged sword. If family was a refuge from the world, it was also a weapon to beat the world. To achieve this the Kennedys had to be trained for it, and it was instilled in them from a young age that they always had to win: coming second was not acceptable. Their competitiveness in all walks of life was renowned. As Eunice Kennedy Shriver told a biographer: 'Daddy was always very competitive. The thing he always kept telling us is that coming in second or third was just no good. The important thing was to win – coming in second or third – that doesn't count – but win, win, win.'

The ultimate prize was the American presidency, but after Joseph Kennedy's tenure as the ambassador to the Court of St James ended following a disastrous interview he gave to a *Boston Globe* reporter in 1940, destroying his presidential aspirations, his hopes transferred to his eldest son, Joe Jr. When he was tragically killed in 1944 while on a secret bombing mission in Europe, his father's hopes and aspirations transferred to his second son.

As a war hero, John Kennedy had a good backstory for a political career. He served in the US Navy in the Pacific during the Second World War, and when his PT boat was sliced in half by a Japanese destroyer he courageously saved the life of one of his injured crew members by using his teeth and a leather strap to tow him to safety on a nearby island.

Ironically, he never envisaged embarking on a political career, assuming that his elder brother would be the politician in the family and that he would pursue a career in journalism or academia. It was only after the death of Joe Jr, and at the insistence of his father, that he was pushed into politics.

In 1946, he was elected a congressman from Boston, being re-elected in 1948 and 1950. He was bored by the work and frustrated, because he could achieve little, as the House of Representatives was governed by the seniority system and as a very junior member his influence was paltry. He was viewed by colleagues as a dilettante with the image of a playboy. In 1952, he took the high risk of challenging the incumbent Republican senator Henry Cabot Lodge for a seat in the US Senate and, in a landslide year for the Republican presidential candidate, Dwight Eisenhower, who won Massachusetts by two hundred thousand votes, he defeated Lodge by just over seventy thousand votes, primarily due to his hard work, Kennedy money and tea parties hosted for women by his mother and sisters.

John used the Senate as a springboard to nurture his presidential ambitions. He nearly died twice, in 1954 and 1955, when two operations on his back were botched, but during his recuperation he wrote a Pulitzer Prize-winning book, *Profiles in Courage*, about eight politicians who at crucial times in American history took unpopular decisions, regardless of the impact on their careers, because they believed it was the right thing to do in the national interest. His bid at the Democratic National Convention in 1956 to be Adlai Stevenson's vice-presidential running mate was ultimately unsuccessful, but his grace under fire won him massive national publicity and catapulted him to becoming a front-runner for the Democratic nomination for president in 1960.

The main challenges facing him in the battle for the nomination were twofold. First, he was a Catholic at a time when there was a deep prejudice against a Catholic becoming president, as it was feared, incredibly, that the Pope would dictate policy to a co-religionist. Second, in 1960 the nomination was determined by the party bosses in most states, as only sixteen of the fifty states held primary elections, and at forty-three years old many feared he was too young to be elected. His strategy was to fight in the primaries and seek to win them convincingly so as to persuade the men in smoke-filled rooms that he was a successful vote getter and winner. His first challenge was to win re-election to the Senate from Massachusetts in 1958 by the largest margin possible to prove his electoral appeal. This was achieved when he was re-elected by a margin of 874,608 votes, the largest margin of victory in a state-wide Massachusetts election up to that point.

Two presidential primary elections in 1960 – Wisconsin and West Virginia – were particularly challenging for Kennedy. If his strategy were to succeed, he knew he had to win all the primary elections he entered or he would be finished. In Wisconsin he won with a credible 56 per cent of the vote, but it turned into a pyrrhic victory when the press interpreted his margin of victory as due to the sizeable Catholic presence going out and voting for one of their own. This compelled Kennedy to enter the next primary, West Virginia, which originally was viewed as an easy state for him to win. It was overwhelmingly Protestant and mired in poverty, and early opinion polls projected Kennedy would win it by a 60:40 margin against Hubert Humphrey, but that was before it was widely known that Kennedy was a Catholic. As the campaign began and more West Virginians learned of his faith, the polls reversed themselves and Kennedy trailed Humphrey by 40:60. The campaign was dirty and gruelling. Kennedy skilfully turned the question of religious bigotry on its head by effectively making it an issue of tolerance versus intolerance and pushing his war record in a state where a disproportionate number of people had or still did serve in the military.

Kennedy also cleverly used Franklin Roosevelt Jr as a surrogate in the campaign. His father had been lionised in West Virginia, and bringing his son into the state to campaign for Kennedy was a smart move. Less honourably, Roosevelt unfairly attacked Humphrey's war record – or rather his lack of one. Humphrey had tried to enlist after Pearl Harbor but was turned down on medical grounds. The scars of this episode were to last long after the election was over.

In the end the Kennedys turned the election around, and on polling day the insurgent beat Humphrey by almost 60 per cent to just under 40 per cent of the vote. By the time Kennedy arrived at the Democratic Convention in Los Angeles in July 1960, despite the last-minute entrance of Lyndon B. Johnson into the race, he had enough votes to win the nomination on the first ballot, and in a politically skilful move that upset his liberal supporters and even his brother, Robert, he made Johnson his vice-presidential running mate.

The outcome of the 1960 presidential election was never going to be a foregone conclusion on either side. The outgoing Republican president, Eisenhower, was still very popular, America was at peace, living standards for the average American had increased dramatically in the last decade and Kennedy's Republican opponent, Vice-President Richard Nixon, was a formidable campaigner. However, there was a mood in the country, encouraged by Kennedy, that the 1950s had been a period of stagnation and that America could do better.

Kennedy won the election by the slimmest of margins, becoming the first, and only, Catholic president until Joe Biden was elected in 2020. Although he won the Electoral College vote convincingly (303 to 219 votes), his victory in the popular vote was minuscule. Out of 64.32 million votes cast, his majority was a mere 112,827 votes (0.17 per cent).

With such a small majority, a number of incidents during the campaign could be used to claim they provided the margin of victory. The reality is that it was a combination of issues that led to Kennedy's win. The first televised debate was a major contributor, as Kennedy appeared fresh and sun-tanned while Nixon, to cover his five o'clock shadow, had used Lazy-Shave makeup that ran under the heat of the television cameras, giving him an appearance of being ill; the telephone call by both Kennedy brothers to Coretta Scott King and the relevant judge, when Martin Luther King was arrested and thrown into jail in October 1960, swayed a significant proportion of African American voters to Kennedy. Also influential was the claim that America was lagging behind the Soviet Union, especially with a missile gap (a claim later found to be incorrect); and the tackling of the Catholic issue head-on by Kennedy early in the general election campaign when he told the Greater Houston Ministerial Association, 'I am not the Catholic candidate for president. I am the Democratic Party's candidate for president who also happens to be a Catholic. I do not speak for my church on public matters – and the church does not speak for me.' Although this did not remove the issue from the minds of some voters, it certainly did reduce the concerns of others. Above all, just as Franklin Roosevelt had recognised the power of radio to influence public opinion, Kennedy understood the importance of television, and with his photogenic looks, charm and wit he embraced the new medium and became the first television candidate and then president.

His inaugural address, probably the second-most-remembered address after FDR's first one in 1933, was a clarion call to Cold War warriors, not only urging the American people to 'Ask not what your country can do for you – ask what you can do for your country', but also warning: 'Let every nation know, whether it wishes us well or ill, that we shall pay any price, bear any burden, meet any hardship, support any friend, oppose any foe to ensure the survival and success of liberty. This much we pledge – and more.'

These tough words reflected the mood of the Americans towards the world situation that Kennedy inherited when he became president. The Cold War was heating up, with the Soviet Union, under the leadership of Nikita Khrushchev, pushing and prodding the Americans by creating flashpoints in Third World countries where they hoped to encourage the spread of communism. The first crisis came in the Congo, where former premier Patrice Lumumba was assassinated, swiftly followed by a crisis in Laos where communist-led forces were close to taking over the country.

Then came Berlin, with the building of the wall to separate East and West Berlin in August 1961.

April 1961 saw the Bay of Pigs, Kennedy's worst foreign policy disaster. Ever since Castro had overthrown the dictator Batista in Cuba in 1959 and turned it into a satellite of the Soviet Union, the Americans had been obsessed with having a communist state only ninety miles off the coast of Florida. Shortly after the presidential election, Kennedy had been briefed on a plan by Eisenhower to land 1,500 Cuban exiles ashore in an amphibious assault on Cuba. They would seize a beachhead and, if they could hold on long enough, the Cuban government-in-exile would be brought in. Alternatively, if it proved impossible to hold the beachhead, the Cubans would disperse to the mountains to wage a guerrilla war. The adventure was a disaster from start to finish, with Castro's army waiting as the forces landed at the Bay of Pigs. The Cuban rebels implored Kennedy to order American air strikes against the Castro forces, but Kennedy refused and the invasion swiftly ended, with all the Cuban rebels being captured or killed. Kennedy took responsibility for the failed invasion and, ironically, his approval ratings increased.

Eighteen months later it was the situation in Cuba again that led to Kennedy's greatest foreign policy success, when the Cuban Missile Crisis brought the United States and the Soviet Union to the brink of nuclear war and, as Secretary of State, Dean Rusk, observed: 'We were eyeball to eyeball and the other side blinked.' Disaster was only averted by the skill Kennedy displayed in dealing with the crisis, resisting the advice of the military to bomb and invade Cuba once the Americans had discovered the Soviet Union was planning to install nuclear weapons on the island, and instead adopting the suggestion of his brother, Attorney General Robert Kennedy, to place a quarantine around the island to stop the ships delivering the weapons to Cuba.

The Cuban Missile Crisis had a sobering effect on Kennedy's thinking, and by the summer of 1963 he had matured from a hard-line Cold War warrior into a more nuanced seeker of a peaceful way to lower the temperature in Cold War rhetoric and actions.

His landmark speech at the American University in Washington in June 1963 showed how far he had evolved following the missile crisis nine months before. He put forward a fundamentally new emphasis on the peaceful and positive aspects of American relations with the Soviets and outlined a plan to curb nuclear arms. The outcome of this bold initiative was that, less than two months after the delivery of his speech, the United States, the Soviet Union and Great Britain had signed the Nuclear Test Ban treaty, which prohibited the testing of nuclear weapons in outer space, underwater or in the atmosphere. It was hailed as an important first step towards the control of nuclear weapons.

Kennedy's intentions concerning Vietnam, and what he would have done had he lived, are still mired in controversy. Under Eisenhower there were just over six hundred American military advisers helping to train the South Vietnamese Army to combat the North Vietnamese military incursions into their country. By the time of his death, Kennedy had more than sixteen thousand advisers there, but he always resisted demands to put American combat troops into the country. In an interview with Walter Cronkite in September 1963, he said: 'It is their war. They are the ones who have to win it or lose it. We can help them, we can give them equipment, we can send our men out there as advisers, but they have to win it, the people of Vietnam.' He is also on record, in private conversations with close and trusted advisers and Senator Mike Mansfield, saying that once the 1964 presidential election was out of the way and he had been re-elected he would withdraw from Vietnam. On balance, that is probably correct, because his understanding of history and his realism told him that the Americans could never win a war in the jungles of Vietnam.

Kennedy's problems with getting his domestic agenda through Congress were, on the face of it, surprising. The Democrats in 1961 had a majority of ninety-one in the House of Representatives and a twenty-eight-seat majority in a hundred-member Senate, which suggested that there should be no problem in getting his programme passed through Congress. However, this failed to take into account the fact that in both houses of Congress the Republican minority was often aided by Southern, conservative Democratic members who were prepared to work with the Republican opposition to thwart passage of Kennedy's more liberal programme.

The record of Kennedy's years in power was not without some

achievements, but there were notable failures as well. The president's power struggle with Congress was almost equal to that of his struggle with communist leaders abroad. He learned early on in his administration that his fundamental weakness as leader was that his party was not united behind him. Although he had some successes with the establishment of the Peace Corps, his trade bill and the Nuclear Test Ban treaty, he was defeated on key legislation that he proposed, such as federal aid for education, Medicare for the elderly and aid to economically depressed areas. His landmark Civil Rights Bill and tax-cutting legislation were posthumously passed in 1964 under the leadership of Lyndon Johnson.

Initially, Kennedy was reluctant to pursue civil rights legislation for fear of antagonising Southern Democrats in the Senate who chaired many of the key Senate committees and could block his domestic agenda. He also needed white Southern votes to win re-election in 1964. However, events in the South forced his hand and he could no longer afford to remain passive. In 1961, the Freedom Riders forced the issue by travelling by bus through the Southern states, challenging the laws of segregation.

In 1962, an African American, James Meredith, attempted (ultimately successfully) to register at the segregated University of Mississippi. In 1963, Governor George Wallace of Alabama had stood in the schoolhouse door in an unsuccessful attempt to stop the registration of African American students. Kennedy's approach to civil rights was viewed by civil rights leaders as non-committal, but following violence in Birmingham, Alabama, in May 1963 he was left with no choice but to alter course, and the next month he took a firm stand, regardless of the political consequences, when he sent a comprehensive Civil Rights Bill to Congress calling for desegregated access to public facilities, voting rights and school desegregation.

Economically, Kennedy pursued conservative policies, possibly influenced by his father. He was a strong believer in personal and corporate tax cuts and keeping inflation low. As a result of his economic policies, in 1966 (which would have been the fifth year of his presidency had he lived) the growth rate in the US was 6.6 per cent and inflation 3.8 per cent.

However, it was his style and grace and his assassination that shaped the image of the Kennedy presidency for a generation. With deft use of television and magazine articles, Kennedy created an image of a young, photogenic family with a beautiful and accomplished wife who completely restored the image and decoration of the White House. Although Kennedy's cultural taste veered on the lowbrow, his sophisticated dinners, for guests ranging from heads of state to Nobel Prize winners, created a style not seen previously in Washington.

But more than anything it was his assassination in Dallas, Texas, on 22 November 1963 that immortalised his position in American history and created the image that his wife insisted on a week after his death of his presidency being 'a brief and shining moment' from Camelot.

The trip to Texas was a political trip to heal wounds caused by a rift between the vice-president, Lyndon Johnson, its governor, John Connally, and Texas senator, Ralph Yarborough, which was threatening to undermine the chances of Kennedy carrying this critical state in the 1964 presidential election.

Accompanied by his wife, Jacqueline, Kennedy was shot dead in a motorcade while driving through downtown Dallas. In keeping with his televisual presidency, the episode was captured on film. A dysfunctional ex-marine, Lee Harvey Oswald, was charged with the murder, but two days later he was shot dead while being moved from Dallas police station to a nearby prison, thereby creating a major industry for conspiracy theorists as to who actually killed JFK, what the motivation was for the killing, and whether one, two or even three people were responsible for the shooting.

The Warren Commission, created by President Lyndon Johnson and headed up by the Chief Justice to investigate the assassination, concluded that it was perpetrated by Oswald, acting on his own, but significant numbers of people have rejected this conclusion. On balance, I suspect that the conclusions of the Warren Commission are correct.

The immortalisation of the Kennedys was further strengthened five years later when Kennedy's brother, Senator Robert Kennedy, was assassinated in Los Angeles, California, while running for the Democratic nomination for president.

Almost seventy years after President Kennedy's assassination, he still enjoys a strong hold on the affections and admiration of many Americans. His presidency is seen as a halcyon few years during which public service was to be admired and governments trusted. Most opinion polls have him in the top ten of great American presidents and even academic surveys of the best American presidents have him in the top half.

The tragedy is that, because his life was cut short, we will never know exactly what Kennedy's presidency would have been like if he had won re-election in 1964 (which at the time seemed likely), but what we do know is that he had matured greatly in the thousand days he was in office, become bolder in fighting for racial justice and tackling the causes of poverty. In all probability he would also have withdrawn from Vietnam, which would have saved America from the divisiveness that tore it apart in the late 1960s and made the possibility of a Nixon presidency in 1969 highly unlikely. Without Nixon there would never have been Watergate.

Sadly, Kennedy's premature death meant that he was unable to realise his potential to become a great president based on a proven record rather than simply an image.

Sir Simon Burns was the Conservative MP for Chelmsford from 1987 to 2017. He was a Government Whip, and served as a minister in the Department of Health and the Department for Transport. He worked as a volunteer on the presidential campaigns of George McGovern in 1972 and Hillary Clinton in 2008 and 2016. He also worked on Senator Ted Kennedy's Senate re-election campaign in 2006 and Congressman Joe Kennedy III's congressional campaign in 2012.

36

Lyndon B. Johnson

22 November 1963 to 20 January 1969
Democrat
Vice-president: Vacant 1963–65, Hubert Humphrey 1965–69

By George Osborne

Full name: Lyndon Baines Johnson
Born: 27 August 1908, Stonewall, Texas
Died: 22 January 1973, Stonewall, Texas
Resting place: Johnson Family Cemetery, Stonewall, Texas
Library/Museum: Austin, Texas
Education: South West Texas Teachers College
Married to: Lady Bird Taylor, m. 1934 (1912–2007)
Children: Two: Lynda and Luci
Quotation: 'We must open the doors of opportunity. But we must also equip our people to walk through those doors.'

L UCI BAINES JOHNSON once told me about the moment she found out that her father had become president.

> Rumours started circulating among us girls at the Cathedral School
> that something terrible had happened. Then our teacher told us
> that Kennedy has been shot. We all left the class in a daze. A man
> in a suit came across the quadrangle and singled me out. I was a
> little embarrassed. He told me he was a secret service agent, and
> that I had to come with him because my daddy was now the
> president.

I have always been fascinated with the life of Lyndon Baines Johnson.
Why? It's an incredible tale, as you'll read; but it's also a timeless
study in politics. Weighing his often gross methods against his
enormous achievements, you are confronted with the perennial
question: when do the ends justify the means?

At its root, the means of LBJ's ascent to power was application.
'If you do everything, you'll win,' was his view. As a result, he put
in longer hours, campaigned harder and buttonholed more people
than anyone around him. He demanded the same of his staff in
every job he had. 'If he caught you taking a crap,' one aide recalled,
'he'd say: "Son, can't you please try a little harder to do that on
your own time?"' But all successful politicians know they benefit
from the misfortune of their rivals. Except in Johnson's case, it
wasn't mere misfortune; it was murder – the most infamous murder
in history.

We are so familiar with what an inauguration of a president
should look like. The beaming candidate, standing on a stage in
front of the Capitol, repeating the words of the Chief Justice before
the Marine Band strikes up and a Lady Gaga takes to the stage.

Now look at the black-and-white photo that is the only image
of Johnson's inauguration. Standing in the stiflingly hot, cramped
cabin of Air Force One as it sits on the tarmac in Texas, alongside
Jackie Kennedy still wearing the dress covered in her husband's
blood, a local federal judge is administering the oath to the grim-
faced thirty-sixth president of the United States. The body of the
thirty-fifth president lies in a coffin out of the camera frame.

The murder of JFK may have been a senseless, random act. No

conspiracy theorist has ever proved otherwise, although Johnson himself had his doubts. But the fact that LBJ was there to take over was not an accident.

Back in 1960 he was asked why he'd give up leadership of the Senate for the powerless job of vice-president. 'Well,' he replied, 'seven of them got to be president without ever being elected.' That's one in five. For a Texan in an America that hadn't elected anyone from the South to the White House since the Civil War, he thought those weren't bad odds. For a boy who had grown up in the isolation and poverty of the Hill Country, they were nothing short of miraculous.

If Abraham Lincoln can still claim the prize of being the man from the humblest origins who made it to the presidency, Johnson comes second. He was born on a hard-scrabble farm near Stonewall on the north bank of the Pedernales River, a day's ride from Austin, on 27 August 1908. As one great biographer of his, Robert Dallek, observes, it would be hard to find a place more 'isolated from early twentieth-century American life'. There were no railways and no paved roads in the Hill Country. There was no electricity either – they would have to wait three decades before Congressman Johnson changed that, and brought the labour-saving devices that rescued thousands of women, like his mother Rebekah Baines, from back-breaking days spent fetching water from the well, scrubbing clothes clean and heating up flat-irons while the men worked in the fields.

Rebekah and Sam Ealy Johnson had nothing in their lives that should have led them to expect something better for their beloved son Lyndon. And yet they did. 'He's going to be governor of Texas someday,' said his father on the day he was born. He grew up with tall stories that the Johnsons and Baineses were different, descended from great pioneering families. 'Listen goddammit,' Johnson once said, 'my ancestors were teachers and lawyers and college presidents and governors when the Kennedys in this country were still tending bar.' It gave him a swagger, and a sense of entitlement, that no one else could comprehend.

There was nothing in Johnson's early life to suggest that his father's prophecy of greatness would be fulfilled. At high school he was quick but got mostly 'Bs'. He left school at sixteen and worked breaking rocks on a road gang. Finally, his parents persuaded him to go to college, and in 1927 he headed off for Southwest Texas State Teachers College at San Marcos.

The American superpower expected their presidents to walk out of Harvard Yard or West Point, not San Marcos Teachers College. But for Lyndon Johnson and his seven hundred fellow students from the farms and small towns nearby it was a route out.

Already, one of the central paradoxes of Johnson's life was beginning to show. The 6-foot-3.5-inch 'big, all-bone Western boy' strutted around campus in a suit with a bow-tie, brown-nosed with the college authorities, and behaved with an arrogance that put off many of his fellow students. But when he couldn't afford the college fees, he took himself off for a year to teach Mexican–American children in a segregated school in 'a little dried up, dying' border town called Cotulla. 'Mired in slums . . . lashed by prejudice . . . buried half alive in illiteracy' is how he described the twenty-eight kids in his class, and they loved him. No one would ever work harder for them. Johnson organised debate classes, baseball and bands. He told them any one of them could be president of the United States. But that was *his* dream.

Johnson already had the political bug. He'd caught it from his father Sam Ealy, who had served occasional terms in the Texas state legislature, and taken his ten-year-old son on the campaign trail down dust farm tracks in a Ford Model T. Leaving college, heading for a teaching job in Houston, he instead ended up landing a job as junior secretary to a local congressman. In November 1931, the twenty-three-year-old Johnson boarded the train to Washington. It would be thirty-eight years before he came back.

Johnson knew no one when he arrived in Depression-era DC. On his first night at his lodgings with other aides, he took four showers; the next morning he brushed his teeth five times. Each visit to the bathroom was simply an excuse to meet new people and build his network, and he was soon effectively running his congressman's district.

Two events then shaped the rest of his life. The first was the election of Franklin Roosevelt as president in 1932. Johnson joined the crowds at the inauguration and forever after he was a New Dealer, a liberal nationalist who believed in the power of the federal government to make lives better for the Americans he had grown up with.

The second was meeting Claudia Alta Taylor in September 1934. Her family called her Lady Bird. She had been born in Karnack, east Texas, had graduated from the University of Texas, and wanted to be a journalist – an ambition few women from her background would have entertained. Twenty-four hours after they'd met, he proposed to her. She thought about it. But she too wanted to go places, and here was the guy who was going to take her there.

The question was: how? Johnson used his emerging political network to land the job as state director of the National Youth Administration, a New Deal programme. Johnson was the youngest director in the country. Again, no one worked harder than he did – driving his staff all hours – and the results showed: he enrolled half a million young Texans on the scheme. From then on, Johnson was FDR's man. When the Tenth District congressional seat (covering Austin) fell vacant, he ran for it – and, although he was the youngest and least known of the candidates, he won.

I've always loved reading about the moments when great figures from history meet without knowing it. On 11 May 1937, the two men who redefined the role of American government in the twentieth century met. The rookie twenty-eight-year-old congressman Johnson joined President Roosevelt, twice his age and contemplating an unprecedented third term in office, as his special train made its way through Texas. When the two-day journey ended, FDR made a prediction to a Cabinet colleague: 'In the next generation, the balance of power will shift south and west, and this boy could well be the first Southern president.'

To become that he had to get on in Congress. He set about becoming the surrogate son of the legendary House Majority Leader Sam Rayburn – joining his cabal of powerful cronies who met every evening for a bourbon in a tiny hideaway room they called 'the Board of Education'.

He also sorted out the money that would bankroll all his future campaigns, and began to lay the foundations of his own personal fortune. Brown & Root was just a small construction company in Austin. Thanks to Johnson, it won contracts to build dams in the 1930s, warships in the 1940s and the whole infrastructure of South

Vietnam in the 1960s. Its nickname became 'Burn & Loot'; the real name was later changed to Halliburton.

Again, the question of means and ends raises itself. Johnson's dealings were corrupt, but the results were transformational for the poor communities he had grown up with. Damming the Lower Colorado River meant electricity for the Hill Country. Farmers could earn a living; their wives were liberated from drudgery. As one of FDR's lieutenants said: Johnson 'was the best congressman for a district that ever was'.

Now he needed a war record without getting himself killed. When FDR dispatched him on a fact-finding mission to the Pacific in 1942, he insisted on taking part in a real combat mission – hitching a ride on a B-26 on a bombing raid over New Guinea. Johnson has been lampooned for the hugely exaggerated stories he later told about his war service, but his life was in real danger. Other planes were shot down; his own, the *Heckling Hare*, was hit many times and lost one engine. 'Cool as ice' was how the crew described their passenger. *He* got the Silver Star, not them.

Equipped with his war story and his medal, Johnson turned his eyes to the Senate. The 1948 race for the Texas Senate seat was one of the closest and most dishonest contests of all time. Johnson faced the near impossible task of defeating the immensely popular former governor and self-styled cowboy Coke Stevenson, who travelled around on a horse. So he hired a helicopter, which he called the Johnson City Windmill, and flew it over astonished crowds across Texas. When the result was a near dead heat, the border bosses provided the votes – and continued to do so days after the polls had supposedly shut. Johnson won with a majority of just eighty-seven. As he used to tell people: 'the first rule of politics is learning to count'.

When the forty-year-old arrived at the Senate, they gave him the disparaging nickname 'Landslide Lyndon'. By the time he left, twelve years later, he had become the most powerful senator in the history of the United States.

In a chamber dominated by length of service, he rewrote the playbook. Within six years, he was Majority Leader. He deployed on fellow senators, officials and journalists what became known as 'The Treatment' – barking, cajoling, threatening, flattering his target while simultaneously enveloping them physically with his gangly arms and pressing his face within millimetres of their own. Ben Bradlee, of *Washington Post* fame, said: 'You really felt as if a St Bernard had licked your face for an hour.' Visit his Texas ranch and he'd manoeuvre you into the deep end of his pool, where he could stand, and have you tread water while he negotiated with you.

In many ways his means were overbearing and grubby. But the ends? His sessions of the Senate passed more legislation than any before them. Major bills on labour, housing and trade that had been blocked for years became law. He was the driving force in the creation of NASA. But his crowning achievement was the passage of the 1957 Civil Rights Act – the first civil rights law to pass the Senate, and overcome the filibuster of the South, since the Civil War.

Johnson's success set him up for his presidential run in 1960. But he was beaten by what he called 'a little scrawny fellow with rickets', Massachusetts senator John F. Kennedy. All his backroom political skills were no match for his younger rival's slick telegenic appeal. He could, however, do one thing that Kennedy desperately needed in a running mate – he could deliver the South.

The first vice-president, John Adams, described his job as 'the most insignificant office that ever the invention of man contrived', and Johnson's efforts to change that failed. 'He looks so sad,' was Kennedy's simple observation. After three miserable years there was speculation that he might be dropped from the ticket in 1964 as scandal brewed. Then came Dallas – and those odds Johnson had calculated on came good.

His memory of 22 November 1963 was of being 'startled' by a 'loud report or explosion' as his limousine trailed behind the president's through the cheering downtown streets. Then the weight of his bodyguard throwing him to the floor of the car. 'I would never forget his knees in my back and his elbows in my back,' he later said. The cavalcade sped off to Parkland Hospital. There, in a small white cubicle, he waited for news. 'Lyndon and I didn't speak,' Lady Bird Johnson recalled. 'We just looked at each other, exchanging messages with our eyes. We knew what it might mean.' At 1:20 p.m. Kennedy's closest aide came in and said simply: 'He's gone.'

No president in American history has taken office in a more desperate, traumatic circumstance. There have been other assassinations: Lincoln, of course. Garfield and McKinley too. But not on television, in replays watched by billions of people. Not in a country whose commander in chief was the most powerful person in the world in the middle of a tense Cold War.

Everyone who dealt with Lyndon Johnson on that chaotic, awful day said the same thing. From the very first moment, he was calm and he was in control. His epic biographer Robert Caro describes the physical transformation that occurred almost immediately. 'The hangdog look was gone.' Lady Bird Johnson looked at her husband and saw 'a face carved in bronze'. Johnson's moment, that he had improbably foreseen all his life, had come.

Like the lives of all governments at all times, you can trace the arc as the Johnson administration rose and fell. Yet rarely in American history has the ascent been so steep, the apogee so high and the descent so deep and painful.

President Johnson's first task was to deal with a nation numb with shock and loss. It is easy with hindsight to underestimate how hard that was. His murdered predecessor cast a long shadow that many would have struggled to escape. He gave space to the Kennedy family to grieve. But the frenzy of calls Johnson made in the hours after assuming office showed a tense, uncertain world that there would be continuity of government.

'All I have I would have given gladly not to be standing here today,' he told Congress five days later, and even the most cynical observers believed him. He then publicly adopted Kennedy's unfinished agenda: advance civil rights, cut taxes to boost the flagging economy, and launch a war on poverty. It was a brilliant stroke. Not only was Johnson honouring the legacy of his dead predecessor but he was laying the foundations of his own.

The first challenge was going to be passing a new civil rights law that would ban segregation of public schools and outlaw employment discrimination. Few this time could see a way through Congress. Johnson found it. One of the mysteries of his life is how a poor white Southern boy came to feel so passionately about helping Black Americans. 'He had no bigotry,' his friends said. 'I'm going to be the president who finishes what Lincoln began,' he told his staff.

With that great achievement under his belt, and the tax cut and a poverty bill passed, Johnson was cruising to re-election in the autumn of 1964. He'd picked the able Hubert Humphrey as his own vice-president, knowing he'd hate it. He didn't care. He summed up his approach to those who served in his administration: 'I want people around me who would kiss my ass on a hot summer's day and say it smells like roses.'

The Republicans helped by choosing the libertarian right-wing Arizona senator Barry Goldwater as their candidate. The Democrats responded with the most famous political ad ever: the little girl counting up to ten as she picks the petals off a daisy, followed by the voice of a man counting down to a nuclear explosion.

The result was one of the biggest victories in American history. Johnson's 61 per cent share of the popular vote was the highest any presidential candidate has ever achieved, before or since. This time he really was 'Landslide Lyndon'.

And yet, as is so often the case in politics, it is at the moments of greatest triumph that the seeds of destruction are sown.

First, only five states other than Arizona hadn't voted Democrat. But they were all in the South. It was a historic shift. Johnson himself had predicted on the night the Civil Rights Act passed that 'we just delivered the South to the Republican Party for a long time to come'. Goldwater himself, though dismissed as 'a crazy', was a presage of a change in the American right that was to lead to Ronald Reagan and ultimately Donald Trump.

Second, an event had taken place on 2 August 1964 – before the election – on the other side of the world that was to consume the Johnson presidency. Three North Vietnamese torpedo boats had apparently attacked the USS *Maddox* in international waters in the Gulf of Tonkin – an event to this day disputed.

The fact the destroyer was there, carrying out clandestine surveillance, was the result of decisions by the Eisenhower and then the Kennedy administrations to support South Vietnam after the defeated French had abandoned their former and now partitioned colonial possession a decade earlier.

Johnson had inherited the policy – and the stellar Kennedy national security team of McGeorge Bundy, Dean Rusk and Bob McNamara who had shaped it. *The Brightest and the Best* was the ironic title of the brilliant book by David Halberstam that chronicles their tragic mistakes.

It is so easy now to see the hubris that would lead to more than a million lives being lost and the humbling of the United States. But I've been in the room when the decisions to intervene in Libya but stay out of Syria were made; I was an MP when the vote on Iraq was held; I see the current talk of 'standing up' to China and Russia, and standing by those countries they threaten; I watch the Afghan defeat. There was no easy path for Lyndon Johnson then, as there isn't for any other president or world leader today.

The president's response to the torpedo boat attack in 1964 was limited air strikes against North Vietnam. He didn't want to escalate the war, but nor could he gift an opportunity to Goldwater by doing nothing. The 'Gulf of Tonkin' resolution authorising the action passed the House of Representatives unanimously and the Senate by ninety-eight votes to two. Johnson called it 'like a grandma's night-shirt – it covered everything'.

It was to be the sole congressional authorisation for the rest of the Vietnam War. Johnson thought he was being smart – limiting the debate, getting the vote, never quite revealing his hand. This was how he had run the Senate. As a result, while large majorities of Americans when surveyed said they supported the war, the implications of it were never explained to them clearly by their president. Peace was always just around the corner, they were told.

Within a year of the resolution, combat marines had been deployed and routine bombing of the North had begun. US force numbers were increased from the 16,000 advisers Kennedy had sent to 125,000. By 1966, that number had risen to 325,000. By the time Johnson left office, it was 536,000.

Fresh from his election triumph in 1964, Johnson would never have predicted that a total of 2.7 million Americans would end up serving in Vietnam – and that 58,000 would die there. He was instead focused on a package of domestic legislation that was to change the role of the federal government in American life forever – and that every Democrat president since has sought to emulate.

He called it the 'Great Society'. The administration began in early 1965 with federal government aid for public education – a holy grail that progressives from FDR to JFK had reached for and failed.

Medicare and Medicaid were to follow. Again, no Democrat had ever been able to get major federal healthcare provision through Congress. Johnson succeeded. What started as $1 billion programmes to provide healthcare to the elderly and the poorest in America are today worth close to $1.5 trillion – and no one dares to suggest repealing them.

Whether this expansion of big government helped combat poverty or instead entrenched it was to become the debate a generation later. At the time, these were the glory months of the Johnson presidency. The man himself was a 'controlled frenzy' of activity – deploying all his skills to get his reforms passed. He returned to civil rights, and the issue most likely to up-end the existing order in the South: the right to vote.

Martin Luther King gave him a shove, leading a campaign of protest in Selma, Alabama – where less than 1 per cent of black citizens were registered to vote. Governor Wallace and his state troopers responded with racist violence that shocked the nation.

Johnson rose to the moment. On 15 March 1964 he spoke to Congress and the nation, declaring that the 'secret heart of America itself' had been 'laid bare'. He told them that the African American cause 'must be our cause' and stunned his audience by adopting the anthem of black protest: 'We Shall Overcome'. Congress responded with thunderous applause, and the legislation passed.

By 1968, almost all the Southern states had registered over 50 per cent of their black residents. Today's controversy over voter registration reminds us that Johnson did not solve the problem, but his highly critical biographer Caro puts it like this: 'Abraham Lincoln struck off the chains of black Americans, but it was Lyndon Johnson who led them into voting booths . . . and made them, at last and forever, a true part of American political life.'

It's hard to see the remaining years of his presidency as anything other than a long, but sad decline from this peak. He pushed on with important reforms in areas like road safety, child nutrition and environmental pollution, but he was slowly running out of capital – political and financial.

Riots in Watts, a black neighbourhood of Los Angeles, in the summer of 1965 – followed by more urban riots the next summer – ended the momentum for civil rights. The poverty and lack of opportunity that fuelled them were precisely the causes Johnson wanted to take up. But white liberal America had taken fright. His appointment of the first black Supreme Court Justice,

Thurgood Marshall, in 1967 was to be a historic but rare advance.

Meanwhile, economic concerns and the enormous costs of the real war abroad meant that the administration could no longer afford its war on poverty at home. By 1967, after the Republicans had made significant advances in the mid-term elections, the administration had to stabilise the economy with austerity measures and tax rises to try to bring the budget deficit under control. As Dallek observes: 'It's a given of US history that war kills reform.' The First World War ended progressivism; FDR's New Deal gave way to the Second World War; Vietnam, far from helping LBJ build a Great Society, created deep divisions within it.

So the question is: why didn't Johnson get out of Vietnam? Why didn't he declare victory and leave? He had plenty of opportunities. He was told by his vice-president that moving to bombing and combat operations in 1965 was one of 'the most fateful decisions of his administration'. In 1966, his political allies warned him about 'getting in deeper and deeper with no end in sight'. In October 1967, Bob McNamara, close to a breakdown, admitted, 'everything I have tried to do since 1961 has been a failure', and he urged the president to pause. Johnson fired him.

The reasons why Johnson persevered in Vietnam are familiar to those of us who have lived through more recent conflicts. First, the nature of the struggle itself was misunderstood. The White House thought they were fighting an ideological conflict for freedom against tyranny, and that they had learned the lessons of Munich and the 'loss of China' that had scarred a previous generation. The Viet Cong were fighting what they saw instead as a war of national self-determination against a foreign oppressor.

Second, the information that the military was providing its commander in chief was mendaciously optimistic. Time and again generals told the president that they were on the verge of a breakthrough. At the end of 1967, General Westmoreland reported that 'we have got our opponent almost on the ropes'. In my personal experience on Britain's National Security Council, military chiefs are rightly cautious of getting into a war, but then rarely want to end one.

Third, national prestige was at stake – and so was personal prestige. This had become 'Lyndon Johnson's war', and he said time and again, 'I'm not going to be the first American president to lose a war.' When a reporter pressed him in private to explain why he was still in Vietnam, 'LBJ unzipped his fly, drew out his substantial organ and declared: "This is why!"'

It led to institutional paranoia. Johnson became convinced that the growing anti-war movement was a fifth column. Thousands of FBI agents were assigned to infiltrate them. The army and the CIA joined in the espionage at home. It's hard to reach a conclusion other than that the president himself had completely lost his calm rationality in a crisis – a quality that had once made him so effective in politics.

Any illusion that the United States was winning in Vietnam was shattered on 30 January 1968, during the Vietnamese new year holiday known as 'Tet'. Dozens of targets were struck simultaneously – from the US Embassy in Saigon to the ancient capital of Hue. While the North's losses were five times higher, the real casualty was American public opinion. It was no longer credible for their president to tell them that the war was being won.

From that point on, Johnson's presidency was effectively over. He had agonised with the question of whether to run for re-election in the autumn. His approval ratings had collapsed, his own health was in doubt, and he now knew he would be contesting Robert Kennedy for his own party's nomination. These two giants of 1960s American liberal politics loathed each other with mutual contempt.

Yes, he doubted he could win. But he also felt that fighting the election would mean he would 'miss or postpone' the opportunity for peace in Vietnam. He had to devote all his energy to saving the reputation of his administration.

So on 31 March 1968, he told the nation: 'I will not seek, and I will not accept, the nomination of my party for another term as your president.' Lady Bird Johnson recalled that he 'bounded from his chair in the Oval Office. His air was that of a prisoner let free.'

Peace was not to be. Though talks started in Paris, Johnson lacked the political strength to deliver the goal he was so desperate for. One of his favourite aphorisms was that 'power is where power goes'.

Nixon beat Humphrey at the election. It was widely seen as a defeat for Johnson too. He made a final farewell address to the Congress he had mastered for three decades and he returned to live on the banks of the Pedernales River where he had been born. There, four years later, just at the end of what would have been another term had he stood and won, he died of a heart attack. He was sixty-four years old.

Forty years later, as Britain's chancellor, I travelled especially to Austin to be shown around the LBJ Presidential Library by his youngest daughter. I had developed a fascination with his presidency. I was not alone. When I hosted a dinner for Robert Caro at Number 11, leading politicians from all our parties pleaded for an invitation.

Why the interest? Hasn't Lyndon Johnson been largely forgotten, squeezed between the martyrdom of Kennedy before him and the ignominy of Nixon who followed? If he's remembered at all, isn't it for the carnage of Vietnam and the division it caused at home? Yes, for many years; but not any more.

When President Biden wants to talk up his early domestic achievements, he encourages comparisons with two predecessors: FDR and LBJ. When the media laments current divisions in Congress, they express admiration for the wheeler-dealing Johnson, 'Master of the Senate'. As Austin booms in the 'new South', those with long memories recall it was Johnson who brought the South back into the mainstream of American life almost a century after the Civil War. The four southern presidents who followed him (Carter, Clinton, two Bushes) are a testament to this, his greatest achievement.

Even on Vietnam, as the West once again contemplates how to contain the ambitions of China and Russia but fears direct confrontation, there is more appreciation of just how difficult – and enduring – were the choices facing the Johnson administration in South East Asia.

Yes, he loved the power. Yes, he made money – many, many millions of dollars – from securing federal contracts and broadcasting licences. But all Lyndon Johnson's flaws and corruption, his bullying and overbearing ambition, were also put to service in his dream of a stronger United States that was fairer to its poorest citizens – the people he had grown up among. Black and white.

Few who have held that highest office after him achieved half so much in that cause. The ends justified the means. That's why Lyndon Johnson is the politician's president.

George Osborne was the UK Chancellor of the Exchequer from 2010 to 2016. He is Chair of the British Museum.

37

Richard Nixon

20 January 1969 to 9 August 1974
Republican
Vice-presidents: Spiro Agnew 1969–73, Gerald Ford 1973–74

By Freddy Gray

Full name: Richard Milhous Nixon
Born: 13 January 1913, Yorba Linda, California
Died: 22 April 1994, New York
Resting place: Richard Nixon Presidential Library and Museum in Yorba Linda, California
Library/Museum: Yorba Linda, California
Education: Whittier College, Duke Law School
Married to: Thelma Catherine Ryan, known as Pat, m. 1940 (1912–93)
Children: Two: Tricia Nixon Cox, Julie Nixon Eisenhower
Quotation: 'People have got to know whether or not their president is a crook. Well, I'm not a crook. I've earned everything I've got.'

Has the reputation of any American statesman been more effectively trashed than that of Richard Milhous Nixon? Donald Trump's, perhaps – certainly the forty-fifth president inspires loathing on a scale matched only by the thirty-seventh.

Nixon and Trump have a few other points in common. Both men built coalitions through appeals to forgotten voters. They spoke to Americans who were frightened by rapid and destructive social and economic change. Both were denounced as fascists and standard bearers of the most reactionary forces in American life, yet in fact both governed with substantial moderation.

Nixon and Trump prove the truth of Marx's quip that history repeats itself first as tragedy, then as farce. Nixon is the tragedy; Trump the farce.

That's why the parallels between the two men only go so far. Nixon was serious, studious and quiet; Trump a loudmouth braggart who revelled in his cartoonish persona. Nobody fought harder to win the presidency than Nixon, who survived two devastating electoral defeats before his ultimate triumph. Trump jumped straight to the presidency with no real political experience and winged everything all the time.

Nixon was laid low by scandal. Trump's shamelessness meant that scandals didn't hurt him. Donald Trump wouldn't have resigned over Watergate; he probably couldn't ever understand why Nixon did.

There is a better comparison: one that Nixon felt himself. It is with the nineteenth-century British prime minister Benjamin Disraeli. The politician, diplomat and sociologist Daniel Patrick Moynihan once recalled giving Nixon a list of his ten favourite political biographies. These included more than four thousand pages of reading on figures as varied as Hitler, Talleyrand and the Mexican revolutionary Emiliano Zapata.

Five weeks later, Nixon had read the lot. His favourite was Robert Blake's magisterial portrait of Disraeli. Nixon could see much of himself in the great Victorian statesman. He had none of Disraeli's flamboyance. Yet, like Dizzy, Dick was an outsider who overcame monstrous obstacles to reach the zenith of power.

'Though I sit down now,' said Disraeli, famously, having been jeered at in his first speech in the House of Commons, 'the time will come when you will hear me.' Those words would have spoken deeply to Nixon, who always felt mocked and shunned by Washington and the respectable classes.

It was from Disraeli that Nixon summoned inspiration for the political vision of his triumphant first term. 'It is the Tory men with liberal policies who have enlarged democracy,' he told Moynihan after finishing Blake's book.

Years later, Nixon openly touted Disraeli as his role model: 'My view, my approach, is probably that of a Disraeli conservative – a strong foreign policy, adherence to basic values that the nation believes in and the people believe in, and to conserving those values, and not being destructive of them, but combined with reform, reform that will work, not reform that destroys.'

Nixon is often called an enigma. Yet he is arguably the president about whom we know more than any other. Thanks to the Watergate tapes, his lengthy memoirs, and his own inclination to mix the personal and political, almost nothing from Nixon's life remains hidden.

His mysteriousness stems from the weirdness of his character. He was an extraordinary mixture of the good and the bad, the heroic and the terrible. He was a man capable of kindness: at law school, for instance, he befriended a disabled man and carried him up the steps to class – yet he could be equally cruel and intensely vicious.

He combined immense self-belief with almost crippling awkwardness, unlike his great rival John F. Kennedy, who valued style over substance. Kennedy represents the sunny image Americans like to project to the world. Nixon is the more troubled reality.

Nixon was born into an America that was still transforming from frontier upstart nation into a global superpower. His nearest home city, Los Angeles, exemplified that transformation. During Nixon's childhood, Los Angeles quadrupled in size and changed from the regional hub of California's rich agricultural lands to the garish heart of the global entertainment industry.

Nixon was not part of that explosive growth. His most formative years were spent a few kilometres away in the quiet Quaker colony of Whittier, where his devout parents ran a small shop. His family suffered great loss. Two of Nixon's brothers died of tuberculosis.

Some of the family believed the deaths to be God's punishment for the Nixons having kept their store open on the Sabbath.

Nixon's early setbacks moulded his character, for better and worse, and instilled in him the fierce resentments that would drive him to the White House. A brilliant boy in high school, he ran for student body president, only to suffer an embarrassing defeat to a jock who seemed to barely want the job. Offered a scholarship to Harvard University out of high school, Nixon was unable to attend due to his older brother's tuberculosis and the need for him to help at the family store.

He attended the local Quaker-affiliated Whittier College instead. Even there, he found himself excluded from the elitist Franklin Society. He founded his own Orthogonian Society as a competitor. After graduation, Nixon attended the brand-new Duke Law School, only then to be rejected by an elite law firm after the hiring partner condemned his 'shifty-eyed' demeanour.

For the rest of his life Nixon would carry that burden of social insecurity. His sense of his own lack of pedigree, or separation from privilege, hardened into a deep distrust of and hostility towards America's elites. Later in life, as he vetted Cabinet picks for his second term after winning re-election to the White House, he told H.R. Haldeman: 'No goddamn *Harvard* men, you understand? Under no condition!' It is worth noting, however, that Nixon's class prejudices were not resolute: the Harvard men of his administration included Defense Secretary James Schlesinger, Health Secretary Caspar Weinberger, Attorney General Elliot Richardson, and his Secretary of State Henry Kissinger.

After graduating, Nixon met Pat Ryan when they were cast together in a local theatre production of comedy called *The Dark Tower* (comical darkness is a strong Nixonian theme). He played the young playwright, she the seductive vamp. Nixon was smitten and he won Pat's heart the way he would later win the presidency: remorselessly. His initial advances rebuffed, he courted her for two years, even driving her to dates with other men, before she finally acquiesced. A very hard worker herself, Pat came to see in young Dick a similar determination to get on and an ambition to achieve great things. They made a formidable pair.

In 1942, Nixon left a bureaucrat's job in Washington for a naval commission and served three years in the South Pacific. He saw some action: at the front on Bougainville Island, near Papua New Guinea, Nixon's hut was destroyed by Japanese artillery as he hid in a nearby foxhole. He also took part in the invasion of Green Island.

It was on Green Island that he discovered the game of poker, an important moment in his life. Gambling, like many other diversions, had been frowned upon in the Nixon home, and by some accounts Nixon never played cards at all before his enrolment. But he mastered the game. He spent hours practising and observing before he risked any of his own money. He then developed a patient strategy that played to his intellect and self-control.

Nixon returned home from war with some $8,000, much of it from poker winnings, and he used this money to finance his first congressional run. He then defeated the Democrat intellectual Jerry Voorhis in the twelfth congressional district of Los Angeles County. His victory was down to his tireless campaigning, backing from local money men, and a touch of cynical 'red baiting' – he success-fully insinuated that Voorhis had ties to communism.

Nixon's political ascent was brisk. He went from congressional neophyte to vice-president in just six years. His career and reputa-tion, for better and for worse, were established in 1948 with his vigorous investigation of Alger Hiss. Hiss was an esteemed State Department veteran and president of the Carnegie Endowment for International Peace, who played a central role at the Yalta Conference and in the establishment of the United Nations. But in 1948, Whittaker Chambers, an editor and writer at *Time*, testified to Congress that in the 1930s he and Hiss had both been communists who spied on behalf of the Soviet Union. Hiss entrapped himself by not only denying the espionage charge, but claiming to have never met Chambers at all. Nixon's vigorous investigation ended with Hiss's conviction for perjury. This destruction of a distinguished public servant has long been regarded as an example of excessive 'McCarthyist' zeal, although Nixon never stooped to Senator McCarthy's low tactics. Later, the fall of the Soviet Union, and the release of the Venona Transcripts, helped establish that Nixon had almost certainly been right.

The Hiss case ensured that Nixon would always be an enemy of the progressive left. Yet the hatred grew even hotter in 1950 after his Senate race against Helen Gahagan Douglas, LBJ's not-so-secret lover and the quintessence of the mid-century bleeding heart. Nixon's smear of Douglas as the communist-sympathising 'pink lady' is well remembered, and the successful campaign won him his 'Tricky Dick' moniker. What is less well known is that Douglas fired the first shot of that bitter clash, accusing Nixon of pushing 'nice, unadulterated fascism'. Similar to America in the Second World War, Nixon did not start the conflict, but was happy to win it with overwhelmingly superior firepower.

Nixon's career nearly ended in 1952, just months after being chosen as Dwight Eisenhower's vice-presidential nominee, when the press targeted him for the existence of a $18,000 political activities fund, paid for by Nixon's donors. The fund gave Nixon the means to travel and build his reputation as a national politician. In fact, Nixon broke no law and never misused the money, nor is there any evidence of political favours granted in exchange for donations. The fund wasn't even a secret, while the Democratic nominee Adlai Stevenson really *did* have a secret slush fund for personal and political expenses.

Nevertheless, a campaign to have Nixon replaced as Eisenhower's running mate was launched. Vipers within the Republican Party lobbied for Nixon's resignation. DNC chairman Stephen Mitchell sneered that men who could not afford to be senators ought not to run for the Senate. Eisenhower himself stood aloof, telling Nixon to save himself if he wished to stay on the ticket.

Nixon did save himself, brilliantly. On 23 September, in a national television address (one of the first of its kind), Nixon laid bare his meagre wealth: he had no inherited fortune like Stevenson, he said, only his $15,000 Senate salary and twice that in debts.

He told America about his 1950 Oldsmobile, the paltry inheritances he'd received, and that he'd never been able to afford a mink coat, so Pat got by with a 'good Republican cloth coat'. He did admit, mawkishly, to accepting one generous donation – the gift of a cocker spaniel, called Checkers, from a man in Texas.

The stunt, now known as the Checkers Speech, struck something deep in the American psyche. Nixon asked voters to decide his fate, and they did: more than four million telegrams, letters and phone calls poured into the Republican National Committee with a 75-to-1 ratio in support of Nixon. Eisenhower and Nixon swept to victory in November.

Nixon's career was saved, but never safe. Four years later, Eisenhower tried to ease Nixon off the ticket by offering him his choice of Cabinet seat. Nixon declined. He had eyes on the White House.

In 1960, he won the nomination and found himself in a battle against JFK, who though Catholic was infinitely more privileged than a WASP (White Anglo-Saxon Protestant). Nixon lost very narrowly, though, unlike Trump, he refused to pursue claims of electoral fraud.

Against his better judgement, Nixon then turned his attentions to the humbler goal of becoming governor of California, only to lose again very narrowly to Pat Brown, a disappointment he marked with a famously bitter speech in which he told the press that they 'don't have Nixon to kick around any more'.

The press did not stop their kicking. Just five days after his defeat, ABC broadcast 'The Political Obituary of Richard M. Nixon', an hour-long special on Nixon's demise, featuring an interview with none other than Alger Hiss.

Humiliation only hardened Nixon's resolve. From that low, he made a Lazarus-like comeback. In 1964, most national Republicans avoided the doomed Barry Goldwater campaign. Nixon, by contrast, campaigned harder for the Arizona senator's candidacy than perhaps Goldwater himself. The effort boosted his reputation and helped make him a favourite for the 1968 election, which he duly won.

A dark legend has built up around that 1968 campaign. The legend accuses Nixon of igniting America's culture wars in his bid for power, and re-founding the Republican Party as a Southern party built on a bedrock of racism, neo-segregation and opposition to civil rights.

This is largely myth. Nixon's political strategy in the South was forthright and stated in his own writings at the time. He wrote in 1966:

The Republican opportunity in the South is a golden one; but Republicans must not go prospecting for the fool's gold of racist votes. Southern Republicans must not climb aboard the sinking

ship of racial injustice . . . Republicans should adhere to the principles of the party of Lincoln. They should leave it to the George
Wallaces and the Lister Hills to squeeze the last ounces of political
juice from the rotting fruit of racial injustice. But respect for human
rights means respect for the laws which protect those rights. The
racial problems which will confront the South in the years ahead
must be settled in the courts – not decided in the streets.

Nixon's pledges to protect law and order were not devious covers
for racism, but a reaction to the genuine terror millions of Americans
felt. America in the late 1960s was convulsed by social trauma. In
August 1965, one week after the passage of the Voting Rights Act,
a black man's arrest for drunken driving caused the Watts neighbourhood in Los Angeles to explode in an orgy of rioting and
looting. Thirty-four were killed, $40 million in property was
destroyed, and 14,000 National Guardsmen were called in to restore
order.

In 1967's 'long, hot summer', more than a hundred and fifty race
riots broke out across the country, claiming more than eighty lives.
In April 1968, Martin Luther King was slain and another wave of
rioting killed forty-three. A month later, Robert Kennedy was shot
and killed in turn. That summer, the Democratic Convention in
Chicago turned into a street war between police and hippie
protesters.

A sense of plunging chaos prevailed. Between 1962 and 1968,
the American murder rate rose by 50 per cent. Robberies and auto
thefts doubled. The liberal project America had voted so enthusiastically for in 1964 seemed to be falling apart.

Nixon didn't appear with a promise to turn back the clock. True
to his idea of benign Toryism, he offered to chart a course for
progress without indulging mayhem. 'In a civilized nation no man
can excuse his crime against the person or property of another by
claiming that he, too, has been a victim of injustice,' Nixon wrote
in Reader's Digest in 1967. 'To tolerate that is to invite anarchy.'

The nation was eager for such a message. Charting a middle path
between Lyndon Johnson's vice-president Hubert Humphrey and
segregationist George Wallace, Nixon won thirty-two states, three
hundred and one Electoral College votes, and the presidency.

Contrary to the 'racist Southern strategy' myth, Nixon lost four of the five Deep South states Barry Goldwater had won in 1964. Segregationists were happily voting for George Wallace's campaign. Nixon's wins in the Carolinas, Virginia and Florida were not built on rural areas, but on voters, many of them transplants, in the South's new cities and burgeoning suburbs.

'Progress without mayhem' effectively became Nixon's mantra, and in office he was much more liberal than the myth surrounding him suggests.

The Supreme Court case *Brown v. Board of Education* had ordered public school desegregation fourteen years earlier, but it took the Nixon administration to carry it out.

When he took office in 1969, more than two-thirds of black children in the South still attended all-black schools. In 1974, that number had fallen to just 8 per cent. Almost all of that shift took place in a mere handful of months in 1970. The policy was not altogether a success, and the issue remains a source of great bitterness, but Nixon skilfully took the political sting out of the integration process by sapping it of drama. Rather than threatening Southern states with harsh federal interventions, Nixon offered the reward of federal education dollars, which would only be available to states and districts making adequate progress on integration.

Nixon knew that the South would never comply if integration seemed a humiliating submission, so instead he offered the Southern states a cooperative path forward with substantial local control. He also made it clear that, if progress wasn't made, his administration would have no choice but to use intrusive federal court rulings.

Bi-racial committees were established for seven holdout Southern states. In contrast to what would be the norm today, the work was not relentlessly promoted to the press. Nixon knew that black members of the committees would fear the 'Uncle Tom' label, while the white members would fear being smeared as 'n_ _ _ _ _-lovers'. A low-key approach was better. The result proved to be one of the rare examples in American history when 'forming a committee' solved a real problem. Hitherto recalcitrant states abolished their two-track school systems.

The integration of America's public schools was arguably the single most dramatic shift in American race relations since emancipation a century before, yet at the time Nixon received little credit, and sought even less. George Romney and Robert Finch were told not to boast about the administration's efforts. Nixon achieved integration without humiliating its opponents, without indulging radicals, without new deployments of federal troops.

He employed similar strategies across a range of divisive issues in American life. His 'New Federalism' devolved federal programmes to decentralised state control via block grants. He made progress steady and deliberate rather than showy and divisive.

Nixon surprised Democrats by stealing the environmental issue from them. Between 1970 and 1973, at Nixon's urging, Congress passed the National Environmental Policy Act, the Ocean Dumping Act, and the Endangered Species Act. It also drastically expanded the Clean Air Act and created the Environmental Protection Agency and National Oceanic and Atmospheric Administration. Internationally, Nixon negotiated the CITES treaty governing international efforts to protect endangered species and prevent their international trafficking.

Some of Nixon's initiatives failed, yet showed vision in the failure. His Family Assistance Plan would have set an income floor for families with children, expanding the social safety net and simplifying the complex morass of federal welfare programmes. However, it was rejected by Congress, as was his bid for universal health insurance, scuttled by Democrats who hoped for a more liberal programme that never came.

Nixon's finest achievements arguably came in foreign policy. 'The greatest honour history can bestow is the title of peacemaker,' he said in his first inaugural address. Nixon didn't carry his Quaker beliefs into adulthood, and he was no pacifist, yet his administration did more than any other in the Cold War to scale back American hostilities abroad.

The obvious exception is Vietnam, which proved as complicated a failure as it was a challenge. Again, though, the image of Nixon as a bloodthirsty maniac is more liberal fantasy than truth.

So enduring is hatred of Nixon that millions today may live under the mistaken impression that he started the Vietnam War, or at least greatly expanded it, and only his downfall finally ended it. The reality is almost the opposite. It is often claimed that Nixon scuppered Johnson's peace talks for electoral advantage – LBJ thought as much – and there is no doubt that he can be accused of playing base politics with American and Vietnamese lives. Still, when Nixon took office, there were 550,000 US combat troops in Vietnam. By the spring of 1973, there were none.

The more controversial actions Nixon took, from increased bombing of the North to attacks on Viet Cong supply lines in neutral Cambodia, were done with the aim of bringing about the 'peace with honour' he had promised America. To achieve that, Nixon needed to bring the North Vietnamese to the negotiating table, which they had abandoned in 1969, promising to stay away until the chairs assigned to them rotted. The bombings, however awful, succeeded in this regard, persuading the North to restart negotiations and, eventually, winning the release of American prisoners of war.

Nixon hated communism and clearly hoped that South Vietnam could be preserved without ever greater American loss. His policy of 'Vietnamization' was meant to do that, gradually withdrawing US forces while bolstering South Vietnamese capabilities and sheltering the country with American airpower.

In the end, Nixon's strategy failed. South Vietnam collapsed two years after America's exit, as Nixon knew it would. 'Peace with honour' is now a term used only sarcastically. But Nixon's record on Vietnam appears considerably more admirable today than, say, George W. Bush's in Iraq and Afghanistan.

When it came to the wider challenge of the Soviet Union, Nixon developed the policy of *détente*, and his efforts bore fruit. His administration negotiated the SALT I agreements in 1969, producing the first limits on the size of nuclear arsenals and restricting the deployment of anti-ballistic missile systems. His unilateral termination of America's biological weapons programme led in turn to the International Biological Weapons Convention three years later.

The march of history has given a sour tinge to what was once almost unanimously regarded as Nixon's greatest diplomatic coup: the rapprochement with communist China in 1972. For decades, the opening of China seemed like the supreme triumph of Cold War realpolitik, an inspired move in the national interest. Nixon's own library treats his China visit as the signature accomplishment of his presidency. Only Nixon could go to China, and go to China Nixon did.

Whether he *should* have gone remains up for debate. When Nixon toasted Mao in Beijing, William F. Buckley wrote that it was 'as if Sir Hartley Shawcross had suddenly risen from the prosecutor's stand at Nuremberg and descended to embrace Goering and Goebbels and Doenitz and Hess, begging them to join with him in the making of a better world'.

China received much from Nixon's initiative: acquiescence to its permanent seat on the UN Security Council, military intelligence on the Soviet Union, access to air and radio technology, and eventually fully normalised relations, all while making no concessions on the freedom of its people or the eventual fate of Taiwan.

At the time, Nixon was praised for opening China to the world with an unpredictable combination of threat and charm.

Today, however, with China poised to match and eventually surpass America as a global superpower, Nixon's victory feels empty. By outsourcing technology and manufacturing in China, Nixon helped kickstart its growth without liberalising the country in the process. The Chinese Communist Party was and still is a despotic regime. But today it is far, far richer.

Nixon himself later acknowledged the peril. Before his death, he reflected that in China, 'We may have created a Frankenstein.'

But no man can see one year into the future, let alone fifty. There were many opportunities to change the nature of China's rise, and later presidents, notably Bill Clinton, failed the world more in that regard. In the 1970s, however, it seemed that Nixon had faced down an enemy and turned it into a partner, thus validating America's role as global peacemaker.

Nixon's re-election year, 1972, saw him at his apex. Hated as he might have been by *Rolling Stone* and the *New York Times*, he remained popular among the public. The war in Vietnam was ending, riots were subsiding, the economy was growing. If crime was still rising, many Americans at least felt the president was on the side of law and order. His electoral matchup with the Democrat George McGovern was a lopsided bloodbath. Nixon won the popular vote by thirty-three points and won every state except

Massachusetts. In nineteen states, McGovern didn't win a single county.

But even at the moment of Nixon's supreme triumph, he had already made the mistakes that would seal his doom. He took his second oath of office with a 67 per cent approval rating, his highest ever. Nineteen months later, he was out of office, disgraced, thanks to Watergate.

To this day, it is unclear what Nixon's underlings hoped to gain by breaking into the DNC headquarters at the Watergate Hotel on 17 June 1972 and bugging its phones. The burglars testified that they were looking to find links between the Democratic Party and communist Cuba, a suitably ridiculous motive for a clownish endeavour. There is no reason to believe Nixon knew in advance of the amateurish plot. But he knew very shortly afterwards that his men were involved. Had he acted swiftly to distance himself and ensure punishment for those involved, he would have saved himself and his presidency.

Why Nixon did not do exactly that is the stuff for decades of historical debate and psychological analysis. Henry Kissinger once suggested, intriguingly, that Nixon possessed an appetite for his own destruction. 'I sometimes had the impression that he invited crisis and could not stand normalcy,' he said. 'Triumph seemed to bring no surcease to this tortured man. It was hard to avoid the impression that Nixon, who thrived on crisis, also craved disasters.'

Psychological mumbo-jumbo, perhaps, but such a mental or spiritual kink might explain Nixon's self-defeating behaviour in 1973. He clumsily tried to hide the links between his aides and the burglary, then he sought to cover up the cover-up.

He may well have survived, had it not been for the spectacular revelation in July 1973 of a secret White House taping system that logged the president's private conversations. The legal battle over the tapes' release continued until July 1974, when the Supreme Court ordered Nixon to release all subpoenaed tapes to investigators. These tapes revealed that Nixon, in flat contradiction of earlier claims, had known immediately after the burglary that his most senior aides were involved, and that he had given politically motivated instructions to the CIA in an attempt to block investigation of the case. Nixon's political support in Congress collapsed, and he resigned on 9 August. Only a pardon from President Ford spared him a likely prosecution.

Never a quitter, Nixon was determined to rebuild after his disgrace. 'This is a test of character and we must not fail the test,' he wrote in his diary. In 1978, he addressed the Oxford Union with the defiant statement: 'You'll be here in the year 2000 and we'll see how I'm regarded then.'

It's tempting to say that Nixon succeeded in his final comeback campaign. There were gains. He was gradually welcomed back into public life. When his library opened in Yorba Linda, President George H.W. Bush attended, and when he died Bill Clinton offered a eulogy. But the year 2000 has come and gone, and Nixon's reputation has never recovered from Watergate. In a 2021 Gallup poll of the American public, respondents ranked him dead last among the past nine presidents.

Perhaps Trump will finally eclipse him there, but for that we may have to wait for Nixon to pass from living memory. His fall was just too ugly.

The Watergate tapes showed the American public not just obstruction of justice, but a more intimate portrait of their president than they cared for. Nixon swore. He reduced everything to politics. He complained about too many Jews in government ('most Jews are disloyal'), called Indian women 'undoubtedly the most unattractive women in the world', and said that he disliked abortion but that it was sometimes necessary 'when you have a black and a white'. Americans crave supermen presidents. Thanks to thousands of hours of tapes, the Nixon the world knows is all too human.

Throughout his career, Nixon allowed ambition to corrode his nobler principles. One of his favourite political tactics was telling small untruths in a way that let him control the narrative. When he accused a rival of voting with President Johnson 98 per cent of the time, and a newspaperman revealed that the truth was just 94 per cent, Nixon was pleased. The small factual correction could be beneficial since it meant his essential point had been made twice. Without Watergate, this fibbery would be a whimsical anecdote of political gamesmanship. But there can be no 'without' Watergate. Nixon, the relentless political animal, sowed his own demise.

Today, though, with greater detachment and greater knowledge, the angst over Nixon's moral failures can feel mildly ridiculous. President Clinton's private moral lapses were more glaring. President Trump's behaviour was far more outlandish. Nixon's personal bigotry was no different from Lyndon Johnson's – and Johnson won his first Senate race through fraud, used lies to launch the Vietnam War and then told more lies to perpetuate it. Nixon's plan to use the Inland Revenue Service to audit his perceived enemies was prompted by the Kennedy administration, which had done the same to him.

Nixon's most ardent defenders could claim he was treated unfairly by a venomous press and hostile establishment that had never accepted him and held him to standards they never applied to themselves. Still, Watergate was not a funds scandal. Nixon was not framed. He destroyed his career and his legacy with an unethical, pointless, stupid act of low political thuggery that diminished the republic he was entrusted to lead. Watergate revealed the pattern of 'dirty tricks' politicking with which Tricky Dick will forever be associated. Nixon showed the Americans how their country was actually run, and it disgusted them.

The president admitted this in 1977, during his televised interviews with David Frost. 'I brought myself down. I gave 'em a sword. And they stuck it in, and they twisted it with relish. And I guess if I'd been in their position, I'd have done the same thing.'

In many ways, Nixon has set the pattern for all the Republican presidents who followed him — especially Reagan, George W. Bush and Trump. All three leaders won through promises to pull back the over-reach of hegemonic liberalism; through appeals to the 'silent majority' (a term Nixon popularised); through electoral coalitions built upon the South rather than the north-east. They governed by accommodating progressive concerns rather than honouring pledges made to the right. (Trump, for instance, made criminal justice reform a centrepiece of his one-term legacy. He never built much of a wall on the border.)

Above all else, Nixon set the tone for the Republicans after him by being *hated*. Nixon was despised by America's most privileged and liberal classes, viscerally, cruelly, irrationally, whether in exile or after winning a forty-nine-state landslide. Watergate vindicated the animosity, but it existed beforehand and would still exist even if Nixon had ended his presidency scandal-free. Hunter S. Thompson, for instance, reserved a special hatred for Nixon, eulogising him after his death as 'a political monster straight out of Grendel', 'a swine of a man and a jabbering dupe of a president', the possessor of an 'ugly, Nazi spirit' casting a toxic pall over all America even in death. 'If the right people had been in charge of Nixon's funeral,' Thompson wrote, 'his casket would have been launched into one of those open-sewage canals that empty into the ocean just south of Los Angeles.' Today, Thompson's tone is the house style of the Twitter blue check. It has been used on Bush, used on Trump, and it will be used on whichever Republican comes next.

American conservatives enjoy quoting film critic Pauline Kael, who supposedly reacted with shock to Nixon's 1972 landslide by saying, 'I can't believe Nixon won. I don't know anyone who voted for him.' The quote is a myth, intended to portray Kael as a Hollywood bubble-dweller. The real quote, however, is even more revealing: 'I only know one person who voted for Nixon. Where they are I don't know. They're outside my ken. But sometimes when I'm in a theater I can feel them.'

There it is. The hatred for Nixon reflects a much more powerful disgust for the man's supporters – for the vast, uncool hordes of proles who gave their ballots to him in a spirit of defiance. These voters – the silent-but-now-not-quite-majority and their children – are one of the few acceptable targets for public bigotry in American society.

How, then, should Nixon's tumultuous presidency be judged? Some day his policies will be more fairly evaluated, but by then their significance will have faded. His Cabinet colleagues and rivals are almost all gone. Even Henry Kissinger (ninety-eight at the time of writing) might die one day.

Sadly, the most lasting legacy of Nixon may be the toxic political culture he inadvertently created. The dreaded Imperial Presidency, the over-reaching executive branch, took on greater form under his watch. And Watergate warped American politics permanently. Distrust of Congress and government became permanently fashionable. Posturing as an 'outsider' and making over-emotional appeals to public sentiment became a necessity for anyone seeking high office.

Worst of all, thanks to Nixon, the press became ever more

astronomically self-important and obsessed with its role as 'guardian of democracy'. Having brought down the most popular presidential winner in history, the hacks of Washington felt they could do it again and again. That's why every scandal, however silly, is now a '-gate'. It's why impeachment, and the threat of impeachment, has become a cheap political weapon.

For a half-century, the shadow of Watergate has hung over America. It lingers still.

Freddy Gray is deputy editor of the Spectator, *and host of the 'Americano' podcast. He's a former deputy editor of the* Catholic Herald *and literary editor of the* American Conservative.

38

Gerald Ford

9 August 1974 to 20 January 1977
Republican
Vice-president: Nelson Rockefeller

By Andy Silvester

Full name: Gerald Rudolph Ford Jr, born Leslie Lynch King Jr
Born: 14 July 1913, Omaha, Nebraska
Died: 26 December 2006, Rancho Mirage, California
Resting place: Gerald R. Ford Presidential Museum, Grand Rapids, Michigan
Library/Museum: Grand Rapids, Michigan
Education: University of Michigan, Yale
Married to: Betty Bloomer, m. 1948 (1918–2011)
Children: Four: Michael, Jack, Steven, Susan
Quotation: 'A government big enough to give you everything you want is a government big enough to take from you everything you have.'

IN THIS LITERARY Mount Rushmore, Gerald R. Ford stands alone in one particular regard: as the only man among these forty-five to have never been elected to national office. Never having sought the highest positions in the land, never having even seemed particularly interested in the big job, Ford remains the accidental president.

His career – as a well-thought-of, cooperative but certainly not flashy congressman – was not supposed to end in the Oval Office.

But unexpected as his ascension to the job was, unusual as the circumstances were, Ford played a key role in holding together the very *idea* of America after the tumultuous 1960s and the twin tragedies of Vietnam and Watergate.

The folksy charm that would later soothe a wounded nation was formed in the American interior. Born to a middle-class mother and an abusive father, he was born Leslie L. King Jr in Omaha, Nebraska. At the age of two, his parents divorced – and mother Dorothy and Leslie moved to her parents' house in Grand Rapids, Michigan. There she fell in love with Gerald Rudolph Ford, the two living together in a rented two-bed apartment. Years later, the future president would be formally renamed after his stepfather.

Ford's adolescence was an all-American affair. An athletic star, he played football in front of a hundred thousand fans at the University of Michigan, and was even offered $2,800 to play for the Green Bay Packers. In his autobiography, Ford credited his sporting youth for giving him a 'thick hide' to face down critics.

But law, rather than the gridiron, seemed his future. Yale beckoned, but after he returned to Michigan to start a small practice, the Second World War intervened. Ford signed up to the navy almost as soon as America declared war.

His time at sea was not without incident – specifically, he had at least one near-death experience, after slipping on the deck of the USS *Monterey* in a Filipino typhoon and hanging on for dear life as the ship came close to capsizing. He dodged death again on rest and recuperation back home in the States, narrowly escaping a crashed plane seconds before it burst into flames. It wouldn't be the last time Ford nearly came to a premature end – later, he was the subject of two close-but-no-cigar assassination attempts, both in California.

Returning from the war determined to do more in public life, his political career began in earnest. An internationalist conservative at heart, he was encouraged by friends in 1948 to take on the isolationist, machine politician Republican incumbent Barney Jonkman for the GOP nomination in Michigan's Fifth District. To Jonkman's dismay, the thirty-four-year-old Ford's energetic campaigning saw him win the primary by a vote of nearly two to one.

The next morning, Ford travelled to a farm in the district and started work at 4:30 a.m. So desperate was he for votes, he'd promised the farm's owners he'd help milk cows for two weeks if he won. It was the toughest electoral fight of his entire political career, until the last year of it.

In a solid safe seat, he won his House of Representatives seat with 60 per cent of the vote and never looked back.

Around the same time, he met and then swiftly married a divorcee by the name of Betty Bloomer. Now Betty Ford, she would be by the president's side – and become an American icon in her own way for her candour and the attention she drew to breast cancer and, later, substance addiction – for the rest of his life.

So began a congressional career of quiet ascent, with friends on all sides. By the early 1960s, he was a respected senior figure within Republican ranks and manoeuvring to become Minority Leader. Ford served as part of the Warren Commission, too, investigating the assassination of JFK. All of his efforts were a step closer to the only job he really wanted: Speaker of the House.

But his folksy demeanour, while warming up congressmen on all sides, didn't come without a downside. It was around the time of Ford's light-hearted joint press conferences with his counterpart in the Senate, Everett Dirksen, that LBJ quipped that Ford was a 'nice guy but he played too much football with his helmet off'. Slightly less wittily, he also said that the Michiganite couldn't 'fart and chew gum at the same time'.

As the vice-presidency of Spiro Agnew began to unravel, with allegation after allegation from his time as Maryland governor, eyes across Washington looked for alternatives. Nixon, who reportedly preferred other candidates to Ford, was already running out of political capital and had to find consensus. Who better than the likeable former sports star who counted senior Democrats such as Tip O'Neill among his close friends?

Ford became the compromise candidate. Though he'd told Betty he planned to quit politics in 1977, he said yes when Nixon asked him to take the role: popular in Congress and plainly without political ambition, the popular Ford was the choice most likely to sail through confirmation hearings. He did.

But even after that, rumours persisted that Nixon may have had a more ulterior motive. They were fuelled by a story that Nixon, pointing to his Oval Office desk, told a guest: 'Can you imagine Jerry Ford sitting in that chair?'

Did Nixon believe Ford was his insurance against impeachment? Perhaps. Did it work? No.

As the Nixon White House fell apart, it became apparent to Ford that life would change. According to his telling, he genuinely believed Nixon's private and public denials of knowledge of Watergate, and felt he needed to serve in his proper constitutional role as vice-president, even to the point of the absurd. With the writing already on the wall, Ford and his wife travelled across Washington to the in-construction vice-president's mansion to discuss interior decoration, curtain choices, and which would be the master bedroom.

He would never sleep there. Nixon told Ford over a seventy-minute meeting that he would become president, urging him to continue a muscular foreign policy and to make the economy – in an awful state – his number-one domestic priority. A day later, Ford took the Oath of Office in the East Wing.

His first speech was arguably his best. After the double-speak of Nixon, his plain candour offered a welcome contrast for a drained public. It was not, he said, 'an inaugural address, not a fireside chat, not a campaign speech – just a little straight talk among friends'.

And then the best line of his presidency: 'My fellow Americans, our long national nightmare is over.'

This was half true. Inflation was running at almost record levels, the stock market jittery and unemployment creeping up. Abroad, America was defeated in Vietnam and its status as world policeman in question.

On the economy, Ford began with a gimmicky, down-home approach to inflation. Fairly or not, his 'Whip Inflation Now' programme (complete with 'WIN' pin badges) was characterised in the press as asking Americans to tighten their belts and scrimp and save their way to recovery. Unsurprisingly, WIN – complete with calls to save petrol and build vegetable gardens in backyards – fell flat.

The whispers that Ford was out of his depth, at least intellectually, were now becoming louder. That tag never quite left him; an unfortunate stumble down the stairs of Air Force One became not just fodder for bored reporters, but eventually even a joke in *The Simpsons* years later.

It was only when Ford pivoted away from his homespun economic mantra towards a more traditional, conservative tax-cutting approach that he began to turn the economic tide. In that effort, he was advised by a young Alan Greenspan – and politically by a young Dick Cheney, too. If the economy had not quite recovered fully by the end of his term, it was at least in convalescence.

Abroad, Ford was perhaps more dynamic. He was desperate to continue the work of previous presidents in forging a more collaborative relationship with the Soviets, while keeping the arm of the US notably well toned.

His first meeting with Soviet premier Brezhnev came in Vladivostok, when the president appeared to win over the General Secretary with sports small talk. They agreed, after much shuttle diplomacy from Henry Kissinger, a raft of reductions on the scale and scope of nuclear weapons – leaving the possibility of wiping each other out only dozens of times, as opposed to hundreds.

And even in frozen Siberia, people warmed to Ford: Brezhnev had been admiring an Alaskan wolf coat that Ford had been wearing during the summit. As the president ascended the steps of Air Force One to fly home, he gave it to Brezhnev as a gift.

He failed to get a further formal agreement on 'SALT II', but elsewhere he had success. He brokered a temporary peace in the Middle East. And when challenged, as he was when Cambodian forces took possession of a US merchant ship and her crew, he responded decisively – winning plaudits at home, and assuring America's allies that Vietnam hadn't completely sated America's appetite for foreign engagements. He surprised foreign leaders, who had perhaps read the American papers, with intelligent conversation on global affairs.

But his presidency was, and is, defined by the signing of one slip of paper just a few weeks into the job: a presidential pardon for his predecessor, Richard Nixon. The decision was Ford's alone, taken largely in secret with only his very closest aides knowing. And to understand why, we must understand what Ford felt his role was.

As he took office, he reflects in his memoirs, the ship of state rather resembled that embattled cruiser in the Philippines. He saw it as his duty to steady that ship – to give America the chance to heal.

There seems little doubt that Ford was personally hurt by Nixon's constant denials of involvement in Watergate, but he wished to put the entire episode behind him. If a later president wanted to 'drain the swamp', Ford wished simply to stop it stinking up the country. He solicited legal advice on how long it would take for a trial of Richard Nixon to be completed – a full year. Press conferences that he chose to attend personally, in a break from Nixon's outwardly hostile relationship with the media, were still dominated by Watergate. Then reports from acquaintances suggested that the former president was not well – distracted, rambling, broken. His emissary to Nixon, lawyer Benton Becker, went as far as to suggest that Nixon would not last the year. Ford made up his mind.

Ford's conditions for a pardon were thus: that all papers and recordings from the Nixon administration be placed under a neutral trust allowing special prosecutors to delve into the facts of cases against others, and that Nixon offer a contrite statement of guilt. The first was simple, the second a struggle. Eventually, Ford accepted a statement in which Nixon offered 'regret' for his 'mistakes'.

Ford announced his decision to the nation: 'I cannot prolong the bad dreams that continue to reopen a chapter that is closed' – but he misjudged the mood. His argument that a 1915 Supreme Court decision meant that Nixon's acceptance of the pardon also meant accepting his guilt may have stood up in a seminar room, but it had no chance in the court of public opinion. Congress was livid. Editorials were scathing. Rumours of secret deals percolated.

But the pardon *did* move America on from Watergate. It pulled hard at the constitutional threads of law and justice, certainly, but those constitutional threads held. The fact that rich and poor alike must surely be held to the same standard in law gives way to realpolitik:

that an America scarred by so much simply needed a rest from high drama, and its break-up from Nixon and Vietnam to be final.

If the pardon allowed America to reset itself, though, it marked Ford. Jimmy Carter, who defeated him narrowly in the 1976 presidential election, used it ad nauseum to tie the honest Jerry Ford to the anything-but Richard Nixon. In truth it would have taken a political superstar to win the 1976 election as a Republican – perhaps only Ronald Reagan, who launched a damaging primary bid from the right of the Republican Party, could have done it. America was underwhelmed by Ford's lack of star power.

But in the grand weighing-up of history, Ford did what he set out to do – to heal a bruised country. And above all? He was decent.

Andy Silvester is a former UK political adviser and is editor of City AM.

39

Jimmy Carter

20 January 1977 to 20 January 1981
Democrat
Vice-president: Walter Mondale

By David Owen

Full name: James Earl Carter Jr
Born: 1 October 1924, Plains, Georgia
Library/Museum: Atlanta, Georgia
Education: Plains High School; Georgia Southwestern College;
Georgia Institute of Technology; US Naval Academy
Married to: Rosalynn Smith, m. 1946 (1927–)
Children: Four: Jack, James III, Donnel and Amy
Quotation: 'I have one life and one chance to make it count
for something . . . My faith demands that I do whatever I
can, wherever I am, whenever I can, for as long as I can with
whatever I have to try to make a difference.'

O N 3 NOVEMBER 1976, Jimmy Carter beat President Gerald Ford in the Electoral College by fifty-seven votes and in the popular vote with only 50.1 per cent. If there had been a combined change of a mere 18,000 votes in the states of Ohio and Hawaii, he would have lost. It was the closest margin of victory since Woodrow Wilson in 1916. By contrast, Joe Biden beat President Trump by slightly bigger margins in the Electoral College by sixty-four votes and in the popular vote with 51.3 per cent with nearly double the number of overall voters, the largest turnout in America's history.

Carter was the first president to be elected from the Deep South since Zachary Taylor in 1848. The first governor elected president since Franklin Roosevelt. He started as governor of Georgia in January 1971, yet his wife, who he describes as his 'best friend and chief adviser', quietly called around in the summer of 1972 to see if her husband might be considered by McGovern when Senator Eagleton stepped down as his vice-presidential candidate. On 17 October 1972, Carter discussed running for president with close advisers in Georgia and the planning began that evening. State law at the time prevented an incumbent governor from running for a second term. He undertook trade trips and joined the Trilateral Commission to extend his personal and international contacts. It was an astonishing personal gamble since most people in America knew nothing about him or vaguely talked about 'Jimmy who?' Yet on the Democratic campaign trail he was surprisingly effective. He destroyed Morris Udall, he beat two other prominent Democrat candidates, Senator 'Scoop' Jackson in Florida by a margin of ten points and Governor George Wallace of Alabama by four points. Governor Wallace had been a candidate in 1964, 1968 and 1972. Belatedly, Wallace endorsed Carter's candidacy, saying, 'It's alright to be a conservative Democrat and vote for Jimmy Carter.'

Amazingly, the first independent full-length biography of Carter only came out in 2020. Fortunately, it was worth waiting for. Jonathan Alter, who has also written on FDR and Obama, has created an excellent book worthy of the man. Yet more than half of it is on winning the presidency. The reason for this unconventional weighting lies in his biographer's words: 'Carter was a historical anomaly – an aberration caused by Watergate and a speed bump in the South's historic transition from solid Democratic to solid Republican.' He was 'a pioneer of centre-left "New Democrat" thinking that would be adopted by Clinton and Obama, though neither would credit him'.

I first met Carter as president when as Foreign Secretary I accompanied Prime Minister Jim Callaghan to Washington from 10 to 12 March 1977. After that visit, Callaghan wrote to his friend Helmut Schmidt, the German Chancellor, that Carter had an 'ordered, well stocked mind . . . quite a formidable person to deal with . . . 'straightforward and not too much artifice'. Callaghan was 'the foreign leader Carter got along with best after Sadat'. Conversely, there was mutual dislike between Schmidt and Carter, who saw Schmidt as 'foul-tempered' and who treated him with 'arrogant disdain'. The reason for the disdain was Carter's wish to ban fast-breeder nuclear reactors and his change of mind over the neutron bomb. Alter reverses Oliver Wendell Holmes's famous description of Franklin Roosevelt and describes Carter as 'a first-class intellect and a second-class temperament'. David McCullough, the historian of many presidents, including most importantly of Truman, saw the naval engineer Carter at his best advocating the Panama Canal treaties and recalls more generally that: 'He didn't seem to have the political adrenaline that one responds favourably to.'

For my part I liked Jimmy Carter and the more I saw of him at NATO and G7 meetings and in the White House the more complex his personality appeared to be. I wrote in retrospect: 'He combines a fundamental decency and good Baptist values with a mean, competitive streak. His "born again" religious views give him a moral certainty which could be unattractive but his interest in facts and his scientific approach to problems counter the fundamentalism, so that there is a greater strength to his decisions than is often at first apparent.' It is noteworthy that Joe Biden, aged thirty-three at the time, was the first senator to endorse Carter in 1976.

In many ways Carter's most formidable achievement was the Panama Canal Treaty. All previous presidents had ducked out of this huge challenge because of the strength of the political opposition. Just before his election, forty-eight senators had signed a resolution saying they would 'never give away the Canal'. Carter seized the moment of his maximum political clout and, as he admitted himself, 'I put my whole life on the line on the Panama Canal Treaty.' It was not primarily even a foreign policy issue. Most Americans simply considered the Canal Zone as American territory and it was this attitude that was so resented in Latin America. During the transition period, Ford had told Carter it was the most important single issue he would face. When people told him it was a second-term issue, he said: 'Suppose there is no second term?' The Joint Chiefs influenced him when they said that it would take at least a hundred thousand troops to defend the Canal if it was sabotaged, which they considered likely. An international treaty needs a two-thirds majority in the Senate, and handling the Panamanians meant it was best to have two treaties. On 18 April 1978, the Senate passed the second treaty by sixty-eight votes to thirty-two, the same margin as on the earlier neutrality treaty. Among the twenty politicians who faced re-election in 1978, and who had supported him, only seven returned to the Senate. Sixteen Republican senators backed him, ten Democrats defied him. The newcomer to Washington had managed a cross-party effort for the national good that was a stunning achievement. His biographer highlights as an example the wooing of Senator Sam Hayakawa from California, whose initial view of the Canal was, 'We stole it fair and square.' Carter lobbied him hard and won him over for the first treaty. On the second treaty he was withholding support. He asked Carter to commit to meeting him for a chat every two weeks. 'Sam,' Carter said, 'I couldn't possibly limit our visits to every two weeks. I might want to hear your advice more often!' Hayakawa voted yes, and that was the last time Jimmy Carter ever spoke to him. Politics is a blood sport and few understood that better than Carter.

After that vote Carter was told by the Republican leaders and Henry Kissinger that they could not and would not give the same level of support for any SALT II treaty. One of the reasons for this stance was they had been very upset by the way Carter had chosen to handle President Ford and Kissinger's Vladivostok agreement with Brezhnev and Gromyko. Instead of going for a quick cross-party ratification of Vladivostok, Carter sent Cyrus Vance to Moscow in the spring of 1977 to say that Carter wanted 'deep cuts' in the number of strategic weapons, which Gromyko later called a 'cheap and shady manoeuvre'; and when Vance explained the alternative approach of proceeding with Vladivostok, Gromyko angrily switched off and cancelled further meetings. The Russians were still nursing their grievance when I saw Brezhnev and Gromyko in Moscow in October and tried to convince them he genuinely wanted a deal. Negotiations over SALT II did resume, but after the Russian invasion of Afghanistan in 1979 further progress in Washington was impossible.

Meanwhile, Carter launched his human rights policies worldwide and carried conviction because he extended rights to his own citizens by selecting more women and blacks as federal judges than all of his predecessors. He was also way ahead of his time on environmental issues, dealing with pollution controls, toxic waste and advanced solar power. In his own admission, 'I put in more time on energy by far than any other issue that I addressed while I was president, domestic or foreign.'

Early on, Walter Mondale as vice-president was sent to confront the South African government over apartheid. For the first time, the US were in the lead over ending the worst abuse of human rights in the world. When Steve Biko, the young black-consciousness leader, was brutally beaten to death in the autumn of 1977, the UN led by the US agreed that the situation in South Africa was a threat to peace and a resolution was passed allowing the application of mandatory sanctions on arms sales. This opened up for the first time the leverage of sanctions on South Africa to make negotiations meaningful in Rhodesia, Namibia and South Africa itself. However, it was not until the US Congress overturned President Reagan's veto on the Comprehensive Anti-Apartheid Act in 1986 that the harshest economic sanctions of international bank loans drying up forced South Africa to start to contemplate releasing Nelson Mandela from prison, and in 1990 President de Klerk agreed to negotiate with him over free elections and the ending of apartheid. If President Carter had not set the pattern of standing firmly against apartheid, the opportunity of Mandela being still young enough to be the great conciliator he was might never have happened. Carter's involvement with Vance and Andy Young helped Rhodesia become independent in 1980 after the Lancaster House constitutional conference chaired by Peter Carrington; and that settlement, though barely admitted, was on the basis of the Anglo-American plan established by Callaghan and Carter at their first meeting in 1977.

Andrew Young, charismatic and a strong influence on Carter

because he had been a huge help in getting him elected, was appointed ambassador to the UN in 1977, and I enjoyed working closely with him over finding a settlement in Rhodesia. But we had one big difference over Mugabe. I had become convinced by 1978 that Mugabe was a zealot. A self-proclaimed Marxist who clandestinely attended Catholic mass in Maputo was a man deeply conflicted. I felt that nothing would stop Mugabe introducing one-party rule in Zimbabwe. Alter has virtually nothing on Africa, but that gap has been very well filled by a book called *Jimmy Carter in Africa: Race and the Cold War*, which does justice to the man and his principled policies. But it stops when Carter leaves office, so there is no mention of when, in 1982, Mugabe was responsible for a genocide in Matabeleland killing twenty thousand people at the hands of Mugabe's 5th Brigade 'special unit', trained and equipped by North Koreans. The world, including the US and the UK, chose to virtually ignore this, as did many human rights supporters.

Carter's other great achievement was the Camp David Accords, for which he deserved the Nobel Peace Prize, which was only given to Anwar Sadat and Menachem Begin. Fortunately, he was given the honour in 2002 for all his many efforts, some successful, some unsuccessful, to promote peace in the world as part of the best record of achievement of any US president out of office, during which time he contributed greatly to many humanitarian projects. I will never forget watching him in Ghana in the 1980s on his knees with a big wooden board in front of him, punctured by six round holes, showing a farm worker how to put one seed in each hole as the best way of ensuring a good crop. Carter, the first US president to be born in a hospital, traces his interest in public service and eradication of diseases to the influence of his mother, a nurse. At the age of 68, Lillian Carter joined the Peace Corps as a volunteer in India.

From the start of his presidency, Carter identified the Middle East as the place to become personally involved. In April, he met with President Sadat of Egypt, who he described in his own memoirs as 'A shining light burst on the Middle East scene for me.' The two religious men bonded and there was mutual respect followed by a real friendship. Carter asked Vance to travel to the region and invite Sadat and Begin, who was now prime minister of Israel, to come later in the year to Camp David. Progress looked blocked until Sadat made his dramatic and very personal move, and flew into Jerusalem on 19 November 1977. Ritually denounced by all the key Arab leaders, Sadat's visit made Begin emotionally engaged. He knew he had to respond, but visiting London soon after in discussions with Callaghan he was still very unsure how he would do so.

The Camp David Summit lasted from 5 to 17 September 1978 and involved twenty-three drafts. Very few presidents would have devoted so much effort and patience to a single foreign policy issue as Carter did during those two weeks. He wrote in his diary the essence of the deal. 'Begin showed courage in Sinai. He did it to keep the West Bank.' For Carter its success was because 'we all shared faith in the same God – we all considered ourselves the sons of Abraham'.

Carter's substantial achievement won him recognition that month in US opinion polls with 58 per cent approval ratings. However, the best lasting recognition is that under the Treaty that followed between Israel and Egypt there has never been any breach and they have never fought each other again.

It is too early, writing in February 2021, to be sure, but Carter's use of the words 'sons of Abraham' was brought to mind when Israel, the UAE, Bahrain and the US signed the Abraham Accords on 15 September 2020 involving a wide range of economic and security cooperation. These Accords, under President Trump, would not have been conceivable had it not been for Camp David over forty years earlier. Yet Egypt and Saudi Arabia have still to become involved.

The biggest crisis in foreign affairs facing Carter during his presidency was Iran. The Shah flew out of the country never to return on 16 January 1979. Then Ayatollah Khomeini flew in to Tehran to a hero's welcome on 1 February. But it was not long before there were predictably widespread killings and very serious abuses of human rights as the zealots took control. In late October 1979 a dying Shah was admitted to a US hospital for cancer treatment. This provoked an outcry back in Iran demanding the Shah's return to be tried. On 4 November the American Embassy was overwhelmed by Islamist students and 52 American diplomats and citizens were held hostage for an eventual 444 days. On 24 April 1980 an abortive attempt by the US military to rescue the hostages had to be aborted when in the Iranian desert three helicopters failed because of mechanical failure. In addition one more helicopter crashed into a tanker aircraft, killing eight US servicemen. The hostage crisis eventually ended with the signing of the Algiers Accords on 19 January 1981 with the hostages being released the following day, minutes after Ronald Reagan became the new American president, having soundly beaten Jimmy Carter in the presidential elections; a calculated insult by Ayatollah Khomeini.

President Carter first encountered the Shah of Iran on 15 November 1977 on his visit to the White House. During a twenty-one-gun salute and as Carter made his welcoming speech, Iranians supporting the Shah and others against him began to fight each other outside the White House perimeter. Police had to use tear gas to break up the disturbance, causing the audience listening a few hundred yards away to cough and splutter. It was a warning that Iran was not a country at peace with itself. The Shah's excessive extravagance – particularly, the party at Persepolis in 1971 to celebrate the 2,500th anniversary of the Persian monarchy, and in 1976 to celebrate the fiftieth anniversary of the Pahlavi dynasty – was becoming deeply resented by many Iranians. The Shah had long had a reputation for being indecisive, but unbeknown to either the Americans or the British, since 1974 he had been secretly treated by French doctors for chronic lymphocytic leukaemia, which progressed to a lymphosarcoma. Had Cyrus Vance and myself known of this in May 1977 when we both visited Tehran for the last CENTO military alliance meeting, we would have stressed the need then to move urgently towards a constitutional monarchy.

By the summer of 1978, the political unrest in Iran led to a popular revolution. Strikes were paralysing the country, including the all-important oilfields. That was the time for the Shah to either use his large army to crush the revolution or to stand down on health grounds and appoint a regency until his son came of age.

The Shah did not fall because of the indecision of President Carter. That is a carefully fostered myth by prominent people who have always known the truth. He fell because of his own chronic indecision, which had become acute by late 1978, almost certainly exacerbated by his progressive blood condition that eventually caused him to die. The

White House became dramatically involved on 2 November 1978 when the US ambassador to Tehran, William Sullivan, sent a telegram to Washington seeking instructions within forty-eight hours, as the Shah wanted to know from the president 'what he should do'.

An account of subsequent events inside the White House has Zbigniew Brzezinski, President Carter's National Security Adviser, saying he did not believe that a civilian coalition government under the Shah would help and claiming that the Iranian ambassador in Washington, Ardeshir Zahedi, agreed. Harold Brown, Secretary of Defense, said that if the Shah opted for a military government, the US should encourage him to form such a government under himself and not without him. On 3 November, Vance, in a press conference, indicated further political liberalisation was just as important as restoration of order. On 6 November, the Shah appointed a military government, although half of its members were civilians. It did reduce the levels of violence, and corrupt officials were arrested, including the head of Savak, the secret police. At this time, Carter's views were closer to those of Vance than agreeing with Brzezinski, who wanted a military clampdown.

On 9 November, Ambassador Sullivan sent a telegram entitled 'Thinking the Unthinkable' – since made famous for describing a parliamentary system with 'Khomeini as spiritual leader in a Gandhi-like role'. In the previous month, the Shah had granted an amnesty to dissidents living abroad, including Ayatollah Khomeini. Sullivan suggested the debate should change from thinking about what the US could do to help the Shah to what the US could do if the Shah fell. Vance disagreed with Sullivan and he, Brzezinski, Mondale and Brown all agreed with Carter that the US should not undermine the Shah's rule. This was also the position of the British government and remained so throughout. We deliberately never made any contact with Khomeini in France as the US did. Ever since September we had felt that only the Iranian military could save Iran. Controversially, I warned publicly on TV that any Khomeini government would be far worse on human rights than the Shah.

On 7 December, Carter was asked at a press breakfast whether the Shah could survive. He replied, 'I don't know. I hope so. It is in the hands of the Iranian people. The US has no intention to intercede in the internal affairs of Iran . . . We primarily want an absence of violence and bloodshed. We personally prefer the Shah maintain a major role in the government, but that is a decision for the Iranian people to make.' This was a very important statement. Carter was ruling out, quite rightly, any US military involvement on the ground.

The American Embassy in Paris was instructed to start talks with Khomeini on 28 December and a telegram was sent to the Shah to end the uncertainty and 'choose without delay an interim military government'.

On 3 January 1979, at a White House meeting, crucial decisions were taken. Vance left the room to arrange a safe haven for the Shah at the Palm Springs home of Walter Annenberg. Vance would not have offered a US residence to the Shah without Carter's agreement, and at that time it would not have been so provocative. One of the few things by then on which the demonstrators in Iran agreed was that the Shah should leave. This was the moment for US firmness, insisting the Shah should fly out immediately. In Paris, Khomeini's people would have seen it as an act paving their way to return. In Iran, the military would have had then an opportunity to use force. General Robert 'Dutch' Huyser, a US Air Force general and Deputy Commander of Allied Forces in Europe, was sent to Tehran. He discovered the Iranian generals were not ready to move. Huyser said, 'I got stern and noisy with the military,' but to no effect. The top generals, he said, were 'gutless'. Huyser met the Shah, who was still in Tehran on 11 January, to ask him how, with four hundred thousand troops, he had managed to lose control. The Shah turned the question around, asking Huyser, 'Could you, as commander in chief, give the orders to kill your own people?' Huyser replied, 'Your Majesty, we are not talking about me, we are talking about you.' The Shah sat silently.

On 16 January, the Shah flew out of Tehran, first for Egypt, and then sought temporary residence in other countries. In September 1979, he sought medical treatment in the US. He had previously been denied entry to the US due to the same fear of hostage taking that had prompted Callaghan and me to refuse him entry to the UK. Unfortunately, Vance and Brzezinski were persuaded by Kissinger and David Rockefeller to let the Shah in, even though Carter had always been against this. He now relented. Why Vance and Brzezinski switched their view I will never understand.

Meanwhile, Callaghan and I were being attacked publicly for refusing the Shah entry by Margaret Thatcher, the leader of the Opposition. The Shah's prolonged stay in New York due to complications led to demonstrations outside his hospital, with students shouting 'Death to the Shah,' and the revolutionary movement in Iran demanding his return. Street protesters invaded and overran the US Embassy, taking US diplomats hostage. Subsequent events are well dealt with by Stuart Eizenstat in his insider biography. The attempt to rescue them by US helicopters was aborted after the first staging post in the Iranian desert due to operational failures and one helicopter crashing. This failure sealed the president's electoral fate.

David Owen, Lord Owen as he is now, was Foreign Secretary from 1977 to 1979. During all of that time Jimmy Carter was president and Cyrus Vance was Secretary of State. The Anglo-American plan for Zimbabwe involved several meetings with the president.

40

Ronald Reagan

20 January 1981 to 20 January 1989
Republican
Vice-president: George H.W. Bush

By Simon Heffer

Full name: Ronald Wilson Reagan
Born: 6 February 1911, Tampico, Illinois
Died: 5 June 2004, Los Angeles, California
Resting place: Ronald W. Reagan Presidential Library, Simi Valley, California
Library/Museum: Simi Valley, California
Education: Dixon High School, Dixon, Illinois; Eureka College, Eureka, Illinois
Married to: Jane Wyman, m. 1940, div. 1949 (1917–2007); Nancy Davis, m. 1952 (1921–2016)
Children: Five: Maureen, Michael, Christine (died in infancy) with Jane Wyman; Patti and Ron with Nancy Davis

Quotation: 'The most terrifying words in the English language are "I'm from the government and I'm here to help."'

R ONALD WILSON REAGAN, in 1981, was inaugurated as the fortieth president of the United States of America. He was born on 6 February 1911 into a lower-middle-class family in an apartment over a shop in Tampico, Illinois, about a hundred and thirty miles west of Chicago near the border with Iowa. His father, Jack Reagan, was a travelling salesman, and the family moved around Illinois during Ronald's childhood. Jack's parents had emigrated from Ireland, and his family was Roman Catholic; Ronald and his brother Neil, who became an advertising executive, were brought up as Protestants under the influence of their mother Nelle (née Wilson), whose ancestry was largely English and Scottish. Her sect was the Disciples of Christ, and she instilled its main tenets into her children: the work ethic; respect for self-starters and for the power of the individual versus that of the state; and a strait-laced approach to moral questions. These ideals would inform her son's political career.

Reagan was known as 'Dutch' to his family and intimates (though later, after a character he played in a film, as 'the Gipper'), because his father thought as a baby he looked like a 'fat little Dutchman'. He attended high school in the small town of Dixon, about thirty miles nearer Chicago, where he made a reputation as a sportsman and developed his interest in drama. In 1927, he started work as a lifeguard and is said to have performed seventy-seven rescues. By now professing a sincere Christian faith that would hold all his life, he went on to a Disciples of Christ college at Eureka, near Peoria in the south of the state, to study economics and social science. He was not an intellectual, but continued to shine in amateur dramatics, captained the swimming team and was elected president of the student union. This was the first evidence of political motivation.

Reagan's ability as a performer did not lead immediately to acting, but to a job after his graduation in 1932 as a sportscaster on radio stations in Iowa. Working in Des Moines in 1937, he served as the announcer for Chicago Cubs, a baseball team. He travelled with them to California that year and while there took a screen test for Warner Brothers. He won a seven-year contract, but was not destined to become the new Clark Gable. His early roles were in B movies and he churned them out; by 1940 (the year he married Jane Wyman, his co-star in the 1938 feature *Brother Rat*), he had made nineteen films, but he was by then appearing in minor parts in star vehicles (films written and produced for a specific acting celebrity to cash in on their fame). His big break was *Dark Victory* (1939), with Bette Davis and Humphrey Bogart, a weepie about an heiress with a brain tumour who goes blind, in which Reagan played a dissolute playboy. Critical views on his performance varied from 'terrible' to 'the best role of his career'; Hollywood leaned towards the latter judgement, and larger roles quickly followed, notably in 1942, which saw him in possibly his best-remembered part, that of Drake McHugh in *Kings Row*, about the sort of turn-of-the-century small town in which Reagan himself had grown up. McHugh suffers injuries that cause a doctor who dislikes him to amputate both his legs unnecessarily, which required Reagan, on coming round, to utter the immortal line: 'Where's the rest of me?'

Kings Row propelled Reagan into the big time. In his next film, *Desperate Journey*, he had joint top billing with Errol Flynn, and Warner's paid him $3,000 a week, three times his previous earnings. But in April 1942, Reagan, in the Army Reserve since 1937, was called up for full-time duty – this was four months after America's entry into the Second World War. Ironically, his keenness to serve his country was thwarted by his poor eyesight, which disqualified him from service abroad. He spent much of the war making training films for the services, and by the time he left the army, in December 1945 in the rank of captain, Hollywood had moved on. He continued to act until 1964, but the momentum acquired with *Kings Row* and *Desperate Journey* would never be regained. His post-war Hollywood career is all too often characterised – or caricatured – by his performance as a psychology professor in *Bedtime for Bonzo* (1951), in which his co-star was a chimpanzee.

Reagan had, though, resumed political activity before being called up, when in 1941 he was elected to the Board of Directors of the Screen Actors' Guild, Hollywood's trade union. He re-joined the Board in 1946 and such was his natural skill at handling political issues that he became president in 1947, re-elected annually and serving until 1952; he was president again in 1959. This was the era of blacklisting actors and studio staff thought to have communist sympathies, and Reagan had to try to steer a satisfactory course through this highly divisive issue. He managed to do this in public; in private he and his wife Jane Wyman were, as documents released many years later showed, supplying the FBI with details of actors they believed to have communist sympathies. Reagan was unhappy to be asked to do this, and asked his FBI contact at one point whether they imagined the Screen Actors' Guild ought to be constituting an FBI of its own to 'determine who is a Commie and who isn't?' When, in October 1947, he had to testify (as president of the SAG) before the House Un-American Activities Committee, and was asked whether he knew of communist activities within the Guild, he replied that such things were 'hearsay'. He also, more mundanely, managed to negotiate fees for his members paid when repeats of their television work were shown, or when their films were shown on television.

Reagan and Wyman were divorced in 1949. She cited his absorption in his SAG work, but they also, ironically, had political differences. She was a registered Republican; he was, then, a Democrat, having been greatly inspired by Franklin D. Roosevelt. The two remained good friends for the rest of their lives, and when Reagan ran for president, Wyman was one of his most vocal supporters. Shortly after his divorce, Reagan met Nancy Davis, an actress, who contacted him in his SAG capacity to get her name removed from the blacklist – she had been mistaken for another Nancy Davis, a communist sympathiser. They married in 1952, and were devoted to each other during their fifty-two-year marriage.

During the 1950s Reagan's acting career moved from film to television. He was host for several years of the hugely popular drama series *General Electric Theater*, which also entailed him trailing round the company's plants in America giving motivational talks: he was well paid for the job, however, and was building up the financial independence he would need for the political career he was starting to contemplate after his success running the SAG. His work for GE also brought him into contact with leading businessmen, notably Lemuel Ricketts Boulware, GE's vice-president, who tutored him in the importance of free market economics, business, deregulation, small government, low taxes and the moral wickedness of communism. This was a Kierkegaardian moment for Reagan, who had rallied Hollywood for Harry Truman in 1948. However, influenced by his new wife, he had moved to the Republican Party by 1952, and campaigned for Eisenhower. After 1954, Boulware's influence on Reagan transformed him into an ideological conservative, and his Republicanism intensified for the rest of the decade. By 1960, he could find nothing in Kennedy to entice him back to the Democrats. 'I didn't leave the Democratic Party,' he would often say in later life. 'The party left me.'

Reagan's public profile as an actor helped him move into politics in a country as large and diverse as America. He enjoyed great brand recognition, which also made him an asset to any party to which he lent his name. He had opposed Richard Nixon in the 1950 Senate race in California, but supported his unsuccessful run against Kennedy in 1960. Thereafter, Reagan became ever more politically active, and militant. He joined the National Rifle Association. When the legislation for Medicare was introduced in 1961, he campaigned against it, saying it would signal the end of freedom in America. He felt similarly about food stamps, saying that such measures would bring in socialism.

His arrival on the national stage as a political activist rather than as an actor came days before the 1964 election, when he supported Barry Goldwater against President Johnson. In a speech that defined his later political career, he told Americans that

> the Founding Fathers knew a government can't control the economy without controlling people . . . to do that it must use force and coercion . . . so we have come to a time for choosing . . . there is no such thing as left or right. There is only an up or down. Up to man's age-old dream – the maximum of individual freedom consistent with order – or down to the ash heap of totalitarianism.

Goldwater lost the election, but Reagan was the new darling of the American right.

The political establishment in his adopted state of California seized upon his newly minted reputation. He won the Republican gubernatorial primary in 1966, and that November defeated Pat Brown, the Democratic governor since 1959, who had defeated Nixon in the 1962 race. Reagan's campaign was based on the slogan of 'send the welfare bums back to work', and a promise to end anti-war protests by students at the University of Berkeley. On a roll, he considered putting himself forward as a compromise Republican candidate for the presidential nomination in 1968 between Nixon and Nelson Rockefeller, but Nixon's support was too strong.

Instead, Reagan had to concentrate on keeping his campaign promises. He reduced California's bureaucracy and balanced the state's budget, even though that meant raising taxes. He sent in first the police and then the National Guard to restore order at Berkeley in 1969: a student died in the action. In 1970, Reagan uncompromisingly said about ending student protests: 'If it takes a bloodbath, let's get it over with. No more appeasement.' After just four months in office, he signed, with admitted reluctance, an abortion bill for the state, which he later said he regretted, and which he professed he would not have signed had he been more experienced as governor; though his son Michael Reagan later claimed that the executive act his father regretted most was signing the bill to legalise no-fault divorce in California. Reagan maintained a strong anti-abortion stance for the rest of his political career. He was also a strong supporter of the death penalty, and was angered when the state Supreme Court annulled all death sentences in 1972. Partly because of these frustrations, he chose not to contest the 1974 gubernatorial election; he felt the time had come to make a serious pitch for the presidency, which he did in 1976.

The Republican Party was still shaken after Nixon's resignation in 1974 over Watergate. Although Gerald Ford had steadied the ship and restored dignity to the highest office, he was deemed uninspiring, and many Republicans felt the party needed a more charismatic, glamorous and overtly conservative figure to stand a chance of retaining the presidency. Reagan had a good run in the primaries but could not even win the state of his birth, Illinois. It was a close-run thing in the end, Ford prevailing by 1,187 votes to Reagan's 1,070. The civilities were observed at the 1976 convention where the result was announced, but a few weeks later Ford lost the White House to Jimmy Carter.

The combination of micro-management and ineptitude that characterised the Carter presidency meant Republican candidates were playing for very high stakes, and the longer the Iranian hostage crisis dragged on, the more apparent it became that, unless Ted Kennedy could seize the democratic nomination from Carter, the Republican candidate would win. Reagan fought a campaign reminiscent of those for the Californian governorship – promising a small state, low taxes and strong defence, with the Soviet Union earmarked as the potential enemy. His most polished opponent in the primaries, George H.W. Bush, a former director of the CIA, attacked Reagan's financial plans as 'voodoo economics', because Reagan had promised to cut taxes and increase revenues: Bush had not understood the supply-side theory that would dominate 1980s economics, where lower taxes did lead to higher revenues because of the reduction of the incentive to evade or avoid taxation and the encouragement low taxation gave to creating businesses and jobs.

Reagan had secured the nomination by 20 May, having won the Michigan and Oregon primaries. Although there was talk of Ford returning as Reagan's running mate, it came to nothing, not least because of the demands of some of Ford's supporters – such as that Henry Kissinger should return as Secretary of State, and Ford's own tactless and impossible suggestion of a 'co-presidency'. At the Detroit convention in July 1980, Reagan nominated Bush as his running mate.

For all Carter's difficulties, not least those caused by divisions within his own party, he came out of the conventions with a lead over Reagan, but Reagan was felt to have thrashed Carter in their sole televised debate, in Cleveland, a week before polling day. He sought to establish that Carter was misleading the American public, and did so by judicious use of the phrase 'there you go again'. Polling suggested Reagan had won the debate by two-thirds to a third. His victory in the election itself was even more devastating: he won forty-four of the fifty states, or four hundred and eighty-nine electoral college votes to forty-nine. He also won the popular vote, not least due to the intervention of an independent candidate, John Anderson. It was clear that many lifelong Democrat voters had switched allegiance to the new president, and yet more would do so in 1984: these were the Reagan Democrats.

At his inauguration Reagan was sixteen days short of his seventieth birthday, at that time the oldest man ever to commence a presidency. His inaugural address, during a general economic downturn throughout the Western world, signified his direction of travel: 'In this present crisis, government is not the solution to our problems; government is the problem.' Moving into the White House, where the private apartments were upstairs, he joked that he was 'living over the store' again – a reference to his childhood home. He appointed an impressive team around him. General Alexander Haig became Secretary of State, though Haig was more adept at giving orders than being a team player and resigned in 1982, to be replaced by the more mandarin George Schultz. Donald Regan, former chairman and CEO of Merrill Lynch, became Secretary to the Treasury, commanded to deliver on Reagan's supply-side economic vision – or what he came to call 'Reaganomics'. Reagan's commitment to boosting defence was left to Caspar Weinberger, a fierce anti-communist who had served in the Nixon and Ford White Houses, had known Reagan since the 1950s, and had chaired the Californian Republican Party during part of Reagan's governorship. The other key appointment, and perhaps the most significant, was that as Chief of Staff of James Baker, a Texas lawyer who had run Ford's presidential campaign in 1976 and Bush's campaign for the nomination in 1980.

Reagan had hardly started work when his presidency almost ended. John Hinckley Jr, an erotomaniac obsessed with Jodie Foster, the film star, shot and wounded Reagan as the president left a speaking engagement at the Washington Hilton on 30 March 1981. James Brady, the president's press secretary, was wounded and brain damaged, and his death thirty-three years later was blamed on the assault. A policeman and a secret service agent were also wounded. The bullet that hit Reagan entered under his left arm, breaking a rib and puncturing a lung. There was uncertainty, after Reagan was bundled into his car, whether he had been shot at all, and his security detail had to decide whether to take him to the White House or to a hospital. He started coughing up blood. Given his internal bleeding, the decision – taken by Special Agent Jerry Parr – to go to a fully equipped hospital with an expert medical team saved his life. On arrival at the George Washington University Hospital, he was believed to be close to death, but he recovered sufficiently to leave hospital twelve days later. When his wife arrived at the hospital, he told her, quoting Jack Dempsey, 'Honey, I forgot to duck.' Although Reagan was livid that his expensively tailored suit was cut off in the search for the wound, the jokes continued: for one of the nurses, he wrote on a piece of paper, quoting W.C. Fields's epitaph, 'All in all, I'd rather be in Philadelphia', and before an operation on his thorax to remove the bullet, he removed his oxygen mask to ask the medical team: 'I hope you're all Republicans.' One of the doctors instrumental in saving Reagan's life, Joseph Gordano, a Democrat, told him, 'Today, Mr President, we are all Republicans.'

Reagan's popularity soared after the assassination attempt. He was back in the Oval Office on 25 April, the first president to survive an attempt at assassination by shooting, and his personal physician declared he had made a complete recovery by October. The incident greatly unsettled his wife, however, who took to consulting an astrologer. Reagan, though, got on with his legislative agenda – his economic Recovery Tax Act of 1981 went comfortably through Congress, not least because of the care he took with more conservative Democrats, usually from the South, to bring them onside. The 1981 Act cut the top rate of tax from 70 per cent to 50 per cent and capital gains tax from 28 to 20 per cent. It also cut corporation tax and raised the threshold on inheritance tax. Reagan was less successful throughout his administrations at cutting spending, especially as he slowly lost the support of some former Democratic admirers. Between his coming to office in 1981 and leaving it eight years later, debt as a proportion of gross domestic product rose from 33 per cent to 53 per cent, and for all his pre-election rhetoric about balanced budgets he never managed this feat once. His particular failure was in cutting the social security bill, which ensured America remained the neo-welfare state he and other conservatives had long claimed it would never be. However, a significant part of his spending rise came in honour of his election promise to improve national security, with defence spending rising by 40 per cent in real terms during his first term.

The economic crisis Reagan inherited eventually disappeared – though the recession did not end until November 1982. Unemployment had peaked at 11 per cent, and 15 per cent of people were, by the standard definition, living in poverty. The Carter presidency ended with inflation at 12.5 per cent; Reagan's last full year in office, 1988, had it at 4.4 per cent. During his eight years in office, GDP grew at an average of 3.4 per cent. In the Reagan years an estimated 16 million jobs were created, and around six million of America's poorer people were removed from paying income tax. Nevertheless, annual federal tax receipts rose from $308.7bn to $549bn during the eight years of his presidency. This represented an annual rise of around 8.2 per cent, though spending annually increased by 7.1 per cent. The government made matters harder for those who conservatives thought were, after the Carter years, getting a free ride on the state. The minimum wage was frozen at $3.35 an hour, and the administration also cut food stamps and Medicaid. Federal funds for state governments were cut, as were housing programmes and rent subsidies. The low tax regime did not last long, however; about a third of the 1981 cut was clawed back by a new finance measure in 1982. Throughout the presidency spending ran far ahead of revenues; the national debt rose from $997bn at the start to $2.85 trillion at the end, something Reagan termed the 'greatest disappointment' of his administration.

America was in a crack cocaine epidemic, with alarming increases in crimes of violence, especially in inner cities, and Reagan announced a 'war on drugs' in 1982, a campaign to which the First Lady lent her name and in which she became highly active. In his second term he earmarked more federal funds for the police operations against drug dealers, and signed legislation introducing mandatory minimum sentences for drug offenders. Evidence suggested the hard line had some success, reducing drug use among young people, but it would take zero-tolerance policing in the 1990s to capitalise on this start, and reclaim the streets in many US cities.

Also on the domestic front, Reagan tried, and failed, to get daily prayers reintroduced into American schools. Civil rights gestures were not important to him, following the great leap forward of the Johnson years, but in 1983 – albeit with some reluctance – he signed into law the annual Martin Luther King Jr Day holiday.

Abroad, although America intervened in the Lebanese civil war in 1983 and sent a force to Grenada the same year at the request of the Organisation of Eastern Caribbean States (but without consulting his close ally, Margaret Thatcher; Grenada was a member of the Commonwealth) to remove a Marxist government, the Cold War dominated Reaganite foreign policy. It was disapproval of the Soviet Union and of its continued occupation of much of Eastern Europe, and, in particular, Afghanistan, that led the agenda. Carter's insipid response to the 1979 invasion of Afghanistan was thought to have contributed heavily to his defeat the following year and Reagan, in concert with Mrs Thatcher, took an unrelentingly hard line on the Soviet Union. In this, they were helped early in Reagan's second term by the generational change that brought Mikhail Gorbachev to power in Moscow.

Much of this hard line concerned the development and deployment of missiles. Reagan resumed the B-1 Lancer programme that Carter had cancelled and stationed Pershing missiles in West Germany. He was informed that the Soviet Union was becoming poorer, was technologically backward and was finding it harder to contain what had for years been schooled to be an obedient society, and he determined to force it to the point where it would face no realistic choice but to dismantle its empire. Visiting Britain in 1982 he made an address to both Houses of Parliament in which he put his prediction of the triumph of the West in more nakedly ideological terms: 'The march of freedom and democracy will leave Marxism-Leninism on the ash heap of history.' It was a year later that he termed the Soviet Union 'an evil empire'; and in September 1983 he brought a programme of financially damaging sanctions into operation against the USSR to punish it for shooting down a Korean Airlines 747 that had accidentally entered its airspace. It had had 289 people on board, one of whom was a Georgia Democratic congressman. Reagan called the incident 'a massacre'. Earlier that year he had announced the Strategic Defense Initiative, which his critics called 'Star Wars', the aim of which was to place a shield of anti-missile defences around America that would nullify any nuclear threat to the country. As things turned out, the Cold War had finished before it was anywhere near being implemented; historians differ about how much its prospect caused the Russians to wind down their hostility to reform.

It was in this climate of unyielding forcefulness against those who would undermine American interests that Reagan embarked upon his campaign for re-election. He announced in November 1983 his intention to seek a second term; there was never any question of his being seriously opposed by a Republican. He was formally nominated as the party's candidate at the Dallas convention in August 1984, with Bush again the vice-presidential candidate; accepting the nomination, Reagan announced that it was 'morning again in America'. The Olympic Games had just finished in Los Angeles – Reagan was the first US president to open them – and America's domination added to the lustre of the moment. The November election was little short of an obliteration of his opponent, Walter 'Fritz' Mondale, Carter's vice-president. In winning forty-nine of the fifty states, Reagan won by 525 Electoral College votes to 13, Mondale carrying just Minnesota, his home state, and Washington, DC; after Roosevelt's crushing of Alf Landon in 1936, it was the greatest margin of victory in history. The 'Reagan Democrats' exceeded their feat of 1980. In winning nearly 59 per cent of the popular vote against Mondale's 40.6, Reagan was supported by a higher proportion of the electorate than any other president except Nixon in 1972.

The president made significant changes to his senior team at the start of his second term, notably swapping James Baker and Don Regan to be Treasury Secretary and Chief of Staff respectively. While continuing the policies of the first term, Reagan also faced new challenges. One was the AIDS epidemic, which he was accused of neglecting in terms of funding research and prevention; and pressure mounted to force an end to apartheid in South Africa. Reagan expressed his opposition to apartheid, but he also opposed disinvestment in the country, claiming US firms there employed 80,000 black people and gave them terms and conditions of service far superior to those endured by their counterparts working in non-US owned concerns. He vetoed the Comprehensive Anti-Apartheid Act, but Congress overturned that veto, and stronger sanctions were enforced.

America's space programme, a source of national pride, continued during the presidency. However, it brought a great episode of national grief in January 1986 when the Space Shuttle *Challenger* disintegrated shortly after lift-off. Reagan made one of his most magnificent speeches in unifying his country in their loss, quoting the sonnet 'High Flight' by the Spitfire pilot John Gillespie Magee, a US citizen who fought and died with the Royal Canadian Air Force: 'The future,' Reagan said, 'doesn't belong to the faint-hearted; it belongs to the brave . . . We will never forget them, nor the last time we saw them, this morning, as they prepared for their journey, and waved goodbye, and "slipped the surly bonds of earth" to "touch the face of God".'

The other foreign policy landmarks of his second term were the air strikes on Libya, made in April 1986 after Libyan terrorists had exploded a bomb at a Berlin discotheque, killing an American serviceman and injuring sixty-three others. American bombers stationed in Britain were used for the raid, Mrs Thatcher giving her agreement under the UN Charter, allowing the US to defend itself.

The attack, concentrated on military targets, was denounced in the UN general assembly by seventy-nine countries, with France a notable critic but with Anglophone countries mostly supporting America. Then, in early 1987, the administration was rocked by what became known as the Iran-Contra scandal, where money raised from selling arms to Iran in its war against Iraq was diverted to the Contra rebels in Nicaragua. This was contrary to an Act of Congress, and Reagan constituted a commission under Senator John Tower to investigate. The president disclaimed all knowledge of it; Washington rumour had it that his vice-president was far better informed. Eleven administration officials were convicted of wrongdoing, and Reagan's popularity sank as his Teflon image of integrity and competence took a battering.

The Cold War, however, allowed him to restore his reputation. Between 1985 and 1988 he held four summit meetings with Gorbachev in Geneva, Reykjavik, Washington and Moscow. At Reykjavik they initially agreed to abolish nuclear weapons, to the world's astonishment; but when Gorbachev asked Reagan to scrap the Strategic Defense Initiative he refused because it was a defensive operation. In Berlin in June 1987, Reagan made a more direct appeal to his Russian counterpart: 'Mr Gorbachev, tear down that wall!' Six months later, when Gorbachev visited Washington, agreement was reached on arms limitation, and this began the Strategic Arms Reduction Talks. By the end of Reagan's presidency in January 1989, the end of what he had termed the evil empire was in sight.

He lived for fifteen years after his retirement. There had been health concerns during his presidency, other than those arising from the attempted assassination: he had had polyps removed from his colon in 1985, and an operation for an enlarged prostate in 1987 (quite routine for a man of seventy-six). In each of those years he had minor operations for the removal of skin cancer cells. He was thrown from a horse in 1989 and sustained a head injury, which some believe was related to his subsequent mental decline. The Reagans moved to Bel Air, Los Angeles, and in 1991 his Presidential Library was opened in Simi Valley in Southern California. Awarded the Presidential Medal of Freedom in 1993, he last spoke in public in February 1994, and was last seen in public at Nixon's funeral that April. That August Reagan published a letter to the American people announcing that he had, like millions of them, Alzheimer's disease. His mental decline from then on was steady, though he played golf until 1999. Two years later, shortly before his ninetieth birthday, he fell and broke his hip, and on 5 June 2004, he died of pneumonia. He was then the longest-lived American president in history; the day of his state funeral, 11 June, was a national day of mourning. Margaret Thatcher was one of those who delivered a tribute.

Reagan's greatest achievement was unquestionably in foreign policy; he consciously increased America's military power, and exploited growing Soviet economic weakness to a point where the 'other' superpower entered an existentialist crisis and had no choice but to back down from its geopolitical strategy over the previous forty-five years and reach an accommodation with its former opponents. His economic policies helped supercharge the American economy after the difficult years of the 1970s and the lack of imagination that accompanied Ford's and Carter's attempts to reboot it after the oil price shock of the early 1970s, even though he failed to cut public spending.

Americans rightly regard Reagan as having been one of their greatest presidents. He took over the White House when national morale was low and the country uneasy because of challenges to the international order from the Soviet Union and Iran. Reagan, through his decisions about US defence expenditure, amply demonstrated his determination that America should be the world's leading power. By January 1989, it was clear to the world that he had succeeded, and that world order was changing in favour of America and the values Reagan had spent most of his political career defending and professing – freedom and democracy. When the Soviet bloc in Europe crumbled, the Berlin Wall came down and the Iron Curtain with it, and the Soviet Union itself dissolved, it was not least Reagan's, and America's, achievement.

Simon Heffer is Professor of Modern British History at the University of Buckingham. He is also a columnist for the Daily *and* Sunday Telegraph *and author of numerous books.*

41

George H.W. Bush

20 January 1989 to 20 January 1993
Republican
Vice-president: Dan Quayle

By Colleen Graffy

Full name: George Herbert Walker Bush
Born: 12 June 1924, second-floor bedroom in the family home on 173 Adams Street, Milton, Massachusetts
Died: 30 November 2018, Houston, Texas
Resting place: George H.W. Bush Presidential Library and Museum, College Station, Texas
Library/Museum: College Station, Texas
Education: Phillips Andover Academy; Yale University, Class of 1948
Married to: Barbara Pierce, m. 1945 (1925–2018)
Children: Six: George Walker, Pauline Robinson 'Robin',

John Ellis 'Jeb', Dorothy Walker 'Doro', Neil Mallon, Marvin
Pierce
Quotation: 'Read my lips, no new taxes.'

THE MOST MEMORABLE line from George Herbert Walker Bush's
acceptance speech at the 1988 Republican National Convention
contained six words that would later undermine his chances of a
second term as president: 'Read my lips: No new taxes.'

The line had been controversial. Aides concerned about the
looming federal deficit wanted it out, but others, like Peggy Noonan,
speechwriter for President Ronald Reagan, felt the more urgent
need was to define Bush and convince conservatives that the vice-
president – suspected of not being a true conservative – was 'one
of them'. The line stayed in.

The virtues that defined the admirable character of George
H.W. Bush, the man, were the same ones that left Bush, the politician, lacking in definition in the eyes of the public. His mother,
arguably the strongest influence on his life, had drilled into her
children to be the best – but never to brag about it. Andover, the
boarding school that he attended from the ages of thirteen to
seventeen, impressed its motto upon the young minds: 'Not for
Self'. The code for life in the Bush family was simple: Honour,
Duty, Country.

Actively promoting himself, therefore, was anathema to Bush –
so it was done for him. He was caricatured as wimpy – he, the war
hero; as privileged – he, the son that eschewed family patronage to
make his own way in West Texas (unlike John F. Kennedy, who
was idolised by the liberal press, Bush noted wryly in his diary);
and as invisible (popularised by cartoonist Garry Trudeau) – a style
Bush had chosen as vice-president out of loyalty and respect for
President Ronald Reagan.

He chose his own path and his own style – sometimes stubbornly
so, but always according to the code. When things didn't break his
way, he never looked back, only ahead.

When the Japanese bombed Pearl Harbor in 1941, the seventeen-
year-old Bush determined that he would serve his country as soon

as possible and was sworn into the US Navy on his eighteenth birthday. Bush was the youngest naval aviator at the time and flew fifty-eight combat missions. He successfully bombed a radio tower on the heavily fortified Chichi-Jima, despite being hit by anti-aircraft fire. Bush parachuted into the ocean, his two crewmates were killed, and he was left drifting in a life-raft towards the island without an oar. Hours later, he was picked up by a US submarine. Awarded the Distinguished Flying Cross for his heroism, he was given the choice to return to the US or re-join his squadron. Bush returned to the squadron.

Bush was smitten by the 'strikingly beautiful' Barbara Pierce at a dance during his last year at Andover. Three years later, while on leave, he returned briefly to the US to marry her. As Bush described his choice for what would be a successful, lifelong partnership: 'I hit the proverbial jackpot.' After the war ended, he went to Yale and completed the four-year degree in two and a half – he was anxious to get on with life. He was married and they were expecting their first child, George Walker Bush.

To the disappointment of family members, Bush turned down their offers of employment after graduation. He did not want to capitalise on his benefits of birth, but was also uninspired by the secure, but unchallenging, future he saw ahead. Instead, he headed to Odessa, Texas, and his first job, selling equipment for oil drilling. In Midland, Texas, Bush started his own business in oil production – now tapping family connections to pitch investments in it. A further move to Houston saw him launch Zapata Petroleum Corporation, pioneers in the new field of offshore drilling. Success mingled with tragedy when the Bushes' three-year-old daughter, Robin, died of leukaemia shortly after the birth of their third child, Jeb (later the two-term governor of Florida). Fifty years later, Bush would still break down in tears recalling her loss.

The family tradition was that those of means give back to society, and, with his business on a sound footing, Bush turned to do just that. His father, Prescott Bush, had been elected as senator from Connecticut and served from 1952 to 1963. The son was courted by both the Democrats and the Republicans. The wiser choice would have been to go with the former – Texas was a Democrat majority state – but Bush stuck with his political philosophy and the Republican Party. He was elected chairman of the Harris County Republican Party in 1963, settling a battle between those who held his traditional Republican values and the far-right-wing John Birch Society. Although Bush won his first election – the Republican primary for a US Senate seat – he lost in the 1964 general election; his opponent benefited from the coat-tails of incumbent Texan Lyndon B. Johnson's win over Barry Goldwater.

Two years later Bush was elected to Congress, one of only two Republicans in the twenty-three-person Texas congressional delegation. But Bush expressed his concerns about elements in the Republican Party: 'When the word moderation becomes a dirty word, we have some soul searching to do.' To the outrage of many of those elements, Bush voted for the 1968 Fair Housing Act, which banned discrimination in the housing market. Further alienating him from the right was his support of Richard Nixon over the conservative's favourite, Ronald Reagan. But the choice proved fateful as Nixon won the nomination and tapped Bush to be one of his key surrogates. Re-elected to the House unopposed, Bush had a good future ahead of him: Nixon was president and he was on the powerful Ways and Means Committee, building up seniority. But Bush didn't want to settle on the easy path and gambled it all on a bid in 1970 for the US Senate, and lost.

President Nixon then appointed Bush as ambassador to the United Nations, during which time China was recognised as a member of the UN – the foreseeable consequence of Nixon's overture to Peking – and Taiwan was ousted, despite Bush's best efforts. After Nixon's landslide re-election in 1972, the president asked Bush to be chairman of the Republican National Committee. Despite Bush's reluctance to take on the RNC position, duty called and he agreed. As the Watergate scandal unfolded, pressure was put on Bush and the RNC to play a role in counterattacking against investigators, but Bush refused. Duty did not put politics above country.

In 1974, President Ford named Bush envoy to the People's Republic of China and then, in 1975, asked him to take over as director of the CIA. At that time, the CIA was embroiled in investigations and Bush viewed the offer as a poisoned chalice and the end of his political career, but, as always, his values dictated what he did, and he accepted. Upon the election of President Jimmy

Carter in 1976, Bush left the CIA position having raised morale and restored the relationship between the intelligence agencies and Congress.

In preparing to run for president in 1980, Bush called upon his good friend, lawyer James A. Baker III, to run his campaign. Baker's focus on organisation and the Iowa caucus paid off and Bush came in first, beating the front-runner, Ronald Reagan. Bush contrasted his youth and vigour against Reagan's age, and attacked Reagan's theory of lower taxes alone as a way to achieve higher revenue as 'voodoo economics'. In the end, however, it was not enough to derail Reagan, who won the Republican nomination. At the Republican Convention in Detroit, after negotiations with former president Gerald Ford as a possible running mate fell through, and at the eleventh hour (literally at 11:37 p.m.), Reagan called Bush to ask him to join the ticket as candidate for vice-president.

Ronald Reagan and George H.W. Bush won in a landslide against Jimmy Carter and Walter Mondale in the 1980 presidential election. Bush, now vice-president, determined that the route to a successful relationship with Reagan would be to gain his trust by never leaking to the press, never distancing himself on unpopular decisions, and never outshining the former Hollywood star and his wife. Reagan and Bush had a scheduled weekly lunch and Reagan included him in all presidential meetings and memos. Bush found that he had a genuine admiration and affection for his former rival.

On 30 March 1981, Bush was in Fort Worth, Texas, unveiling a plaque where John Kennedy spent the night before his assassination, and Reagan was in Washington, DC, giving a speech at the Washington Hilton. As the vice-president's plane was departing for another venue, word arrived that Reagan had been shot and Bush headed back to Washington. After he landed at Andrews Air Force Base, Bush's staff pressed him to take a helicopter to the South Lawn at the White House (usually a prerogative of the president) to avoid the rush hour traffic from the vice-president's residence to the White House, but Bush demurred. A dramatic landing would be good television for Bush but would make the president look weaker. Pressed again, Bush replied, 'Only the president lands on the South Lawn.'

Bush's firm, but low-key, handling of affairs until Reagan's recovery won him respect by all and the confidence of Reagan. The president assigned Bush the task of turning European audiences back towards the US position on placement of Pershing II missiles in Europe. Initially, Europe had welcomed the protection the missiles would provide, but the image of Reagan as a trigger-happy cowboy and the growing anti-nuclear movement now threatened the deployment of the intermediate-range nuclear forces (INF). The INF installation was critical to Reagan's 'zero-zero option' to force the Soviets to withdraw their nuclear weapons. The 1983 mission took Bush to seven countries in eleven days. His ability to listen, combined with his calm and measured demeanour, reassured Europeans that, despite Reagan's harsh rhetoric, the US was committed to peace through strength, and the deployment remained on course, along with the alliance.

One of the jobs delegated to a vice-president is to represent the president at funerals. Bush's attendance at those of Soviet leaders alone was so frequent (Brezhnev 1982, Andropov 1984, Chernenko 1985) that, in typical self-deprecating humour, he would quip (privately): 'You die, I fly.' The chore had the advantage, however, of exposing Bush to world leaders, in particular, Mikhail Gorbachev, and helped form friendships that would serve him well as president.

After the Reagan–Bush victory over Mondale–Ferraro in the 1984 presidential election, Bush's thoughts turned to a possible run for president in 1988. Complicating matters was the news that the US had sold arms to Iran via Israel in an attempt to free American hostages. Bush's instinctive loyalty to Reagan initially had him denying the story, but he later focused on the arms sales as a strategic way to open channels with Iran (then fighting a war against Iraq) rather than as a ransom for hostages (which was contrary to US policy). Because Bush had not echoed the Secretaries of State and Defense when they had objected to the plan, he was vulnerable (although Chief of Staff Don Regan later stated that Bush had expressed reservations about the arms sales, in private, with the president).

In addition to persuading Jim Baker, then Secretary of the Treasury, to be his campaign manager, Bush brought in 'street fighters' Lee Atwater and Roger Ailes to bolster his election chances. Ailes was one of the few who could coax Bush into adjustments to improve his image on television. Together, they convinced a reluctant Bush to go negative against his primary opponent, Bob Dole. Bush's characteristic decency prevented many such attempts, but his competitiveness (often unrecognised) would prevail in the end if that was what it took.

Pat Robertson, the televangelist who was also in the primary, was rallying the religious conservatives behind him; they were still suspicious of Bush's credentials as a 'true' conservative. Reflecting on the post-convention work that would be needed to unify the party, Bush was prescient in his diary observations: '[T]hey're religious fanatics and they're spooky. They will destroy this party if they're permitted to take over.'

Bush prevailed over his rivals and, on the final day of the Republican Convention, gave 'the speech of his life' to rally and unify the party, including: 'Read my lips: No new taxes.' Bush picked a young senator from Indiana, Dan Quayle, to be his running mate and they won a resounding victory against Democrats Michael Dukakis and Lloyd Bentsen in the 1988 election.

President Bush followed through on his campaign promise to create equal opportunities for the disabled and passed the landmark Americans with Disabilities Act. He had promised to tackle acid rain, a problem that had bedevilled Congress for twelve years, and did so by introducing market-based solutions of 'cap and trade', an emissions trading scheme, in place of the 'command-and-control' strategy of the past. The Clean Air Act Amendments passed in 1990. Bush sought to reduce America's dependency on foreign oil and diversify energy sources. The Energy Policy Act of 1992 used market-based incentives and deregulation to promote competition and energy conservation.

The jury was out on Mikhail Gorbachev: some considered him a genuine reformer, others saw his actions as a ruse. Because Bush knew him, he believed the former. He advanced a new vision for NATO at its fortieth Anniversary Summit in Brussels: a substantial reduction of conventional armed forces in Europe – to be matched by the Soviets, thereby eliminating the need for NATO's unpopular short-range nuclear forces. Bush spoke of the 'seeds of democracy' that were 'buried under the frozen tundra of the Cold War'. 'The world has waited long enough,' he said. 'The time is right. Let

Europe be whole and free.' Sixteen years later, when I served in the State Department, under Condoleezza Rice (who served on the National Security Council under President G.H.W. Bush), our policy towards Europe remained (and remains) similar: to work for a Europe that is 'whole, free . . . and at peace'.

On 9 November 1989, the Berlin Wall fell. Bush was cautious; he had witnessed the Chinese response to Tiananmen Square and worried that the Soviets would respond similarly. When urged, then, to go to the Wall, he was dismissive. 'I'm not going to dance on the wall,' he insisted. He viewed such gloating as pouring gasoline on the embers of the Soviet Union and potentially igniting hardliners. Although wise, his low-key response deepened the perception that he had been inadequate to the moment, and he was unfavourably compared to the Great Communicator, Reagan.

In December 1989, after the death of a US marine in Panama and other difficulties there under the leadership of Panamanian dictator Manuel Noriega, Bush had had enough. He dispatched significant troops to depose him, and the issue was resolved. The event showed that Bush might be cautious, but not timid, and that restraint was not reluctance on his part but strategic – even if the media rarely acknowledged that.

Bush understood that to destabilise Gorbachev was to risk losing the venture of democracy in the Soviet Union. Recalling Hungary in 1956, he was determined not to give false hopes and to avoid bloodshed. In Kiev, Ukraine, Bush warned that 'freedom is not the same thing as independence' and that the US would not support independence in order to replace a far-off tyrant with a local despot (the situation in Georgia). The media dismissed this as timidity in support of the status quo and dubbed the speech, 'Chicken Kiev'. Bush was not equivocal about the reunification of Germany and stood firm against a sceptical Margaret Thatcher and François Mitterrand for a united Germany within NATO.

On 1 August 1990, Iraq invaded Kuwait. In impromptu remarks, Bush stated simply, 'This will not stand.' His clarity of purpose stemmed from his view that Saddam Hussein's aggression would threaten a peaceful post-Cold War world if not challenged. Bush believed in 'personal diplomacy' and drew from his years of practising it to create a coalition of support from thirty-five disparate nations that included the Soviet Union, China and Arab nations. Constitutionally, Bush did not need authorisation from Congress for military action, but politically, he did. Protests of 'No Blood for Oil', and projections of 'thousands of body bags' made getting the authorisation challenging, but Bush was convinced that Saddam would only understand force. Not known at the time was that Bush was willing to act without congressional approval even though it might result in his impeachment. In the end, he got it. With Vietnam in mind, Bush's approach was to define the mission, then apply overwhelming force to carry it out. The result was a spectacular victory. There was a clamouring to depose Saddam, but Bush believed that the mission was to restore sovereignty to Kuwait only. To act further would go against the UN Resolution, split the coalition, turn the Arab world against the US and create 'an unwinnable urban guerrilla war' in Baghdad.

Bush's domestic priority was to get the budget deficit under control. 'George,' Nixon said to him before the 1980 election, 'you know you were right about "voodoo economics", don't you?' The law demanded a balanced budget, but with a Democratic majority in both Houses, there was little room to manoeuvre. Without a balanced budget, the Federal Reserve Chairman, Alan Greenspan, would not lower interest rates even as the economy was sliding into a recession. Democrats refused to agree to spending restraints unless Bush agreed to raise taxes. For Bush, compromise was at the core of sound governance, and, faced with the possibility of shutting down the government and a worsening economy, he took his 'no new taxes' pledge off the table. What might have been inconsequential for many politicians – going back on a pledge – was not true of Bush, who had run on character. Doubling the damage was his stubborn belief that results mattered more than rhetoric or framing the issues for public consumption. Had he articulated the dilemma at the start – as he had for the Gulf War – or held off announcing the new taxes until they were woven into a package deal showing political gains, he might have been forgiven. But he did not.

Not appreciated at the time was Bush's 'pay-as-you-go' formula that required new appropriations to be paid for by specific revenues rather than by more borrowing. This, and other controls on spending, created budget stability and created the conditions for surpluses (under Clinton), but the green shoots of the recovery started too late to help Bush in the election.

Bush's heart did not seem to be in the campaign. Perhaps it was because appreciation for his deft global diplomacy had faded (he had an 89 per cent approval rate after restoring Kuwait – the highest poll rating of any previous president, surpassed only by his son's 90 per cent after 9/11) and his domestic achievements, despite Democratic majorities, were under-appreciated. Or perhaps it was due to a thyroid condition (Graves' disease) that was diagnosed the year before. Bush's lacklustre campaign was further hampered by a third-party candidate, Ross Perot, as well as by the ability of Bill Clinton – the talented governor of Arkansas – to 'feel the pain' of voters that the empathetic Bush was incapable of expressing.

The characteristics that made George H.W. Bush a great man, father and husband were not enough to make him a great president. His flaw was to under-appreciate the importance of image and communications in the modern TV age. He expressed himself beautifully in writing, but was unable to do so in person to project 'the vision thing', and his garbled syntax launched many comedy careers. Although not one of the 'greats', Bush was better than average, and most put him in the second quartile for his role in reunifying Germany, ending the Cold War and creating a coalition to liberate Kuwait. True, he was a one-term president, but he had already gone against history by being the first incumbent vice-president to be elected president in over one hundred years.

I got a sense of the patrician family and its values when I squired Bush's sister, Nancy Bush Ellis, around London in 2004. A lifelong Democrat, she had come to campaign for her nephew, Bush's son, President George W. Bush, who was seeking re-election (and for whom I later worked). Her Katharine Hepburn demeanour reinforced the feeling of a bygone era, one of service and country and family – above politics. An era that many now look back on, like her brother, with greater appreciation.

Colleen Graffy is a former Deputy Assistant Secretary of State for Europe and Eurasia and a law professor at Pepperdine University, Caruso Law School.

42

William Jefferson Clinton

20 January 1993 to 20 January 2001
Democrat
Vice-president: Al Gore

By Poppy Trowbridge

Full name: William Jefferson Clinton (born William Jefferson Blythe III)
Born: 19 August 1946, Hope, Arkansas
Library/Museum: Little Rock, Arkansas
Education: Georgetown University, Oxford University, Yale University
Married to: Hillary Rodham, m. 1975 (1947–)
Children: One: Chelsea
Quotation: 'I did not have sexual relations with that woman, Miss Lewinsky.'

BILL CLINTON WENT into politics because he didn't think he could do anything else as well. In his memoirs, he describes his political motivation as wanting to 'keep things moving in the right direction'. This vastly underplays his successes, the largest of which was economic. During the eight years of his presidency, the economy expanded by 50 per cent in real terms, he achieved budget surplus, and grew America's gross national product to one-quarter of the entire world economic output. Welfare rolls declined, unemployment dropped to a forty-year low, and by the end of his tenure, the booming US economy delivered a measure of economic benefit across the income spectrum.

Abroad, Clinton is credited with enhanced multilateral cooperation, even if he struggled to implement his own 'Clinton Doctrine' of conscious intervention at times. A centrist and a globalist, he embraced free trade and sought to expand the ecosystem of market democracies and multilateral peacekeeping efforts by ensuring the US set a leading example. His presidency has been ranked among the highest of the past century, and his successful domestic and foreign policy influenced successive British prime ministers. With his zeal for modern management techniques, he became a mentor to Third Way progressives, who assumed this model of managerial liberal capitalism was irrevocably the developed world's norm. Nominally, Clinton's presidency ushered in the twenty-first century, yet it is better described as 'the end of an era'. He was the last leader of a certain generation that was pre-9/11, pre-social media and pre-Columbine, although his presidency presaged the impact these events would have on American society. He declared Al Qaeda an enemy of the USA several years before the 9/11 attacks; the Monica Lewinsky scandal was the first truly global news story to break over the internet; and Clinton took on the gun lobby years before the wave of mass school shootings began in 1999.

A deeply religious Southern Democrat, Clinton wanted to leave Washington with intense change and modern practices as his legacy. Instead, he became synonymous with a sex scandal. One of the youngest presidents in US history, his youth was a selling point at the start. His inexperience and country ways endeared him to many as he rose to the White House, but they would prove a weakness in office. Once there, Clinton was slow to learn to wield the power of the presidency and slow to spot the lessons of his mistakes. Arguably, some he never learned. Those who've met him will recount his hypnotic ability to engage with individuals as if they are alone in the room with him. Yet he could lie readily – to his colleagues, his aides, his family, the press, the public. Stories of affairs with women would surface during his rise to the Oval Office, and throughout the eight years he occupied it. Remarkably, his presidency is not remembered as much for these sins as it is for the cover-up. He left office with some of the highest approval ratings ever, despite the very public sexual impropriety. I suspect that the man himself would not get such a free pass nowadays. The dreamer would be tested by practicalities sooner. The leader, who sought forgiveness so frequently, would not find it so forthcoming today.

Bill Clinton had a traumatic childhood. His early life was turbulent, and at times violent. His mother was a nurse. She had married a travelling salesman named William Blythe, who was killed in a car accident when his wife was six months pregnant with their son. William Jefferson Blythe III was born on 19 August 1946 in Hope, Arkansas, and so began life with a father he would never know, and a brother he didn't yet know existed. Billy Blythe's early teenage years would, at times, be filled with 'uncertainty, anger and a dread of ever looming violence'. Unusually, as a leader Clinton shared this suffering openly and acknowledged the impact it had on his impulses, insecurities and decisions.

Clinton's family were Democrats in the segregated South, from a town that was legally dry. His mother was a professional who cared about his education and her own, leaving a very young Billy to be raised by his maternal grandparents in Hope, so she could finish nursing school. When he was aged six, the two of them moved to Hot Springs, Arkansas, after the widowed Virginia married Roger Clinton, whose name the young boy was to formally take as a teenager. With a step-father whom he loved, but who drank and abused his mother, church provided an outlet for the popular, musical, well-read teenager. Young Clinton took himself off to church service and Sunday school alone every week. His parents only joined him at Christmas and Easter. The politician who would come to crave the human connection and contact of the campaign trail began seeking it out as a child under the developing shadow of alcoholism and domestic abuse.

While his religious faith would remain a lifelong source of succour,

447

an attraction to politics also took root early on. As a ten-year-old child who'd just received his first television, Clinton binge-watched the Democrat and Republican conventions of 1956. By the age of sixteen he had decided upon a career in elected public service and first went to Washington on a young leaders programme while still in high school. There, thirty years before he became president, Bill Clinton was filmed in the Rose Garden shaking John F. Kennedy's hand, rapt by the youthful president who would remain symbolic for Clinton – as a model for his own ambitions and administration many years later. This encounter wasn't destiny, it was priming.

In the mid-1960s, the draft was the prevailing challenge facing all young American men of his generation. Campuses across America were crucibles of activity against the war in Vietnam, but in a fairly conservative move, Clinton chose Georgetown University for his undergraduate degree – a decision designed to get him back to Washington, where he became freshman class president. Clinton held a student clerking job with the Committee on Foreign Relations, in which role he inadvertently had access to confidential casualty lists of men from his home state of Arkansas killed in the ongoing military action. One day he spotted the name of his childhood friend, Tommy Young, among them. After Georgetown, a two-year Rhodes scholarship at Oxford followed, and in April of his first year, Clinton would receive his own draft notice. It arrived in England via surface mail nine days after he was required to present for induction. Luckily, the rules at the time allowed students to finish their academic term first. A subsequent change allowed him to finish both years of his scholarship and enrol in law school with a commitment to join the Army Reserve Officers' Training Corps to fulfil his military obligations. Clinton always opposed the war but was largely silent about it as a student. He admits to a lifelong 'Vietnam guilt' that stems from his success in utilising education to avoid the draft. He would eventually become the first American president since the Second World War who'd never worn a military uniform and he would be ridiculed as commander in chief for not knowing how to salute properly.

He continued his policy studies at Yale Law School, where he met fellow student Hillary Rodham. By graduation the two were inseparable and Clinton took Hillary back to Arkansas to prepare for political life, accepting a temporary teaching job at the university. In 1974, Bill Clinton was twenty-eight when he entered, and lost, his first professional political race for Congress, for Arkansas' third district, against the incumbent John P. Hammerschmidt. Demonstrating a resilience that would become a trademark political asset, Clinton reportedly reappeared in the town square the morning after his loss to greet anyone he could stop. Thirty years later, Clinton would reflect that if he'd won this first race, he'd have never been elected president. It would have deprived him of the political education the next two decades in Arkansas would provide.

Losing aside, campaigning left Clinton, in his own words, 'higher than a kite' and gave him exposure to the middle-class voters' appetite for the sober pairing of 'opportunity with responsibility' that would form part of his presidential platform eighteen years later. He and Hillary were married the following year in the living room of a small brick house in Fayetteville by a Methodist minister friend whose wife had worked on Clinton's losing campaign.

In 1976, Clinton ran for State Attorney General. This time he won. Two years later, he became the governor of Arkansas with 60 per cent of the vote. He promised kindergarten for every child in the state; education – a theme from his childhood – was a key component of his campaign. But once in office, his focus dissipated as he tried to do too much, too fast – a sabotaging trait that would re-emerge in his first term as president. Clinton's determination to take on vested interests and hike taxes to pay for his grand transformation plans proved very unpopular. He was not re-elected as governor in 1980. The leftist reformer had come up against the limits of that strategy. This setback was unlike his first. New parents to baby Chelsea, the Clintons, now a professional duo, took this loss to heart. They understood that it wasn't due to the new candidate's political obscurity, like in 1974, but to his policy mistakes and poor decisions. Clinton spent a long time studying the statistics of his defeat, resolved to win back what he'd lost. With Hillary in charge of his next campaign, he did just that in 1982. Clinton's journey to the political centre had begun.

As a young family man, politically established in his home state of Arkansas, Clinton was first advised to run for president in 1987 at the age of just forty. But it was on a family holiday to Vancouver several years later that eleven-year-old Chelsea encouraged him to finally go for it. On 3 October 1991, in Little Rock, Arkansas, Bill Clinton announced his candidacy for president of the United States with a message of youthful change, economic renewal and a promise to look out for the 'forgotten middle classes'. Stories about Clinton and his affairs with women were widely known well before he decided to run for high office, his aides have recounted. One said that he'd initially believed Clinton to be 'too smart and too ambitious' to be so self-destructive as to jeopardise his position by conducting affairs, but he was quickly proven wrong.

Bill Clinton became president in 1992, benefiting from a power vacuum. As the Republican incumbent President Bush seemed indestructible after executing the Gulf War, Democrat big beasts Mario Cuomo and Jesse Jackson did not run. The lesser-known Clinton was able to easily defeat other rivals in the primaries despite embarrassing stories about his infidelity, marijuana consumption and draft dodging emerging in the process. Early forecasts had put him in third place and he himself 'didn't trust exit polls', so the newly elected President Clinton had to be convinced by aides that he had indeed secured an Electoral College vote majority and won the three-man race for the White House. Independent candidate Ross Perot had captured 19 per cent of the vote, leaving Clinton with 43 per cent to Bush's 37 per cent. It was a solid, but not sweeping, victory to become the youngest US president since his idol John F. Kennedy.

The new president had chosen the young moderniser, Al Gore, as running mate. Clinton knew economics, agriculture, crime, welfare, education, healthcare and foreign policy. Gore brought expertise in energy policy, the environment, technology and national security. He also understood Congress and Washington better than Clinton, which the president would come to rely upon. The country welcomed this fresh, youthful, Democratic duo after twelve years of Republicans in the White House. The inauguration celebrations showcased pop stars Diana Ross and Bob Dylan, and Clinton's address hinted at his New Democrat political philosophy, promising to 'offer more opportunity to all and demand more responsibility from all'.

Clinton brought a young family and an informality to the White House. He and his wife worked as a policy team and kept late hours. Renowned for dominating long, rambling Oval Office meetings, he tended in his first months in the White House – as staff later recalled

– to get lost in details and insist on exploring every policy nuance, to the detriment of decision-making. Clinton's process was a lot messier than what Washington was used to and distracted colleagues from his superior analytical talent and ability to relate to individuals. A confidential briefing note for Prime Minister John Major from the British embassy in Washington at the time reported that the new Clinton administration 'remains chaotic' and that the new president 'enjoys thinking about, discussing and talking issues to death. He tries not to make up his mind until the last possible moment.'

The campaign mission statement that propelled him to the presidency had three tenets, but the one most quoted from the 1992 election is: 'It's the economy, stupid.' Voters had chosen him because of their concerns about the economy. There was widespread frustration among the public that the incumbent Bush administration had failed to prevent or address economic recession. They responded to Clinton's campaign promise of an economic plan to 'get the country moving again'. The agenda was an enticing – and improbable – combination of deficit reduction, middle-class tax cuts and increased spending. However, Clinton had been left with large budget deficits from the Reagan and Bush administrations and addressing this swiftly became the singular economic priority during his first months in office. To succeed, he eventually cut spending and raised taxes by a quarter of a billion dollars each. Achieving his first major piece of legislation this way brought consequences – a fracturing of support from his own side. Republicans, unsurprisingly, hated the tax hikes and his own party were angered by the broken promise to invest in the middle classes. In the process of trying to secure every single Democratic vote, Clinton was forced to strong-arm, cajole and charm to get the bill passed, thereby getting his first taste of the practical implementation of some of his newfound power. The Budget bill passed in the Senate by just one vote, a tiebreak cast by Vice-President Gore.

In terms of policy implementation, a pattern of ground-breaking intent, coupled with disappointing delivery, was beginning to emerge. The 'Don't ask, don't tell' compromise that Clinton agreed, after having promised to end the ban on homosexuals serving in the military, was another textbook example of this. He vastly underestimated the negative reaction it would provoke from both the Pentagon and

Congress. So, when the watered-down proposals were introduced in July 1993, they did little to diminish the scepticism with which the new president was viewed within the military.

In a more deliberate move, Clinton took early action on gun control. On his first campaign trip for governor of Arkansas in the 1970s, Clinton was marked by an encounter with one of his constituents – a shop owner from whom a customer purchased a pistol, claiming that he wanted to use it for target practice, but who instead shot six people the following day. The shooter had just escaped from a federal mental health facility. Nineteen years later, eleven months into his presidency, Clinton signed the Brady Handgun Violence Prevention Act, which required a background check for gun purchasers. He went on to advocate for childproof trigger locks and to block the importation of millions of assault weapons in his second term.

Having won the Oval Office with promises on the economy and healthcare, the latter was the chief area where Clinton himself believed his personal legacy would rest. He was determined to make early headway, but didn't fully grasp the challenges of massive expansion of the welfare state. When Clinton took office, one-fifth of American adults lacked health insurance. In his first week, he announced a task force to create a plan that would provide for universal healthcare. Very controversially, it was chaired by his wife Hillary, whom Clinton believed brought the brainpower and background experience to define the initiative. Initially, this move was a popular one. Polls showed strong public support, but progress was slow and her unprecedented appointment riled traditionalists, who worried that universal reforms were being drawn up by the closed and secretive group of Washington wonks she led. Not until 1994 did Congress even begin considering Clinton's proposal. By then, much of the public pressure for reform had disappeared and Republicans were deeply opposed to the legislation, which ran to over one thousand three hundred pages. Rather than delivering universal coverage and cost control, the complicated proposals came across as a textbook example of big-government blindness, dictating and restricting medical choices. In the initial euphoria of taking office, Clinton had reverted to type, as the grandiose leftist reformer. After admitting his deep regret for his failure to deliver far-reaching reform, for the rest of his tenure he only pursued smaller, more specific health policy initiatives.

Clinton's first year was a mixture of pointed policy successes, clumsy over-reaching missteps and searing press coverage. At the end of 1993, he ratified the North American Free Trade Agreement into law, removing barriers to intra-continental commerce between the USA, Canada and Mexico. Against strong opposition from within his own party, he pushed through a trade deal. A globalist and advocate of world trade, he would continue to open the US to foreign markets and support the establishment of the World Trade Organization (WTO). As part of this effort, Clinton also granted China temporary most-favoured-nation status, minimised tariff levels on Chinese imports and eventually, in 2000, granted permanent normal trade relations to China.

Despite a formidable opposition in Washington and teething problems passing legislation, internationally the Clinton presidency was ripe with a sense of the possible. Russia was subdued, America was a thriving benevolent hegemon. Clinton himself would grow into the role of patron, able to bring together ancient adversaries around the world. Sinn Féin leader Gerry Adams visited the United States in early 1994 when Clinton controversially approved a visa. As Adams had not actually renounced violence, this enraged the British government. Prime Minister Major refused to take Clinton's phone calls in the days following the decision. But according to Adams, the visit was one of the pivotal moments that paved the way for the IRA ceasefire.

Bill Clinton had won the election against an opponent considered a brilliant foreign policy guy, George Bush Sr, precisely because of his focus on the domestic problems of everyman. Foreign affairs were also of keen interest to Clinton, but he didn't have much hands-on experience. As president, he would learn two lessons in quick succession. The risk of military action (in Somalia), and the risk of doing nothing (in Rwanda). His predecessor, Bush, had sent 25,000 troops to Somalia in support of the UN peacekeeping mission there, and Clinton inherited the situation with civil war still raging and several thousand men and women on the ground. Believing he was supporting the humanitarian nature of the UN mission, Clinton allowed US special forces to launch an attempt to capture a warlord who'd attacked UN forces. It failed and eighteen Americans were killed, eighty-four more injured – a humiliating incident for America and the president.

Clinton eventually removed US forces from the country, but bore the brunt of the negative feeling and went on to place limits on the deployment of his troops. So when the Hutu of Rwanda began attacking the minority Tutsi, killing up to 800,000 in a matter of months, the Clinton administration did very little to intervene. The US had no economic interests in the region at the time, but Clinton later defined this moment as one of the worst mistakes of his presidency.

Clinton's inexperience in Washington meant he had to learn on the job. The tendency to serve up huge, sweeping bills gave way to proposals for specific, focused, digestible portions of policy change – an approach dubbed 'get into our knickers' by one of his Republican Senate colleagues. Embracing 'the politics of the possible' allowed Clinton to make the most of the middle-class initiatives that he'd promised in the presidential race. From being an inexperienced Southern hick, charming but one-dimensional, he emerges halfway through his first term as a pragmatic president and a skilled compromise-maker, with an understanding that part of his job was to manage Washington itself. To survive in office, Clinton had grasped that he needed to focus, not on what he wanted, but on what would actually work.

When the political landscape in America shifted sharply to the right and both the House and Senate went to the Republicans in the 1994 mid-term elections, Clinton was better prepared to navigate the competing agendas. Speaker of the House Newt Gingrich wanted a conservative revolution that would implement tax cuts, welfare reform and major domestic spending reductions. In a creative response, Clinton co-opted some Republican ideas – notably welfare reform. When the Republican Congress presented a budget plan that cut Medicare spending and instituted major tax cuts for the wealthy, which, if not agreed to, would force a temporary government shutdown, Clinton was able to tap into his newfound spirit of creative compromise.

He presented his own plan, which did not include cuts to Medicare but offered to balance the budget. Still, the ensuing back-and-forth over the details left major portions of the government suspended for months. With public sympathy favouring Clinton, and in danger of being seen as extremists, Republicans eventually accepted Clinton's budget, when one of their leaders, Bob Dole, marshalled enough votes in the Senate to reopen the government, fearing damage to his own presidential plans. The government shutdown disrupted Clinton's momentum in one other respect. While almost all government employees stayed home, interns were allowed to come in to work at the White House. On the second day of the shutdown, President Clinton met Monica Lewinsky.

Republicans had long since homed in on a provincial Arkansas land deal, enacted early in the Clintons' marriage. He and Hillary had purchased land along the White River with a lawyer friend of theirs, with the intention of developing it for sale. Their business partner became mired in financial controversy, which included complicated connections to Hillary's legal practice, and the opaque arrangements became an obsession with Clinton's Republican opponents. While not otherwise very concerned for Clinton, John Major told the president, 'I sympathise with you about the Whitewater stuff. I'm sorry it keeps coming up. You don't need that sort of rubbish.' In an effort to cauterise a constant line of Republican attack after a bruising first year in office, Clinton had agreed to appoint a special prosecutor to examine the Whitewater issue. The investigation would be expanded to include, and focus almost exclusively on, the Lewinsky affair. While the Clintons always believed a 'vast, right-wing conspiracy' was determined to use his personal indiscretions to drive them from political office, the reality depends more on timing and technology.

The internet took the Lewinsky scandal global. When renowned magazine *Newsweek* spiked their scoop on the affair, the story was given to an internet publication run by Matt Drudge. It became the first global news story to break over the internet and be accessible to news outlets and readers around the world instantaneously. For days after the news broke, Clinton continued to deny the affair. He gave a television statement: finger pointing, his voice rhythmic, banging the desk with each word, he uttered the sentence, 'I want you to listen to me, I am going to say this again, I did not have sexual relations with that woman, Miss Lewinsky.' He insisted on the same lie to his wife and colleagues. Disbelieving that the president would jeopardise his leadership this way, Secretary of State Madeleine Albright and a number of Cabinet members said publicly that they didn't believe the allegations. Yet Clinton had even commissioned a pollster to test whether he could just go public with the details of the relationship. The numbers revealed he'd be forgiven the sex and the infidelity, but not the lying. Lewinsky herself eventually agreed an immunity deal, forcing Clinton to admit the truth.

As the investigation came to a head in his second term, the Clinton administration focused on keeping the Middle East peace talks moving towards an agreement between Israeli prime minister Benjamin Netanyahu and Palestinian president Yasser Arafat. Clinton was also working closely with Tony Blair on both the Irish peace initiative and to build support for air strikes against Iraq, which had expelled UN inspectors. The Clintons and Blairs were close friends, and Tony and his wife Cherie provided comfort and light relief to the couple on a state visit to Washington at the height of the unfolding scandal.

The Whitewater investigation took four years, cost a reported $40 million and became a case against the president for perjury, abuse of office and obstruction of justice charges. It was presented to Congress on 9 September 1998 and was nearly five hundred pages. The report marked a surprising turning point in public opinion for the beleaguered Clinton. He was viewed as finally taking responsibility – 'a sinner asking for redemption', as his press secretary observed. The Republican persecution was perceived as wasteful and their insistence on impeachment divisive. Still, in December of 1998, Clinton became the second US president to be impeached on counts of obstruction of justice and perjury. He was acquitted by the Senate a few months later, and would serve out his full eight years.

The bloody war in Yugoslavia dominated the mid-1990s foreign policy arena. In May 1994, after Serb forces invaded safe zones established by UN troops, Clinton authorised air strikes against Serb positions. This intervention didn't end Serb advances, and the following year the Srebrenica massacre took place. He was initially wary of sending troops; Clinton aides recall the president declaring, 'I'm not going to go into my own Vietnam.' But under pressure from the international community and the American press, Clinton would eventually spearhead European leaders' support for a major NATO air campaign. Peace talks followed and the subsequent 1995 Dayton Agreement ended the Bosnian War by dividing Bosnia into two autonomous regions. According to one of Clinton's national security coordinators at the time, this exercise marks the point that the president had become rational and comfortable with the use of force in his role as commander in chief. His foreign policy was fomenting around a guiding maxim of 'conscious intervention' to protect America's interests abroad. Known as the Clinton Doctrine, this approach was articulated by the belief that 'where you can make a difference you should'. In an extension of this attitude, Clinton's foreign policy prioritised the expansion of NATO into former Eastern Bloc countries in Eastern Europe. He believed that NATO would provide a stabilising influence on these countries.

In Clinton's first presidential campaign, Republicans had tried to label him as a skirt-chaser and draft-dodger, giving him the nickname 'slick Willie'. But by his second election, it was the powerful Republican Congress, led by Newt Gingrich, that appeared reckless and irresponsible for frustrating the legislative process. By contrast, the president's handling of the budget and the Bosnian War had improved his standing. The public had got to know Bill Clinton, and on a personal level he was increasingly popular despite stories of his extramarital relationships.

In the 1996 election, Bill Clinton became the first Democratic president to win a second term since Franklin D. Roosevelt, with 70 per cent of the Electoral College votes. There was an aura of untapped potential at the start of Clinton's second presidential term. Western democracies were enjoying the rise of the internet, the American economy was healthy, and unemployment was low. Clinton planned to balance the budget by 2002 and complete the process of welfare reform initiated as he campaigned for re-election. By the end of his presidency, he would indeed deliver the first federal budget surplus since the 1960s.

Clinton's contribution to global trade culminated in the passing of the Global Agreement on Tariffs and trade (GATT) in the final months of 1997, eliminating $740 billion in tariffs worldwide and taking American products into new markets. The Clinton administration would also help broker a peace accord in Northern Ireland the following year and successfully strike Iraq's nuclear, chemical and biological weapons programmes. Clinton asserted America's power abroad by issuing an order to destroy Al Qaeda and Osama bin Laden following a series of bombings at US embassies attributed to the terror group. He pushed for the expansion of NATO, and the United States led the NATO effort to end ethnic cleansing in Kosovo in 1999. The following year he came close to bringing Yasser Arafat to agreeing a peace deal with Israel, and registered a budget surplus of more than $200 billion. But by this point, Clinton was also exhausted by the sex scandal and Republican wrangling.

Every two-term American president struggles to have much momentum or impact in their final two years. The race has already begun to succeed them and the attention is firmly on the next potential leader of the free world. Within the Clinton family, the political momentum had now swung towards Hillary. She began her campaign for a New York Senate seat and won. Waltzing his wife down the long, central corridor, Bill Clinton danced out of the White House in January 2001, and the new millennium was truly underway. Nine months later, the Twin Tower attacks would permanently alter the America that Bill Clinton had governed.

Still, elements of the centrist Clinton legacy lived on for nearly another decade in the New Labour governments in Britain. He and Tony Blair knew each other well in their respective positions and maintained a strong personal friendship that continued after office. Clinton's New Democrat approach cut a path for Blair's Third Way. A year out of office, Clinton would warn against any action his friend might consider taking in Iraq, speaking publicly about the consequences of military intervention. But they nonetheless shared a worldview, a commitment to centrist government and an informality that allowed them much intimacy.

Bill Clinton, unlike Tony Blair, left office popular and remained so. As his presidency ended, Hillary had become the elected Clinton – as senator from New York – and Bill moved there to be with her, and took up the role of supportive spouse. He fulfilled this role for the next fifteen years, throughout the 2008 Democratic primaries, her tenure as Secretary of State to President Obama, and eventually also his wife's own presidential campaign against Donald Trump in 2016.

Described as 'bulky and butter-cheeked' in 1991 when he was preparing to run for president, Clinton would experience health concerns that would lead to heart surgery, weight loss and a commitment to veganism in the years just after leaving office. But he remained active in public life through the Clinton Foundation, a non-profit organisation created in his name committed to humanitarian causes including HIV/AIDS initiatives and global warming. He developed a professional friendship with his predecessor, George Bush Sr, and the two worked together closely to support the recovery efforts following the Asian tsunami and Hurricane Katrina. Their combined work to support rebuilding won them the 2006 Philadelphia Liberty Medal. Clinton would go on to become a UN special envoy to Haiti, overseeing aid and reconstruction in the wake of the devastating earthquake that struck that country in January 2010.

Like all presidents, he fulfilled his immediate duties of completing his presidential library in Little Rock, Arkansas, and writing his memoirs, but unusually Clinton's autobiography set a worldwide sales record upon publication. He has remained popular on the lecture circuit, where he earns six-figure fees, and continues to write, including two fictional, political thrillers. While his political life followed a pattern of loss and recovery, his post-presidential work is more constant. His main contribution to Democratic politics after the presidency was in support of Hillary's campaigns, but he addresses the Democratic National Conventions regularly. Clinton's cultural influence on politics has waned in recent years as centrism has given way to populism. The #MeToo movement has now cast Clinton's sexual transgressions in a more perverse and unforgiving light. More recently, Clinton has acknowledged travelling on convicted sex offender Jeffery Epstein's plane for work connected to his foundation in the early 2000s.

Clinton was a man almost biologically suited to life in politics because politics is ultimately about people. He couldn't resist other people. The personal success of his presidency was that he was able to work through his human nature, not around it. Politically, he was a superior operative of persuasion, compromise, fiscal responsibility and multilateralism. We have learned in the decades since his presidency that these qualities are not always in fashion in political life. Clinton was a man of many personal contradictions, but he knew how to fashion conflicts into conversations that led to compromises. Stripping away the complications, the most reductive description of Bill Clinton's life is still that he was a small-town boy who rose to become leader of the free world. In this sense, he is America incarnate.

Poppy Trowbridge is a journalist and broadcaster. She served as Special Adviser to the UK Chancellor of the Exchequer, Philip Hammond, from 2016 to 2019.

43

George W. Bush

20 January 2001 to 20 January 2009
Republican
Vice-president: Dick Cheney

By Christopher Meyer

Full name: George Walker Bush
Born: 6 July 1946, New Haven, Connecticut, USA
Library/Museum: Dallas, Texas
Education: Yale, Harvard
Married to: Laura Welch, m. 1977 (1946–)
Children: Two: Jenna and Barbara
Quotation: 'He's one cold dude.' (Bush on Putin in conversation with Tony Blair at Camp David, February 2001)

TWO MEMORIES OF the forty-third president of the United States stand out for me: his laughing uproariously throughout a showing at Camp David, the presidential retreat, of the Robert De Niro/Ben Stiller comedy *Meet the Parents*; and, nine days after 9/11, his astonishingly relaxed calmness at a meeting in the White House with Tony Blair just before he was to give the speech of his life to a joint session of Congress.

But I am getting ahead of myself.

I arrived in Washington, DC in October 1997 to take up the post of British ambassador to the US. It was a good three years before the next presidential election. But my mind was turning already to the 2000 campaign.

A presidential election is the supreme challenge for an ambassador in Washington. In short order your government wants you to forecast accurately the outcome; to be already on good terms with the new president-elect; to be familiar with those who will be his closest advisers; to start influencing the new team in a way congenial to your national interest; and, last but not least, to set up as soon as possible after Inauguration Day in early January a meeting between your prime minister and the brand-new president.

The so-called Special Relationship between Britain and the United States – to which British governments attach inordinate importance even if most Americans have never heard of it – places yet another burden on your shoulders. This is to ensure that the prime minister is the first head of state or government to be invited to meet the new president on American soil. In February 2001 I got Tony Blair in to see George W. Bush at number two, having been pipped at the post by the Mexican president. But all Señor Fox had to do was nip over the border to meet George W. in his home state of Texas.

When I moved into our residence on Massachusetts Avenue, the assumption was that Al Gore, President Bill Clinton's vice-president, would be the Democratic candidate for the presidential race in 2000. Most Washingtonian pundits also thought him favourite to win the presidency, if only because of Clinton's coat-tails, albeit somewhat soiled by the Lewinsky affair. Polling told us that had Clinton been allowed to run a third time for president, he would have won handily. In reality, Clinton and Gore were not that close, personally or politically.

The more interesting question for me was the Republican

candidate. There was no odds-on favourite. President George H.W. Bush had been beaten by Clinton in 1992 after only one term. That was some achievement for a youngish governor from the deeply unfashionable state of Arkansas. But more senior Democratic politicians who might have expected precedence over Clinton as the party's candidate – Senator Jay Rockefeller, Congressman Dick Gephardt, to name but two – had been deterred from running by Bush's sky-high ratings immediately after the first Iraq war.

So, there was some talk of Bush getting his own back and taking another crack at the presidency. This withered rapidly on the vine. Bush had led a pretty competent administration, full of experienced people. But in 1992 he was not a happy campaigner, a tad too patrician for many Americans' taste, as his very public difficulties paying at a supermarket revealed. Nor had he helped himself by looking at his watch in a live televised debate with Bill Clinton. More importantly, he had made the cardinal strategic error of letting himself be outflanked on the right, so allowing the ultra-conservative Texas billionaire, Ross Perot, to split the Republican vote and let in Clinton. It was a lesson his oldest son, George W. Bush, did not forget. Steve Forbes, another ultra-conservative billionaire, tried a similar tactic against Bush junior in 2000 but gained little traction.

Not long after my arrival in DC I had a bit of luck. At a reception I ran into George Shultz, who had been Secretary of State under Ronald Reagan. Our Foreign Secretary for most of that time had been the late Sir Geoffrey Howe, later to become Lord Howe. I was Howe's press secretary for four years and went with him on all his travels. These had included frequent meetings with Shultz (who died only in 2021 at the age of a hundred). It had been a time of very close cooperation between Thatcher and Reagan.

Though Shultz had left public office by the time I arrived in Washington, he remained enormously influential in the Republican Party and was something of a kingmaker. An ex-marine, well over six feet, he was a formidable, even intimidating, presence. I asked him who would run for his party in 2000. With that low rumbling voice, so similar to Howe's that their conversations were almost inaudible to the naked ear, including each other's, he said that it was too soon to say. But if ever I was in Texas, I could do worse than pay a call on Governor Bush. His piercing blue eyes briefly twinkled.

You don't ignore a hint like that. I started to do some digging, but was unable to find out much. One of my predecessors, after meeting George W., had left a note on the Embassy files saying he was 'very smart'. This was not an opinion widely shared in DC, a largely Democratic town. Bush, said the chattering classes, was amiable but not very bright. He had a dubious past of carousing and drunkenness. He was a draft-dodger, who, thanks to his family connections, had found refuge from service in Vietnam in the Texas and Alabama Air National Guard. He had been an oilman and part-owner of a baseball team. He was married to Laura with twin daughters, Jenna and Barbara.

The more snide among his critics added that, like his father, he was not a real Texan at all, but the scion of a long line of East Coast patricians. Sure, he grew up in Midland, Texas, and went to school there for a while. But then for high school he reverted to type and attended the posh boarding school, Phillips Academy, in Andover, Massachusetts. For college it was Yale and Harvard, where else? And the family holidayed every summer in Kennebunkport, Maine, where they owned a compound by the sea, just like the Kennedys down the coast in Hyannis Port.

Not long after my conversation with George Shultz, Catherine and I set off for the Lone Star State to find out for ourselves. In the first months of our time in the US, we needed anyway to visit all the UK's consular districts as soon as possible. Texas was the headquarters of one of the most important.

We stayed in Houston at the home of our consul general, Peter Bacon, and his wife, Valerie. It was Peter's job to look after British interests in Texas and a handful of contiguous states. These interests boiled down to trade, investment and British citizens in distress. But he was also interested in local politics, which was not something you could always say about our consuls general. The portrait he painted of Governor Bush was very different from that presented to me in DC.

Bush, said Peter, was an experienced and successful politician. He had at the first attempt defeated the formidable Democratic incumbent, Ann Richards, in the 1994 Texas gubernatorial election. It was she who had memorably said, in reference to Bush senior's patrician pedigree and verbal stumblings, that he had been born with a 'silver foot in his mouth'.

What was more, George W.'s success was in sharp contrast to his supposedly brighter younger brother, Jeb, who had failed in the same year to capture the governorship of Florida. The expectation that it would be Jeb, not George W., who would have greater political success was a widely shared view that reached into the Bush family itself. The family matriarch, Barbara Bush, a woman of remarkable forcefulness and candour, once told my wife and me that it was Jeb who was destined for higher things. She was wrong. George W. was a two-term president. Jeb's aspirations to the presidency went down in flames in 2016, the year of the Trump ascendancy.

We travelled from Houston to the state capital of Austin to meet the governor – and to call first on Karl Rove. It was a compulsory stop if you wanted to know what was going on in the Bush family and the Texas Republican Party. Working out of a modest, untidy office, behind an enormous barricade of files, Rove was the most influential political consultant in Texas. He had been Bush's campaign manager in his victory over Ann Richards and in winning a second term. He had known the Bush family for decades and would be intimately involved in George W.'s decision to run for president. In due course, Bush would make Rove deputy chief of staff in the White House, in effect his principal political *consigliere*. He is still active in Republican Party politics to this day.

I asked this jovial, round-faced Texan, with his swept-back sandy hair, the key question: would the governor run? Nothing was decided, he replied. But Rove clearly expected him to do so. He gave us a detailed prospectus of Bush's fitness for high office, emphasising his success and long experience in politics, for which he had a natural talent. Yes, he had failed in the late 1970s to get a seat in the US House of Representatives. But that had been at the beginning of his political career. He had learned a lot from the experience. He had also learned much from working for his father on several Texas campaigns, going back to 1964 when he was only eighteen and his father was making his first run for the Senate. He had been deeply involved in his father's failed presidential campaign. A few years later, in 2001, when Tony Blair first met Bush at Camp David, the presidential retreat, Bush entertained us with tales from the campaign trail.

My wife and I met Governor Bush in his office in the fine, domed Austin Capitol building. He was friendly, open and unpretentious.

He was smart. We could see immediately why he was such a hit with people on the campaign trail. We came away impressed. Catherine is usually a better judge of people than I. On the same trip to Texas, we had paid a call on the late founder of the now-defunct Enron corporation, Ken Lay, in his palatial Houston office. I was impressed by Lay; she was not. She was right, I was wrong. But we both agreed on 'Dubya', as some called him.

A large part of his appeal was his candour, much like his mother. He and Rove went out of their way to emphasise that he was more like her than his father. We were complete strangers to him. But he made no bones about having had a drink problem, which he had overcome. He also admitted to having been abroad on very few occasions. These included holidays in Scotland when he was a child. He would wave to tourist buses full of Americans and they would wave back. Little did they know that he was not a cute little Scottish boy.

At that first meeting Bush was non-committal about the presidency. But it was obvious he was weighing the pros and cons. We had had drinks with his parents the night before in Houston. His father had said that his son was worried about the disruptive impact that the presidency would have on his young daughters. He was right to be. His mother brushed all this aside. The girls were already living in the public eye and would soon get used to it. You could understand why he wanted to be seen as his mother's son.

We returned to Texas a year later and once again went to see the governor. An announcement that he would run for the Republican nomination was expected any day. Karl Rove confirmed it. George W. all but did so.

Bush's demeanour was altogether more serious and purposeful than on our visit the previous year. He told us two interesting things. If he became president, he would make up for his ignorance of foreign policy by surrounding himself with experts. He would create a team led by Condoleezza Rice, a Russian specialist (and family friend) who had worked in his father's administration; and by Paul Wolfowitz, former US ambassador to Indonesia and now the Dean of the Paul Nitze School of Advanced International Studies (of which I am an alumnus). Rice would become Bush's national security adviser and then, in his second administration, secretary of state. Wolfowitz, a leading 'neocon' who believed Saddam Hussein should be removed without delay, would become Deputy Secretary for Defense. The group of experts became known as the Vulcans, all of whom found berths in George W.'s first administration.

He then tried out on us a little speech. It said in essence that the US's role in the world was to spread democracy and freedom. Bush delivered it with some feeling. He asked us what we thought. I made approving noises. Actually, I found it banal, pure motherhood and apple pie. I forgot about it after we returned to Washington. I should not have done. Because this simple belief, magnified a thousand times by the shock of 9/11, was to become for Bush one of the mainsprings, perhaps *the* mainspring, of American action in Afghanistan, Iraq and the wider world.

I came to appreciate this fully a few years later at a meeting in September 2002 between Bush and Blair at Camp David. They had just agreed to make one last effort to bring Saddam Hussein to heel through the United Nations. Yet we still seemed to be drifting inexorably towards war in Iraq. The pips were starting to squeak on both sides of the Atlantic. As we were waiting to get on helicopters to return to Washington, Bush suddenly said to no one in particular that putting young men in harm's way was the greatest responsibility of all for an American president. But if the result was a victory for liberty and democracy, future generations would thank us. As he said this, there were tears in his eyes.

When the battle for the presidency was joined in 2000 – through the long primary season and then the election proper – *bien-pensant* opinion on both sides of the Atlantic, fuelled by the Gore campaign and Clinton's Third Way politics, began immediately to trash George W.'s abilities. It noticed the verbal stumbles (inherited from his father) and the near-death experience inflicted on him in the Republican primary contest by the wily maverick senator, John McCain. By contrast, Gore had disposed of his primary rival, Senator Bill Bradley, without too much difficulty. Things reached such a pass that when George W. won the Republican nomination, the French newspaper *Le Monde* talked of the 'cretinisation' of American politics.

But my wife and I knew that Bush was quick-witted and no fool. He would be a formidable presidential candidate. Bill Clinton himself told Tony Blair not to underestimate Bush. I began to wonder whether the *bien-pensants* were making the same mistake as they had made with Ronald Reagan in 1980: to underestimate the power of simple messaging and personal affability, underpinned by long experience of politics. Too many people had seen in Reagan only a mediocre Hollywood actor, when he had shown serious political smarts as California governor and head of the Screen Actors' Guild.

As the presidential campaign moved towards its climax in November, my political staff – bright young officers who accompany the candidates on the campaign trail – were coming back to base with eyewitness reports of how well George W. was doing on the stump. Al Gore, by contrast, was stiff and wooden without Bush's personal touch. The three televised debates presented a similar contrast in styles. I could not in all honesty say that Gore 'won' any of them. When we reported to London that it should prepare for the possibility of a Bush victory, this was not a message well received by a New Labour government invested in the Clinton legacy.

I still thought Gore would shade it. I was wrong. After a month's delay to resolve the contested vote in Florida – the notorious episode of the 'hanging chads' – Bush won the presidency by the whisker handed him by the US Supreme Court's decision not to allow a recount.

The rest, as they say, is history. And that, of course, is where the problems lie for President George W. Bush's reputation and legacy. Few occupants of the Oval Office have had to confront such a variety of crises as George W. They started with 9/11 in his first year in office, passing through the invasion of Afghanistan, the second Iraq war, Hurricane Katrina and the banking crisis of 2008. His approval ratings went from the stratospheric nineties after 9/11 to a historic low in the twenties as he left the White House.

Bush's presidency was unusual in another way. A conventional analytical framework would compare and contrast his two terms. That is still useful, up to a point. But the true watershed was not his re-election in 2004, but the destruction of the World Trade Center by Osama bin Laden's men in hijacked aircraft less than a year into his first term as president. As Bush himself said in his memoirs: 'In a single morning the purpose of my presidency had become clear . . . it redefined my job.'

That job, as Bush saw it, was to become leader of a global war on terror. That little speech he had read to my wife and me in 1998 in the Austin Capitol had been heavily infused with moral purpose.

It was not a difficult jump to see himself as God's instrument to rid the world of terror. It was what you would expect from someone who had been brought back to the paths of righteousness and sobriety with the help of the famous evangelist preacher, Billy Graham.

The events of 9/11 gave Bush the finest moment of his presidency, when, standing on a mound of rubble at Ground Zero a few days later, he took a bullhorn and rallied the workers around him and the nation beyond. The passages in his memoir, *Decision Points*, describing those days, when fear of a second terrorist attack was all-pervasive, are quite gripping and often moving. His critics have never cut Bush any slack for the near-intolerable stress and shock of the moment. The fact that, in the next seven and a half years of his presidency, America never again suffered a successful terrorist attack allows Bush to conclude in his book that 'this was my most meaningful accomplishment as president'.

But the heroic moral certainty of that moment passed as fleetingly as it had come, to be replaced by the ambiguities and dilemmas of policy-making. To the disgust of many, Bush continued to justify 'water-boarding', while acknowledging the painful tension between protecting the country and preserving civil liberties. In his book, Bush invokes a higher power in the great struggle between tyranny and freedom. He speaks of the 'transformative power of liberty'. It is a Manichean vision, brooking no nuance. It carries him to Afghanistan and to Iraq. And he takes with him Tony Blair, no mean Manichean himself.

New Labour had neither wanted nor expected Bush to win. His victory caused a fair degree of consternation in No. 10. At the end of 2000, I invited Karl Rove for a drink and asked him if Blair's close personal and political ties to Clinton were going to be a problem for the prime minister's relations with Bush. 'By your works shall ye be known,' came Rove's typically Texan biblical reply. 'The president-elect is very pleased that Britain and America have been close over the last eight years. He wants to establish something similar – on its own merits.'

The two men met for the first time at Camp David in February 2001. With their respective retainers, they sat opposite each other across the lunch table. We were about a dozen in all. The dress was casual. As the African American waiters poured iced tea, Bush said:

'Welcome to Camp David, Tony – may I call you, Tony? – it's great to have you here.' Without missing a beat, Blair replied: 'Thanks, George – may I call you, George? – it's great to be here.' And off they went in a business-like, no-frills way, starting, if I remember rightly, with the Middle East. I heard the rapid cracking of ice. I heaved a sigh of relief. You know immediately if the chemistry is going to work. They enjoyed each other's company. Blair, too, had a black-and-white vision of the world's troubles. For better or for worse, this was going to work.

But it was the fires of Ground Zero that truly forged the relationship like tempered steel. Blair expressed sympathy and support for the US in its hour of need with an eloquence and emotion that could not have been better crafted to resonate with Americans and George W. personally. 'This is not a battle between the United States of America and terrorism but between the free and democratic world and terrorism . . . We were with you at the first. We will stay with you to the last.'

And so it came to pass. That's when things started to go wrong, first of all in Afghanistan.

What had started out in late 2001 as a punitive expedition against Al Qaeda and the Taliban in Afghanistan was allowed, foolishly, to morph into regime change and nation building. Clausewitz, the great Prussian general, had written in the nineteenth century that war was the extension of politics by other means. But nation building in the Western liberal mould went against the grain of Afghan culture. The US and the UK had set themselves a political goal that was unachievable by military means. The British, who had fought three largely futile wars against the Afghans in the nineteenth and twentieth centuries, should have known better. Winston Churchill himself had warned at the end of the nineteenth century of the pointlessness of fighting in Afghanistan. Today, twenty long years after the invasion, the US and its allies are about to withdraw their troops from Afghanistan, mission unaccomplished. You have to ask yourself how many Western reforms, bought so dearly in blood and treasure, will survive the withdrawal. The slaughter by the Taliban of scores of Hazara schoolgirls in May 2021 looks like a grim harbinger of things to come. It is another defeat inflicted by the old, unfathomable Afghanistan to add to those suffered by the Soviet Union, Britain and Alexander the Great.

It was always a fool's errand to imagine that Western liberal democracy would take root in Afghanistan's arid and alien soil. Much the same could be said about the invasion of Iraq, another door opened by 9/11. I remember having my head bitten off by Condi Rice in late 2002, when I wondered whether Iraq was ready for parliamentary democracy. Yet, today, we can see how political parties have entrenched ethnic and sectarian divisions, including the influence of Iran, the main strategic beneficiary of the invasion. Corruption and bad government are the result.

Like Tony Blair, Bush is unrepentant about removing Saddam Hussein, but a good deal franker in *Decision Points* about what went wrong. It was a 'big mistake' to declare 'Mission Accomplished' after the taking of Baghdad. The US was not adequately prepared for the disorder that followed. It was a mistake to disband the Iraqi Army. Above all, the intelligence on weapons of mass destruction was false, 'a massive blow to our credibility – my credibility . . .'

Bush's presidency remains defined by 9/11 and the misfortunes of war in Afghanistan and Iraq. Equally prominent in the debit column is Hurricane Katrina, a Category 5 storm that ravaged New Orleans early in Bush's second term in 2005. The catastrophic floods killed almost two thousand people and drove thousands more from their homes. African Americans bore the brunt of the disaster. The response of the federal authorities was generally considered slow and incompetent. The president was personally tainted – Katrina damaged his reputation as much as his Ground Zero speech four years earlier had boosted it.

These great events have all but wiped from the memory George W.'s achievements in domestic politics: notably, the massive $1.3 trillion tax cut of 2001, early in his presidency, which absorbed so much political effort that many thought his administration had run out of steam by the summer; the No Child Left Behind Act of the same year, which aimed to set high, measurable targets in elementary and secondary education; and, at the very end of his presidency, TARP, the Troubled Asset Relief Program, authorising the purchase of toxic assets to address the banking crisis of 2008.

Few remember today Bush's initiative in his second term to provide AIDS relief to Africa, even though it exists to this day and has disbursed billions of dollars to help in particular children who have lost parents to the disease.

George W. saw himself as the decision-taking president. It is the *leitmotiv* of his memoirs, as their title suggests. The fourteen chapters rotate around the most important decisions of his life and presidency. This allows him, time and again, to present himself as he would like to be remembered: a leader unafraid to take tough decisions. Along the way, Bush denies a number of charges: that he was in competition with his father; that he sought to dodge the draft; that he is incurious and does not read books. He professes a love for history and discloses that he and his political *éminence grise*, Karl Rove, used to compete over how many history books each could read. In one year, Rove won by 110 to Bush's 95.

George W. finds redemption in the precedent of President Harry Truman, who succeeded Franklin Roosevelt after the latter's death in 1945. He sees himself as a president in Truman's mould. 'The man from Missouri knew how to make a hard decision and stick by it. He did what he thought was right and didn't care much what the critics said. When he left office in 1953, his approval ratings were in the twenties. Today he is viewed as one of America's great presidents.'

Bush looks similarly to history for his vindication, which, he confesses in his book, will not come in his lifetime. If fifty years hence, Iraq is a stable and prosperous democracy, the agony of its birth pangs will, he thinks, be seen as a price worth paying for the removal of Saddam Hussein. At which point, though he does not say it in these terms, he will assume his rightful place in the pantheon of great American presidents alongside Harry Truman.

That may or may not happen. Since leaving office he has kept out of the limelight. But his courteous affability, his sense of humour and his willingness to call a spade a spade still cut through. According to Hillary Clinton, he described Donald Trump's Inauguration speech as 'some weird shit'.

Meanwhile, his ratings have crept up into the thirties. That's at least a start on the long road to the pantheon.

Sir Christopher Meyer is a former British ambassador to the US and Germany. He spent thirty-seven years in the Diplomatic Service, with postings to Moscow (twice), Madrid, Brussels (EU), Bonn, and Washington, DC (twice). He is a director of the Arbuthnot Banking Group.

44

Barack Obama

20 January 2009 to 20 January 2017
Democrat
Vice-president: Joe Biden

By Toby Harnden

Full name: Barack Hussein Obama II
Born: 4 August 1961, Honolulu, Hawaii
Library/Museum: Chicago (under construction)
Education: Occidental University, Columbia University, Harvard Law School
Married to: Michelle LaVaughn Robinson, m. 1992 (1964–)
Children: Two: Malia and Natasha (known as Sasha)
Quotation: 'Change will not come if we wait for some other person or some other time. We are the ones we've been waiting for. We are the change that we seek.'

Barack obama's place in history is secure. He was the first black president of the United States and his election in 2008 at the age of just forty-seven marked a symbolic break with America's past of slavery and segregation. The heady optimism and soaring eloquence of his campaign – replete with slogans such as 'Yes, We Can' and 'Change We Can Believe In' – however, led to expectations he could never fulfil.

Obama was the first Democrat since Franklin Roosevelt to win two elections with majorities of the popular vote, but he could not maintain his party's majorities in Congress or its grip on the White House in 2016. While his vision of national unity was bold, he proved unable to work across the aisle with Republicans and appeared to disdain seeking compromise with opponents. His failure to secure bipartisan legislation led to a reliance on executive actions that his Republican successor cast aside. The post-racial future seemingly promised by his election has been clouded by the racial tumult in the United States since he left office. For the time being, the historic significance of Obama's election victories has overshadowed his achievements. The shocking election of Donald Trump as his successor led to an almost instant nostalgia for Obama's personal qualities and intellect; it also imperilled his legacy and left a sense of regret for what might have been.

The modern political history of the United States – a nation almost evenly divided between two political tribes, the coasts and the heartland, liberal and conservative – has been punctuated by the swinging of the pendulum from one extreme to the other every four or eight years. In 2009, it seemed hardly possible for the country's new president to be more different than his predecessor. Obama had based his campaign on opposition to the Iraq war, which George W. Bush had launched in 2003. Whereas Bush was – for all his Texas mannerisms – the scion of a political dynasty and a glad-handing politician who acted from the gut, Obama came from a modest background and was cerebral and ice cool. Later, the contrast between Obama and his successor Trump, however, was even more startling. Trump's candidacy was a rejection of everything Obama stood for, even who he was. It was foreshadowed by Trump's peddling of the racist 'Birther' conspiracy that Obama was born in Kenya rather than Hawaii. It remains to be seen whether the election to president in 2020 of Obama's vice-president, Joe Biden, will be a de facto restoration that will render the Trump era an aberration.

By any standards, Obama's political rise was meteoric. Before entering the 2008 presidential race, he had been a senator for Illinois for just two years and, before that, a state senator for eight years, when he also taught constitutional law part time at the University of Chicago. He was the first person elected to the presidency without any executive experience since John F. Kennedy – also a senator – in 1960. At the outset, Hillary Clinton, wife of Bill Clinton and a senator for New York, was the overwhelming Democratic party establishment favourite. Many believed Obama was running with the goal of being Clinton's vice-president, and that he would wait his turn for a serious tilt at the top job.

In early 2006, Obama ruled out running, but he changed his mind, picking up on widespread resistance to the notion of two political dynasties occupying the White House for twenty-four years; if the former First Lady had won in 2008, the victors' list from 1988 onwards would have been Bush, Clinton, Clinton, Bush, Bush, Clinton. There was also the question of the Iraq war, then seen as a disastrous failure. Hillary Clinton had voted for it. Obama, in line with his liberal constituents in Hyde Park, Chicago, had given an impassioned speech against it in October 2002, declaring: 'I am not opposed to all wars. I'm opposed to dumb wars.' While Clinton was a wooden, uninspiring campaigner, Obama's youth and sparkling tongue made him someone altogether more exciting. He had become a star in his party at its 2004 convention, when he denounced the idea of red states and blue states, proclaiming: 'There is not a Black America and a White America and Latino America and Asian America – there's the United States of America.'

Obama's race and life story were central to his appeal. Clinton based her campaign on the idea that she would make history as the first woman president. But Obama, nearly fifteen years her junior, could go one better: the son of a white woman from Kansas and a Muslim former goat-herder from Kenya, he would be the first black president. Obama had barely known his father and had grown up in Hawaii and Indonesia, raised by a single mother and her parents. He had grown up outside the core Black American experience – he had no ancestors who were slaves – and, as he noted in his lyrical 1995 memoir *Dreams from My Father*, 'learned to slip back and forth between my black and white worlds'. Democratic consultants soon realised that this made him attractive to white voters who might have felt threatened by the likes of Jesse Jackson and Al Sharpton. Joe Biden, then a rival candidate to Obama, put his foot in it by expressing this out loud, saying: 'I mean, you got the first mainstream African American who is articulate and bright and clean and a nice-looking guy. I mean, that's a storybook, man.'

Obama had bolstered his black identity by marrying Michelle Robinson, whose family had experienced discrimination on Chicago's South Side and had lived through the civil rights era. On his campaign plane in 2007, he told me: 'Part of me settling in Chicago and marrying Michelle was a conscious decision to root myself. There's a glamour, there's a romance to that nomadic kind of life and there's a part of that still in me. But there's a curse to it as well. You need a frame for the canvas, because too much freedom's not freedom.' He then laughed and added: 'I'm waxing too poetic here.'

By the time he declared his candidacy in Springfield, Illinois – home of Abraham Lincoln – on a February day in 2007 that was so cold I could barely write, Barack Obama was electric. With equal parts sham humility and self-regarding grandeur, he promised that his campaign would not 'only be about me' but would represent 'the occasion, the vehicle of your hopes, and your dreams'. More than fifteen thousand people turned out for an event that had more than a whiff of history. The American press, tired of the Clintons, lapped it up. As a British correspondent travelling on the campaign plane – soon dubbed Obama One – I found myself being told by my news desk that Americans would never elect a black president and later on, more darkly, that if they did he would be assassinated. From the outset, it appeared to me that Obama had a very real chance; Kennedy's 1960 campaign seemed a reasonable comparison. The threat of any candidate or president being gunned down is always a serious concern and Obama received Secret Service protection at an early stage. When he spoke in Chicago's Grant Park after his presidential election victory, he was flanked by two huge sheets of bullet-proof glass.

For all his highbrow and somewhat vague rhetoric, Obama proved to be a tough and resilient campaigner. He had shown he had the killer instinct in his first campaign in 1996 for an Illinois state senate seat, when he mounted legal challenges to the signatures gathered by incumbent Alice Palmer and three other rivals; he was successful and was elected unopposed. He had also experienced defeat, losing by more than thirty points in a 2000 congressional race for a seat held by Representative Bobby Rush, a former Black Panther. Rush had cut through Obama's CV as a community organiser and first black president of the *Harvard Law Review* by asking during a debate: 'Just what's he done? I mean, what's he done?'

When Hillary Clinton tried a similar tack, Obama was ready. 'Talking tough and tallying up your years in Washington is no substitute for judgement, and courage, and clear plans,' he shot back. For most of the primary campaign, Clinton was ahead. Although it might seem surprising in hindsight, the black vote was far from assured for Obama. In part that was due to the goodwill engendered by Bill Clinton, who had been a Southern governor and was described by the writer Toni Morrison as 'our first black president'. Some Clinton backers were less than helpful on this score. Andrew Young, US ambassador to the United Nations in the Carter administration, quipped: 'Bill is every bit as black as Barack. He's probably gone with more black women than Barack.' Black voters wanted to be sure that Obama had the potential to win. Once that became clear, they swung behind him in record numbers.

When talk-show queen Oprah Winfrey described Obama as 'the one', Clinton supporters and Republicans began to mock the deification of the young senator. An aide to a rival Democratic candidate told me, with a hint of jealousy, that Obama events were like a 'Second Coming'. Obama never lacked belief in his own ability and had come to see himself as a transcendent figure. When I asked him in Los Angeles about how he saw his candidacy, he answered in starkly self-referential terms: 'As somebody who myself lived overseas for a time, the world would see me as a different kind of president, somebody who could see the world through their eyes,' he said mellifluously.

And so if I go to a poor country to talk about how the United States and that poor country can cooperate I'd do so with the credibility of somebody who has a grandmother who lives in a poor village in Africa. If I convened a meeting with Muslim leaders around the world to discuss how they can align themselves against terrorism . . . I'd do so with the credibility of someone who has lived in a Muslim country. All these things can make a difference.

The primary race went almost all the way to the party convention in August and there was much bad blood. At one point Clinton parodied an Obama speech: 'Let's just get everybody together. Let's get unified. The sky will open. The lights will come down. Celestial choirs will be singing and everyone will know we should do the right thing and the world will be perfect.' Loose remarks by Obama at a San Francisco fundraiser nearly sank him, and revealed what his opponents argued was an elitist contempt for working-class Americans. Referring to job losses in ailing industrial towns, he said: 'They get bitter, they cling to guns or religion or antipathy to people who aren't like them or anti-immigrant sentiment or anti-trade sentiment as a way to explain their frustrations.' Just as Trump supporters would embrace the term 'deplorables' in 2016, there were soon 'bitter clinger' t-shirts and bumper stickers being sold. One of the nails in Clinton's coffin was the full-throated endorsement of Obama by Senator Ted Kennedy – the seal of an American dynasty that easily eclipsed the Bushes and the Clintons.

Some tough primary battles leave the winner damaged and ener-vated. In 2008, Obama's contest with Clinton made him a presidential election candidate forged in fire who had campaigned in almost all fifty states. With Bush's popularity ratings in the doldrums, it always appeared that the Democratic nominee would prevail, and McCain, the Republican nominee, never seemed a match for Obama. After a lacklustre campaign, McCain's last throw of the dice was to choose Sarah Palin as his vice-presidential nominee – she proved to be almost comically out of her depth, though her fervent support from conservatives was an early demonstration of a phenomenon later tapped into by Trump. While on his way to a seven-point victory over McCain – translating into a 365 to 173 Electoral College landslide – Obama displayed signs of hubris. When it was clear his victory over Clinton was assured, he had declared that future generations would recognise this as 'the moment when the rise of the oceans began to slow and our planet began to heal'. Rather than Obama accepting the Democratic nomination on the convention stage in Denver, his campaign spent $3 million to switch it to a sports stadium, where 75,000 people watched him speak in front of a *faux* Greek temple.

Perhaps Obama's greatest accomplishment was saving the American economy, which was on its knees amid a global financial crisis when he took office. By the end of his second term, the US had experienced seventy-five consecutive months of employment growth and 156,000 new jobs were created in his final full month. Through a $787-billion stimulus package, relief for banks and investment firms, and a bailout of the car industry, Obama restored economic stability. He rejected, however, the advice of Christine Romer, chair of his Council of Economic Advisers, who proposed a much larger package of $1.8 trillion. Rather than depleting his political capital to fight for a larger stimulus that focused on jobs, he chose to spend it on healthcare reform. 'Obamacare' – as the Affordable Care Act he sponsored came to be known – became his principal legislative victory, but it was secured without a single Republican vote in Congress and came at an enormous political cost. Passed in March 2010, Obamacare was the most significant overhaul of the US healthcare system since 1965, slashing the uninsured population by half, to around 20 million people. But many Americans were happy with their existing healthcare arrangements and Obama's promise that 'If you like your doctor, you will be able to keep your doctor' turned out to be untrue – the non-partisan PolitiFact site later made that statement their 'Lie of the Year'.

In the 2010 mid-term elections, Republicans campaigned on the slow recovery, the unpopularity of Obamacare, and the perception that the stimulus favoured Wall Street over ordinary Americans. The Democrats were routed, as Republicans regained control of the House of Representatives by netting sixty-three seats – the biggest mid-term gains for the opposing party since 1938. Shortly after taking office, Obama had told Republicans that 'elections have consequences', adding: 'I won.' These words came back to haunt him in 2010. Democrats managed to cling on to the Senate for another two years, but Obama had lost the unified power he had enjoyed in Washington. The era of the Tea Party was ushered in

– a precursor to Trump's 2016 victory – with a wave that sent to Congress a group of conservative radicals determined to oppose everything Obama did. For all his appeals for unity and bipartisanship, Obama proved ill-suited to the kind of congressional horse-trading that could produce results. Although a keen golfer, he almost invariably played with close aides rather than inviting potential allies like John Boehner, the new Republican Speaker of the House, to join him. As well as being an avid golfer, Boehner, a cigar-smoking, Merlot-quaffing dealmaker, was implacably opposed to the Tea Party wing of his party. But Obama appeared uninterested in wooing the Speaker. Even Democrats on Capitol Hill found Obama aloof and unapproachable. Obama's aides argued that obstructionist Republicans would never have worked with him, but some members of the president's own party yearned for the kind of relationship Ronald Reagan, a Republican president, enjoyed with Tip O'Neill, a Democratic Speaker.

Obama was often criticised for his professorial manner and a tendency to conduct policy as if it were part of an academic seminar. He could be condescending, with an outlook that at times was a stereotype of what one would expect from a habitué of an Ivy League common room who viewed those who disagreed with him as stupid or ill-informed. Sometimes, he neglected to bring the country with him. His switch to supporting gay marriage was broadly reflective of how American society had changed, but his party's swift embrace of the idea that anyone who opposed it was a bigot alienated many in what liberals derided as the 'flyover states'. After all, Obama himself had opposed gay marriage during the 2008 campaign, and lighting up the White House in rainbow colours in 2015 seemed unnecessarily triumphalist to social conservatives.

On foreign policy, Obama represented much less of a break in continuity with his predecessor George W. Bush than had been expected. Ironically, Obama had been awarded the Nobel Peace Prize just nine months into his presidency, and shortly after he announced he was sending 30,000 more troops to Afghanistan. The timing of the prize was almost comically premature, and the award seemed to have been bestowed almost solely because he was not Bush. There was much more of a multilateral gloss to his actions and Obama normalised relations with Cuba after fifty-four years of enmity and struck an international nuclear deal with Iran, though the latter was jettisoned by Trump. He shared Bush's global approach to terrorism, however, massively increasing the number of drone strikes. Obama had denounced the CIA's 'torture' – the agency preferred the term 'enhanced interrogation techniques' – programme, but critics argued that killing terrorist suspects was hardly morally preferable and made it harder to glean human intelligence. On Iraq, Obama followed through on his campaign promise to bring American troops home. Unfortunately, declaring the war to be over neglected the fact that the enemy had a say in this, and ISIS used the resulting power vacuum left at the end of 2011 to grow into a global threat. In contrast, Obama viewed Afghanistan as a 'war of necessity' and increased US troop numbers to 100,000 in 2009 – similar to the number the Soviet Union had used to invade in 1979. Some of Obama's top aides, including Biden, believed the president had been 'rolled' by American generals, whose perennial advice tends to be that a few tens of thousands more troops will do the trick. Even in announcing the surge at the end of 2010, Obama seemed to have doubts himself, deciding at the last minute to simultaneously declare there would be a withdrawal beginning in 2011. The Taliban appeared to get the message that it was just a matter of time before the Americans, like the Russians before them, would leave.

Obama intervened in Libya to help overthrow Muammar Gaddafi, but managed to replace him with little more than chaos and, in so doing, alienated Russia. In Syria, Obama announced a 'red line' over the use of chemical weapons, but decided not to act when President Bashar Assad crossed it in 2013. Having pursued a Libya policy described by one anonymous adviser as 'leading from behind', Obama was a bystander over Syria, watching as Assad committed mass murder of his own people and the Russians intervened in a civil war that left more than four hundred thousand people dead. Obama received adulatory press coverage for announcing that the Guantanamo Bay detention camp would close within a year; by the time he left office after eight years, it remained open. Obama's Justice Department pursued journalists and those who leaked secrets – most notably the intelligence analyst Edward Snowden – with a fervour that shocked civil libertarians.

One of the crowning moments of Obama's presidency was his decision to launch the raid to kill Osama bin Laden. The escape of the Al Qaeda leader at Tora Bora in late 2001 had been a major setback for the Bush administration. By tracking a pair of couriers, the CIA located a compound in Abbottabad, just north of the Pakistan capital Islamabad, that was occupied by a tall man and his family. It was far from certain, however, that the tall man was bin Laden. Launching a raid was an extremely risky enterprise because it involved breaching Pakistani sovereignty – the country's intelligence service was too close to Al Qaeda to be trusted. The safer option would have been to use a drone to strike the compound, but that meant possibly never truly knowing the identity of those killed. Politically, a botched operation could have been catastrophic for Obama. The disastrous 1980 Desert One operation to rescue American hostages in Iran was widely seen as a factor in Jimmy Carter's election defeat that year. Despite some advisers, the most prominent of whom was Biden, counselling against the raid, Obama gave the CIA and US Navy SEALs the green light. Bin Laden was shot dead and his body secretly buried at sea. Obama was re-elected in November 2012, inoculated from claims that he was weak on foreign policy – normally a potent Republican argument against a Democratic incumbent. 'For the first and only time in my presidency, we didn't have to sell what we'd done,' he later noted.

Having telegraphed on the campaign trail that he felt he could shift the country largely through the sheer force of his personality, Obama encountered the limits of the office of the presidency and his own appeal. Nowhere was this more apparent than on the issue of guns. He called the 2012 mass shooting at Sandy Hook elementary school, when twenty small children and six staff were murdered, 'the worst day of my presidency', and four years later wept publicly when calling for gun control. Although Obama was a supremely self-disciplined and usually undemonstrative politician – campaign aides wore 'No Drama Obama' t-shirts – on occasion he channelled the emotions of Americans as effectively and genuinely as the famously empathetic Bill Clinton or easy-to-tears George W. Bush. Delivering a eulogy in Charleston, South Carolina, at the funeral of a pastor of a black church who had been among nine murdered by a white supremacist, Obama began singing 'Amazing Grace';

soon, the entire congregation, and much of the country, was singing along with him.

One of the tragedies of Obama's presidency, and something that was almost certainly largely beyond his control, was that racial divisions appeared to grow during his eight years in office rather than heal, as he had intended. Before he was elected, his campaign had been buffeted by the emergence of fiery, anti-American sermons delivered by the Reverend Jeremiah Wright, minister at the church in Chicago's South Side attended by Obama. The reality was that Obama, whose mother was an atheist, seemed to have few religious convictions; later, he seldom attended church. But in 2008, even a Democrat was expected to be a staunch Christian, anti gay marriage, and pro death penalty. Publicly, Obama ticked all three boxes. If he'd been present at the church for any of Wright's sermons, Obama might have nodded off; but having presented himself as Born Again, he couldn't admit to that.

That left Obama trying to draw the line under the fuss about Wright by giving a speech on race in Philadelphia. It was soaring oratory and deeply personal. His white grandmother, he said, 'who loves me as much as she loves anything in this world, [was] a woman who once confessed her fear of black men who passed by her on the street'. He would not renounce Wright, he insisted, because 'I can no more disown him than I can disown the black community. I can no more disown him than I can disown my white grandmother.' He added: 'I will never forget that in no other country on Earth is my story even possible. It's a story that hasn't made me the most conventional of candidates. But it is a story that has seared into my genetic makeup the idea that this nation is more than the sum of its parts – that out of many, we are truly one.'

In office, Obama resolutely tried to be a president for all Americans, once stating: 'I can't pass laws that say I'm just helping black folks – I'm the president of the United States.' When he did weigh in on race, it came back to bite him. When asked for his views on a black Harvard professor being arrested outside his own home after a neighbour had called 911 suspecting he was a burglar, Obama said he thought the local police had 'acted stupidly'. As he recounted in his memoir, the fallout from those words was that his standing among white voters dropped more precipitously than at any other point in his eight years as president. It was an indication, he reflected, that the issue of black people and the police was more polarising than almost any other aspect of American life. The episode, he wrote, 'seemed to tap into some of the deepest undercurrents of our nation's psyche'.

After 2010, Obama increasingly turned to executive action in order to push through his agenda. He enacted meaningful reforms on immigration policy, climate change and mass incarceration – an area where there was potential for common ground with Republicans – but these reforms were open to being undone by his successor. Obama had made a convincing case in 2008 that Hillary Clinton was an unimaginative, conventional politician who was too close to corporate interests. In a somewhat ostentatious nod to Lincoln's 'Team of Rivals', he made her his Secretary of State; in part because he judged she would be less of a threat to him if she were inside his tent. It was remarkable that he later anointed Clinton as his successor during the 2016 presidential race, dissuading other Democrats from running, most notably Joe Biden. Obama chose Biden – a notoriously long-winded thirty-six-year senator – as his running mate in 2008 because he was an older, white man with Washington experience who could never outshine Obama. It was always presumed he would be too old to run for president in 2016, a plus because he would not be distracted by his own White House run, as Bill Clinton's Veep Al Gore had been. Privately, Obama viewed Biden as gaffe-prone and second tier – he had dropped out of the 1988 presidential race after being caught plagiarising British Labour Party leader Neil Kinnock, and twenty years later called it quits when he secured less than 1 per cent of the vote in Iowa. So, Obama bypassed Biden, who could probably have beaten Trump, and instead used his political clout to leave Hillary Clinton an almost clear primary field. Underscoring Obama's grave miscalculation, Clinton lost to Trump. Indeed, four months before the election, a senior Trump aide told me: 'He may be the only candidate who could lose to her, but she's the only candidate who could lose to him.'

In putting his thumb on the Democratic Party scale for Clinton in 2016 – to the lasting chagrin of supporters of the socialist senator Bernie Sanders – Obama made a catastrophic error. It may be that he favoured Clinton rather than a new-generation candidate because he felt that she would be a safe pair of hands who would protect his legacy without the lustre of his star power. Instead, the country was left with Donald Trump. In the third sentence of the first volume of his memoirs, Obama could not bring himself to mention his successor by name – 'someone diametrically opposed to everything we stood for' is as far as he goes. But Trump's presence on that first page is testament to the sense of failure Obama feels that he, like most of the rest of the country, never felt it possible that such a candidate could win.

When asked in 1972 about the impact of the French Revolution nearly two centuries earlier, Chinese premier Zhou Enlai reputedly responded: 'Too early to say.' With barely five years elapsing since Obama left the White House, any verdict on his presidency would certainly be premature. In one sense, the wild ride of Trump's four years, culminating in an attack on the US Capitol that was one of the most shameful episodes in modern American history, has only made a majority of Americans more wistful for the Obama years. Obama managed to serve eight years with no scandal to speak of, maintaining a dignified and even reverential approach to the office of the presidency while at the same time modernising it. Joe Biden, treated as an amiable but not entirely serious figure by many within the Obama White House, looks likely – he is more than eighteen years older than Obama – to be a one-term president whose main aim is to return the US to something resembling normality. There are some early signs, however, that Biden and his staff are prepared to be bolder than Obama, who was a much more conventional president than many predicted. The most stalwart of Obama defenders blame recalcitrant Republicans for the legislative gridlock of 2009 to 2017 or even a deep-seated racism in the country that led much of the country to refuse to accept a black president. How much Biden is able to achieve will offer important perspective on those contentions.

At just sixty years old this year, Obama is a young former president and projects the sense that he yearns for a global role beyond even the one previously offered by the White House. In the shadow of the Trump era, Obama engaged in Tony Blair-style hobnobbing with the ultra-rich. He was photographed on David Geffen's yacht in French Polynesia and kite-surfing with Richard Branson off Necker Island, as well as rafting with his family in Bali, and hanging out with Bruce Springsteen. Obama and his wife Michelle, who supplanted Angelina Jolie as the world's most admired woman in 2019, according to YouGov, secured a reported $60 million in book advances. In 2019, they bought an $11.75-million home on Martha's Vineyard, a favourite haunt of the Clintons. Naturally, there have been paid speeches – $400,000 for an address to Wall Street bankers and an estimated $3.2 million for an appearance at a food summit in Milan. He has held sessions with groups of young people in Brazil, Indonesia, New Zealand and Singapore and delivered a lecture in Johannesburg to commemorate the hundredth anniversary of the birth of Nelson Mandela. There are projects such as the Obama Presidential Center, to be built on Chicago's South Side, and the Obama Foundation.

For now, Obama appears to be biding his time as the country – and the world – recovers from the tumult of the Trump years. Obama himself appears to view Trump less as an aberration than as a sign of America's ills. At the same time, Obama's long-held optimism about the broader trajectory of his country appears unshaken. When he was first elected, he spoke of America as 'a place where all things are possible', where people could 'put their hands on the arc of history and bend it once more toward the hope of a better day'. Despite all that has happened since and the some-times grinding and dispiriting experience of his own eight years in office, one senses that Obama still believes that to be true. While never the transformational president he sought to be, Obama will be remembered as an inspirational one – though principally for who he was rather than for his record in office.

Toby Harnden is a writer based in McLean, Virginia, who spent sixteen years covering US politics for British newspapers. He is the author of Bandit Country *(1999),* Dead Men Risen *(2011) and* First Casualty *(2021).*

45

Donald J. Trump

20 January 2017 to 20 January 2021
Republican
Vice-president: Mike Pence

By Justin Webb

Full name: Donald John Trump
Born: 14 June 1946, Queens, New York City
Education: Fordham University, University of Pennsylvania
Married to: Ivana Marie Zelnickova, m. 1977, div. 1992 (1949–);
Marla Maples, m. 1993, div. 1999 (1963–); Melania Knavs, m.
2005 (1970–)
Children: Five: Donald Jr, Ivanka, Eric, Tiffany, Barron
Quotation: 'I alone can fix it.'

NOTHING ABOUT THE presidency of Donald J. Trump was
normal. He was, to his supporters, a glorious rebel, an iconoclast,

a saviour. To his opponents, he was simply contemptible; from his policies to his character, he stank, debasing the office of the presidency and the conduct of public affairs. He was impeached twice, he failed to attend the inauguration of his successor, and he made repeated claims about electoral fraud that were untrue. He was an earthquake in human form. He shook everything and everyone.

When he first thought of standing for the Republican nomination in 2016, few took him seriously. When I interviewed him about his golf business two years earlier, I had tacked on to the end of our conversation a question about whether he might run. He had done it before, in 2000, for the Reform Party set up by the businessman Ross Perot, qualifying for two primary contests but pulling out in February of that year without ever being seen as much more than a showman in search of publicity.

'I may well run,' he told me. 'People are telling me I should.'

When the item was broadcast on the *Today* programme many in the audience were unimpressed, suggesting that we had wasted airtime on the ramblings of a self-publicist and we should be more discerning.

The failure of otherwise politically aware people to take Trump seriously is one of the key features of his rise to power. Nowhere was this better exemplified than on the prestigious ABC News TV programme *This Week*, in July 2015, by which time Donald Trump was a rambunctious outsider now threatening the Republican elite. A senior Democrat, the then Congressman Keith Ellison, told the programme's host that Trump might well be the GOP candidate in 2016 and could win. 'This man has got some momentum,' Ellison said, 'and we better be ready for the fact that he might be leading the Republican ticket.'

The reaction sums up American politics in the pre-Trump era. The other guests – all of them experts – burst into uproarious laughter. One of them was so racked with giggles that she could not speak. The host – the former Clinton-era White House aide George Stephanopoulos – chided Ellison: 'I know you don't believe that.'

Before they moved on to other candidates, Ellison gave it one more shot: 'Stranger things have happened.'

Donald J. Trump was born in Queens, a New York city suburb,

on 14 June 1946, the fourth child of the real-estate tycoon Fred Trump. He grew up wealthy and, according to those who knew him at the time, badly behaved. His father was a disciplinarian, but Donald could not be controlled, even by him: 'I used to fight back all the time,' he told a biographer. Friends remember a boy often in trouble; Trump himself has talked of giving a teacher a black eye, 'because I didn't think he knew anything about music'.

Eventually his father – who seems to have respected his son's waywardness but wanted it controlled as well – sent him to the New York Military Academy, a boarding school for boys. Donald Trump excelled in the hyper-competitive, sometimes violent atmosphere of the school. A teacher remembers: 'He would do anything to win.'

Trump attended the Wharton Business School at the University of Pennsylvania. He has said he went to 'the hardest school to get into, the best school in the world', calling it 'super genius stuff', and that he graduated at the top of his class. Wharton is indeed prestigious but it's not clear that Trump got in on his own merit – his father was involved in the process – or that he did well while he was there. The difference between his memory, his claims and those of others who were present began with his university education and was to become a feature of Donald Trump's entire life.

A life dominated not by politics but by property and television. Donald Trump inherited his father's property empire and changed its focus from relatively down-at-heel housing in the New York City suburbs to signature real-estate in Manhattan. He bought towers and he built towers. His signal achievements: transforming the run-down Commodore Hotel into the Grand Hyatt and erecting the most famous Trump property, the sixty-eight-storey Trump Tower on Fifth Avenue.

Along with property came the acquisition of a range of money-making enterprises that suited his outsized personality. From 1996 until 2015, he was an owner of the Miss Universe, Miss USA and Miss Teen USA beauty pageants. In 2003, he began an NBC reality television show called *The Apprentice*, in which contestants competed for a shot at a management job within Mr Trump's organisation. He hosted the show for fourteen seasons, making the catch-phrase 'You're fired!' famous and making himself millions of dollars in fees and publicity.

He also lost money, sometimes staggering amounts. And when he lost, it often seems to be other people, with fewer resources, who suffered. The Taj Mahal Casino in Atlantic City was an eye-catching example. It was the city's biggest, when it was opened in 1990.

'We're calling it the eighth wonder of the world,' said Donald Trump of his creation. 'I think it's going to do huge numbers. The overall majesty of the building is what's going to attract people. People are just amazed at the opulence.'

A year later it went bust along with an airline shuttle Trump ran between New York and Washington. Six thousand people lost their jobs, but Donald Trump somehow convinced his bankers that he could walk away and prosper in the future. Which he did. As he put it once to an incredulous lawyer in a court deposition: 'My net worth fluctuates, and it goes up and down with the markets and with attitudes and with feelings, even my own feelings.'

Donald Trump's self-belief never wavered. There are some who wonder whether he intended his run for the presidency in 2016 to be a publicity stunt, which went horribly wrong when he actually won. There are eyewitness accounts of some shock in the Trump camp on the night that the election was called.

But the mistake many made was in thinking that there might be a point when Donald Trump would call it a day, stepping back and accepting that his Democratic opponent Hillary Clinton would win, or, once he was president, transforming himself into someone more conventional. One of the best Donald Trump biographies from his pre-political days is entitled *Never Enough*. It's a good title. It sums up the man and it should have served as a warning to those who expected him to fade away.

Donald Trump has an instinct for verbal assassination. He also took on board what Karl Rove, George W. Bush's former political adviser and electoral campaign strategist, claimed was the best way to defeat your opponents. Don't attack their weaknesses, attack their strengths!

He deployed it with devastating effect in the Republican primary in 2016. He blamed George W. Bush not just for the Iraq war disaster but for the terrorist attacks of 9/11 during which most people had thought the former president had performed admirably.

Thus Trump undermined the entire Bush enterprise. George's brother Jeb Bush, the amiable moderate whom many expected to win the nomination, became 'low-energy Jeb'. Other potential threats were seen off with similar jujitsu moves; Senator Marco Rubio, young looking and earnest, became 'Little Marco', and Senator Ted Cruz, a highly able politician with a strong evangelical Christian following, became 'Lyin' Ted'.

Trump blew them out of the water. And then he turned his attention to Hillary Clinton. Mrs Clinton was in many ways highly qualified to be president, having been First Lady, a senator, and then Secretary of State under Barack Obama. But she was hopelessly exposed in a contest with a man as unconventional as Trump. He called her 'crooked Hillary', in reference to controversies surrounding a private email server that she had set up when she became Secretary of State.

It was not a big deal compared with the business practices of Donald Trump, but he made it a deal. It was peculiarly effective as a campaign slogan. To the horror of the political class, he openly called for this opponent to be 'locked up'. Like so much of Donald Trump's political appeal, it was to the emotions, to the gut, rather than the brain. Years later, David Beaver, a professor of linguistics at the University of Texas at Austin, provided an interesting commentary on why the Clinton attack, and so many other Trump tropes, worked so well. He told the influential *Columbia Journalism Review* that the sentence '"Hillary is crooked' goes into our brains through the intellect: so we are allowed the space to weigh whether it's true or not. The epithet "Crooked Hillary", on the other hand, presupposes the truth of the crookedness. "Crooked Hillary" is emotional, it has this visceral way of just grabbing you.'

Grabby but not true. In July of 2016, an FBI investigation concluded that no 'reasonable prosecutor' would bring a criminal case against Mrs Clinton, but that she and her aides were 'extremely careless' in their handling of classified information. But then, goaded by Trump and probably seduced by the belief that Clinton would anyway win, the FBI announced just eleven days before the poll that it was examining newly discovered emails sent or received by Mrs Clinton. Even more confusingly, two days before voting booths opened across the nation, FBI Director James Comey announced he was standing by his original assessment – that Mrs Clinton should not face criminal charges. But the damage was done.

Donald Trump had suffered a setback of his own in the last days of the campaign when a tape was revealed of a conversation he had had in 2005 in which he described what he believed was his animal attraction to women, 'When you're a star, they let you do it. You can do anything. Grab 'em by the pussy. You can do anything.'

It added to a widely held perception of Trump as being too coarse for the job. He was already accused of being openly racist following his campaign launch where he said of immigration on the southern border, 'When Mexico sends its people . . . They're bringing drugs. They're bringing crime. They're rapists.'

Now he was accused of misogyny. Several senior Republicans, including his vice-presidential running mate Mike Pence, criticised Trump for the grabbing pussy comments and some expected that he would step down in favour of Mr Pence. Mr Trump apologised, but once again demonstrated the ability he had in his business career to shake off disaster, to rise from ashes, to reinvent himself. On the afternoon of 8 October 2016, Mr Trump sent a tweet: 'The media and establishment want me out of the race so badly – I WILL NEVER DROP OUT OF THE RACE, WILL NEVER LET MY SUPPORTERS DOWN!'

He was, on this occasion, as good as his word.

Donald Trump went on to win the presidency by a wide margin, 304 Electoral College votes to 227. He lost the popular vote but he had easily done enough to win in the battleground states of the 'rust belt'. And not only did Trump win, but Republicans retained their House and Senate majorities, leaving Democrats out of power in Congress. It left many Democrats in tears, of anguish, of rage, of disbelief.

Donald Trump had taken control of a political party, and now taken control of the levers of power in Washington, DC. He was the least conventional candidate in modern history to enter the White House, but for that very reason he came to Washington with a groundswell of support from many Americans, particularly poorly educated rural white people, who felt that they had lost control of the culture of the nation and Trump might help them win it back.

His first task was to reorder America's foreign priorities, or as he put it in typically pithy forthright terms: 'America First'.

America withdrew from the Paris Climate Accords, and later from the Iran Nuclear Agreement. In a fraught meeting with his top national security staff, the president shocked those present by wondering about the whole range of American commitments to the world, demonstrating – according to those present – that he had no understanding of or feeling for America's post-war role. It was left to Theresa May, the British prime minister visiting Washington, to try to force the recently elected president into publicly backing NATO – he did it, but with no enthusiasm. He was much keener on strong leaders of undemocratic states: Crown Prince Mohammed bin Salman of Saudi Arabia, Vladimir Putin of Russia, President Xi Jinping of China (until the relationship soured) and strangest of all, the North Korean despot Kim Jong-un.

Trump and Kim held two summits, one in Singapore and the second in Vietnam; this one cut short when no agreement could be reached. But they nonetheless had a relationship that was as odd as it was unproductive. Mr Trump seemed to like the North Korean leader or his flattery, telling a rally in West Virginia: 'He wrote me beautiful letters, and they're great letters. We fell in love.' Critics of Trump's foreign policy point out that he gave succour to some of the world's worst leaders and caused dismay and discord among America's allies.

But what Donald Trump did *not* do is involve America in more wars. For all his rhetoric, he was cautious about the use of American power. He wanted to end the war he inherited – Afghanistan – and his decision to pull all troops out was not subsequently altered by the Biden administration.

Donald Trump's China policy was governed by his sense that the Chinese were undercutting American industry and doing so unfairly, without ever being asked to pay a price. This was a view that plenty of economists shared. Where they differed was in the imposition of a trade war, which they felt would impoverish both sides. But Donald Trump took no notice; he levied tariffs on billions of dollars of Chinese goods, sparking a trade war that stretched on for most of his presidency.

The greatest domestic achievement of the Trump administration was a successful first step at least in an attempt to turn the tide against the liberal progressive orthodoxy imposed on Americans – so many believed – by their political and cultural leaders: the values of New York City and of Hollywood. A man who was, by his own admission, sexually incontinent and entirely metropolitan in focus became the man who fought for the rubes.

No actions by the Trump presidency have any chance of outlasting it and guaranteeing its impact as much as the successful appointment of three Supreme Court Justices. The first, Neil Gorsuch, was a cautious replacement for a conservative justice; he did not change the balance of the court. But the appointment of Brett Kavanaugh in 2018 replaced a swing voter on the court with a firm conservative. And then in 2020, just as his presidency was slipping away, Trump provided the coup de grace. He appointed Amy Coney Barrett to replace the most liberal justice, Ruth Bader Ginsburg, and thus give the court a conservative majority for years, perhaps decades to come.

The importance of this cannot be overstressed. People often wondered how it could be that God-fearing folk could turn in such large numbers to Donald Trump. How could they forgive him his multiple marriages, his disregard for propriety, his obvious personal dishonesty? The answer is the court. He promised to deliver conservative justices and he did. Of course, the longer-term question is whether they in turn deliver an America that is more hostile to abortion and gay rights, more sympathetic to guns and Christianity. When Donald Trump, during the chaotic end to his presidency, wanted his court to back him in his effort to stay in office, they stayed properly and silently out of the fight. They are still judges with a belief in the rule of law. It is not clear whether they will exercise similar restraint in the future.

Indeed, the Trump-appointed justices may bring to a head arguments about the over-domination of American politics by small states and small populations living in economically inactive places. There may be pressure for change – to the court, to the Senate, to the electoral college. When Donald Trump lost in 2020, he left a court in which fifteen of the last nineteen justices had been nominated by Republican presidents despite the fact that the Democrats won the popular vote in seven of the last eight presidential elections. He went for broke, as was his constant habit, but in doing so may have over-reached.

What else did he achieve? He claimed to revitalise the economy and it is true that his reduction in red tape and in tax helped fuel a blue-collar boom. On a reporting trip in Pennsylvania in 2018, I met dozens of people – electricians, plumbers, builders – who felt that the Trump economy was good for them. And it was: Trump was an expansionist. He ran the economy hot, with none of the traditional Republican concern for balancing the books. Wages rose; the national unemployment rate flirted with a fifty-year low. Companies became increasingly desperate, dropping educational requirements, waiving criminal background checks and offering training packages and other inducements to potential workers. Again, the question is asked of Americans who are not racist or sexist how they could have supported him – the answer is that he appeared to them to be delivering things that they needed in a way other presidents of both parties could not or would not.

Above all: to many of these people he was delivering dignity. It feels strange to say this of a president who was so personally unpleasant about large groups of people, and sometimes about individuals as well; a president who seemed to find it difficult to say kindly or gentle things about anyone except himself; a president who tried to ban people from majority Muslim nations from coming to America, who mocked the weak around the world and admired the strong. And yet for many of his lowliest supporters he was a champion. They loved his use of coarse basic language, his lack of interest in subtle diplomacy, his willingness, in their eyes, to 'tell it like it is'. They had noticed a truth too: that the promise of America had been stolen in recent decades by the upper middle classes who insulated themselves from the rest, sending their children to the best universities, living apart, and then lecturing everyone else on how they should be more inclusive, less sexist, more tolerant. All the time hectoring, lecturing from on high: don't use this word or that. Be aware of your ingrained unconscious racism. Be ashamed. Be reduced.

People were utterly sick of being told by the established wealthy classes that they were, to use the catastrophic word used in the campaign by Hillary Clinton, 'deplorable'. To large numbers of

Americans this felt like an attack on legitimately lived lives, and voting for Donald Trump was their angry riposte. It emerged after 2020 that the strongest predictors of a Trump vote, apart from a lack of formal education, were to do with poor health. People with fewer opportunities and more difficult lives were drawn to Trump throughout his presidency and, crucially, even when their lives did not noticeably improve. President Trump was too ill-disciplined to govern effectively as a populist – his threats, for instance, to take on the pharmaceutical industry over drug prices never really got off the ground – but politically this hardly mattered. He kept his core supporters to the end.

They were certainly unimpressed by his first impeachment. In 2019, Donald Trump was impeached by the House of Representatives after they found that he had put pressure on the president of Ukraine to investigate Joe Biden for fraudulent involvement in the politics of the European nation. The senate threw out the conviction, so Mr Trump stayed in office. He was defiant and it seemed strange to many that the focus had been on Ukraine rather than on the two-year investigation into Russian election meddling by Robert Mueller, the special counsel, or what the *New York Times* called 'the seemingly endless series of other accusations of corruption and misconduct that have plagued this White House: tax evasion, profiting from the presidency, payoffs to a pornographic film actress and fraudulent activities by his charitable foundation'.

The impeachment felt lame to many and it left the president essentially undamaged. But heading still for a clash that would shake the foundations of the nation. In a sense the end, a year later, was entirely predictable. Indeed, it was predicted by people who could be counted as backers of Trump.

Victor Davis Hanson is a classicist who has written positively about Trump. He compares the president – seriously – to Ajax, the creation of Sophocles: 'Ajax's soliloquies about a rigged system and the lack of recognition accorded his undeniable accomplishments is Trumpian to the core,' Hanson says. 'Tragic heroes are often unstable loners. They are aloof by preference and due to society's understandable unease with them.'

If Trump as hero makes you queasy, try the Steve Bannon take.

The man who helped make Trump powerful – he was a key aide until they fell out – talked to the author Michael Wolff.

Bannon, we are told, in Wolff's book *Siege*, was asked by a friend how the Trump presidency ends. Wolff takes up the story:

> 'Well he won't go out classy,' replied Bannon.
>
> 'If you think about it American history doesn't have many unseemly moments. Even bad guys, looking at the end, take their medicine,' Bannon tells his friend. Even Nixon was classy and smart when it became obvious the game was up.
>
> 'But we don't have classy and we don't have smart.'
>
> 'This is not going to be like that. This is going to be very . . . Unseemly.'

It was worse than that. Donald Trump was probably on course to win a second term when the year 2020 began. The Democrats held a shambolic first caucus in Iowa and seemed unsure of what they wanted to be, which part of their wide coalition their candidate would represent.

Then came Covid-19. President Trump tried first to minimise its importance. He seemed concerned about its effect on the stock market rather than on lives. Repeatedly, and erroneously, he claimed that the crisis was over or about to be over. He did establish an effort to find a vaccine – an effort for which he has perhaps been given less credit than he deserves – but his overall response was unconvincing to put it mildly.

When the Democrats chose Joe Biden to run against him, Trump tried to fight back but found it difficult to grapple with an opponent who needed to stay quiet and largely confined to his basement to protect his own health. Trump was flummoxed by Biden's lack of aggression.

And then, weeks before the election, he caught Covid himself. Just how ill he was is not clear, but he was taken to hospital and it seems that his blood oxygen levels were causing genuine concern. His reaction was, typically, defiance and self-aggrandisement. He told his supporters that they could beat the virus as he had: 'As your leader, I had to do that. I knew there's danger to it, but I had to do it. I stood out front, and led.' Among his actions was an unnecessary car ride to see his supporters outside the Walter Reed military hospital, a ride in which secret service men had to travel inside the sealed car with the president. James Phillips, an attending physician at Walter Reed, called the stunt 'insanity'.

The election in November 2020 was always going to be a bare-knuckle fight. It was, in the event, close to being a disaster for America and for democracy. Donald Trump did well. In particular, he increased his support among Hispanic voters, the largest of America's minority blocs. The accusations of racism made against this president throughout his time in office did not put them off voting for him. The early returns suggested that Mr Trump was on course to win. But a large postal vote needed to be counted and that vote, in several key states, went overwhelmingly to Biden. So the Trump confidence in the early hours of the count turned to dismay, and anger. And then: denial.

Donald Trump claimed, repeatedly and falsely, that he had won and that widespread fraud had robbed him of the victory. He refused to concede, although he had lost by 306 to 232 Electoral College votes.

It is alleged that some of his aides, at a meeting in the White House on 18 December, discussed the idea of overturning the election by invoking martial law and rerunning the poll in several swing states under military supervision. The president called it 'fake news', but whether or not that is true, something provoked the Army Secretary Ryan McCarthy and Army Chief of Staff General James McConville into issuing a joint statement saying: 'There is no role for the U.S. military in determining the outcome of an American election.'

There was one more twist to come.

Donald Trump addressed his supporters in front of the White House shortly before Congress convened for a joint session on 6 January 2021 to confirm the Electoral College vote won by President-elect Joe Biden. It should have been a formality. But dozens of Republican House and Senate members disputed the poll results of several swing states, in a show of loyalty to Trump.

And then a large group of his supporters stormed the building in an effort to get the vote stopped. Lawmakers had to run to escape the mob. The police were unprepared and overwhelmed.

More than a hundred and forty people were injured. Five people died either shortly before, during or after the event, including a woman shot dead by police.

The distinguished White House historian Michael Beschloss told Americans: 'That was a terrorist attack on our Congress today and our U.S. Capitol.'

Donald Trump told his supporters to go home. It was the end of the road for him. A week before he left office, he was impeached for a second time by the House of Representatives on charges of incitement of insurrection. Ten Republican representatives voted for the impeachment, the most pro-impeachment votes ever from a president's party. Again, though, the Senate, controlled by the Republicans, voted not to convict, so he was not removed from office.

Mr Trump did not attend the inauguration of his successor. He was banned from Twitter and Facebook and shunned by some senior members of the party. He and members of his family went off to live in Florida and consider their next moves. The nation, shakily, got on with its business. Mr Trump's voice was occasionally heard but he was a diminished figure, perhaps more so than he or his backers expected.

The earthquake had come to an end. It was time to rebuild.

Justin Webb is a presenter of the BBC's flagship news programme, Today. *He was the BBC's first North America Editor and writes about US politics for a range of outlets including* The Times *and* UnHerd.

46

Joe Biden

20 January 2021–
Democrat
Vice-president: Kamala Harris

By Andrew Adonis

Full name: Joseph Robinette Biden Jr
Born: 20 November 1942, Scranton, Pennsylvania
Education: University of Delaware (BA), Syracuse
University (JD)
Married to: Neilia Hunter, m. 1966 (1942–72); Jill Jacobs, m.
1977 (1951–)
Children: Four: Joseph Robinette 'Beau' Biden III, Robert
Hunter, Naomi Christina, Ashley Blazer
Quotation: 'I think you're a damn war criminal and you should
be tried as one.' (To Slobodan Milošević, dictator of Serbia)

FROM THE MOMENT John F. Kennedy said, 'Ask not what your country can do for you – ask what you can do for your country,' the eighteen-year-old Joe Biden wanted to be a future president, emulating such an image of youthful dynamic leadership. It didn't happen when he was young, but the supreme office came to him six decades later when he was inaugurated as the forty-sixth and oldest president on 20 January 2021.

Born in 1942 to an Irish Catholic family in small-town Pennsylvania, Biden's early years were as turbulent as the Kennedys'. His father Joseph Biden Sr suffered agonising downward mobility working for an uncle's unsuccessful armament business. At one time the Bidens were living with Joe's maternal grandparents until Joe Sr managed to drag the family back into the middle class as a car salesman in Scranton, Pennsylvania, and then just across the state border in Wilmington, Delaware.

As a student at the University of Delaware in the early 1960s, Biden was described by a friend as 'a coat-and-tie guy' who 'would do everything correctly'. He became a trial lawyer, doing just that after law school at Syracuse University in upstate New York and politically registered as an independent. He voted for a Republican state governor in 1968 and his first wife, Neilia, was also a Republican. Only in 1969, a year before fighting his first election in then fairly conservative Delaware, did he register as a Democrat for the first time.

Elected to one of Delaware's three local councils at age twenty-seven in 1970, Biden went on to pull off a spectacular and unexpected victory over the state's popular Republican Senate incumbent just two years later, becoming one of the youngest senators in US history and inaugurating a seven-term thirty-six-year Senate career. He was only able to serve because his thirtieth birthday fell between the election and the commencement of the new Congress in January 1973. 'I'm like the token black or the token woman; I was the token young person,' he noted chippily in a 1974 interview.

Within weeks of his election, Biden's first wife Neilia and newly born daughter were killed when a truck smashed into their car on the way to buy a Christmas tree. His two young sons, Beau and Hunter, were injured but survived, and Biden took the oath of office from their hospital room. Over the following decades, Biden's personal trials and tribulations became integral to his public life. From the death of Neilia to his own brain aneurysm shortly before his 1988 presidential bid, and later his son Beau's death from brain cancer in 2015, he became a tragic hero, 'a man of sorrows, acquainted with grief' embodying American perseverance against tremendous adversity.

Religion also became integral to brand Biden. In the footsteps of JFK, he is America's second Catholic president. He wears his dead son Beau's rosary around his wrist, calling it his connection with his lost son, and quotes Kierkegaard: 'faith sees best in the dark'. Morbidity as charisma is a rare and strange thing. It has been Biden's political shield and sword over a political career spanning half a century.

Dynamic, if sometimes erratic, centrism has been Biden's abiding political philosophy. From the outset of his political career, he straddled both Democratic and Republican positions on controversial issues, often simultaneously, although generally without appearing excessively hypocritical or contradictory. In the 1960s, he was against the Vietnam War, but opposed amnesty for draft dodgers. In the 1970s, he was against criminalising abortion, but opposed federal funding for abortion. He was against racial segregation, but opposed desegregated bussing to create racially mixed schools. In the 1980s, as chairman of the Senate Judiciary Committee, Biden initially supported the hard-line conservative Robert Bork's appointment to the Supreme Court, then became his most passionate opponent. 'I didn't want to be a little asterisk in history,' he said when the extent of Democrat hostility to an ultra-conservative judge on the Supreme Court became apparent.

During the Clinton era, Biden backed welfare reforms that limited welfare and was denounced as 'the new Jim Crow' for the 1994 Crime Act – his biggest legislative legacy in the Senate – which dramatically increased black incarceration. He even boasted that 'the liberal wing of the Democratic Party' was now for '60 new death penalties, 70 enhanced penalties, 100,000 cops and 125,000 new state prison cells'.

In the mid-1990s, as Chairman of the Senate Foreign Relations Committee, he agitated for Clinton's US intervention to stop Milošević's tyranny, winning him plaudits on left and right. In the early 2000s, he voted for George Bush's war in Iraq, then quickly became its most vociferous critic. 'I do not believe this is a rush to war,' he said in the October 2002 Senate debate. 'I believe it is a march to peace and security.' Even at the time, few saw it like that, but by such stratagems Biden sustained a centrist reputation and appeal. He also consciously straddled the aisle in personal alliances and friendships, and never more so than when in 2018 he spoke at the funeral of John McCain, Republican war hero turned senator, who became a close friend, beginning his eulogy with: 'My name is Joe Biden. I'm a Democrat. And I love John McCain.'

From his earliest days in Delaware politics, this almost feline shape-shifting was crucial to Biden's political survival. It is highly unlikely that he would have been elected during the Nixon landslide of 1972, or re-elected in the Carter mid-term of 1978, but for his opposition to school bussing, teaming up with Delaware's Republican senator, William Roth, in a bid to ban federal funding for it. But there were progressive causes too. Alongside his support for parsimonious welfare reforms, he led the charge on fiscal stimulus and against tax cuts for the rich in response to both the financial crash and the Covid-19 pandemic.

Prior to serving as Obama's vice-president in 2008, Biden had never held any Cabinet position or executive role; indeed, besides chairing the Senate Foreign Relations and Senate Judiciary Committees, Biden held no other senior office in the public or private sectors until the age of sixty-six. Yet from tiny Delaware, a state with less than half the population of Houston, he established himself as a national political leader. His Washington-based longevity, latency and centrism became defining assets for first the vice-presidency and then the presidency after the millennium.

Biden's first one hundred days as president have been some of the most successfully assertive of any president since FDR. He made tackling Covid-19, reviving the economy and reversing the 'worst' of Trumpism his hallmarks from day one.

On his first day in office, Biden signed an executive order taking the United States back into the Paris Climate Change Agreement. Further expanding on his green agenda, he revoked the permit that Trump had granted for the controversial Keystone Pipeline and symbolically ended funding for the wall along the Mexican border.

He took America back into the World Health Organization as part of a Covid-19 strategy that saw the US rapidly move from a death toll higher than every American war combined to rolling out on average 1.7 million vaccinations per day. The first major bill he signed into law was a $1.9 trillion stimulus – the American Rescue Plan Act 2021 – one of the biggest Keynesian acts since Keynes himself and an even greater cash injection into America's ailing economy than FDR's New Deal. When declining an EU request to export supplies of vaccine, Biden exclaimed: 'I said we had to treat this like a war.'

Other 'first 100 days' actions included reviving the Deferred Action for Childhood Arrivals (DACA) programme for immigrant children, which the previous administration sought to abolish, an immigration bill to provide green-card eligibility for the 'Dreamers' (minors whose parents brought them to the US illegally) and the promotion of a route to citizenship for undocumented immigrants. After his first stimulus package, Biden proposed a $2 trillion infrastructure plan.

Biden's Cabinet is the most diverse in American history. Trump's Cabinet was 82 per cent white and 82 per cent male, Biden's 55 per cent non-white and 45 per cent female. Yet while diverse, his team is equally strong on Biden's 'tough moderate' and 'competent' brand of progressivism. Vice-president Kamala Harris personifies both strands: a woman of colour yet also an aggressive former California state prosecutor. Lloyd Austin, the black four-star general appointed Defence Secretary, served with Biden's son Beau in Iraq. Secretary of State Antony Blinken, a throwback to Cordell Hull, the longest-ever holder of the post under FDR and 'father of the United Nations', is a long-experienced diplomat who served as Biden's Foreign Relations Committee adviser going back four decades, travelling back and forth to Iraq and across central and eastern Europe in the 1990s and 2000s as Biden passionately argued for the eastern expansion of NATO and military intervention to stop Milošević's outrages in the Balkans. Blinken went on to become Obama's Deputy Secretary of State under John Kerry – himself a long-time Senate buddy of Biden's, now reincarnated as climate envoy. Biden's Transportation Secretary is 'Mayor Pete' Buttigieg, a gay, energetic young Democrat; his Attorney General is Merrick Garland, Obama's eminent Supreme

Court pick, who was denied Senate confirmation by then Republican majority leader Mitch McConnell at his most partisan; and his Treasury Secretary is Janet Yellen, former chair of the Federal Reserve, described as 'Keynesian to her fingertips'.

By the summer of 2021, the pre-war FDR template of the Biden presidency had become steadily clearer. Massive energy and focus were devoted to state-led jobs growth, infrastructure and social welfare. The initial Covid-19 stimulus measures were followed by the successful passage by September of a $1 trillion infrastructure bill and a $3.5bn federal budget boost for health, children and social outlays. Biden's Congressional skills were on full display in an audacious bipartisan deal with Republicans, including minority leader Mitch McConnell in the Senate, to enact the first of these and enable the second to pass on a narrow party vote as part of a package. The splitting of the Republicans was facilitated by Trump's bizarre determination to continue disputing the 2020 election, and by Biden's skill in playing to the centre, or into touch, on divisive cultural and non-economic issues. 'Amtrak Joe', the man who commuted from Delaware to Washington via train each day he was in the Senate, pledged to rebuild America's middle class, and he may prove to be America's most powerful social reformer from the centre-left since his heroes FDR and LBJ.

However, also with echoes of pre-war FDR, and in stark contrast to LBJ, foreign policy was handled with great caution and risk aversion bordering on isolationism. A scuttle of American forces from Afghanistan in August 2021, implementing a deal with the militant Taliban agreed a year previously by Trump, ended 20 years of military engagements begun by George W. Bush. The withdrawal enjoyed strong popular support but the legacy was the same instability and Islamic extremism which, allied to terrorism, precipitated the original invasion. Time will tell whether the terrorist threat has abated, and whether the twin perils of Russia and China were contained or exacerbated by a president determined at the start of his presidency to fight at home rather than abroad.

Lord Adonis is a Labour peer and political biographer and served in Prime Minister Gordon Brown's Cabinet as Secretary of State for Transport from 2009 to 2010.

Ranking the Presidents: The Promise and Limitations of Presidential Ratings

By Alvin S. Felzenberg

COMPARING A PRESIDENT'S performance in office with those of other political actors is as old as the American republic. It may have commenced with Henry ('Light Horse Harry') Lee's observation that George Washington was 'first in war, first in peace, and first in the heart of his countrymen'.

The practice of rating a president's legacy against those of his predecessors and successors (a luxury Mr Lee did not have) is now a common occurrence. In a 1941 editorial in *Life* magazine, press magnate Henry R. Luce proclaimed the twentieth century the 'American century'. Within the American political system, beginning in the Progressive era, presidential powers expanded to the point at which they seemed to dwarf those customarily bestowed upon Congress, the courts, other levels of government, and the private sector. The centralisation of power in the presidency and the uses presidents made of it to win two world wars, emerge from the Great Depression, create the welfare state, and exert responsible control of nuclear weapons changed public expectations of what the federal government could achieve.

In the years after the Second World War, government was increasingly regarded as a force for good. The United States and its allies had defeated Nazism, Italian fascism and Japanese militarism. American leadership, in concert with other democratic nations, built the diplomatic, military and economic architecture that held the Soviet Union at bay in the darkest years of the Cold War and contributed to the ultimate demise of an 'evil empire'. These were the years when polio and other diseases were eradicated and opportunities for higher education were greatly expanded. These events spawned an unprecedented period in which Americans and their well-wishers thought anything was possible and that government could achieve it. This was the time when, as presidents and others repeatedly pointed out, the United States 'landed a man on the moon'.

In both the international and domestic arenas, presidents compared programmes they sought to enact to great undertakings of recent memory. They envisioned programmes on a 'scale of the Marshall Plan' to build housing, repair infrastructure and reform education. They declared 'wars' on poverty, illiteracy, cancer and other maladies that cried out for public attention and investment. It would take some time, and some failures in both policy outcomes and presidential performance, for expectations about government and what it could achieve to change. Scepticism set in during the aftermath of Vietnam and Watergate, which gave rise to cynicism, only to be challenged again by occasional sparks of idealism. With all of these shifts in expectations, it is not surprising that historians, seeking to put the present in perspective, began to 'rate' the performance of presidents past.

The first venture into 'the presidential rating game' began when historian Arthur M. Schlesinger Sr asked fifty-five colleagues to place American presidents into one of five categories: great, near great, average, below average and failure. (They exempted from the grading William Henry Harrison and James A. Garfield, who died shortly after taking office, and the then incumbent, Harry Truman.) Schlesinger did not provide jurors with guidance as to criteria they should use in rendering judgements. Nor did he assure for diversity in opinion, area of specialisation, or personal distinctions among deliberators. Placing in the highest ('great') category (I list them chronologically) were Washington, Jefferson, Jackson, Lincoln, Wilson and Franklin D. Roosevelt. Just missing out on the highest honour were the 'near greats': John Adams, James K. Polk, Grover Cleveland and Theodore Roosevelt. (Modern-day readers will be surprised at Andrew Johnson's appearance among the 'average' grouping. He was to fall steadily in subsequent surveys. This certainly results from reappraisals historians have made of post-Civil War reconstruction, which Johnson worked to thwart.) Grant and Harding were placed at the bottom of Schlesinger's survey as 'failures'. *Life* magazine published the results of the survey on 1 November 1948, on the eve of a presidential election.

Schlesinger discerned a commonality among those receiving the highest scores. All were presumed to have increased the powers of the president and federal intervention in the economy. Polk's appearance among the 'near greats', which came as a surprise to many readers, resulted from his handling of the US–Mexico war. (Time will tell whether and how current research on this period will affect his future ratings.) Grant's and Harding's scores, Schlesinger and others attributed to the corruption that characterised their administrations.

Schlesinger replicated his poll in 1962. He had increased the number of jurors to seventy-five and assigned each president a numerical rating, but the results remained largely unchanged. The poll's rating of the then recently retired Eisenhower, whose approval ratings remained above 50 per cent during his eight years in office, raised some eyebrows. The architect of the interstate highway, who redesigned the nation's defences and ended legal segregation in much of the country, was placed in the twenties, a notch above Chester A. Arthur. One conspicuous change in Schlesinger's 1962 poll from its 1948 predecessor was the fall of Grover Cleveland from 'near great' to 'average'. (This coincided with the academy's embrace of Keynesian economics over the '*laissez-faire*' stance towards the economy that Cleveland pursued.)

In 1996, Schlesinger's son and fellow historian replicated his father's survey. Again, results were similar, but with a few changes. Arthur Schlesinger Jr, expert on Jackson and FDR and adviser to Kennedy, voiced surprise that Eisenhower came in ninth. (Most recent surveys rank him fifth.) The younger Schlesinger's poll ignited controversy with its rating of Reagan. In spite of a few holdouts, who self-identified as 'conservatives', his panel placed Reagan one notch *beneath* Mr Arthur – not far away from where Ike had once been. Schlesinger Jr noted the 'progressive' tilt of his 1996 poll, with the highest grades going to presidents who had expanded the scope of the federal government. He advised the recently re-elected Clinton that he might raise his grade by moving left.

Readers of the younger Schlesinger survey will be forgiven for wondering whether in his rush to praise government activism per se, Schlesinger awarded greater priority to competence and process than to the merits of policy. Yes, his hero, Jackson, through his successful veto of the Second Bank of the United States, prevailed over Congress and humbled the financial community, but at the cost of producing the second most destructive depression in US history. And, yes, Jackson showed considerable legislative skills to assure passage of the Indian Removal Act of 1832. His 'victory', the product of his mowing down of some institutional checks on his power and ignoring of others, produced one of the greatest violations of human and constitutional rights in American history. (Schlesinger belatedly showed some sympathy for this view. A life-long advocate of an activist presidency, he was one of the first to warn of an 'imperial presidency', as Congress and the courts sought to hold presidents accountable during the Vietnam War and in the course of the Watergate scandal.)

To his and his thirty-two jurors' credit, Schlesinger wondered out loud whether violations of the Constitution constituted graver presidential failures than the transitory (and sometime petty) scandals of Grant and Harding. These two former 'failures' have seen their ratings rise in recent years because of their espousal of increased racial justice and reconciliation.

The most obvious defect in early efforts to rank presidents was the ideological bias of the evaluators. If only participants in these surveys and those publicising them had born in mind an admonition Calvin Coolidge (in my view, a much under-rated president) made in 1926: 'Unfortunately, not all experts are entirely disinterested. Not all specialists are without guile.' With or without the presence of guile among the evaluators, ideological bias is among the defects detected in early surveys that are the easiest to remedy. More recent surveys took pains to include jurors with greater diversity of opinion, life experience, professional expertise, areas of specialisation, and personal background. As new issues come to the fore and as older ones are re-evaluated, surveys will always tell those who behold them as much, if not more, about the evaluators and their times than about the presidents and theirs. The good news for present and future students of the presidency is that, in recent years, the tendency has been to grade presidents according to specified criteria. (Gone are the arbitrary boxes with their 'pin the tail on the donkey' approach.)

Still, there remain unavoidable defects inherent in any survey that any perceptive student of politics, past and present, should be aware of. The first and most obvious is the use journalists, textbook writers, museum curators and commentators make of them. The mere transmittal of surveys' results can lead to a 'freezing of debate'. In some quarters, these surveys have taken on an air of authority that can crowd out views contrary to the consensus among 'experts'. What serious reader, other than the most diehard contrarian or specialist on a particular president, would dare make the case for lowering or raising a presidential grade after having been repeatedly told that the 'experts' have spoken? On the other hand, with revisionism having become a constant in historical studies, each new survey can spur on additional and welcome research.

Another shortcoming inherent in the rating process, as the late Fred Greenstein pointed out, is the diversion of attention from the 'full range of presidential experience'. Great presidents made mistakes. Failed ones were not without their achievements, some of them noble. Lessons can be learned from all of them.

Perhaps the greatest challenge facing those who seek to rank presidents is that all presidents are not equally good or bad in all things. It will come as no surprise to readers of this volume that Lyndon Johnson possessed extraordinary skills in his handling of Congress, which he amply demonstrated in the passage of civil rights and voting rights legislation. It is also no secret that his handling of the Vietnam War left a permanent scar on his place in history. Similar observations might be made about other presidents (Jefferson, Wilson and Nixon to name just three). Political scientist James MacGregor Burns suggested that this dichotomy might lead evaluators to 'average' such a president's performance (balancing an 'A' here with an 'F' there). But the one thing historians of all persuasions say about LBJ is that there was nothing 'average' about him.

After reading Arthur M. Schlesinger Jr's 1996 survey (published in 1997), I suggested a way in which scholars and lay people alike might be able to access presidential strengths and weaknesses across time and administrations in the hope that they come away from their reading of the past better informed about it and more able to form an opinion as to how prospective presidents might perform in office. I suggested giving every president a grade in six categories. (Others suggest as many as ten or twelve.) Three of the categories I selected were internal to each president: character, vision and competence. Three considered their handling of three issues no president can avoid: the economy; preserving and extending liberty; and national security, defence and foreign policy.

Character, as Heraclitus declared, is a person's 'fate'. While good character does not assure presidential success, it can be a precursor. (And, while it is true that some with character failings can and have succeeded as president some of the time, this deficiency caused them difficulties they did not need.) Under this category fall all the precepts parents have tried to instil in their young since the beginning of time: *honesty* (doing what one said one would do, or explaining why unforeseen circumstances necessitated a change in course); *courage* (meeting adversity head-on, often at political or personal risk); and *integrity* (placing the interests of one's country ahead of personal convenience or interests, *or* those of one's associates).

Most who have run for president articulated in their campaigns a *vision* for the nation they hoped to lead. While most presidents came to office with at least an idea of what they hoped to achieve, the American people elected few visionaries. Those they did tended to temper some of their convictions with more than occasional pragmatism. While they kept their eyes fixed on their ends, they compromised over means and prioritised between what was essential to their goals and what would be nice to have. Some who had not articulated a sense of vision in their campaigns developed one in response to the emergence of unforeseen issues in their response to crises. Surely, some presidents contented themselves to sit back and respond to events. Others pursued a vision historians have since judged to have been wrong for the country at the time they were in office. Presidents who performed in these latter two ways failed to attain greatness.

Competence is the ability to achieve one's policy objectives and respond to unanticipated events. In order to succeed, presidents must be able to communicate effectively to the public and persuade others within and outside government to follow their lead. Often, presidents must navigate through, circumvent or bridge inherent institutional barriers in the American political system. 'Influence' that presidents exert flows from their ability to persuade would-be allies and adversaries to take the president's preferences into account as a means of advancing their own. (To observe this process at work, readers of this book will find no better guide than Richard E. Neustadt's *Presidential Power*.)

Under the assumption that readers will have a common understanding of what is meant by 'managing the economy' and 'safeguarding the nation's security', a word needs be said about 'preserving and extending liberty'. 'Liberty' connotes what the framers said were 'rights' assured to all Americans that governments were obliged to protect. While their concept of this was restricted to a small set of people within their lifetime, that they proclaimed these rights to be universal led others they had excluded or never considered to lay claim to them over time. (The Revd Martin Luther King Jr referred to this process as demanding payment on a promissory note proclaimed years earlier, before the world.) In the international arena, this has meant standing up for victims of human rights abuses abroad and, on occasion, has been part of the nation's justification for going to war.

I ended my book with precepts that the electorate, the ultimate selector of future presidents, might use as guide posts in making its selections. I list them here.

On the Upside of the Ledger:

- Scout out a sense of purpose.
- Examine how candidates handled adversity or hardship.
- Look for broad life experiences.
- Probe for a natural (and an intellectual) curiosity.
- Seek a well-developed sense of integrity.
- Crave humility.
- Award extra credit for a sense of humour, often spontaneous and self-deprecating.

On the Precautionary Side:

- Watch out for cynicism and complacency.
- Stay away from whiners.
- Keep away from know-it-alls.
- Steer clear of candidates with a narrow focus.
- Be leery of unrelenting ideologues.
- Stand guard against bearers of grudges.
- Eschew tendencies towards bald assertions of power.

Rank	President	Character	Vision	Competence	Economic Policy	Preserving and Expanding Liberty	Defence, National Security and Foreign Policy	Average Score	First Year
1	Lincoln	5	5	5	5	5	5	5.00	1861
2	Washington	5	4	5	5	4	5	4.67	1789
3	Roosevelt, T.	4	5	5	5	3	5	4.50	1901
3	Reagan	5	5	3	5	4	5	4.50	1981
5	Eisenhower	5	3	5	4	4	4	4.17	1953
6	Roosevelt, F.	3	4	5	3	4	5	4.00	1933
7	Taylor	5	4	4	3	4	3	3.83	1849
7	Grant	4	5	3	3	5	3	3.83	1869
7	McKinley	5	3	4	4	2	5	3.83	1897
7	Truman	5	4	4	2	4	4	3.83	1945
7	Kennedy	3	4	4	4	4	4	3.83	1961
12	Coolidge	5	3	4	4	4	2	3.67	1923
13	Harrison, B.	5	3	3	3	4	3	3.50	1889
13	Obama	5	3	3	3	4	3	3.50	2009
15	Adams, J.	5	3	3	3	2	4	3.33	1797
15	Jefferson	3	4	4	3	3	3	3.33	1801
15	Monroe	3	4	4	1	3	5	3.33	1817
15	Adams, J. Q.	5	3	3	3	3	3	3.33	1825
15	Wilson	3	4	3	4	2	4	3.33	1913
15	Bush, G. H. W.	5	2	3	3	3	4	3.33	1989
21	Polk	1	2	5	4	2	5	3.17	1845
21	Ford	5	2	3	3	3	3	3.17	1974
23	Taft	5	3	2	3	2	3	3.00	1909
23	Clinton	2	3	3	4	3	3	3.00	1993

25	Arthur	3	2	3	3	3	3	2.83	1881
25	Cleveland	5	2	3	2	2	3	2.83	1885
27	Harding	2	3	2	3	4	2	2.67	1921
28	Jackson	3	2	5	1	1	3	2.50	1829
28	Johnson, L.	2	3	2	2	5	1	2.50	1963
30	Madison	5	2	1	1	4	1	2.33	1809
30	Hayes	3	2	2	3	1	3	2.33	1877
30	Carter	5	2	2	1	3	1	2.33	1977
30	Bush, G. W.	3	2	1	2	3	3	2.33	2001
34	Van Buren	2	2	3	1	1	3	2.00	1837
34	Fillmore	2	1	2	3	1	3	2.00	1850
34	Trump	1	3	1	4	1	2	2.00	2017
37	Tyler	2	1	2	2	1	3	1.83	1841
37	Hoover	4	1	1	1	2	2	1.83	1929
37	Nixon	1	2	2	1	2	3	1.83	1969
40	Pierce	1	1	1	3	1	3	1.67	1853
40	Johnson, A.	2	1	1	2	1	3	1.67	1865
42	Buchanan	1	1	1	2	1	3	1.50	1857

Schlesinger's 1996 poll generated multiple criticisms from many directions. Most focused on the ideological imbalance of the jurors, of whom only three self-identified as conservatives, and in the lack of diversity among the panellists. Although some news organisations had intermittently commissioned surveys of presidential performance before the publication of Schlesinger's poll, these surveys proliferated afterwards.

Among them, C-SPAN, the non-profit public affairs channel on US cable television, has produced the most credible and prestigious. Begun in 2000, the C-SPAN poll has been replicated three times (2009, 2017, and 2021). Its creators took pains to assure ideological balance on its panel and diversity in the personal backgrounds of its jurors. Each president (save W.H. Harrison and J.A. Garfield) received grades in *ten* categories, as opposed to my original six. The categories were: public persuasion, crisis leadership, economic management, moral authority, international relationships, administrative skills, relations with Congress, vision (setting an agenda), pursuit of equal justice for all and performance within the context of their times. I had subsumed the first, the fifth and the sixth categories under the broader heading 'competence.' All but C-SPAN's final category overlap with those I used (character, vision, economic management, and defence and foreign policy, and preserving and extending liberty). Disclaimer: I was among C-SPAN's 142 jurors.

The significance of the C-SPAN poll and, I hope, of my book, was less where any particular president placed, but the extent to which it encouraged discussion among lay readers as well as scholars and students about the reasoning that lay behind the grades and whether it was correct. As C-SPAN is aware, as suggested by its tenth category, '"within the context of their times'," both presidential ratings and the categories we use to assess them change over time. Thus, the truism, that such surveys are as much about us and the values we hold as they are of the presidents.

The results of the most recent C-SPAN survey are below:

President	2021 Final Score	Overall Rankings			
		2021	2017	2009	2000
Abraham Lincoln	897	1	1	1	1
George Washington	851	2	2	2	3
Franklin D. Roosevelt	841	3	3	3	2
Theodore Roosevelt	785	4	4	4	4
Dwight D. Eisenhower	734	5	5	8	9
Harry S. Truman	713	6	6	5	5
Thomas Jefferson	704	7	7	7	7
John F. Kennedy	699	8	8	6	8
Ronald Reagan	681	9	9	10	11
Barack Obama	664	10	12	NA	NA
Lyndon B. Johnson	654	11	10	11	10
James Monroe	643	12	13	15	14

Woodrow Wilson	617	13	11	9	6
William McKinley	612	14	16	16	15
John Adams	609	15	19	17	16
James Madison	604	16	17	20	18
John Quincy Adams	603	17	21	19	19
James K. Polk	599	18	14	12	12
William J. Clinton	594	19	15	14	21
Ulysses S. Grant	590	20	22	23	33
George H. W. Bush	585	21	20	18	20
Andrew Jackson	568	22	18	13	13
William Howard Taft	543	23	24	24	24
Calvin Coolidge	535	24	26	26	27
Grover Cleveland	523	25	23	21	17
Jimmy Carter	506	26	27	25	22
James A. Garfield	506	27	29	28	29
Gerald R. Ford	498	28	25	22	23
George W. Bush	495	29	33	36	NA
Chester A. Arthur	472	30	35	32	32
Richard M. Nixon	464	31	28	27	26
Benjamin Harrison	462	32	30	30	31
Rutherford B. Hayes	456	33	31	33	25
Martin Van Buren	455	34	34	31	30
Zachary Taylor	449	35	32	29	28
Herbert Hoover	396	36	36	34	34
Warren G. Harding	388	37	40	38	38
Millard Fillmore	378	38	37	37	35
John Tyler	354	39	39	35	36
William Henry Harrison	354	40	38	39	37
Donald J. Trump	312	41	NA	NA	NA
Franklin Pierce	312	42	41	40	39
Andrew Johnson	230	43	42	41	40
James Buchanan	227	44	43	42	41

Acknowledgements

This is the fourth in a series of five books of biographical essays. In 2018 and 2019, I published a two-volume set of biographies of every woman to have been elected to the House of Commons. Then, in November 2020, Hodder published my book *The Prime Ministers 1721–2020*. An updated paperback edition will be published in May 2022. Despite the pandemic and the fact that bookshops have been forced to shut their doors, *The Prime Ministers* has been a massive seller, and to my absolute delight it won the Best Political Book by a Non-Parliamentarian at the 2021 Parliamentary Book Awards. It seemed natural, given the increased interest in American politics, to tackle *The Presidents* for my next book, and here we are. As you will have seen, it's identical in format to *The Prime Ministers*, with forty-six different essayists, and I am grateful to each of them. Choosing who should write about each president was certainly more of an art than a science. Everyone wanted to write about Obama, Bush or Clinton. James Buchanan, less so.

I am indebted to Rupert Lancaster at Hodder & Stoughton for commissioning this book, as part of a two-book deal. *Kings & Queens* will follow in late 2023. Rupert is a prince among publishers and has been a pleasure to work with. He's willing to consider new (and sometimes wacky) ideas and is such an enthusiast. His team at Hodder include Cameron Myers, Ciara Mongey, Sahini Bibi, Zakirah Alam, Ian Wong, Catriona Horne, Steven Cooper and Dominic Gribben. Nick Fawcett copyedited the MS and Jacqui Lewis was the proofreader.

A huge thank-you to Zoom Rockman, who has drawn all the images of the forty-six presidents. I really think they add something to the book. And if you would like to buy a set of presidential mugs or playing cards that accompany the book, just go to www.politicos.co.uk.

I owe a huge debt to my literary agent Martin Redfern from

Northbank Talent Management. He has now negotiated four book deals for me, and I can honestly say that none of them would have happened without him. He knows the world of political publishing better than anyone in the business and, just as importantly, he's an absolute pleasure to do business with – unusual in an agent!

This book is also available as an audiobook, read by me. Please look out as well for the podcast series *The Presidents* in which I will interview all the contributors concerning the president they have written about. And if you enjoy these podcasts, please do also download *The Prime Ministers* podcast too.

I hope you have enjoyed the book. I take full responsibility for any mistakes, but please do let me know if you spot any so that we can correct them for future editions. You can reach me at iain@iaindale.com or via social media.

If you have enjoyed the book, please do tell your friends and colleagues, because as I always say, the best form of marketing is by word of mouth. Yours.

Iain Dale
Tunbridge Wells, September 2021

Index

Adams, Abigail Smith 18, 21–2,
  25, 26
Adams, Charles 22, 25
Adams, Elihu 16
Adams, Gerry 453
Adams, John 6, 11, 61, 70, 177,
  378
  and Declaration of
    Independence 20–1, 29
  diplomatic career 22, 71
  early life, beliefs and influences
    16–17
  as first vice-president 22–3
  law, politics and Revolution
    18–19
  legacy and reputation 21, 26–7
  marriage 17–18
  presidential career 23–5, 38, 53
  retirement and death xiii, 25–6
  and slavery 16
  and Thomas Jefferson 23, 26,
    33, 38, 42
  and title of 'Mr President' xvii
Adams, John Quincy 25–6, 111,
  113, 177, 192
  death of 76
  diplomatic and political career
    63, 65–6, 72–3, 75–6
  early life, experiences and
    beliefs 22, 71–2
  and James Madison 72
  marriage 75
  and the Monroe Doctrine 73

and Native Americans 65
presidential career 67, 71, 73–5,
  83, 96
reputation and legacy 70–1,
  76–7
and slavery 70–1, 76
and William Henry Harrison
  106
Adams, John Snr 16
Adams, Louisa Johnson 75, 76
Adams, Peter 16
Adams, Susanna Boylston 16
Afghanistan xxvi, xxix
African Americans xxiv, xxv, xxvi,
  214
  and Benjamin Harrison 230
  Black Lives Matter movement
    12
  and Chester A. Arthur 209, 211
  and Dwight D. Eisenhower 357
  and Franklin D. Roosevelt 325,
    331
  and James A. Garfield 199–200
  and John F. Kennedy 369
  and Lyndon B. Johnson 369,
    378, 379, 382–3
  and Richard Nixon 393, 394–5
  and Rutherford B. Hayes ('Jim
    Crow' measures) 190, 193,
    195
  and Theodore Roosevelt 255
  and Ulysses S. Grant 183–4, 185
  and William Howard Taft 264

African Americans (*cont'd*)
  and Woodrow Wilson 270, 274,
    282
  see also slaves, slavery
Agnew, Spiro 405
Ailes, Roger 440–1
Albright, Madeleine 455
Alexander, General William 60
Alter, Jonathan 411
American Civil War 8, 65, 103,
    110, 118, 124, 129, 130, 148,
    154–5, 158, 163, 165, 166,
    168, 170, 174, 179, 182–3,
    191, 199, 205, 217, 227, 237,
    274
American War of Independence
    (Revolutionary War) 3, 4–5,
    9, 11, 18–19, 35, 50, 60, 80,
    126, 214
Anderson, John 427
Andropov, Yuri 440
Annenberg, Walter 419
Apotheosis of Washington, The
    (Brumidi fresco) 12
Arafat, Yasser 456, 458
Armistead (John Tyler's personal
    black slave) 114
Arnold, Benedict 5, 33
Arthur, Chester A. 260
  achievements, reputation and
    legacy 204–5, 211–12
  civil rights and immigration
    209, 210, 211
  and the civil service 194, 206
  death of 211
  description of 208
  early life and influences 205, 209
  marriage 205
  and Native Americans 210
  and the navy 207–8
  political career 205–6
  presidential career 206–11
  and slavery 205
Arthur, Ellen Herndon 205, 209
Arthur, Malvina Stone 205
Arthur, William 205
Ashburton, Lord 113
Assad, Bashar 480
Atwater, Lee 440
Austin, Lloyd 503
Available Man, The (Sinclair)
    286

Babbitt (Lewis) 292
Bacon, Peter 463
Bacon, Valerie 463
Baker, James 428, 432, 439, 440
Ballinger, Richard 264
Bannon, Steve 495–6
Barkley, Alben W. 337
Bayard, James 38
Bayard, Thomas F. 215, 217
Beaver, David 490
Beckwith, Robert Todd Lincoln
    167
Begin, Menachem 415–16
Bentsen, Lloyd 441
Berlin, Irving 312
Bernanke, Ben 343
Bernstein, R.B. 19, 24
Beschloss, Michael 498
Biddle, Nicholas 88
Biden, Beau 500, 501, 503
Biden, Hunter 500
Biden, Joe xxxi, xxxii, 385, 411,
    483
  achievements and reputation
    502–4
  and Barack Obama 475, 483
  character and description 335,
    501
  and COVID-19 502, 503, 504

domestic policies xxxii–xxxiii,
  501, 502, 503, 504
and Donald Trump 495, 497
early life and influences 500,
  501
family tragedies 500–1
foreign policy 501–2, 503, 504
green agenda 502
and Osama bin Laden 481
political career 412, 500–2
presidential career xviii, 365,
  502–4
Biden, Joseph Snr 500
Biden, Neilia Hunter 500
Biko, Steve 414
Birchard, Sardis 190
Birx, Dr Deborah xxxi
Bismarck, Otto von 187
Blaine, James G. 191, 216–17, 229,
  231
Blair, Tony xxix, 456, 458, 461,
  464, 466, 468–9
Blake, Robert 387, 388
Blinken, Antony 503
Blythe, William 447
Boehner, John 479
Bogart, Humphrey 423
Boies, Horace 221
Bolingbroke, Henry St John, 1st
  Viscount 34–5
Booth, John Wilkes 242
Booth, Wilkes 167
Borah, William 309, 310
Bork, Robert 501
Bosnian War 456, 457
Boulware, Lemuel Ricketts 424,
  425
Bradlee, Ben 378
Bradley, Omar 352
Brady, James 428
Branson, Richard 485

Brezhnev, Leonid 407, 413, 414,
  440
Brightest and the Best, The
  (Halberstam) 380
Britton, Elizabeth 285
Britton, Nan 285, 290
Brogan, Denis 264
Brooke, Field Marshall Alan 351
Brown, Harold 418
Brown, Pat 392, 425
Bryan, William Jennings 238, 241,
  248, 262, 272, 273
Brzezinski, Zbigniew 418, 419
Buchanan, James 145, 214
  and Abraham Lincoln 156
  achievements, reputation and
    legacy 150, 155–6
  early life and influences 150
  political career 150–1
  presidential career xix, 147–8,
    151–4
  retirement and death 154–5
  and slavery 150, 152, 153
Buckley, William F. 397
Bunau-Varilla, Philippe 254
Bundy, McGeorge 380
Burchard, Samuel G. 216
Burleston, Albert S. 274
Burns, James McGregor 509
Burr, Aaron 25, 37, 49
Bush, Barbara Pierce 437, 463,
  464
Bush, George H.W. 399, 462
  achievements and legacy 444
  and Bill Clinton 459
  character and description 335,
    436, 441, 444
  and the CIA 438–9
  domestic policy xxvii, 441,
    443–4
  early life and influences 436–7

Bush, George H.W. (*cont'd*)
  foreign policy (including Berlin
    Wall, Gulf War) 442–3, 450,
    453
  marriage 437
  and Mikhail Gorbachev 440
  military service 436–7
  and paradox of insecurity xxvii
  political career 427, 437–41
  presidential career 441–4
  and Richard Nixon 443
  and Ronald Reagan 439–40
Bush, George W. xiv, 192, 437
  9/11 and the War on Terror
    xxviii–xxix, 466, 467, 468,
    469–70, 473, 504
  achievements, reputation and
    legacy 467, 468, 470, 471
  character and description 335,
    460–1, 465
  and Donald Trump 489–90
  early life 463
  political career 461–7
  presidential career 467–71
  and Tony Blair 461, 464, 466,
    468–9
Bush, Jeb 437, 464, 490
Bush, Jenna 463
Bush, Laura 463
Bush, Prescott 437
Bush, Robin 437
Butcher, Harry C. 358
Butler, Nicholas Murray 292
Buttigieg, Pete 503

Calhoun, John C. 63, 65, 84, 85,
  86, 96, 99, 101, 115, 128
Callaghan, James 412, 416, 419,
  420
Campbell, Revd Archibald 60
Cannon, Newton 119

Capone, Al 312
Carlisle, John G. 222
Caro, Robert 379, 382
Carranza, Venustiano 276, 278
Carrington, Peter 414
Carter, Jimmy xxv, xxvi, 426, 427,
  438–9, 439
  achievements, reputation and
    legacy 412–15, 471
  character and description 335,
    412, 471
  foreign policy (including
    Panama Canal Treaty, Camp
    David, Shah of Iran)
    412–20
  and Gerald Ford 409
  human rights policies 414
  presidential career 411–12
Carter, Lillian 415
Cass, Lewis 128
Castro, Fidel 367
Cheney, Dick xxix, 407
Chernenko, Konstantin 440
Chernow, Ron 7, 8, 10
Churchill, Winston 322, 328,
  329–30, 332, 339, 341, 351,
  469
Civil Disobedience (Thoreau) 122
Clark, Mark 349
Clay, Henry 55, 82, 83, 86, 88, 89,
  96, 107, 113, 120, 128, 135
Clemenceau, Georges 278,
  279–80, 282
Cleveland, Ann Neal 214
Cleveland, Frances Folsom 218
Cleveland, Grover 228, 232
  achievements, reputation and
    legacy 214, 218, 224–5
  character and description 216,
    217, 218
  domestic policy (including civil

service, economy, strikes)
217, 218–19, 223–4
early life and influences
214–15
foreign policy 224, 232
legal career 220–1
marriage 218
political career 215–17
presidential career 214, 217–20,
221–4, 233
as public executioner 214–15
retirement and death 224
Cleveland, Richard Falley 214
Cleverly, Joseph 17
Clinton, Bill 190, 399, 400, 466
achievements, reputation and
legacy 446, 447, 458–9
character and description 335,
458
domestic policy (including
taxes, health care) 446,
451–2, 454
early life and influences 446–9
foreign policy (including
Rwanda, Yugoslavia) 317,
446, 453–4, 456–7, 457–8
humanitarian work 458–9
and John F. Kennedy 448
Lewinsky affair, impeachment
and the internet xxviii, 446,
455–6, 461
marriage 449
political career 446, 449–50
presidential career xxvii–xxviii,
449–58
Thatcher's comment on xiii
and Tony Blair 456, 458
Clinton, Chelsea 449
Clinton, DeWitt 55, 95
Clinton, Hillary Rodham xvi, 335,
448–9, 452, 455, 458, 459,

471, 474, 476, 477, 483–4,
490–1, 494
Clinton, Roger 447
Clinton, Virginia 447
Coffelt, Leslie 338
Cold War xxiii, xxvi, xxvii,
366–8, 395, 430–1, 433,
441–2
Collazo, Oscar 338–9
Comey, James 490–1
Coney, Amy 493
Congressional Politics (Wilson) 270
Conkling, Roscoe 191, 201, 205–7
Connally, John 370
Conner, Major General Fox 348
Continental Congress (First and
Second) 4, 19, 20, 29, 31,
32, 33, 35, 50, 61
Conway, Ed 344
Coolidge, Abigail 297
Coolidge, Calvin xxi, 284, 288,
289
character and description
295–7, 298, 302
death of 295, 303
early life and influences 296–7
marriage 297–8
and Native Americans 296, 299
political career 297, 298–9
presidential career 295–6,
299–303
Coolidge, Calvin Jnr 298, 300
Coolidge, Grace Anna Goodhue
296, 297–9, 302
Coolidge, John 297, 298
Coolidge, Victoria 297
Cornwallis, General 5
Cortelyou, George 240
Coughlin, Father Charles 323
Cox, James M. 289, 318
Crawford, William 63, 64, 96

Cronkite, Walter 368
Cruz, Ted 490
Cuney, N. Wright 230
Cuomo, Mario 450
Custer, General 187
Czolgosz, Leon xxi, 242

D-Day Plus Twenty Years (docu-
    mentary) 359
Dallek, Robert 374, 383
Dana, Francis 71
Darlan, Admiral 249
Darwin, Charles 168
Daugherty, Harry M. 285, 288,
    290
Davis, James J. 302
Davis, Jefferson 129
Davis, John W. 300–1
Davis, Richard Beale 63
Davis, Sarah Taylor 129
Dawes, Charles 300, 303
Day, William 265
De Gaulle, Charles 350
Debs, Eugene V. 291
Decatur, Captain Stephen 40
Dempsey, Jack 428
Devis, Bette 423
Dewey, Thomas 332, 335, 337–8
Dirksen, Everett 405
Disraeli, Benjamin 387–8
Dole, Bob 335, 441, 455
Donelson, Andrew 89
Douglas, Helen Gahagan 391
Douglas, Stephen 145, 147, 154,
    155, 164
Douglass, Frederick 230
Dreams from My Father (Obama)
    475
Drudge, Matt 455
Dukakis, Michael 441
Dylan, Bob 450

Eagleton, Thomas 411
Earp, Wyatt 204
Eaton, John 80, 82–3, 84–5
Eaton, Peggy O'Neill 84–5
Eaton, William 40
Edison, Thomas 195, 284
Edwards, Jonathan 49
Eisenhauer, Nikolaus 351–2
Eisenhower, David Jacob 347
Eisenhower, Doud 348
Eisenhower, Dwight D. 365
    achievements and legacy 358–9
    and African Americans 357
    character and description 349,
        354, 358, 359
    death of 359
    domestic policy 356–7
    early life and influences 347
    foreign policy (including Suez,
        Hungary and NATO) 352–3,
        355
    and Herbert Hoover 313
    and the hydrogen bomb xxiv
    and McCarthyism 354
    marriage 348
    military career 347–52
    as painter and writer 348, 350
    presidential career 353–9, 363
    and Richard Nixon 353, 355,
        391, 392
Eisenhower, Dwight David II
    353
Eisenhower, Ida Elizabeth Stover
    347
Eisenhower, John 348
Eisenhower, Mary 'Mamie'
    Geneva Doud 348
Eisenhower, Milton 347
Eisenhower, Paul 347
Eizenstat, Stuart 420
Ellis, Nancy Bush 444

Ellison, Keith 487
Epstein, Jeffery 459

Face the Music (musical, Berlin) 312
Fall, Albert Bacon 285
Fauci, Dr Anthony xxxi
Fauquier, Francis 31
Federalist Papers (Madison & Hamilton) 52
Feldstein, Martin 343
Fields, W.C. 428
Fillmore, Abigail Powers 133, 137, 138
Fillmore, Catherine Carmichael McIntosh 139
Fillmore, Mary 133, 138
Fillmore, Millard 335
  character and description 132, 133, 138–9
  early life and influences 132–3
  joins the Know-Nothing Party 139
  marriages 133, 139
  political career 133–6
  presidential career xix, 136–9
  reputation and legacy 132, 139–40
  retirement and death 139
  and slavery 134, 135, 136–8
Fillmore, Millard Jnr 133
Fillmore, Nathaniel 132
Finch, Robert 395
Firestone, Harvey 284
First World War 257–8, 307–8, 335
Fishing and Shooting Sketches (Cleveland) 224
Fitzgerald, F. Scott 292–3
Flynn, Errol 423
Foraker, Joseph B. 260, 261
Forbes, Robert 65

Forbes, Steve 462
Ford, Betty Bloomer 405, 406
Ford, Dorothy 404
Ford, Gerald xxv, 426, 427
  achievements 404, 409
  assassination attempts 404
  character and description 404, 405
  domestic policy 406–7
  early life and influences 404–5
  foreign policy 407, 413
  and George H.W. Bush 438
  marriage 405
  military service 404
  political career 405–6
  presidential career 399, 406–9
  and Richard Nixon 399, 405–6, 408–9
Ford, Gerald Rudolph 404
Ford, Henry 284, 300
Founding Fathers 2, 7, 13, 16, 26, 51, 70, 110, 173, 227, 425
Franklin, Benjamin 20–1, 22, 33
Franz Ferdinand, Emperor 279
Fraser, Sir Bruce 342
French Revolution 6, 34, 37
Frost, David 400

Gaddafi, Muammar 480
Gallatin, Albert 39–40
Gardiner, David 114–15
Garfield, James A. 196
  achievements, reputation and legacy 198, 202
  and African Americans 199–200
  assassination of xx, 198, 201, 206
  and the civil service 201
  early life and influences 198–9
  'front porch' campaign 200, 246
  military career 199

Garfield, James A. (*cont'd*)
    political career 200
    presidential career 200–1
    and Roscoe Conkling 201
Garland, Augustus H. 217
Garland, Merrick 503–4
Garner, John Nance 319, 327
Geffen, David 484–5
Genêt, Edmond-Charles 37
George III 3, 5, 10, 22, 31
George VI 351
Gephardt, Dick 462
Gerard, James W. 318
Gerry, Elbridge 24
Gingrich, Newt 457
Ginsburg, Ruth Bader 493
Goldwater, Barry 380, 392, 394,
    425, 438
Gone with the Wind (film & novel)
    179, 247
Gorbachev, Mikhail xxvi, 431,
    433, 440, 441, 442
Gordano, Joseph 429
Gore, Al 335, 450, 451, 461, 466,
    467, 483
Gorsuch, Neil 493
Gould, Jay 186, 248
Gould, Lewis L. 242, 243
Graffy, Colleen xiv
Grant, Julia 181, 186
Grant, Ulysses S. xx, 176, 191,
    208
    achievements, reputation and
        legacy 179–80, 184, 185–6,
        188
    and African American civil
        rights 183–4, 185
    and Andrew Johnson 183
    character and description 179
    death of 187
    early life and influences 180–1

and expulsion of Jews (General
        Order No. 11) 183
    marriage 181
    military career 180–1, 182–3
    and Native Americans 187
    presidential career 184–7
    and slavery 181–2
Great Gatsby, The (Fitzgerald)
    293
Greeley, Horace 186
Greenberg, David 300
Greenberger, Scot S. 211–12
Greene, Nathaniel 33
Greenspan, Alan 343, 407, 443
Greenstein, Fred 509
Gresham, Walter Q. 222
Grey, Edward 279
Gromyko, Andrei 413–14
*Guide to the American Battle Fields
    in Europe, A* (Eisenhower)
    348
Guiteau, Charles J. 198, 206
Gutt, Camille 344

Haig, General Alexander 428
Halberstam, David 380
Haldeman, H.R. 389
Hamilton, Alexander 6, 7–8, 34,
    51, 61
    early life and influences 35
    economic and fiscal vision 34,
        35, 36
    and James Madison 52
    and Thomas Jefferson 34, 36,
        37, 39, 42
    and Whiskey Rebellion 9–10
Hamilton, The Musical 11
Hammerschmidt, John P. 449
Hancock, Winfield Scott 200
Hanna, Mark 239, 249, 250, 251
Hanson, Victor Davis 495

Harding, Florence Mabel Kling
    284, 285, 287, 288–9, 292
Harding, Phoebe 286
Harding, Tryon 286
Harding, Warren G.
    achievements, reputation and
        legacy 284–6, 289–90, 291–3
    and African Americans 291
    character and description 284,
        285, 287–8, 292
    death of xxi, 7, 284, 292, 299
    early life and influences 286–7
    and Herbert Hoover 286, 288,
        290, 308
    newspaper career 286–7, 289,
        291
    presidential career 288–92, 298,
        318
    and the Teapot Dome scandal
        xxi, 285, 290
    and William Howard Taft
        265
Harris, Kamala xvi, 503
Harrison, Benjamin 223
    achievements, reputation and
        legacy 233–4
    and civil rights 230
    defeat, retirement and death
        222, 232–3
    early life and influences 227
    'front porch' campaign 228, 246
    marriages 227, 233
    military career 227–8
    pan-American ventures and
        foreign policy 231–2
    presidential career 192, 214,
        220, 228–32
    and veteran welfare 230–1
    and William Howard Taft 261
Harrison, Benjamin (Founding
    Father) 105, 227

Harrison, Caroline Lavinia Scott
    227, 233
Harrison, Elizabeth 227
Harrison, John 227
Harrison, Mary 228
Harrison, Mary Lord Dimmick
    233
Harrison, Russell 228
Harrison, William Henry
    death of xix, 105, 108, 112, 227
    early life and influences 105
    and John Quincy Adams 106
    legacy of 108
    and Native Americans 105–6,
        112
    political career 106–8
    presidential career 102, 108
    and slavery 106
Haugen, Gilbert 301
Hawley, Willis C. 310
Hawthorne, Nathaniel 142
Hay, John 250, 254
Hayakawa, Sam 413
Hayes, Lorenzo 190
Hayes, Lucy Ware Webb 190, 195
Hayes, Rutherford B. 100, 208
    achievements, reputation and
        legacy 190–1, 193–6
    and African Americans 190,
        193, 195
    and disputed election xx
    early life and influences 190
    and federal workforce 194
    military career 191, 237
    political career 191
    presidential career 191–3, 237
    retirement and death 196
    and Roscoe Conkling 206
    and Theodore Roosevelt 247
Hays, Will 286, 290
Hearst, William Randolph 239

Hemings, Sally 44
Hendricks, Thomas A. 215, 218
Henry, Patrick 31
Heraclitus 510
Herring, George 339
Hill, David B. 221
Hinckley, John Jnr 428
Hiroshima xxiii
Hiss, Alger 353, 390–1, 392
Hitler, Adolf 326–7, 328
Holmes, Oliver Wendell 412
Hoover, Herbert xxi
  achievements, reputation and
    legacy 305, 310, 313–14
  and African Americans 310
  and Calvin Coolidge 302, 303,
    308
  character and description 313
  death of 313
  and Dwight Eisenhower 313
  early life, beliefs and influences
    306–7
  and the First World War 307–8
  and Franklin Roosevelt 305,
    308, 320
  and Harry S. Truman 313
  and the Hoover Dam 305, 308
  industrial and economic policy
    (including the Wall Street
    Crash) 310–12
  marriage 306
  and Native Americans 310
  political career 286, 288, 290,
    308–9
  presidential career 284, 303,
    309–13, 319
  and Prohibition 312
  and the Teapot Dome scandal
    310
  as traveller, consultant and
    humanitarian 307–8

  and Warren Harding 286, 288,
    290, 308
  and William Howard Taft 266
Hoover, Huldah 306
Hoover, J. Edgar 344
Hoover, Jesse 306
Hoover, Lou Henry 306, 309
Hopkins, Harry 321, 324, 326
House, Edward M. 273–4
Houston, Sam 114
Howe, Geoffrey 462
Howe, Louis 317, 318
Huerta, General Victoriano 276
Hughes, Charles Evans 266, 290,
    325
Hull, Cordell 503
Humphrey, Hubert 364, 365,
    379–80, 384, 394
Hussein, Saddam xxviii, xxix, 442,
    466, 468–9, 470, 471
Huyser, General Robert 'Dutch'
    419

Ickes, Harold 300, 305, 320
Iran-Contra scandal xxvii
Islamic Revolution xxv–xxvi

Jackson, Andrew xv, 150, 170,
    190
  character, reputation and legacy
    79–80, 81, 82, 83, 90–1, 98
  and creation of Democrats and
    Whigs 106–7
  early life 80
  failed assassination attempt
    89–90
  fiscal policy and the 'Bank War'
    87–9, 99–100, 101–2
  and James Monroe 82
  and James Polk 119
  and John Eaton 82–3

and John Quincy Adams 75
and John Tyler 111–12
marriage 80–1
and Martin Van Buren 96–102
military career 65, 80, 81–2
and Native Americans xix, 81,
    82, 86–7, 89, 90, 119
and the Petticoat Affair 84–5
political career 81–4
presidential career xix, 79,
    84–90, 98–101, 119, 151
retirement and death 90
and slavery 79, 82, 85–6, 90,
    91, 100
and Thomas Jefferson 82
Jackson, Henry M. 'Scoop' 411
Jackson, Jesse 450, 475
Jackson, Rachel Donelson
    Robards 80–1, 83, 84, 90
James, Henry 251
Janin, Louis 307
Jay, John (and Jay Treaty) 9
Jefferson, Jane Randolph 30
Jefferson, Martha Wayles Skelton
    31–2, 33
Jefferson, Peter 30
Jefferson, Thomas xiii, 6, 7–8, 11,
    20, 25, 110, 258
    and Alexander Hamilton 34,
        36, 37, 39, 42
    and Andrew Jackson 82
    death of 26
    early life, beliefs and influences
        29–31, 42–3
    fiscal policy 39–40
    foreign policy (including
        Louisiana Purchase) xviii,
        xix, 40–2, 53–4, 62
    and James Madison 33, 36, 37,
        52, 53
    and James Monroe 61, 62

and John Adams 23, 26, 33, 38,
    42
legacy of 45–6
marriage 31–2
political and diplomatic career
    32–8
presidential career 25, 38–46
and slavery 43–5
writes the Declaration of
    Independence 20–1, 29, 32,
    44
Jefferson's Manual (Jefferson) 31
Jennings, Lizzie 205
*Jimmy Carter in Africa: Race and the
    Cold War* (N. Mitchell) 415
John Adams (HBO mini-series) 20
Johnson, Andrew xv
    achievements, reputation and
        legacy 170–1, 177
    character and description of
        170
    death of 177
    early life and influences 171–2
    impeachment of xx, 176–7
    political career 172–3
    presidential career 173–7
    and slavery 171, 173–4
    and Ulysses S. Grant 183
Johnson, Boris xxxi
Johnson, Eliza McCardle 172
Johnson, Hiram 300
Johnson, Lady Bird (Claudia Alta)
    Taylor 376, 379, 384
Johnson, Lyndon B. 359, 391, 425,
    438, 504
    achievements and legacy 378,
        379, 381–2, 385
    domestic policy (civil rights,
        healthcare) 369, 378, 379,
        381–2
    early life and influences 374–6

Johnson, Lyndon B. (*cont'd*)
  foundation of personal fortune
    (Brown & Root) 376–7
  and Franklin Roosevelt 375–6,
    377
  and Gerald Ford 405
  marriage 376
  military service 377
  political career 365, 370, 375–8
  presidential career xxv, 373–4,
    378–85
  retirement and death 384–5
  and Vietnam 380–1, 383–4, 385
Johnson, Rebekah Baines 374
Johnson, Richard Mentor 101
Johnson, Sam Ealy 374, 375
Jonkman, Barney 405

Kael, Pauline 401
Karabell, Zachary 208
Kavanagh, Brett 493
Kellogg, Frank 303
Kelly, Ed 327
Kennedy, Edward 361, 362, 426,
  477
Kennedy, Jacqueline 110, 348, 370,
  373
Kennedy, Joe Jnr 363
Kennedy, John F. 46, 176, 242,
  354, 359, 474
  achievements, reputation and
    legacy xxiv–xxv, 368–71
  assassination of xxiv, 369–71,
    373, 378–9, 439
  and Bill Clinton 448
  character and description 335,
    361–2, 363, 388
  and civil rights 369
  and the Cold War 366–8
  and Cuba xxv, 367
  domestic policy 368

  early years and influences 362–3
  foreign crises 366–8
  and James Buchanan 155–6
  military service 363
  political life 363–4
  presidential career 364–70, 378,
    392
  and Vietnam 368, 371
  writes Putlitzer Prize-winning
    book 363–4
Kennedy, Joseph Snr 362
Kennedy, Robert 361, 365, 367,
  370, 393
Kerry, John 335, 503
Keynes, J.M. 341, 344
Khomeini, Ayatollah 416, 417, 418
Khrushchev, Nikita 355, 366
Kierkegaard, Søren 501
Kim John-un 492
King, Coretta Scott 366
King, Martin Luther 366, 393,
  430, 511
King, Rodney xxvii
King, Rufus 63
King, William Rufus 151
Kinnock, Neil 483
Kipling, Rudyard 254–5
Kissinger, Henry 389, 401, 407,
  413, 419, 427
Kitchener, Lord 308
Klerk, President de 414
Kling, Amos 290
Knox, Philander 252
Korean War 340, 352, 359
Krueger, Alan 343
Ku Klux Klan 185, 186, 296

La Follette, Robert 300–1
Laden, Osama bin 457, 469–70,
  481
Lafayette, Marquis de 34

Lafitte, Jean 82
Lamar, L.C.Q. 217
Lamont, Daniel S. 222
Landon, Alf 325, 432
Lane, Harriet 151
Lasker, Albert 286
Laski, Harold 263
Lawrence, Richard 89–90
Lay, Ken 465
Lazear, Eddie 343
Lee, Arthur 257
Lee, General Charles 60
Lee, Harry 55, 505
Lee, Robert E. 129, 179, 182
Leuchtenberg, William 320
Lewinsky, Monica 446, 455–6
Lewis, Sinclair 292
Lili'uokalani, Queen 232, 240
Lincoln, Abraham xiv, xv, xxxii,
    39, 90, 128, 258, 475
  achievements, reputation and
    legacy xx, 158–9, 166, 168
  assassination of xx, 158, 167–8,
    183
  character and description
    160–1, 163, 335
  and Civil War 148, 158, 165,
    166
  and creation of the Secret
    Service 167
  deaths of his children 167
  early life, beliefs and influences
    158, 161, 162–3, 165–6
  health of 160–1
  and James Buchanan 156
  and James Polk 122
  marriage 161–2, 164, 167
  military service 163
  oratorial skill 164–5
  political career 163–5
  presidential career 154, 181–2
  and slavery xix, 159, 164, 165,
    166
  and Ulysses S. Grant 183, 187
Lincoln, Abraham (Lincoln's
    grandson) 167
Lincoln, Eddie 167
Lincoln, Mary Todd 161–2, 164,
    167, 183
Lincoln, Nancy Hanks 161
Lincoln, Robert 167
Lincoln, Sarah 161
Lincoln, Sarah Johnston 162
Lincoln, Tad 167
Lincoln, Thomas 160, 161, 162
Lincoln, Willie 167
Lindbergh, Charles 296
Lipmann, Walter 302
Livingston, Robert R. 20, 41
Lloyd George, David 256–7, 278,
    279–80, 282
Locke, John 49
Lodge, Henry Cabot 281, 298,
    353, 354, 363
Long, Huey 323
Longworth, Alice Roosevelt 300
Louis XVI 8, 61
Lowry, Edward 295
Luce, Henry R. 505
Lumumba, Patrice 366

McAdoo, William Gibbs 273, 287
MacArthur, Douglas 340, 342,
    348, 352
McCain, John 335, 466, 477, 502
McCarthy, Joe 342–3, 354, 391
McClure, Alexander K. 204
McConnell, Mitch xxxi, 21, 504
McCullough, David 16, 412
McElroy, Mary Arthur 209
McGinnis, Schuyler 245
McGovern, George 398, 411

McKinley, Ida 237
McKinley, Ida Saxton 237, 238
McKinley, Katie 237
McKinley, William 233, 335
  achievements and legacy 242–3
  assassination of xxi, 236, 241–2,
    250–1
  description of 238
  early life and influences 236–7
  foreign policy xx, 239–41
  'front porch' campaign 238, 246
  marriage 237
  military career 237
  political career 237–8
  presidential career 238–41, 249
  and William Howard Taft 260,
    261–2
McNamara, Bob 380, 383
McNary, Charles 301
Madison, Dolley Payne Todd 52–3
Madison, James 6, 7, 8, 11, 23, 24,
    110, 126
  and Alexander Hamilton 52
  defends the Constitution 42
  description of 48, 50, 335
  early life, beliefs and influences
    48–50
  as first wartime president 55
  and James Monroe 61, 62
  and John Quincy Adams 72
  legacy 48, 57–8
  marriage 52–3
  political career and ideology
    50–4
  presidential career xviii–xix,
    54–7, 61
  retirement and death 67–8
  and Thomas Jefferson 33, 36,
    37, 52, 53
Madison, James Snr 48
Madison, John 48

Magee, John Gillespie 432
Main Street (Lewis) 292
Major, John 451, 453, 455
Mandela, Nelson 414
Mangum, Willie P. 101
Manning, Daniel 215
Manning, David 217
Mansfield, Mike 368
Mao Zedong 397
Marcos, Ferdinand xxvi
Marcy, William 127
Marshall, Edward 249
Marshall, George C. 339, 348,
    349, 351, 352, 354
Marshall, John 23–4, 60
Marshall, Thomas 258
Marshall, Thurgood 383
Martin, Revd Thomas 48
Marx, Karl 387
Maury, Revd James 30
May, Gary 116
May, Theresa xxxi, 492
Meacham, John 89
Mellon, Andrew 290, 291, 301,
    309
Mencken, H.L. 302
Mercer, Lucy 318, 336
Meredith, James 369
Merkel, Angela xxxi
Merry, Robert W. 243
Mexican-American War 76,
    122–3, 127, 136, 144, 164,
    181
Meyer, Sir Christopher xiv
Mills, Roger Q. 219
*Missouri Compromise and Its
    Aftermath: Slavery and the
    Meaning of America, The*
    (Forbes) 65
Mitchell, Stephen 391
Mitterand, François 442

Mondale, Walter 'Fritz' 335, 414, 418, 431–2, 439
Monroe, Eliza 61
Monroe, Elizabeth Kortright 61, 68
Monroe, James xiv, 41, 95, 110
 and Andrew Jackson 82
 domestic legacy 66–8
 early life, beliefs and influences 60–1
 foreign policy (including Monroe Doctrine) xxiii, 60, 65–6, 73
 and George Washington 61–2
 and James Madison 61, 62
 marriage of 61
 military service 60
 and Native Americans 65
 political and diplomatic career 61–3
 presidential career (including three major crises) xix, 63–8
 and slavery 64–5
 and Thomas Jefferson 61, 62
Monroe, James Jnr 61
Monroe, Maria 61
Montgomery, Bernard 'Monty' 350, 351
Morgan, H. Wayne 243
Morgan, J. Pierpont 252, 253
Morgan, William 133
Morgenthau, Henry 326
Morrison, Toni 483–4
Morton, J. Sterling 222
Morton, Levi P. 220, 228, 233
Moynihan, Daniel Patrick 387, 388
Mueller, Robert 495
Mugabe, Robert 415
Murray, Joe 247–8

Napoleon Bonaparte 41, 55
Napoleonic Wars 53–5, 71–2, 75

Nasser, Gamal 355
Native Americans xx
 and Abraham Lincoln 163
 and Andrew Jackson xix, 81, 82, 86–7, 89, 90, 119
 and Calvin Coolidge 296, 299
 and Chester Arthur 210
 and George Washington 3, 7, 86
 and Herbert Hoover 310
 and James Madison 56
 and James Monroe 65, 66
 and James Polk 122, 123
 and Martin Van Buren 99, 102
 and Ulysses S. Grant 187
 and William Henry Harrison 105–6, 112
 and Zachary Taylor 126
Nelson, Horatio 40
Netanyahu, Benjamin 456
Neustadt, Richard E. 510
Never Enough (M. D'Antonio) 489
New Deal xxii, xxiii
Nixon, Julie 353
Nixon, Pat Ryan 389–90, 391
Nixon, Richard xi, 21, 425, 426
 achievements, reputation and legacy 390–2, 400–2
 and African Americans 393, 394–5
 character and description 388, 389, 390, 399–400
 death of 399
 description of 335
 and Donald Trump 387, 392, 399, 400
 and Dwight D. Eisenhower 353, 355, 391, 392
 early life and influences 387–90

Nixon, Richard (*cont'd*)
  foreign policy (including
      Nixon, Vietnam and China)
      xxv, 395–7, 438
  and George H.W. Bush 443
  and Gerald Ford 405–6
  marriage 389–90
  military service 390
  pardoned by Gerald Ford 399,
      408–9
  political career 353, 355, 365,
      390–4
  presidential career 394–8
  racist beliefs 399
  and Watergate xxv, 398–9, 400,
      401, 402, 408
Noonan, Peggy 436
Noriega, Manuel 442
Notes on Virginia (Jefferson) xx, 31,
      44

Obama, Barack xvi, 210
  achievements, reputation and
      legacy 473–4, 478, 484–5
  and Andrew Jackson 91
  character and description 335,
      475–6, 479
  domestic policy (including
      healthcare, gun control) 478,
      481
  and Donald Trump 483–4, 485
  early life and influences 473,
      474–5, 482
  as first Black president xxix, 473
  foreign policy (including
      Osama bin Laden,
      Guantanamo) 474, 479–81
  and Hillary Clinton 483–4
  invective, conspiracy theory and
      social media against xxx
  marriage 475

  political career 474–8
  post-presidential interests 484–5
  presidential career 478–83
  and racism 482–3
  receives Nobel Peace Prize 479
  and the Tea Party 478–9
Obama, Michelle Robinson 475,
      485
O'Bannon, Lieutenant Presley 40
Olney, Richard 223
O'Neill, Peggy 84
O'Neill, Tip 405, 479
Oswald, Lee Harvey 242, 370
*Our Chief Magistrate and His
      Powers* (Taft) 264
Owen, David xiv

Paine, Thomas 4–5, 61
Palin, Sarah 477
Palmer, Alice 476
Parker, Alton B. 251
Parker, Dorothy 295
Parr, Jerry 428
Patton, S. 348
Pence, Mike xxxii, 491
Pendergast 336
Perkins, Frances 320
Perot, Ross 444, 450, 462, 487
Pershing, General John J. 277, 348
Phillips, Carrie 289
Pierce, Benjamin 142
Pierce, Benny Franklin 146
Pierce, Frank 144
Pierce, Franklin 138
  achievements, reputation and
      legacy 142, 148
  deaths of his children 143, 144,
      146
  early life and influences 142
  and James Polk 143–4
  marriage 142–3

political career 143–6
presidential career xix, 146–8
retirement and death 148
and slavery 143, 146–7
Pierce, Jane Appleton 142–3, 144,
145, 146, 148
Pinchot, Forester 264
Pinckney, Charles C. 23, 37, 54
Pinochet, Augusto xxvi
Platt, Thomas 250
Polk, James K. 115, 128
achievements, reputation and
legacy 118, 121–4
and Andrew Jackson 119
charmless character of 121
death of 124
early life, beliefs and influences
118–19
and Franklin Pierce 143–4
and Native Americans 122, 123
political career 119–20
presidential career 120–4, 151
and slavery 123–4
and Zachary Taylor 127
Polk, Sarah 124
Porter, General 182
Preble, Commodore Edward 40
Presidency
development of xviii–xix, 6,
7–8, 10–11
expansive xxi–xxviii
ranking of Presidents 505–15
recovering xx–xxi
rising anew xxxii–xxxiii
uncertain xxviii–xxxii
Presidential Power (Neustadt) 510
Presidential Problems (Cleveland)
224
President's Daughter, The (Britton)
285
Preston, Diana 342

Proctor, Redfield 229
Profiles in Courage (Kennedy)
363–4
Putin, Vladimir 492
Putnam, James 17

Quayle, Dan 441
Quincy, Hannah 17
Quincy, Josiah 17

Randolph, Isham 30
Randolph, Peyton 31
Rayburn, Sam 337, 376
Reagan, Jack 422
Reagan, Michael 426
Reagan, Nancy Davis 424
Reagan, Neil 422
Reagan, Nelle Wilson 422
Reagan, Ronald xvi, 225, 333,
380, 436, 438, 462, 479
achievements and legacy 434
acting career 422–5, 467
assassination attempt 428–9,
439–40
character and description 335,
467
and the Cold War xxvii, 430–1,
433
domestic policy (including
drugs, civil rights, and
AIDS) xxvi, 429–30, 432
early life and influences 422,
424, 425
foreign policy 430–1, 432–3, 440
and George H.W. Bush 439–40
marriages 424
political career 424–7
presidential career 417, 422,
427–33, 439–40
retirement and death 433–4
space programme 432

Reed, Thomas B. 231
Reeves, Thomas 204
Regan, Donald 428, 432, 440
Reid, Whitelaw 233
Reiss, Mitchell xiv
Rice, Condoleezza xxviii, 442,
    465, 470
Richards, Ann 463, 464
Richardson, Elliot 389
Richie, Thomas 97
Ridgway, Matthew 352
Robertson, Donald 48
Robertson, Pat 441
Rockefeller, David 419
Rockefeller, Jay 462
Rockefeller, John D. 252, 253
Rockefeller, Nelson 426
Romer, Christine 478
Romney, George 395
Roosevelt, Alice Hathaway Lee
    247, 248
Roosevelt, Alice Lee 248
Roosevelt, Archie 257
Roosevelt, Bamie 248
Roosevelt, Edith Carrow 248
Roosevelt, Eleanor 317–18, 337
Roosevelt, Elliott 317
Roosevelt, Franklin Delano 10,
    90, 258, 288, 303, 411, 412,
    471, 504
  achievements, reputation and
    legacy 316, 321–2, 333
  and African Americans 325, 331
  character and description 318,
    335
  contracts poliomyelitis 318
  death of xxii, 332–3, 336–7, 340
  domestic policy 321–6, 350–1
  early life and influences 316–17
  and fear itself speech xxii, 321
  and Harry S. Truman 336

  and Herbert Hoover 305, 308,
    320
  and Jewish refugees 331
  Lend-Lease programme 328
  and Lyndon B. Johnson 375–6,
    377
  and the Manhattan Project 340
  marriage 317
  and the 'New Deal' xxii, 274,
    305, 316, 321, 322–6, 333
  political career 317–20
  presidential career xxi–xxii, 313,
    320–32, 375
  and Prohibition 322
  radio 'Fireside Chats' xxii, 321,
    328
  and the Second World War
    316, 325–31, 332–3
  and the United Nations 328,
    331, 332, 333
Roosevelt, Franklin Jnr 365
Roosevelt, James 316
Roosevelt, James Jnr 319
Roosevelt, Martha Bulloch 247,
    248
Roosevelt, Quentin 257–8
Roosevelt, Sara 316, 317, 318
Roosevelt, Theodore 21, 215, 287,
    288, 316
  achievements and legacy 258
  and African Americans 255
  assassination attempt 257
  death of 258
  description of 246, 247
  domestic policy (based on the
    'square deal') xxi, 252–3
  early life and influences 246–7
  foreign policy (including
    building of Panama Canal)
    253–4
  and Franklin Pierce 148

marriages 247, 248
military career xxi, 245–6, 249
political career 247–50, 256–8
presidential career 242, 250–6,
    263
receives Nobel Peace Prize 254
and Rutherford B. Hayes 247
and William Howard Taft 260,
    262, 264
Roosevelt, Theodore Snr 246–7
Ross, Diana 450
Ross, Edmund 176
Roth, William 502
Rouse, Ceci 343
Rove, Karl 464, 465, 468, 471,
    489
Rubio, Marco 490
*Rules of Civility and Decent Behavior
    in Company and Conversation*
    (Washington) 2, 10
Rush, Bobby 476
Rusk, Dean 367, 380
Russo-Japanese war 254
Rutledge, Ann 161

Sadat, Anwar 415–16
Salisbury, Lord 241
Salman, Crown Prince
    Mohammed bin 492
Salomon, Edward S. 183
Schlesinger, Arthur M. Jnr 507–8
Schlesinger, Arthur M. Snr 506–7
Schlesinger, James 389
Schmidt, Helmut 412
Schultz, George 428, 462
Scott, Dred 152
Scott, Winfield 127, 128, 154
Second World War xxii, 258,
    277–81, 316, 325–31, 332–3,
    339, 340–2, 347, 349–51, 363,
    377, 390, 404, 436–7

Seward, William 134, 135
Seymour, Horatio 183
Shah of Iran 416–20
Sharpton, Al 475
Sheehan, William F. 'Blue-eyed
    Billy' 317
Sherman, General 182
Sherman, John 200, 238
Sherman, Roger 20
Shlaes, Amity 295, 298
Shriver, Eunice Kennedy 362
Simpson, O.J. xxviii
Sinclair, Andrew 286
Sitting Bull 187
'Sketches of American Statesmen'
    (Davis) 63
slaves, slavery xv, 6, 13
    and Abraham Lincoln xix, 159,
        164, 165, 166
    and Andrew Jackson 79, 82,
        85–6, 90, 91, 100
    and Andrew Johnson 171,
        173–4
    and Barack Obama 475
    and Chester A. Arthur 205
    and Franklin Pierce 143, 146–7
    and George Washington 6, 11,
        13
    and Henry Clay 128
    and James Buchanan 150, 152,
        153
    and James Monroe 64–5
    and James Polk 122, 123–4
    and John Adams 16
    and John Quincy Adams 70–1,
        76
    and John Tyler 110, 111, 112,
        114, 115, 116
    and Millard Fillmore 134, 135,
        136–8
    and Thomas Jefferson 43–5

slaves, slavery (*cont'd*)
  and Ulysses S. Grant 181–2
  and William Henry Harrison
    106
  and Zachary Taylor 128–9, 135
  see also African Americans
Small, William 31
Smith, Alfred E. 309, 319
Smith, Hoke 222
Smith, Margaret Bayard 84
Smithson, James 76
Smoot, Reed 310
Snowden, Edward 480
Social Contract (Rousseau) 49
Somoza, Anastasio xxvi
Sousa, John Philip 228
Spanish Civil War 326
Spanish-American War xx, xxi,
  239–40, 245, 249
Spirit of Law, The (Montesquieu)
  49
Stalin, Joseph 329, 332, 339, 340–1
Stanford, Leland 306
Stanton, Edwin 175, 183
Stephanopoulos, George 487
Stevens, Thaddeus 175, 176
Stevenson, Adlai E. 221, 233, 354,
  356, 391
Stevenson, Coke 377
Stiglitz, Joseph 343
Stimson, Harry 340, 341
Stone, Harlan F. 266, 337
Stuart, Gilbert 12
Sullivan, William 418
*Summary View on the Rights of
  British America, A* (Jefferson)
  32

Taft, Alphonso 260
Taft, Helen 'Nellie' Herron 260,
  261, 263

Taft, Senator 352–3
Taft, William Howard 240, 287
  acheivements and legacy 266–7
  administrative career 260, 262
  and African Americans 264
  death of 266
  early life and influences 260
  gets stuck in his bathtub xxi,
    266
  legal career 260–2, 265–6
  marriage 260, 261
  presidential career 256, 260,
    262–4, 274
  and Theodore Roosevelt 260,
    262, 264
  and Warren Harding 265
  and William McKinley 260,
    261–2
Taft-Hartley Act xxiii
Talleyrand, Charles Maurice de
  24
Tallmadge, James 64
Taney, Roger 152
Tanner, Corporal James R. 230–1
Tarleton, Lt-Col. Banastre 33
Taylor, James C. 25
Taylor, Zachary 411
  achievements, reputation and
    legacy 126, 129–30
  death of 129, 136
  early life and influences 126
  military career 126–8
  and Native Americans 126
  presidential career 128–9, 135,
    151
  and slavery 128–9, 135
Tecumseh (Shooting Star) 105
Thatcher, Margaret xii–xiii, 29,
  318, 430, 432, 434, 442
Thoreau, Henry David 122
Thurman, Allen G. 219

Thurmond, Strom 337
Tiffany, Louis C. 208
Tilden, Samuel J. 192, 215
Tillman, Bill 223
Torresola, Griselio 338
Tower, John 433
Trudeau, Garry 436
Trudeau, Justin xxxi
Truman, Anderson Shipp 335
Truman, Elizabeth 'Bess' Wallace
    335, 337
Truman, Harry 506
Truman, Harry S. xiv, 425, 471
    achievements and legacy 343–5
    assassination attempts 338–9
    and the atomic bomb 340–2
    character and description 335,
        338, 343
    and Dwight D. Eisenhower 352
    early life and influences 335–6
    establishes the CIA 339
    and Franklin D. Roosevelt 331,
        336
    and Herbert Hoover 313
    and Joe McCarthy 342–3
    and the Korean War 340
    marriage 335
    and the Marshall Plan 339
    military service 335–6, 347
    and NATO 339, 352
    political career 336
    presidential career xxii–xxiii,
        336–44
    retirement and death 335,
        344–5
    and the Second World War
        340–2
    and the Truman Doctrine
        339–40
Truman, Mary Margaret 335
Trump, Donald xiv–xv, xxx–

xxxiii, 90, 177, 192, 380,
    411, 471
    achievements, reputation and
        legacy 486–7, 492–3, 494
    and attack on Capitol building
        xviii, xxxii, 497–8
    and Barack Obama 473–4,
        483–4
    business and television career
        488–9
    character and description 335,
        489–90
    and Covid-19 xxxi–xxxii,
        496–7
    divisive and chaotic 12, 487,
        492, 493, 495, 496–8
    domestic policy (including
        Supreme Court justices) 194,
        492–4
    early life and influences 487–8
    foreign policy 480, 492, 504
    and George W. Bush 489–90
    and Hillary Clinton 490–1, 494
    impeachment 487, 495, 498
    and Joe Biden 495
    marriages 493
    misogyny of 491, 493
    presidential career 491–8
    racism of 491, 494
    and Richard Nixon 387, 392,
        399, 400
    rise to power xxx, 487, 489–91
    and Steve Bannon 495–6
Trump, Fred 488
Tubman, Harriet 91
Twain, Mark 204, 211, 246
Tyler, John
    achievements, reputation and
        legacy 110, 113–14, 116
    and Andrew Jackson 111–12
    and campaign song

Tyler, John (con't)
'Tippecanoe and Tyler Too'
108, 112
early life, experiences and
influences 110–11
first vice president to become
president 110, 112–13
foreign policy 113–14
marriages of 110, 113, 115
political career 111–12
presidential career 112–15
retirement and death 115–16
and slavery 110, 111, 112, 114,
115, 116
Tyler, Julia Gardiner 115
Tyler, Letitia 113
Tyler, Mary Armistead 111
Tyler, Pearl 110

Udall, Morris 411
United Nations (UN) xxiii
Upshur, Abel 115

Van Buren, Abraham 93
Van Buren, Martin 119, 120
and Andrew Jackson 96–102
and the 'Bank War' 99–100
death of 103
early life, experiences and
influences 93–4
legacy of 93, 96–7, 103
and Native Americans 99, 102
political career 94–101
presidential career 90, 101–2,
107
and slavery 65, 95, 102
Vance, Cyrus 413, 415–16, 417,
418, 419
Vegetable, The (Fitzgerald) 293
Victoria, Queen 132, 139, 187,
241

Vietnam War xxv, 368, 371,
380–1, 383–4, 385, 395–6,
400
Villa, Francisco 'Pancho' 277
Voorhis, Jerry 390

Wallace, George 369, 394, 411
Wallace, Henry A. 327, 331, 336,
337
Walpole, Robert 34
War of 1812 55–7, 58, 65, 81, 95,
111
Washburn, W.D. 232
Washington, Booker T. 255
Washington, George 1, 33, 34, 52,
71, 110, 335, 505
achievements, reputation and
legacy 5, 10–14
character and beliefs 2, 11–12
early life, experiences and
influences 2–3
elected as first president 5–6, 22
establishes presidential norms 6,
7–8, 10–11, 255–6
fiscal policy 7–8, 36
foreign policy 6–7, 8–9
initiates first Thanksgiving Day
holiday 6
and James Monroe 61–2
Jay Treaty and Whiskey
Rebellion 9–10
and Native Americans 7, 86
and North-South divide 6, 8
presidential challenges, crises
and solutions xix, 6–10
as reluctant revolutionary 4–5
retirement and death 11, 37
and slavery 6, 11, 13
sour expression on $1 bill due
(perhaps) to new set of
dentures 12

Washington, Martha Custis 3
Weaver, James B. 221, 222
Webster, Daniel 101, 113, 114, 128
Weems, Mason 12
Weinberg, Caspar 428
Weinberger, Caspar 389
Westmoreland, General 383
White, Edward 265
White, Harry Dexter 344
White House xiii
   alcohol-free 190, 195
   burning of 56, 63, 82
   creation of the Library 133
   dedicated space for journalists
     in 239
   Hoover's changes to 309
   informality in 450
   menagerie of animals at 228,
     301
   near-Riot at 84
   as official title of the president's
     home 251
   Oval office added 251
   redecoration and refurbishment
     110, 208
   supporters of Andrew Jackson
     march on 175
White, Lawson 101
White, William Allen 246, 287
Whitney, William C. 215
Wilcox, Ansley 251
Wilhelm II, Kaiser 279
Wilkes, John 167
Willkie, Wendell 328
Wilson, Ellen Louise Axson 270
Wilson, Jesse 269
Wilson, Joseph Ruggles 269
Wilson, Woodrow 214, 288, 411
   academic career 270–1

achievements and legacy 269
and African Americans 270,
   274, 282
and Calvin Coolidge 298
and creation of the League of
   Nations 269, 279–81
domestic policy 274–5
early life and influences
   269–70
foreign policy (including First
   World War) 276–81, 290
and Franklin D. Roosevelt 318
marriage 270
political career 271–3
presidential career xxi, 257, 264,
   273–82
receives Nobel Peace Prize 281
retirement and death 282
Windom, William 230
Winfrey, Oprah 476
Wirt, William 63
Witherspoon, John 49
Wolfowitz, Paul 465
Wright, Revd Jeremiah 482
Wyman, Jane 423, 424
Wythe, George 31

Xi Jinping xxxi, 492

Yarborough, Ralph 370
Yellen, Janet 343, 504
Yeltsin, Boris xxvii
Young, Andrew 414–15, 476
Young, Brigham 152–3, 210
Young, Solomon 335
Young, Tommy 448

Zhou Enlai 484
Zimmerman, Arthur 278